XML Developer's Guide

Fabio Arciniegas A.

McGraw-Hill
New York San Francisco Washington, D.C.
Auckland Bogotá Caracas Lisbon London Madrid
Mexico City Milan Montreal New Delhi San Juan
Singapore Sydney Tokyo Toronto

McGraw-Hill
A Division of The McGraw-Hill Companies

1 2 3 4 5 6 7 8 9 0 AGM/AGM 0 5 4 3 2 1 0

P/N 0-07-212646-9
Part of ISBN 0-07-212648-5

The sponsoring editor for this book was Rebekah Young and the production manager was Clare Stanley. It was set in New Century Schoolbook by Patricia Wallenburg.

Printed and bound by Quebecor Martinsburg.

This book is printed on recycled, acid-free paper containing a minimum of 50% recycled, de-inked fiber.

To My Mother

"A book is made up of signs that speak of other signs, which in their turn speak of things."

Umberto Eco in *The Name of the Rose*

Contents

Introduction

What Is This Book About?

This book is about XML Technologies from the perspective of the software developer. It deals with all major current problems in XML development, from the very basics of the language to advanced uses in areas such as wireless, databases, and vector graphics.

What Makes This Book Unique?

Three main features characterize this book:

- **Completeness**—This book covers all the major W3C standards and programming techniques available for XML development today (XML, DOM, XPath, XPointer, XSLT, etc.), as well as the most relevant standard XML applications (XHTML, SVG, WML).
- **Environment independence**—The book is focused on application development, without compromising any particular operating system, vendor, language, or implementation.
- **High-end techniques, abundant examples**—The book is based on the premise that you are looking for practical, serious development with cutting-edge technologies and sound methodologies. Every chapter illustrates its theory with non-trivial, real-life examples (their complete code and auxiliary tools can be found on the CD).

Who Should Read This Book?

This book is written for software developers. It is meant to be a clear and complete guide to XML technologies and techniques, not a compendium of brochure descriptions.

This book focuses on technology, design, and implementation issues for real applications. That is why it will be most useful if you are interested in software construction.

How Is The Book Structured?

The book is divided into five parts:

1. **XML Structure, Syntax, and Uses**—Discusses XML 1.0 syntax, semantics, and best practices. It deals with the concepts and applications of well-formed XML, DTDs and namespaces. It is composed of Chapters 1 through 3.
2. **Parsing and Programmatic Manipulation of XML**—Discusses DOM (level 2), SAX (versions 1 and 2) and several design techniques for making the most out of them in real-life applications. It is composed of Chapters 4 through 7.
3. **XML Related Technologies**—Discusses the rest of the core XML family of technologies and their application.[1] It is composed of Chapters 8 through 14.
4. **Key XML Applications**—Discusses fundamental XML applications such as WML (WAP's markup language), SVG, SOAP, and databases.
5. **Comprehensive Case Studies**—Presents the application of the concepts and technologies of the previous four parts in light of the design and implementation of fully functional applications.

How Should I Read this Book?

The book can be read fluently either from cover to cover or using one of the following tracks (sets of chapters), according to your specific needs:

- **XML Basics (Chapters 1 through 6)**—Gives a complete overview of the tools and techniques to manipulate XML 1.0.
- **XML and Web Development (Chapters 11 through 16)**—All the key technologies for Web development are presented here. Please make sure to complement this with the final examples of Part 5.
- **Advanced XML (Chapters 1 through 13)**—Gives a complete overview of the tools and techniques to manipulate XML 1.0 and all key members of the XML family of specifications.
- **XML and Java Programming (Chapters 4 through 7 and 16)**—Discover all facets and techniques for common Java programming and XML.

[1] Chapter 1, fundamental for all reading tracks, explains the structure of the XML family of specifications.

- **XML and Wireless (Chapters 1 through 3 and 15)**—Covers Wireless Application Protocol (WAP), WMLScript, VoiceXML, and all you need to know to start developing XML based Wireless applications.
- **XML Data Modeling (Chapters 1 through 3, 13 and 14)**—Presents theory and praxis of data modeling with XML DTDs and schemas.
- **XML Key Vocabularies (Chapters 1 through 3 and 15 through 18)**—Presents key XML applications every developer should be aware of.
- **XML E-Commerce (Chapters 1 through 3, 16 and 17)**—Addresses key XML components for B2B and B2C applications.

Regardless of the particular track, it is recommended that you take a good look at the basics and the example applications: they will provide foundation and inspiration for successful projects of your own.

Requirements

This book has been developed with a strong devotion to open standards and diversity, so it assumes no particular working environment (such as a particular browser or operating system). The only platform requirement for the examples on the book is a modern PC capable of running a Java environment. The CD contains the programs and pointers needed for each topic and chapter in the book (see figure on next page).

A basic understanding of the concepts of Object Oriented programming is expected as well as some familiarity with Java. Whenever possible non-vendor-specific implementations have been used for the examples. *No ASP or Visual Basic knowledge is expected or required.*

Questions and Feedback

The author is available for comments and questions in the following addresses:

faa@thefaactory.com and faa@fabioarciniegas.com

A guide to updates of the programs included on the CD can be found on http://www.thefaactory.com/xmldevguide.

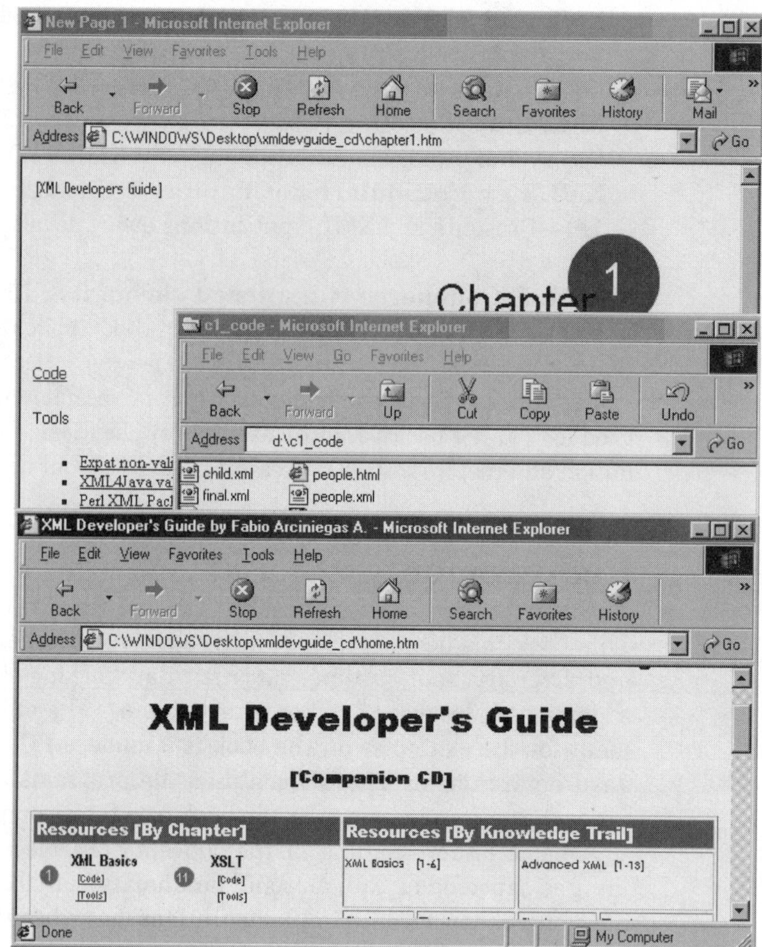

Figure 1
CD contents.

PART 1

XML Structure, Syntax, and Uses

CHAPTER 1

XML Fundamentals

Introduction

This chapter explores the fundamentals of XML as a language. It is an essential chapter to review for some readers, and should be mastered before continuing with the rest of the book. Readers who are particularly experienced, however, or those who already have a solid understanding of XML, should skip this chapter and return if necessary.

The chapter is divided into two parts: one is mostly historical and conceptual background while the other is purely technical. The first part deals with the history and definitions of XML, while the second part dives directly into the syntax and semantics of XML as a language.

De-mystifying Markup

It is not unusual to hear *definitions* of XML such as the following:

- XML is a *subset of SGML*, the Standard Generalized Markup Language.
- XML is a *generalized markup language*.
- XML is a *metalanguage* to create *markup languages*.

One key difference between using buzzword quotations and really mastering a technology is the proper understanding of foundations and terminology. So, before we start, let's review where these definitions come from and how they are really applied to XML.

What is Markup?

Markup is a term applied to any set of codes or tags added to the contents of a document in order to indicate its meaning or presentation.

Pre-markup and Specific Markup Languages

Without markup, documents are limited to the mere presentation of content data. No structure is explicit in the document and any special meaning or process that may be applied to the data must be encoded outside of it.

Markup allows the inclusion of metadata in the document itself. However, this doesn't imply that the document will be semantically richer, or easier to work with, as myriad proprietary markup mechanisms have shown.

Proprietary markup mechanisms have been around for a long time, each adopting different conventions and meanings for the vocabularies they define. Consider for example the piece of RTF (Rich Text Format), shown in Windows WordPad in Figure 1.1.

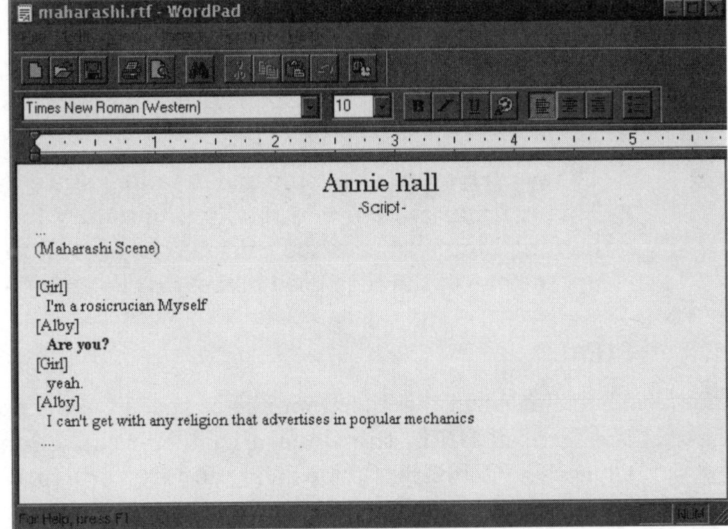

Figure 1.1
A simple document in WordPad.

In order to produce the output that you see in the figure, the RTF document intersperses special markup with the content data, instructing the viewer (WordPad) to perform special actions, such as to show some parts in bold, or start a new paragraph. The following is the source RTF code for the document in Figure 1.1:

```
{\rtf1\ansi\ansicpg1252\deff0\deflang1033{\fonttbl{\f0\froman\fpr
q2\fcharset0 Century Schoolbook;}{\f1\fswiss\fprq2\fcharset0
AvantGarde Bk BT;}{\f2\froman\fprq2\fcharset0 Times New
Roman;}{\f3\fnil\fcharset0 Times New Roman;}}
\viewkind4\uc1\pard\qc\f0\fs28 Annie hall\f1\fs20\par
-Script-\par
\pard\f2 ...\par
(Maharashi Scene)\par
\par
[Girl] \par
I'm a rosicrucian Myself\par
[Alby]\b\par
```

```
Are you?\b0\par
[Girl]\par
yeah.\par
[Alby]\par
I can't get with any religion that advertises in popular mechan-
ics\par
 ....\f1\par
\f3\par
}
```

Non-standardized markup such as the above has many disadvantages:

- Poor problem-domain semantics: The markup shown here is concerned with things like making paragraphs bold and not defining the structure of the dialog. It has nothing to do with the structure of the data.
- The markup is cumbersome and definitely hard to read.
- This markup structure is totally proprietary to a particular application: nothing else uses the conventions of RTF to mark anything else up, so none of the code used to treat RTF can be reused anywhere.

SGML

The solution to the shortcomings of specific markup languages came in the form of GML, the Generalized Markup Language developed by Charles F. Goldfarb, Ed Mosher, and Ray Lorie in 1969.

The ideas brought by GML were seminal:[1]

- Each document type must be able to represent the markup significant to its domain.
- All document types share formalism for the representation of their tags.

The creation of a metalanguage that creates markup languages was the major achievement of the 1970s in terms of text processing. This work was so important it was later formalized as an international standard (ISO 8879): *The Standard Generalized Markup Language* (SGML).

SGML is a metalanguage; it defines a set of rules that apply to all the languages created as applications of SGML. For example, it defines the markup form of tags, how these tags should be nested, etc. By complying with the markup rules defined by SGML, while inventing one's own set

[1] GML and SGML brought many more ideas to the table, including character handling, the notion of entities, etc., which we will discuss later in relation to XML.

of tags, one can create a personalized markup language. Such a language, by virtue of complying with the rules of SGML, will be an *application of SGML*.

The applications of SGML span many industries and purposes. For example, the following two pieces of code show documents that are instances of SGML applications. The first is a document describing the data on the previous movie script (note the semantic improvement here—now a computer can recognize the title of the movie, instead of trying to figure it out by the position of the characters).

```
<script>
    <movie_title>Annie Hall
    <scene number="34">
       <dialog>
            <persona name="Rolling stone Girl">I'm a Rosicrucian
             myself
            <persona name="Alby">Are you?
            <persona name="Rolling stone Girl">Yeah.
            <persona name="Alby">I can't get with any religion
that advertises in popular mechanics
       </dialog>
    </scene>
</script>
```

The second example shows a simple mathematical operation, tagged using SGML:

```
<math_formula>
     <!-- This is a comment -->
     <!-- This SGML document shows one way to tag the expression
     (2+6)*4 -->
    <times>
       <plus><term>2</term><term>6/term></plus>
       <term>4</term>
    </times>
</math_formula>
```

These documents and the applications that process them are significantly different in nature. The first is likely to be used in a system that ends up printing a hard copy of the script, while the second might be the input for a calculating program that computes a numeric result (32). However, both languages share several important rules, including the way the tags are written, and the fact that there is one "root" tag that contains the rest. This has several consequences:

- It permits the reuse of libraries to parse both documents.

- It permits the creation of a common conceptual model, in which a document is created by nested elements.
- It permits the interoperability of the document, as its metadata no longer depend on system-specific additions.

In short, the creation of a metalanguage, with which all languages comply, brings *interoperability* and *reusability* to the world of markup.

HTML

One application of SGML is the most successful markup language in history, HTML. We do not need to discuss what HTML looks like here. It is, however, important to keep in mind that HTML is merely a presentation language, a set of fixed tags designed to tell a browser how to display a page, *not* the structure of the data on the page.

Consider for example an HTML page presenting people data such as the following:

```
<html>
<head>
<title>People</title>
</head>
<body>
<h1>People</h1>

<p><b>Wolfgang Amadeus Mozart (1756-91)</b>
<br>By the age of six Mozart had become an accomplished performer...

<p><b>Cole Porter (1893-1964)</b>
<br>Famous American Composer who...

</body>
</html>
```

Even though this page is suited for rendering on a browser (Figure 1.2), it is totally inappropriate for anything that has to do with the data. There is absolutely nothing in the markup indicating that a certain string is a name, or a date; there are only instructions about setting characters in bold or creating new paragraphs.

If we are to create a database of people out of this document, if we want a computer to easily reorder the elements chronologically, or if we want to do anything else related to the fact that these are data about *people*, we must begin tagging the data in a way that reflects the *structure* of the document.

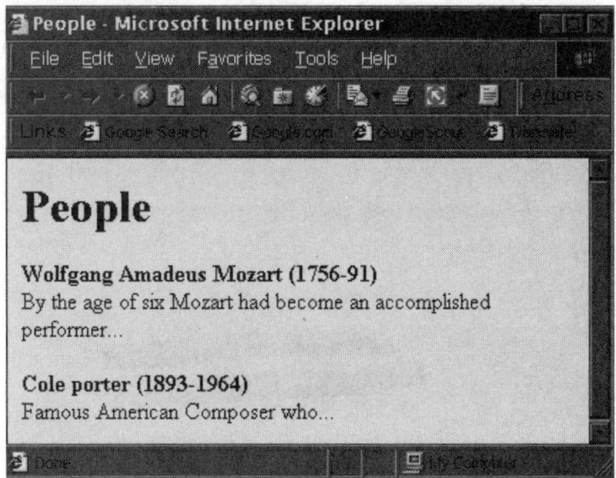

Figure 1.2 HTML output.

What we want is to create our own language, where the tags are representative of our problem domain. With such a language, we could encode the data above in the following way:

```
<people>
   <person>
     <name>Wolfgang Amadeus</name>
     <surname>Mozart</name>
     <born-year>1756</born-year>
     <dead-year>1791</dead-year>
     <description>By the age of six....</description>
   </person>
   <person>
     <name>Cole</name>
     <surname>Porter</name>
     <born-year>1893</born-year>
     <dead-year>1964</dead-year>
     <description>Famous American Composer....</description>
   </person>
</people>
```

As the Web evolves, the need for richer languages, which express the particular needs of industries and individuals, has become apparent. Simple as it is to learn and useful as it has been, HTML fails to represent correctly the structure and semantics of the data needed.

XML

SGML, a generalized markup metalanguage that allows people to create their own tags to describe their own data, was clearly a necessity, but it was too complicated for most purposes. That is why, in September 1998, a special W3C (the World Wide Web Consortium) group headed by Jon Bosak began working on a simplified version of SGML, which could capture most of its power, while avoiding the complications that made it unpopular until then. The result was the eXtensible Markup Language, XML. Colloquially, XML is said to capture 80 percent of SGML power with a mere 20 percent of its complexity. Figure 1.3 shows the evolution of markup languages.

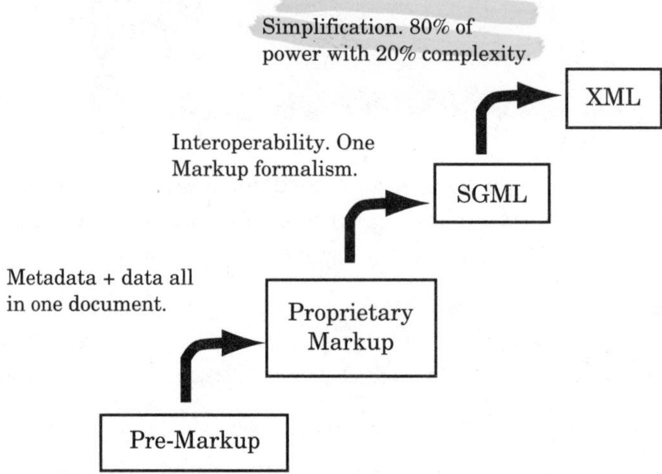

Figure 1.3 The evolution of markup.

XML Defined

As we saw, XML is a metalanguage for constructing markup languages that reflect individual needs. However, different groups see XML in different ways for two main reasons:

- XML uses cover an amazingly wide spectrum of applications. A person using XML to represent relational tables is bound to perceive the language differently from a person using XML for graphic data interchange.
- XML, as a standard, is not alone; it's complemented by numerous other specifications that allow such things as linking, querying, and transformation of XML documents. Depending on whether we refer to the *XML family* of specifications, or to XML 1.0 (just XML), our definitions may vary.

The following paragraphs give several definitions of XML from different points of view. Depending on your interests and problems, you will find some more suitable than others.

A Strict Definition

The eXtensible Markup Language (XML 1.0) is a subset of SGML. It is a metalanguage that describes the concepts and rules for the creation of specific markup languages.

A Web-Oriented Definition

Given more specific standpoints, other, less formal definitions are common. For example, the following is a typical description of the XML family from the Web point of view: XML is the foundation technology for the next generation of the WWW. XML allows for the creation, manipulation, and display of data tagged according to particular domain problems.

A Data-Oriented Definition

From the data standpoint, XML is the ASCII of the new century: an independent, global way to express any kind of information using constructs that can be accommodated to fit particular needs. Because the language shares common structures and concepts, it permits the interoperability and reuse of software that reads them.

A Map of the XML Family

As mentioned before, XML is more than the XML 1.0 specification. An important number of additions have been completed around it. When taken as a whole, they form what is commonly called the XML family.

Some of these additional specifications enhance XML 1.0 to include abilities such as linking, transformations, and advanced data modeling; these will be called *core* or *fundamental specifications*. Some other specifications build sophisticated and widely used markup languages as applications of XML 1.0; these will be called *application specifications*.

Truly understanding XML means acquiring knowledge of the fundamental specifications, as well as some familiarity with the languages in use, plus the skills and guidelines to create your own applications. This book tackles these three goals by guiding you through the XML family of specifications as shown in Figure 1.4.

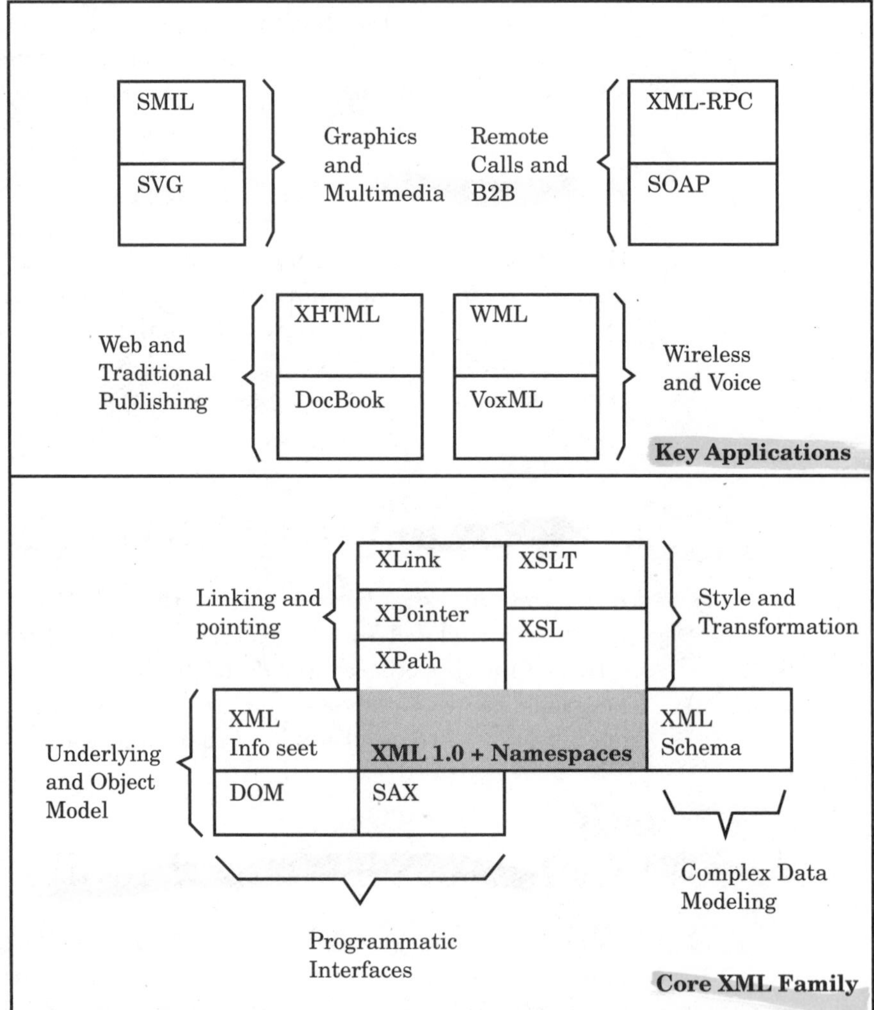

Figure 1.4 A map of the XML family.

Naturally, the place to start our study of this collection of powerful tools is XML 1.0.

XML Syntax and Key Concepts

This section starts our study of the XML language itself. It presents the basic concepts and syntactic constructs of XML.

A Hands-on Introduction

In order to introduce the basic concepts, let's examine the following XML document, which encodes a tiny part of the *Divine Comedy* (Canto V of Inferno) as XML:[2]

```
<?xml version="1.0"?>
<canto number="5">
  <!-- (this is a comment) other verses here -->
  <verse number="34">
  Love, which permits no loved one not to love,
  took me so strongly with delight in him
  that we are one in Hell, as we were above.
  <note>The Temptation of many readers is to interpret the line
  romantically: i.e. that the love of Paolo and Francesca
  survives Hell. The more Dantean interpretation, however, is
  that they add to one another's anguish</note>
 </verse>
 <!-- more verses here -->
</canto>
```

Small as it is, this XML document illustrates instances of almost every important concept for well-formed documents. Let's review each of them in an informal way, before we tackle the precise definitions in the next section.

Elements and Tags

Elements are the basic content unit in XML. They are delimited by tags and may contain other elements or character data. Consider for example the note element inside verse: it is delimited by the *start tag* <note> and the *end tag* </note>, and it contains only character data. Other elements may contain only elements; others will contain nothing at all (*empty elements*), and many others—called *mixed-content elements*—will contain a mixture of both (like the verse element, which contains characters and the note element).

The following lines show examples of the three kinds of elements:

[2] From the John Ciardi translation (Modern Library).

```
<!-- non-empty element with element content -->
<foo>
   <bar>
      <f>
      </f>
   <bar>
</foo>

<!-- empty element -->
<bar/> <!-- this is equivalent to <bar></bar> -->

<!-- mixed-content element -->
<foo>Character data and then <an_element/>, more characters and
then
   <more>
      <and_more>elements</and_more>
   </more>
</foo>
```

Well Formedness: Correct Nesting

The main condition for well formedness is the correct nesting of elements. Simply put, correct nesting means that every element in the document must have its end tag inside the same element where it has its start tag.

The following code shows an example of a non-well-formed document:

```
<foo>
<bar>
</foo>
</bar>
```

The XML Declaration

It is an option for the first line of the XML document to be an XML declaration. The declaration states the version of XML being used, as well as in which character encoding the document is written (see Chapter 2 for a discussion of character encodings). The following document, for example, states that the document is an instance of XML 1.0,[3] written using the very popular UTF-8:

```
<?xml version="1.0"?>
```

[3] There is no version of XML other than 1.0 at present. This is only included for compatibility with future versions (if they ever appear).

XML: A Detailed View

By now, you have a basic notion of how XML documents look. Now it is time to review in detail the concepts and rules behind them.

Document Structure

An XML document is mainly composed of the following parts:

- An optional (and recommended) *prolog*, which includes the XML declaration and document type definition.[4]
- A *root element* (also called *document element*), which contains all other markup and character data in the document.
- An optional (and not recommended[5]) *miscellaneous* collection of comments and other non-element markup after the end of the root element.

Figure 1.5
The document parts.

Prolog
```
<?xml version="1.0"?>
<!DOCTYPE play SYSTEM "play.dtd">
<!-- This is an XMl version of Richard the Second-->
```

Root element (and its contents)
```
<play>
 <title>King Richard the Second</title>
 <author>William Shakespeare</author>
 <published year=1595"/>
 <act number="1">
  <scene number="1">
   <directions>
    Enter King Richard, John of Gaunt, with other nobles
    and attendants
   </directions>
   <!--many more elements with the dialog should go here-->
  </scene>
 </act>
</play>
```

Misc
```
<!-- This is a totaly superfluous comment-->
```

[4] The syntax and uses of the document type definition (DTD) will be explained in Chapter 2. For now, it is enough to understand that there is a mechanism by which a document can explicitly state it belongs to a certain type of document.

[5] The fact that there might be comments and other markup after the end of the root element is commonly regarded as a design error in the XML specification. For most practical purposes (as reflected in the vast majority of documents), one can safely think of an XML document as only prolog + root element.

Some of the available literature will refer to these parts as prolog, body, and epilogue; however, we will use the formal terminology of the XML 1.0 spec for the sake of consistency and clarity.

Text: Character Data + Markup

Physically, an XML document is made out of pieces of text. This text is composed of character data and markup. Instances of the following constructs are considered markup:

- Start tags
- End tags
- Empty element tags
- Attributes
- Comments
- Processing instructions
- CDATA section delimiters
- Entity references
- Character references
- Document type declarations

All text that does not fall in the above categories, is considered character data (Figure 1.6).

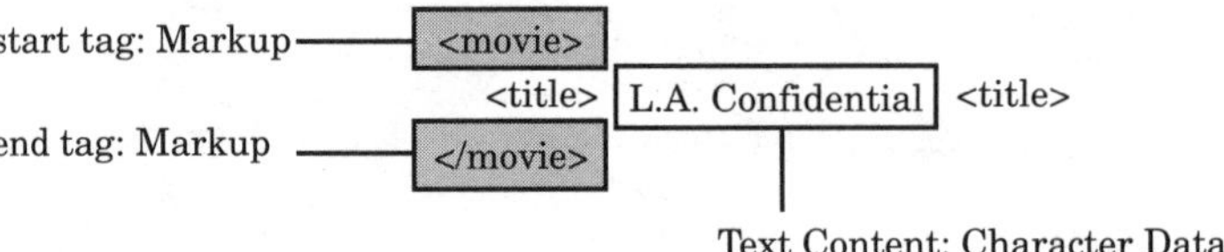

Figure 1.6 A simple case of character data versus markup.

Let's review these constructs one by one and see how they fit in the scheme of our document structure.

Start Tags

Start tags delimit the beginning of a non-empty element. They enclose the name of the element within brackets as follows:

```
<elementTypeName>
```

There are three important things to note about start tags (actually, about tags in general):

- Tags are case sensitive; the following start tags are all different:

```
<Dialog>
<DIALOG>
<dialog>
```

- Tags must start with a letter (for a precise definition of what a letter is, consult the *Characters* section in this chapter) and may be followed by any name character. This includes numbers, but not spaces.
- Tag names are not restricted to ASCII; they can contain any valid name character (as defined in the *Names* section). This includes accented letters and even ideographic characters. The following are examples of valid start tags:

```
<aStartTag>
<españa>
<Σ>
```

End Tags

Every non-empty element must be closed by an end tag. End tags must contain an element type name that exactly matches the one in the start tag. The following examples show the corresponding end tags for the start tags above:

```
</aStartTag>
</españa>
</Σ>
```

Everything between the start tag and the end tag is considered the element's content. This may include character data, other elements, and other types of markup such as processing instructions and comments.

Empty Element Tags

For the special case of elements with no content, such as the following:

```
<an_element_with_no_content></an_element_with_no_content>
```

XML 1.0 has provided an abbreviated mechanism called empty element tags. These contain the name of the element, followed by a slash (/):

```
<an_element_with_no_content/>
```

Attributes

Start tags and empty element tags can be enriched by the use of attributes. Attributes contain data better represented as an aspect, or characteristic of the element, as opposed to a component of the element. Consider for example the problem of marking certain products in a list as sold out. The original list might look as follows:

```
<list>
   <product>
      <manufacturer>ACME</manufacturer>
      <name>Flying Kit</name>
      <description>Rubber-based Flying kit…</description>
   <product>
   <product>
      <manufacturer>ACME</manufacturer>
      <name>Bird Seed</name>
      <description>Toxic Bird Seed…</description>
   <product>
<list>
```

Now we want to mark some of the products as sold out. One alternative is to include an extra element on the content of each product stating this condition:

```
<product>
   <sold_out>yes</sold_out>
   <manufacturer>ACME</manufacturer>
   <name>Flying Kit</name>
   <description>Rubber-based Flying kit…</description>
<product>
```

Another, more sensitive approach, would be to add a `soldOut` attribute to the product element. This will take the form of an attribute name plus attribute value pair in the start tag:

```
<product soldOut="yes">
   <manufacturer>ACME</manufacturer>
   <name>Flying Kit</name>
   <description>Rubber-based Flying kit…</description>
<product>
```

In general, attributes take the form of name-value pairs within start and empty element tags. The value of an attribute is separated from its name by the equals sign (=) and must be enclosed by either single or double quotes (it makes no difference which you ones you use, as long as you use them consistently). The following element illustrates the syntax of attributes:

```
<movie year="1962"
      rated='R'>
   <title>A Clockwork Orange</title>
</movie>
```

There are two additional important issues to highlight about attributes:

- The attribute name must be a letter, followed by any other valid name character, including numbers (see the section on *Names* for a precise definition).
- The attribute value cannot contain either of the characters < or &. These characters are reserved to indicate the beginning of special constructs in XML (elements and references, respectively).[6]

Comments

We have already introduced comments in XML in the examples above. Simply enough, anything between `<!--` and `-->` is considered a comment. Comments may contain any combination of characters except the string --.

The following is a valid example of an XML comment:

```
<!-- Author: Sir Ignace I. Bofa
     Description: A Foucault's Pendulum Dictionary on XML
     $Id: foucaults_pendulum.xml,v 1.1 2000/08/12 02:25:12
     Default Exp $
-->
```

Comments are not part of the document's character data; instead, they are considered markup.

Processing instructions

Even though XML documents are not concerned with *how* they should be treated, but rather with the description of *what* type of data they contain, sometimes it is necessary to instruct the application directly to perform some action or customization.

Traditionally, HTML developers circumvented this problem by abusing the comment mechanism (i.e. wrapping scripts in comments). Now, since the XML 1.0 specification allows, but does not require, the parsers

---

[6] The idea of character and entity references will be presented later in this chapter. For now, you can consider this an arbitrary restriction of the language.

to return XML comments, a particular application cannot rely on comments to pass information to the application. Instead, the processing instruction mechanism must be used.

Processing instructions are very simple syntactically:

```
<?target instruction?>
```

`target` is an arbitrary XML name, used to identify the application to which the *Processing Instruction* (PI) is directed. The `instruction` can be any collection of characters, as long as it doesn't contain the string `?>`, which marks the end of the instruction. The following is an example of a valid PI:

```
<?use_processor "xst"?>
```

Only two important features of PIs are left to mention:

- The semantics of the PIs are not restricted in any way by the XML 1.0 specification.
- Even though the only technically invalid names for targets would be "XML" and any other case combination of the string "xml," it is an extremely poor idea to name PI targets with strings that start with xml, since all such names are reserved for future standard purposes (e.g. the xml-style sheet PI is used to associate a style sheet with a particular document[7]).

CDATA Sections

Sometimes it is necessary to avoid large chunks of text containing markup. Consider, for example, the problem of writing a document that explains the syntax of start tags. At some point, an example will be necessary and you will need to include—as character data, not as markup—a string such as:

```
<example> This illustrates start and end tags syntax </example>
<another_example/>
```

One solution[8] would be to escape the whole block using a CDATA section. CDATA sections are delimited by the strings `<![CDATA[` and `]]>`.

---

[7] See Chapter 15 for examples of this particular PI.

[8] The other solution would be to use character references to escape individual characters such as < to replace <. A complete explanation of character references is included later in this chapter.

Everything between those sections is interpreted and passed to the application as *character data*.

CDATA sections may contain any combination of characters, except of course for the string `]]>`, which delimits the end of the section. CDATA sections *cannot* be nested. The following example shows a valid CDATA section:

```
<![CDATA[<example> This illustrates start and end tags syntax
</example>
<another_example/>]]>
```

After we presented the XML document structure, we mentioned that text is divided between markup and character data. Ten forms of markup were mentioned, six of which have been defined already. Before continuing with the rest of the markup constructs (entity and character references and Document Type Declaration), is important to define precisely the concepts of character, white space, and entity.

Characters and Encodings

One of the most common sources of confusion for new XML users is SML's utilization of Unicode as the standard for characters, and the notion of encodings. In this section we will see these notions in detail.

CHARACTERS VS. GLYPHS

A character is the atomic unit of text. It is an abstract concept, an instance of the *smallest semantic unit in a writing system*.

Glyphs, on the other hand, are the *representations* of characters. There can be many glyphs for a particular character; for example, the character *heh* in Arabic has four very different representations, but they all still refer to the same character. Figure 1.7 shows some of the different glyphs used to represent the letter *e* (a unique character).

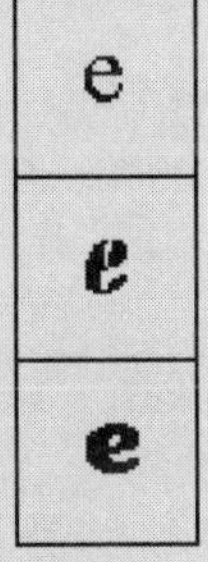

Figure 1.7 Different glyphs for the letter e.

The Unicode and ISO 10646 Standards deal with characters, not glyphs.

ENUMERATING CHARACTERS: UNICODE

The function of the Unicode Standard is simple: provide a unique number for each character, regardless of the platform or language used, thus alleviating the burden brought by the plethora of incompatible and provincial standards of the past (such as the 7-bit ASCII, which can only represent a minuscule portion of the characters in use today).

In order to enumerate all the characters in use, Unicode uses a 16-bit code for each of them, which amounts to 65,535 possible characters. In written media (books, the Unicode Standard, etc.) Unicode characters are often referred to by naming their hexadecimal value; for example, the following figure is an entry from the Unicode standard showing the number of a particular character and a sample glyph for it:[9]

Figure 1.8
A Unicode character point and its sample glyph.

UNICODE ORGANIZATION: BLOCKS

Unicode organizes groups of related characters in blocks. Examples of such blocks are the Greek and Coptic block (from character 0370 to 03FF)[10], mathematical signs block (from 2600 to 26FF), and the Arabic characters block (0600 to 06FF), etc.

An enumeration of each block would be out of place here, but you are welcome to try the Unibook software by the Unicode Consortium, which allows you to navigate each block and character, showing not only character properties such as name, but also sample glyphs that will help you familiarize yourself with the standards. Figure 1.9 shows a snapshot of the tool while displaying a list of all the blocks by name.

---

[9] This character was taken from the Unicode Standard 3.0 book, a must-have book for anyone seriously interested in international development.

[10] The use of extra zeros at the left is only a matter of convention. Simply saying 370 to 3FF would represent the same hexadecimal values.

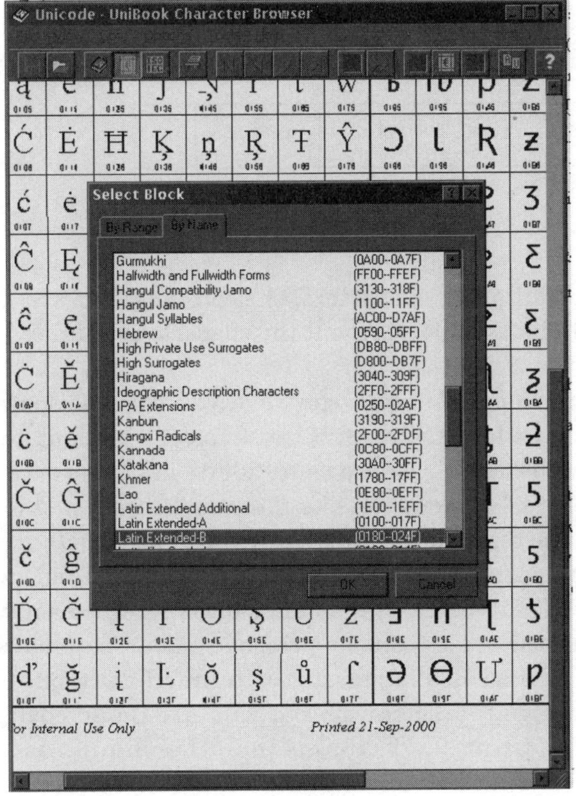

Figure 1.9
Unibook showing the blocks of Unicode.

ENCODINGS: CHARACTER POINTS VERSUS CHARACTER POINTS REPRESENTATIONS

The Unicode Standard defines a unique, 16-bit value for each character, but that does not mean all computer representations of these characters must be 16 bits long. Let us illustrate this with an example: suppose you want to create a representation of Unicode characters but you know you would be using English characters most of the time. ASCII English characters are located at the beginning of Unicode (that is, they have values that go from 0000 to 007F[11]). Such values can be easily represented in only one byte, so you decide to adopt the following conventions:

- If a character is within the values of 0000 and 00F7, it will be represented in only one byte, where the left-most bit is zero and the other 7 bits represent the character value. Thus, in order to represent charac-

[11] 0 to 127 in decimal.

ter number 00F7, we would have a single byte as shown in Figure 1.10.

0	1	1	1	1	1	1	1

Figure 1.10 Representing character 00F7 in a single bit.

- For all other characters, the left-most bit will be 1 and more bytes will be used to represent the character value.

This representation can save you a lot of space if you are dealing mostly with ASCII data, because instead of using two bytes to represent every character, you are using additional bytes only when needed.

A set of conventions like those just mentioned for the representation of character values is commonly called an *encoding*.

XML parsers are only required to understand two encodings: UTF-8 and UTF-16 (UTF stands for Unicode Transformation Format). UTF-8 shares the same economy principle as our example above. It is very useful if you are dealing mostly with ASCII data, but not as ideal for treating foreign characters, since it will take up to 5 bytes to represent a particular point. UTF-16, on the other hand, uses a 16-bit value to represent each 16-bit character.

Many other encodings are available and most parsers will support a wide variety of them. Sticking with UTF-8 or UTF-16, however, might be a good idea, since it ensures the portability of your document across parsers.

UNICODE SURROGATE BLOCKS

Even though 65,535 is a quite a big number, enough to store most of the current characters in the world today, it was clear that it would not be enough to represent all the characters in less-common, but important alphabets such those of some ideographic and dead languages (e.g. Egyptian hieroglyphics).

In order to cope with this problem, Unicode reserves two blocks, called *surrogate blocks* (one from d800 to dbff and the other from dc00 to dfff). Values on these blocks do not represent characters; instead, they are used as the first part of a value that consists of two 16-bit values. In other words, Unicode may represent some characters outside the basic set (called the *Basic Multilingual Plane* [BMP]) by using two 16-bit characters, the first within the surrogate blocks, and the second with an arbitrary value. Characters that use the surrogate blocks are not valid within XML.

Whitespace

Whitespace is defined as any combination of the following characters:

TABLE 1.1
Whitespace characters.

Unicode Character name	Unicode Character number
SPACE	0020
CARRIAGE RETURN	000D
LINE FEED	000A
HORIZONTAL TABULATION	0009

Even though many other characters in the Unicode standard are associated with whitespaces (e.g. 000B for vertical tabulation), only the ones listed in Table 1.1 are considered within XML. The rules for the handling of whitespace are as follows:

- All spaces that are part of the character data must be passed to the application, which will decide whether to keep them, condense them, or ignore them.
- The parser can ignore all spaces within markup. They are, by definition, insignificant whitespaces.

An important consequence of this is the ability to use indentation in XML documents. Consider, for example, the following XML document with two identical elements, one with good indentation (by combining the whitespace characters above) and the other without it.

```
<reviews>
   <movie>
      <name>Eyes Wide Shut</name>
      <review rating="5"
         author="LDM">A powerful movie...</review>
   </movie>
<movie><name>Eyes Wide Shut</name><review rating="5"
author="LDM">A powerful movie</review></movie>
</reviews>
```

Naturally, the readability of the first element is much higher, and while the two elements are syntactically identical, the first option is a much better choice.

THE XML:SPACE ATTRIBUTE

The XML specification allows the inclusion of the special `xml:space` attribute to signify the intention of whitespace within an element. For example, the following element represents a poem's verse,[12] in which whitespace is quite significant. Therefore, the `xml:space` attribute is included with a value of `preserve`, thus hinting to the application about the treatment of whitespace within the element:

```
<verse xml:space="preserve">
   Ein Geschlecht, das mir gleich sei,
   Zu leiden, weinen,
   Geniessen und zu freuen sich,
   Und dein nicht zu achten,
   Wie ich.
</verse>
```

NOTE

For other elements, where there is no need to signal any whitespace preservation intention, the value "default" can be used.

Names

XML names are strings of characters that begin with a letter or an instance of a few punctuation characters (namely _ and :), and continue with any combination of letters, digits, hyphens, underscores, colons, or full stops, together known as name characters. Names beginning with any capitalization variation of "xml" (i.e. "XML", "xMl", etc.) are reserved.

Character references

Character references are the mechanisms by which a particular character may be included in the document, using its numeric value within Unicode. Character references can take two forms:

---

[12] From Goethe's *Prometheus*. A German example was chosen in order to recapture it when we talk about language identification with XML.

- The string `&#` followed by a decimal numeric value and a colon (e.g. @).
- The string `&#x` followed by a hexadecimal numeric value and a colon (e.g. N).

In both cases, the semantics are the same: when a parser encounters a character reference, it must replace it with the appropriate character.

One important use of character reference is the inclusion of characters that are not available in input devices such as keyboards. For example, the following character references,

```
&#x00E5; &#x00BC; &#x00AE;
```

if interpreted with an application that is capable of displaying glyphs for them (e.g. a Web browser[13]) will be transformed to the following characters:

```
å ¼ ®
```

Entity References

For the purposes of this chapter, we will define an entity as a storage unit, a physical collection of data. Entity references allow the inclusion of an entity value in the document. Some of these entities are predefined and recognized by all parsers. Table 1.2 summarizes the predefined entities, their replacement value, and some common uses.

TABLE 1.2 Predefined entities, replacement values, and common uses.

Entity	Replacement	Usage
&	&	Used to escape the ampersand, which would otherwise be interpreted as markup (beginning of a reference)
<	<	Used to escape the < character, which would otherwise be interpreted as the beginning of a tag
>	>	Used to escape the > character, which could be misinterpreted as the end of a CDATA section if it follows the string]]
'	'	Used to escape this delimiter character in string literals such as attribute values
"	"	Used to escape this delimiter character in string literals such as attribute values

[13] One good way to experiment with character references is to create a dummy HTML document and include them. Most modern Web browsers will show you an appropriate glyph.

Back to the Prolog

Now that we have covered all the markup that can appear in the body of the document (i.e. on the root element), it is time to go back to the XML prolog, those important first lines which declare the nature of the document.

The XML prolog is composed of three things:

- The XML declaration
- An optional document type declaration
- An optional set of arbitrary comments and processing instructions

THE XML DECLARATION

The XML declaration indicates explicitly that the document is an XML instance. It is composed of the following three elements:

- A mandatory XML version information, of the form `version="1.0"`.
- An optional *encoding declaration*, stating the name of the encoding used for the document. This declaration takes the form `encoding="encodingName"` (e.g. `encoding="UTF-16"`).
- An optional *standalone declaration*, stating that the document is a self-contained unit, with no markup declarations outside it (more on the standalone declaration will be presented in Chapter 2, after we study DTDs).

The following are correct examples of XML declarations:

```
<?xml version="1.0" encoding="UTF-8" standalone="yes">

<?xml version="1.0"?>
```

Finally, it is important to note that the XML declaration, if it exists, must be at the very beginning of the document.

DOCUMENT TYPE DECLARATIONS

The document type declaration contains or points to the markup declarations that form the Document Type Definition (commonly known as DTD). In order to make this clear, we most first see what a DTD is.

A VERY BRIEF INTRODUCTION TO DTDS

A complete explanation of DTDs is found in Chapter 2, but for the moment we can sketch some of the key concepts behind them. A DTD is a collection of markup declarations, or rules that specify what elements are valid in a particular type of document, how they nest within each other, and what attributes they possess.

For example, the following set of markup declarations state that there can be a `person` element, which may contain only one instance of `name` as well as zero or more instances of the `child` element. The name element may contain only character data:

```
<!ELEMENT person (name,child*)>
<!ELEMENT child (name)>
<!ELEMENT name(#PCDATA)>
```

A valid document, conformant with this DTD (suppose the previous declarations were stored in a file called `person.dtd`) will look like the following:

```
<?xml version="1.0"?>
<!DOCTYPE person SYSTEM "person.dtd">
<person>
   <name>Jacopo Belbo</name>
   <child>
      <name>le nalp</name>
   </child>
</person>
```

The document type declaration (second line of the example above) can point to an external collection of markup declarations (called the external DTD subset) and can include some markup declarations of its own (in what is called the internal DTD subset). The DTD of the document is the union of both subsets.

MISCELLANEOUS CONTENT IN THE PROLOG

An XML document may include arbitrary comments and processing instructions before the root element. These are the third and final component of the XML prolog.

Validity versus Well-formedness

The concept of DTD brings with it one of the most fundamental distinctions among XML documents: well formedness vs. validity. Basically a document is well formed if it follows the syntax rules of the XML specification, and the elements within it are correctly nested and part of a unique root.[14]

---

[14] See Chapter 2 for more formal and complete definitions of validity and well formedness. They require thorough explanations of entities and DTDs.

A document is valid if it is well formed and conforms to the markup declarations of a provided DTD.

PARSERS: VALIDATING VS. NON-VALIDATING

A parser is a piece of software that reads the XML document on behalf of an application. Parsers are either validating and non-validating:

- Non-validating parsers check that the document is well-formed XML.
- Validating parsers also check that the document conforms to a given DTD.

On the companion CD you will find several parsers (both validating and non-validating), as well the instructions for their installation and use. Before you continue to the next chapter, we recommend that you install and test at least one of them.

Putting It All Together: A Sample XML Document

The following code shows a well-formed XML document with instances of all the constructs presented in this chapter. It may serve as a review of the syntax we just covered:

```
<?xml version="1.0" encoding="iso-8859-1"?>
<!DOCTYPE booknotes SYSTEM "booknotes.dtd">
<--
   $Id: foucaults_pendulum.xml,v 1.1 2000/08/12 02:25:12 Default
   Exp $
-->


<booknotes>
   <originalworkinfo>
      <title>Il pendolo di Foucaoult</title>
      <author>Umberto Eco</author>
      <date month="jan" year="1988"/>
   </originalworkinfo>
   <notesinfo>
      <title>English Dictionary to Foucault's Pendulum</title>
      <author>Fabio Arciniegas A.
      &lt;faa@fabioarciniegas.com&gt;</author>
   </notesinfo>
```

```
      <!-- many other entries here -->
      <entry type="term" id="pantarei">
      <name>Panta Rei</name>
      <explanation><p>Panta Rei is a greek expression used by
      <see also="heraclitus">Heraclitus &#x03A8; </see> to
      express the concept of <emphasis>perpetual change</empha-
      sis> in the universe. According with Heraclitus, the only
      constant in the universe is change. Panta Rei means
      "<emphasis>everything flows</emphasis>".</p></explanation>
      <?dictionary "search google for related data"?>
      <!--A sample PI -->
   </entry>
</booknotes>
```

Summary

This chapter presented the background history of markup and the relationship among XML, HTML, and SGML. It also presented the basic constructs of XML, as well as some examples of their use. The tools and concepts discussed here (i.e., the syntax and semantics of well-formed XML documents) are fundamental and will be reused in every chapter, as we explore the whole family of XML specifications and the way they fit together. The following chapter explores DTDs and entities in detail.

CHAPTER 2

DTDs: Features and Techniques

Introduction

In the previous chapter, we explored the fundamentals of XML, showing the components of well-formed documents. In this chapter we will expand that knowledge, presenting the remaining XML notions, focusing on the concept of validity and *Document Type Definitions*.

This chapter is divided in two main sections; the first presents a hands-on explanation of element and attribute declarations, entities. and the rules of validity, and wraps up with a complete example. The second section explores all the details behind each type of declaration while pointing to some of their advanced uses. Several sample DTDs (their code available also on the CD) are provided.

An Introduction to DTDs

Before jumping into formal definitions, it is important that we have a solid understanding of the structure and usage of DTDs.

DTDs and Documents

Document Type Definitions are the means by which we can restrict the structure of a class of XML documents. DTDs specify which components are available for a particular type of document (e.g. a *catalog* document has items, prices, descriptions, etc.) and the way those components can be mixed in order to produce a valid instance (e.g. each item has only one description and one price; there can be many items in a catalog).

A natural analogy for the DTD-document relationship is the relationship between class and object. A class defines the types and names of a certain group of objects. The objects themselves have all types of different data, but they all comply with the rules stated by the class.

The XML 1.0 specification provides the syntax for the creation of DTDs and rules for the behavior of XML parsers that *validate* XML documents against them. In the sections below we will see a practical introduction to DTD construction.

Declaring Elements

Documents—or instances[1]—are mainly composed of elements, therefore the first feature of DTDs we shall explore are *element type declarations*. An element declaration specifies what kind of content a particular element may have.

As an example, let's construct a very simple *film list DTD* that reflects the following design decisions:

- A film list is a collection of films.
- Each film has a name and a director.
- Names and directors contain only raw character data such as "Taxi Driver."

The first requirement can be expressed by the following element declaration:

```
<!ELEMENT film_list (film*)>
```

An element declaration specifies the name of the element and its *content model*, that is, what content is valid inside it. In the above case we stated that a `film_list` may contain zero or more films.

As you have already noted, we specified cardinality by using the asterisk, which, like the other modifiers shown in Table 2.1, retains the semantics that are usually associated with it in regular expressions.

TABLE 2.1
Modifiers.

Modifier	Semantics
*	Zero or more occurrences of the preceding term
+	One or more occurrences of the preceding term
?	Zero or one occurrences of the preceding term (i.e. optionality)

The next requirement is implemented with an element type declaration using *sequences*:

```
<!ELEMENT film (name,director+)>
```

[1] From now on, the two terms will be used interchangeably.

A sequence or list of comma-separated terms, indicates the sequential order of its components. In our case, it means that all films will have one name and at least one director.

Finally, our third requirement (textual content inside name and director elements) is implemented by the following declarations:

```
<!ELEMENT name (#PCDATA)>
<!ELEMENT director (#PCDATA)>
```

`#PCDATA` stands for *parsed character data*: textual content that will be read by the parser and passed to the application (e.g. for rendering). Note that unlike a programming language like Java, XML doesn't strictly specify the kind of textual data that can be included. It is simply PCDATA, not a string, not a number, with no restrictions on its length, or the kind of words that it must contain.[2]

Before we add new requirements, it is important to make a reality check and validate instances of the elements just presented.

Compliant Instances

A compliant instance of the type we just defined is an XML document that looks like the following:

```
<?xml version="1.0"?>
<!DOCTYPE film_list SYSTEM "films-1.dtd">
<film_list>
  <film>
    <name>Taxi Driver</name>
    <director>Martin Scorsese</director>
  </film>
  <film>
    <name>La cité des enfants perdus</name>
    <director>Marc Caro</director>
    <director>Jean-Pierre Jeunet</director>
  </film>
</film_list>
```

Besides the fact that the document complies with the rules specified by the DTD we have created, the only remarkable fact is the use of the *document type declaration*[3] at the prolog of the file. The document type declaration above states three things:

---

[2] This, of course, can turn out to be a real shortcoming for some applications. Later we will see tools and techniques to alleviate this problem.

[3] This is not to be confused with the Document Type *Definition* we just created.

- The intention of the document to be considered a valid instance of some type, not just well-formed XML.
- The type of the root element (`film_list`).
- A pointer to the DTD that specifies the rules for the type. In this case, that pointer comes in the form of a system identifier—including the keyword SYSTEM followed by the quoted name of the file that contains the DTD.

NOTE

Remember that XML is case sensitive, so just as any other keyword, `DOCTYPE` *must be strictly used in capitals.*

Testing the Validity of the Document

While all the XML literature in the world talks about validation, there is little mention of the simple but important process of validating your document in real life. This is a process you will repeat thousands of times, so we'll mention some key tools.

For the purpose of validating documents, you can use the built-in capabilities of any XML editor, or you can use simple applications that internally utilize XML parsers to read a document and output the error messages that occur during the process. Such tools[4] include:

- **SAXCount, Java, and C++ versions**—These simple tools (included with almost every major parser toolkit) are used to count the elements and attributes in a particular document. When used with the `-v` switch they will turn validation on and list any issues with the input files.
- **nsgmls**—This traditional SGML tool by James Clark can be used to do extremely fast XML validation. Use the `-wxml` switch to indicate that you are doing XML validation, not SGML.
- **Validate**—This visual tool is extremely useful for Windows developers.[5] It provides a graphical front end to the parser messages (including highlighting of illegal lines). Figure 2.1 shows Validate at work.

---

[4] See the CD for their installation instructions.

[5] At the time of this writing only Windows versions of Validate are available. However, there are plans for a port to Java.

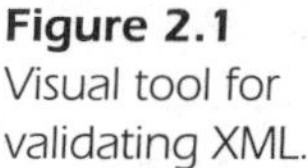

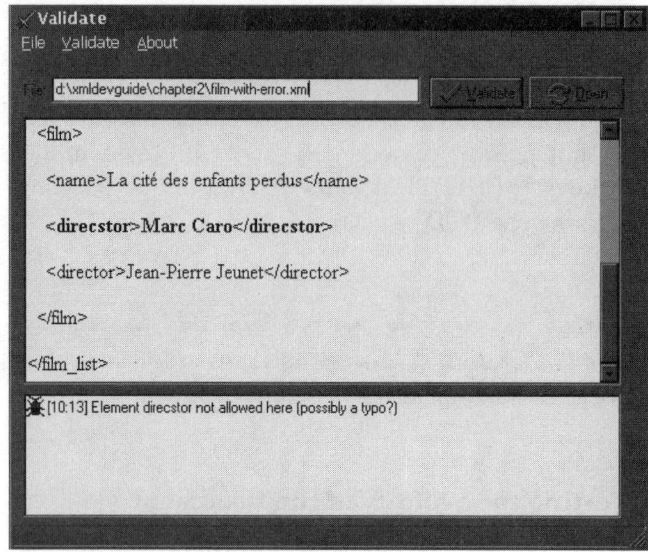

Figure 2.1 Visual tool for validating XML.

Declaring Attributes

So far, we have documented only the use of elements. In order to introduce the use of attributes, we will implement the following two requirements for our existing list:

- Every film must have a unique identifier.
- Every film must have a rating, which must be one of the following values: G, PG, PG13, R, or NC17.

The first item is an interesting requirement that could not be expressed completely if we decided to deal with elements only. Here is why: as you remember, one can just state that an element contains textual data, but there is no way to constrain it any further, so we could only hope that the data inside a hypothetical `id` element is indeed unique, but there would be no check of this on the parsing level.

```
<film>
  <id>1234</id>
  <name>Taxi Driver</name>
  <director>Martin Scorsese</director>
</film>
```

The whole idea of DTDs is to restrict the structure of the documents so they can syntactically reflect our design decisions, enforcing them as much as the DTD syntax allows; trying to implement the first requirement with elements would be a mistake.

Instead, we will use attributes. When we declare an attribute we specify, among other things, its type. In particular, one possible type is `ID`,[6] a unique name ID for the element that contains it.

In order to specify attributes for a particular element, *attribute list declarations* are used. An attribute declaration states which attributes a particular element has, their types, and whether they are required or not.[7] The following attribute list declaration states that the film element has an attribute associated to it, that its name is *identifier* and that it is of type `ID` (i.e. its value is a unique name). It also states that this attribute is required for all the instances of the element.

```
<!ATTLIST film
          identifier     ID     #REQUIRED>
```

As you can see, declaring attributes is as easy as declaring elements. Now let's complete the list with the second requirement: a movie classification attribute.

The first interesting feature of the movie classification attribute is that it can only take values out of a very specific set (PG, PG13, G, R, NC17). For cases like this, the attribute list notation allows the creation of *enumerated types* (a pipe-separated list of the allowable values), such as the one in the following declaration:

```
<!ATTLIST film
          identifier        ID     #REQUIRED
          classification    (G|PG|PG13|R|NC17)     #IMPLIED >
```

The other important fact is that this attribute is optional; that is, not all the instances of the movie element must have one. This is reflected by the keyword `#IMPLIED`.

Finally, we could add a default value for the attribute (i.e. if an element in the document doesn't specify that attribute, the validating parser will act as if there were an instance of it, with a value equal to the default). For our case, let's assume that the value by default is `R`:

---

[6] The complete list of attribute types will be presented later, when we introduce the formal descriptions.

[7] The declarations also can include a default value for the attribute, but since we are talking about an attribute that expresses a unique identifier, it really makes no sense to think of that now.

```
<!ATTLIST film
        identifier      ID    #REQUIRED
        classification  (G|PG|PG13|R|NC17)    "R">
```

So far, if we enhance the director element to have a more refined content, our DTD looks like the following:

```
<!-- A simple DTD for films -->
<!ELEMENT film_list (film*)>
<!ELEMENT film (name,director+)>
<!ATTLIST film
        identifier      ID    #REQUIRED
        classification  (G|PG|PG13|R|NC17) "R" >
<!ELEMENT name (#PCDATA)>
<!ELEMENT director      (firstname,midinitial?,lastname)>
<!ELEMENT firstname     (#PCDATA)>
<!ELEMENT midinitial    (#PCDATA)>
<!ELEMENT lastname      (#PCDATA)>
```

An instance of this document could look like the following:

```
<?xml version="1.0" encoding="iso-8859-1"?>
<!DOCTYPE film_list SYSTEM "films-1.dtd">
<film_list>
  <film identifier="ole" classification="R">
    <name>Taxi Driver</name>
    <director>
      <firstname>Martin</firstname>
      <lastname>Scorsese</lastname>
</director>
  </film>
  <film identifier="enf">
    <name>La cité des enfants perdus</name>
    <director>
      <firstname>Marc</firstname>
      <lastname>Caró</lastname>
    </director>
    <director>
      <firstname>Jean-Pierre</firstname>
      <lastname>Jeunet</lastname>
    </director>
  </film>
</film_list>
```

Now that we have seen the basic syntax for elements and attributes, let's see more about entities and how to make them reusable tools.

Declaring Entities

An XML document is made out of storage units called entities. The basic idea of entities is that they can be defined once and then reused (possibly many times) within the document, as the following examples show.

Entities as Reusable Tools

Suppose we are including every single Stanley Kubrick movie in our XML document. Even though the title for each movie changes, the following elements remain the same for each film:

```
<firstname>Stanley</firstname>
<lastname>Kubrick</lastname>
```

What we will do is create an *internal general entity* that contains these elements and then reference it in our document as many times as we like. The following is the required declaration for the DTD:

```
<!ENTITY  kubrick        "<firstname>Stanley</firstname>
                          <lastname>Kubrick</lastname>">
```

In the document, all we need to do is to create a reference to it, using the notation `&entityname`, as follows:

```
<?xml version="1.0" encoding="iso-8859-1"?>
<!DOCTYPE film_list SYSTEM "films-1.dtd">
<film_list>
  <film identifier="lol">
    <name>Lolita</name>
    <director>&kubrick;</director>
  </film>
  <film identifier="fmj">
    <name>Full Metal Jacket</name>
    <director>&kubrick;</director>
  </film>
  <film identifier="so">
    <name>2001: A Space Odysey</name>
    <director>&kubrick;</director>
  </film>
</film_list>
```

Entitites as Modularity Tools

Since the replacement text of a particular entity can be stored in a different physical unit (i.e. in another file), entities can also be used as a modularization mechanism.

In order to create an *external general entity*, all one needs to do is provide an identifier (either public or local to the system) that can be used to fetch the replacement text for the entity. The syntax is simple and can be illustrated with the following example, which indicates that the replacement text for the entity `foo` can be found in the file `foo.xml`:

```
<!ENTITY foo SYSTEM "foo.xml">
```

In order to put this to work in our example, let's create several files like the following, one for each director we want on the list:

```
<!-- beginning of kusturica.xml -->
  <film identifier="AZ" classification="R">
    <name>Arizona Dream</name>
    <director>
      <firstname>Emir</firstname>
      <lastname>Kusturica</lastname>
    </director>
  </film>
  <film identifier="und" classification="R">
    <name>Underground</name>
    <director>
      <firstname>Emir</firstname>
      <lastname>Kusturica</lastname>
    </director>
  </film>

<!-- end of kusturica.xml -->
```

Using files like this, we have just modularized the document, making it easier to maintain and expand. All that is left now is to declare those files as the replacement text of entities in our DTD, and use them in the document. Here is the final version of the DTD, with the appropriate entity declarations:

```
<!ELEMENT film_list (film*)>
<!ELEMENT film (name,director+)>
<!ATTLIST film
          identifier        ID     #REQUIRED
          classification    (G|PG|PG13|R|NC17) "R" >
<!ELEMENT name (#PCDATA)>
<!ELEMENT director        (firstname,midinitial?,lastname)>
<!ELEMENT firstname       (#PCDATA)>
<!ELEMENT midinitial      (#PCDATA)>
<!ELEMENT lastname        (#PCDATA)>

<!ENTITY  kubrick         "<firstname>Stanley</firstname>
                           <lastname>Kubrick</lastname>">
```

```
<!ENTITY  Emir_Kusturica   SYSTEM "kusturica.xml">
<!ENTITY  Stanley_Kubrick  SYSTEM "kubrick.xml">
```

Finally, provided the existence of the files `kusturica.xml` and `kubrick.xml` (as portrayed above), the XML document will be as simple as the following:

```
<?xml version="1.0" encoding="iso-8859-1"?>
<!DOCTYPE film_list SYSTEM "films-1.dtd">
<film_list>
  &Emir_Kusturica;
  &Stanley_Kubrick;
</film_list>
```

DTDs in Depth

In the previous pages we've provided a hands-on introduction to DTDs. This introduction, though useful, must be complemented by more precise definitions (a complete list of attribute types, a taxonomy of entities, etc.).

Element Type Declarations

An *element type declaration* is composed of a name and a content model specification. It takes the form depicted in Figure 2.2.

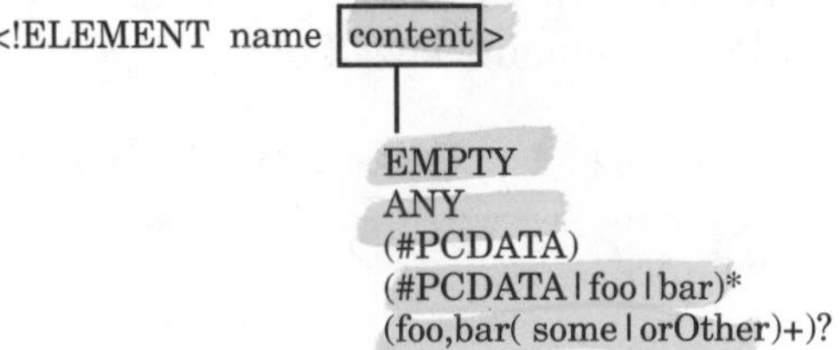

Figure 2.2 Element type declaration structure.

The name of the element must be a correct XML name (i.e. a letter, semicolon, or underscore, followed by any name character); the content model specification must have one of the following forms:

- **EMPTY**—In this case, the element is declared to be an empty one—no content allowed. The following is an example of an element declaration for an empty element:

```
<!ELEMENT cartesian_point EMPTY>
```

and an instance of such an element is:

```
<cartesian_point/>
```

- **ANY**—In this case, the element is allowed to have any element or character data as its content, in any order.[8] Here is an example declaration:

```
<!ELEMENT unorganized ANY>
```

and an example:

```
<unorganized> We are assuming the element <whatever/> was
previously declared
</unorganized>
```

- **(#PCDATA)**—In this case, the only valid content for the element is character data. Here are some declarations:

```
<!ELEMENT emphasis (#PCDATA)>
<!ELEMENT important (#PCDATA)>
```

and an instance:

```
<emphasis> this is some character content with character
references such as &#xd7; and &#00F6; </emphasis>
```

- **"Mixed content"**—In this case, character data can be intermingled with the children elements specified:

```
<!ELEMENT paragraph (#PCDATA|emphasis|important)*>
```

Here is an instance:

```
<paragraph><important>It is important to see that no
particular order is imposed.</important> The content of this
paragraph could very well have started with <emphasis>an
emphasis child</emphasis></paragraph>
```

---

[8] ANY is sometimes a useful construct, but is generally a sign of poor design. The section on DTD design practices and common errors will address this further.

- **"children elements only"**—In this case, only the child elements specified can appear as content of the element. Using parentheses, commas (","), pipes ("|") and the modifiers shown in Table 2-1, the ideas of sequence, alternative, and cardinality can be expressed. Following is a more detailed look:
  - **Sequence in content models**—Sequence is denoted by commas, as in the following example:

```
<!ELEMENT x (a,b,c)> <!--element x must have an element a,
                    followed by a b, followed by a c -->
```

  - **Choice in content models**—Choices are denoted by pipes, as the following declaration shows:

```
<!ELEMENT y (a|b|c)> <!--element x must have an element a,
                    or an element b, or a c -->
```

  - **Combining choice and sequence**—It is possible to combine both sequence and choice, as in the following example, in which **x** can have either a **y** or a **z**, followed by a **d**, followed by either:

```
<!ELEMENT x ((y|z),v,(y|z))>
<!ELEMENT y EMPTY>
<!ELEMENT z EMPTY>
<!ELEMENT v EMPTY>
```

    The following `x` elements are all conformant with the declaration:

```
<x><y/><v/><y/></x>
<x><z/><v/><y/></x>
<x><z/><v/><z/></x>
```

  - **Modifying models with *, +, and ?**—In order to express the idea of cardinality, we must use these three modifiers. `?` stands for "zero or one instances" (i.e. optional), `*` stands for "zero or more," and `+` stands for "one or more." Some examples will clarify their use:

```
<!ELEMENT section1 (section2+,comments*)>
<!-- A section one must have at lease one section2, after
  which, it may have zero or more comments -->

<!ELEMENT section2 (paragraph|note)*>
<!-- A section two is composed by any number of
  paragraphs and notes -->
```

```
<!ELEMENT note (author?,(rant|cheer)+)>
```

NOTE

A `note` *can be anonymous. It must have at least one* `rant` *or* `cheer`*, followed by any number of other items.*

The following is a compliant instance of the `section1` element:

```
<section1>
    <section2>
      <paragraph>The Earth Is Round</paragraph>
      <note>
      <author>Cristopher Columbus</author>
      <cheer>Sure. you can get to Asia from Spain
      by going around it.</cheer>
      </note>
    </section2>
    <comments>No comments &#x263A;.</comments>
  </section1>
```

In this section we have covered all the varieties of element declarations specified by XML 1.0. Exhaustive as this list is, there are some final points that are worth mentioning, because even though they can be deduced from the above, they are not always evident.

Some Final Remarks about Content Models

The following points should be noted about element declarations.

LIMITATIONS OF MIXED CONTENT

Note that content models (aside from `EMPTY` and `ANY`) can only specify a combination of children, or have mixed content, with no particular order between the markup and the character data. There is no middle point where one can define a certain order between the markup and the characters of a particular element. In other words, it is not possible to do a declaration such as the following:

```
<!ELEMENT aWrongElement (anElement,(#PCDATA|b))>
<!-- This is wrong -->
```

At first, this may seem an unnecessary restriction, perhaps an oversimplification. But the history of SGML has taught us that allowing any other mechanism of controlling mixed elements can be costly.

LIMITATIONS OF CARDINALITY

Note that there are important restrictions to cardinality. There is no easy mechanism to specify that an element should, say, appear fewer than 20 times in a document, or more than 3 times in a particular element, or any other refined restriction beyond the broad ones already mentioned (zero or one, one or many, zero or many).

For most applications, this restriction is not a crucial one and, provided good documentation, it is quite easy to overcome. However, for some applications that really need a syntactic check of more specific cardinality, it can become a problem; in that case it is necessary to implement a type definition mechanism beyond DTDs.[9]

LIMITATIONS OF CONTENT TYPE

Perhaps the most evident shortcoming of DTDs is the lack of typing for character data. There is no way to specify that the content of an element is going to be a decimal number, or a certain type of string (e.g. a phone number); there is only `#PCDATA`.

This problem has two consequences. Since there is no syntactic on the character data, an element intended for a particular purpose may be misused in a way not checkable by the parser. Take, for example, the following elements:

```
<phone>202-463-2222</phone>
<phone>Are African sparrows migratory?</phone>
```

Even though the misuse of the phone elements is evident here to us, this is purely a semantic issue. From the perspective of the parser, both elements are equally valid and conformant with the element declaration:

```
<!ELEMENT phone (#PCDATA)>
```

The problem of stronger syntactic enforcement on character data is one of the motivators of XML schemas. Before jumping to them, however, we must take into account that DTDs are the one and only type definition mechanism specified in XML 1.0, and the benefits of their widespread use and support must be weighed against their shortcomings.

The second problem imposed by the lack of stronger character restrictions is related more to us. DTDs not only serve as syntactic restrictions,

---

[9] Chapter 13, XML schemas, treats this problem. Schemas are a much more complex (and less universal) way to specify document type rules.

but they are also a tool that helps us communicate about the purpose of a particular type. If we are able to specify a more significant name for #PCDATA (even if no particular check is really enforced), we can tremendously improve the readability and usability of a document type.

In order to achieve that aliasing of #PCDATA, we use parameter entities. The complete concept and syntax of entities will be explained in their own section, but for now, let's just illustrate with an example of how one may overcome the readability problem of #PCDATA by using correct documentation and entities:

```
<!--
    A DTD for expressing data about the U.S. public debt
-->

<!ENTITY % float      "#PCDATA">
<!ENTITY % integer    "#PCDATA">

<!ELEMENT points (point+)>
<!ELEMENT point  (year,debt)>

<!ELEMENT year   (%integer;)>
<!ELEMENT debt   (%float;)> <!-- The value of the national debt
                                 in billions of dollars -->
```

The following instance, of course, would have been just as valid if we had used simple #PCDATA (i.e. <!ELEMENT debt (#PCDATA)>), but the readability improvements to the DTD are evident.

```
<?xml version="1.0"?>
<!DOCTYPE points SYSTEM "debt.dtd">
<points>
  <point>
    <year>1845</year>
    <debt>2.68</debt>
  </point>
  <point>
    <year>1919</year>
    <debt>25.5</debt>
  </point>
  <point>
    <year>1944</year>
    <debt>260.12</debt>
  </point>
  <!-- better stop here...
       by the 1980s it was already a trillion
   -->
</points>
```

Now that we have thoroughly analyzed element declarations, we'll complement them with attribute lists.

Attribute List Declarations

Attribute lists define which attributes may be associated with a particular element. For each attribute, they specify a name, a type, whether the attribute is optional, required, or fixed, and possibly a default. The general structure is shown in Figure 2.3. The complete details are explained below.

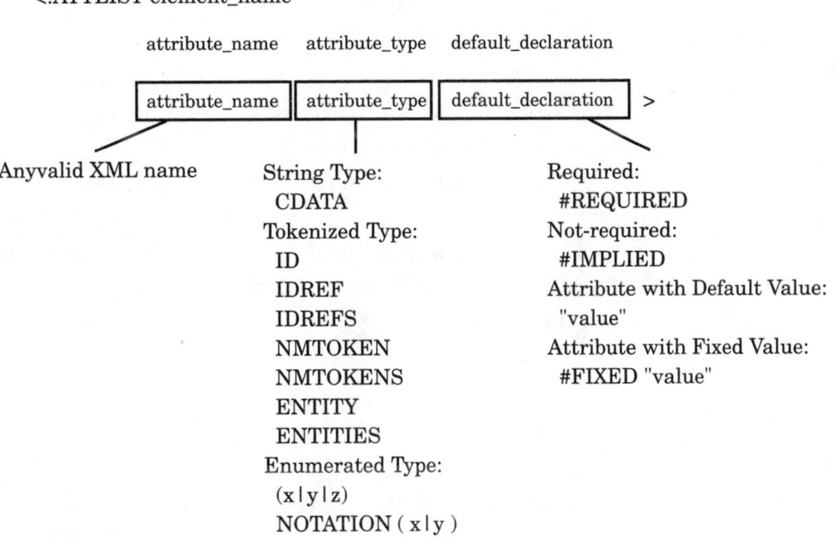

Figure 2.3
Element declaration structure.

Attribute Names

Attribute names share the same restrictions as any other name in XML: they must start with either a letter or one of a few punctuation signs (_ or :) and be followed by name characters, which include the digits, point, hyphen, underscore and letters.

The following are all examples of valid attribute names:

```
point
volonté
xmlns  (since it begins with xml, it is a reserved name)
λ
xmlns:ψ
```

Attribute Types

Figure 2.3 shows how an attribute list is constructed of triplets that are associated to a certain element name. The second component of the triplet, the topic of this section, is the attribute type, an important yet somewhat obscure aspect of XML.

If you are only interested in a basic knowledge of XML, you probably want to skip the details about attribute types (just make sure you read about string types, ids, and idrefs).

Attribute types can be categorized in three groups:

- String type
- Enumerated types
- Tokenized types

STRING TYPE

The easiest and probably most common type of attribute is the *String type*. A String type attribute can have as a value, any string, as long as it doesn't include the characters `<` or `&` (which are reserved to delimit the beginning of tags and entity references, respectively).

The following piece of DTD shows an element declaration for the element `country` and an attribute list declaration with a required string attribute called `population`:

```
<!ELEMENT country (#PCDATA)>
<!ATTLIST country
          population CDATA #REQUIRED>
```

An instance of this element could be:

```
<country population="3617104">
      Lithuania (Lietuvos Respublika)
</country>
```

or:

```
<!ELEMENT cartesian_point EMPTY>
<!ATTLIST cartesian_point
          x CDATA #REQUIRED
          y CDATA #REQUIRED>
```

with the instance:

```
<cartesian_point x="3.4" y="2"/>
```

ENUMERATED TYPES

Enumerated types are tremendously useful when one needs to represent data that can only take values from a small set of possibilities. Examples for such values are data such as priorities (i.e. only a value from 1 to 5), boolean values (yes, no), and flag values (soldOut, onRequest, preOrder).

Enumerated Types explicitly state the set of possible values an attribute may take. Each attribute is a `nmtoken`, an arbitrary string whose only restriction is to be composed of name characters (that is, tokens that need not to start with a letter).

The following example shows an attribute list for an `email` element, adding an attribute priority with the possible values `high`, `normal`, and `low`:

```
<!ATTLIST email
          priority ( high | normal | low )  #required>
```

An instance of this element mail looks like the following:

```
<email priority="high">
  <to>leni@riefenstahl.com</to>
  <from>faa@thefaactory.com</from>
  <content>&#x2665;</content>
</email>
```

NOTATIONS

There is another type of enumerated attribute type, the notation enumeration. Before we can tackle it, we must understand the concept of notation. This is a fairly advanced and somewhat infrequent feature, so please feel free to consider this section optional.

Notations are a way to identify by name a non-XML format. They are used to inform the parser about the type of data a part of the document contains or points to. One very common example would be the declaration of a JPEG notation that is later used to inform the parser that a certain piece of data is a JPEG graphic file.

As mentioned before, a notation is nothing but a name for a particular type or application. The following `notation` declaration shows how to describe a notation for each version of VRML:

```
<!NOTATION vrml2 PUBLIC "VRML 2">
<!NOTATION vrml1 PUBLIC "VRML 1">
```

This notation can later be used in a *notation enumeration* in order to signify that the content of the element is not only text, but it is text of a special kind. Following is the declaration:

```
<!ATTLIST three_dimensional_map
          type NOTATION (vrml1 | vrml2) #REQUIRED>
```

Using instances of this declaration, a `three_dimensional_map` element will be able to announce what type of VRML is the character data it contains. In order to see this clearly, please review the complete DTD that follows:

```
<!NOTATION vrml2 PUBLIC "VRML 2">
<!NOTATION vrml1 PUBLIC "VRML 1">


<!ELEMENT country (#PCDATA|three_dimensional_map)*>
<!ATTLIST country
          population CDATA #REQUIRED>

<!ELEMENT  three_dimensional_map  (#PCDATA)>
<!ATTLIST  three_dimensional_map
           type NOTATION (vrml1 | vrml2) #REQUIRED>
```

and the instance:

```
<?xml version="1.0"?>
<!DOCTYPE country SYSTEM "country.dtd">
<country population="3617104">
   <three_dimensional_map type="vrml2">
   ElevationGrid {
   xDimension 6
   zDimension 6
   xSpacing 5.0
   zSpacing 5.0
   height [ 1.5, 1, 0.5, 0.5, 1, 1.5,
            1, 0.5, 0.25, 0.25, 0.5, 1,
            0.5, 0.25, 0, 0, 0.25, 0.5,
            0.5, 0.25, 0, 0, 0.25, 0.5,
            1, 0.5, 0.25, 0.25, 0.5, 1,
            1.5, 1, 0.5, 0.5, 1, 1.5]
   }
   ... and all the rest of the vrml document
   </three_dimensional_map>
</country>
```

Notation enumerations are a useful, yet rarely used type of attribute. Rare as they may be, keep them in your toolbox, because they can make a big difference between professional DTDs and under-specified first approximations.

TOKENIZED TYPES

Tokenized types are the last main group of attribute types. The following particular types are considered part of the tokenized type group:

- ID
- IDREF
- ENTITY
- ENTITIES
- NMTOKEN
- NMTOKENS

ID

IDs are one of the (if not *the*) most useful tokenized types. They are names (with the restrictions mentioned before) that cannot be repeated as values of another ID element. In other words, ID values uniquely identify the elements that hold them.

The following example shows a document type that makes use of ID attributes to identify entries in a list of artists:

```
<artist_list>
  <artist id="mondigliani">
    <name>
      <firstname>Amedeo</firstname>
      <lastname>Mondigliani</lastname>
    </name>
    <bio>Along with two other Jewish artists émigrés,
    (Chaim Soutine and Marc
    Chagall), Mondigliani appeared in Paris in the dawn of the
    century... </bio>
  </artist>
  <artist id="picasso">
    <name>
      <firstname>Pablo</firstname>
      <lastname>Picasso</lastname>
    </name>
    <bio>No comments.</bio>
  </artist>
</artist_list>
```

IDREF

An IDREF must be a name that matches some name specified as an ID of another element. It is often used to create relationships/pointers between elements. The following code extends the artist example to show the use of IDREF.

```
<!ELEMENT artist      (name,bio,influenced*)>
<!ATTLIST artist
          id            ID       #REQUIRED>

<!ELEMENT influenced     EMPTY>
<!ATTLIST influenced
          by            IDREF      #REQUIRED>

<!-- Rest of the DTD just as above -->
```

Here is a modified instance example that makes use of the `influenced` element. (The application that uses this document could use it, for example, to show a clickable link between Mondigliani and Picasso.)

```
<?xml version="1.0" encoding="iso8859-1"?>
<!DOCTYPE artist_list SYSTEM "artists.dtd">
<artist_list>
  <artist id="mondigliani">
    <name>
      <firstname>Amedeo</firstname>
      <lastname>Mondigliani</lastname>
    </name>
    <bio>Along with two other Jewish artists émigrés,
    (Chaim Soutine and Marc
    Chagall), Mondigliani appeared in Paris in the dawn of the
    century... </bio>
  </artist>
  <artist id="picasso">
    <name>
      <firstname>Pablo</firstname>
      <lastname>Picasso</lastname>
    </name>
    <bio>No comments.</bio>
    <influenced by="mondigliani"/>
  </artist>
</artist_list>
```

NMTOKEN AND NMTOKENS

`NMTOKEN` attribute values must be name tokens, that is, arbitrary strings of characters without spaces within them.

Since `NMTOKENs` do not have the starting restrictions imposed on names (start with a letter), the following declaration and instances are perfectly valid:

```
<!ELEMENT born          EMPTY>
<!ATTLIST born
          year           NMTOKEN       #REQUIRED>
```

Instance:

```
<born year="1934"/>
```

In the case of NMTOKENS, the value of the attribute must simply be a list of NMTOKENs separated by white space. The following declaration and instance show an example:

```
<!ELEMENT livedin       EMPTY>
<!ATTLIST livedin
          city          NMTOKENS      #REQUIRED>
```

ENTITY AND ENTITIES

These are the less-known and less-used types of elements in XML 1.0. However, they can sometimes be useful if you want to create pointers to non-XML data outside your document (e.g., a graphic) and be very precise about its nature.

The idea behind ENTITY values is simple: they must correspond to the name of an unparsed entity previously declared. They are simply pointers to predeclared non-XML data.

In order to use entity names as values in ENTITY-type attributes,[10] one must undergo four steps:

- Declare a notation that describes the format.
- Declare an unparsed entity that uses that format.
- Declare an attribute of type ENTITY.
- Use an instance of that declaration to insert the name of the unparsed entity, creating an explicit relation between the document and the entity.

The following declaration shows the first three steps:

```
<!NOTATION jpeg  PUBLIC "JPEG">
<!ENTITY unicorn
      SYSTEM "http://www.thefaactory.com/unicorn.jpg" NDATA jpeg>
<!ENTITY dragon
       SYSTEM "http://www.thefaactory.com/dragon.jpg" NDATA jpeg>

<!ELEMENT mythologicalAnimal (#PCDATA)>
<!ATTLIST mythologicalAnimal
       image ENTITY #REQUIRED>
```

---

[10] The only advantage of doing this as opposed to having character data that state the name of the file you want, is that the parser could know the type of the data, because it was previously specified by a notation.

The actual instance shows the fourth:

```
<mythologicalAnimal image="dragon"/>  <!-- Valid -->
<mythologicalAnimal image="unicorn"/> <!-- Valid -->
<mythologicalAnimal image="banshee"/> <!-- Invalid, no such
entity -->
```

Naturally, some applications will do better with just CDATA stating the name of the file, and leaving the responsibility of finding the type to the application (or to an agreement). But knowing the existence of the language features is always a benefit.

The case of the `ENTITIES` type is analogous to that of `NMTOKENS`; they must contain a whitespace-separated list of names identifying predeclared unparsed entities.

Attribute Default Declarations

Taking another look at Figure 2.3, we see that two-thirds of all the details behind attribute lists have been covered. Now we must see that last component, the *attribute default declaration*.

The attribute default declaration is used to define whether an attribute is required or not, if it has a default value, or if it has only a fixed value. The possible forms of the declarations are:

- **#REQUIRED**—The attribute is required. Every instance of the enclosing element must have this attribute.
- **#IMPLIED**—The attribute can be omitted.
- **"default"**—The attribute may or may not appear in the element. If it doesn't explicitly appear, the parser will act as if it would have appeared with this value.
- **FIXED "value"**—The attribute must always have this value.

The following attribute declaration presents each case:

```
<!ELEMENT dvd (#PCDATA)>
<!ATTLIST dvd
          id        ID              #REQUIRED
          features  NMTOKENS        #IMPLIED
          rating    (G|PG|PG13|R)   "R"
          onStock   CDATA           #FIXED "yes">
```

The following instance conforms to the declaration:

```
<dvd id="timNBC"
```

```
features="widescreen english spanish"
rating="PG"
onStock="yes">The Nightmare Before Christmas</dvd>
```

Single or Double Quotes

It is worth noting that there is no difference between using single or double quotes to delimit attribute values (as long as you are consistent, of course).

A Closer Look at Entities

So far we have explored elements, attributes, and notations. We have also touched on the concept of *entity*, a physical and reusable container of data, usable as part of an XML document. In this section we will see a taxonomy of entities, their declarations and uses.

Types of Entities

Entities can be classified either by the way a parser looks at them (parsed or unparsed) or by their function (parameter entities or general entities). Furthermore, general entities, that is, pieces of text that can be reused inside the document, can be divided into internal and external entities. Before getting to the details of each, let's see this classification in Figure 2.4.

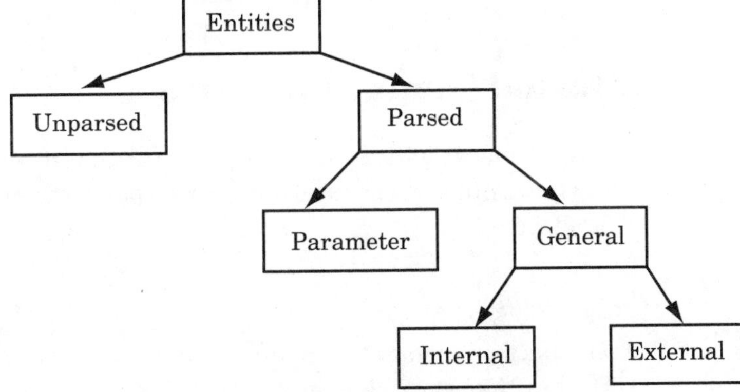

Figure 2.4 A taxonomy of entity types.

External General Entities

External general entities are pieces of text that can be replaced *inside the document*. They mainly serve as modularization mechanisms, since they allow the contents of a document to be spread among many physical pieces (files).

Declaration

A general external entity is declared in one of the following forms:

- `<!ENTITY name  SYSTEM "systemID">`
- `<!ENTITY name  PUBLIC "publicID" "systemID">`

`SystemID` identifies the entity by directly pointing to it (i.e. by saying the name of the file or giving a URL to it). `PublicID`s, on the other hand, use well-known arbitrary strings that must be resolved to system identifiers (e.g. using a catalog).

The following example declares the `products` external general entity:

```
<!ENTITY  products SYSTEM "products.txt">
```

Usage

The use of external general entities is simple; they are referred to by name at any point within the document (naturally, it only makes sense to put them where the content will not ruin the well-formedness of the document):

```
<?xml version="1.0" encoding="iso8859-1"?>
<!DOCTYPE dvds SYSTEM "dvds.dtd">
<dvds>
   &products;
</dvds>
```

Internal General Entities

Internal general entities can also be replaced at any point in the document, but unlike their external counterparts, their definition is inside the DTD itself.

Declaration

Since the replacement text of internal general entities is inside the DTD, they take the following form:

```
<!ENTITY name   "replacement text">
<!ENTITY version "$Id 1.0 'baseline 1'$">
```

Usage

This type of entity, as the examples in this book will show, is extremely useful for improving modularization and reusability in XML documents. The syntax for their use is identical to that of any other general entity:

```
&name;
&version;
```

Unparsed Entities

In order to use unparsed entities, one must go through the process of declaring a notation for them, and then use an entity attribute. The details are explained in the `ENTITY` attributes section.

Parameter Entities

Parameter entities are the main readability and reusability enablers in DTD creation. They allow you to name pieces of text that can be reused inside the DTD, not the document, thus enabling aliasing of XML types and the reuse of pieces of content models, etc.

Declaration

Parameter entities are declared using the following syntax:

```
<!ENTITY % name     "replacement text">
```

Usage

Parameter entities can be used only within the DTD. References to them take the following form:

```
%name;
```

Example

Suppose you have many elements that need a month attribute. Instead of retyping in all of them an enumerated type with the names of months, you can easily modularize it using parameter entities:

```
<!ENTITY % months_att      "(jan|feb|mar|apr|may|jun|
                             jul|aug|sep|oct|nov|dec|
                           1|2|3|4|5|6|7|8|9|10|11|12)">
<!ELEMENT born_date EMPTY>
<!ATTLIST born_date
          %months_att;>
<!ELEMENT dead_date EMPTY>
<!ATTLIST dead_date
          %months_att;>
```

We improved not only readability, but also maintainability. Now any change in the month representation can be easily performed in only one place.

Since parameter entities are so important for DTD construction, the following section shows a library of them which you can reuse in your own DTDs (this is also included on the companion CD).

A Useful Collection of Parameter Entities

```
    <!ENTITY % string_att      "CDATA">
    <!ENTITY % letter_att      "CDATA">
    <!ENTITY % number_att      "CDATA">

    <!ENTITY % string          "#PCDATA">
    <!ENTITY % character       "#PCDATA">
    <!ENTITY % letter          "#PCDATA">



<!-- ***** Parameter entities and elements for date
representation ***** -->

    <!ENTITY % year_att        "CDATA">
    <!ENTITY % day_att         "CDATA">
    <!ENTITY % months_att      "(jan|feb|mar|apr|may|jun|
                                jul|aug|sep|oct|nov|dec|
        1|2|3|4|5|6|7|8|9|10|11|12)">

    <!ENTITY % description     "#PCDATA">

    <!ELEMENT date             (%description;)>
    <!ATTLIST date
         day    %number_att;        #IMPLIED
         month  %months_att;       #IMPLIED
         year   %number_att;        #REQUIRED>
```

```
    <!ATTLIST date
           year       %year_att;          (%description;)>

    <!ELEMENT datefrom              (#PCDATA)>
    <!ATTLIST datefrom
        day    %number_att; #IMPLIED
        month  %months_att;   #IMPLIED
        year   %number_att;   #REQUIRED>

    <!ELEMENT dateto              (#PCDATA)>
    <!ATTLIST dateto
        day    %number_att;   #IMPLIED
        month  %months_att;   #IMPLIED
        year   %number_att;   #REQUIRED>


<!-- ***** Parameter entities and elements for time
representation ***** -->

    <!ENTITY % sec_att       "CDATA">
    <!ENTITY % mili_att      "CDATA">
    <!ENTITY % min_att       "CDATA">
    <!ENTITY % hour_att      "CDATA">

    <!ELEMENT time           (%description;)>
    <!ATTLIST time
        hour    %hour_att;       #IMPLIED
        min     %min_att;      #IMPLIED
        sec     %sec_att;        #IMPLIED
        mili    %mili_att;       #IMPLIED>

<!-- ***** Parameter entities for common Language Attributes
***** -->
<!-- Use inside ATTLIST declarations -->

    <!ENTITY % english_def "xml:lang    NMTOKEN    'en'">
    <!ENTITY % french_def  "xml:lang    NMTOKEN    'fr'">
    <!ENTITY % german_def  "xml:lang    NMTOKEN    'ge'">


<!-- ***** Parameter entities and elements for text-oriented
problems ** -->
    <!ELEMENT p           (#PCDATA|emphasis|important)*>
    <!ELEMENT emphasis    (#PCDATA)>
    <!ELEMENT important   (#PCDATA)>


<!-- ***** Parameter entities and elements for name
representation ***** -->

    <!ELEMENT name          (firstname,midinitial?,lastname)>
    <!ELEMENT firstname     (%string;)>
    <!ELEMENT midinitial    (%letter;)>
```

```
     <!ELEMENT lastname       (%string;)>
     <!ATTLIST name
             %english_def;>

<!-- ***** Parameter entities and elements for simple links *****
-->
     <!ELEMENT a              (ANY)>
     <!ATTLIST a
          xlink:type (simple)  #FIXED   "simple"
          xlink:href CDATA     #REQUIRED
       %languageattribute;>


<!-- ***** Parameter entities and elements for images ***** -->
     <!ELEMENT img        (#PCDATA)>
     <!ATTLIST img
             xmlns:xlink CDATA
"http://www.w3c.org/1999/XLink"
             xlink:type  (simple)  #FIXED   "simple"
             xlink:href  CDATA     #REQUIRED>
```

Conditional Sections

One final advanced feature of DTDs is the use of conditional sections. Conditional sections allow you to include/exclude chunks of the DTD by enclosing them in the following special markup:

```
<![INCLUDE[
<!-- this section of DTD gets included -->
<!ELEMENT foo (bar)>
]]>

<![IGNORE[
<!-- this section of DTD does not get included -->
<!ELEMENT bar (foo)>
]]>
```

Internal and External DTD Subsets

All the examples in this chapter assumed the complete DTD was on a separate file, which was referred to by the document using either a public or system identifier (i.e. `<!DOCTYPE x SYTEM "s.dtd">` or `<!DOCTYPE y PUBLIC "..." "s.dtd">`).

The truth of the matter is that this is only a special (though very common) method. The general method encompasses two subsets of the DTD:

one is the *external subset*, defined in another file and referred to via the doctype declaration, and the other, an *internal subset*, enclosed in brackets in the doctype declaration itself.

They both contain the same type of data (declarations) but generally the internal subset includes declarations that are less general (more document oriented) than those in the external subset. The following document expands the example in the first section to show the use of both subsets:

```
<?xml version="1.0" encoding="iso-8859-1"?>
<!DOCTYPE film_list SYSTEM "films-1.dtd"
[
<!ATTLIST film_list
          author  CDATA #IMPLIED>
<!ENTITY document_author  "Uther P."> <!-- very local -->
]>
<film_list author="&document_author;">
  &Emir_Kusturica;
</film_list>
```

Summary

This chapter presented the syntax, rationale, and techniques for DTDs in XML. DTDs allow the creation of valid documents, with stronger checks than mere well-formed instances. DTDs present certain limitations, some of which can be fixed by correctly documenting the document and using features such as parameter entities. Other limitations require the use of more powerful formalisms.

Knowing DTDs is of paramount importance since they are the mechanism for type definition in XML 1.0. But other techniques may be needed for complex problems with very precise data representation requirements. Chapter 13 continues this discussion with the presentation of XML schemas.

CHAPTER 3

Namespaces and Introduction to XML Processing

Introduction

This is in part a transitional chapter. It combines Parts 1 and 2 (XML structure and XML processing) by presenting the last advanced feature of XML as a language—namespaces—and then uses it to explain the history and basics of XML manipulation.

Namespaces

Definition and Example

Reuse is one of the key goals of software engineering; it is pervasive in all mature technologies and languages in one way or another (e.g. as function libraries in procedural languages like C, as classes in OO, even as patterns in software design).

As XML grew, the need to reuse *markup vocabularies* (i.e. particular combinations of elements and attributes) became apparent. However, as we will illustrate, the XML 1.0 specification lacked the mechanisms to support—in a standard way—the mixture of dialects.

To see the difficulties imposed by the use of multiple vocabularies, consider the following example, the creation of a music review system on top of an XML vocabulary for the description of CDs. Imagine you already have a vocabulary for the description of CDs. A file compliant with that vocabulary may look like the following:

```
<?xml version="1.0"?>
<!DOCTYPE cd_collection SYSTEM "cd.dtd">
<cd_collection>
  <title xml:space="preserve">A sample cut of a CD
collection</title>
  <cd id="a9362-43515-2">
    <title xml:space="preserve">In our sleep</title>
    <author>Laurie Anderson &amp; Lou Reed</author>
    <producer>Brian Eno</producer>
    <year>1995</year>
    <track number="1">In our sleep</track>
    <track number="2">...</track>
  </cd>
  <cd id="a9233-436432-3">
    <title xml:space="preserve">Trans-Europe Express</title>
    <author>Kraftwerk</author>\
    <producer>Kraftwerk</producer>
```

```
    <year>1978</year>
    <track number="1">Europe Endless</track>
  </cd>
  <!-- ... more cds here ...-->
</cd_collection>
```

Suppose you want to create files that contain user reviews of each CD. You add tags for components like user comments, other recommendations, etc., and you end up with files like the following:

```
<?xml version="1.0" standalone="yes"?>
<cd_review>
    <author>Clark Evans</author>
    <score points="8" out_of="10"/>
    This album reflects... blah blah… clearly
<author>Lamb</author> is one …
    <cd id="a9362-43515-2">
     <title xml:space="preserve">Undone</title>
     <author>Lamb</author>
     <producer>Moby</producer>
     <year>2000</year>
     <track number="1">...</track>
     <track number="2">...</track>
   </cd>
</cd_review>
```

It all looks fine, until you realize there can be problems with the `author` element: it is not the same to be the author of a review as it is to be the author of an opera! But this is not only a conceptual problem; it will also get in your way when you process the document. For example, when you decide to insert these data into a relational database, how is your program going to decide whether "Puccini" is an author or a reviewer? In which table should it go?

This is where namespaces enter the picture. An XML namespace is a collection of names, used as element types or attribute names. Using namespaces, you can "qualify" your elements as members of a particular namespace, thus eliminating the ambiguity and enabling namespace-aware applications to process your document correctly.

The following section presents the solution to our problem.

An Example

Including namespaces in your document is a fairly simple process that consists of two steps: the namespace declaration itself and the use of qualified names. Before investigating the details of each, let's review the solution of our CD review problem as an example.

To create our namespace-aware document, we start, as usual, by providing the XML prolog:

```
<?xml version="1.0" encoding="utf-8"?>
```

Now, we need to specify that we will use names from different namespaces. (This will eliminate the ambiguity between a CD author and a review author.) We do this via *namespace declarations*:

```
<review:cd_reviews
xmlns:review="http://www.cdreviews.net.df/cdrev"
                    xmlns:cd="http://www.cdreviews.net.df/cd/">
```

The rest is just the use of the declared namespaces identifiers (CD and review), into *qualified names*:

```
<?xml version="1.0" standalone="yes"?>
<review:cd_reviews
xmlns:review="http://www.cdreviews.net.df/cdrev"
                    xmlns:cd="http://www.cdreviews.net.df/cd/">
    <review:author>Matthew Jhonson</review:author>
    <review:score points="8" out_of="10"/>
    This album reflects... blah blah… clearly
<cd:author>Lamb</cd:author> is one …
    <cd:cd id="a9362-43515-2">
     <cd:title xml:space="preserve">Undone</title>
     <cd:author>Lamb</cd:author>
     <cd:producer>Moby</cd:producer>
     <cd:year>2000</cd:year>
     <cd:track number="1">...</cd:track>
     <cd:track number="2">...</cd:track>
   </cd:cd>
 </review:cd_reviews>
```

NOTE

We don't have to redeclare the namespace identifiers in each child element—we just use the prefixes (A and B) because namespace declarations propagate among subelements. This and other technical details of namespaces are discussed later.

Namespace Declaration

There are two types of namespace declarations. In one, a namespace declaration is a special attribute that binds a prefix to a given namespace name. The general form of a namespace declaration is:

```
xmlns:prefix = "name"
```

The prefix can be any string starting with a letter, followed by any combination of digits, letters, and punctuation signs (except, for the colon ":" since it is used to separate the mandatory string "xmlns" from the prefix).

The *namespace name*, which is the attribute value, must be a valid, unique URI. However, since all that is required from the name is its uniqueness, a URL such as "http://music.massiveattack.com/schema" also achieves the goal. Note that this doesn't have to point to anything in particular (that is the first common misconception), it is merely a way to uniquely identify a set of names.

Given the previous rules, the following are examples of valid namespace declarations:

```
<someElement xmlns:panda="http://www.thefaactory.com/panda">
   <!--now, all the sub elements can use the panda prefix -->
</someElement>

<xsl:transform xmlns:xsl="http://www.w3.org/1999/XSL/Transform"
               version  ="1.0"
               id       ="FAA-XLink2HTML"
                >
```

NOTE

The xsl prefix can be used on the element in which it is defined.

In the second form, a namespace declaration is a special attribute that binds a name to the *default namespace*. The effect is that all nonqualified elements belong, by default, to that particular namespace. Following are some examples:

```
<someElement xmlns="http://www.w3.org/2000/XNL/X">
      <X>
```

`X` belongs to the default namespace (even `someElement` does).

```
      </X>
</someElement>

<xii:old_book
xmlns:xii="http://www.thefaactory.com/literature/xii_century"

xmlns:xx="http://www.thefaactory.com/literature/xx_century"
             xmlns="http://www.foo.org/xyz">
```

NOTE

Naturally, the default namespace declaration can be applied even if there are more declarations around.

Now that we have seen the first part of the process (the actual namespace declaration), it is time to explore its consequences in the use of qualified names.

Qualified Names

Qualified names can take one of two forms:

1. A string containing a prefix (a predefined namespace prefix), and a name (called the local part), separated by a colon. For example, `xslt:x` or `foo:y`
2. Just a local part, such as `myAttribute`

Qualified names appear as element and attribute names, and map to *universal*, unique names used by applications to unambiguously identify a particular component. The XMLQuickViewer application (Figure 3.1), provided on the companion CD, will show you the universal name of any given element or attribute of a namespace-aware document.[1]

Structural Details

So far, we have seen all the basics of namespaces. However, in anticipation of common questions that will arise with the use of namespaces in your XML documents, this section discusses advanced structural issues like scoping and validity of namespace-aware documents.

Scope

Namespace *scoping* is governed by two rules:

[1] The XMLQuickViewer application uses one of two common representations of universal names: the namespace URI is included between braces and the local part is concatenated without them, {http://panda.org/panda}labella. This notation was initially proposed by James Clark.

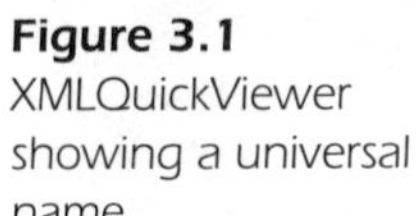

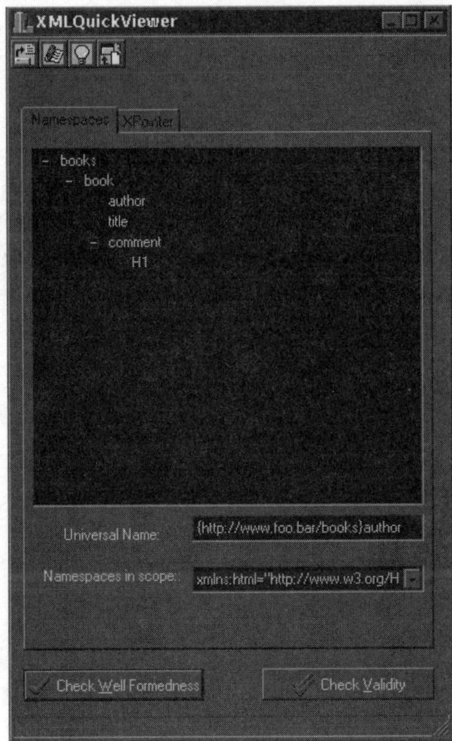

Figure 3.1 XMLQuickViewer showing a universal name.

1. A namespace declaration is considered to apply to the element where it is specified and all the elements within the content of that element unless...
2. The namespace declaration is redefined by another declaration with exactly the same prefix.

The following document illustrate these rules:

```
<?xml version="1.0" standalone="yes"?>
<xsl:transform xmlns:xsl="http://www.w3.org/1999/XSL/Transform"
               xmlns="http://www.thefaactory.com/panda"
               version  ="1.0">
<history xmlns:xsl="http://www.thefaactory.com/panda/historynotes">
        <!-- the xsl namespace is redefined here -->
     <xsl:note year="1307">Arrest of the Templars</xsl:note>
</history>
```

Once again, the `xsl` prefix is bound to the original URI "http://www.w3.org/1999/XSL/Transform".

```
<xsl:include href="../foo.xsl"/>

</xsl:transform>
```

Defaults

Most of the relevant discussion about default namespaces has taken place already. However, there are two important issues still to cover: elimination of the default namespace and the attribute's defaults.

The elimination of default namespace occurs when the default namespace is set to the empty string:

```
<?xml version="1.0" standalone="yes"?>
<xsl:transform xmlns="http://www.thefaactory.com/panda"
                version  ="1.0">
<history xmlns="">
        <!--no default namespace here -->
</history>
</xsl:transform>
```

The effect of such a declaration is that of having no default namespace within the scope of the declaration. Note also that the same mechanism cannot be applied to namespaces other than the default (i.e. one cannot "nullify" a namespace prefix). Therefore, the following is an error:

```
<?xml version="1.0" standalone="yes"?>
<foo xmlns:X="http://www.thefaactory.com/panda"
                version  ="1.0">
<history xmlns:X="">  <!--ERROR -->
</history>
</foo>
```

The second default-related issue is the treatment of attributes. Unlike elements, attributes are not bound by default to any particular namespace; therefore, in the following code, A and B are bound to certain namespaces, but C is not.

```
<?xml version="1.0" standalone="yes"?>
<X xmlns="http://www.thefaactory.com/panda"
   xmlns:history="http://www.thefaactory.com/history"
   version  ="1.0">
<A history:B="foo"
          C="bar"/>
```

In terms of Universal names we have:

{http://www.thefaactory.com/panda}A

```
{http://www.thefaactory.com/history}B
C

</A>
</X>
```

Note, however, that two different namespace prefixes can point to the same URI, thereby allowing you to express something like the following:

```
<?xml version="1.0" standalone="yes"?>
<X xmlns="http://www.thefaactory.com/history"
   xmlns:history="http://www.thefaactory.com/history">
<A history:B="foo"/>
```

NOTE

Both A and B belong to the same namespace.

```
</A>
</X>
```

Attribute Uniqueness

Along with the concept of defaulting comes the precise definition of *uniqueness*. With XML namespaces, no tag may contain two attributes with the same Universal names. That is, no tag may contain two attributes that have:

- The same name, or
- Equivalent qualified names—that is, the same local parts and prefixes that map to the same URI.

Following these rules, both the following elements (X and Y) are in error:

```
<x xmlns:n1="http://www.thefaactory.com"
   xmlns:n2="http://www.thefaactory.com " >
  <X a="1"     a="2" />
  <Y n1:a="1"  n2:a="2" />
</x>
```

On the other hand, since the default namespace does not apply to attributes, the following elements (X and Y) are correct:

```
<x xmlns:n1="http://www.thefaactory.com"
   xmlns="http://www.thefaactory.com" >
```

```
  <X a="1"     b="2" />
  <Y n1:a="1"  a="2" />
</x>
```

Some Common Misconceptions

To end our discussion about namespaces, we will enumerate the three most common misconceptions about them, in the hope of avoiding any future problems.

Misconception #1: A Namespace URI Points to a Schema

This is probably the most common error among new users of namespaces. The reality, however, is quite simple: A namespace URI does not have to point to *anything*. A namespaces is just a mechanism to render names unambiguous in XML documents. The only reason we use URIs is because they are unique and normally associated with company or other representative group names (e.g., http://www.w3.org).

Misconception #2: Namespaces Enhance the Notion of Validity

Namespaces do not redefine validity. The notion of validity, as defined in the specification of XML 1.0, remains the same. Using two different namespaces like:

```
<?xml version="1.0"?>
<n1:X xmlns:n1="http://foo.bar"
      xmlns:n2="http://bar.foo">
   <n2:Y/>
</n1>
```

does not mean that X will be validated against one DTD and Y against some other. Furthermore, the following is also invalid:

```
<?xml version="1.0"? standalone="yes">
<!DOCTYPE n1:X [
   <!ELEMENT n1:X  (#PCDATA)>
   <!ATTLIST n1:X
             xmlns    CDATA #FIXED "http://some.com"
             xmlns:n1 CDATA #FIXED "http://some.com">
]>
<X>
```

NOTE

This is not a valid document. Even though n1:X and X would have the same Universal name (i.e. {http://some.com}X), the XML 1.0 spec defines validity in terms qualified names, so X is not equal to n1:X.

```
</X>
```

The reality behind this somewhat unexpected behavior is that XML 1.0 validity is defined in terms of qualified names. That fact is unlikely to change in the future because validity in terms of DTDs must be backward compatible with SGML. In later chapters we will discuss other forms of schema definition and how they react to the same problem.

Misconception #3: There is a Null/base Namespace

Some programming languages provide a default namespace for variables without a specifically declared one. This is probably why people expect to have a "base" or "null" namespace for elements without one (i.e., unqualified name elements in a point where no default namespace has been declared).

There is no null/base namespace, and the fact that some applications use the `null` value to signify the absence of a namespace is irrelevant to the namespace discussion.

We have now covered the last advanced feature of XML as a language: namespaces. The next part of the book will concentrate on programmatic XML processing. Throughout XML history different paradigms of manipulation have arisen and key features of the language have shaped them. We have chosen to treat namespaces in this chapter because they are arguably the most important characteristic in the evolution of the different XML processing models.

The next section will give a basic map of the options available for XML processing before we get into the details in Part 2.

Processing Models

XML manipulation programs may use different paradigms to access the data contained in XML documents. This section introduces the main paradigms for XML parsing/processing, and the features (such as namespaces) that each can express.

Paradigms

The first, and probably most general way to categorize XML processors is by the paradigm behind them. Commonly, XML parsers are said to be either event-oriented or object-model–oriented.

Event-oriented Paradigms

In the event-oriented paradigm, a processor reads an XML document sequentially and issues calls to special functions called event handlers. The parameters of these functions contain the data of the current part of the document. For example, if the parser finds a line with such as:

```
<A>
```

it must generate a call to the start-element handler:

```
startElement("A")
```

The body of that method may do whatever it wants with that information; for example it might just print it back:

```
void startElement(String name)
{
  System.out.println("I saw an element named " +name);
}
```

The general form of a program in the event-oriented paradigm is:

1. Instantiate a parser
2. Register the handlers with the parser
3. Begin reading the XML document
4. Wait for the parser to issue the calls to the appropriate handlers.

Object-model Oriented Paradigm

The object-model paradigm differs greatly from the event-oriented view. In the object-model approach, the program doesn't have access to the XML data until the whole document is read. Furthermore, the result of parsing a document is not a set of calls, but a complete object tree (hence the name), with attributes and methods to call: a complete representation of the document as a tree of objects.

In this model, the general form a program takes is:

1. Instantiate a parser
2. Begin reading the XML document
3. Traverse the result tree, looking for and manipulating the information.

Both these paradigms will be treated in detail in Part 2. Before we jump into the next chapter, we must also examine the features exposed in Part 1, like validity and namespaces.

Features

The following is a list of the main features parsers may provide. These features are orthogonal to the paradigms: both event-oriented and model-oriented parsers may expose them.

Validation

The ability to validate against a DTD is the first and most-used feature when comparing parsers. Validation, while desirable in many cases, imposes a footprint in performance time just as object construction implies a cost in memory. Therefore, event-oriented, non-validating parsers such as libxml for linux, tend to be the fastest.[2]

Namespace Awareness

Next to validation, the most important feature a parser may provide is namespace awareness. The ability to determine the namespace URI of an element or attribute has been such a growing need in XML programs, that since the publication of namespace recommendation the two standards for each paradigm (SAX and DOM) have been forced to produce new versions with namespace awareness.

Chapters 4 through 7 will show, among other things, the inner workings of namespace manipulation on each paradigm.

XML Schema Support

A less- (but increasingly) required feature is XML schema validation support. XML schemas—analyzed in detail in Part 3—are a sophisticated way to express the rules behind a particular XML vocabulary. A

---

[2] The fastest XML processor at the moment of this writing is James Clark's expat, a non-validating, event-oriented, pure C parser.

growing number of advanced applications are in need of the extra power over DTDs that schemas provide; therefore, their relevance as keys features can only grow in the future.

A Note about Paradigms, Features, and Parsers

Finally, it is important to note that the parsers contained on the CD span all the previous paradigms and features. Feel free to explore and make sure you follow the special comparison/benchmarking trail on the CD, once you have covered Part II; it is sure to prove useful as a general decision-making tool when you are choosing parsers for your project.

Summary

This chapter showed the last, and probably most important advanced feature of XML as a language: namespaces. It presented a preliminary view of the main paradigms in preparation for Chapters 4 through 7, which will cover in detail the mechanisms, strategies, and design techniques of XML processing programs.

PART 2

Parsing and Programmatic Manipulation of XML

CHAPTER 4

SAX and SAX2 (Versions 1.0 and 2.0)

The Rationale Behind SAX and SAX2

In the process of parsing an XML document, different parsers can use dissimilar ways to tell the application about events. Consider, for example, the problem of reporting a new start tag and its attributes; the following are some of the possible methods a parser designer could use:

```
// Option 1 - A simple option using two arrays
void startElement(String tagName,
                  String[] attributeNames,
                  String[] attributeValues) { … }
// Option 2 - Using an extra class defined elsewhere
void startElement(String tagName,
                  AttributeList atts) { … }

// Option 3 - An awkward option
void startElement(String tagName,
                  Vector attributeNames) { … }
```

The lack of a standard interface for processing XML documents would mean the destruction of portability of code among parsers—the XML portion of your application would have to be rewritten every time to accommodate each parser.

The Simple API for XML (SAX) is an open standard that solves the problem of parser dependence by defining a common set of interfaces for XML processors. David Megginson and the XML-DEV community originally developed SAX in 1998. SAX2, the second version, was released in May 2000.

The original specifications of SAX/SAX2 included only interfaces for Java. However, SAX is supported in virtually all languages for which there are XML processors (except for functional languages like scheme or lisp).

This chapter will explore SAX2, its structure, basic ways to create SAX2 applications, and advanced strategies for developing high quality, successful programs.

SAX 1.0 /SAX2 Uses

SAX is an event-oriented API; therefore, the typical SAX parser follows the same behavior as any of the parsers explored in the previous chapter:

- Create a parser instance
- Create instances of handlers
- Register handlers with parser
- Start parsing
- Receive events on the handlers.

An important, distinguishing characteristic of SAX is that it has been conceived within the object-oriented paradigm. This implies two important consequences:

- Unlike most other event-driven APIs (e.g., that of expat, in Chapter 3), highly related handler methods are grouped aside in separate interfaces.
- Subclassing/implementation of base handlers is the expected, basic way for behavior implementation.

These two aspects are fundamental to both the structure and the use of SAX; in the next sections, we will explore each and the best ways to make the most out of them.

A Simple SAX Program

Before getting to the structure of each SAX interface, let's review a simple Java program that illustrates the basics.

Our goal will be to implement a SAX application that can read movie reviews and print the average rating of each film. The following code shows the DTD and a sample XML instance, respectively.

```
<!-- A simplified DTD for movie reviews -->

<!ELEMENT reviews (movie)+>
<!ELEMENT movie   (name,review+)>
<!ELEMENT name    (#PCDATA)>
<!ELEMENT review  (#PCDATA)>
<!ATTLIST review
          rating  CDATA  #REQUIRED>
```

An instance document conformant with this DTD would look like:

```
<?xml version="1.0" ?>
```

```
 <!DOCTYPE reviews SYSTEM "reviews.dtd">
<reviews>
 <movie>
    <name>Eyes Wide Shut</name>
    <review rating="5">A powerful movie...</review>
    <review rating="5">... ... ...</review>
    <review rating="4.6">...</review>
    <review rating="4">...</review>
 </movie>
</reviews>
```

The process of creating a simple SAX application involves the following steps.

Define Your Handlers

In this simple application, we must do two things: look for the data located in an attribute value of a certain element (the rating attribute of the review elements); and watch out for the end of an element so we know the process is over and we can print the results. The following code[1] defines a handler that accomplishes our objective.

```
import org.xml.sax.Parser;
import org.xml.sax.HandlerBase;
import org.xml.sax.AttributeList;
import org.xml.sax.SAXException;
import org.xml.sax.SAXParseException;
// *******************************                Class Definition
public class SAXMoviesHandler extends HandlerBase
{
// *******************************            SAX specific methods
/**
 * Since the ratings are expressed as an attribute of the review
 * element, All we have to do is check the startElement method
 * @see DocumentHandler
 */
public void startElement(String name, AttributeList atts)
    {
     if(name.compareTo("review") == 0)
         average = (numberOfReviews*average +
                        new Integer(atts.getValue(0)).intValue())
                        +numberOfReviews;
       // A purist may argue that this is an indecent way to
       // calculate the average because of precision issues.
       // However, our focus here is on SAX, not on Numeric
```

[1] This sample code uses SAX version 1.0. Version 2 code can be found on the companion CD.

```
        // Analysis, so simplicity takes precedence! :)
    }
    public void endElement(String name)
    {
     if(name.compareTo("") == 0)
        System.out.println("The average rating for this movie is "
+ average);
    }
    private float average;          // for the movie
    private int   numberOfReviews;  // for the movie
};
```

Register Your Handlers with the Parser and Start Parsing

The next step is to register our handler with the parser.

```
SAXCountHandlers handler = new SAXCountHandlers();
try {
        parser.setContentHandler(handler);
        parser.parse(xmlFile);
}
catch (SAXException e)
{
   System.out.println("Error parsing " + xmlFile);
}
```

Both of the methods overwritten in our handler class are part of the ContentHandler Interface. If we would have been interested in treating information about other events such as parsing errors we should have also registered our handler using the setErrorHandler method.

```
The average rating for this movie is 4.25
```

This simple, two-step approach to SAX parsing is a good start because it summarizes what is syntactically required to start developing SAX applications. However, it is not representative of real-life SAX development. In order to master SAX we must know two things: the capabilities of each interface, so we can treat our XML documents in a proficient manner; and correct ways to design our handlers so the union of them and the rest of the application result in as elegant and efficient solution as possible. These two goals are the subject of the remainder of this chapter.

SAX2 Structure

The contents of the SAX2 distribution (included on the companion CD) can be logically classified in four groups:

- **Handler interfaces**—They define cohesive groups of methods that can be implemented to deal with events during the parsing of an XML resource (e.g. `ContentHandler` and `ErrorHandler`).
- **Helper interfaces and classes**—They provide the handler classes with the auxiliary definitions they need in order to complete their tasks (e.g. `AttributeList`, Locator).
- **SAX2 sources**—They define the interfaces for sources of SAX events (e.g. `XMLReader`, `XMLFilter`). Instances of handler classes hook up with instances of SAX sources in order to receive event notifications.
- **Adapter and filter interfaces and classes**—They define wrappers that allow compatibility with SAX version 1. They are used when SAX2 sources must work with SAX 1 handlers (e.g. `XMLReader` Adapter).

What follows is a more in-depth description of the main SAX2 interfaces and the methods they provide. For full coverage of the parameters and details of each method, please refer to the API documentation on the companion CD.

SAX Interfaces

ContentHandler

This interface is the core interface for application writers. It implements methods that allow a handler to be notified about basic parsing events such as the start and end of elements.

This interface replaces the SAX1 `DocumentHandler` interface. The following are the methods `ContentHandler` provides:

public void startDocument()
This method is called once, at the beginning of the document in order to let the handler know that the parsing of the document has started.

public void startElement(String namespaceURI, String localName, String rawName, Attributes atts)

This method is called whenever a new element is found. The semantics of the parameters are simple:

- `namespaceURI` contains a string identifying the namespace URI
- `localName` contains the element name without the namespace prefix
- `rawName` contains the element name with prefix
- `atts` contains the collection of attributes encapsulated in an instance of the SAX-defined class *Attributes*.

For example, given the following document:

```
<a xmlns:h="http://www.kerouac.org/ontheroad">
   <h:b foo="bar"/>
</a>
```

When the parser reaches element b, a call to `startElement` will be issued with the following parameters:

- `namespaceURI`—"http://www.kerouac.org/ontheroad"
- `localname`—"b"
- `rawname`—"h:b"
- `atts`—an attribute object containing foo="bar"

For more information about namespaces see Chapter 3.

characters(char []ch,int start,int length)

This method gets called when character data are found within the document. Parameter start indicates the index of the array where the data begin and length indicates how many positions of the array should be read.

Two important aspects of this method are:

- SAX parsers are not required to return all the character data of an element in one call (even if that is all the element contains), therefore, no assumptions about the completion of the character data should be made inside the implementation of this method
- One of SAX's primary goals is to be efficient, thus the implementation of character notifications is not—as some may have expected—based on `java.lang.String`. The burden of creating strings out of a portion of the array—if at all necessary—is left to the application.

endElement(String namespaceURI, String localName, String rawName)
This method is called whenever an element ends. The semantics of its attributes are the same of those in `startElement`.

startPrefixMapping(String prefix, String uri)
This is a seldom-used method of notifying the handler of the start of a new prefix–URI Namespace mapping.

For example, given the element

```
<artist xmlns:warhol="http://www.andywarhol.org"> … </artist>
```

A call to this method would be issued, using "`warhol`" as the value of the first argument and "`http://www.andywarhol.org`" as the value of the second.

This apparently useless method (because `startElement` already gives us this information for each element) is used on the rare occasion when the application needs to use the prefixes in character data or in attribute values. It should normally be ignored.

endPrefixMapping(String prefix)
This ends the scope of a prefix–URI Namespace mapping. It is rarely used and should normally be ignored.

endDocument()
This method is called once, when the document ends.

ignorableWhitespace(char[] ch,int start, int length)
This method uses the same mechanism as the `characters` method to inform the handler about contiguous ignorable whitespace (see Chapter 2 for a complete discussion on whitespace). It is important to note that all the whitespace may not be returned in one single piece (just as all the character data are not required to be returned in one call to the `characters` method).

processingInstruction(String target, String Data)
This method will be invoked each time a processing instruction is found. The semantics of the parameters are just what could be expected from their names. In the event of a processing instruction with no data, the second parameter will be null.

Two important aspects of this method should be noted, in order to avoid common programming errors:

- Processing instructions may occur outside the main document element.
- Neither the text declaration nor the XML declaration can be reported by a SAX parser using this method.

setDocumentLocator(Locator loc)

In order to provide information about the localization of the data that spawned each event (e.g. the line and column number of a start tag), SAX parsers provide locator objects. This method is called by the parser and is used to set the locator for upcoming events. Events such as the notification of character data or whitespaces are guaranteed to provide information that comes from the same external entity, so the locator provides useful information.

Using ContentHandler—An Example

The following code is part of a collection of handlers that serialize their own input into well-indented, good-looking XML (together with the other handlers on this chapter, it forms an XML equivalent to the Unix command *indent*, used to format C programs).

```
// import clauses and other details ommited. please look at the
// companion cd for the complete code

public class PrettyPrint extends DefaultHandler
{
```

Processing instructions and Document Start code is as follows:

```
public void processingInstruction(String target, String data) {
      out.print("<?");
      out.print(target);
      if (data != null && data.length() > 0) {
          out.print(' ');
          out.print(data);
      }
      out.print("?>");
     }
  public void startDocument() {
      if (!canonical) {
          out.println("<?xml version=\"1.0\"
                      encoding=\"UTF-8\"?>");
      }
  }
```

Element methods (Xerces notation used—at the time of this writing there are no pure SAX2 implementations available) are the following:

```
public void startElement(String uri, String local, String
                            raw, Attributes attrs) {
    out.print('<');
    out.print(raw);
    if (attrs != null) {
        attrs = sortAttributes(attrs);
        int len = attrs.getLength();
        for (int i = 0; i < len; i++) {
            out.print(' ');
            out.print(attrs.getRawName(i));
            out.print("=\"");
            out.print(normalize(attrs.getValue(i)));
            out.print('"');
        }
    }
    out.print('>');
}
```

For character treatment, note that the current distribution of Xerces only supports UTF-8 and UTF-16 encodings. Note also that a generalized writer like this has no means of knowing what is ignorable whitespace and how to treat it, so it simply dispatches it to the `characters` method.

```
public void characters(char ch[], int start, int length) {
        out.print(normalize(new String(ch, start, length)));
    }
public void ignorableWhitespace(char ch[], int start, int length)
{
        characters(ch, start, length);
    }
```

Finally, following is the `endElement` method of `ContentHandler`:

```
public void endElement(String uri, String local, String raw) {
    out.print("</");
    out.print(raw);
    out.print('>');
} // endElement(String)
```

For space reasons, helper functions like `normalize` are not included in the text. Please refer to the CD for the complete code.

ErrorHandler

During the processing of an XML file, a SAX parser (`XMLReader`) may find three kinds of special issues: normal errors, fatal errors, and warnings. If the application wants to be notified about such issues, it must implement a handler that realizes the `ErrorHandler` interface and register it with the parser using the `setErrorHandler` method. The `ErrorHandler` interface defines the following methods:

public void error(SAXParseException exception) throws SAXException

This method is called whenever a recoverable error arises. An error reported via this method does not indicate that the parsing should stop; however, the final logic to decide the usefulness of the remaining data depends on each application. The usual behavior for such errors is to ignore them.

Note that the only parameter to the error method is an exception. Code equivalent to an `ErrorHandler` can be written by catching parsing exceptions like:

```
try {
   parser.parse(xmlFile);
}
catch(SAXParseException e) {
   // determine the type of error and decide what to do
}
```

Nevertheless, the Handler approach is preferred because it keeps the style of the application congruent, improving readability and maintainability.

public void fatalError(SAXParseException exception) throws SAXException

After a fatal error, the application must assume the document is unusable. A SAX parser may continue to keep processing the document, but only for the gathering of more errors. The `fatalError` method is called upon the encounter of violations to well-formedness requirements (such as the incorrect nesting of elements).

public void warning(SAXParseException warning) throws SAXException

Warnings are similar to non-fatal errors in the sense that is possible for the application to continue processing the document after receiving one. Warnings are defined in SAX as "conditions that are not errors or fatal errors"; in practice the definition of what is reported is dependent on the SAX implementation.

Using ErrorHandler—An Example

The following code complements the `ContentHandler` example in order to provide error counts.

```
public class PrettyPrint extends DefaultHandler
{
   // Some simple variables to keep track of the number of errors
   int fatal = 0;
   int non-fatal = 0;
   int warnings = 0;
   // Insert ContentHandler example code here
```

`ErrorHandler`-specific methods are the following:

```
public void error(SAXParseException exception)
{
    non-fatal++;
}
public void fatalError(SAXParseException exception)
{
     fatal++; // Remember the parser may continue even after a
              // fatal error in order to find more errors.
}
public void warning(SAXParseException warning)
{
     warning++;
}
```

Rewrite `ContentHandler::endDocument` so it includes the error count as a comment at the end of the file.

```
public void endDocument ()
{
    if( fatal + non-fatal + warnings > 0)
    out.print("<!-- Errors were found (this document " +
             "may not be well-formed!)");
    out.print("Warnings              : " + warnings);
    out.print("Non Fatal Error       : " + non-fatal);
    out.print("Fatal Erros           : " + fatal + " -->");
}
```

DTDHandler

The `DTDHandler` interface is used only by those applications that need information about notations and unparsed entities. All the `DTDHandler` events will occur between the `startDocument` and the first `startElement` events.

The normal process for an application interested on those events would be to store the values reported via this interface (e.g. notation names) and later on, use them when an attribute makes reference to them. In our sample application we use the `DTDHandler` interface only for statistical purposes.

The `DTDHandler` interface defines the following methods:

notationDecl(String name, String publicId, String systemId)

This method is used to inform the application about the existence of a notation declaration. Note that there is no guarantee about the order in which these calls are made (the only assurance is that every call will happen before the first `startElement`).

For example, given a notation declaration like

```
<!NOTATION ISO3166 PUBLIC
     "ISO/IEC 3166:1993//NOTATION
      Codes for the Representation of Languages//EN">
```

the parser (`XMLReader`) must make a call to this method using the following values:

- `name`—"ISO3166"
- `publicId`—"ISO/IEC 3166:1993//NOTATION
  Codes for the Representation of Languages//EN"
- `systemId`—NULL

unparsedEntityDecl(String name,String publicId, String systemId, String notationName)

This method is used to report unparsed entity declaration events. For example, given the following declaration:

```
<!ENTITY 2001-soundtrack
         SYSTEM "../kubrick/ThusSpakeZ.mp3"
         NDATA  mp3 >
```

this method must be called by the parser, using the following arguments:

- `name`—"2001-soundtrack"
- `publicID`—NULL
- `systemId`—"../kubrick/ThusSpakeZ.mp3"
- `notationName`—"mp3"

Note also, that if this is needed, it is the application's responsibility to keep track of the entity declarations (as well as of the notation declarations) for future use.

Using DTDHandler—An Example

The following code complements our example in order to provide entity and notation declarations:

```
public class PrettyPrint extends DefaultHandler
{
     // Some simple variables to keep track of the number of
     // unparsed entities and notation declarations. For a more
     // interesting example of DTDHandler see the section on
     // Little languages on the next chapter
public void unparsedEntityDecl(String name,String publicId,String
systemId, String notationName)
{
    out.print("<!ENTITY " + name + " " );
    if(publicId!= null)
       out.print("PUBLIC \"" + publicId + "\"");
    if(systemId!= null)
       out.print("SYSTEM \"" + systemId + "\"");
    out.print(" " + notationName + ">");
}

public void notationDecl(String name, String publicId, String
systemId)
{
    out.print("<!NOTATION " + name + " " );
    if(publicId!= null)
       out.print("PUBLIC \"" + publicId + "\"");
    if(systemId!= null)
       out.print("SYSTEM \"" + systemId + "\"");
    out.print(">");
}
```

DeclHandler

In the previous section we saw `DTDHandler`, an interface for the report of data-related DTD declarations (i.e. unparsed entitites and notations). Now we will see `DeclHandler`, an interface used to provide information about non-data DTD declarations, such as element and attribute list declarations. Unlike the previous interfaces, `DeclHandler` is not a core interface but an extension, which means that a SAX2 XML Reader is not required to support it.

The `DeclHandler` interface defines the following methods:

public void elementDecl(String name, String model) throws SAXException

This method is used to inform the application about element declarations such as:

```
<!ELEMENT  movie (director, actor*)>
```

It is important to note that SAX was designed under the idea of making data *available*, not necessarily on the *perfect form* for each application, so the level of abstraction of methods like `elementDecl` is quite low.

Almost every application interested in doing anything useful with element declarations will have to provide an extra layer above it in order to get meaningful and easy-to-manipulate data. For a complete example of how to build a graph representation of content models out of `DeclHandler`, see "Building Little Languages."

public void attributeDecl(String eName, String aName,String type, String valueDefault, String value)

This method is used to inform the application about the contents of attribute list declarations, such as the following:

```
<!ATTLIST movie
          year      CDATA              #IMPLIED
          rated     (PG | PG13 | R)    "R" >
```

For the previous declaration, two calls to `attributeDecl` will be issued. One of them will contain the following parameters:

- `eName` (element name)—"movie"
- `aName` (attribute name)—"year"
- `type` (attribute type)—"CDATA"
- `valueDefault` (attribute default)—"#IMPLIED" (note that this parameter defines the attribute default—i.e. either #IMPLIED, #REQUIRED, or #FIXED—not the attribute default *value*—null on this case)
- `value` (attribute default value)—null

The other call will contain the following parameters:

- `eName`—"movie"
- `aName`—"year"
- `type`—"PG|PG13|R" (note that all whitespace has been removed from the original type declaration)

- valueDefault—"#REQUIRED"
- value—"R"

Just as with the DTDHandler methods—and the other DeclHandler members—there is no guarantee about the call order of attributeDecl.

public void internalEntityDecl(String name, String value) throws SAXException

This method returns the name and value of each internal entity declaration such as the following:

```
<!ENTITY   bulletType     "circle">
```

- name—"bulletType"
- value—"circle"

An important design decision is that there is no separate method to report parameter declarations, such as:

```
<!ENTITY % operator " not | and | or ">
<!ENTITY % expression " #PCDATA | %operator ">
```

Parameter declarations will be reported also using the internalEntityDeclaration method, leaving a leading '%' character in the *name* parameter. The most important consequence of this is that it shifts the responsibility of checking the nature of the entity to the handler (for more examples of forced delegation of responsibilities, see "GRASP Patterns" in Chapter 12).

Using DeclHandler—An Example

The following handler complements the DTDHandler of the previous section, acquiring statistics about element and attribute declarations. For a complex example of DeclHandler, see the "Little Language Pattern" section in the next chapter.

```
public class PrettyPrint extends DefaultHandler
{
   // Some simple variables to keep track of the number of errors
   int elements = 0;
   int attributes = 0;
   int internal-entities = 0
  // Insert ContentHandler example code here
  // Insert ErrorHandler example code here
```

DeclHandler-specific methods:

```
public void attributeDecl(String eName, String aName,String type,
String valueDefault, String value)
{
    attributes++;
}
public void elementDecl(String name, String model) throws
SAXException
{
    elements++;
}
```

Rewrite ContentHandler::endDocument so it includes the declaration count as a comment at the end of the file.

```
public void endDocument ()
{
    out.print("<!-- DTD statistics ");
    out.print("Elements           : " + elements);
    out.print("Attributes         : " + attributes);
    out.print("Internal Entities : " + internal-entities);
    out.print(" -->")
}
```

As mentioned previously, the DeclHandler interface is not a core handler, therefore the mechanism to hook the example above with an XMLReader differs from that of more conventional handlers such as ContentHandler. A detailed and working example of how to register the DeclHandler can be found on the section "Putting It All Together" later in this chapter.

XMLReader

XMLReader is probably the most important of all interfaces in SAX, since it is the interface that a SAX2-compliant parser must implement in order to:

- Register handlers
- Get and set features and properties such as namespace support
- Parse a document

XMLReader replaces the SAX1 Parser interface, adding two key aspects: the ability to set and get properties and features in a standard way, and namespace support (a feature itself). Before we dive into the list of the methods XMLReader provides, we must see what **features** and

properties are so we can better appreciate what SAX2 contributes to previous versions.

FEATURES AND PROPERTIES

Within SAX, *features* are capabilities that an `XMLReader` may or may not possess (e.g. validation, namespace support, etc.). Features are identified by fully qualified URIs (e.g. "http://xml.org/sax/features/namespaces") so an `XMLReader` may be queried about its capabilities in an unambiguous and standard way.

Features can only be turned on and off (e.g. one can ask an `XMLReader` to turn the validation feature on). That is why the following definition is common: "A feature is a Boolean aspect of an `XMLReader`, identified by a fully qualified URI."

Different `XMLReader`s may recognize different features; however, two features are always required to be recognized by SAX2 compliant parsers:

- http://xml.org/sax/features/namespaces
- http://xml.org/sax/features/namespace-prefixes

The next section explains the details of setting and getting feature values and the rules governing SAX2 feature compliance.

Properties, on the other hand, are not Boolean, but arbitrary objects used to extend the capabilities of SAX2 in an organized way. The most common and useful examples of properties are extended handlers such as `DeclHandler`.

Properties are also identified using URIs, so the application could try to set a property using something like:

```
MyParser p = new MyParser(); // all try/catch blocks deliberately
ommited
DTDGraphBuilder myDeclHandler = new DTDGraphBuilder();
// DTDGraphBuilder implements the DeclHandler interface
p.setProperty("http://xml.org/sax/handlers/DeclHandler",
myDeclHandler);
// as opposed to the registration of core handlers such as
// p.setContentHandler(foo)
```

If the parser does not support, or does not even recognize, declaration handlers (i.e. it does not recognize the URI) it will throw an exception. Details on the types of exceptions and the rules for properties on SAX2 can be found in the next section.

Now that we know what properties and features are, we are ready to explore the list of the methods `XMLReader` provides.

Handler setters and getters

A SAX2-compliant `XMLReader` must provide methods to register and query the types of handlers defined in the previous sections of this chapter. The general form of each setter is:

```
public void set[TYPE]([TYPE] myHandler);
```

where `[TYPE]` can be `ContentHandler`, `DTDHandler`, or `ErrorHandler`.

Analogously, the general form for getters is:

```
public [TYPE] get[TYPE]();
```

public boolean getFeature(String name) throws SAXNotRecognizedException, SAXNotSupportedException

This method is used to query the status (true or false) of a feature. Each feature is identified by a fully-qualified URI (the only parameter of this method).

If an `XMLReader` does not recognize a particular URI, it will throw a `SAXNotRecognizedException`. Since it is possible for a reader to recognize a feature name but be unable to determine its value, this method can also throw a `SAXNotSupportedException`.

As mentioned above, `XMLReader`s are required to recognize the following features:

- http://xml.org/sax/features/namespaces
- http://xml.org/sax/features/namespace-prefixes

public void setFeature(String name, boolean value) throws SAXNotRecognizedException, SAXNotSupportedException

This method is used to request the change of status of a feature. The same rules for recognition and support exceptions that were described for `getFeature` apply here, however, they are complemented by three addenda:

- All `XMLReader`s are required to support setting http://xml.org/sax/features/namespaces to true
- All `XMLReader`s are required to support setting http://xml.org/sax/features/namespace-prefixes to false, and

- There is no guarantee that a supported feature can change its value at a given point (some features are immutable, some can only be changed before starting parsing, etc.); therefore, depending on the time it is invoked, this method may throw an exception even if the feature is indeed supported.

public Object getProperty(String name) SAXNotRecognizedException, SAXNotSupportedException

This method returns the current value (if any) of a property identified with the URI *name*. The same rules for exception throwing used for `getFeature`, apply to this method.

public void setProperty(String name, Object value)

This method sets the value of the property identified with the URI *name*. Naturally, the same rules for exception throwing used for `setFeature` apply to this method.

Using XMLReader—An Example

The following code glues together all the examples of previous sections to complete the application.

```
XMLReader r = new MySAXDriver();

PrettyPrint myHandler = new PrettyPrint();
try {
   r.setFeature("http://xml.org/sax/features/validation", true);
   // register event handlers
   // remember DeclHandler must be registered as a property
   r.setProperty("http://xml.org/sax/features/
                DeclarationHandler", MyHandler);
   r.setContentHandler(new myHandler());
   r.setErrorHandler(new myHandler());
 } catch (SAXException e) {
   System.err.println("XML exception setting handlers.");
 }

  try {
   r.parse("http://www.foo.com/mydoc.xml");
 } catch (IOException e) {
   System.err.println("I/O exception reading XML document");
 } catch (SAXException e) {
   System.err.println("XML exception reading document.");
 }
```

Advanced Aspects of SAX2

In the section titled "Structure of SAX" we classified the contents of SAX as: 1) handler interfaces, 2) helper interfaces and classes, 3) SAX2 sources, and 4) adapters.

So far, we have covered a vast part of the distribution: all the handler interfaces were dissected, helper interfaces (such as `Locator`) were also presented where appropriate along with the handlers discussion, and `XMLReader` (the main SAX2 source) was introduced.

We have, two topics left to discover in SAX2: `XMLFilters` (the other possible SAX2 sources) and adapters. Both of these topics can be considered advanced and/or ancillary aspects, so this section may be safely skipped; however, filters and adapters are as simple as the rest of SAX2 and can be of great value in applications that cooperate with other SAX2 sources. Therefore, the reading of this section is recommended.

Filters

Many systems (most notably Unix) have benefited for years from the concept of filters and pipes. The idea, formalized as an architectural form, is quite simple: there are processing units called filters that communicate with others using communication channels called pipes as shown in Figure 4.1

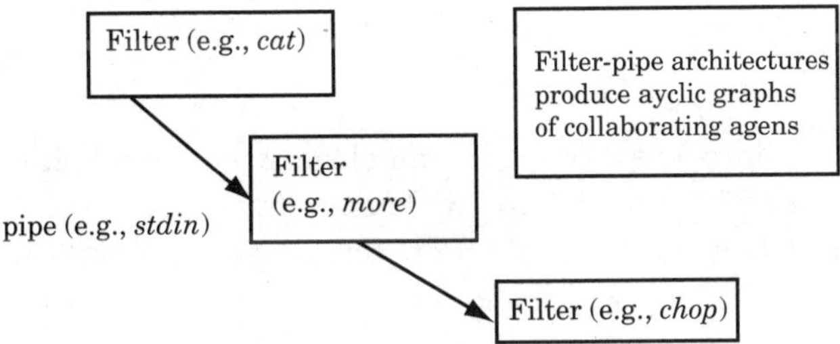

Figure 4.1
The filter/pipe architectural style.

The filter/pipe architecture can be used in SAX2 applications by using the output of `XMLReader`s as the input of other `XMLReader`s (which must also implement handler capabilities). These hybrid objects that can act both as handlers and as sources of SAX2 events are called `XMLFilters` and sit between `XMLReader` and the application handlers in order to perform intermediate tasks and re-raise events transparently.

The following example uses `XMLFilters` filter to log errors:

```
public class ErrorFilter extends XMLFilterImpl
{
  // XMLFilterImpl is analogous to DefaultHandler in the sense
  // that it provides an empty behavior for all the methods of a
  // filter
  public ErrorFilter ()
  {
  }
```

Filters provide the ability to specify the source of the SAX events:

```
  public ErrorFilter (XMLReader parent)
  {
    super(parent);
  }
```

`ErrorHandler`-specific methods include:

```
public void error(SAXParseException exception)
{
   // On each method, simply send the exception to the stream.
    outError(exception);
}
public void fatalError(SAXParseException exception)
{
     outError(exception);
}
public void warning(SAXParseException warning)
{
     outError(exception);
}
```

Filters are a common and elegant way to add intermediate functionality to SAX applications without compromising the cohesion of an application (e.g., without mixing heterogeneous goals such as logging and object construction, which should each be performed by a different handler).

Adapters

Adapter is a structural design pattern that treats the problem of converting the interface an object provides into another interface a client expects, as shown in Figure 4.2.

An adapter is a wrapper over an object. It offers the methods the client expects and delegates them internally to the original object.

Adapters are used in SAX2 to make old SAX1 parsers look like SAX2 `XMLReader`s.

Even though, for the most part, the adapter strategy works well for SAX2 purposes, one must keep in mind some limitations:

- Requests about arbitrary parser features and properties are not supported (e.g. the SAX1 parser object cannot set/unset the validation feature).
- No special properties are supported at the moment.
- Only namespace and namespace-prefix features can be set.

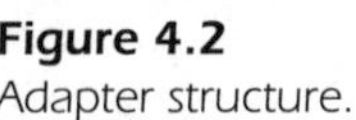

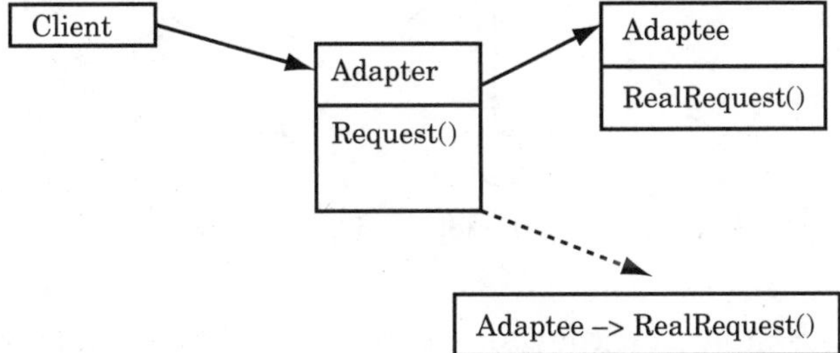

Figure 4.2 Adapter structure.

Common Design Errors in SAX Applications

Below you will find a list of the most common errors on SAX applications and recommendations for avoiding them. Use this section as a check list for quality issues on your SAX projects.

Using Noncohesive Handlers

The most common error on SAX applications is to make handlers that attempt to do many unrelated things at one time. Noncohesive handlers are tempting because they are easy to write; however, since they broke the fundamental principle of separation of concerns, they are as dangerous and undesirable as having all the code for your program in one big piece inside `public void main()`!

One useful heuristic is to determine how many different tasks are being executed by each method. If there are more than two different tasks on more than two handler methods, a filter for that handler is probably worth considering.

Overusing DefaultHandler

`DefaultHandler` is a useful shortcut for writing simple handler implementations. Since `DefaultHandler` provides a void implementation for every SAX2 handler, the process of implementing the SAX2 portion of your program is reduced to overwriting the methods you are interested in (Figure 4.3).

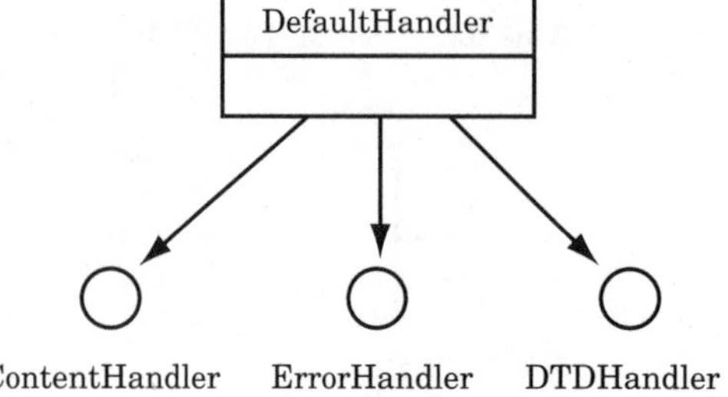

Figure 4.3 DefaultHandler structure

Simple and convenient as it may be, `DefaultHandler` has an enormous disadvantage for serious projects: lack of traceability. When a developer encounters a well structured, explicit handler such as:

```
import org.xml.sax.ErrorHandler;
import org.xml.sax.SAXException;

public class FooErrorHandler implements ErrorHandler {…}
```

he will, from the very first line, get an idea of the purpose and origins of this class. On the other hand, when faced with code like:

```
import org.xml.sax.*;
public class Foo extends HandlerBase {…}
```

that knowledge will not be immediate. He will eventually find out what the class is really implementing, and to which interfaces each method originally belongs, but it will cost time and readability (a cost that will be paid by each person who reads the code).

Development and readability costs tend to grow exponentially in large projects, so whenever you are writing any serious SAX2 code[2], the time invested in stating explicitly which interfaces you implement will definitely pay off.

[2] Anything that compromises more than an isolated 100 LOC program.

Direct Modification of Data State (When History is Required)

Often, the events received by handlers must be interpreted as commands:

```
<?xml version="1.0"?>
<drawing>
   <circle radius="1.3">
      <x pos="3"/>
      <y pos="2"/>
   </circle>
   <!-- … other drawing directives- ->
</drawing>
```

The easiest way to implement the behavior, of course, would be to change the canvas directly according to the type of element, as follows. This solution is fast and convenient as long as you don't need to keep track of the history of changes.

```
public void startElement(…)
{
   if(name.equals("x"))
      canvas.movePen(atts.getElement(0).value());
  // … other direct modifications
}
```

If the history of changes should be maintained (which is often the case), a better approach would be to use command objects to encapsulate each action, as shown below. Each object will contain a do/undo set of methods that will allow the application to execute the changes, but also to keep track of what has happened.

```
public void startElement(…)
{
   if(name.equals("x"))
   {
     Command c = new MoveCommand(MoveCommand.XPOS,
                                     atts.getElement(0).value());
     commandManager.queue(c);
   }
   // … other command creations
}
```

The command pattern is a powerful and heavily used alternative in event-oriented processing. For details about constructing commands (and combining them with other useful patterns) please see Chapter 5, "Command Pattern in SAX2 Applications."

Summary

In this chapter we covered the complete SAX2 distribution, its structure, common uses, advanced features, and common pitfalls. In the next chapter we will see advanced techniques and patterns for treating complex problems using event-based interfaces.

CHAPTER 5

Advanced Design with SAX and SAX2

Introduction

In the previous chapter we explored the syntax and basic uses of event-driven standards for the processing of XML. Even though the uses shown so far are representative of a large number of simple applications, they fall short of showing the complexity of advanced development with SAX/SAX2.

In this chapter we will see three key advanced uses of SAX2[1] in the form of patterns that will guide you through the process of creating efficient and elegant XML programs. The techniques discussed here require a basic understanding of the principles of Object Oriented programming. If you are not familiar with OO, please refer to Appendix C for the information necessary to understand this chapter.

A Word On Patterns

A *design pattern* is the description of a common problem in a context, together with a common solution and its consequences. Patterns are neither recipes nor magic formulas; they are only molds that formalize our knowledge about typical solutions to typical problems.

Traditionally, a pattern has been presented as the union of four elements:

1. **Pattern name**—Pattern names are vital because they build a common vocabulary that empowers our communication. Suddenly, thanks to patterns, you will find yourself expressing complex designs better, conveying whole chunks of design rationale with just a pattern name.
2. **Context and problem description**—Patterns are not universal solutions. They are confined to specific contexts, which must be presented as part of the pattern itself. Since we are concerned with the use of these patterns in SAX2 applications, our contexts and problems will be directly related to XML.
3. **Solution**—The solution describes the template, the general structure of the design that tackles the problem. This includes the objects that participate, their relationships and collaborations.

[1] From this point on, for brevity, we will refer only to SAX2, however, the principles presented apply to both SAX version 1.0 and SAX2.

4. **Consequences**—By applying a pattern we are adhering to a whole set of decisions that will bring certain trade-offs and effects. The enumeration of the consequences of a pattern is vital to its description since it will allow us to evaluate when to use the pattern.

In this chapter, we will explore three key design patterns in the light of SAX2 processing. Each section contains the foregoing components of a pattern as well as a synopsis, motivation and complete examples of its use on a complete application.[2]

Builder Pattern in SAX2 Applications

Usage

Builder Pattern is used in SAX2 handlers that incrementally construct complex objects using SAX2 events as prime matter. The main concern is to decouple the SAX2 construction from the actual product the client application requires.

Example

Suppose you have a program that deals with black and white pictures. A black and white picture can be represented in memory by a data structure called a *quadtree*, which is formed by nodes that can be black, white, or gray. Each node represents some area on the screen[3] according with the following rules:

- If a node is black, the whole area it represents is black on the image.
- If a node is white, the whole area it represents is white on the image.
- If a node is gray, it has four children, each representing one quadrant of its area.

Using these rules, one may compose the following pictures and their quadtree (Figures 5.1 and 5.2) representations:

---

[2] Embedded sample code is mostly Java. C++ and Perl equivalents can be found on the companion CD.

[3] For simplicity's sake, in this example we will assume the picture is square.

Figure 5.1 A black and white picture and its quadtree representation.

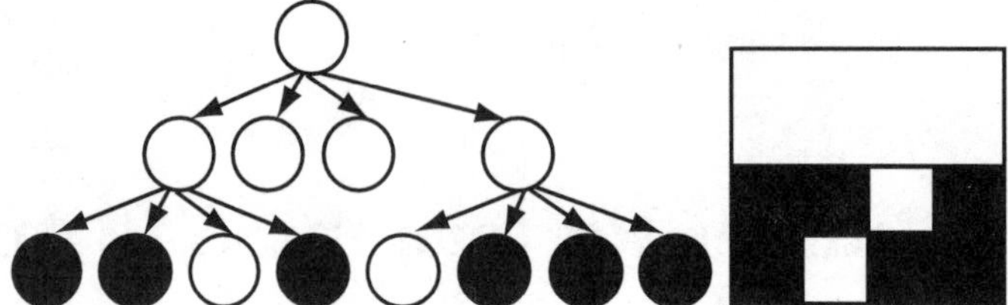

Figure 5.2 A slightly more complex picture and its quadtree representation.

For the application itself, being able to manipulate large images in memory is a key requirement, so the program that manipulates these structures may have a very efficient way to represent quadtrees in memory. For example, the C++ version of the content presented here[4] represents the whole quadtree using just an array of bits (see Figure 5.1).

The quadtree in the C++ version is represented as a collection of bits divided into 4-bit control nodes for gray nodes and 1-bit data nodes for the actual black and white nodes. Using this compact representation, the Marilyn picture (Figure 5.3) can be represented in only 678 bytes. For details about this representation see the documentation of `quadtree.cpp`.

The quadtree in the C++ version is represented as a collection of bits divided into 4-bit control nodes for gray nodes and 1-bit data nodes for the actual black and white nodes. Using this compact representation, the Marilyn picture on the left can be represented in only 678 bytes (!). For details about this representation see the documentation of quadtree.cpp.

Figure 5.3 A black and white picture and its extremely compact internal representation.

[4] Available on the companion CD under applications/SAX2/quadtree.

However, for the disk persistence and transfer of the images, considerations such as portability, readability, and clarity can be much more important, so we decide to use XML as our file format for quadtree representation.

The DTD for representing quadtrees is quite simple:

```
<!ELEMENT quadtree (node) >
<!-- the size of the image: -- >
<!ATTLIST quadtree
          size   CDATA  #REQUIRED>
<!ELEMENT node      (node)* >
<!ATTLIST node
          value (BLACK |  WHITE | GRAY) #REQUIRED>
```

Using this DTD, an XML document representing Figure 5.1 looks like the following:

```
// Include file quadtree.xml here
<!DOCTYPE quadtree [

<!ELEMENT quadtree (node)>
<!ATTLIST quadtree size CDATA #REQUIRED>
<!ELEMENT node      (node,node,node,node)? >
<!ATTLIST node      value  (BLACK | WHITE | GRAY) #REQUIRED>]>
<!-- could also have been just (node)* but this emphasizes the
intent of the element -->

<quadtree size="256">
  <node value="gray">
    <node value="gray">
      <node value="black">
      </node>
      <node value="black"/> <!-- this style is also valid -->
      <node value="white"/>
      <node value="white"/>
    </node>
    <node value="white"/>
    <node value="white"/>
    <node value="gray">
      <node value="white">
      </node>
      <node value="black">
      </node>
      <node value="black">
      </node>
      <node value="black">
      </node>
    </node>
  </node>
</quadtree>
```

Our goal is to implement a module that isolates the complexities of building the memory-efficient representation (excellent for the program) out of the XML representation (excellent as a standard persistence format). How the XML-related module (a SAX handler, naturally) constructs the quadtree is irrelevant for the main program. We want to give it the illusion of simplicity, so the whole process—from the client point of view—should be as easy as the following:

```
//Create a director
XMLToQuadtree myDirector = new XMLToQuadtree();
// Ask the creator to make a quadtree out of an XML file
Quadtree myTree = myDirector.readFromXMLFile("marylin.xml");
```

The solution to this problem (i.e. the implementation of `XMLToQuadtree`) is what we will call Builder Pattern: create a *director* class that feeds a *builder* with the prime matter (SAX events) and return the final *product* to the client, without involving it on the incremental process that is taking place.

Before getting to the details of our solution for our quadtree reader, we should examine the general structure of the builder pattern.

Structure

The structure of Builder Pattern, which is shown in Figure 5.4, compromises four elements:

- **Client**—This object requires a product. It doesn't know how to create it, or even who really produces it, but it knows a director to whom it can delegate the task.
- **Director**—This constructs an object by feeding the `ConcreteBuilder` class with the prime matter it needs to incrementally create the product.
- **ConcreteBuilder**—This class encapsulates the logic needed to create the product. It acts only on behalf of director.
- **Product**—This is the final result of the process. Director returns it to the Client.

SAX2 Builder Structure

Since our interest is centered on the XML application of the pattern, let's examine its structure in the light of SAX2 elements (Figure 5.5).

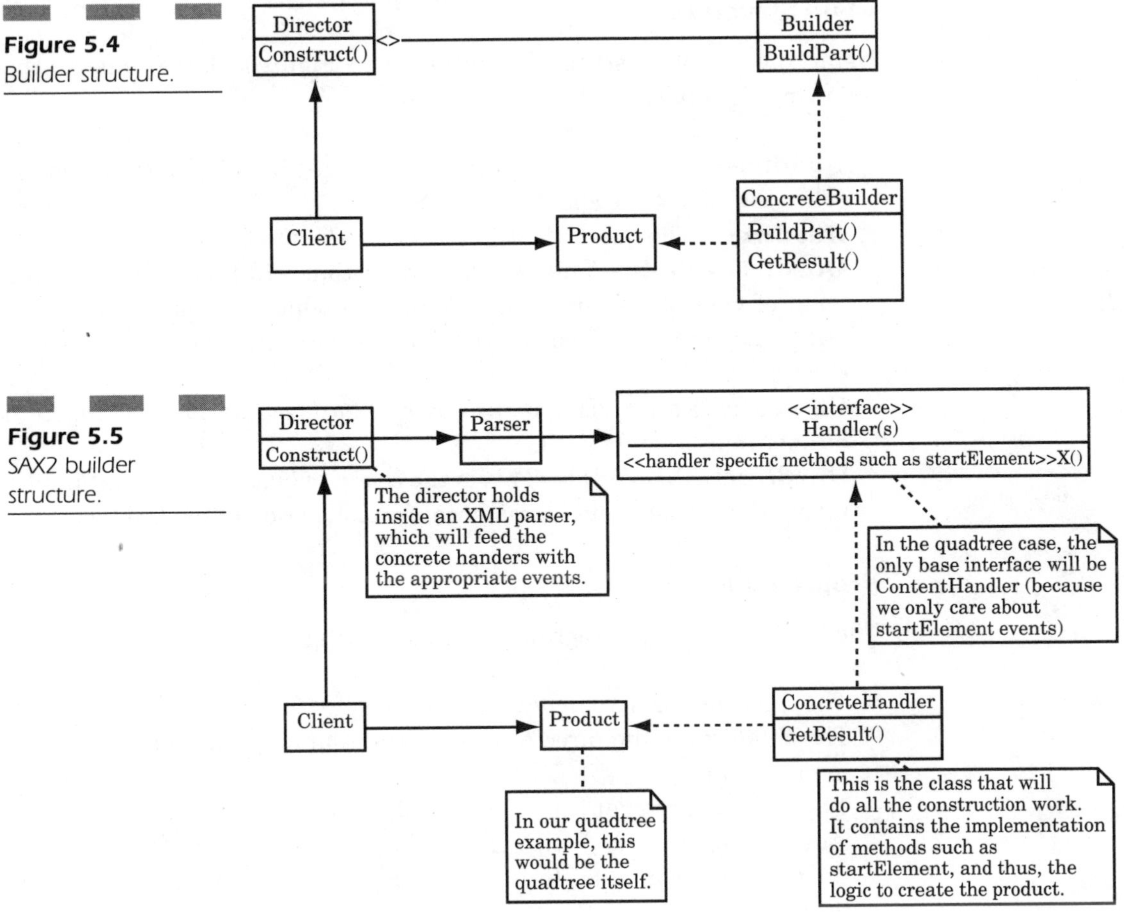

Figure 5.4 Builder structure.

Figure 5.5 SAX2 builder structure.

As you can see, the nature of SAX2 fits perfectly into builder architecture, providing us with a natural way to construct domain specific objects out of XML. Now that we have this general structure, let's go back to our initial example.

Example

Back at our quadtree example, we have a `client` (the main application), which needs to create a meaningful `product` (the quadtree itself) out of a `prime` matter he does not understand (XML). This is a typical scenario for Builder Pattern.

Class Structure

Using the template structure presented in Figure 5.5, we come to the following class diagram for our problem:

- **QuadtreeViewer**—The main application that displays the image takes the role of the *client*.
- **Quadtree**—The quadtree itself is the *product* to be built.
- **QuadtreeToXML**—This is the *director* that will take care (from the point of view of the client) of creating a product. It contains an internal parser that will feed the constructor with the *prime matter* (SAX events).
- **ContentHandler**—This is the *abstract builder* interface the concrete builder must comply with.
- **QuadtreeSAXBuilder**—This is the *concrete builder* class that implements the actual—and incremental—construction of the product.

Program Flow

The key points in our program are the following:

- The *client* builds a *director* (`XMLToQuadtree`).
- The client gives the director the information necessary to start creating a *product*.
- The director creates and feeds the appropriate *builder* (`QuadtreeSAXBuilder`) with chunks of *prime matter* (SAX2 events) as they become available. In other words, we begin normal SAX2 parsing.
- The director returns the complete product to the client.

Code

The design in the previous two sections materializes into the following classes (only the most relevant pieces of code are shown here. Complete code can be found on the CD).

QUADTREEVIEWER (CLIENT)

```
public class QuadtreeViewer
{
    public static void main (String args[])
    {
     // Get the xml file name from the command line arguments
     String filename = args.lenght == 1 ? args[0] : null;
```

```
    if(filename == null)
        System.out.println("Usage: java QuadtreeViewer
                            [filename]");
    // Construct a builder
    // Note that this main class doesn't know anything about
    // XML, the concrete builder or anything else... It just
    // cares about the product it must receive and the director
    // that can provide it.

    //Create a director
    XMLToQuadtree myDirector = new XMLToQuadtree();
    // Ask the creator to make a quadtree out of an XML file
    try {
        Quadtree myTree = myDirector.readFromXMLFile("filename");
    }
    catch (CreationException e){
        System.out.println ("Unable to create quadtree from " +
                            filename);      }
    // Display the quadtree image of the appropriate
    // size on the 0,0 coordinate
    displayQuadtree(myTree,0,0,myTree.getSize());
    }
    /*
      ... other methods like graphic initialization, etc
    */
    // A recursive display procedure
    public void displayQuadtree(QuadTree q,int x,int y,int size)
    {
     if(q.getRoot() == QuadTree.WHITE) { // this is just a leaf in
                        the tree putSquare(x,y,Color.WHITE,size);
        return;
     }
     if(q.getRoot() == QuadTree.BLACK) { // this is just a leaf in
                        the tree putSquare(x,y,Color.BLACK,size);
        return;
     }
     // Then it is gray and the method should be called again for
     // each quadrant.
     displayQuadtree(q.getQuadrant(1),x,y,size/2);
     displayQuadtree(q.getQuadrant(2),x+size/2,y,size/2);
     displayQuadtree(q.getQuadrant(3),x+size/2,y+size/2,size/2);
     displayQuadtree(q.getQuadrant(4),x,y+size/2,size/2);
    }
}
```

XMLTOQUADTREE (DIRECTOR)

```
public class XMLToQuadtree
{
    public static void readFromXMLFile (String filename) throws
CreationException     {
try
```

```
    {
      // Create an XML parser
      XMLParser myParser = new XMLParser();
      Parser.setValidation(true);
      //register the appropriate handlers
      QuadtreeSAXBuilder h = new QuadtreeSAXBuilder();
      Parser.setContentHandler(h);
      //Start Parsing
      Parser.parse(filename);
      // get product and return it to the client
      return h.getProduct();
    }
    catch (SAXException e) {
     log(e);
     throw new CreationException();
     }

     /*
       ... other methods like log
     */
}
```

QUADTREE (PRODUCT)

In order to emphasize the difference between the XML representation, I have decided to include the bit-based C++ implementation here (complete Java code is available on the CD). However, the code for this product is extremely low level and can be safely ignored since it doesn't illustrate any SAX/XML feature.[5]

```
enum QuadColor {BLACK | WHITE | GRAY};
#define Q1_CONTROL (myBits[0]>>4)&1
#define Q2_CONTROL (myBits[0]>>5)&1
#define Q3_CONTROL (myBits[0]>>6)&1
#define Q4_CONTROL (myBits[0]>>7)&1
class QuadTree {
public:
  inline QuadTree *getQuadrant(int i);
  inline QuadTree *setNextQuadrant(QuadTree *newQuadTree);
  inline QuadTree(QuadColor color = GRAY);
  inline ~QuadTree();
protected:
  inline char *getImplementationBits();
private:
  inline unsigned int getImplementationLength();
  char *myBits;
  short int currentQuadrant = 1;
  unsigned int insertionPoints[4];
  unsigned int pictureSize;
```

[5] The implementation of Quadtree is an exercise in bitwise operations.

```
}
inline QuadTree *getQuadrant(int i)
{
 /* quadtrees are represented like patterns of bits like this:
000101100001010
   *** THIS COMMENT IS BY NO MEANS RELEVANT TO THE XML CONTENT OF
       THE EXAMPLE. PLEASE READ ONLY IF YOU ARE INTERESTED ON A
       BIT MANIPULATION PROBLEM ***
 The first four bits indicate whether the component quadrants are
gray or not. In this case, we indicate the first quadrant may be
black, the second may be black or white, the third may also be
black or white and the fourth is gray. This is call a gray
control.
     The bits following the gray control are the actual content
of the node. For a black node or white node, we simply include a
0 or a 1 respectively. For a gray node, a new, embedded gray
control and its content is included.
     Therefore, the pattern of bits above represents the
     following figure:
      * * * * * * * *
      * * * * * * * *
      * * * * * * * *
      * * * * * * * *
      * *
      * *
         * *
          * *
  */
  // initialize insertion point so its ready for the next
insertion
  insertionPoints[0] = 5;
  // Getting quadrant i
 return (i > 0 && i < 4) ? new QuadTree(myBits[starts[i]]) :
null;
}
// pre: always called in order
inline QuadTree *setNextQuadrant(QuadTree *newQuadTree)
{
  //Change the gray control
  // if it is the first quadrant
 insertionPoint[currentQuadrant] =
insertionPoint[currentQuadrant-1] +
newQuadTree->getImplementationLength();
 if( (implementationLength + newQuadTree-
>getImplementationLength()) >      strlen(myBits)*CHAR_BIT)
 myBits = (char *)realloc((strlen(myBits) +
EXTRA_SIZE)*CHAR_BIT);
 strcat(myBits[insertionPoint[currentQuadrant-1]],
       newQuadTree->getImplementationBits());
}
// … other methods
```

QUADTREESAXBUILDER (BUILDER)

```
package xmldevguide;
import org.xml.sax.Parser;
import org.xml.sax.HandlerBase;
import org.xml.sax.AttributeList;
import org.xml.sax.SAXException;
import org.xml.sax.SAXParseException;
public class QuadTreeSAXBuilder extends HandlerBase
{
/**
 * Since the colors are expressed as an attribute of the node
 * element, All we have to do is check the startElement method
 * @see DocumentHandler
 */
public void startElement(String name, AttributeList atts)
    {
     if(name.compareTo("node") == 0)
     {
          if(atts.getValue(0).compareTo("BLACK") == 0)
           current.setQuadrant(currentQuadrant++,
                      new Quadtree(Quadtree.BLACK));
          else if(atts.getValue(0).compareTo("WHITE") == 0)
            current.setQuadrant(currentQuadrant++,
                         new Quadtree(Quadtree.WHITE));
          else {
           Quadtree child = new Quadtree(Quadtree.GRAY);
             current.setQuadrant(currentQuadrant++,child);
             current = child;
           }
          // Make sure we don't try to set Quadrant 5 next time ;)

           currentQuadrant = currentQuadrant%4;
     }
    }
   protected Quadtree getProduct()
   {
        return productHead;
   }
    Quadtree productHead = new Quadtree(); // The product to
return
    Quadtree current = null;
    int currentQuadrant = 0;
};
```

Consequences

Using Builder Pattern in XML-based applications that need to construct domain specific objects has a number of important consequences:

- It isolates the logic for constructing an object from the logic to manipulate it.
- It isolates the logic for construction from the logic of presentation.
- In programs with more builders (e.g., a quadtree builder that uses a stream of bytes as its input), it permits viewing the XML persistence as just *another* builder, instead of an esoteric module.
- It allows complex objects to be created in a way that is both elegant and sensible for the problem domain.

Command Pattern in SAX2 Applications

Usage

Use Command Pattern to encapsulate operations as objects, allowing the program to queue, log and undo requests.

Example

Suppose you are writing a chess program that supports saving the moves of a whole game as an XML file. Among other requirements, your program must fulfill the following:

- The program must be able to present the board.
- Given a valid XML file—conforming to our `ChessXML` DTD below—the program must be able to show a list of all the moves in the play.
- The user must be able to go back and forward through the list of moves, seeing how they apply to the state of the game.

Basically, your application must look like that in Figure 5.6.

As we mentioned previously, we want the games to be recorded in XML. Our natural first step is to create a DTD that rules our XML files. It looks like the following:

```
<!-- A Typical header/body DTD structure -->
<!ELEMENT chess (gameinfo,moves)>
<!ELEMENT gameinfo (title,playerA,playerB)>
<!ELEMENT title (#PCDATA)>
```

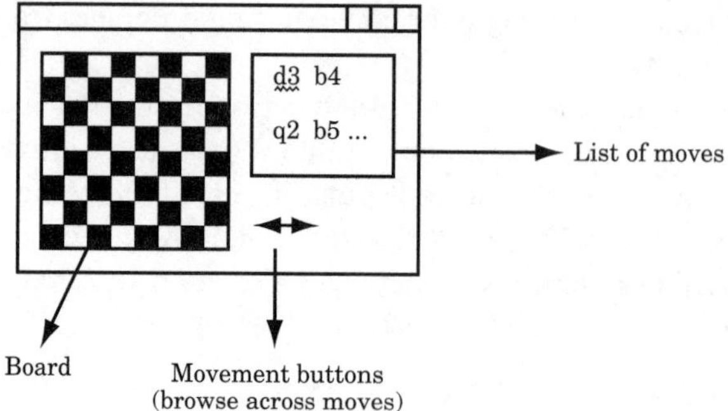

Figure 5.6 A chess game browser application.

```
<!ELEMENT playerA (#PCDATA)>
<!ELEMENT playerB (#PCDATA)>
<!ELEMENT moves (move)+>
<!ELEMENT move  empty>
<!ATTLIST move  from    CDATA  #required
                to      CDATA  #required>
```

A recorded game will then look like the following:

```
<chess>
  <gameinfo>
    <title>An imaginary game of ambient chess</title>
    <playera>R. Lichtenstein</playera>
    <playerb>J. Cage</playerb>
  </gameinfo>
  <moves>
    <!-- The following moves contain arbitrarly wrong moves.
         This doesn't affect at all our Command SAX example, but
         will serve us later when we introduce XML Schemas and
         compare this DTD with its equivalent XSchema. -->
    <move from="x2" to="b7">
    <move from="j2" to="l2">
    <move from="k3" to="l1">
    <move from="o2" to="c2">
    <move from="e2" to="d3">
  </moves>
</chess>
```

As you can see, our files are classic examples of XML being used to express actions: there is an implicit model (the board and the pieces), and all the XML says is how to transform that model, one step at a time.

In some cases, performing the action expressed in an element is enough. For example, if we were creating a *very* simple music box that received elements like the following:

```
<note value="C"/>
<note value="D"/>
<note value="A"/>
```

we could simply embed the logic of playing the note on the handler itself, with the following `startElementHandler` method:

```
public void startElementHandler(String name, AttributeList atts)
{
   if(name.compareTo("note") == 0
     && atts.getValue(0).compareTo("C"))
     playSound(440,1);
}
```

In other cases, however, performing the action itself is not enough. That is why, if you are dealing with XML data that represent actions, it is vital to know the Command Pattern. Command Pattern will let you encapsulate the actions represented as XML elements as objects inside your program, thus allowing you to queue them, log them, undo them, or perfor any other activity beyond simply executing the action.

Before continuing with the final solution for our chess program, let's take a look at the general structure for Command Pattern.

Structure

Command Pattern structure (shown in Figure 5.7) compromises five elements:

- **CommandProducer**[6]—This object knows who will be the receiver of the action. It knows how to create concrete commands, but it doesn't execute them.
- **Command**—This defines an interface for executing an operation.
- **ConcreteCommand(s)**—These classes encapsulate the concrete actions. They comply with the interface defined by command, so they can all be called uniformly, no matter what they do (i.e., they all provide `do()` and `undo()` methods).
- **Receiver**—This is the final destination of the action.
- **Invoker**—This object takes care of the order of execution of the commands. It is the invoker that maintains the queue of commands and is responsible for calls to the `do()` and `undo()` methods).

---

[6] In several pattern books you will find this class as "Client." I chose to call it `CommandProducer` here because it better encapsulates the spirit of what we are achieving.

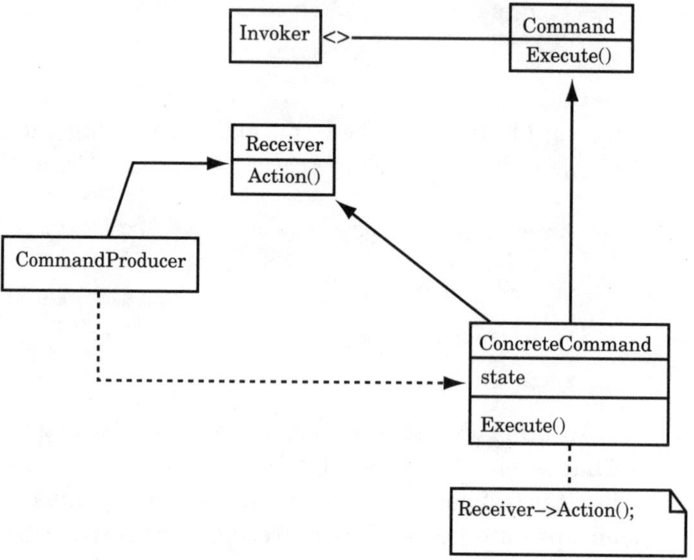

Figure 5.7 Command structure.

SAX2 Command Structure

In light of the SAX2 applications, Command Pattern takes the form depicted in Figure 5.8.

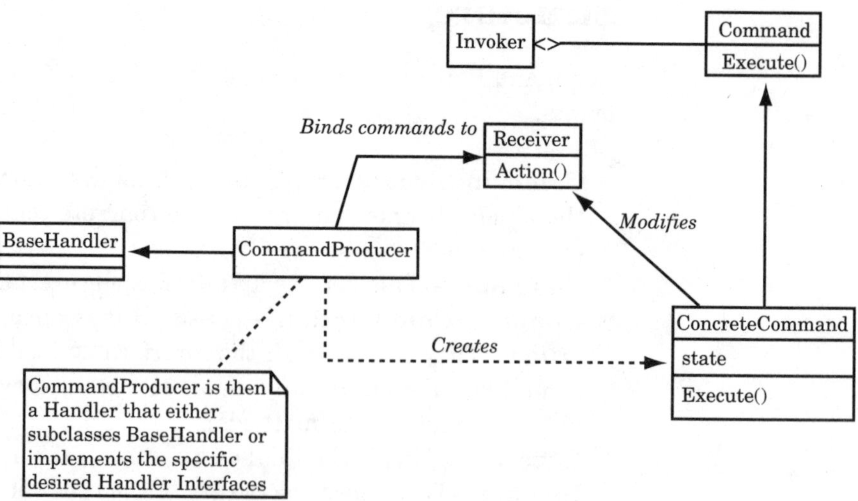

Figure 5.8 SAX2 Command Pattern structure.

Now that we have this general structure, let's go back to our initial example.

Example

Let's reiterate the state of our chess example:

- We have a *receiver*.
- *Receiver* is affected by changes triggered by an *invoker* (in this case, tied to the user interface in the form of a list of chess moves).
- The user can browse back and forth in the moves, so they must be represented as *command* objects, not just calls to methods in the receiver.
- Finally, the source of the commands is an XML file.

Given this situation *the SAX module on the program must be the bridge between the XML representation of an action and its* ***creation*** *inside the program as an object, not its* ***execution***. This scenario exemplifies a very common situation in dealing with XML files that represent actions. In these cases, mastering Command Pattern applied to SAX handlers is often the difference between a powerful and extensible program and one that is not.

Class structure

Using the template structure presented in Figure 5.8, we come to the following class diagram for our program, shown in Figure 5.9.

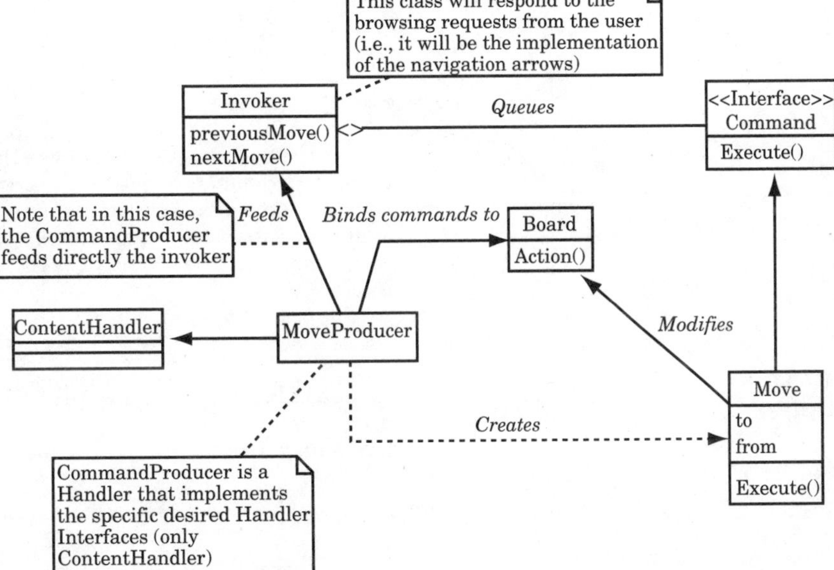

Figure 5.9 Quadtree reader class diagram.

Code

The final code for the creation and execution of the movements on our chess program follows. (Only the most relevant pieces of code are shown here. Complete code, including GUI, can be found on the CD.)

MOVEPRODUCER (SAX HANDLER ACTING AS A COMMAND PRODUCER)

```
public class SAXCommandProducer implements ContentHandler
{
      AbstractCommand current = null;
      Invoker myInvoker = null;
     // Note that from the point of view of the invoker, this is
     // an application of the Builder pattern of the previous
     // section. However, what is important in this method is
     // that is not a modifier, it is a constructor of modifier
     // objects
     public void startElementHandler( String name,
                                     AttributeList atts)
     {

        if(name.compareTo("Move") == 0)
         {
          String from = atts.getValue(0);
          String to = atts.getValue(1); // Note that for brevity,
                              // we are assuming a certain order on
                              // the attributes.
            current = new MoveCommand(from,to);
         }
     }
     public void endElement(String name)
     {
        // The element is totally parsed. Send the command to the
        // queue. Note that all the information needed to
        // construct a Move Command was contained on the start
        // tag, so we could have queued the command in
        // startElement. However is far better to do it here
        // because of extensibility reasons: in the future one
        // may want to have commands represented as elements with
        // subelements.
        myInvoker.queueCommand(current);
        current = null;
     }
     public MoveProducer(Invoker newInvoker)
     {
         myInvoker = newInvoker;
     }
}
```

INVOKER (INVOKER TIED TO USER ACTIONS)

Invoker is a simple class that keeps track of the current move and allows the movement among commands.

```
public class Invoker
{
    Vector myCommands = new Vector();
    int currentIndex = -1;
    // Execute the next command
    public void goForward()
     {
```

NOTE

Note how it doesn't matter what the command does. We have a generic do/undo mechanism.

```
((AbstractCommand)myCommands.elementAt(++currentIndex)).do();
     }
     // undo the current command and go back
     public void goBack()
     {
          ((AbstractCommand)myCommands.elementAt
                                        (currentIndex--)).undo();
     }
}
```

Consequences

Using Command Pattern in applications that use XML to represent actions has a number of important consequences:

- It decouples the action creation from its execution.
- It allows the easy and extensible creation of do/undo features.
- It provides extensibility in terms of the actions (adding a complex new command does not imply the rewriting of the receiver or the invoker).
- It provides extensibility in terms of the sources of actions (the invoker receives commands, not XML files; thus you can seemlessly add another source of commands, e.g. a human player).
- Since it clearly separates concerns, it makes the program more maintainable.

Chain of Responsibility

Usage

Use Chain of Responsibility when more than one handler must be used as the target of an event, or when the handler to use should be specified dynamically.

Example

Sometimes, a single XML source must be used in many ways. Consider, for example, the problem of analyzing the following XML file that contains the logs of your Web server:

```
<log>
  <entry date="30/05/2000" time="23:03">
          <action type="GET">home.html</action>
          <from>192.168.0.155</from>
   </entry>
</log>
```

The treatment of such a file is not trivial since it may include tasks as diverse as the following:

- Draw a diagram of usage of the server.
- Calculate the average number of hits in a given period (e.g. weekends).
- Discover the peak hours.
- Determine the most popular page (i.e. the one with the highest number of hits).

Furthermore, according to the preferences of each user, you may want to turn on and off some of these capabilities at runtime. On top of this, you know you will have to provide new features in upcoming versions. Whichever solution you implement must be not only robust and efficient but also easily extensible.

Before examining the solution proposed by the Chain of Responsibility pattern, let's look at other options and their consequences.

Error-prone Solution #1: The Big Case Statement

The first, inelegant and error-prone solution would be to put all the code in the handler itself, methods like the following:

```
public class uglyHandler1 implements ContentHandler
{
   String currentElement = new String();
   public void characters(char []characters, int start, int length)
  {
     if(currentElement.compareTo("action")) { … }// do something
     if(currentElement.compareTo("from")){ … } // do something else
     if(currentElement.compareTo("entry")){ … }// do yet something else
     // In short, create a big case statement
  }
  public void startElement(String name, AttributesList atts)
   {
      currentElement = name;
   }
}
```

This is not a good choice since it mixes many different concerns in one place (lack of cohesion) and makes it difficult to extend the solution—you would actually have to touch the files that contain code totally unrelated to your goal, in order to add functionality.

Furthermore, this kind of code doesn't even meet the objective of dynamic selection and loading of different behaviors; it can merely simulate this using an inelegant set of additional variables.

Let's try a more structured approach:

Error-prone Solution #2: Calling External Classes

A second approach (better, but far from optimal) would be to have handlers that act merely as stubs between the parser and the objects that contain the real behavior:

```
public void characters(char []chars, int start, int length)
   {
      if(currentElement.compareTo("action"))
        { ActionManager = new ActionManager(chars,start,length }
   }
```

This solution is more aesthetically appealing, but is only a prettier form of the previous one: you would still have to modify the handler's code to add new behavior, and, what is worse, the ability to dynamically change and load actions is still lacking.

To clarify why this is not a good choice, imagine if the user could specify the *order* in which the actions take place. You would have to write $n!$ (factorial of n, where n is the number of actions)[7] different cases in order to simulate each order selection. That kind of bloated solution is definitely not an option.

The solution proposed by Chain of Responsibility is to encapsulate each requirement in a handler while making it reissue its input to other handlers, thus enabling the application to arbitrarily interchange them (Figure 5.10).

No matter what they do internally, all the blocks of the chain are interchangable. Messages pass across them until they find the correct handler(s).

Figure 5.10 Interchangeable handlers.

The next sections examine the details of the pattern, preparing us to give a correct solution for our example.

Structure

The structure of Chain of Responsibility (Figure 5.11) is simple and uses the following three elements:

- **Client**—This object knows the available handlers, decides which are part of the chain and their order.
- **Handler(s)**—Each handler performs some action, but is also capable of re-throwing its input, so it can be fed to the next handler in the chain.
- **AbstractHandler**—This interface is included in order to make sure all the parts of the chain are compatible. Since all the handlers implement this interface, the client can change the order seamlessly without worrying about differences in the way the input is treated.

[7] The number of possible combinations among n elements is n! That is, with five elements we would have 5! = 5*4*3*2*1 =120 combinations.

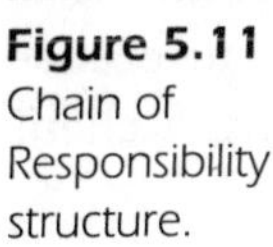

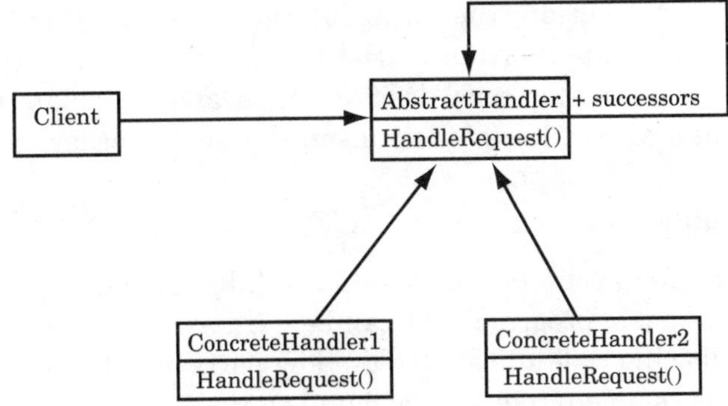

Figure 5.11 Chain of Responsibility structure.

SAX2 Chain of Responsibility

In the light of SAX2 applications, the Chain of Responsibility pattern makes use of filters (presented in Chapter 4), as in Figure 5.12.

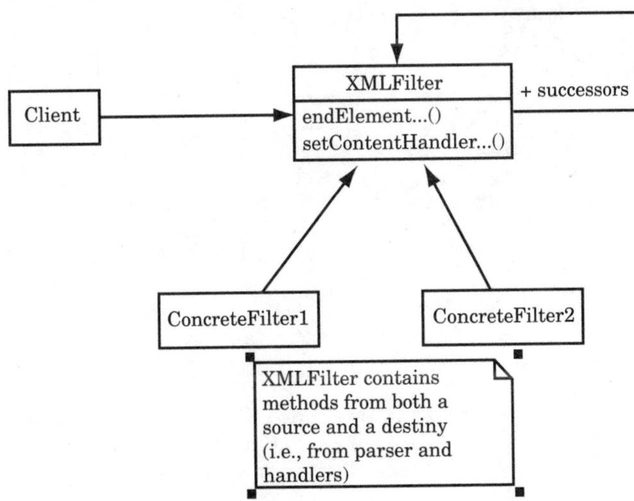

Figure 5.12 SAX2 Chain of Responsibility structure.

Keeping this structure in mind, let's go back to our initial example.

Example

Our problem consisted of several actions over an XML log file. Such actions included tasks as dissimilar as making averages and constructing a visual representation of the data. Also, we wanted to give the user the option of choosing which of these activities would be executed and in what order.

Our solution, the encapsulation of each action as a SAX2 filter, is a direct application of the Chain of Responsibility pattern: create `XMLFilters` for each desired action and articulate them using a client class, responsible of their instantiation and order.

Code

The final code for our solution fulfills all the requirements, making an extensible program that can be used as a base for any SAX2 chain. The following code illustrates the key parts of both the client and the filters (the complete code can be found on the CD).

CHAINCLIENT

```
public class ChainClient
{
     XMLParser current = null;
     XMLParser first = null;
     public static void main(String []args)
      {
        The first argument will be the file to treat. From
        there, each argument will be the name of a handler
        class, so all the client has to do is instantiate each
        class and glue them together
       if(args.length < 2)
         System.out.println("Please specify at least one handler
                                class.");
       else
       {
           first = current = new XParser();
           for(int j = 1; j < args.length; j++)
            {
               XMLFilter next = class.forName(args[j]);
               current.setContentHandler(next);
               // current.setErrorHandler, etc.

               // Now make the new piece, the current slave.
               current = next;
            }
           // The chain is ready. Parse the file
           first.parse(args[0]);
       }
     }
}
```

AVERAGEFILTER

Including a handler to compute the average is not necessary here. You already have enough experience with simple `ContentHandlers` like this.

However, code for this and several other pluggable filters is provided on the CD (samples/SAX2).

A simple use of the final program (found under apps/SAX2Chain), would be the following command line:

```
$ java com.xmldevguide.samples.Chain myLogFile.xml Print Average
Display
```

Note also that the program is independent not only of the handlers it uses, but also of the log files. Since it receives an arbitrary list of handlers in the command line, you can use this program as a generic chain composer (see ChainSamples.bash in apps/ChainOfResponsibility).

Consequences

Using Chain of Responsibility in SAX2 applications that perform many actions using one XML source has a number of important consequences:

- A single message can be targeted to many destinations.
- Chain of Responsibility cleanly encapsulates each action while making it compatible with the rest of the actions.
- It allows the easy and elegant change of logic pieces.
- It eliminates the need to read the XML source more than once.
- It provides extensibility and elegance to the problem of multiple actions over a single SAX2 event.

Summary

In this chapter we covered key techniques for the development of efficient, high-quality SAX2 programs. In the next chapter we will discuss DOM, the alternative to event-based processing and the criteria for deciding when to use each.

CHAPTER 6

The Document Object Model Level 2 (DOM 2)

Introduction

In the previous chapters we explored the structure and principles of event-driven interfaces. In this chapter we will see an alternative approach: the Document Object Model (DOM).

When the DOM is used, the result of parsing an XML file is not the emission of events (a la SAX), but a generic[1] object tree similar to that in Figure 6.1.

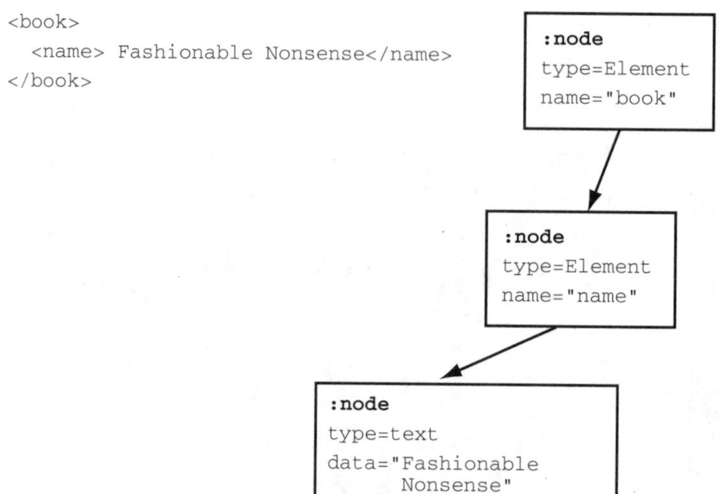

Figure 6.1
An XML fragment and its DOM representation.

Note that by using this model, you are adhering to a whole different set of structures and processing styles. Consider, for example, the following implications:

- Before you are able to see the content of even the first element, the whole document is loaded in memory.
- The object structure reflects the view of your XML file as a *document* object, not as a *domain-specific* object.
- You can easily go back and forth in the tree, visiting elements and attributes more than once (instead of receiving a unique notification when they are found).
- The process of manipulating your XML is now based on the traversing and manipulation of objects, not on the handling of events.

[1] Generic in the sense that the type of the objects is not meaningful to your problem.

Whether or not this model of processing is better depends on the problem at hand (see the section "Deciding between SAX and DOM" in Chapter 7). This chapter will focus on showing you the structure and the most convenient ways to use this model so you have a complete set of tools when faced with XML processing problems.

DOM History

Back in the early days of the Web, people started to realize the need to manipulate the content and presentation of HTML pages on the client side. This involved the creation of scripting languages that could manipulate the document, and of course, some program-accessible representation of the document itself.

As is usual in polarized markets with time constraints, the first approach to the problem was the creation of proprietary, browser-specific solutions. Both Netscape and Microsoft came up with their own "Object Document Models."[2]

With those document models, developers were then able to manipulate HTML in the client side using what was called *Dynamic HTML*. Due to differences between the models exposed by each browser, developers had to replicate code (or what was worse, restrict some applications to a particular browser).

The Document Object Model is the result of efforts to standardize a common document view of HTML and XML documents. Despite its origins, the uses of DOM are not restricted to Web browsers and the current recommendation (Level 2) includes interfaces not only for HTML but also for CSS, stylesheets, user interface events, and generic XML.

What DOM Is

The DOM recommendation defines an API (Application Programmer Interface) for the description and manipulation of HTML/XML documents.[3] It is said to be an "Object Model" because it describes an object view of the components of the document (see Figure 6.2).

---

[2] Note that this refers to the differences between object views of the HTML source. The differences between the HTML sources they supported (like the famous blink tag) are a whole different history of disagreement.

[3] From this point on, we will only refer to the XML capabilities of the DOM, even though many of the interfaces apply to both XML and HTML.

Figure 6.2
A DOM tree.

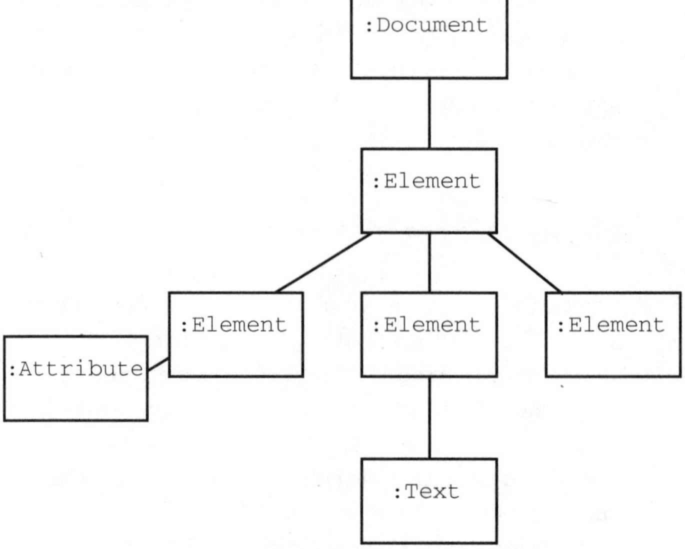

The DOM specification itself only defines the interfaces that will be used to represent an XML document, by presenting one abstraction for each of the components of a document (e.g. the `CharacterData` of Figure 6.3 is used to represent simple character text element).

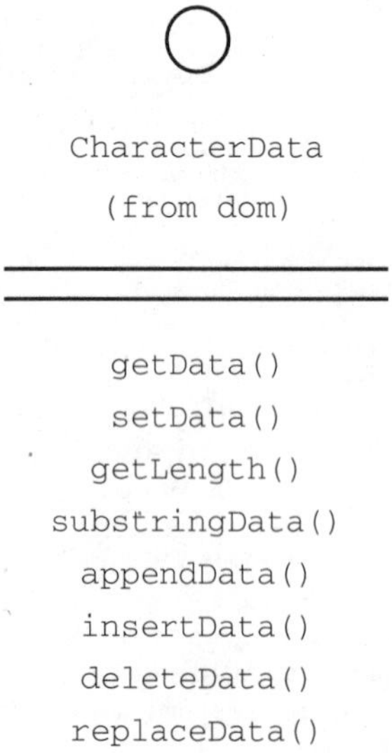

Figure 6.3
The attribute class.

CharacterData
(from dom)

getData()
setData()
getLength()
substringData()
appendData()
insertData()
deleteData()
replaceData()

Using the DOM classes, one can represent almost any XML data[4] as a *DOM tree*. Note, however, that the DOM tree is an object representation of your *XML document*, not an object representation of the *data* contained in it (Figure 6.4).

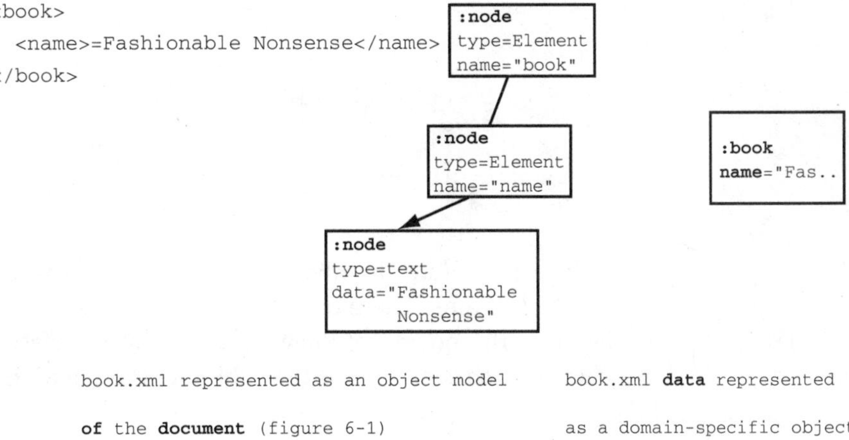
<book>
<name>=Fashionable Nonsense</name>
</book>
:node
type=Element
name="book"
:node
type=Element
name="name"
:node
type=text
data="Fashionable Nonsense"
:book
name="Fas..
book.xml represented as an object model of the document (figure 6-1)
book.xml data represented as a domain-specific object

Figure 6.4 Document representation vs. Data representation.

In order to represent any document, the DOM must provide well-defined, standard interfaces to all the possible components. Those interfaces must be very specific since they are the key to parser independence (if all parsers agree on the interface they provide, you can switch them at will).

Not only must the DOM be precise in order to assure parser independence, but it also must assure implementation language independence (There should be no need to create different models for each language.) Therefore, DOM is not specified in any particular programming language; instead, it is written using a neutral *Interface Definition language (IDL)*. For example, the following is the definition of the attribute interface:

```
interface Attr : Node {
  readonly attribute DOMString        name;
  readonly attribute boolean          specified;
           attribute DOMString        value;
  readonly attribute Element          ownerElement;
};
```

For each common programming language, there is a particular binding that rules how to translate the IDL types to meaningful language-

[4] Except for the internal and external DTD subsets.

specific types. For example, using Java Binding, the previous IDL is converted to the following Java code:

```
public interface Attr extends Node {
    public String getName();
    public boolean getSpecified(); // Note that no setSpecified
                                      is produced
                                   // since in the IDL
                                      "specified" is readonly
    public String getValue();
    public void setValue(String value)
                              throws DOMException;
    public Element getOwnerElement();
}
```

Interfaces like the above are going to be the building blocks of your DOM programs. Therefore, the process of mastering the DOM applications becomes the process of knowing the DOM interfaces and the best ways to manipulate them. That is the subject of the remainder of this chapter.

A Small DOM Application

Before jumping to the definition of each DOM interface, let's examine a sample DOM application.

The Problem

Suppose you have XML documents that represent magazine articles. The DTD for such documents looks like the following:

NOTE

More than one element can have the same type of metadata. It is a good idea to encapsulate it in an entity.

```
<!ENTITY % metadata "author,date,keywords*">
```

An `Article` is composed by metadata and paragraphs with images .

```
<!ELEMENT article  (%metadata;,para+)>
```

```
<!ELEMENT para      (#PCDATA,image,a)*>
<!ELEMENT a         (#PCDATA)>
<!ATTLIST href       CDATA   #REQUIRED> <!--simple links -->
<!ELEMENT image     (%metadata;)>
<!ATTLIST image     src     CDATA   #REQUIRED>
```

An article, then, may look like the following:

```
<article>
  <author>Grimm, Wilheim</author>
  <date>03,29,1800</date>
  <para>King Thrushbeard has announced the official ....
     <image src="king.jpg">
      <author>Grimm, Jacob</author>
      <date>03,29,1800</date>
      <keywords>Grimm, Thrushbeard, King, Princess</keywords>
    </image>
     ...
  </para>
</article>
```

Now suppose you want to write a "crawler" DOM application that looks for pictures with particular words on their description and saves them on your hard drive. The basic strategy is the following:

- Scan the document for pictures and links.
- If a picture is found, see if its description contains the desired words. If so, fetch the picture and save it.
- If a link is found, visit it in search of new pictures.[5]

The Solution

Solving our problem is an exercise in DOM tree traversing, a simple process we will perform many times: take a node; see if it matches the criteria; move to the next node. The following code implements the most relevant parts of our application (the complete code, including GUI is on the CD).

```
import org.w3c.dom.Attr;
import org.w3c.dom.Document;
import org.w3c.dom.Node;
import org.w3c.dom.NodeList;
```

[5] Of course, considerations like avoiding loops and having a limit of searches must be taken into account.

```
public class DOMCrawler {

    //... methods to read the file, main, etc. can be found on
the CD version
   public void search(Node node) {

        // This is a  recursive method. Is there something to do?
        if (node == null)
         return;

        int type = node.getNodeType();


     if(// We only care about element nodes...
           type == Node.ELEMENT_NODE &&
        // specifically keyword elements...
           node.getNodeName().compareTo("keyword") &&
        // but only those that are part of an image element!
           node.getParentNode().getNodeType() ==
           Node.ELEMENT_NODE &&
        node.getParentNode().getNodeName().compareTo("image")
          )
        {
         // Voila!. We found a candidate keyword node. Scan it.
         if(nodeMatchesKeyword(node))
          getImage(node);
         return;
     }
```

NOTE

This is not a keyword or link node... keep searching on its children.

```
        NodeList children = node.getChildNodes();
        if (children != null) {
          int len = children.getLength();
            for (int i = 0; i < len; i++)
             search(children.item(i));
        }
    }


    // Precondition: the node being passed is a Keyword Element
    private boolean nodeMatchesKeyword(Node node)
    {
```

NOTE

Since this is a keyword element, all of its children must be text elements.

```
        NodeList children = node.getChildNodes();
        if (children != null) {
          int len = children.getLength();
            for (int i = 0; i < len; i++)
          if(children.item(i).getValue().contains(keyword))
               return true;
        }
    return false;
    }
    String keyword;
```

The keyword is initialized in the constructor. The current version looks only for one keyword.

```
}
```

Given the parameters shown in Figure 6.5 (keyword=Burton, depth= 4 and start = http://www.thefaactory.com/massive/chap6news), our application will find 13 pictures and save them on your disk.[6]

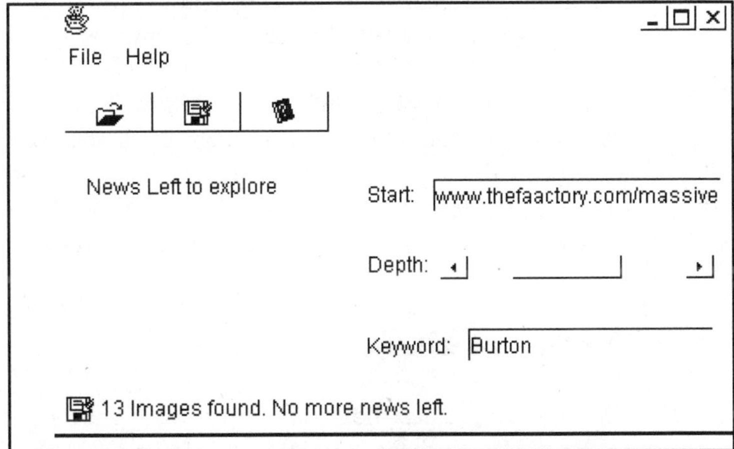

Figure 6.5 The DOMCrawler application.

DOM Structure

Now that we have a basic idea of how the DOM looks, let's review its formal structure. DOM Interfaces are grouped in eight categories:

[6] In order to see which pictures, you will have to actually run the program.

- **Core interfaces**—These define the core interfaces needed for XML processing, including the Document, Node, NodeList, and text interfaces.
- **HTML**—This module extends the core interfaces to represent objects particular to HTML.
- **Views**—After a stylesheet is applied to a source document, a view (i.e. a presentation) of the document is produced. The interfaces in this module include the basics to manipulate those results.
- **Stylesheets**—Generic stylesheet information (type, owner, etc.) may be exposed to the application via these interfaces.
- **CSS**—This module is used to expose Cascading Stylesheet information to the application.
- **Events**—These are attempts to define a general model for event/handler notification and standardize a subset of the event models used by dissimilar browsers.
- **Traversal**—This module defines a set of optional[7] interfaces for traversing DOM trees using TreeWalkers and NodeIterators (somewhat in the spirit of STL iterators).
- **Range**—This module, also optional, defines a Range interface used to represent the content between two boundary points in the document.

Most of the extra modules in DOM Level 2 deal with HTML and presentation problems. Since our interest is the use of DOM within the realm of XML, we will concentrate only on the interfaces directly related to it (i.e., those included in the Core module). The following sections will introduce each main interface, as well as Java examples of their use.

A Map of DOM

The following class diagram (Figure 6.6) shows the structure of all the Core DOM interfaces. The diagram layout is indeed similar to that of a map, divided in four quadrants, with Node in the center. This organization will help familiarize you with the dozen core interfaces.

[7] That is an application does not need to implement them to be DOM Level 2 compliant.

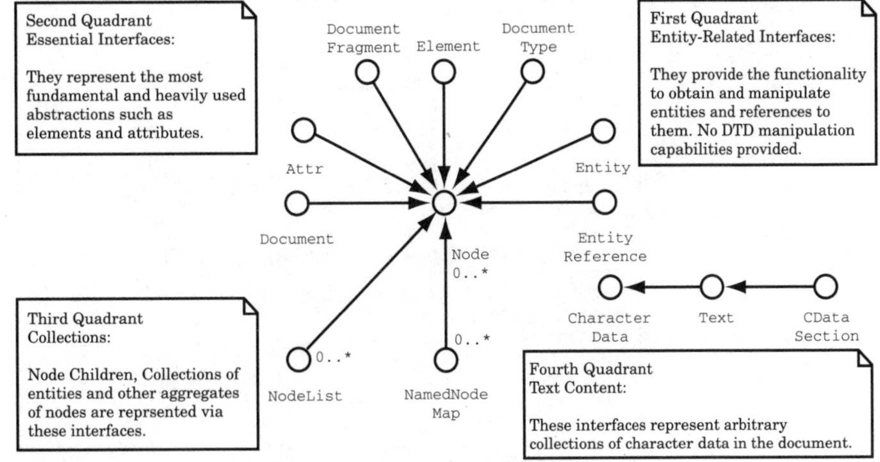

Figure 6.6 DOM Level 2 core map.

Core DOM Interfaces

In this section we will investigate the features and uses of each of the main core DOM interfaces (those depicted in quadrant two of our map). In order to avoid saturation, instead of presenting each method on the core (nearly a hundred), we will look at a static diagram of each interface,[8] a description, and finally an example that illustrates its use. For a method-by-method description of the interface please refer to the javadoc documentation on the CD.

Node

`Node` (Figure 6.7) is the base interface for the whole DOM. It defines the set of methods necessary to navigate, inspect, and modify any node (e.g. `getChildren`, `removeChild`, `getFirstChild`).

Nodes are the basis of all DOM trees, in the sense that every object in a DOM Tree is an instance of a class that implements the `Node` interface (see map in previous section). However, some methods on the `Node` interface are not meaningful for certain types of nodes; for example, *Text* nodes never have children.

In case a particular method is irrelevant for some kinds of node (e.g., `getChildren` on a *Comment* node), the general rule is to simply return `null`. On the other hand, if the method is irrelevant and is attempting to

---

[8] If you are not familiar with UML class diagrams, please see Appendix B.

Figure 6.7
The Node interface.

```
<<Inface>>
Node
(from dom)

getNodeName() : String
getNodeValue() : String
setNodeValue(nodeValue : String) : void
getNodeType() : short
getParentNode() : Node
getChildNodes() : NodeList
getFirstChild() : Node
getLastChild() : Node
getPreviousSibling() : Node
getNextSibling() : Node
getAttributes() : NamedNodeMap
getOwnerDocument() : Document
insertBefore(newChild : Node, refChild : Node) : Node
replaceChild(newChild : Node, oldChild : Node) : Node
removeChild(oldChild : Node) : Node
appendChild(newChild : Node) : Node
hasChildNodes() : boolean
cloneNode(deep : boolean) : Node
normalize() : void
supports(feature : String, version : String) : boolean
getNamespaceURI() : String
getPrefix() : String
setPrefix(prefix : String) : void
getLocalName() : String
```

modify the node (e.g. `appendChild` on a *Text* node), an exception will be raised.

USING NODE—AN EXAMPLE

NOTE

Using Nodes only as such (i.e. without taking into account the fact that they might be elements or text, etc.) should only be done during traversals like the following code:

```
void traverse(Node *myNode)
  {
      short int j = 0;
      NodeListImpl *children = myNode->getChildNodes();
      for(;j < children->length();j++)
         traverse(children[j]);
  }
```

Element

The `Element` interface represents an element in the XML document. It contains methods to access and manipulate the name and attributes of the element, as well as the inherited methods of the `Node` interface (as shown in Figure 6.8).

Figure 6.8
The DOM Element interface.

```
<<Interface>>
Element
(from dom)

getTagName() : String
getAttribute()name : String) : String
setAttribute(name : String, value : String) : void
removeAttribute(name : String) : void
getAttributeNode(name : String) : Attr
setAttributeNode(newAttr : Attr) : Attr
removeAttributeNode(oldAttr : Attr) : Attr
getElementsByTagName(name : String) : NodeList
getAttributeNS(namespaceURI : String, localName : String) : String
setAttributeNS(namespaceURI : String, qualifiedName : String, value : String) : void
removeAttributeNS(namespaceURI : String, localName : String) : void
getAttributeNodeNS(namespaceURI : String, localName : Sring) : Attr
setAttributeNodeNS(newAttr : Attr) : Attr
getElementsByTagNameNS(namespaceURI : String, localName : String) : NodeList
hasAttribute(name : String) : boolean
hasAttributeNS(namespaceURI : String, localName : String) : boolean
```

The functionality of `Element` is simple and can be characterized as the following:

- Get and set attributes of the element
- Get and set subnodes

However, as you can see in Figure 6.7, this functionality comes in several flavors, depending on the level of complexity of the input data. The options provided by `Element` are the following:

SIMPLE "VANILLA" GETTERS AND SETTERS

These refer to attributes by simple, unqualified name strings and treat their value as mere strings.

```
String getAttribute(String name);
String setAttribute(String name, String value); // Some vanilla
methods
```

These methods are very helpful in applications that don't need the advanced features of the `Attr` interface (e.g., all the programs that deal only with HTML). Their use however, is not encouraged in general-purpose XML applications that may need more complex treatment of attributes.

ATTR-BASED GETTERS AND SETTERS

The value of a given attribute can be expressed in an `Attr` object (the details of `Attr` are explained in the following section). `Attr` objects provide additional functionality over the simple getters and should be preferred in general-purpose applications dealing with arbitrary XML. The Attr-based version of the attribute getters and setters looks like the following:

```
Attr setAttributeNode(Attr newAttr);
Attr removeAttributeNode(Attr oldAttr); //Some Attr-based methods
```

NAMESPACE-AWARE GETTERS AND SETTERS

Attributes can be qualified by Namespaces (as seen in Chapter 3), therefore the Element interface provides namespace-aware versions of both the string-based and Attr-based methods. The namespace-enhanced methods are analogous to those seen above except that they allow you to specify the namespace that qualifies each attribute:

```
String getAttributeNS(String namespaceURI, String localName);
Attr   getAttributeNodeNS(String namespaceURI, String localName);
// String and Attr getters with Namespace support
```

As shown in Figure 6.8, the Element interface provides extra methods to verify the existence of an attribute and to get the list of subelements. Because of their intuitiveness, they are not discussed here; please see the CD for a detailed description.

USING ELEMENT—AN EXAMPLE

```
// Printing an empty element
void printEmptyNode(Node node)
{
            out.print('<');
            out.print(node.getNodeName());
            Attr attrs[] = sortAttributes(node.getAttributes());
            for (int i = 0; i < attrs.length; i++) {
                Attr attr = attrs[i];
                out.print(' ');
                out.print(attr.getNodeName());
                out.print("=\"");
                out.print(attr.getNodeValue());
                out.print('"');
            }
            out.print('>');
}
```

Attr

The Attr interface represents an attribute/value pair. Attr objects are not considered subnodes of the tree (even though Attr descends from

Node) but rather mere attributes of the element in which they appear. Consequently, the only way to get Attr objects is by calling the Attr-based methods in Element nodes.

As shown in Figure 6.9, besides the intuitive getters and setters, Attr also provides a getSpecified() method, used to determine whether the attribute was given an explicit value in the document or not. The example in the previous section about Element also illustrates the use of Attr.

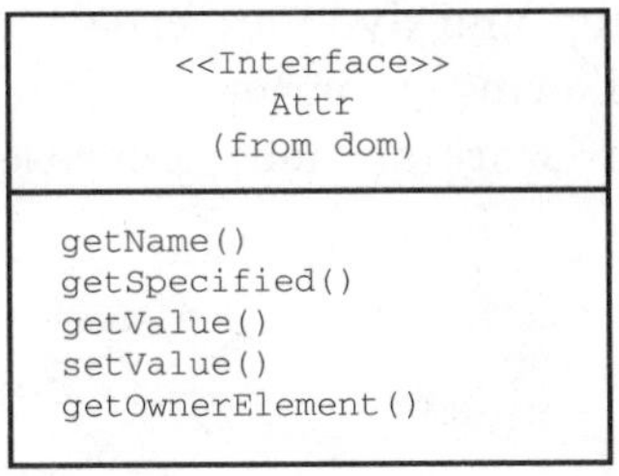

Figure 6.9
The Attr interface.

```
<<Interface>>
Attr
(from dom)

getName()
getSpecified()
getValue()
setValue()
getOwnerElement()
```

Document

The Document interface serves a double purpose: first, it represents the whole XML document and is therefore the root of the DOM tree. Second, it provides the factory methods used to create elements and attributes programmatically. The following diagram (Figure 6.10) illustrates the structure of Document:

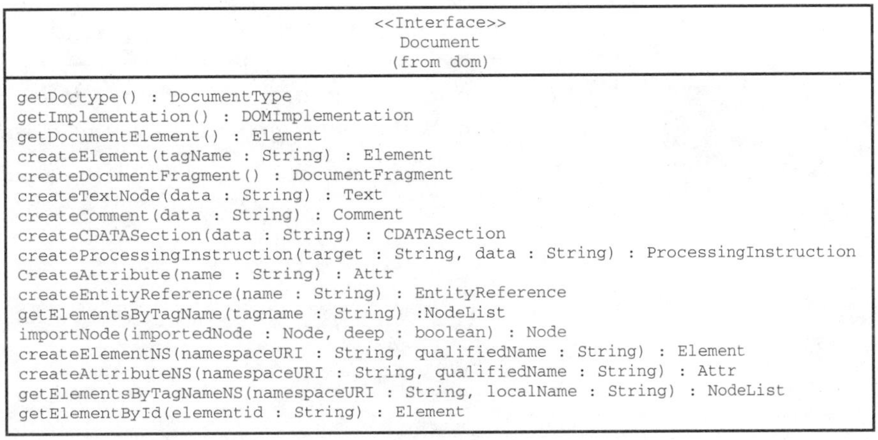

Figure 6.10
The Document DOM interface.

```
<<Interface>>
Document
(from dom)

getDoctype() : DocumentType
getImplementation() : DOMImplementation
getDocumentElement() : Element
createElement(tagName : String) : Element
createDocumentFragment() : DocumentFragment
createTextNode(data : String) : Text
createComment(data : String) : Comment
createCDATASection(data : String) : CDATASection
createProcessingInstruction(target : String, data : String) : ProcessingInstruction
CreateAttribute(name : String) : Attr
createEntityReference(name : String) : EntityReference
getElementsByTagName(tagname : String) :NodeList
importNode(importedNode : Node, deep : boolean) : Node
createElementNS(namespaceURI : String, qualifiedName : String) : Element
createAttributeNS(namespaceURI : String, qualifiedName : String) : Attr
getElementsByTagNameNS(namespaceURI : String, localName : String) : NodeList
getElementById(elementid : String) : Element
```

The methods in the Document interface are numerous and dependent on the rest of DOM interfaces. Instead of trying to explain them all in prose, it is time to jump to a complete example that will introduce not only the nuances of `Document`, but also the remaining core members of the DOM.

A Comprehensive Example

Now that we have a relatively complete view of the structure of the DOM, it is appropriate to introduce a complex example. In order to illustrate both the reading and dynamic creation capabilities of the DOM, let's imagine the following scenario:

Suppose you have your working hours represented as XML documents like the following:[9]

```
<?xml version="1.0"?>
<!DOCTYPE timetrack [


<!-- Time spans  -->
<!ELEMENT init (#PCDATA)>
<!ELEMENT end  (#PCDATA)>
<!ELEMENT timedesc (#PCDATA)> <!-- a description of the time span
e.g. "morning" -->
<!ELEMENT interruption (#PCDATA | init | end)*>


<!-- Essential elements definition -->
<!ELEMENT timetrack (
init,end,timedesc,interruption*,goal*,activity*,timetrack*)>
```

NOTE

A goal has an id (so activities can reference to it), a priority, possibly a reference to a higher level goal (thus being a subgoal) and a status expressed as a percentage.

```
<!ELEMENT goal (#PCDATA)>
<!ATTLIST goal
          id          ID                 #REQUIRED
          priority    (1|2|3|4|5|6)      "2"
          towards     IDREF              #IMPLIED
          status      CDATA              #IMPLIED >
```

[9] Actually, I keeps my hours this way. In the extras directory of the CD you can find an emacs module to manipulate files like this and a little Perl program to port them to Palm Pilot notes.

```
<!ELEMENT activity  (#PCDATA | init | end | timedesc)*>
<!ATTLIST activity
          towards    IDREF             #IMPLIED
          status     CDATA             #IMPLIED >

]>

<timetrack>
  <init>01/08/00</init>
  <end>07/08/00</end>
  <timedesc>First week of August</timedesc>
  <goal id="joyce-ulysses">Write essay about Ulysses.</goal>
  <goal id="foo-database">Finish regresion tests for the foobar
database</goal>
  <!-- ... -->
  <activity towards="joyce-ulysses">
     <init>01/08/00 4:40 PM</init>
     <end>01/08/00 10:20 PM</end>
     <timedesc>Whole afternoon</timedesc>
     Write first part of the essay.
  </activity>
  <activity>
     <init>01/08/00 10:20 PM</init>
     <end>01/08/00 11:32 PM</end>
     Write tests scripts 1 through 5.
  </activity>
</timetrack>
```

Given a file like the above, suppose you want to create a tool to help you calculate and enrich your data with all sorts of statistics about your work. The requirements for the tool are:

- Present a visual tree of the data, categorized by time periods (year contains months, months contain weeks, weeks contain days, and days contain activities).
- Whenever the user chooses a period, the consolidated data about that period must appear (e.g. how much time was invested in each goal).
- Finally, if the user chooses to generate all the statistics, the document must be enhanced with nodes that represent the consolidated data as follows:

NOTE

Nodes like the following must be added to the document, as the final node of each time track:

```
<statistics>
   <total_hours>4.6</total_hours>
   <addressed goal="foo-database" completed="yes"
              hours="3.4" activities="1"/>
   <addressed goal="joyce-ulysses" completed="no"
              hours="1.2" activities="2"/>
</statistics>
```

Our solution has four parts that illustrate all the activities that can be performed in DOM programs:

- Create the visual representation (DOM reading).
- Create the statistics at user request (DOM traversing and modification).
- Create new nodes for the statistical data (DOM node creation and deletion).
- Revert the total document to file (DOM writing).

The following sections illustrate the key code. For the complete application (and source, of course) please see the CD.

Create the Visual Representation: DOM Reading and Traversing

In order to show a tree like that in Figure 6.10, we must read the XML file and walk the tree once, creating not only the visual representations, but a structure that allows us to map the visual tree to the actual DOM nodes (this is necessary, in order to enable the fast lookup of DOM nodes when the user chooses a particular visual node).

The visual tree creation is encapsulated in the `createVisualTree` method:

```
import java.io.OutputStreamWriter;
import java.io.PrintWriter;
import java.io.UnsupportedEncodingException;

import org.w3c.dom.Attr;
import org.w3c.dom.Document;
import org.w3c.dom.NamedNodeMap;
import org.w3c.dom.Node;
import org.w3c.dom.NodeList;

public class DOMHours {

    public static void main(String args[])
    {
```

NOTE

This code is abridged (no main or helpers methods included). The complete code is on the CD.

First read the document, creating a DOM tree in the variable `myDocument`. Then begin the visual representation by calling `createVisualTree`.

```
createVisualTree(myDocument);
}
public void createVisualTree(Node node)
{

    // is there anything to do?
 if (node == null)
      return;

    int type = node.getNodeType();
    JTree current = null;

    switch (type)
     { // find what type of node we are dealing with

     case Node.DOCUMENT_NODE: {
```

NOTE

`addVisualNode` *adds a node to the visual representation using a given icon and a certain string.*

```
current = addNewVisualNode("Your times", ICON_1);
```

Make a key,value pair on the table stating that the current visual node is tied to the DOM node. That way, when the user clicks the visual node we can find out what DOM node he is talking about.

```
 tieVisual(current,node);
 break;
}

// print element with attributes
case Node.ELEMENT_NODE: {
 if(node.getNodeName().compareTo("timedesc"))
      {
```

NOTE

The description text is actually the first son of this element.

```
        Node myDescription text =
             node.getChildNodes().item(0).getValue();
        current = addNewVisualNode(myDescription,
              icon_time);
        tieVisual(current,node);
       }

  if(node.getNodeName().compareTo("activity"))
       {
```

NOTE

The description text is actually the first son of this element.

```
        Node myDescription text =
             node.getChildNodes().item(0).getValue();
        current = addNewVisualNode(myDescription,
              icon_activity);
        tieVisual(current,node);
       }
  //... other analogous rules for activity and goal nodes
  break;
 }
 }
```

Now recurse through the children nodes.

```
        NodeList children = node.getChildNodes();
        if (children != null) {
         int len = children.getLength();
             for (int i = 0; i < len; i++)
          createVisualTree(children.item(i));
        }
    }

    Document DOMTree;
    JTree    visualTree; // A graphic tree for the UI
    JImage   icon_calendar; // An icon for a calendar
    HashTable visualToDOM = new HashTable();
    // ... other private data
}
```

Gathering the Data for the Statistics—More Traversing (and a Nifty, Common Trick)

Each time the user selects a Node two actions must be performed:

- Find out which DOM Node correspond to the clicked visual node.
- Traverse that section of the tree and show the calculated statistics.

The above functionality is encapsulated in the `findNode` and `calculateStatistics` methods:

```
public Node findNode(JTreeNode visual)
{
```

NOTE

Since we took the precaution of mapping each visual node to its corresponding DOM Node this method becomes trivial (and quite efficient).

```
 return (Node) visualToDOM(visual);
}
```

NOTE

Calculate statistics is a simple traverse similar to the visual creation and other examples in this chapter. The complete code can be found on the CD.

Create New Nodes for the Statistical Data (DOM Node Creation and Deletion)

In what is probably the most interesting operation of our program, when the user hits the **save enhanced file** button, the whole tree must be processed, recursively creating the consolidate statistics nodes.

This functionality is embedded in the `createStatistics` method. This code (while accessible on the CD and in Chapter 7) is not shown here because it involves concepts that have not been treated yet—in particular, the creation aspect of this method. This could be implemented by calling the `Document` factory methods (e.g. `createElement`), it is coded using `Visitor` and `Strategy` patterns. We will start Chapter 7 by reviewing them.

Summary

This application is not only a solution for our statistics problem, but is also a good representative of DOM use. It shows some of the tradeoffs that DOM imposes (e.g., the whole tree is loaded into memory, thus expending much more memory than SAX; on the other hand, arbitrary access to particular nodes is instantaneous).[10]

Finding out exactly what the tradeoffs are and how best to exploit them using advanced patterns is the subject of Chapter 7.

[10] For readers familiar with Big O notation, the cost of accessing a node in our DOM program is O(1), unlike the sequential, O(n) search of event-based interfaces.

CHAPTER 7

Advanced Design With DOM2

Introduction

In the previous chapter we explored the structure and principles of the Document Object Model.[1] In this chapter we will see advanced design techniques that will empower designs, providing quality approaches to common problems with DOM manipulation.

The programs in this chapter use both server-side implementations of the DOM (i.e. Java and C++ interfaces) and browser implementations (manipulated via JavaScript), thus covering all the uses of DOM. All the necessary tools for the compilation and use of these applications are on the CD, along with the code for the complete, working programs.

Visitor Pattern in DOM2 Applications

The DOM2 structure lends itself naturally to many traditional behavioral patterns. In this chapter we explore three fundamental design techniques that cover practically every use of a DOM tree. The first of them is the *visitor pattern*.

Visitor Pattern Usage

Visitor pattern is used to encapsulate operations over an object structure. Visitor lets you code new behavior over a hierarchy without changing the classes that constitute the hierarchy itself. The main concern is to allow the organized creation of new ways to manipulate the DOM, without having to subclass its structure.

Example

Quality object-oriented programming and design combines, among others, two key concepts: *cohesion* and *encapsulation*.

---

[1] Even though we use the latest W3C recommendation, that is DOM level 2, we consistently use the term DOM to refer to the set of interfaces.

Cohesion can be described as a measure of the closeness in relationship among the elements of a given group. For example, the class in Figure 7.1 is said to be uncohesive because it mixes date-related functions (that should be there) with absolutely unrelated items like a method for calculating the days between today and the author's birthday.

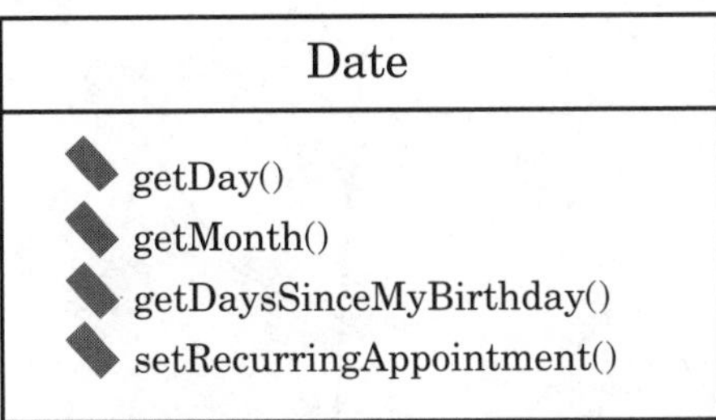

Figure 7.1 An uncohesive class.

Encapsulation is a far better-known quality: an object can be queried and modified only via the interface it provides to the outside world. Its internal workings and representation are unknown to the other classes. The clients of the object don't know anything about *how* things are made, they just *invoke* the appropriate methods.

These two qualities are fundamental to quality OO design and they usually complement each other fairly well (see Figure 7.2); but what happens when they collide?

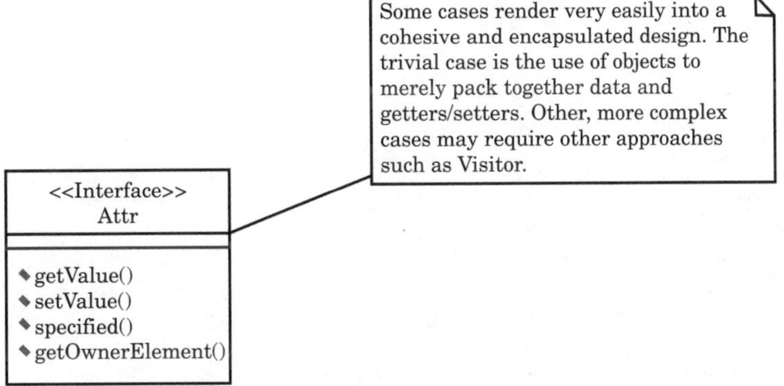

Figure 7.2 A typical, unchallenging case.

Consider, for example, the problem of merging DOM nodes (Figure 7.3) according to some criteria—e.g. merge all contiguous "paragraph" nodes.

At first glance it seems as though there would have to be a tradeoff between encapsulation and cohesion: if you add a `mergeNodesWithSameName` method to the DOM Node class you are breaking the class cohesion by inserting your own problem into a general-purpose class. On the other hand, if you take the code out and put the logic in the client, which needs the modified tree, you would be breaking the encapsulation of the model. The client should only know *what* it wants, not the logic to actually do it.

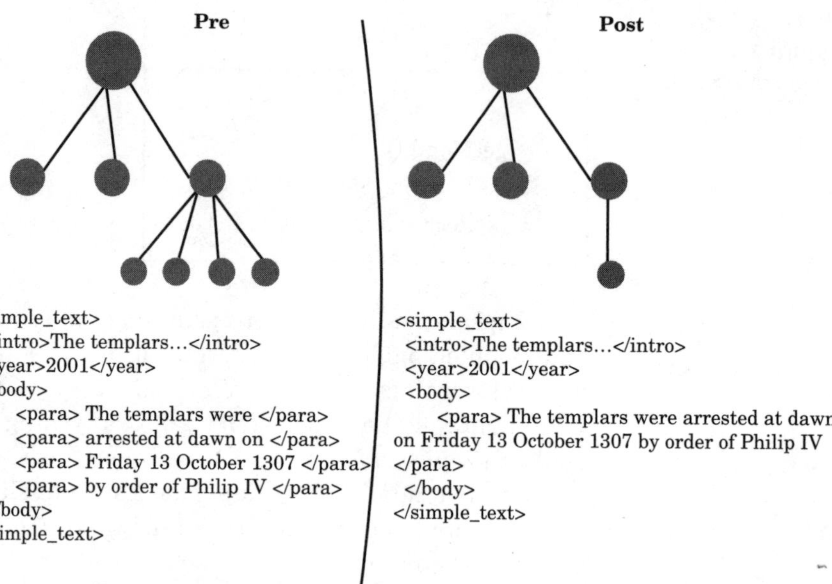
Pre
Post
<simple_text>
<intro>The templars...</intro>
<year>2001</year>
<body>
<para> The templars were </para>
<para> arrested at dawn on </para>
<para> Friday 13 October 1307 </para>
<para> by order of Philip IV </para>
</body>
</simple_text>
<simple_text>
<intro>The templars...</intro>
<year>2001</year>
<body>
<para> The templars were arrested at dawn on Friday 13 October 1307 by order of Philip IV </para>
</body>
</simple_text>

Figure 7.3 Merging DOM nodes.

```
 // Breaking encapsulation and cohesion
 // ----------------------------------

import org.w3c.dom.Document;
import org.w3c.dom.NodeList;

// NodeMergerClient is a program that needs to apply the
// mergeNodesWithName functionality (among many others)to DOM
// Nodes. Since such functionality is not found on the DOM
// classes, it decides -poorly-to implement it as part
// of its methods.
public class NodeMergerClient__Broken
{
    public static void main(String args[])
    {
      // ... Check parameters
      if(readCommandLineOptions() == false)
        return usageMessage();
```

```
      // ... Read FileName
        DOMParserWrapper parser =
         (DOMParserWrapper)MyParserWrapper.newInstance();
        Document document = parser.parse(uri);

    // ... Do many other operations
    // Traverse the tree, merging contiguous nodes with the same
        name mergeNodesWithName(document,"para");

    // ... Do many other operations
    }

    // The following method shouldn't be here! This is an mistake
    // not in the sense that the DOM tree gets violated,but in
    // the sense that this *client* is getting to know way too
    // much about *how* things are done, instead of just knowing
    // what it wants and who to invoke-.

    // It also is a cohesion error. This client should have a
    // main method, a method to print the program usage, and
    // probably a method for parsing command line options.But it
    // should not have methods with DOM traversing logic!

    // In short, the following behavior should be encapsulated
    // elsewhere.
    private void mergeNodesWithName(Document doc, String name)
    {
     // ... See the complete logic to merge nodes with the same
     // name in the final result, after applying the pattern.
    }
}
```

Visitor pattern deals precisely with this problem: the clean encapsulation of behavior outside the target object model. The approach proposed is to encapsulate each new behavior as a new class conforming to some interface known to the client (see Figure 7.4).[2]

This way, the client may use the operation without knowing how it is implemented. Furthermore, new "black-boxed" operations that deal with every type of node can be inserted and used without changing anything on the model or the client, thus achieving the desired encapsulation without compromising our cohesion.

Every visitor has code to deal with every type of node (even if "dealing" with some types of nodes means ignoring them). This logic may be expressed explicitly (many methods like `visitElementNode`, `visitAttrs`, etc.) or implicity as shown below (simply having a single visit method that takes care of the relevant types and ignores the rest).

---

[2] Figure 7.4 is included for the sake of congruency with the rest of the patterns presented. However, its intent may not be obvious before you read the structure section and the code.

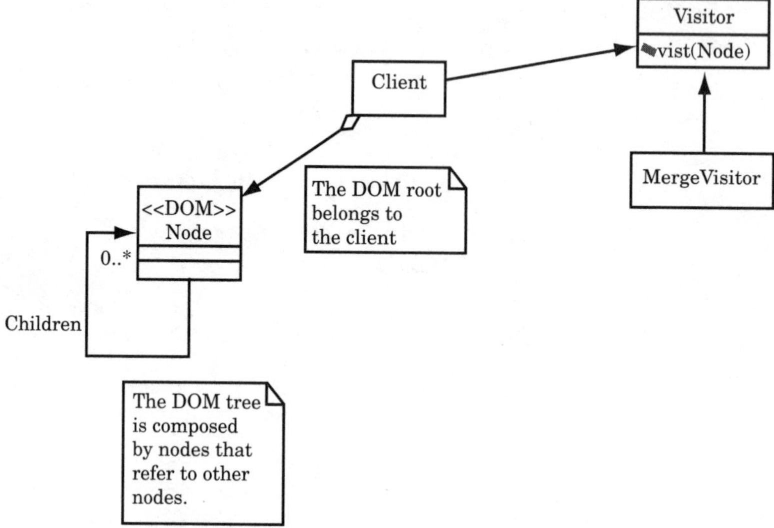

Figure 7.4 Using Visitor in the merge problem.

The following is a nice way to encapsulate the merge functionality: `Visitor` (only the key functionality is presented—i.e., `DOMVIsitor` and `MergeVisitor`). For the client class please refer to the CD).

```
// DOMVisitor
import org.w3c.dom.Node;

// Defines a common interface for visitors of DOM trees

public interface DOMVisitor
{
    public void visit(Node current);
}

// MergeVisitor
import org.w3c.dom.Attr;
import org.w3c.dom.Node;
import org.w3c.dom.NamedNodeMap;
import org.w3c.dom.Element;
import org.w3c.dom.NodeList;
import java.util.Vector;

public class MergeVisitor implements DOMVisitor
{
```

Construct a new visitor that will merge contiguous elements with the specified name. Merging two nodes A and B consists of two things: 1) uniting attributes and 2) uniting subnodes. Uniting subnodes is simple:merely append to A all subnodes of B. Uniting attributes also requires duplicate checks.

```
public MergeVisitor(String name)
{
 searchName = new String(name);
}

public void visit(Node current)
{

   if(current != null)
   {

 // Did we find a candidate for merging?
 if(current.getNodeType() == Node.ELEMENT_NODE &&
    merging != null)
     {
      if(current.getNodeName().compareTo(searchName) != 0)
      {
       merging = null; // Stop merging
      }
      else   // merge!
      {
       // First, copy attributes
       NamedNodeMap atts = current.getAttributes();
       for(int i = 0; i < atts.getLength(); i++)
```

NOTE

Before inserting an attribute check there are no duplicates.

```
       if(merging.getAttribute(atts.item(i).getNodeName()).
          length() == 0)
       {
        merging.setAttribute(atts.item(i).getNodeName(),
                         atts.item(i).getNodeValue());
       }
      }
```

Now, copy subnodes:

```
       NodeList children = current.getChildNodes();
       if(children != null)
       {
           int len = children.getLength();
           for(int i = 0; i < len; i++)
           {
            merging.appendChild(children.item(i));
           }
       }
```

Finally, get rid of the merged element:

```
        current.getParentNode().removeChild(current);
        }
       }
       else if(current.getNodeType() == Node.ELEMENT_NODE &&
               merging == null &&
               current.getNodeName().compareTo(searchName) == 0)
       {
        merging = (Element)current;
       }
```

Now keep visiting nodes:

```
   NodeList children = current.getChildNodes();
   if(children != null)
   {
       int len = children.getLength();
       for(int i = 0; i < len; i++)
       {
        nodesToVisit.addElement(children.item(i));
       }
   }
     } // if != null
   if(nodesToVisit.size() > 0)
   {
       Node next = (Node)nodesToVisit.elementAt(0);
       nodesToVisit.removeElementAt(0);
          visit(next);
   }
  }
  Vector nodesToVisit = new Vector(); // Nodes left to visit in
                                      // the level by level
                                      // traverse.
  String searchName;  // Name of elements to merge
  Element   merging = null; // Contains the previous element
                            //  node iff it had a name equal to
                            //  _searchname_. null otherwise.
}
```

When applying this visitor to merge the p elements of the following document (to the DOM tree that represents this document, to be precise):

```
<?xml version="1.0" standalone="yes"?>
<!DOCTYPE letter [
<!ELEMENT letter (p*,confidential)>
<!ELEMENT confidential (p*)>
<!ELEMENT p (#PCDATA|from)*>
<!ELEMENT from EMPTY>
<!ATTLIST from
          codename     CDATA  #IMPLIED
```

```
            private      (yes)  #FIXED   "yes">
]>
<letter>
  <p>A </p>
  <p>word of advise </p>
  <confidential>
    <p><from codename="Artephius"/> ... having no
    </p>
  <p>Ariadne's thread to lead him out.</p>
  </confidential>
</letter>
```

the result is the following (note how the `p` elements get merged regardless of their depth in the tree):

```
<?xml version="1.0"?>
<letter>
  <p>A word of advise </p>
  <confidential>
    <p><from codename="Artephius" private="yes"></from> ...
    having no Ariadne's thread to lead him out.</p>
  </confidential>
</letter>
```

The following sections will discuss the detailed structure and consequences of `Visitor` in DOM applications.

Structure

The classic structure of the `Visitor` pattern is shown in Figure 7.5.

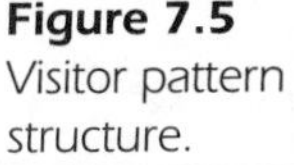

Figure 7.5
Visitor pattern structure.

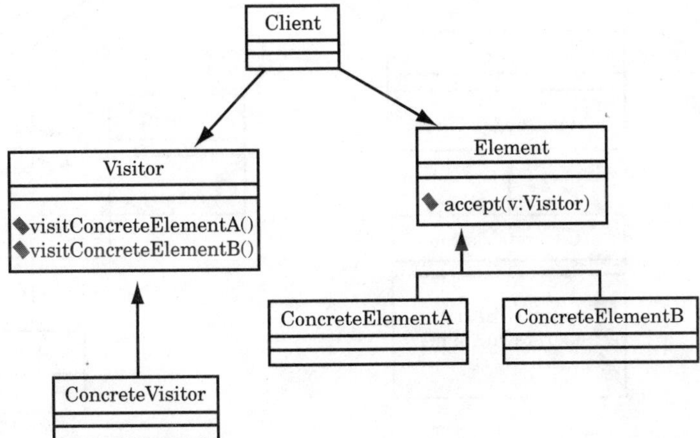

Note the use of a previously unseen accept method. This was originally included in the definition of the pattern in order to have a way to inform the Visitor about the concrete type of element that was being visited. In other words, the implementation of accept was merely the following:

```
public class A extends HierarchyElement {
  public void accept(Visitor v) {
     v.doSomethingForA();
  }
}
// or, in the case of some other concrete class
public class B extends HierarchyElement {
  public void accept(Visitor v) {
     v.doSomethingForB();
  }
}
```

Such a method is not needed when treating DOM trees because each node is guaranteed to have a getNodeType function from which the visitor can deduce the correct logic to apply. Given this difference, a general visitor pattern for DOM2 structures takes the form shown in Figure 7.6.

Figure 7.6 DOM2 Visitor structure.

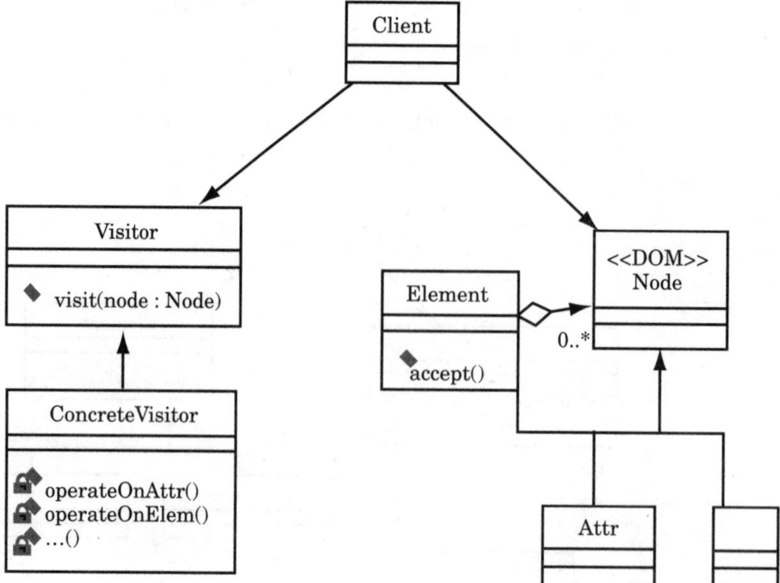

DOM2 Visitor Structure

Visitors in the context of DOM have the following elements/participants:

- **Client:** The client owns the DOM tree and knows what it wants to do, but it doesn't know *how* to do it. It creates instances of `ConcreteVisitors` to work on the tree. Sometimes the client can have the logic for the traversal, and sometimes it may be embedded on another class (even on the visitor itself, as we saw on the previous example).
- **Nodes:** The collection of nodes forms the DOM tree. Since each node has a `getNodeType` method, there is no need for the classical `accept` method, as explained previously.
- **Visitor:** This defines an interface for all visitors, so the client may interchange them freely.
- **ConcreteVisitor:** This encapsulates the logic to treat every type of node. This logic may be expressed in the form of several methods (as portrayed) or implicity, as in our merging example.

Example

In the first example we saw a Visitor that implicitly treated some node types (by ignoring them). In this example we will see a more common use of the structure shown in the previous section: a `DOMWriter`.

A `DOMWriter` is a classical application that can be found in almost every toolkit that contains a DOM implementation. It is the perfect example of Visitor because in order to print the DOM, it must treat every single type of element.

A `DOMWriter` class. Please look in the CD for variations of this class and toolkit-specific versions.

```
import org.w3c.dom.Attr;
import org.w3c.dom.Document;
import org.w3c.dom.NamedNodeMap;
import org.w3c.dom.Node;
import org.w3c.dom.NodeList;

public class DOMWriter extends Visitor{

    /** Prints the resulting document tree. */
    public static void visit(String uri)
    {
        try {
```

```
            DOMParserWrapper parser = new MyParser();
            Document document = parser.parse(uri);
            // decide which visit method to use and apply it
            // (see cd for the gory details)
        }
        catch (Exception e) {
            e.printStackTrace(System.err);
        }
    }

    /** Prints the specified node, recursively. */
    public void visitDocument(Document node) {
          out.println("<?xml version=\"1.0\"
encoding=\"UTF-8\"?>");
    }
    public void visitElement(Element node)
    {
              out.print('<');
              out.print(node.getNodeName());
              Attr attrs[] = sortAttributes(node.getAttributes());
                 for (int i = 0; i < attrs.length; i++) {
                     Attr attr = attrs[i];
                     out.print(' ');
                     out.print(attr.getNodeName());
                     out.print("=\"");
                     out.print(normalize(attr.getNodeValue()));
                     out.print('"');
              }
                 out.print('>');
                 NodeList children = node.getChildNodes();
        // Visit each child.
    }
}
```

For the complete code (including the other visit methods and a main) please refer to the CD.

Consequences

The use of Visitor pattern in applications that use DOM has a number of important consequences:

- **Improved cohesion:** Each visitor contains a well-defined, elegant operation.
- **Extensibility:** Employing visitor makes the creation and use of new algorithms over the DOM an easy task.

Iterator Pattern in DOM2 Applications

In the previous section of this chapter we saw a way to isolate new behavior over a DOM tree. This section will show how to isolate the way we *move* through the tree by introducing a new logical layer between the methods of the DOM and what the client sees.

Iterator Usage

Iterator provides a way to isolate the sequential traversal of a structure from its internal representation. It allows the client to behave in terms of abstractions such as "the next element" without knowing the internal process to get it.

Example

Preliminary Concepts

Before we start, let's review some key concepts[3] that are shown in Figure 7.7.

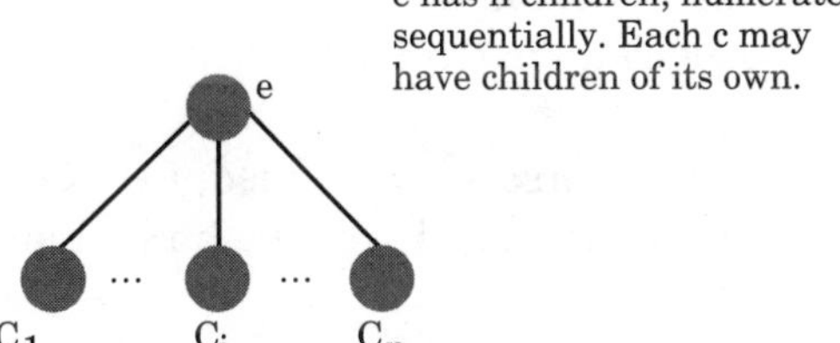
e has n children, numerated
sequentially. Each c may
have children of its own.
e
...
...

Figure 7.7
An arbitrary tree.

Given any tree (see Figure 7.7) we define the *main traversals* as follows:

- **Preorder:** Visit the current node, then each of the children (c1 through cn) applying the same algorithm.

[3] Please skip this section if you are either (1) not going to read the code on the example section in detail or (2) already familiar with traversal of tree structures in classical computer science.

- **Inorder:** Visit the first child (c1), then the current node (e), and finally the remaining children (c2 through cn) applying the same algorithm.
- **Postorder:** Visit each of the children and finally the node.

Thus, if we have a tree such as the one in Figure 7.8,

Figure 7.8 A tree and its traversals.

preorder= e, preorder(c1)...preorder(cn)

inorder= inorder(c1),e,inorder(c2)...inorder(cn)

postorder= postorder(c1)...postorder(cn),e

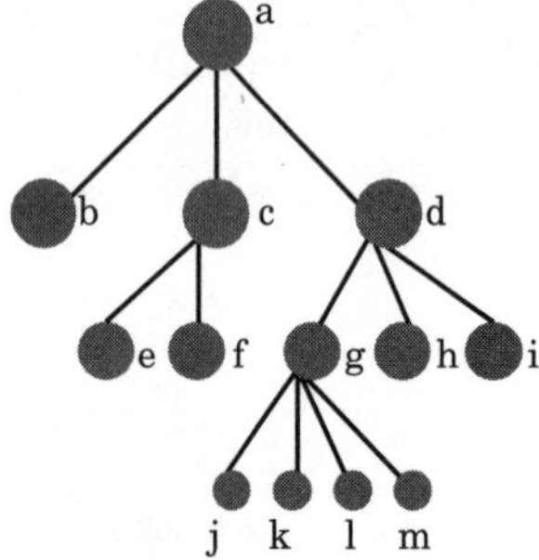

its main traversals would be:

- **Preorder:** a b c e f d g j k l m h i
- **Inorder:** b a e c f j g k l m d h i
- **Postorder:** b e f c j k l m g h i d a

Of course, other traversals are defined; for example, a level traversal would give use the sequence: a b c d e f g h i j k l m.

Different Problems Mean Different Objectives and Different Traversals

Suppose you are implementing a search engine on top of a collection of XML documents. These documents include definitions and references to explain terms and concepts in a book. In short, you are implementing a searchable XML dictionary.

Three parts will comprise the system: The XML documents themselves, a search engine, and the GUI (see Figure 7.9). For the purposes of this chapter, we will concentrate on these first two items.

The XML documents we are going to search are collections of entries. Each entry has a name, an explanation, and a list of references. Our XML dictionary document therefore looks like the following[4]:

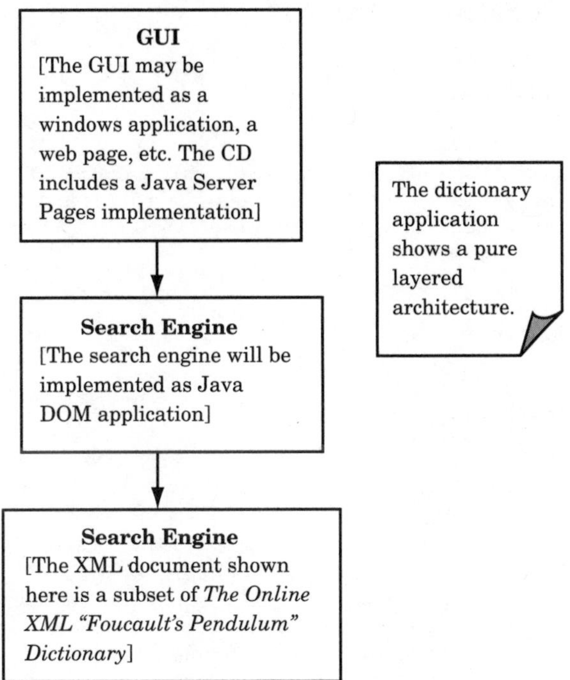
GUI
[The GUI may be implemented as a windows application, a web page, etc. The CD includes a Java Server Pages implementation]
Search Engine
[The search engine will be implemented as Java DOM application]
Search Engine
[The XML document shown here is a subset of *The Online XML "Foucault's Pendulum" Dictionary*]
The dictionary application shows a pure layered architecture.

Figure 7.9 XML Dictionary application architecture.

```
<booknotes xmlns:xlink="http://www.w3.org/1999/xlink"
                    xmlns="http://www.thefaactory.com/booknotes">
  <originalworkinfo>
    <title xml:lang="en">Il pendolo di Foucaoult</title>
    <author>Umberto Eco</author>
    <date month="jan" year="1988"></date>
  </originalworkinfo>
  <notesinfo>
    <title xml:lang="en">English Dictionary to Foucault's Pendulum</title>
    <author>Fabio Arciniegas A. &lt;faa@fabioarciniegas.com&gt;</author>
    </notesinfo>
  <entry type="term" id="pantarei">
    <name>Panta Rei</name>
    <explanation><p>Panta Rei is a greek expression used by <see
    also="heraclitus" xml:lang="en">Heraclitus</see> to express the concept
    of <emphasis>perpetual change</emphasis> in the universe. According with
```

[4] The document presented here is a small subset of the actual "Online XML 'Foucault's Pendulum' Dictionary [http://www.thefaactory.com/foucault]."

```
    Heraclitus, the only constant in the universe is change. Panta Rei means
    "<emphasis>everything flows</emphasis>".</p></explanation>
    <references>
      <appearsin directly="yes" chapter="1" xml:lang="en"/>
      <relatedoutsidereferent type="book" xml:lang="en">On Nature, by Heraclitus
      of Ephesus</relatedoutsidereferent>
    </references>
  </entry>
  <entry type="concept" id="ensof">
    <name>En-Sof</name>
    <explanation>
      <p>In the Hebrew Kabalah tradition, En-sof, which could be translated
      as "<emphasis>Infinite</emphasis>", is the primordial and perfect form
      of God, from which the ten <see also="sefirot" xml:lang="en">
      Sefirot</see> derive.</p>
    </explanation>
    <references>
      <appearsin directly="yes" chapter="1"/>
    </references>
  </entry>
  <entry type="person" id="heraclitus">
    <name>Heraclitus of Ephesus</name>
    <daterange>
      <datefrom year="540?"/>
      <dateto year="475?"/>
    <explanation>
      <p>Heraclitus of Ephesus was one of the founders of greek
      <emphasis>Methaphysics</emphasis>. His philosophy is based on the
      principle of perpetual change, immanent to all things. His vision was
      later oppossed by that of Parmenides, who argued the Universe is an
      indivisible and constant whole and any reference to change is
      self-contradictory.</p></explanation>
    <references>
      <appearsin directly="no" chapter="1"/>
    </references>
  </entry>
  <entry type="concept" id="sefirot">
    <name>Sefirot</name>
    <explanation>
      <p>...<img xlink:href="sefirot.jpg" xlink:title="the 10 Sefirot"/></p>
    </explanation>
    <references>
      <appearsin directly="yes" chapter="1"/>
    </references>
  </entry>
</booknotes>
```

Our search engine may offer many kinds of searches:

- Search by name for a particular entry
- Search for text in any point (i.e. as an entry name, as an entry explanation, as references, and even in the image URLs)

- Search for terms in a particular chapter
- Search for all other entries related to a particular entry
- Search for an image that has something to do with a term or name (i.e. an image contained in an entry with that name, or referred to in an entry with that name).

Note that each of these searches tackles a different subset of the whole DOM. The first one only cares about `name` elements; the second one must look at every single node; and the third one should only care about `chapter` attributes in `appearsin` nodes, etc.

Furthermore, if we look closely, we'll see that some traversals (Figure 7.8) apply better than others to each of these searches. For example, we know that `name` elements are always going to be located at the same level in the tree. Therefore it would be silly to do a complete postorder traversal in search of them (naturally, the correct approach is a bi-level traversal).

In summary, different searches mean different objectives and different traversals. Our goal is to find the best way to implement the multitude of searches on the engine, in a readable, cohesive, and extensible way.

A naïve attempt to put the logic for every single type of traversal/search on the main class would lead to a bloated, hard-to-maintain, and even harder-to-extend code. Furthermore, it would fail to see an intuitive nature of the problem: from the point of view of the main class, the search process is always the same.

```
get the initial node
see if it meets the criteria
3. get the next suitable node and repeat #2
```

The key to an elegant solution is the encapsulation of the logic needed to find the `next suitable` node. This includes encapsulating the correct way to traverse the tree for each problem, and the hiding of irrelevant nodes. Providing such an elegant and efficient interface is the job of the `Iterator` pattern (shown in Figure 7.10).

Iterator Pattern Structure

Iterator pattern is composed of the following participants:

- **Client:** The client owns the Aggregate (DOM tree) and needs to traverse in different ways, without coding any logic other than a seemingly sequential walk, such as the following:

```
Iterator i = myConcreteIterator();
for (i.first(); !i.isDone(); i.next())
{
    doSomethingWithThisElement(i.currentItem());
}
```

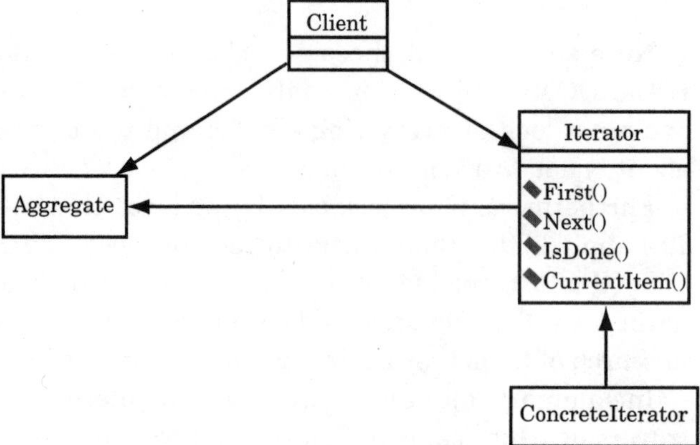

Figure 7.10 Iterator pattern structure.

- **Aggregate:** This is the collection of objects to be traversed. Traditionally, Iterator pattern is presented with an `aggregate` that is capable of creating its own `iterators`. However, since that will be not translatable to our case (we can't change the DOM interface), that option has been omitted.
- **Iterator:** This defines an interface for all iterators, so the client may interchange them freely. It provides methods for sequentially accessing the aggregate
- **ConcreteIterator:** Implements the `Iterator` interface in order to give sequential access to the aggregate without exposing the underlying logic of the traversal.

DOM2 Iterator Structure

Applying the general structure of Figure 7.10 to the context of DOM manipulation is straightforward and shown in Figure 7.11.

Example

In our example we now need to encapsulate the different traversals of the tree and give the client the impression that it is just a sequential access of the relevant elements. Naturally, Iterator is the correct pattern to apply.

The following code shows the `Iterator` and `LevelsElementsOnly Iterator` classes, as well as part of the client class. (The complete application can be found on the companion CD.)

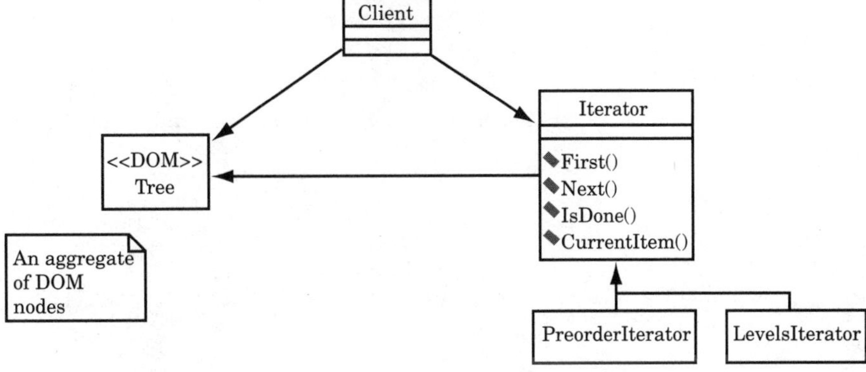

Figure 7.11 DOM2 iterator structure.

```
// Iterator Interface
// ----------------------
public interface DOMIterator
{
/**
 * Go to the first item of the collection
 */
public void first();

/**
 * Indicate whether the end has been reached
 */
public boolean isDone();

/**
 * return the next item of the collection
 */
public void next();

/**
 * return the current item
 */
public Node currentItem();
}
```

`LevelsElementOnlyIterator` implements a by-level traversal over the element nodes of a document, ignoring other nodes such as processing instructions and text nodes. The complete implementation on the

CD shows the use of this class in a server-side JavaBean implementation of the search engine.

```
import org.w3c.dom.Node;
import org.w3c.dom.Document;
import org.w3c.dom.NodeList;
import java.util.Vector;

public class LevelsElementOnlyIterator implements DOMIterator
{

/**
 * Constructor. Takes a document and initializes the iterator so
it is
 * ready to begin the traversal
 */
public LevelsElementOnlyIterator(Document doc)
{
    childrenLeft = new Vector();
    firstElement = doc.getDocumentElement();
    first();
}

public void first()
{
    current = firstElement;
}

/**
 * Indicate whether the end has been reached
 */
public boolean isDone()
{
    return current == null;
}

/**
 * return the next item of the collection
 */
public void next()
{
    NodeList candidates = current.getChildNodes();
    if(candidates != null)
    {
        int len = candidates.getLength();
     for(int i = 0; i < len; i++)
     {
       if(candidates.item(i).getNodeType() == Node.ELEMENT_NODE)
         childrenLeft.addElement(candidates.item(i));
     }
    }
    if(childrenLeft.size() > 0)
    {
       current = (Node) childrenLeft.elementAt(0);
       childrenLeft.removeElementAt(0);
```

```
        }
        else
         current = null;
    }


    public Node currentItem()
    {
        return current;
    }

    Node   current;
    Node   firstElement;
    Vector childrenLeft;
    }
```

Note how all gets simplified for the client by using Iterators:

```
 // Client fragment - space considerations.
 // A hypothetical client that for some reason needs level
 // traversal.(For a complete -and longer example- see the search
 // for chapter in the dictionary example on the CD).
    public static void hypotheticalSearch(String searchString) {
          DOMIterator i = new LevelsElementOnlyIterator(document);
          for (i.first(); !i.isDone(); i.next())
              {
                 if(i.currentItem().getNodeName().
compareTo(searchString))
                    doSomethingWithThisElement(i.currentItem());
              }
    }
```

Consequences

The use of Iterator has several positive consequences; the main one already discussed is that it enables the implementation of different traversals of the DOM without any overhead on the client. Others include maintainability and readability.

Mediator Pattern in DOM2 Applications

As discussed in Chapter 6, one of the advantages of the DOM specification is that it is language independent. So far, the examples have shown the Java implementation as applied on server-side and standalone programs; in this chapter, the JavaScript implementation is shown, as we discover a browser-based application of Mediator pattern.

NOTE

It is worth noting that there are no major complications of the JavaScript syntax and even though pointers to JavaScript learning resources are provided, they should not be necessary to understand this section.

Usage

Mediator factorizes common behavior among numerous objects in order to reduce the coupling between them. In the context of DOM processing it is often used as a way to express dependency constraints between elements.

Example

Different objects often need to know about each other's interfaces or states in order to do their job. This is inevitable to some extent, and even desirable, as the work gets distributed among many "individuals."

However, sometimes the number of relationships among objects goes beyond what is easy to maintain. The result can be hard to read, and it can be even harder to understand the mix of objects, in which everyone needs to know about everyone else to do their jobs.

This situation[5] is not unusual with dynamic manipulation of DOM trees. Consider, for example, the problem of writing a simple XHTML form[6] for the purchase of mail labels (see Figure 7.12).

The request form (Figure 7.13) will have the following fields and restrictions:

---

[5] This extreme of high coupling (illustrated in Figure 7.14) is sometimes referred to as a form of "ravioli programming—an untraceable mix of little boxes—", since it brings confusing code out of the misuse of the OO paradigm just as "spaghetti programming" did with other paradigms in the past.

[6] There is no need to consult Chapter 11 (XHTML) for this example, since it is readily applicable to HTML as supported by current browsers. The snapshots presented in this chapter are from the HTML/JavaScript implementation of the program described.

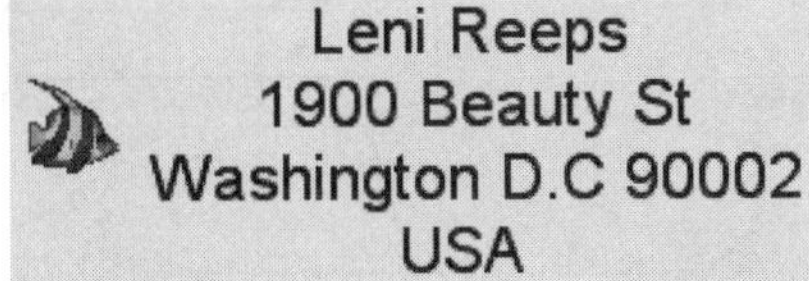

Figure 7.12
A mail label.

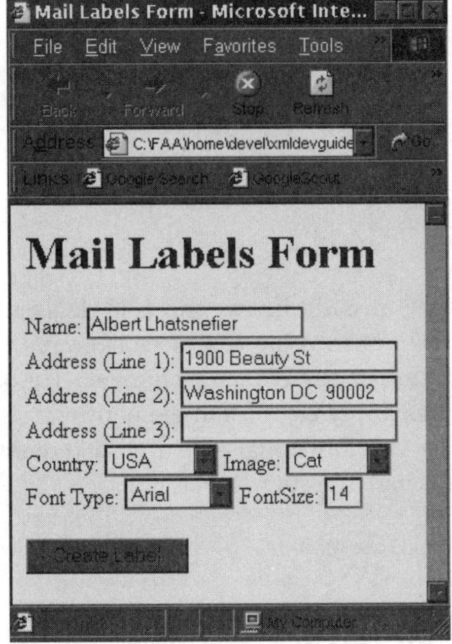

Figure 7.13
The mail label request form.

- Name
- Address line 1 and 2
- Address line 3 (only available if font size less than 20 and Country equals "USA")
- Country (has impact on the number of lines and fonts available)
- Font type (restricts fonts according to the country, in order to avoid offering fonts that don't support certain characters)
- Font size (must be less than 24)
- Picture (only available if font size is less than 20)

In order to implement the above elements and the behavior specified, each time an element gets changed, the effects must be propagated and the rest of the objects must be updated. This leads to the set of dependencies like the one depicted in Figure 7.14.

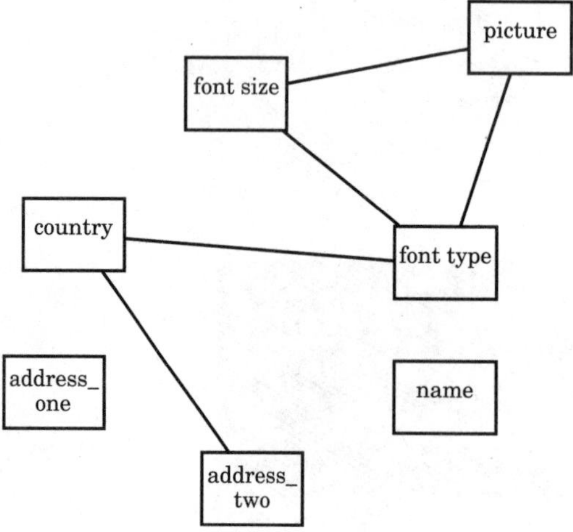

Figure 7.14 Dependencies among form components (abridged).

As you probably already know, the HTML form elements contain a `onchange` attribute whose value is a piece of scripting code that gets executed when the state of the element changes. The first approach would be to code the rules applying to each element on the value of this attribute. For example, the following code would implement the fourth element above (font type) and its restrictions:

```
<form action="labelgenerator.cgi" method="post">
```

NOTE

Only onchange methods for country and font are shown. This code illustrates a highly coupled, hard to maintain code that spawns even a simple functionality between too many individuals.

```
Name: <input type="text" name="name"> <br/>
Address (Line 1): <input type="text" name="address1"> <br/>
Address (Line 2): <input type="text" name="address2"> <br/>
Address (Line 3): <input type="text" name="address3"> <br/>
Country:
<select name="country"
        onchange="
            if(children[1].selected ||    //If either germany or
                children[2].selected)  //iceland are selected...
              {
                  address3.value = '[disabled]'; // Disable 3rd
                                                 // line
                  address3.disabled = 'disabled';
                    // note how the disabling functionality
```

```
                    // gets an ugly split between the following line
                    // and the code in the font type _onchange_ attr.
                         font.children[2].text = '[disabled]';
                }
            else
            {
                        address3.value = '';
                        address3.disabled = '';
                          font.children[2].text = 'Stencil';
                }
          ">
<option name="USA">USA
<option name="Germany">Germany
<option name="Iceland">Iceland
<option name="Italy">Italy
</select>
Image:          <select name="image">
<option>Cat
<option>Penguin
<option>Bat
</select><br/>
Font Type:
<select name="font"
        onchange="
           if(country.children[1].selected ||
              country.children[2].selected)
              {  // Don't allow Stencil to be chosen
                  if(children[2].selected)
                  {
              children[2].selected = false;
              children[0].selected = true;
                  }
              }
         ">
<option name="Verdana">Verdana</option>
<option label="Arial"/>Arial
<option label="Stencil"/>Stencil
</select>
FontSize: <input type="text" maxlength="2" size="2"><br/>
<br/>
<input type="submit" value="Create Label">
</form>
```

Note that by implementing rules this way, we will arrive at a clumsy solution. Each element must know about almost every other node in order to implement the restrictions, which is not only hard to read but also hard to maintain and extend (not to mention the fact that even the simplest things get distributed among more than one `onchange` method).

In order to implement a robust and extensible solution for our problem, it is necessary to separate the change rules from the objects themselves. One way to achieve this is to create a mediator object between them, one that is ready to listen to changes and apply the correct measures to update the state (as shown in Figure 7.15).

Before continuing with the implementation of this solution, let's review the general structure of the Mediator pattern and its DOM2 form.

Structure

Mediator is structurally very simple. Each coordinated item (colleague) reports to a mediator, which keeps the responsibility of updating every other involved item. Figure 7.15 shows the classical structure of Mediator.

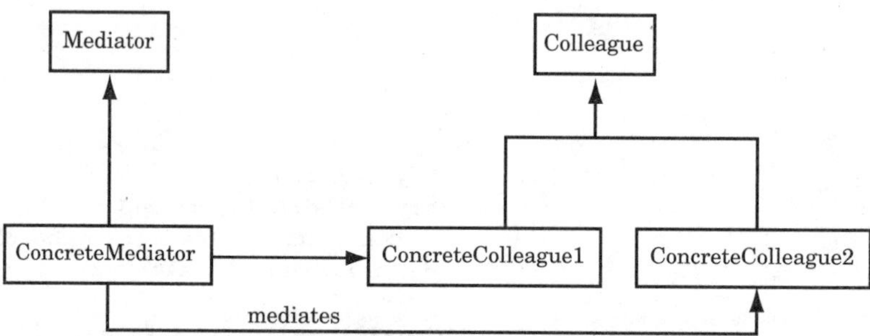

Figure 7.15 Mediator pattern structure.

DOM2 Interpreter Structure

In the context of DOM2, the structure remains virtually unchanged. The only detail worth mentioning is that this pattern is quite common in situations where only scripting—not very object-oriented—languages are available. In this case the mediator may take the simplified form of an outside, shared function.

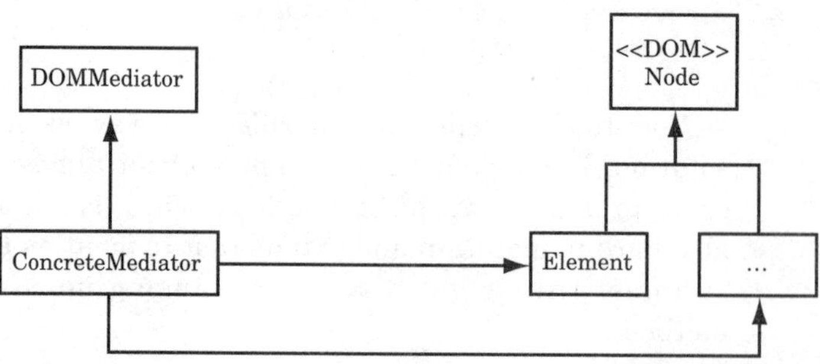

Figure 7.16 DOM2 mediator pattern structure.

Example

The conclusion of our example is natural: create a mediator that knows the rules involved in changing the form state and connect every `onchange` method to it, so it can verify the correctness of each change and propagate the necessary changes.

The following code shows the JavaScript implementation of the restrictions, as well as the complete form that uses them.

```
<html>
<head>
<!-- Mediator: Factorizes the dependencies among the components
of the
     form. It improves readability and maintanability
-->
<script language="JavaScript">
<!--Begin

var thirdLine;

function checkState()
{
      thirdLine = true; // begin by assuming 3rd line will be on
      // Check each set of restrictions.
      // Note how it all gets encapsultated in very readable and
      // cohesive functions.
      checkFontSizeRestrictions();
      checkCountryRestrictions();
      if(!thirdLine)
      {
          labels.address3.value = '[disabled]'; // Disable 3rd
                                                // line
          labels.address3.disabled = 'disabled';
      }
      else
      {
         labels.address3.value = '';
      labels.address3.disabled = '';
      }
}

function checkCountryRestrictions()
{
    // All Country-related restrictions are here, in an
    // encapsulated, accessible place. Much better than the
    // previous attempt.

       if(labels.country.children[1].selected ||  //If either
          labels.country.children[2].selected)    //germany or
                                                  //iceland are
```

```
                                                    //selected...
      {
         thirdLine = false;

         // Now, if there is a country restriction, don't let
         // unfit fonts to be chosen

         labels.font.children[2].text = '[disabled]';
         if(labels.font.children[2].selected)          {
            labels.font.children[0].selected = true;
         }
      }
      else
      {
        labels.font.children[2].text = 'Stencil';
      }
}

function checkFontSizeRestrictions()
{
      if(labels.fontsize.value > 24 || labels.fontsize.value < 0)
      {  // Don't allow sizes above 24
         labels.fontsize.value = 24;
      }
      if(labels.fontsize.value >= 20)
      {
         thirdLine = false;
         labels.image.disabled = 'disabled';
      }
      else
      {
         labels.image.disabled = '';
      }
}
-->
</script>
```

The invocation of each mediator is reduced to the following code in each element of the form (check the CD for all the HTML).

```
<select name="country"
        onchange="checkState()">
<option name="USA">USA</option>
<option name="Germany">Germany</option>
<option name="Iceland">Iceland</option>
<option name="Italy">Italy</option>
</select>
```

Consequences

Mediator has three main consequences:

- It simplifies complex multi-object interaction by breaking dependencies and other disperse behavior into factors.
- It improves readability and maintainability by putting a certain logic in an easy-to-locate and change bundle.
- It centralizes control. This means a tradeoff between complexity of object communication and complexity of the mediator. Mixed strategies can be feasible.

Summary

This chapter explored advanced techniques for the application of DOM2 in server-side, standalone and client-side applications. This concludes the exploration of direct, API-based XML programming. The next chapter is the first in Part 3, which is devoted to XML-related standards and other non-API ways of processing XML.

PART 3

XML Related Technologies

CHAPTER 8

XPath—The XML Path Language

Introduction

As XML evolves, the number of specifications and tools that focus around it grows. Some of these specifications are considered "fundamental," as they provide extensions and frameworks for XML to model itself; others are "application specifications" and build upon the fundamental blocks in order to provide languages for specific industries or tasks. Namespaces and XLink (Linking over XML) are examples of the fundamental specs of the XML family, just as XHTML and SMIL (Synchronized Multimedia Language) are examples of application specifications. Understanding and mastering the fundamental specifications of the XML family is key not only to thoroughly understanding application specs, but also to create your own.

The first fundamental specification is namespace (covered in Chapter 3) and the second is XPath. The XML Path language determines *a data model and a syntax to address parts of an XML document* and is therefore the building block for other specifications such as XSLT. Its syntax, data model, and tools are all explored in this chapter.

XPath—The Empirical Approach

A Preliminary Note on Style

XPath has been specified in a very precise way; however, simply following the layout and details of the specification is probably not the best way to learn. That is why this section provides a learn-by-example approach to the language. The next section complements this with a more theoretical approach for those interested in formal definitions.

XPath Basics

Goal and Basic Structure

The goal of XPath is to define a language that addresses parts of XML documents. In order to accomplish this goal, the XPath specification defines two main components: an expression syntax that allows the descriptions of *paths* to parts of the XML document, and, in support of those expressions, a basic set of functions—such as `count()`—known as the XPath core library.

Context and Data Model

XPath does not operate in terms of the XML syntax of the document. Instead, it views the document as a tree and operates over its nodes. This view is based on the XML Infoset[1] and even though it is somewhat similar to the DOM, it is not an object model: it is an abstraction of the document in terms of behaviorless nodes.

Figure 8.1 The XPath data model.

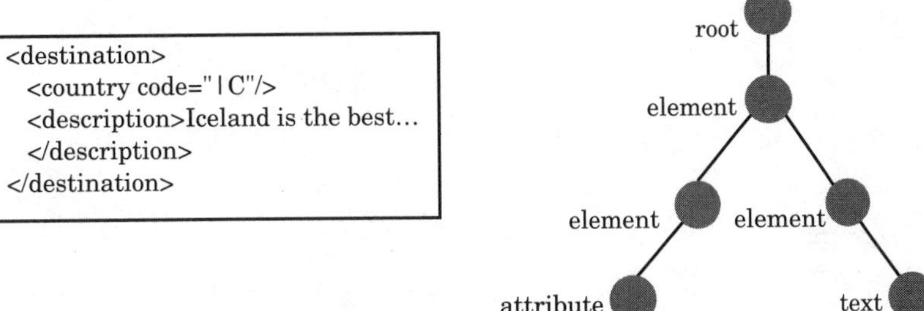

Note: See how the node for "destination" is not the root node on the tree.

As we see in Figure 8.1, each node on the tree can be of one of the following types:

- Root nodes
- Element nodes
- Text nodes
- Attribute nodes
- Namespace nodes
- Processing instruction nodes
- Comment nodes

Location Paths

A location path is an XPath expression that refers to a node or group of nodes. Location paths are constructed by concatenating steps separated by '/'. They are very similar to normal directory paths in file systems.

Location paths can use either a verbose or an abbreviated syntax. All the examples here are presented using both.

---

[1] There is no need to refer to the chapter on the Infoset to understand XPath. At this point, it is enough to understand that XPath works over the document as a tree, and not over the XML syntax.

Addressing Child Elements/Text

The first, and simpler, location path on XPath is the selection of subelements. Just like directory paths in your system, XPath expressions can be absolute (akin to `/usr/bin/perl`) or relative to a node (akin to '`bin/perl`' if you are on the '`/usr`' dir).

Before beginning, suppose you have a document like the following, and *your current node is the* `historicaldates` *element node.*

```
Historical Dates DTD
<!ELEMENT historicaldates (author,description,entry+)>

<!ELEMENT author (#PCDATA)>
<!ELEMENT description  (#PCDATA)>
<!ELEMENT entry  (date,description)>
<!ATTLIST entry
          country    CDATA   #IMPLIED
          city       CDATA   #IMPLIED
>
<!ELEMENT date  (#PCDATA)>
<!ENTITY  % number              "CDATA">
<!ENTITY  % month
"(1|2|3|4|5|6|7|8|9|10|11|12|jan|feb|mar|apr|may|jun|jul|aug|sep|oct|nov|dec)">
<!ATTLIST date
          day    %number;         #IMPLIED
          month  %month;          #IMPLIED
          year   CDATA            #REQUIRED>


An instance of historical dates
<?xml version="1.0" encoding="iso-8859-1" ?>

<!-- A simplistic document to log important dates -->
<!DOCTYPE historicaldates SYSTEM "history.dtd">

<historicaldates>
  <author>La countess de Pandesquieau</author>
  <description>Some notable imprisonments</description>

  <entry country="france">
    <date day="13" month="oct" year="1307"/>
    <description>The Templars are captured by orders of Philip IV</description>
  </entry>

  <entry country="england">
    <date day="2" month="may" year="1536"/>
    <description>Anne Boleyn is imprisioned under the charges of adultery with her
    brother and high treason.</description>
  </entry>

  <entry country="france">
    <date year="1430"/>
```

```
    <description>Joan of Arc, the maid of Orléans, is captured by Bourguignon
    soldiers</description>
  </entry>

</historicaldates>
```

The following examples illustrate the selection of subelements using the unabbreviated syntax:

- `child::author` selects the author element (remember that the context is historical dates node):

```
<author>La countess de Pandesquieau</author>
```

- `child::author/text()` selects the text nodes of the author element:

```
La countess de Pandesquieau
```

- `child::description` selects the document description (but not any of the `child::entry/description`):

```
<description>Some notable imprisonments</description>
```

- `descendant::description` selects all the document descriptions under historical dates:

```
<description>Some notable imprisonments</description>
     <description>The Templars are captured by orders of Philip
IV</description>
      <description>Anne Boleyn is imprisioned under the charges
of adultery with her
      brother and high treason.</description>
      <description>Joan of Arc, the maid of Orléans, is
captured by Bourguignon
      soldiers</description>
```

- `child::entry/child::date` selects all the dates:

```
<date day="13" month="oct" year="1307"/>
<date day="2" month="may" year="1536"/>
<date year="1430"/>
```

- `child::entry[position() =2]/child::date` selects only the date of the second entry:

```
<date day="2" month="may" year="1536"/>
```

All the previous examples can be easily abbreviated into the following forms:

- `author` is equivalent to `child::author`
- `author/text()` is equivalent to `author/text()`
- `descendant::description` is equivalent to `//description`
- `child::entry[position() =2]/child::date` is equivalent to `entry [position()=2] /date`

Accessing Attributes

For this section the context node is `/historicaldates/entry [position()=1]`, that is, the following element:

```
<entry country="france">
  <date day="13" month="oct" year="1307"/>
  <description>The Templars are captured by orders of Philip
IV</description>
  </entry>
```

- `attribute::country` and its abbreviated version `@country` select the value of the country attribute of the current node:

  ```
  france
  ```

- `child::date/attribute::year` or `date/@year`:

  ```
  1307
  ```

- Note how the previous attribute is different from `date[@year]`, which selects any date that is a child of the current node and has a year attribute:

  ```
  <date day="13" month="oct" year="1307"/>
  ```

  In general, you can think of the expression `foo/bar` as "every bar inside a foo" and `foo[bar]` as "every foo that complies with the bar condition."

- `child::date/attribute::*[position() > 1 and position() != last()]` all the attributes, except the first and the last, of the date child, regardless of their name:

  ```
  oct
  ```

Accessing Siblings, Descendants, and Ancestors

So far all the examples have addressed ways to access descendants of the context node. In this set of examples, the access to siblings, ancestors, and far descendants (Figure 8.2) will be explored.

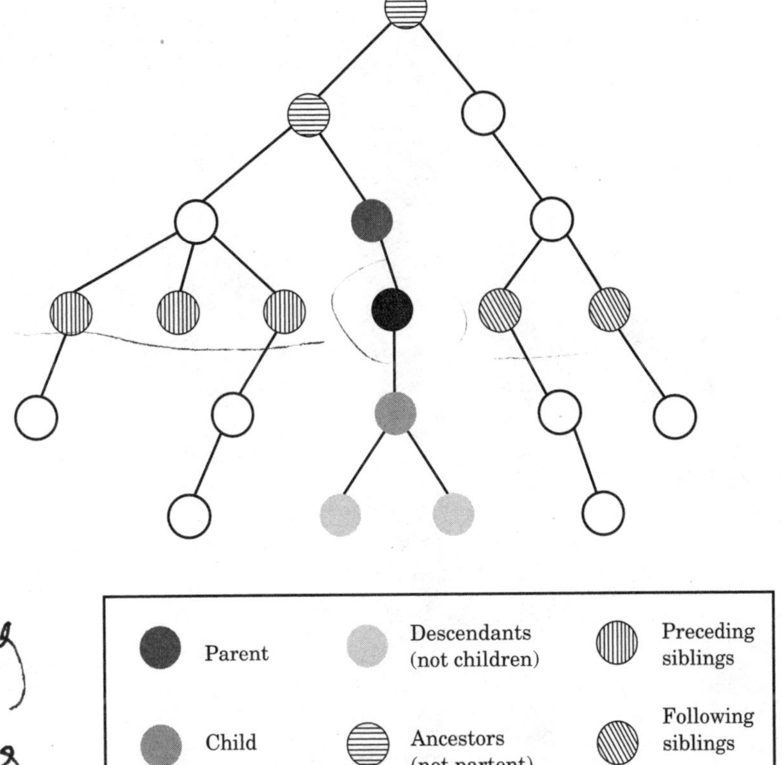

Figure 8.2
Node relationships.

For the upcoming expressions, assume we are treating the following document:

```
<?xml version="1.0" encoding="iso-8859-1"?>
<record xmlns:html="http://www.w3c.org/1999/xhtml">
   <player>Martina Hingis</player>
   <year>2000</year>

<tournament type="carpet">
```

```
    <name>Pan Pacific Open</name>
    <bye   round="1"/>
    <match round="2">
       <opponent>Raymond</opponent>
       <result win="yes">
           <set p="6" o="3"/>
           <set p="7" o="5"/>
       </result>
       <html:p>Some comment about the Raymond/Hingis game, with
<html:em>elements
       in the html namespace</html:em></html:p>
    </match>
    <match round="QF">
       <opponent>Kournikova</opponent>
       <result win="yes">
           <set p="6" o="0"/>
           <set p="6" o="2"/>
       </result>
       <html:p>Hingis beats Kournikova with an amazing
(...)</html:p>
    </match>
    <match round="SF">
       <opponent>Rubin</opponent>
       <result win="yes">
           <set p="7" o="6"/>
           <set p="6" o="4"/>
       </result>
    </match>
    <match round="F">
       <opponent>Testud</opponent>
       <result win="yes">
           <set p="6" o="3"/>
           <set p="7" o="5"/>
       </result>
    </match>
</tournament>
 <!-- insert other tournaments here... -->
</record>
```

Furthermore, assume the current node is the match against Anna Kournikova (which could be selected `/record/tournament[child::name = "Pan Pacific Open"]/match[position() =2]`, for example).

- `descendant::set` selects all the sets in the match, even though they are not direct children of the match:

```
<set p="7" o="6"/>
<set p="6" o="4"/>
```

which is equivalent to `.//set`.

- `ancestor::tournament` or `//tournament/.` selects all the ancestor tournament elements (just the parent in this case). An small variation of this construct is `ancestor-or-self`. In the following document, for example,

```
<a>
  <b>
    <c>
     <b>Let's say this is the context</b>
    </c>
  </b>
</a>
```

the expression `ancestor-or-self::b` (with `/a/b/c/b` as context) would evaluate to a node set that includes both the outermost and innermost `b` elements:

```
<b>
    <c>
     <b>Let's say this is the context</b>
    </c>
</b>
<b>Let's say this is the context</b>
```

- `following-sibling::*[@round = "F"]` selects following matches only if they are finals:

```
<match round="F">
      <opponent>Testud</opponent>
      <result win="yes">
          <set o="3" p="6"/>
          <set o="5" p="7"/>
      </result>
</match>
```

- Finally, `preceding-sibling::match`, selects all the previous matches in the same tournament (i.e. the `bye` element is omitted, even though is a preceding sibling):

```
<match round="2">
      <opponent>Raymond</opponent>
      <result win="yes">
          <set o="3" p="6"/>
          <set o="5" p="7"/>
      </result>
    <html:p>Some comment about the Raymond/Hingis game, with
      <html:em>elements in the html namespace</html:em>
```

```
        </html:p>
    </match>
```

Accessing Namespace Information

Sometimes it is useful to know at some arbitrary point the list of visible namespaces. This list can be accessed using the `namespace::*` expression.

Also, particular namespace identifiers can be included. For example, on the `/record` element of the tennis record example, the value of `namespace::html` is:

```
http://www.w3c.org/1999/xhtml
```

Functions

In the previous sections some functions of the Core Library have been presented (e.g. position, last). The vast majority of these functions are quite intuitive; however, the following list presents a description of each and examples of their use.[2] Even though this section could be read sequentially, it is mainly intended as a reference and it is recommended that you first play with the programs in the tools section of this chapter.

NODE SET FUNCTIONS

- `number position()` returns the position of a member in a node set. See examples of it above.
- `number count(node-set)` returns the number of nodes in the node set. Given the following document:

  ```
  <!DOCTYPE people [
  <!ELEMENT  people (person+)>
  <!ELEMENT  person (#PCDATA)>
  <!ATTLIST  person
             id     ID       #REQUIRED>
  ]>
  <people>
    <person id="a1">Terry Gilliam</person>
    <person id="a2">John Cleese</person>
    <person id="a3">Graham Chapman</person>
  </people>
  ```

  The expression `count(//people/person)` will evaluate to `3`.

---

[2] Note that these descriptions are, just as the rest of their section, informal. For a more precise presentation of function semantics, please go to the next section.

- `number last()` returns the position of the last member of the context (*not* the last member). Note that since the positions are counted from 1 (not from 0 like in many languages), the number returned is equal to that of `count()`. See the previous examples.
- `node-set id( object )` returns a node set of the objects with the specified ID. Note that `id` returns an node set an not a node. This is because more than one ID may be specified in the parameter (thus, resulting in many objects).

  ```
  id('a1') will evaluate to <person id="a1">Terry
  Gilliam</person> if people is the current node.
  ```

- `string local-name(node-set?)` returns the local part of the expanded name of the node. If no node-set is given, it returns the local part of the context node's name. For a node with:

  `the expanded name {http://www.thefaactory.com/panda}Panda`, local-name would return Panda.

- `string namespace-uri(node-set?)` returns the namespace URI of the expanded name. For a node with the expanded name:

  `{http://www.thefaactory.com/panda}Panda`, namespace-uri would return http://www.thefaactory.com/panda.

- `string name(node-set)` returns the qualified name representing the name of the node.

STRING FUNCTIONS

- `string concat(string, string, string*)` returns the concatenation of 2 or more strings.

  ```
  concat("gn","at","noop") returns gnatnoop
  ```

- `boolean starts-with(string,string)`

  ```
  starts-with("wilde","wild") returns true
  starts-with("wilde","ilde") returns false
  ```

- `boolean contains`

  ```
  starts-with("wilde","ilde") returns true
  ```

- `boolean substring-before(string,string)` returns the substring of the first argument that precedes the occurrence of the second argument.

```
substring-before("Lou Reed"," ") returns Lou
```

- `boolean substring-after(string,string)` returns the substring of the first argument that follows the occurrence of the second argument.

```
substring-before("Reed"," ") returns Reed
```

- `string substring(string, number, number?)` returns the substring between the positions and offset specified. Note that unlike languages such as Java or C++, the positions in the string are counted from 1 and not from 0.

```
substring("Foucault",2,2) returns "ou"
```

  If no offset is specified, all the character to the end of the string are included:

```
substring("Foucault",2,2) returns "oucault"
```

- `number string-length(string?)` returns the length of the given string.

```
string-length("Sabato") returns 6
```

  If no argument is provided, the string value of the context is taken by default.

- `string normalize-space(string?)` strips all leading and trailing whitespace and condenses every sequence of whitespace characters to a single space.

```
normalize-space("    M o l     o   k    o  ") returns "M o l o
k o"
```

- `string translate(string,string,string)` returns a modified version of the first argument, by replacing characters that appear on the second string with the characters in the same position on the third string. An example should make things clearer:

```
translate("tree", "aeiou", "AEIOU") returns "trEE"
```

```
translate("tree", "xyzt", "opqf") returns "free"
```

If there is no target in the third string for a character in the second (i.e. if the second string is larger than the third), the character is removed:

```
translate("tree", "blahe" "BLAH") returns "tr"
```

BOOLEAN FUNCTIONS

- `boolean boolean(object)` converts its argument to a boolean object according to the following rules:
  1. A number is converted to true if it is different than zero. Otherwise (including the special value `NaN` –Not a Number-) it is converted to false.
  2. `boolean(-2)` returns true.
     `boolean(0)` returns false.
  3. A node set is true if and only if it is non-empty.
  4. `boolean(/)` returns true for any well formed document.
  5. A string is converted to true if and only if it is not empty.
  6. `boolean("")` returns false.
- `boolean false()` always returns false.
- `boolean true()` always returns true.
- `boolean not(boolean)` returns the negation of its argument.
- `boolean lang(string)` returns true if the language of the context node is the same or a sublanguage of the one specified in the argument. For example, given the following element as the context node:

```
<name xml:lang="GE">
     Johann Wolfgang von Göthe
</name>
```

The value of lang("FR") would be false.

NUMBER FUNCTIONS The last category of functions in the core is the number functions. They provide basic numeric abilities. They are seldom used within the context of location paths, but can be very helpful when developing numeric-oriented XSLT stylesheets (see the XSLT chapter for examples).

- `number number(object?)` returns a number for the string representation of the object. As the examples below show, the conversion is fairly intuitive. For details about the conversion and the IEEE 754 mathematic rules please refer to the spec ([XPath]).

```
number("  -234") returns -234
number(false) returns 0
number(true) returns 1
```

- `number sum(node-set)` returns the sum of the number representations of each node on the node set. For example, given the Martina Hingis record example of a few pages ago, the following expression:

```
sum(/record/tournament/match/result/set/@p)
```

would evaluate to the sum of point scored by Martina on every set of every tournament listed—or 51.

- `number floor(number)` returns the largest integer number that is no greater than the argument.

```
floor(6.5) returns 6
floor(6.99999) returns 6
```

- `number ceiling(number)` returns the smallest integer number that is greater than the argument.

```
ceiling(6.5) returns 7
ceiling(6.000001) returns 7
```

- `number round(number)` returns the integer number closest to the argument.

```
round(7.7) returns 8
round(-1.1) returns -1
```

If there are two numbers equally close to the argument (e.g., 7 and 8 in the case of 7.5), the biggest number is taken.

```
round(5.5) returns 6
```

XPath Tools

As mentioned earlier, most current XPath uses are within the context of XSLT stylesheets. However, in some cases, being able to play with XPath expressions outside the scope of stylesheets can be highly useful, not only for learning purposes but also for the actual coding and debugging of applications.

This section shows three tools that will prove useful (maybe to a surprising extent) during your XPath-related projects, including the coding of XSLT Stylesheets.

XPath Location Path Tester

The first tool is the XPath Location Path Tester, a set of JavaServer Pages that receive a file from the client, an XPath expression for the context, and another XPath expression to evaluate (Figure 8.3).

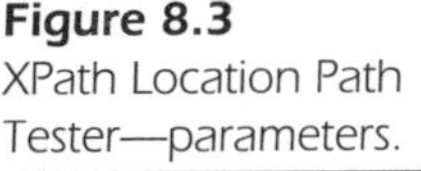

Figure 8.3 XPath Location Path Tester—parameters.

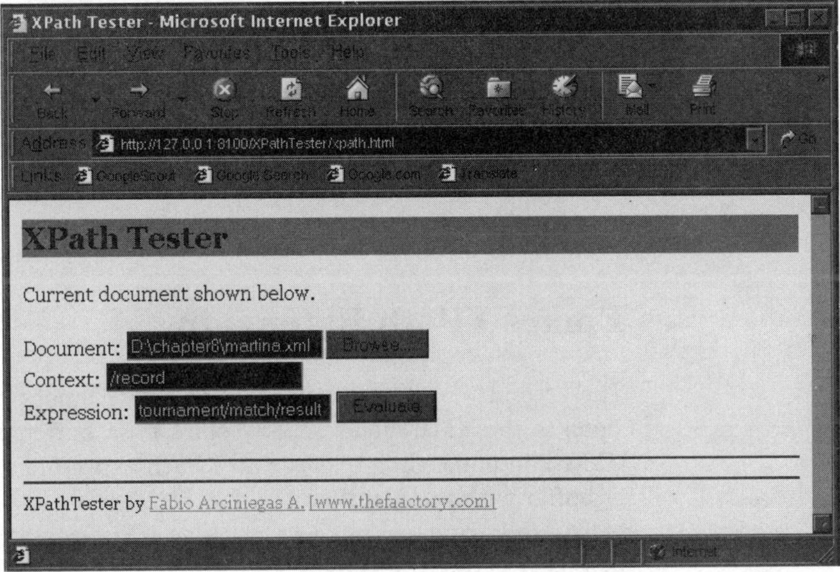

The result is the collection of nodes selected by the given location path (Figure 8.4).

This application is particularly useful when you want to see the result of a certain XPath expression without having to write a stylesheet, or—as it is more frequently the case—when stylesheet debugging is needed and you need to test a particular XPath.

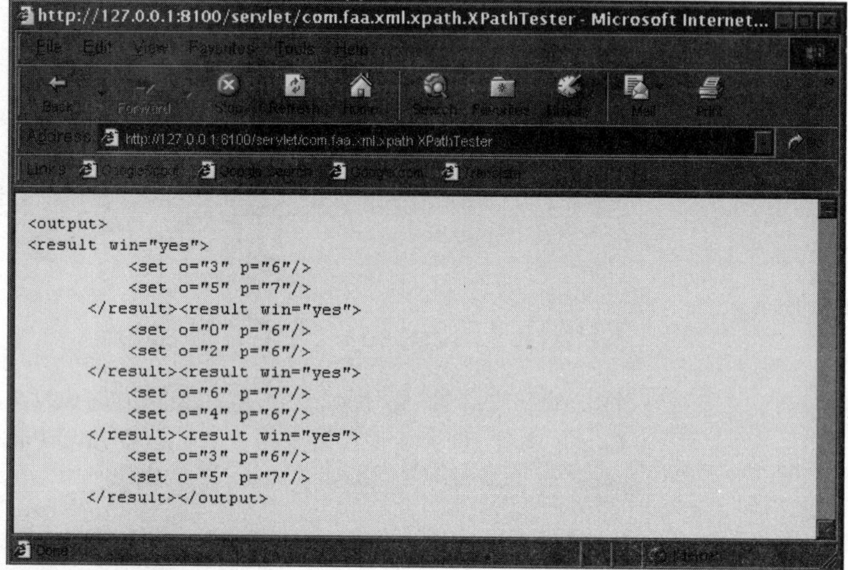

Figure 8.4
XPath Location Path Tester—result.

NOTE

The application (including source code) is distributed on the CD and can be freely installed on any JSP-capable server.[3] *If you don't have a Web server on your machine, you can use it online at* ***http://www.thefaactory.com/xpathtester***.

Emacs XPath Extension

The second tool is an invaluable friend of emacs users:[4] XPath extensions to the XML mode. At any point on a buffer press, **Control-Alt-X** (**C-M-x** in emacs lingo), enter an XPath expression, and then see another buffer with the results.

The following screenshots of emacs (Figures 8.5 and 8.6) show this tool used to find the sum of points in a match. Note how there is no need to specify a context node since it is deduced by the position of the cursor.

---

[3] This application was written by the author of this book and is distributed as open-source software under the Mozilla license.

[4] Emacs is an extremely powerful text editor with—among many others—extensions for XML. The emacs extension mentioned was also written by the author and distributed under the Mozilla license.

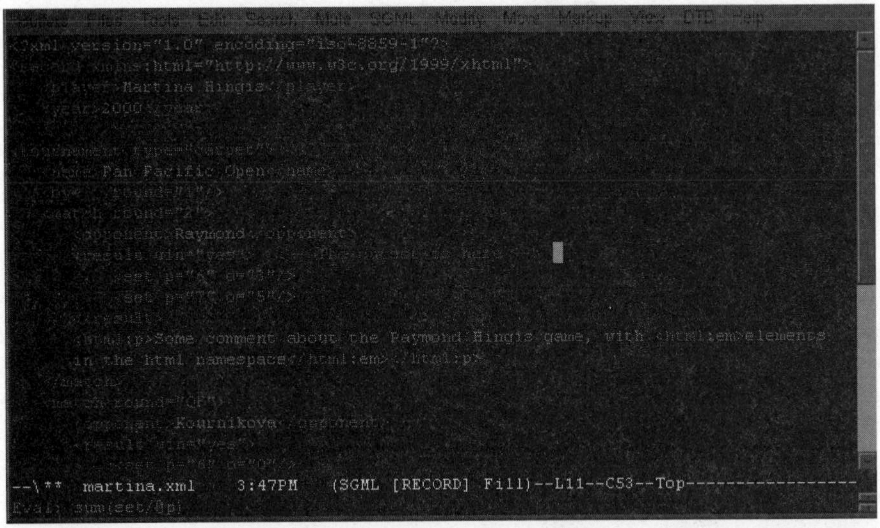

Figure 8.5
Emacs XPath extension—parameters.

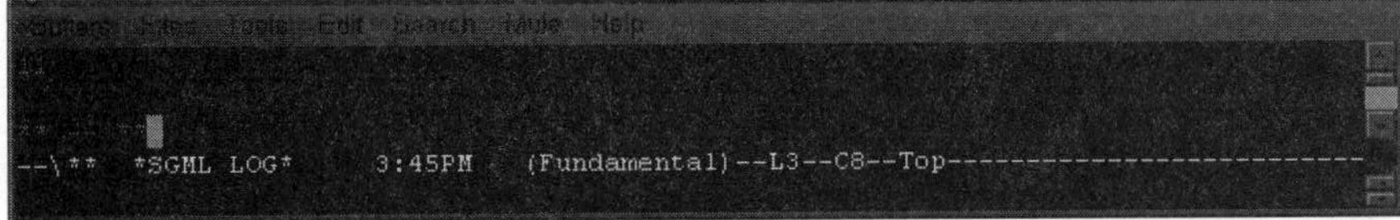

Figure 8.6
Emacs XPath extension—result.

Libraries

One final set of tools (also included on the accompanying CD) for the use of XPath expressions is XPath Libraries. Even though there is no standard API, several XML toolkits include functions for the evaluation of XPath expressions.

One notable example is the Xerces XPath library, over which the XPath Location Path Tester is implemented. The following section shows its use by presenting the XPath related code for that application.

Using XPath Programmatically

Even when the programmatic use of XPath outside XSLT is not very common, and the Java/C++ APIs for XPath are far from being standardized, it is always useful to know examples of what can be achieved by using XPath in the context of traditional application programming.

This section shows the XPath-relevant snippet of the Location Path Tester as a small example of the use of an XPath Library (Xalan[5]). Please refer to the CD for further insight on the API and more examples.

```
Node root = parser.getDocument().getDocumentElement();
Node context;
NodeList nl;
out.println("<output>");
try
{
    // Use the simple XPath API to select a node.
    context = XPathAPI.selectSingleNode(root, contextXpath);
    nl = XPathAPI.selectNodeList(context, xpath);

    // Use some of the nice Xalan classes to print the document out
    FormatterToXML fl = new FormatterToXML(out);
    TreeWalker tw = new TreeWalker(fl);
    int n = nl.getLength();
    for(int i = 0; i < n; i++)
    {
      tw.traverse(nl.item(i));
      fl.flush();
      fl.flushWriter();
    }
}
catch (Exception e)
{
    System.err.println("Exception finding: " + xpath + " " +
                e.toString() +
                " [Probably no nodes were returned] ");
    e.printStackTrace();
    return;
}
out.println("</output>");
```

Some XPath Details

For everyday use of XPath, the coverage in the previous sections of this chapter should prove more than enough. However, the following section is provided for those interested in a more formal view of the definitions and constructs of XPath. In order to avoid redundancy, only special, not previously mentioned aspects of each topic will be covered.

---

[5] Xalan is a very complete XSLT toolkit by the Apache Project. It includes an XPath API as well as an XSLT translator and numerous examples.

Location Paths

A location path is the most common type of expression in XPath. Location paths come in two versions: absolute and relative.

A *relative location path* is a sequence of one or more location steps separated by a /. Each step selects a set of nodes relative to a context node.

```
foo/bar is a relative location path with two steps
```

An *absolute location path* always starts from the root node. It is the connection of / and an optional relative path.

Steps

A step is composed of three parts:

- An *axis*, which specifies the relationship between the selected nodes and the context.
- A *node test*, which specifies the name of the nodes selected.
- An *optional set* of predicates, which can further refine the node set selected by the step.

```
child::music[@type = "blues"] is composed by the child axis,
the music node test and the [@type = "blues"] predicate.
```

Axes

XPath defines the following 13 axes:

- Ancestor
- Ancestor-or-self
- Attribute
- Child
- Descendant
- Descendant-or-self
- Following
- Following-sibling
- Namespace
- Parent

- Preceding
- Preceding-sibling
- Self

For examples and definitions of each axis (except *preceding* and *following*), refer to the section "Accessing Siblings, Descendants, and Ancestors" in this chapter.

Preceding and *following* refer to the nodes before and after the context, given the *document order*. The document order is defined as the order in which the first character of each node appears in the XML representation of the document after the expansion of general entities.

Abbreviated Syntax

The following are the rules governing syntax abbreviation (there are examples for all the abbreviations in the previous sections):

- `child` is the default axis, therefore `child::` can be omitted from a location step
- `attribute::` can be abbreviated by `@`
- `/descendant-or-self::node()/` can be abbreviated by `//`
- `/self::node()/` can be abbreviated by `.`
- `parent::node()` can be abbreviated by `..`

Summary

XPath, the XML Path language, is a powerful (and sometimes complex) means of addressing parts of an XML document. It is composed of a step-like syntax for location paths, similar to that of directories in file systems (`c:\foo\bar`) and a core library with numeric, boolean, and node-based functions.

Subsequent chapters will make extensive use of this essential specification, which is a keystone for XPointer and XSLT.

CHAPTER 9

XPointer

Introduction

XPointer defines a standard for fragment identifiers in URI references. This means XPointer provides a language for pointing to the internal structures of XML documents, and expressions of this language can be used as parts of a URI reference. This allows applications, such as browsers, to have a direct notation for specific nodes and ranges within XML documents.

XPointer is based on the XPath specification (covered in Chapter 8) and even though it is inspired by today's Web requirements, it is not restricted to presentation or linking purposes.

In addition to XPointer, this chapter also covers XML Base, a small specification for the resolution of relative URI pointers.

XPointer Basics

You have probably come across URIs such as the following while working with HTML:

```
<A HREF="http://www.metropolis.com/desc.html#actors">…</a>
```

This means "go to the point marked as `actors` within the `desc.html` document." In HTML, such a point is marked by a tag, such as the following, inside the archive:

```
<A NAME="actors"/>
```

This mechanism is not only provincial, but totally unsuited to the growing needs of an XML world, due to the following flaws:

- In order to be able to point to a particular location in the document, the document itself must be marked up in anticipation.
- The fragment-addressing portion of the URI (`#actors`) can only direct to particular points, not ranges.
- The fragment-addressing portion of the URI is not based on the structure of the document, but rather on a convention over a particular element (A).

Clearly, a mechanism for fragment addressing in XML documents must do better than this and provide, among other things, the following:

- The ability to specify more than document point, that is, the ability to specify whole ranges, as well as particular nodes
- A structure-based syntax for pointing to fragments of the document, thus relieving the need for "signaling" mark-up on the target
- A syntax configured so that expressions of the language can be included as the fragment portion of an URI.

The XPointer specification builds upon XPath to provide a structure-based fragment addressing language for XML documents.[1] The sections of this chapter will explain the syntactic and semantic additions to the XPath model after we first review basic terminology that will be used throughout the chapter.

XPath Concepts and Terms

The following concepts are key to the XPointer specification (the basis for the following definitions are included in the XPointer spec):

- **Sub-resource**—The portion of an XML resource that is identified by an XPointer; for example, the whole resource being referred to is an XML document, but a sub-resource might be a particular element inside the document. Following a link to such a sub-resource might result, for example, in highlighting that element or scrolling to that point in the document.
- **Point**—A position in XML information. The term *point* is introduced in XPointer in order to be able to talk about fragments such as the position before a certain character, while avoiding ambiguities with the term *position* as defined in XPath (i.e. the index of a node in a node-set).
- **Range**—An identification of a contiguous selection of all the XML information between two given points
- **Location-set**—An ordered list of document nodes, points, and/or ranges such as those produced by an XPointer expression; this is analogous to the node-set that is produced by XPath expressions except for the generalization to include points and ranges.

---

[1] The XPointer specification formalizes this idea by stating that "XPointer defines the basis of fragment identifiers only for the `text/xml` and `application/xml` media types."

We will also cover less fundamental XPointer concepts in this chapter.

XPointer Model and Language

Like XPath, XPointer works on an abstract view of the document, in terms of nodes, not in the syntax of its XML representation. Also like XPath, XPointer works by selecting portions of an XML document by means of an expression.

A Brief Review of Logical Paths

Since most of the time XPointer expressions use XPath logical paths, a brief review of this concept is worthwhile.

A *logical path* is an XPath expression, which is composed of steps, separated from each other by /; each has the following elements:

- An *axis*, which specifies the relationship between the selected nodes and the context.
- A *node test*, which specifies the name of the nodes selected.
- An *optional set* of predicates, which can further refine the node set selected by the step.

For example:

```
child::X[@type = "Y"] is composed by the child axis, the X node
test and the [@type = "Y"] predicate.
```

Forms of XPointer

XPointer expressions come in three flavors: one full form and two shorthand forms. Since the two shorthand forms can be defined as abbreviations of the full form, the full form will be presented first.

Full XPointers

A full XPointer is a collection of *XPointer parts*, optionally separated by whitespace. Each part starts with the string `xpointer` and is followed by an XPath expression enclosed in parentheses:

```
xpointer(id("aParticularId"))
```

To be precise, the XPointer specification states that each XPointer part must be preceded by a scheme, i.e., a particular string that governs the notation that is going to be used on the part. So, in theory one could have XPointers that look like:

```
Mp3SpecialScheme(…)
```

However, the only scheme at the moment of this writing is XPointer.

One final note about XPointers concerns *parenthesis escaping*, in which the end of the full XPointer is marked by a final closing parenthesis ")" that is matched by the corresponding opener at the beginning. Any *unbalanced* parentheses inside the expression, even if part of a literal, must be escaped using a circumflex "^." If the circumflex itself appears in the expression, it must be escaped with an extra ^, that is ^^.

Note, however, that balanced parentheses are allowed, so there is no need to escape function calls such as:

```
xpointer(id("bru")) xpointer(id("haha"))
```

Bare Names

The first form of abbreviated XPointer is designed to mimic the convenience of traditional HTML fragment identifiers.

In this form, an XPointer is merely a name, and is treated as the argument of the ID function that constitutes the whole logical path. In other words, the following two lines identify the same XPointer, the first in the "bare names" abbreviated form, and the second in the full XPointer form.

```
aleph

xpointer(id("aleph"))
```

Child Sequences

The "child sequence" abbreviation locates an element by a sequence of integers separated by slashes. Each integer n designates the nth child element of the previously located element.

For the following document,

```
<?xml version="1.0" encoding="iso-8859-1" ?>
```

```
<!-- A simplistic document to log important dates -->
<!DOCTYPE historicaldates SYSTEM "history.dtd">

<historicaldates>
  <author>Elizabeth Tudor</author>
  <description>Some notable imprisonments</description>

  <entry country="france">
    <date day="13" month="oct" year="1307"/>
    <description>The Templars are captured by orders of Philip
IV</description>
  </entry>

  <entry country="england">
    <date day="2" month="may" year="1536"/>
    <description>Anne Boleyn is imprisioned under the charges of
adultery with her
    brother and high treason.</description>
  </entry>

  <entry country="france">
    <date year="1430"/>
    <description>Joan of Arc, the maid of Orléans, is captured by
Bourguignon
    soldiers</description>
  </entry>

</historicaldates>
```

the child sequence

```
/1/2
```

would point to the document description:

```
<description>Some notable imprisonments</description>
```

As an option, the first step can be replaced by the name of the document element, in this case *historical dates*:

```
/1/6/4
```

```
is equivalent to
```

```
historicalDates/6/4
```

Finally, note that this can be formalized as a logical path for which each numerical step with value *n* can be replaced with `*[n]` or `*[position() = n ]`.

```
historicalDates/6/4
is equivalent to

xpointer(/historicalDates/*[6]/*[4]
```

XPointer Escaping

XPointer is designed to work as part of URI references. After all, it has been created to have a fragment identifier language for XML. This fact has several consequences related to character escaping:

- As part of an URI, an XPointer must undergo URI escaping.
- Since most of the time those URIs are going to be used within XML documents, XPointers also undergo certain XML escaping rules.
- XPointer itself has escaping rules of its own.

XPointer URI Reference Escaping

XPointer can be expressed with any valid character in the Unicode standard; however, since XPointers are used as fragment identifiers, they must be converted so they don't include characters invalid in a URI.

The invalid characters are non-ASCII and non-printable ASCII characters[2] plus special characters like [and] that get converted to an escaped numeric sequence of the form %HH. One fairly common example of this mechanism is applied in URLs when spaces are found (see Figure 9.1).

Figure 9.1
Escaping spaces with the URI mechanism.

2 Plus others including those listen on the IETF RFC 2396. For a complete list see the Specification, but the above subset is more than enough for most applications.

Formal URI Escaping

This optional section enumerates the steps involved in escaping a disallowed character in a URI reference:

- Each disallowed character is converted to UTF-8 as one or more bytes.
- Any octets corresponding to a disallowed character are escaped with the URI escaping mechanism (that is, converted to %HH, where HH is the hexadecimal notation of the byte value).
- The original character is replaced by the resulting character sequence.

The following example illustrates the point by showing a complex XPointer and its appearance as a URI reference:

```
xpointer(id('historicalDates')) xpointer(//*[@id='Ré'])
the previous xpointer could be used as a document fragment in the
following uri:

myDates.xml#xpinter(id('historicalDates'))%20xpointer(//*%58@id='
R%C3'%5D)
```

When used as a link on a (hypothetical) XPointer-aware browser, this link could bring the following element, part of a `historicalDate` document like that treated in the previous chapter:

```
<entry place="Re">
    <date year="1577"/>
    <description>English subsidies and volunteers are sent to the
islands
    of Ré and Oléron and the port of La Rochelle, France, to aid
the Huguenots
   </description>
  </entry>
```

XPointer XML Escaping

When used within XML documents, XPointers must escape occurrences of left angle brackets (<) and ampersands (&) to avoid introducing malformed markup into the document (the < would be mistakenly taken as the beginning of a new element, and the & would be interpreted as the beginning of an entity reference).

The easiest way to avoid these errors is by escaping these characters with the following entities: < for left bracket and & for ampersand.

```
xpointer(historicalDate position () < 3)
```

would be converted to

```
xpointer(historicalDate position lt; 3)
```

NOTE

It is also important to note that if the XPointer is used within the XML document as part of an URI (e.g., if it is the value of an href *attribute), it must also undergo the escaping described in the previous section.*

XPointer Escaping

XPointer defines two rules of its own for character escaping. Both have been previously mentioned: the first is the escaping of unbalanced parentheses by using ^. The second is the escaping of loose carets by appending an extra ^ (i.e. representing single-caret literals as ^^).

XPointer Extensions to XPath

Now we have covered the whole syntax of XPointer: there are full XPointers and two flavors of abbreviations. All XPointers contain XPath expressions and may be escaped if used as fragment identifiers in a URI and/or if used within an XML document.

Now it is time to see how XPointer extends XPath to create even more powerful expressions for fragment addressing. This section is divided into the kinds of additions that XPointer makes to XPath: concepts/constructs and functions.

New Concepts Added by XPointer to XPath

The Problem of Locations and Ranges

As we saw in Chapter 8, XPath deals with collections of nodes that represent elements, text, etc. XPath provides a language for dealing with nodes and node-sets in a concise way. This goes a long way, but is not enough for the behavior expected from XPointer.

One typical example of a document portion that should be addressable by XPointer, but cannot be addressed by XPath (since it is not a proper node or node-set) is an *arbitrary selection* like the one shown in Figure 9.2.

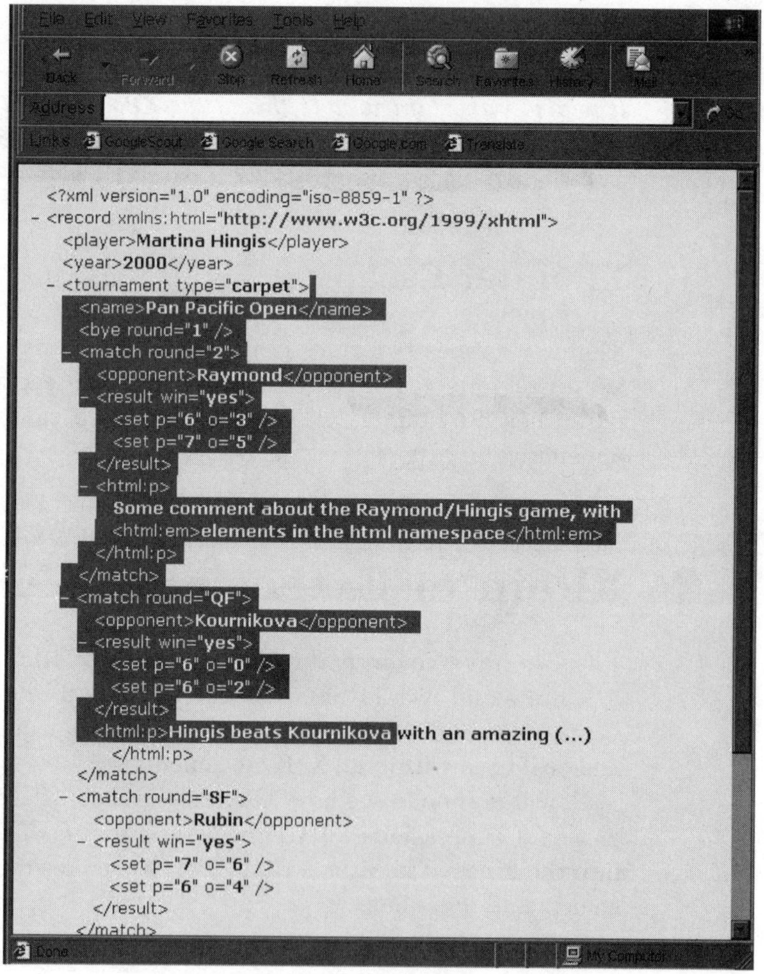

Figure 9.2
An arbitrary user selection on an XML document.

```
  <?xml version="1.0" encoding="iso-8859-1" ?>
- <record xmlns:html="http://www.w3c.org/1999/xhtml">
    <player>Martina Hingis</player>
    <year>2000</year>
  - <tournament type="carpet">
      <name>Pan Pacific Open</name>
      <bye round="1" />
    - <match round="2">
        <opponent>Raymond</opponent>
      - <result win="yes">
          <set p="6" o="3" />
          <set p="7" o="5" />
        </result>
      - <html:p>
          Some comment about the Raymond/Hingis game, with
          <html:em>elements in the html namespace</html:em>
        </html:p>
      </match>
    - <match round="QF">
        <opponent>Kournikova</opponent>
      - <result win="yes">
          <set p="6" o="0" />
          <set p="6" o="2" />
        </result>
        <html:p>Hingis beats Kournikova with an amazing (...)
          </html:p>
      </match>
    - <match round="SF">
        <opponent>Rubin</opponent>
      - <result win="yes">
          <set p="7" o="6" />
          <set p="6" o="4" />
        </result>
      </match>
```

Note how the beginning and ending points of the selections fail to coincide with element tags or text boundaries. Note also how the start and end of the selection are within elements that are not children of the same parent.

XPointer must not only be able to address this kind of document portion, but it must do so in a manner consistent with XPath. That is why two new constructs are introduced as node types: *point* and *range*.

Points

Points are arbitrary positions within XML data. A point is described by (but not necessary implemented by) a *container node* and a non-negative integer called the *index*.

When the container node can have children (e.g. element nodes), the index specifies the child number. In this case, the point is called a *node-point*.

When the container node cannot have children (e.g. text nodes and comments) the index specifies a character within its content. In this case, the point is called a *character-point*.

One important difference between node-points and character-points is that node-points are zero based (i.e. the first child is number 0) while the character-point nodes are one based (i.e. the first child is number 1). Keep this in mind, as it is the source of many errors in the creation of XPointers.

Ranges

A range is the arbitrary XML structure and content between two points. This is different from any list of nodes and characters because some nodes might be chopped (only one part of them might be included). It is important to realize that the XML representation of a range may not be well-formed XML.

NOTE

It must be noted—even though it may appear obvious—that the start and end point of a range both must be inside the same document.

Extending the Notion of Node and Node-set

XPointer extends the notion of a node, as it appears in the XPath specification, to include points and ranges as node types.

```
NodeType    ::=     'comment'
    | 'text'
    | 'processing-instruction'
    | 'node'
    | 'point'
    | 'range'
```

This decision, even when it seems somewhat unclear (we stated before that a range is *not* a node) is useful for the syntax of XPointer since it allows the construction of XPath expressions that treat the new types as "normal" nodes.[3] Because of this, the idea of a node as the addressable unit of the XPath catalog gets expanded to the concept of *location*, that is, either a node, a point, or a range. Analogously, the node-set concept gets updated to *location-set*, a collection of locations.

New Functions Added by XPointer to XPath

The following functions must be provided by XPointer-aware applications in addition to those in the XPath core library. This section is provided mainly as a reference. You should browse through it to see the functions available, but careful study can be delayed until you are actually implementing XPointer-related software.

range-to

```
location-set    range-to    (expression)
```

For each location in the context, the range-to function returns a range that goes from the context location to the point that results from evaluating the expression.

```
xpointer(1/range-to(id("tunel")))
```

NOTE

This `xpointer` *locates the range that goes from the document element to the element with ID equal to "tunnel."*

string-range

```
1")/range-to(id("chap2")))
```

```
location-set  string-range  (location-set, string, number?,
number?)
```

`string-range`, a useful yet sometimes complex function, returns a location-set that is a collection of substrings. When called with just two argu-

[3] This avoids, among other things, syntax bloating.

ments (the required location-set and string arguments), each location on the location set attribute is analyzed in search of the string parameter. If that is found, the range that goes from the first character of the string to the last (that is, the string match) is inserted in the result.

The following:

```
string-range(//fight/champion,"Ali")
```

returns all the occurrences of `"Ali"` that appear in champion elements. When it is called with four arguments, the last two specify the range of the substring to be returned. The first number will mark the index and the second will mark the length. The following:

```
string-range(//fight/champion,"Ali",1,2)
```

returns the first two letters of all the occurrences of `"Ali"` that appear in champion elements (remember that the first character in strings is 1).

range

```
location-set    range    (location-set)
```

A *covering-range* is a range that completely covers a location. The range function provides a covering range for each location in its location-set attribute.

range-inside

```
location-set    range-inside    (location-set)
```

The `range-inside` function returns a range for each location on its argument. If a particular location on the argument is a range, the location is copied to the return value. If the location is *not* a range, then it is used as the context of range that includes all its children.

start-point and end-point

```
location-set   start-point    (location-set)
location-set    end-point    (location-set)
```

For each location on the argument, these functions return a point that marks the start or the end of the location, respectively.[4]

---

[4] At the time of this writing the XPointer specification presented inconsistencies in the definition of those functions. Refer to the spec if implementing any of them.

here

```
location-set here()
```

The here function returns a location-set with only one element. This element is the node that contains the XPointer itself.

unique

```
boolean unique()
```

The unique function returns true only if the context size is equal to 1. It is shorthand for the XPath expression count()=1.

Summary of Additions to XPath

The XPointer specification adds the following to XPath:

- Two new location types, point and range, that can appear in location-set results; as well as tests for these location types.
- A generalization of the XPath concepts of nodes and node-sets to the XPointer concepts of locations and location-sets which include nodes, points and ranges.
- Rules for establishing the XPath evaluation context (outside the scope of the chapter).
- The functions string-range and range-to, which return the range location type for selections that are not single XML information-set nodes.
- The functions here and origin,[5] which provide for the relative addressing of the location of an XPointer expression itself, and the point of origin for hypertext traversal when XPointers are used in that application domain.
- The functions start-point and end-point, which address the beginning and ending locations that bound another location such as a node or range.
- The predicate function unique, which enables testing whether an XPointer expression or sub-expression finds a singleton rather than multiple locations, or no locations at all.

[5] The origin function is directly related with XLink, and its presentation will be delayed until Chapter 11, after the XLink concepts are presented.

XPointer Tools

Even though tools for XPointer are scarce at the moment, it is probable that this situation will change as soon as major browsers begin to support XLink.

The current tools are mostly within the development toolkit area and include the following (these are on the enclosed CD):

- Parser for XPointer Language (0.3) by Patrice Bonhomme
- XLink/XPointer test by W. Eliot Kimber
- XPath/XPointer tester by Fabio Arciniegas.
- psgml-xpointer.el, an add-on to PSGML (the emacs module for SGML/XML discussed in previous chapters) by David Megginson

psgml-xpointer.el shows an XPointer for any point in an XML or SGML document. The Figures 9.3 and 9.4 show a sample run of psgml-xpointer when the cursor is standing at the beginning of the author element.[6]

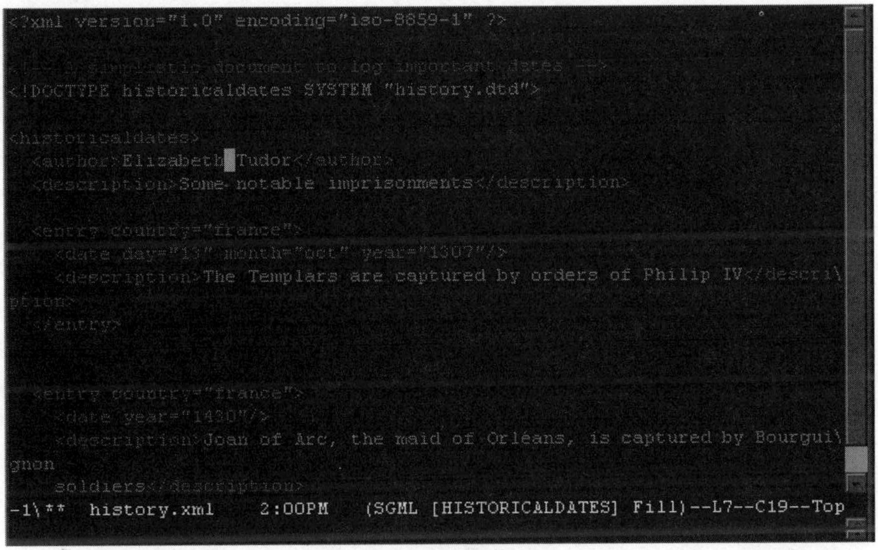

Figure 9.3
A sample document for psgml-xpointer.

```
<?xml version="1.0" encoding="iso-8859-1" ?>

<!-- A simplistic document to log important dates -->
<!DOCTYPE historicaldates SYSTEM "history.dtd">

<historicaldates>
  <author>Elizabeth Tudor</author>
  <description>Some notable imprisonments</description>

  <entry country="france">
    <date day="13" month="oct" year="1307"/>
    <description>The Templars are captured by orders of Philip IV</descri\
ption>
  </entry>



  <entry country="france">
    <date year="1430"/>
    <description>Joan of Arc, the maid of Orléans, is captured by Bourgui\
gnon
    soldiers</description>
-1\** history.xml    2:00PM   (SGML [HISTORICALDATES] Fill)--L7--C19--Top
```

[6] Note that psgml-xpointer uses child statements of the form `child(number,type,name)`, which could be translated to the more traditional form `./type::name[number]`.

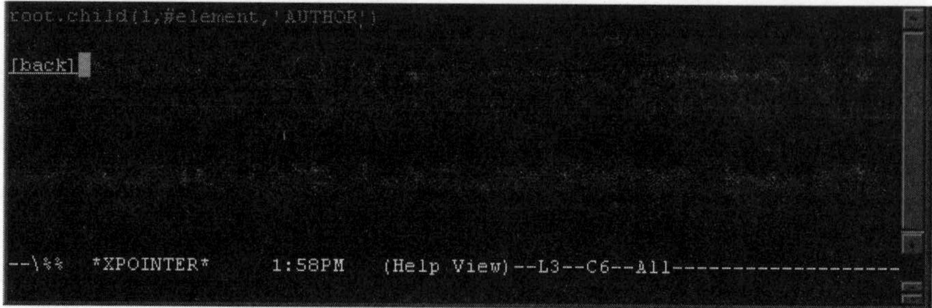

Figure 9.4 psgml-xpointer output.

Summary

This chapter presented the syntax and semantics of the XPointer language, an XPath-based mechanism that addresses fragments in XML documents. XPointer adds to XPath a set of concepts (point, location, range, and location-set), as well as a number of functions that can be used in XPath predicates.

CHAPTER 10

XLink

Introduction

To discuss the historical importance of HTML and its linking mechanism via the <A> tag, would probably be a waste of time. Almost every developer has come across this HTML construct, and its use is pervasive on the Web. A much more interesting topic is the analysis of its shortcomings and the challenges that an XML-based world of information presents to the problem of linking. That is the focus of this chapter.

XML provides us with the means to create meaningful and clear representations of data. These data can be not only complex, but also related in complex ways to other resources. The ability to express those relationships in a clear and semantically rich way is the goal of XML Linking.

XLink allows the marking of arbitrary elements as *linking elements*, which can bind together any number of local and remote resources. This chapter presents both the practical application and the theory of XLink, and discusses its implications for XML projects.

Relationships Between XML Data

To see some of the problems associated with linking in XML, consider a collection of documents like the following:

```
<person>
 <name xml:lang="en">
   <firstname>Wolfgang</firstname>
   <midinitial>A</midinitial>
   <lastname>Mozart</lastname>
 </name>
 <borndate day="22" month="jan" year="1756"/>
 <deaddate day="5"  month="dec" year="1791"/>
 <p>Born in Salzburg (...)</p>
</person>

<person>
 <name xml:lang="en">
   <firstname>Richard</firstname>
   <lastname>Wagner</lastname>
 </name>
 <borndate day="22" month="may" year="1813"/>
 <deaddate day="13" month="feb" year="1883"/>
 <biography>
   <p>This Leipzig genius (...)</p>
 </biography>
</person>
```

```
<person>
 <name xml:lang="en">
   <firstname>Anna</firstname>
   <midinitial>M</midinitial>
   <lastname>Mozart</lastname>
 </name>
 <borndate day="25" month="dec" year="1720"/>
 <deaddate day="3"  month="jul" year="1778"/>
 <biography>
   <p>Mother of Johann Chrysostom Wolfgang Gottlieb.</p>
 </biography>
</person>
```

The great advantage of writing these data as XML is that the data can be encoded with meaningful tags and attributes: semantically rich pieces of metadata that make all the difference between an extensible and strong solution and the following:

```
<html>
  <h1>Anna M. Mozart</h1>
  <p>
     <b>25/dec/1720</b>
     <b>3/jul/1778</b>
  </p>
</html>
```

Suppose you want to express the fact that a person might be bound to another by a relationship such as "motherhood" or "friendship". One way to represent this would be by mimicking the HTML `<A>` element, by implementing documents such as this:

```
<!-- mozartmom.mxl -->
<person>
 <name xml:lang="en">
   <firstname>Anna</firstname>
   <midinitial>M</midinitial>
   <lastname>Mozart</lastname>
 </name>
 <borndate day="25" month="dec" year="1720"/>
 <deaddate day="3"  month="jul" year="1778"/>
 <biography>
   <p>Mother of Johann Chrysostom Wolfgang Gottlieb.</p>
```

NOTE

Note that these links are unidirectional, one-ended, and semantically poor.

```
    <A href="mozart.xml>Mozart's mom</A>
    <A href="mariaanna.xml>She was Maria Anna's mom too</A>
    <A href="mozartdad.xml>Anna Maria was married to Leopold
Mozart</A>
  </biography>
 </person>
```

The real strength of XML wasn't utilized in this solution: instead of having meaningful markup to express the nature of the link, there is merely a URL and some textual data. Is it a motherhood relationship? Is it a marriage relationship? Could you determine programmatically how many children this woman had? How many husbands? Regrettably, there are no metadata here to tell us such things, so there is no way to know. A poor solution like this one can negate the power behind XML. It did so in one of the points where we needed its clarity the most: the problem of relationships of data.

The need to create meaningful and complex XML links is the focus of the XLink specification and of this chapter.

XLink Elements

Before jumping into concrete examples and definitions, let's take a moment to discuss the nature of XLink. XLinks can be summarized as follows:[1] An XLink linking element defines relationships between resources. A resource can be anything addressable on the net, including of course, XML data internal to the resource itself. Elements used to point to external resources are called *locators*. Finally, the relationships among resources are defined by *arcs* (see Figure 10.1).

```
<impossibilities xlink:type="extended">
```
[2]

NOTE

By virtue of having an `xlink:type` *with the value extended, this element is now an Extended element (assume the declaration of the XLink namespace).*

[1] Do not worry about the conciseness of these definitions, there are many examples ahead.
[2] These few examples are taken from work by the masters Diotavelli and Belbo (Foucault's pendulum).

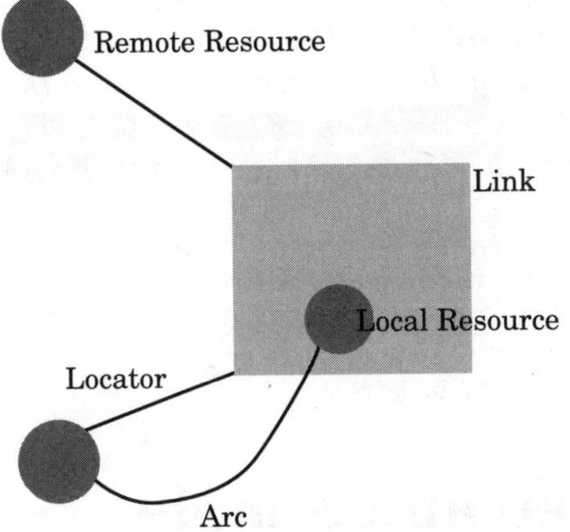

Figure 10.1
The parts of an extended link.

```
<term xlink:type="resource"
      xlink:role="oxymonoric">
      Urban Planning for Gypsies
</term>
<term xlink:type="resource"
      xlink:role="impossibilia">
      Babilonic philately
</term>
<term xlink:type="resource"
      xlink:role="oxymonoric">
      Democratic Oligarchy
</term>
```

NOTE

These terms are actually local resources which will be later bound to other resources by arcs.

```
<definition xlink:type="locator"
            xlink:role="impossibilia-faculty"
            xlink:href="impossibilia.xml"/>
<definition xlink:type="locator"
            xlink:role="oximoronic-faculty"
            xlink:href="oximoronic.xml"/>
```

The previous faculty definitions are locators. They identify an external resource by pointing to it with an `xlink:href` attribute.

```
<assignment xlink:type="arc"
            xlink:from="oximoronic"
            xlink:to="oxymoronic-faculty"/>
```

NOTE

An arc, identified by the value of "arc" on the `xlink:type` *attribute, defines relationships between resources. Note that unlike traditional links in HTML, an XLink can relate many resources with just one arc. Above and below, the assignment arc is binding two terms to a faculty.*

```
   <assignment xlink:type="arc"
               xlink:from="imbossibilia"
               xlink:to="impossibilia-faculty"/>
</impossibilities>
```

Extended and Simple XLinks by Example

In order to introduce the basic concepts behind XLink, this section will construct an example using complex and semantically rich links. The next section will present a formal view of XLink and the details of the specification.

We previously discussed the shortcomings of the HTML linking within XML by presenting the problems of relationships between *person* elements (motherhood, marriage, etc.). In this section we revisit this difficulty, but just to make things more interesting, we deal with a slightly more complex version: relationships between mythological figures.

Example Structure

This example is divided into four parts: basic DTD construction, where non-XLink structures will be defined; basic instance construction, where a non-linked set of figures will be coded; XLink DTD extensions; and XLink instance extensions, in which the model and the instance will be enhanced to reflect XLink constructs.

Even though figures are presented, the rationale behind the presentation of the results will be delayed until the end of the chapter, when more subtle issues of the language are introduced.

Basic (Non-XLink) DTD Declarations

The basic DTD declarations provide the elements and attributes for plain description of mythological figures.

PARAMETER ENTITIES

```
<!ENTITY % defaultLang        "xml:lang    NMTOKEN    'en'">
<!ENTITY % numberAtt          "CDATA">
<!ENTITY % monthAtt
"(jan|feb|mar|apr|may|jun|jul|aug|sep|oct|nov|dec)">
```

BASIC TYPE DECLARATIONS

```
<!ELEMENT date                      (#PCDATA)>
<!ATTLIST date
          day    %numberAtt;      #IMPLIED
          month  %monthAtt;       #IMPLIED
          year   %numberAtt;         #REQUIRED>

<!ELEMENT description (p+)>
<!ELEMENT p           (#PCDATA|emphasis|important)*>

<!ELEMENT emphasis   (#PCDATA)>
<!ELEMENT important  (#PCDATA)>



<!ELEMENT compilationInfo     (title,author,date)>
<!ELEMENT title               (#PCDATA)>
<!ATTLIST title
          %defaultLang;>
```

Change the values of draft and final to include alternative definitions of elements, such as name:

```
<!ENTITY % draft "INCLUDE">
<!ENTITY % final "IGNORE">

<![%draft;[
  <!ENTITY % name "#PCDATA">
]]>

<![%final;[
  <!ELEMENT firstname        (#PCDATA)>
  <!ATTLIST firstname
          %defaultLang;>

  <!ELEMENT middle           (#PCDATA)>
  <!ELEMENT surname          (#PCDATA)>
  <!ATTLIST surname
          %defaultLang;>

  <!ENTITY % name "firstname,middle?,surname">
]]>
<!ATTLIST name
```

```
        %defaultLang;>

<!ELEMENT author            (%name;)>
```

DOCUMENT AND KEY COMPLEX TYPES

```
<!ELEMENT myths          (compilationInfo,mythFiguress)>
<!ELEMENT mythFigures    (figure|story)+>
<!ELEMENT figure         (name,date?,description)>
<!ELEMENT story          (name,date?,description)>
```

Basic Instance Construction

The following document shows an instance of the type defined in the previous section. This small collection of Norse figures will later be complemented with family and battle relationships expressed as XLinks.

```
<?xml version="1.0" encoding="iso8859-1"?>
<!DOCTYPE myths SYSTEM  "myths.dtd">
```

A short collection of Norse mythology figures is:

```
<myths>
  <compilationInfo>
    <title xml:lang="en">Norse Mythology</title>
    <author>J.P. Castel</author>
    <date day="22" month="jan" year="2001"/>
  </compilationInfo>
  <mythFigures>
    <figure>
      <name xml:lang="is">Loki</name>
      <description>
     <p>Loki is one of the most prominent and interesting
figures in Norse Mythology. Initially recorded as a very
ambivalent god, akin   to the Jungian archetype of
<important>Trickster</important>, he is later deformed into a
totally evil figure, closer to the medieval lucifer.</p>
```

A link to the `trickster` (an external document) is needed.

```
<p>
```

We will add an image reference here.

```
Loki -according to some traditions, <emphasis
xml:lang="is">Ódinn</emphasis>'s brother- was twice responsible
for the death of Baldr, for (1)initially was him who tricked
```

```
Hodur into killing him and (2)when Hel agreed to free Baldr from
death if every creature cried for him, he refused to do so in the
figure of the old woman <emphasis>Thok</emphasis>.</p>
```

Links to `Baldr` and `Ódinn` are obviously needed. They must reflect the nature of the relationships:

```
</description>
  </figure>

  <figure>
   <name xml:lang="is">Balder</name>
   <description>

   <p>Balder, all light and purity was the proud son of Ódinn and
Frigga. He lived in his gold and silver palace
<emphasis>Breidablik</emphasis>, where he lived with his wife
Nanna.</p>
<p>During Ragnarok he will rise from the dead to fight bravely on
the Aesir side.</p>
```

NOTE

At this point, the necessity to expand our DTD to include narrations like the Ragnarok, is evident. Among other things, a narration could have links to participants. Furthermore, the idea of different families in battle suggests a possible complex "battle" link that would tie all the members of each side together.

```
      </description>
    </figure>
```

Other entries for `Ódinn`, `Frigga`, etc., follow.

```
    <story>
      <name>Ragnarok</name>
      <description>
     <p> Ragnarok, also called Gotterdammerung,
     means the end of the cosmos in Norse mythology. It will be
       preceded by  Fimbulvetr, the winter of winters. Three such
winters will follow each other with no summers in between.
[EMY]</p>
      </description>
    </story>
    <story>
      <name>Aesir</name>
      <description>
     <p>The collective name for the the principal race of Norse
gods; they who lived in Asgard, and with the All-Father Odin,
ruled the lives of  mortal men, the other was the Vanir.
```

```
      </p>
    </description>
  </story>
```

Other descriptions, for giants, etc., follow.

```
  </mythFigures>
</myths>
```

XLink DTD Modifications

Now it is time to enhance the DTD so each participant may be identified correctly as either a resource, a locator (a pointer to an external resource), or an arc.

ADDING THE XLINK NAMESPACE

The first step to enable XLink in a document is the inclusion of the XLink namespace. Processors will correctly identify XLink attributes only if this namespace agrees to the one specified by the XLink recommendation. The XLink namespace is identified by the following URI:

```
http://www.w3.org/1999/xlink
```

In order to add the XLink namespace we introduce the following fixed attribute to the root element (so it gets included even if the attribute is not specified in the instance document). Document and key complex types are as follows:

```
<!ELEMENT myths (compilationInfo,mythFigures)>

<!ELEMENT mythFigures       (figure|story)+>
<!ATTLIST mythFigures
          xmlns:xlink   CDATA   #FIXED
"http://www.w3.org/1999/xlink"
          xlink:type          (extended)   #FIXED "extended">
```

NOTE

The mythFigures *element itself has been turned into an XLink. This will allow the binding between figures and race descriptions.*

ADDING THE "FAMILY" ROLE TO EACH RESOURCE (FIGURE AND STORY ELEMENTS)

Each figure in Norse mythology can be classified as part of a family (i.e. a character can be either a giant or an aesir (god), or an elf, etc.). A role attribute will be added to each figure, so it can be identified as a member of a particular family. Similarly, the role attribute will be added to story, so—depending on its value—we can identify certain stories as family descriptions.

Later on, this information will be used as the basis for a character-to-family arc (Figure 10.2).

```
<!ELEMENT figure      (name,date?,description)>
<!ATTLIST figure
          xlink:type           (resource)    #FIXED "resource"
          xlink:role           NMTOKEN       #REQUIRED
          xlink:title          CDATA         #IMPLIED
>
```

NOTE

A `title` *attribute was also added to the list. This attribute will be used later when a list of the participants on the link is presented.*

```
<!ELEMENT story       (name,date?,description)>
<!ATTLIST story
          xlink:type           (resource)    #FIXED "resource"
          xlink:role           NMTOKEN       #REQUIRED
          xlink:title          CDATA         #IMPLIED
>
```

CREATING SIMPLE LINKS: ADDING AN IMAGE ELEMENT

One of the most common applications of external resources pointed out from an XML attribute are images (Figure 10.3). Let's add a simple linking element that allows the reference to external images (pretty much in the way HTML does now).

```
<!ELEMENT image (#PCDATA)>
<!ATTLIST image
          xlink:type  (simple)    #FIXED "simple"
          xlink:href  CDATA       #REQUIRED>
```

Now, let's update the `update` element so it can have images:

```
<!ELEMENT p           (#PCDATA|image|emphasis|important)*>
```

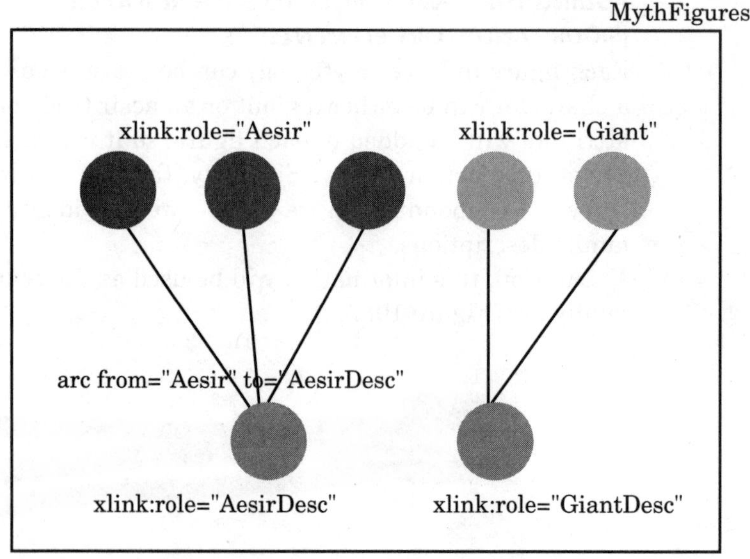

Figure 10.2 Inline link between figures and families (see DTD and document).

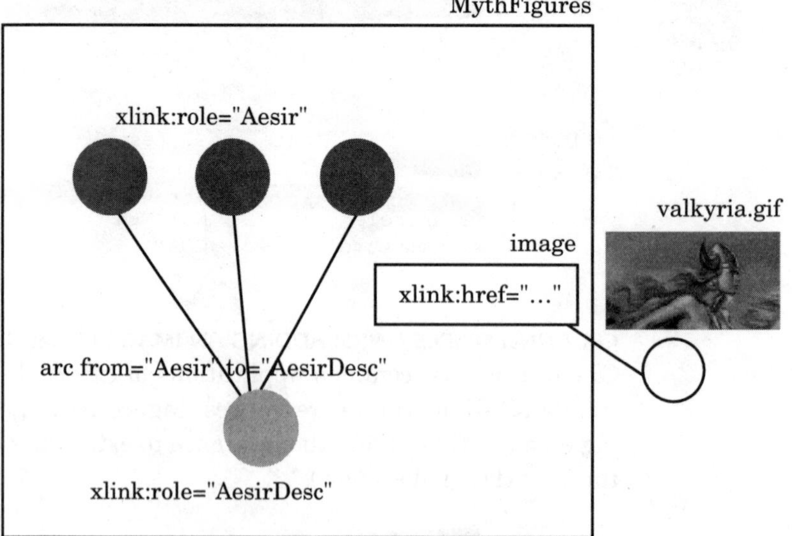

Figure 10.3 The image element as simple link inside an extended link.

FINALLY LAYING THE UNIONS: ARC DECLARATION

In order to express the union between families and individuals, an `arc` element is needed. Arcs create relationships between resources with certain roles.

```
<!ELEMENT family EMPTY>
<!ATTLIST  family
        xlink:type  (arc)           #FIXED          "arc"
        xlink:from   NMTOKEN        #IMPLIED
        xlink:to     NMTOKEN        #IMPLIED
        xlink:title  CDATA          #IMPLIED>
```

Not all the stories are descriptions of families; therefore it makes sense to make a more general relationship to bind a figure to a story: the `appearsin` `arc` element:

```
<!ELEMENT appearsin EMPTY>
<!ATTLIST appearsin
        xlink:type   (arc)          #FIXED          "arc"
        xlink:from    NMTOKEN       #IMPLIED
        xlink:to      NMTOKEN       #IMPLIED
        xlink:title   CDATA         #IMPLIED>
```

Naturally, the `mythFigures` element must be updated to allow these arcs:

```
<!ELEMENT mythFigures       (figure|story|appearsin|family)+>
```

The XLink-Aware Instance

The code for the new and XLink-enhanced document follows. Note how the `xlink:type` of the elements is not included (and thus does not pollute the document) because it is a fixed attribute that will get included when the document is validated.

Some of the parsed character data in the document have been abridged to avoid redundancy and all the XLink-related parts have been set to bold.

```
<?xml version="1.0" encoding="iso8859-1"?>
<!DOCTYPE myths SYSTEM  "myths.dtd">
<myths>
  <compilationInfo>
    <title xml:lang="en">Norse Mythology</title>
    <author>J.P. Castel</author>
    <date day="22" month="jan" year="2001"/>
  </compilationInfo>
  <mythFigures xmlns:xlink="http://www.w3.org/1999/xlink"
               xlink:type="extended">
```

NOTE

`mythFigures` is now an XLink.

```
<figure xlink:type="resource"
     xlink:title="loki"
        xlink:role="aesir">
```

NOTE

`Figure` is a resource (including `xlink:type` and is optional since it was specified as a fixed attribute with a default value in the DTD).

```
<name xml:lang="en">Loki</name>
      <description>
     <p>... A description of Loki ...</p>
      </description>
    </figure>
    <figure xlink:type="resource"
         xlink:title="balder"
            xlink:role="aesir">
      <name xml:lang="is">Balder</name>
      <description>
     <p>... A description of Balder ...</p>
      </description>
    </figure>
    <figure xlink:title="freya"
            xlink:role="vanir">
      <name xml:lang="en">Freya</name>
      <description>
     <p>Freya is a goddess of love and fertility, and the most
beautiful and propitious of the goddesses. She is the patron god-
dess of crops and birth, the symbol of sensuality and was called
upon in matters of love. She loves music, spring and flowers, and
is particularly fond of the elves (fairies). Freya is one of the
foremost goddesses of the Vanir.
```

Now add an image for Freya:

```
        <image xlink:type="simple" xlink:href="freya.gif">Freya
the beautiful</image>
        </p>
      </description>
    </figure>
    <story xlink:type="resource"
       xlink:title="Ragnarok"
          xlink:role="ragnarok_battle">
```

```
      <name>Ragnarok</name>
      <description>
     <p> ... A Description of the Ragnarok ...
```

Now add an image for the Ragnarok:

```
        <image xlink:type="simple" xlink:href="ragnarok.gif"/>
      </p>
      </description>
    </story>
    <story xlink:type="resource"
        xlink:title="Aesir Description"
           xlink:role="aesir_desc">
      <name>Aesir</name>
      <description>
     <p>The collective name for the the principal race of Norse
gods; they who lived in Asgard, and with the All-Father Odin,
ruled the lives of  mortal men, the other was the Vanir.
        </p>
      </description>
    </story>
    <story xlink:type="resource"
        xlink:title="Vanir Description"
           xlink:role="vanir_desc">
       <name xml:lang="en">Vanir</name>
       <description>
         <p>In Norse myth, the Vanir are originally a group of
wild nature and fertility gods and goddesses, the sworn enemies
of the warriorgods of the Aesir. They were considered to be the
bringers of health, youth, fertility, luck and wealth, and
masters of magic. The Vanir live in Vanaheim.[EMY]</p>
       </description>
    </story>
    <family xlink:type="arc"
         xlink:from="vanir"
         xlink:to="vanir_desc"
            xlink:title="Vanir Family"/>
```

The previous arc links *all* the vanir to their description as a family:

```
    <family xlink:type="arc"
         xlink:from="aesir"
         xlink:to="aesir_desc"
            xlink:title="Aesir Family"/>
  </mythFigures>
</myths>
```

This section provides an in-depth look at the structure and usage patterns of XLink. While the previous section may have touched some of the issues behind the everyday use of XLink, understanding this section is crucial for any serious development.

XLink Markup

As we mentioned before, instead of imposing a particular new element, the XLink strategy is to provide *global attributes* that mark *any* element as a linking element.

Every linking element, regardless of its function on the link (i.e. whether it is an arc, a resource, a locator, etc.) is marked by an `xlink:type` attribute. By convention, an element that holds a value *X* for its `type` attribute, is called an *X-type-element*. Therefore, in subsequent sections we will refer to *extended-type-elements*, *arc-type-elements*, etc., regardless of the actual name of the elements mentioned.

Extended Links

The most important construct in XLink is the *extended link*. An extended link is mainly a named container for resources, locators, and arcs. More formally, an extended link is marked by an extended-type-element and may contain the following subelements:

- Zero or more local resources (i.e. resource-type subelements).
- Zero or more locators (i.e. locator-type subelements that point to remote resources; the image element of the myth section is an example of such an element).
- Zero or more arcs binding resources (whether local or remote) based on their role information.
- An optional title.

In order to see this description more clearly, let's analyze each component.

Local Resources

Local resources are marked by resource-type elements. The complete element marked with `xlink:type="resource"`,[3] with all its attributes and subelements, is considered the local resource; however, the contents of such an element are not restricted by the XLink specification.

[3] The prefix of this name could be anything else as long as it is bound to the XLink namespace (e.g. If there is an xmlns:foo="http://www.w3c.org/1999/xlink" declaration, the name foo:type is also perfectly valid). The use of the XLink prefix is customary.

```
<A xlink:type="resource">
    <B> The contents of this resource-type element are
        not restricted.
        <C/>
    </B>
</A>
```

A resource-type element only has XLink significance if it is a child of an extended link. Within the link, the resource plays some role—it has some semantics. In order to make explicit those semantics, a resource-type element may use the `xlink:role` and `xlink:title` attributes.

The `xlink:role` attribute provides a name that identifies its nature within the link. The `xlink:title` provides a more verbose and descriptive value that is commonly aimed at the human user.

Since some of these global attributes often have fixed values for all the instances of a given element type (e.g. all the `cat` elements will have a `mammal` role), it is a customary good practice to reflect it on the DTD, and not in the instance:

```
<!ELEMENT cat                         (#PCDATA)>
<!ATTLIST xmlns:xlink      CDATA          #FIXED
"http://www.w3.org/1999/xlink"
          xlink:type       (resource)     #FIXED "resource"
          xlink:title      CDATA          #IMPLIED
          xlink:role       NMTOKEN        "mammal">
```

Since both the role and type of the resource are fixed from the DTD, the instance can be as unpolluted as:

```
<cat xlink:title="Calvin"> Calvin </cat>
```

Remember that the XLink prefix must be bound to the XLink namespace if we expect this to have any significance at all to an XLink-aware tool.

Remote Resources

Not all the resources involved in a link are local. Some of them reside not only outside the link, but possibly even outside the document itself. In order to point to such remote resources we use *locator-type-elements*. These must use the locator attribute `xlink:href` attribute to refer to the remote resource. The value of this attribute is a URI reference such as "http://www.davidbyrne.com/". In addition to the required `xlink:href` attribute, a locator-type element may have both an `xlink:role` and a `xlink:title` attributes. The semantics of these attributes are the same as for the *resource-type-elements*.

Just as with local resources, a good amount of saturation can be taken off by factorizing some attribute values on the DTD as follows:

```
<!ELEMENT mammal_facts  (foo,bar)>
<!ATTLIST mammal_facts
          xlink:type  (locator)  #FIXED      "locator"
          xlink:href  CDATA      #REQUIRED
          xlink:title            CDATA       #IMPLIED
          xlink:role             NMTOKEN     "mammal_facts">
```

NOTE

Note how the locator-type-element can include elements totally unrelated to XLink.

The following is a *resource-type-element* instance of the previous definition:

```
<mammal_facts xlink:title="Life Expectancy"
              xlink:href="expectancy.xml">
```

Locator-type elements are not links themselves; they are pointers to the remote resources. By including a locator-type element we have just declared the fact that such a resource may be a participant, but the actual description of how it is linked to other resources has not been given yet.

Traversal Rules

In order to establish how resources (whether local or remote) refer to each other, we need traversal rules.

A specifications of how certain resources relate to others. They take the form of arcs:

```
<arc xlink:from="mammal" xlink:to="mammal_fact"/>
```

This arc specifies a traversal rule between all mammals (local resources) and all `mammal_facts` (remote resources).

Arcs go from resources marked with certain roles (starting or source resources) to resources marked with others (ending or target resources). In order to specify the source and target groups, the `xlink:from` and `xlink:to` attributes are used (hence their collective name traversal attributes). The value of a *traversal attribute* must be the name of a role within the same extended link.[4]

Aside from traversal attributes, arc-type elements may have other XLink constructs known as *behavior attributes*. These hint to the client about the presentation of each arc. In particular, they determine (or, more precisely, suggest) two things: *how* to show the ending resource, and *when* to do so.

The behavior attributes are `xlink:show` and `xlink:actuate`. The `show` attribute is used to determine the desired presentation of the ending resource. Its possible values are "`new`" (open a new window and show the resource there); "`replace`" (load the pointed resource in this same window); "`embed`" (embed the pointed resource—a sound, for example); "`none`" (unrestricted—application dependent); and "`other`" (this special value means that the presentation is unrestricted by the XLink spec, but the application should look into the sub-elements for further information instead of arbitrarily taking a decision).

The `actuate` attribute is used to determine the timing of traversal to the ending resource. Its possible values are "`onLoad`" (load the ending resource as soon as the start resource is found), "`onRequest`" (load the ending resource only when the client explicitly asks for it—the user clicks the link), "`other`", and "`none`" (those two retain the same semantics as in `xlink:show`).

The following element declaration creates an *arc-type-element*:

```
<!ELEMENT facts_arc EMPTY>
<!ATTLIST facts_arc
          xlink:type        (arc)              #FIXED "arc"
          xlink:title       CDATA              #IMPLIED
          xlink:show        (new | replace |
                             embed | other |
                             none)             #IMPLIED
          xlink:from        NMTOKEN            #IMPLIED
          xlink:to          NMTOKEN            #IMPLIED>
```

The following element links all mammals to all the mammal facts by creating one single arc-type element, which is an instance of the previous declaration. The element also specifies that each fact should be shown on a new window, and only when the user clicks a starting resource.

---

[4] One very important restriction of XLinks is that there may not be duplicate arcs. Only one arc per extended link may have each combination of values for its `xlink:from` and `xlink:to` attributes.

```
<facts_arc xlink:from="mammal"
           xlink:to="mammal_fact"
          xlink:show="new"
           xlink:actuate="onRequest"/>
```

NOTE

Only one arc-type element is enough to specify every arc from each mammal to each `mammal_fact`. *If we have four cats, four dogs, and four facts about mammals, we have already made 8*4 = 32 arcs in just one element.*

TITLE ELEMENTS

The last kind of XLink element, the title-type element, has a double function that can be categorized as both semantic and presentational. A title-type element serves the same purpose as its attribute counterpart (see examples above): it gives a user-oriented description of another element.

To be significant as an XLink element, a title-type element must be a direct child of the element it describes. The following two instances illustrate the point:

```
<iceland xlink:type="locator"
         xlink:label="country"
         xlink:href="ytuaeb.xml">
<title xlink:type="title"> ICELAND! </title>

<somethingElse>
    <yetAnotherElement/>
<somethingElse>
</iceland>
```

This is a perfectly valid usage of a title-type element, since it is a direct child of the locator it is describing.

```
<usa     xlink:type="locator"
         xlink:label="country"
         xlink:href="llud.xml">
<somethingElse>
    <title xlink:type="title"> ICELAND! </title>
    <yetAnotherElement/>
<somethingElse>
</iceland>
```

In this case the title element will not be interpreted as an XLink element.

The rationale behind having a seemingly redundant type for elements is simple: some applications of XLink may need complex titles that cannot be represented as attributes. One important and frequent case is that of titles composed by XML elements such as the following:

```
<iceland xlink:type="locator"
         xlink:label="country"
         xlink:href="ytuaeb.xml">
<title xlink:type="title">
    <H1>Reykjavik &amp; Beyond!</H1>
</title>

</iceland>
```

This concludes our exploration of XLink extended links. The next section will treat simple links, a small abbreviation for simpler linking cases.

Simple Links

Even though the extensibility and power of extended links is an advantage in many cases, it is also clear that sometimes all that's needed is a simple element akin to HTML <A>. In order to provide the concise functionality of those links, XLink provides simple-type elements whose role is the functionality of a resource, a locator, and an arc, all in one. Their structure is very similar to that of links in applications such as HTML.

A simple XLink follows:

```
<anchor xlink:type="simple"
        xlink:href="sallinger.html">
   The Catcher In the Rye
</anchor>
```

Naturally, all simple elements could be rewritten as extended links with only one resource, one locator, and one arc. The following code shows the extended equivalent to the previous link:

```
<anchor xlink:type="extended">
  <resource xlink:type="resource"
            xlink:label="asource">
    The Catcher In The Rye
  </resource>

  <locator xlink:type="locator"
           xlink:label="atarget"
```

```
             xlink:href="sallinger.html"/>

  <arc xlink:from="asource"
       xlink:to="atarget"/>
</anchor>
```

Within simple-type elements, one can use behavior attributes to control the appearance of the link. The following example shows an anchor attribute that would embed a sound into the document as soon as the link is encountered:

```
<anchor xlink:type="simple"
        xlink:href="sallinger.html"
        xlink:actuate="onLoad"
        xlink:show="embed">
    The Catcher In the Rye
</anchor>
```

XLink Representation

Even though the XLink specification has many presentation-oriented aspects, the current support for XLink in browsers is quite limited. We hope that efforts toward generalized XML-based browsers can soon become a reality and that there will be general support for transforming XLink into a presentational standard. In the meantime, however, the reality is that the Web is mainly an HTML-oriented media in which XML is preprocessed in order to have an HTML representation.

XLink2HTML is an XSLT tool that allows the conversion from XLinks to a sensible HTML representation. It allows extended and simple links to be translated into HTML and JavaScript that is interpreted correctly by all modern browsers.

XLink2HTML is a fairly elaborate application of XSLT stylesheets, so the details of its inner workings will be reserved until the XSLT chapter. However, the following two quick views will illustrate some of the functionality of XLink2HTML applied to some of the extended links created in this chapter.

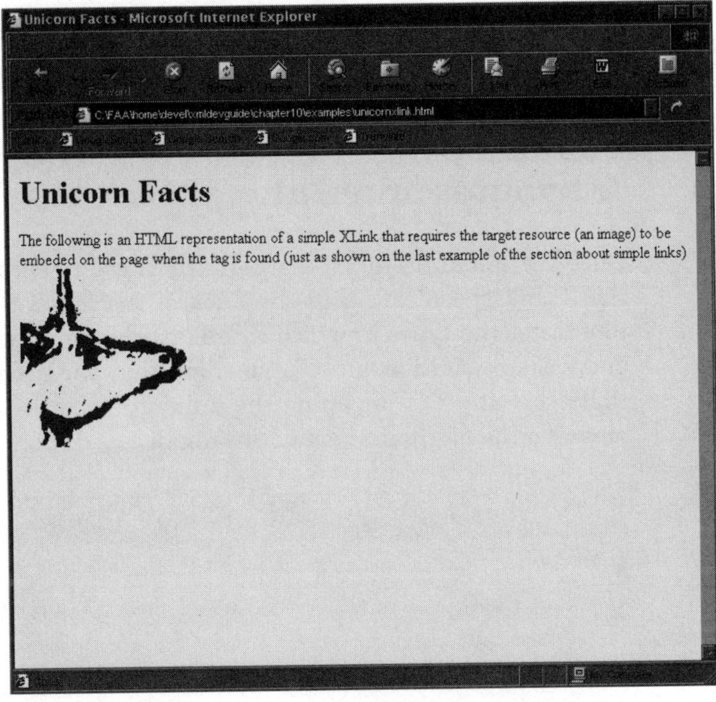

Figure 10.4 An HTML representation of a simple XLink—XLink2HTML generated.

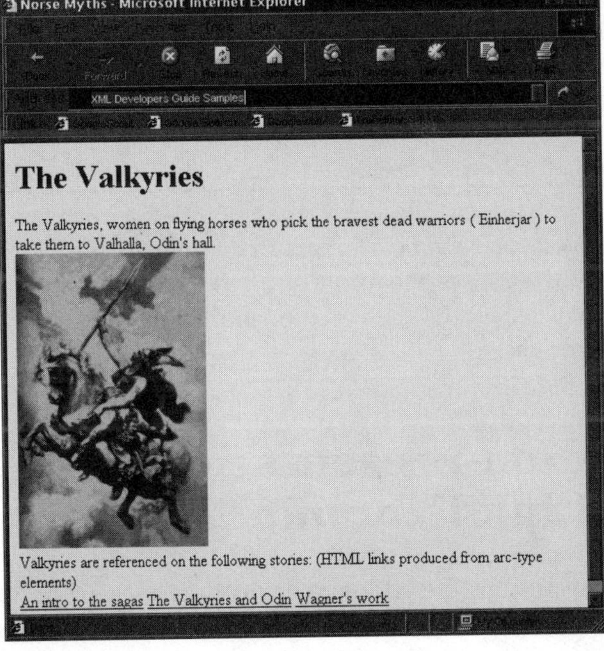

Figure 10.5 HTML output of the Viking example (Image Artist Unknown)—XLink2HTML generated.

The XLink2HTML stylesheets, complete instructions, and more samples can be found on the companion CD.

Summarizing: Taxonomy of XLink Global Attributes and Rules of Use

Once the semantics of XLink definitions are understood, we can look at the XLink specification in the form of the following tables. Table 10.1 illustrates the types in which XLink attributes may be applied. For each entry there is either an "R", meaning that the attribute is required for that type, an "O", meaning the attribute is optional, or a blank space, meaning the attribute may not be applied.

TABLE 10.1
XLink attribute usage.

	simple	extended	locator	arc	resource	title
type	R	R	R	R	R	R
href	O		R			
role	O	O	O		O	
title	O	O	O	O	O	
show	O			O		
actuate	O			O		
label			O		O	
from				O		
to				O		

As mentioned before, within any particular XLink element, only a few child types are meaningful for XLink purposes (the others are irrelevant). Table 10.2 shows the significant child types for each XLink element type.

A Non-presentational XLink Example

Even though the XLink specification is clearly oriented toward linking items such as hypertext, there is an important application of XLink outside of presentational and document-oriented areas. In order to illustrate how to take advantage of XLink outside the presentational domain, the next example shows how to make an XML representation of a directed graph, useful to share graph information among different languages and internal representations.[5]

TABLE 10.2 XLink significant types.

Parent type	Significant child types
simple	none
extended	locator, arc, resource, title
locator	title
arc	title
resource	none
title	none

Graph Concepts

A directed graph is a structure formed by a set of nodes and arcs between them (Figure 10.6).

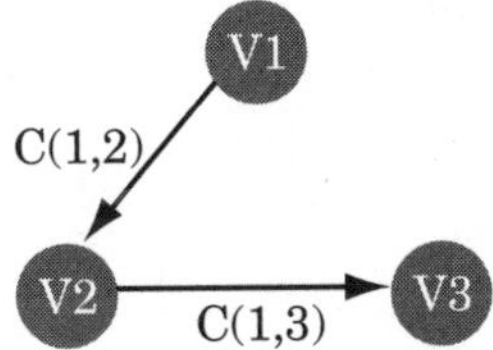

Figure 10.6 A simple directed graph.

Each node (marked V_1 through V_n, where n is the number of nodes) has associated information, while every arc has a direction and a cost—shown in the figure as c(1,2) meaning "the cost of going from V_1 to V_2." The direction of the arc in the picture is denoted by the arrow that represents it.

Directed graphs have one important restriction: there can only be one arc between each two nodes for each direction. Figure 10.7 illustrates two graphs; one is a valid example of directed graphs and the other is not.

[5] This section is optional; however, it is representative not only of XLink programmatic treatment outside hypertext, but also of SAX code.

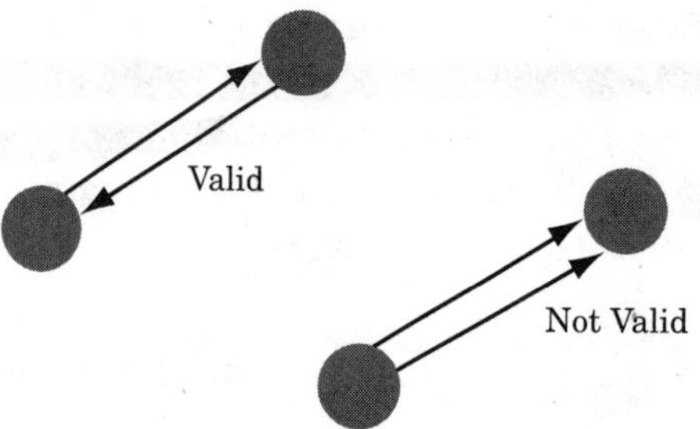

Figure 10.7 Directed graph restrictions.

Modelling Directed Graphs in XML Using XLink

The very definition of the concept of graph is a hint about how naturally it could be represented in XML using XLink: there is a set of resources (nodes), each with a certain content and each marked with a certain role (V_1 through V_n). Among those resources, arcs are laid down, with a certain direction (specified by *from* and *to*).

Specifying a directed graph using XLink is not only feasible but also natural. The following DTD specifies the element types needed:

```
<!ELEMENT graph (node*,arc*)>
```

Because graph is not only the root element, but also an extended XLink, we must put the namespace declaration here:

```
<!ATTLIST graph
          xmlns:xlink  CDATA
                       #FIXED "http://www.w3.org/1999/xlink"
          xlink:type  (extended) #FIXED "extended">
```

NOTE

Nodes are modeled as resources.

```
<!ELEMENT node  (#PCDATA)>
<!ATTLIST node
          xlink:type (resource) #FIXED    "resource"
          xlink:label  NMTOKEN   #REQUIRED >

<!ELEMENT arc  (#PCDATA)>
<!ATTLIST arc
          xlink:type (arc) #FIXED    "arc"
```

```
xlink:from     NMTOKEN       #REQUIRED
xlink:to       NMTOKEN       #REQUIRED
xlink:title    CDATA         #IMPLIED>
```

The following instance represents in XML the graph of Figure 10.8.

```
<?xml version="1.0"?>

<!DOCTYPE graph SYSTEM "graph.dtd">
<graph xmlns:xlink="http://www.w3.org/1999/xlink"
xlink:type="extended">

  <node xlink:type="resource" xlink:label="v1">A</node>
  <node xlink:type="resource" xlink:label="v2">B</node>
  <node xlink:type="resource" xlink:label="v3">C</node>
  <node xlink:type="resource" xlink:label="v4">D</node>
  <node xlink:type="resource" xlink:label="v5">E</node>

  <arc xlink:type="arc" xlink:from="v1" xlink:to="v5">5</arc>
  <arc xlink:type="arc" xlink:from="v2" xlink:to="v5">4</arc>
  <arc xlink:type="arc" xlink:from="v3" xlink:to="v5">6</arc>
  <arc xlink:type="arc" xlink:from="v4" xlink:to="v5">6</arc>

  <arc xlink:type="arc" xlink:from="v1" xlink:to="v1">3</arc>
  <arc xlink:type="arc" xlink:from="v5" xlink:to="v5">9</arc>

  <arc xlink:type="arc" xlink:from="v2" xlink:to="v1">2</arc>
  <arc xlink:type="arc" xlink:from="v3" xlink:to="v4">1</arc>
</graph>
```

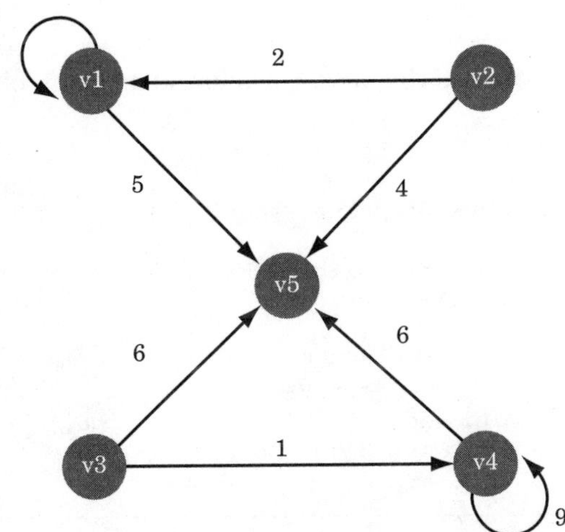

Figure 10.8
A directed graph.

Modeling Graphs in Java

As mentioned in Chapter 5, there can be big differences between the way data are represented in XML and the way they are modeled inside a program.

As a result of performance issues, the graph data can be better modeled as objects with two attributes:[7] first, a vector with the values of each node, and second, a matrix in which each intersection indicates the cost of the arc that joins the two nodes. The following diagram (Figure 10.9, a visual representation of the Java graph object for our example) will make things clearer.

Figure 10.9
A Java graph object

myGraph : An instance of the Graph Class

Arc Costs

	v1	v2	v3	v4	v5
v1	3				5
v2	2				4
v3				1	6
v4				9	6
v5					

NodeData

v1	A
v 2	B
v3	C
v4	D
v5	E

The following is the Java class for such graph objects:[8]

```
import java.util. Vector;

public interface GraphInterface
{
    // It is quite probable that all
    // values will turn out to be ints, but using Object is more
general
    public void setNodeData(int      nodeNumber,
                   Object Value);
    public void setArcCost(int sourceNode,
                  int targetNode,
```

7 The term attribute is used here in the traditional object-oriented sense of "member data."

8 The class structure proposed here is just one of many possible representations for graphs. Please refer to your toolkit to see how graphs are implemented.

```
                   int Value);

    // The most likely implementation would have something like
the following
    // private Vector nodeData;
    // private int[][] arcCost;
}
```

Concealing the two representations (each of them adequate for its own purpose), is the job of a third party: the *XML To graph builder*.

Constructing Java Graphs out of XML Graphs

On the one hand, a compact matrix representation is adequate for the performance purposes of graph-manipulation programs. On the other, an XML XLink-aware representation is ideal for graph persistence and transport.

In order to account for and take advantage of both methods, Chapter 5 introduced the concept of an XML builder, an object whose only purpose is to create a program-sensible representation out of XML data within a particular domain.

The code that implements a SAX handler for the creation of graph objects out of Graph XML documents is rather verbose; it could be better classified as a SAX example, and is therefore reserved for the CD. The XML graph toolkit (also on the CD) shows implementation of some classic graph algorithms.

Summary

XLink defines a powerful and standard method of making links in HTML. XLink defines extended links based on resources, locators, and arcs, as well as simple links that resemble the structure of traditional HTML linking.

XLink-aware documents can be represented in HTML by using transformation packages (included on the CD). XLink can also be used to solve linking issues outside the presentation domain in cases where the problems lend themselves naturally to a node/arc representation.

CHAPTER 11

XSLT: Transforming XML

Introduction

XML manipulation frequently involves transforming a source XML document into something else, for instance HTML, to present it in a browser, or maybe a PDF report, or even an image on a screen.

This chapter addresses the XML Stylesheet Language Transformations (XSLT), a language for transforming XML documents. The chapter is divided in two parts: the first presents a practical approach to the language, focusing on a simple example in which only the basics are introduced. The second part presents all the features of the language in a more formal manner, while introducing a complex example. This chapter is complemented by the advanced examples found in Chapter 12.

A Hands-on Overview

The Basics

XSLT transformations are not expressed in a programming language such as Java. Instead, they are specified in XML documents called *stylesheets*, composed of a set of rules. Each rule (also called a *template*) is defined by a pattern and a body, such as the following:

```
<xsl:template match="item"> <!--the pattern is "item"-->
   <xsl:text>Saw an item!</xsl:text> <!-- this the body -->
</xsl:template>
```

The basic processing model for XSLT stylesheets (Figure 11.1) is simple: an *XSLT processor* reads a source document, going node by node, testing whether there is a template to apply. If there is such a template, its body is instantiated.

The contents of a template are the combination of well-formed XML that doesn't belong to the XSLT namespace, and specially treated XSLT elements (i.e. meaningful elements qualified within the XSLT namespace). The following example shows a simple document and an XSLT stylesheet, and the result of passing them through an XSLT processor.

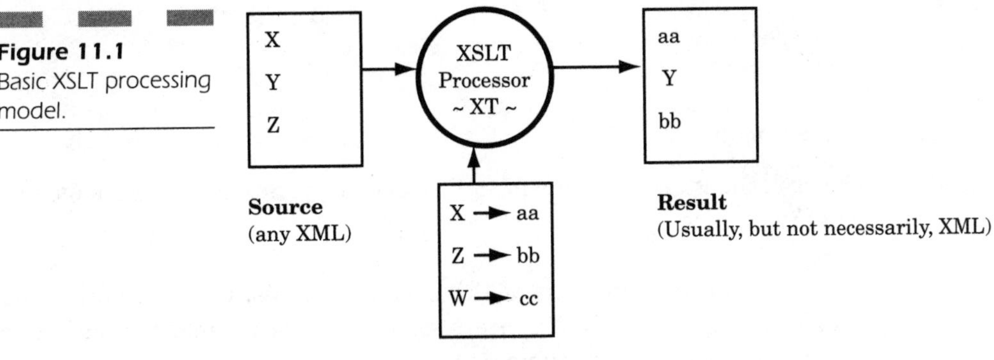

Figure 11.1 Basic XSLT processing model.

A Simple XSLT Transformation

The Source

The source document is collection of statistics about Nobel literature prizes in the twentieth century. It includes the number of prizes awarded to American writers in each decade.

```
<?xml version="1.0"?>
<!DOCTYPE nobeldata [

<!ELEMENT nobeldata (prizes+)>
<!ELEMENT prizes          EMPTY>   <!-- Prize summary by
continent -->

<!ATTLIST prizes
          continent    (africa|america|asia
                        |europa|australia)         #REQUIRED
          prizes       CDATA                       #REQUIRED
          decade       (1900s|1910s|1920s|1930s|
                        1940s|1950s|1960s|1970s|
                        1980s|1990s)               #REQUIRED>
]>
<nobeldata>
  <!-- Number of American prizes(literature) in the 20th century
-->
  <prizes continent="america" prizes="0" decade="1900s"/>
  <prizes continent="america" prizes="0" decade="1910s"/>
  <prizes continent="america" prizes="0" decade="1920s"/>
  <prizes continent="america" prizes="3" decade="1930s"/>
  <prizes continent="america" prizes="2" decade="1940s"/>
  <prizes continent="america" prizes="1" decade="1950s"/>
  <prizes continent="america" prizes="2" decade="1960s"/>
  <prizes continent="america" prizes="3" decade="1970s"/>
```

```
  <prizes continent="america" prizes="3" decade="1980s"/>
  <prizes continent="america" prizes="2" decade="1990s"/>
</nobeldata>
```

The Stylesheet

The stylesheet used to transform this document into an HTML page is a set of two rules:

1. When the root element of the document is found (the appropriate XPath expression is "/"), insert some basic HTML markup such as a paragraph as well as some text.
2. When each prize element is found (i.e. for each decade), include a row in a table.

The actual XSLT stylesheet looks like the following (the explanation of each important element is included below):

```
<?xml version="1.0"?>
<xsl:stylesheet    xmlns:xsl="/1999/XSL/Transform">

   <xsl:template match="/nobeldata">
     <html>
```

NOTE

Non-XSLT Elements are simply copied.

```
<head>
     <title>Nobel Literature Prizes</title>
      </head>
      <h1>Nobel Literature Prizes</h1>
      <p>Number of American Nobel Awards by decade</p>
      <table border="1">
     <tr>
          <th>Decade</th> <!-- table headers -->
          <th>Awards</th>
        </tr>
```

Now find templates to transform all my children:

```
<xsl:apply-templates select="*"/>

      </table>
    </html>
  </xsl:template>
```

```
  <xsl:template match="prizes"> <!-- For each decade... -->
    <tr> <!-- add a row to the table -->
      <td>
```

Now, add the value of the decade attribute:

```
     <xsl:value-of select="@decade"/>
      </td>
      <td>
     <xsl:value-of select="@prizes"/>
      </td>
    </tr>
  </xsl:template>
</xsl:stylesheet>
```

The Result

When the source document and the stylesheet are fed to an XSLT processor, the HTML page shown in Figure 11.2 is produced.

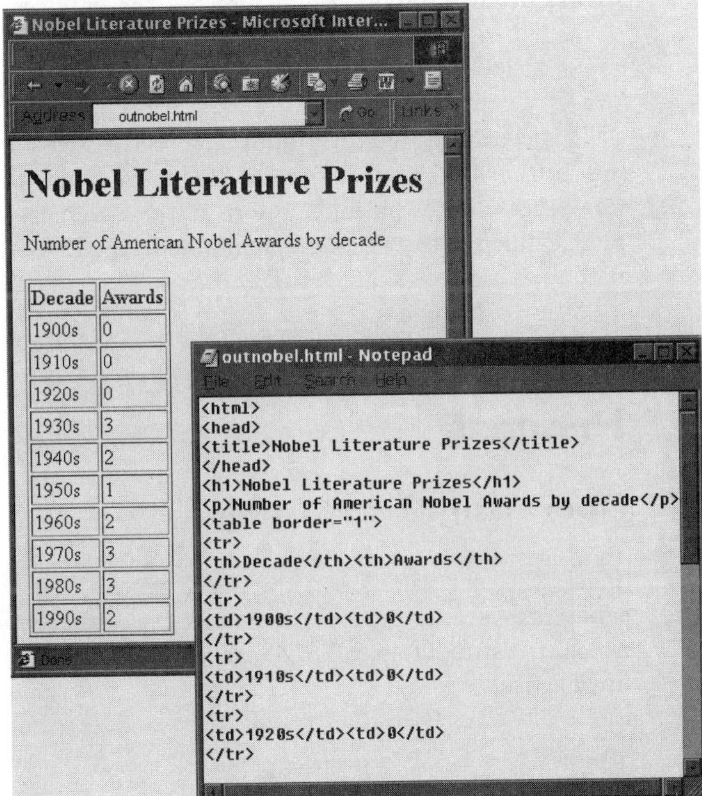

Figure 11.2 An HTML transformation of the Nobel data.

Some Important Points

Several things about our simple stylesheet should be pointed out. These items will be addressed later in the chapter.

- The root element of the stylesheet includes the XSLT namespace.[1] This is essential for the whole process because it allows the distinction of XSLT elements, which must be interpreted by the processor, and non-XSLT elements, which are simply copied to the output.
- Each template has a `match` attribute, the value of which is an *XPath expression*.[2] The XSLT processor goes node by node on the source tree; if the pattern of a given template matches the current node, the body of the template is applied.
- When a node matches a template, it becomes the context for XPath expressions within the template; thus, when the `xsl:value-of` element requests the value of the expression "`@decade`," the correct value for each element is presented.
- Once the processor finds a matching template, it needs to be explicitly instructed to go down and process the children of this template via the `xsl:apply-templates` element. If this element were not included, the XSLT processor would never visit any `prizes` element.

This concludes our first approach to the XSLT language. The following section will show a more detailed view of how the actual transformation process takes place, before continuing to more examples and a complete catalog of the elements available in the XSLT specification.

More on the Transformation Process

Operating Over Nodes

XSLT does not work upon the XML syntax of a document. Instead, it constructs a tree representation of its input, and operates over the nodes. Let's update our XSLT processing model to reflect this fact (Figure 11.3):

---

[1] For more information about namespaces see Chapter 3.
[2] XPath is covered in Chapter 8.

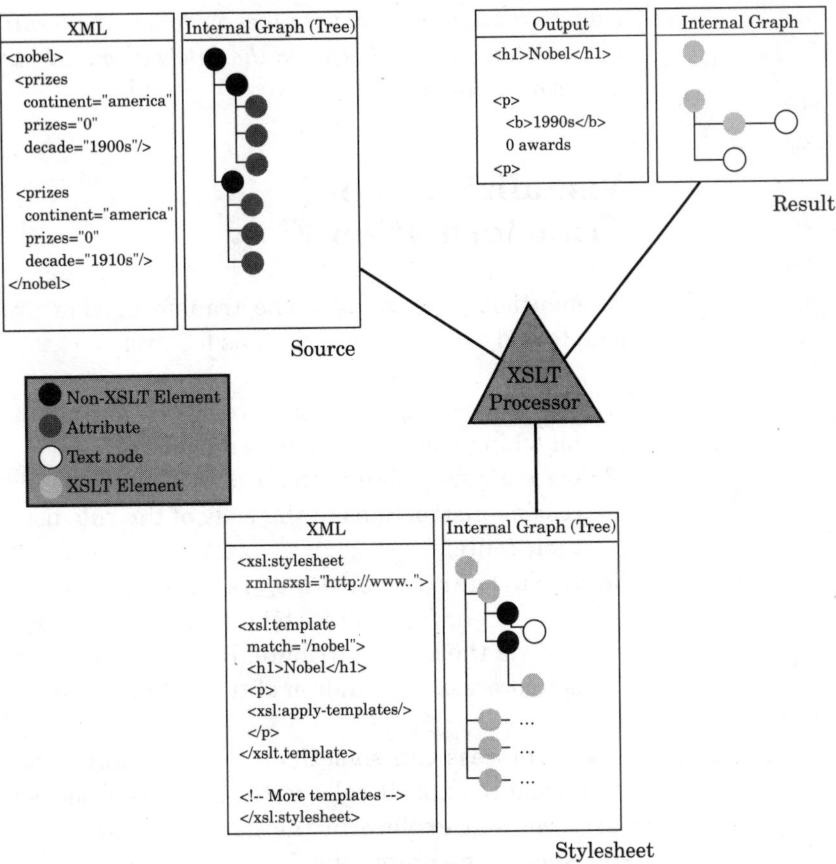

Figure 11.3
The XSLT processing model.

Our new model not only reflects the fact that XSLT processors act upon nodes, but also shows two very important aspects:

- The output of the transformation can be something other than well-formed XML. In the case of Figure 11.3, the output is malformed XML because there is no root node (both `h1` and `p` are at the root level).
- The internal model is not necessarily a tree. In fact, in the general case, it is a graph (i.e. a set of nodes and arcs) that might very well be comprised of unconnected nodes as presented in Figure 11.3.

NOTE

Some of the available literature will refer to this internal model as a grove, *a special kind of graph used to represent data according to a set of rules specified in a document called a* property set. *An XSLT processor can make good use of a grove to represent internally the output of the transformation, so it is not an error to use the term; however, for the sake of exactitude, we will refer to the internal model simply as a* graph *since this is all it has to be.*

Visualizing the Transformation Flow

As mentioned previously, the transformation process is conceptually simple and can be summarized as follows:

1. The process starts by traversing the document tree, trying to find a matching rule for each visited node.
2. Once a rule is found, the body of the rule is instantiated. XSLT processing instructions in the body of the rule use the matching node as their context.
3. If further processing is desired, the XSLT instruction `apply-templates` must be included. The nodes to process are specified via the `match` attribute. If `match` is omitted, the default behavior is to process the children of the current node.

This process can sometimes become more complex, especially when we introduce explicit calls to templates and loops (two of the many features we will explore in the next section). In time, as you see more stylesheets, the processing flow will become natural and obvious; however, if you like a visual track of what's happening in the processor you can use a tool like XSLTrace from IBM (Figure 11.4).

For the latest version of XSLTrace, please see the companion CD.[3]

XSLT Processors

Before going any further, it is advisable to install and run the initial example with at least one XSLT processor. Table 11.1 lists the best-known XSLT tools. The CD includes pointers to the installation and usage instructions for each of them.

[3] XSLTrace is, at the time of this writing, beta software. Expect bugs.

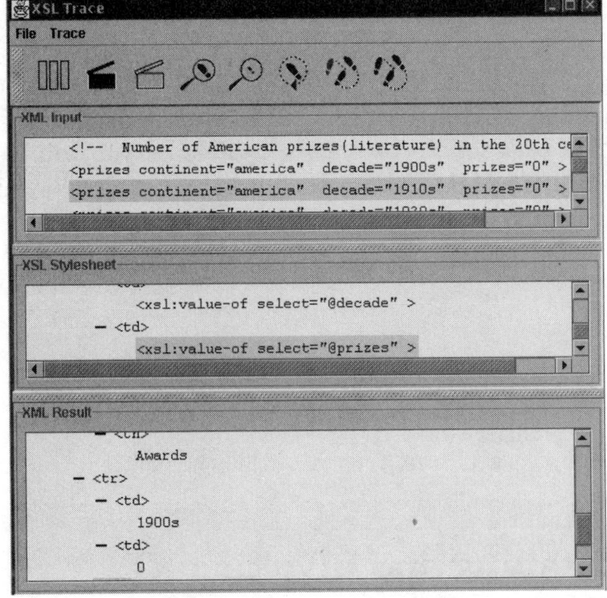

Figure 11.4 Visualizing the XSLT transformation flow with XSLTrace.

TABLE 11.1 Well-known XSLT Processors

Processor	Implementation language(s)	Author
XT	Java	James Clark
Xalan	C++ and Java	IBM/Apache project
Oracle XSLT processor (not on the CD)	C++ and Java	Oracle
Saxon	Java	Michael Kay
MSXML (**Important:** at the time of this writing, the MS processor implemented an archaic version of the XSLT recommendation.)	C++	Microsoft
XML::XSLT	Perl	SourceForge

The examples used here have all been successfully tested with both XT and Xalan for Java (two very stable and complete implementations). These are both recommended, although the invocations shown in this chapter are all for Xalan (Java).

Installing and Invoking Xalan

Installing Xalan requires JDK 1.2 or higher. To install Xalan, unpack the zip distribution, and add xalan.jar to your CLASSPATH (since Xalan uses the Xerces parser by default, you will have to add the xerces jar too, if you have not done so already). The following line will take care of the process under Windows:

```
SET CLASSPATH=%CLASSPATH%;C:\programs\xalan\xalan.jar
SET CLASSPATH=%CLASSPATH%;C:\programs\xalan\xerces.jar
```

To use Xalan, invoke it from the command line as follows:

```
java org.apache.xalan.xslt.Process -IN nobel.xml -XSL nobel.xsl -
OUT nobel.html
```

Installing and Invoking XT

Installing XT is quite similar:

```
SET CLASSPATH=%CLASSPATH%;c:\lib\java\xt\xt.jar;c:\lib\
java\xt\sax.jar
```

To use XT, invoke it, passing the names of the source file, the XSLT stylesheet, and an optional output file (in that order). Also, since XT can be used with any SAX-compliant processor to parse the files, you must also specify the parser class to use. The complete invocation looks like the following:

```
java -Dcom.jclark.xsl.sax.parser=com.jclark.xml.sax.Driver
com.jclark.xsl.sax.Driver nobel.xml nobel.xsl nobel.html
```

The Windows-only version of XT can be invoked by typing `xt` and the file parameters. This is very convenient; however, the Windows version is not immediately updated as new releases of XT become available, so staying with the Java version is probably wiser.

To add the benefit of the short invocation to the Java distribution, you can use a batch file such as the following (copy this text to a file named xt.bat and put it in a place visible to your PATH):

```
@java -Dcom.jclark.xsl.sax.parser=com.jclark.xml.sax.Driver
com.jclark.xsl.sax.Driver %1 %2 %3
```

Now that the environment is set and the basic ideas behind XSLT are presented, it is time to explore all the constructs of the language.

The Complete XSLT Language

The XSLT language is composed of seven parts, each explaining the instructions relevant to a particular type of functionality (inserting text, conditionals, etc.).

Each part of this section presents an example that adds some utility to the task of creating a small Web site out of a single XML document. The companion CD includes files for each step so you can test each construct as soon as it is presented.

The Source

The following is the source document that will be used for the examples in this section. It is an XML document with information about the best English novels of the twentieth century.[4] It will be used to create several pages, including a graphic with statistics about their distribution in time.

```
<bestnovels>
  <!-- a list of the best novels of the 20th century -->
<book year="1922">
  <title>Ulysses</title>
  <author><name>James</name>
  <surname>Joyce</surname></author>
</book>
<!-- … -->
<book year="1916">
  <title>A Portrait of the Artist as a Young Man</title>
  <author><name>James</name>
  <surname>Joyce</surname></author>
</book>
<book year="1955">
  <title>Lolita</title>
  <author><name>Vladimir</name>
  <surname>Nabokov</surname></author>
</book>
<book year="1932">
```

[4] As classified by the Modern Library.

```
  <title>Brave New World</title>
  <author><name>Aldous</name>
  <surname>Huxley</surname></author>
</book>
<book year="1961">
  <title>Catch-22</title>
  <author><name>Joseph</name>
  <surname>Heller</surname></author>
</book>
<book year="1949">
  <title>1984</title>
  <author><name>George</name>
  <surname>Orwell</surname></author>
</book>
<book year="1961">
  <title>The Moviegoer</title>
  <author><name>Walker</name>
  <surname>Percy</surname></author>
</book>
<book year="1951">
  <title>From Here to Eternity</title>
  <author><name>James</name>
  <surname>Jones</surname></author>
</book>
<book year="1957">
  <title>The Wapshot Chronicles</title>
  <author><name>John</name>
  <surname>Cheever</surname></author>
</book>
<book year="1951">
  <title>The Catcher in the Rye</title>
  <author><name>J. D.</name>
  <surname>Salinger</surname></author>
</book>
<book year="1962">
  <title>A Clockwork Orange</title>
  <author><name>Anthony</name>
  <surname>Burgess</surname></author>
</book>
 <!-- … many books more …-->
<book year="1949">
  <title>The Sheltering Sky</title>
  <author><name>Paul</name>
  <surname>Bowles</surname></author>
</book>
<book year="1934">
  <title>The Postman Always Rings Twice</title>
  <author><name>James M.</name>
  <surname>Cain</surname></author>
</book>
</bestnovels>
```

Inserting New Elements and Attributes

The first and most common thing to do in a stylesheet is to create new elements and attributes. The following subsections show two possible ways to do it.

Inserting Literal Result Elements

Inserting literal elements is something we have seen already: if an element is not an XSLT instruction, it gets copied to the output tree. The following example uses literal result elements to create the headers for our result page.

```
<?xml version="1.0"?>
<xsl:stylesheet xmlns:xsl="http://www.w3.org/1999/XSL/Transform">
   <xsl:template match="/">
     <html>
       <head>
      <title>Best Novels of the 20th Century</title>
       </head>
       <h1>Best Novels of the 20th Century</h1>
       <hr/>
     </html>
   </xsl:template>
</xsl:stylesheet>
```

NOTE

Since there are no calls to `xsl:apply-templates` *within the template, the book elements never get visited and nothing but the HTML is output.*

xsl:element and xsl:attribute

The other way to create new elements and attributes in the output tree is by using the XSLT instructions `xsl:element` and `xsl:attribute`. The `xsl:element` has only one required attribute, the `name` of the output element. The contents of `xsl:element` are interpreted and incorporated as the contents of the output element. For example, the following instruction would create two nested elements with some interspersed text:

```
<xsl:element name="paragraph">
    Speak to this gentle hearing kind commends.
    <xsl:element name="emphasis">
         [To Aumerle]
    </xsl:element>
    We do debase ourselves, cousin, do we not,…
```

```
</xsl:element>
```

The result of evaluating the above within an XSLT template is:

```
<paragraph>
    Speak to this gentle hearing kind commends.
    <emphasis>
        [To Aumerle]
    </emphasis>
    We do debase ourselves, cousin, do we not,…
</paragraph>
```

Similarly, the `xsl:attribute` will create an attribute with the given `name` if used inside an `xsl:element`.

```
<xsl:element name="title">
     <xsl:attribute name="xml:lang">fr</xsl:attribute>
     Bouvard et Pécuchet
</xsl:element>
```

will create the output element:

```
<title xml:lang="fr">
     Bouvard et Pécuchet
</title>
```

It is important to note that instances of the `xsl:attribute` element will only produce the desired output if they are inserted as children of an element.

Nice, but Why?

By now, you are probably wondering why you would want to go through the trouble of `xsl:element` and `xsl:attribute` if you can directly write literal values. The answer is simple: sometimes you don't know in advance what the contents of an element will be. `xsl:attribute` and `xsl:element` allow you to create new nodes whose values are dependent on the output and deduced only at run time. The following example illustrates the point.

Let us make an HTML page with search references for each book. The goal of our stylesheet will be to provide a link to a google.com search such as the following for each author listed:

```
<a href="http://www.google.com/search?q=james+joyce>James
Joyce</a>
```

Since the value of the href attribute is dependent on the input, we must use xsl:attribute to produce it. The following template implements the goal:

```
<xsl:template match="book"> <!-- apply this to every book -->
    <br/>
    <xsl:element name="a">
      <xsl:attribute name="href">
        http://www.google.com/search?q=
            <xsl:value-of select="author/name"/>
        +
            <xsl:value-of select="author/surname"/>
  </xsl:attribute>
   <xsl:value-of select="author/name"/>
   <xsl:value-of select="author/surname"/>
    </xsl:element>
</xsl:template>
```

The result of our template can be appreciated on Figure 11.5 (note the address in the status bar).

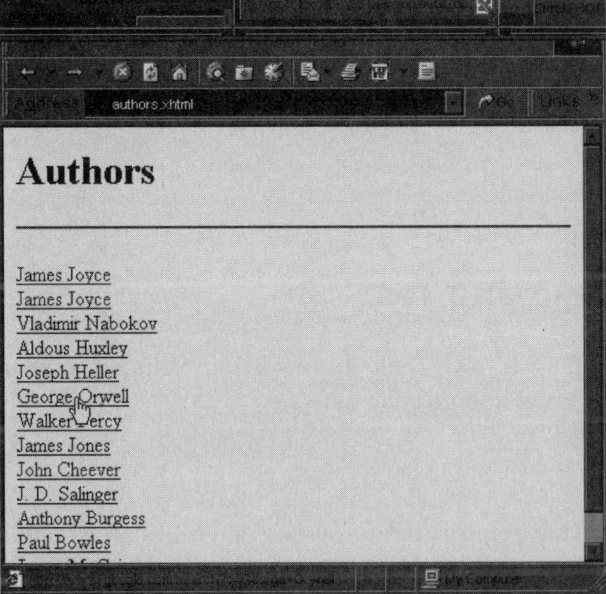

Figure 11.5 Result of using xsl:element and xsl:attribute.

There are three important things to note about the above template:

- For readability purposes, the contents of xsl:attribute were indented, but in real life they should not be, for a simple reason: attribute values cannot contain new line characters, so the XSLT processor will automatically escape them. Even though the google search works including the escaped characters, it is important to be clear about this: in real life, the contents of our `xsl:attribute` would have to be a less-than-beautiful, long string like the one below.

```
<xsl:attribute
name="href">http://www.google.com/search?q=<xsl:value-of
select="author/name"/>+<xsl:value-of select="author/sur-
name"/></xsl:attribute>
```

- The `xsl:value-of` instruction will be explained in the next section. However, in the meantime, the intuitive description is sufficient: insert the value of evaluating the expression in the `select` attribute.
- The previous template is only part of a bigger stylesheet, such as the following:

```
<?xml version="1.0"?>
<xsl:stylesheet  xmlns:xsl="/1999/XSL/Transform">
   <xsl:template match="/">
     <html>
       <h1>Authors</h1>
         <xsl:apply-templates/>
     </html>
   </xsl:template>
   <xsl:template match="book">
         <!-- contents of this template already shown -->
   </xsl:template>
</xsl:stylesheet>
```

Inserting Text

So far we have seen the insertion of literal text by including it within output elements such as:

```
<H1>Authors</H1>
```

Another approach to the problem is to include it by using the `xsl:text` element:

```
<xsl:text>A sample string</xsl:text>
```

One important use of the `xsl:text` instruction is the disabling of output escaping, which allows the inclusion of characters that otherwise would be impossible to include in the document. Suppose, for example, that we need to output the string <<<<<<< : Including the string as a literal is not possible because it would damage the well-formedness of the XSLT stylesheet:

```
<xsl:template match="*">
     <<<<<<<  <!-- wrong! < indicates the beginning of a new
element-->
</xsl:template>
```

Using the character reference < will not work either because of output escaping:

```
<xsl:template match="*">
    &lt;&lt; <!-- this will only print &lt;&lt; -->
</xsl:template>
```

Using the disable-output-escaping attribute of xsl:text, the correct result is achieved:

```
<xsl:text disable-output-
escaping="yes">&lt;&lt;&lt;&lt;</xsl:text>
```

This code effectively prints <<<< to the output.

Inserting Generated Text

The previous sections have presented examples of generated text by using the xsl:value-of instruction. xsl:value-of is useful since it is simple: it requires only one parameter, called select, whose value is an XPath expression. The output text inserted into the tree is the string representation of the result.

The following example shows a simple stylesheet that outputs a text file with all the titles:

```
<?xml version="1.0"?>
<xsl:stylesheet xmlns:xsl="http://www.w3.org/1999/XSL/Transform">

   <xsl:output method="text"/> <!-- we don't want xml output -->

   <xsl:template match="book">
         <xsl:value-of select="title"/>
   </xsl:template>

</xsl:stylesheet>
```

Note the use of the xsl:output element.[5] In this case it instructs the processor to output raw text, not XML. Among other consequences, this means no prologue is included in the output text. The following is the output thrown by Xalan:

```
Transforming...
Ulysses
A Portrait of the Artist as a Young Man
Lolita
Brave New World
Catch-22
1984
The Moviegoer
transform took 70 milliseconds
```

Copying

Perhaps the most common instruction besides xsl:value-of is xsl:copy. It creates a shallow copy of the current node in the output tree, plus all the namespace nodes visible at that point in the source.

One very important aspect to keep in mind is that xsl:copy does not copy subelements or attributes by default. The following example shows a stylesheet that produces a copy of the source document (remember that the XPath expression attribute::* can be abbreviated by @*):

```
<?xml version="1.0"?>
<xsl:stylesheet xmlns:xsl="http://www.w3.org/1999/XSL/Transform">
   <xsl:template match="@*|node()">
      <xsl:copy>
          <xsl:apply-templates select="@*|node()"/>
      </xsl:copy>
   </xsl:template>
</xsl:stylesheet>
```

Numbering

If you take a good look at our initial source, a fatal design flaw becomes evident: the actual classification of the novels is not marked up, but rather implied by the order of the elements. In order to fix this error we will produce a new document in which every book element has a rated

[5] This is defined in the “selecting output preferences” section.

attribute that explicitly shows the classification number of the novel. This can be accomplished via the `xsl:number` instruction.

`xsl:number` outputs the numeric value of an expression specified in its `value` attribute. A first example would be the following stylesheet, which counts the number of elements in the source document:

```
<xsl:stylesheet xmlns:xsl="http://www.w3.org/1999/XSL/Transform">
   <xsl:output method="text"/>
   <xsl:template match="/bestnovels">
     <xsl:text>There are </xsl:text> <xsl:number
value="count(*)"/>
     <xsl:text> elements in the source document.</xsl:text>
   </xsl:template>
</xsl:stylesheet>
```

The following text shows the result of invoking this stylesheet using Xalan:[6]

```
C:\xmldevguide\examples> xalan -IN best100abridged.xml -XSL nov-
els-7.xml
========= Parsing file:novels-7.xml ==========
Parse of file:novels-7.xml took  770 milliseconds
========= Parsing best100abridged.xml ==========
Parse of best100abridged.xml took 110 milliseconds
=============================
Transforming...
There are 13 elements in the source document.transform took 50
milliseconds
XSLProcessor: done
```

One common usage of `xsl:number` is enumeration. That is why the `value` attribute defaults to the relative position of the node within nodes of the same name, allowing the creation of stylesheets such as the following:

```
<?xml version="1.0"?>
<xsl:stylesheet xmlns:xsl="http://www.w3.org/1999/XSL/Transform">

  <xsl:template match="book"> <!-- apply this to every book -->
     <xsl:copy>
       <xsl:attribute name="rated"><xsl:number/></xsl:attribute>
       <xsl:apply-templates select="@*|node()"/>
```

[6] Note that a stylesheet like this can only serve educational purposes, since from the performance perspective, it is a terrible alternative to a SAX-based program. In the author's machine (a 1GHz Pentium III) the SAXCount program shown in Chapter 4 takes only 5 milliseconds to count all the elements of the source document, while the stylesheet alternative takes 885!

```
    </xsl:copy>
  </xsl:template>

  <xsl:template match="/bestnovels">
    <xsl:copy>
      <xsl:apply-templates/>
    </xsl:copy>
  </xsl:template>

  <xsl:template match="@year|name|surname|title|text()">
    <xsl:copy> <!--simply copy all the rest of nodes in the
document -->
      <xsl:apply-templates/>
    </xsl:copy>
  </xsl:template>

</xsl:stylesheet>
```

The outcome of processing the initial source with this stylesheet is a corrected version of the document with the explicit `rated` attribute for each book:

```
<?xml version="1.0" encoding="UTF-8"?>
<bestnovels>
<book rated="1" year="1922">
  <title>Ulysses</title>
  <name>James</name>
  <surname>Joyce</surname>
</book>
<book rated="2" year="1916">
  <title>A Portrait of the Artist as a Young Man</title>
  <name>James</name>
  <surname>Joyce</surname>
</book>
<!--and all the other books…-->
```

Aside from the attributes shown here (and in examples to come), the `xsl:number` instruction provides numerous attributes to tailor the outcome of enumerations. See the reference guide at end of Chapter 12 for a list of the available attributes and the XSLT specification (see the CD) for a more formal explanation of each.

Conditionals

XSLT provides the ability to do conditional processing via the `xsl:if` and `xsl:choose` constructs. Both behave pretty much like their counterparts in traditional procedural languages such as C. `xsl:if` takes a single attribute called test and evaluates the Boolean expression inside it, while xsl:choose provides a series of alternatives that are matched against the current node; whichever evaluates to true is instantiated.

The following code shows how to use xsl:if to test whether a book was made in the Fifties or not:

```
<?xml version="1.0"?>
<xsl:stylesheet xmlns:xsl="http://www.w3.org/1999/XSL/Transform">

   <xsl:template match="book">
   <!-- maybe do some other things with the rest of the data -->
     <xsl:apply-templates select="@year"/>
   </xsl:template>

  <xsl:template match="@year">
```

NOTE

The default argument for string() *is the current node.*

```
<xsl:value-of select="string()"/>
      <xsl:if test="contains(string(),'195')">
          <xsl:text> this book was written in the 50s </xsl:text>
     </xsl:if>
  </xsl:template>
</xsl:stylesheet>
```

The following is a piece of the result of interpreting this stylesheet against our book collection:

```
1949
1961
1951 this book was written in the 50s
1957 this book was written in the 50s
```

Similarly, the xml:choose construction can be used to create a table of books against decades, such as the one shown in Figure 11.6.

```
<xsl:stylesheet xmlns:xsl="http://www.w3.org/1999/XSL/Transform">

   <xsl:template match="/bestnovels">
     <html>
       <head>
      <title>Books vs decades</title>
        </head>
        <h1>Books vs decades</h1>
        <hr/>
```

```
        <table border="1">
          <tr>
             <th>Book</th>
             <th>1940s</th><th>1950s</th><th>other</th>
          </tr>
          <xsl:apply-templates select="book"/>
        </table>
      </html>
    </xsl:template>

    <xsl:template match="book">
        <tr>
           <td><xsl:value-of select="title"/></td>
           <xsl:apply-templates select="@year"/>
        </tr>
    </xsl:template>

    <xsl:template match="@year">
           <xsl:choose>
             <xsl:when test="contains(string(),'194')">
                <td><img src="check.gif"/></td><td/><td/>
             </xsl:when>
             <xsl:when test="contains(string(),'195')">
                <td/><td><img src="check.gif"/></td><td/>
             </xsl:when>
             <xsl:otherwise>
                <td/><td/><td><img src="check.gif"/></td>
             </xsl:otherwise>
           </xsl:choose>
    </xsl:template>

</xsl:stylesheet>
```

Loops

In XSLT, explicit loops come in the form of instances of the `xsl:for-each` instruction. The semantics of `xsl:for-each` are very simple: this element provides an attribute named `select` whose value is an expression that evaluates to a node-list. The contents of the element are instantiated for each node on the list.

The following template shows how to use `xsl:for-each` to print all the first names of authors:

```
<xsl:template match="book">
  <xsl:for-each select="author/name">
      <xsl:text>First Name: </xsl:text>
      <xsl:value-of select="."/>
  </xsl:for-each>
</xsl:template>
```

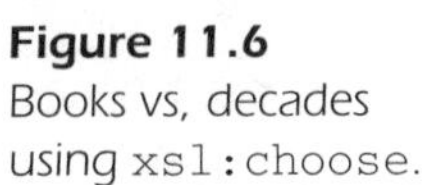

Figure 11.6 Books vs, decades using `xsl:choose`.

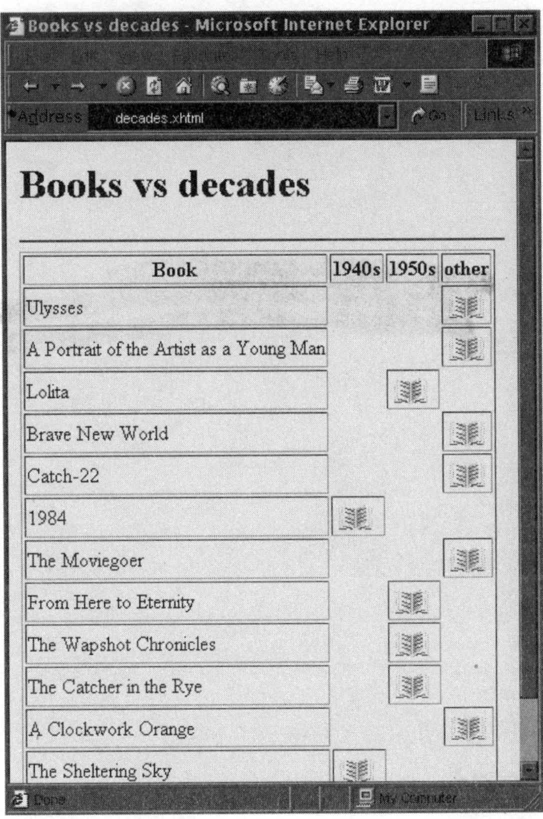

Sorting

`xsl:sort` provides the ability to rearrange the order of a node-list before any other processing takes place. In this section we will use it to create two different documents out of our source: one will list the books, sorting them by author surname and then by author name; the other will list the books by title.

Here is the appropriate stylesheet (note that only one stylesheet is needed to output both HTML pages):

```
<?xml version="1.0"?>
<xsl:stylesheet xmlns:xsl="http://www.w3.org/1999/XSL/Transform"
                xmlns:xt="http://www.jclark.com/xt"
                extension-element-prefixes="xt">

   <xsl:template match="/bestnovels">
    <xt:document method="html" href="novelsbyauthor.html">
     <html>
```

```
      <head>
     <title>Books by Author</title>
      </head>
      <h1>Books by Author</h1>
      <hr/>
       <table border="1">
          <tr>
             <th>Book</th>
             <th>Author</th>
          </tr>
          <xsl:for-each select="book">
               <xsl:sort select="author/surname"/>
               <xsl:sort select="author/name"/>
               <tr>
                 <td><xsl:value-of select="title"/></td>
                 <td><xsl:value-of select="author/name"/>
                      <xsl:text> </xsl:text>
                      <xsl:value-of select="author/surname"/>
                 </td>
               </tr>
          </xsl:for-each>
       </table>
    </html>
   </xt:document>

   <xt:document method="html" href="novelsbytitle.html">
    <html>
      <head>
     <title>Books by Title</title>
      </head>
      <h1>Books by Title</h1>
      <hr/>
       <table border="1">
          <tr>
             <th>Book</th>
             <th>Author</th>
          </tr>
          <xsl:for-each select="book">
               <xsl:sort select="title"/>
               <tr>
                 <td><xsl:value-of select="title"/></td>
                 <td><xsl:value-of select="author/name"/>
                      <xsl:text> </xsl:text>
                      <xsl:value-of select="author/surname"/>
                 </td>
               </tr>
          </xsl:for-each>
       </table>
    </html>
   </xt:document>
  </xsl:template>
</xsl:stylesheet>
```

Figures 11.7 and 11.8 show the two files resulting from our stylesheet.

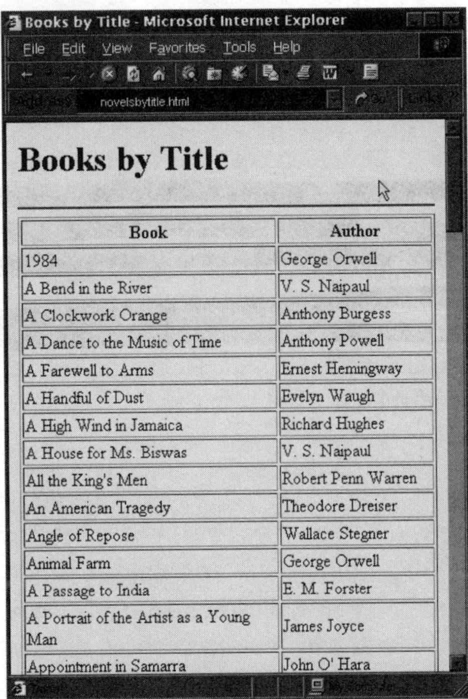

Figure 11.7
Sorting by title.

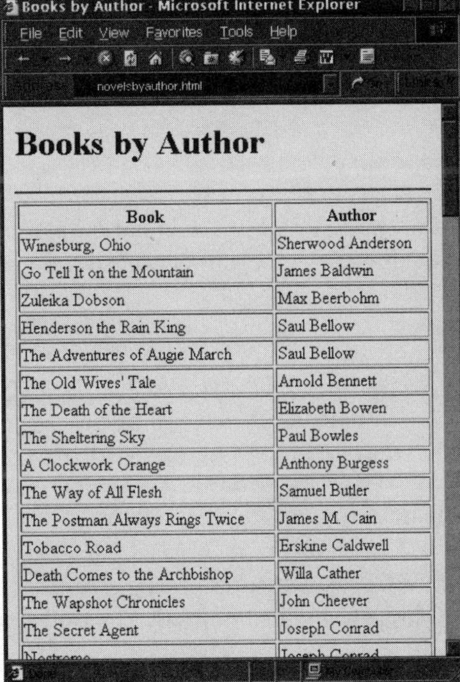

Figure 11.8
Sorting by author surname and author name.

Important details to note about this example include:

- The output of more than one document is not a standard ability of XSLT 1.0. It will be standardized (most likely with the syntax shown here) in version 1.1, which is currently under production.
- The `xsl:sort` element is only meaningful if it is included within `xsl:for-each` or `xsl:apply-templates` elements. It pre-orders the nodes that these instructions select before any other action takes place.
- If there is more than one instance of `xsl:sort`, the order in which they are written indicates the order in which they are applied. For example, in the first document, books are sorted first by the author's last name, and then by first name.

Variables

Variables simplify and empower stylesheets by providing a short name for a particular value. Variables in XSLT are defined using the `xsl:variable` element, which permits three types of initialization:

- If the content of the `xsl:variable` element is empty, and the `select` value holds an expression, the value of the variable is the result of evaluating such an expression:

```
<xsl:variable name="x" select="position()"/>

<xsl:variable name="y" select="hello"/>
```

- If the content of the `xsl:variable` is not empty, *and* there is no `select` attribute, the value of the variable is set to the content of the element:

```
<xsl:variable name="long_word">paranguatirimicuaro</xsl:
variable>
```

- Finally, if there is neither a `content` nor a `select` attribute, the variable is initialized to an empty string:

```
<xsl:variable name="x" select="''"/>
```

The usage of XSLT variables is pretty straightforward. To obtain the value of a variable, precede its name by the dollar sign, as shown in the following example:

```
<xsl:template match="book">
  <xsl:variable name="y" select="@year"/>
  <xsl:for-each select="author/name">
      <xsl:if test="contains($y,'196')">
        <xsl:text>This is a 60's author</xsl:text>
      </xsl:if>
  </xsl:for-each>
</xsl:template>
```

Note how the use of a variable simplified this stylesheet by saving one extra template for year attributes.

Now consider the problem of outputting the value of a variable that contains a node such as:

```
<xsl:variable name="message">
    <b>This is a 60's author</b>
</xsl:variable>
```

One cannot simply put `$message` in the body of a rule. It would simply output the string `$message`. The option of using `xsl:value-of` is also incorrect, because it would output the string value of the variable, which is "This is a 60s author."

The correct answer is the use of a new instruction: `xsl:copy-of`, which has one single attribute called `select`:

```
<xsl:template match="book">
  <xsl:variable name="y" select="@year"/>
  <xsl:variable name="message">
      <b>This is a 60's author</b>
  </xsl:variable>
  <xsl:for-each select="author/name">
      <xsl:if test="contains($y,'196')">
         <xsl:copy-of select="$message"/>
      </xsl:if>
  </xsl:for-each>
</xsl:template>
```

An Important Note on Variables

The term *variable* in XSLT can be somewhat misleading, because variables are in fact immutable objects. This means that once their value has been initialized, there is no way to assign a new value to them.

There is no assignment operator in XSLT, and getting used to thinking of "variables" as immutable place holders may take a while, but that does not mean they are useless. In Chapter 12 you will find many more examples of how to put variables to practical use.

Named Templates

One requisite for encapsulation and reuse is the existence of syntactic constructs that allow the naming and calling of portions of code. In traditional procedural programming, these constructs are functions. In XSLT, they are *named templates*.

A named template is defined by using the name attribute of the xsl:template instruction. The following is a simple example showing the creation of an HTML image within a CSS layer:[7]

```
<xsl:template name="point">
  <xsl:element name="img">
    <xsl:attribute name="src">point.gif</xsl:attribute>
    <xsl:attribute name="style">
        {position: absolute; left: 34pt; top: 34pt;}
    </xsl:attribute>
  </xsl:element>
</xsl:template>
```

When instantiated using the xsl:call-template instruction like this:

```
<xsl:call-template name="point"/>
```

the following output is produced:

```
<img src="point.gif" style="{position: absolute; left: 34pt;
top: 34pt;}&#10;"/>
```

Named templates are a key aid to stylesheet reuse. Try to use them often and wherever there is a need for future reuse.

Passing Parameters to Templates

The last tool we will see in this chapter, before jumping to the advanced examples in Chapter 12, is the use of parameters in templates. Parameters in templates are akin to arguments in traditional functions. However, like variables, they are immutable and share their initialization

[7] In case you are not familiar with Cascading Style Sheets (CSS) it will be explored in detail in the XHTML chapter. For our immediate purposes, it is sufficient to understand that CSS allows an element to float in a layer, allowing the superimposition of images in the browser.

rules. Parameters are defined by using `xsl:with-parameter` and must be used as direct children of `xsl:call-template`.

For example, the following instruction calls the `point` template with a parameter named `x` with value `60`:

```
<xsl:call-template name="point">
   <xsl:with-param name="x" select="60"/>
</xsl:call-template>
```

In order to provide default values, a named template may use the `xsl:param` element with a `select` attribute. Using the parameter inside the template is as simple as referring to it with the `$` sign:

```
<xsl:template name="point">
  <xsl:param name="x" select="0"/>
  <xsl:element name="img">
    <xsl:attribute name="src">point.gif</xsl:attribute>
    <xsl:attribute name="style">
         <xsl:text>{position: absolute; left:</xsl:text>
         <xsl:value-of select="$x"/>
       <xsl:text>pt; top: 34pt;}</xsl:text>
    </xsl:attribute>
  </xsl:element>
</xsl:template>
```

The output of the invocation is:

```
<img src="point.gif" style="{position: absolute; left:60pt; top:
34pt;}"/>
```

An Attractive Finale

Note that by outputting many points like the one above, and plotting them over a graphic of the Cartesian coordinates, we can create a good visual representation of the time distribution of our famous books.

Our goal is to show for each book, a point in a graphic of books vs. years. The first step is shown in the following template, which refines the `point` template above to allow a Y coordinate:

```
<xsl:template name="point">
  <xsl:param name="x" select="0"/>
  <xsl:param name="y" select="0"/> <!-- add the Y coord -->
  <xsl:element name="img">
    <xsl:attribute name="src">point.gif</xsl:attribute>
    <xsl:attribute name="style">
         <xsl:text>{position: absolute; left:</xsl:text>
         <xsl:value-of select="$x"/>
```

```
      <xsl:text>pt; top: </xsl:text>
       <xsl:value-of select="$y"/>
      <xsl:text>pt;}     </xsl:text>
    </xsl:attribute>
  </xsl:element>
</xsl:template>
```

The next step is to create an `img` element that point to the background image:

```
<xsl:stylesheet    xmlns:xsl="http://www.w3.org/1999/XSL/Trans-
form">
<xsl:template match="/">
 <html>
   <body background="white">
      <img src="cartesian.gif"/>
   </body>
  </html>
 </xsl:template>
</xsl:stylesheet>
```

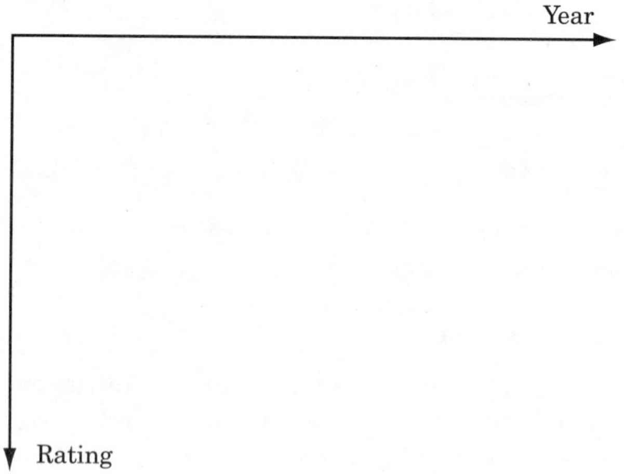

Figure 11.9 A blank set of coordinates.

Obviously, the output of this stylesheet alone is not too exciting (Figure 11.9), but if we use the `point` template to superimpose points over it, like in the following stylesheet:

```
<?xml version="1.0"?>
<xsl:stylesheet xmlns:xsl="http://www.w3.org/1999/XSL/Transform">

   <xsl:template match="/bestnovels">
    <html>
      <body bgcolor="#FFFFFF">
```

```
      <img src="cartesian.gif"/>
    </body>

    <xsl:for-each select="book">
      <xsl:call-template name="point">
        <xsl:with-param name="x" select="@year"/>
        <xsl:with-param name="y" select="@rated"/>
      </xsl:call-template>
    </xsl:for-each>

  </html>
 </xsl:template>



 <xsl:template name="point">
   <xsl:param name="x" select="0"/>
   <xsl:param name="y" select="0"/> <!-- add the Y coord -->
   <xsl:element name="img">
     <xsl:attribute name="src">point.gif</xsl:attribute>
     <xsl:attribute name="style">
          <xsl:text>{position: absolute; left:</xsl:text>
          <!-- if a book is rated 10, the point is 30 -->
          <xsl:value-of select="substring($x,3)*5-30"/>
         <xsl:text>pt; top: </xsl:text>
          <!-- if a year was written in 1940, the point is 40 -
->

          <xsl:value-of select="30+$y*10"/>
         <xsl:text>pt;}     </xsl:text>
     </xsl:attribute>
   </xsl:element>
 </xsl:template>


</xsl:stylesheet>
```

We have created a nice representation for our data.[8] The final result is shown in Figure 11.10.

Summary

This chapter has shown all the instructions and basic techniques of XSLT along with some advanced tricks. The following chapter continues the ideas presented here by analyzing several examples of complex stylesheets and the advanced XSLT uses they exhibit.

---

[8] Chapter 12 shows how to create graphics also, not only superimpose them.

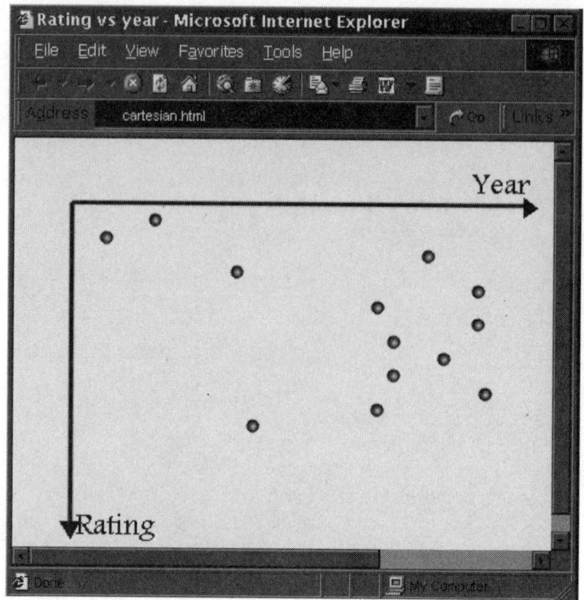

Figure 11.10
A visual representation of book year vs. rating.

CHAPTER 12

XSLT: Advanced Uses and Techniques

Introduction

The previous chapter introduced the main constructs of XSLT as well as some examples of its use. This chapter builds upon the functionality shown in Chapter 11 by presenting advanced techniques and uses of XSLT. The chapter has four sections. The first two show important forms of XSLT transformations via advanced examples.[1] The third section shows how to expand XSLT, and the fourth presents a complete map of XSLT that can be used as an instant reference for the contents of Chapters 11 and 12.

From Structure to Presentation: Functional Requirements

Perhaps the most common and important form of XSLT transformation is that from structure-oriented XML to presentational formats. Some presentational formats—like XHTML or graphics encoded with SVG—are XML based, others, like PDF, are not. This section explores the problem of transforming a purely structural piece of XML into a presentational format, namely XHTML pages.

Requirements

Developers are continually dealing with the problem of solving software requirements. Gathering, managing, maintaining, and enhancing requirements is a complex and crucial activity that can make the difference between a successful project and a nightmare.

From the development point of view, the expression and maintenance of requirements can be greatly helped if we encode them in XML. After all, a requirement is a collection of very specific data (e.g. a description, a priority, etc.) that can be easily and effectively modeled in XML.

On the other hand, a requirement is also a communication tool among people. Requirements define the extent of the work, acting as contract terms with a client who does not necessarily share the technical back-

---

[1] Reading Chapter 11 is a prerequisite for these examples, as they concentrate on showing advanced uses of the XSLT functionality, not the basics of the language.

ground of the developer. This means that they must be presented in a clear way that everyone, not only the development team, can understand.

The XML documents presented here, and, of course, the XSLT transformations based upon them, bring together a solution that meets our needs: the data will be represented in our own, specially tailored XML vocabulary, which is the ideal way of encoding this kind of information, and it will also be presented in a variety of forms better suited for general output, such as Web pages.

Modeling the Information

The first step is to find a suitable XML representation for the functional requirements of a system. Functional requirements are the clear expression of what a system *must do* (not *how* to do it, or where it should run, etc.), and can be expressed as the union of the following components:

- A name and an unique identifier
- A version
- A description
- An indication of whether the requirement is merely optional or a necessity
- A priority
- Inputs and outputs
- A list of other requirements related to it
- Acceptance criteria.

A Sample Requirement

To see how functional requirements capture the high-level abstractions of what a system must do, the following table shows an example of a document as it would be presented to the final reader. (Actually, the table in Figure 12.1 was automatically produced from an instance of the XML vocabulary that we are about to create, so it also serves as an example—and a promise—of the final goal to achieve via XSLT transformations.)

The Functional Requirements DTD

In order to express functional requirements in XML, we shall create a vocabulary for a class of documents that express particular requirements in terms of the information items presented above.

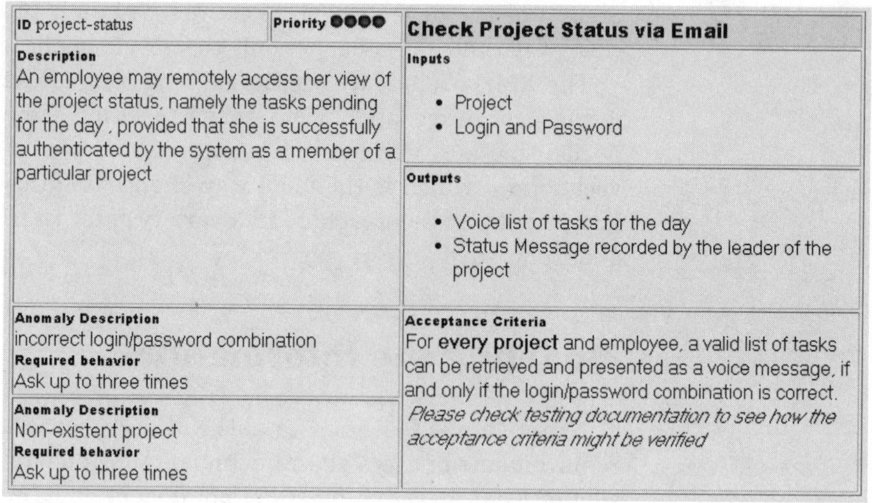

Figure 12.1 The final presentation of a single requirement.

ID project-status **Priority** ●●●●	**Check Project Status via Email**
Description An employee may remotely access her view of the project status, namely the tasks pending for the day , provided that she is successfully authenticated by the system as a member of a particular project	**Inputs** • Project • Login and Password **Outputs** • Voice list of tasks for the day • Status Message recorded by the leader of the project
Anomaly Description incorrect login/password combination **Required behavior** Ask up to three times **Anomaly Description** Non-existent project **Required behavior** Ask up to three times	**Acceptance Criteria** For **every project** and employee, a valid list of tasks can be retrieved and presented as a voice message, if and only if the login/password combination is correct. *Please check testing documentation to see how the acceptance criteria might be verified*

The following DTD defines such a class of documents:

```
<!ELEMENT fr (header,requirement+)>

<!ELEMENT header (author*,version?,project,description)>


<!-- ******** Metadata about the requirements ********** -->
<!ENTITY % string       "#PCDATA">
<!ENTITY % character    "#PCDATA">
<!ENTITY % letter       "#PCDATA">
<!ENTITY % number_att   "CDATA">

<!ENTITY % english_def "xml:lang    NMTOKEN    'en'">

<!ELEMENT author        (firstname,midinitial?,lastname)>
<!ELEMENT firstname     (%string;)>
<!ELEMENT midinitial    (%letter;)>
<!ELEMENT lastname      (%string;)>
<!ATTLIST name
         %english_def;>

<!ELEMENT version (#PCDATA)>

<!ATTLIST version
          release       %number_att;    #IMPLIED
          subordinate   %number_att;    #IMPLIED>

<!ELEMENT project (%string;)>


<!-- **** Type definition for requirements **** -->
<!ELEMENT requirement (name,description,
```

```
                        uses*,extends*,
                        input,output,
                        anomaly,acceptance+)>

<!ATTLIST requirement
          id        ID              #REQUIRED
          optional  (yes|no)        #REQUIRED
          priority  (0|1|2|3|4|5)   #REQUIRED
>
<!ELEMENT name  (%string;)>

<!-- a description is composed by paragraphs, describing
     the problem
-->
<!ELEMENT description (p+)>
<!ELEMENT p          (#PCDATA|b|i*>
<!ELEMENT b          (#PCDATA)> <!-- bold -->
<!ELEMENT i          (#PCDATA)>
```

NOTE

A requirement may use or extend others (see example).

```
<!ELEMENT uses EMPTY>
<!ATTLIST uses
          req  IDREF #REQUIRED>

<!ELEMENT extends EMPTY>
<!ATTLIST extends
          req     IDREF #REQUIRED>

<!ELEMENT input  (entry*)>
<!ELEMENT output (result+)>

<!ELEMENT entry  (%string;)>
<!ELEMENT result (%string;)>

<!ELEMENT anomaly (description,behavior)>
<!ELEMENT behavior (p+)>

<!-- The description of the acceptance criteria -->
<!ELEMENT acceptance (p+)>
```

An Instance of the Functional Requirements DTD

The following document is an abridged version of a real-life instance of the functional requirements document type (it is a valid document, but it only contains one requirement).

```
<?xml version="1.0"?>

<!DOCTYPE fr SYSTEM "fr.dtd">

<fr>
  <header>
    <project>Intranet Voice Server</project>
    <description>
      <p>The Intranet Voice Server gives a phone-based
         interface to our company's intranet (...) </p>
    </description>
  </header>
  <requirement id="messages" optional="no" priority="2">
    <name xml:lang="en">Message Retrieval</name>
    <description>
      <p>An employee may access her voice messages remotely,
      provided that she is successfully authenticated by the
      system as the owner of a particular phone extension.</p>
    </description>
    <input>
      <entry>The phone extension</entry>
      <entry>A voice or numeric password</entry>
    </input>
    <output>
      <result>The collection of new messages for the particular
      extension.</result>
    </output>
    <anomaly>
      <description>
     <p>The password given does not match the particular
     extension.</p>
      </description>
      <behavior>
     <p>The connection is terminated.</p>
      </behavior>
    </anomaly>
    <acceptance>
      <p>Every extension on the company must be accessible via
      this mechanism.</p>
    </acceptance>
  </requirement>
</fr>
```

This previous document is a classic example of the strength of XML to encode data in a structured way that reflects the nature of the problem domain. The next step is to apply XSLT to produce a format that reflects the needs of all readers.

Transforming to XHTML

XHTML (as mentioned in previous chapters) is an XML version of HTML. It provides a collection of elements that reflect one by one those of HTML 4.0, in a manner that is pure XML (not SGML).

XHTML can be interpreted by current browsers and therefore is our choice for the Web-based presentation of functional requirements.

Creating a List of the Requirements

The first issue in the creation of a Web-based interface to a large number of requirements is an exercise in XSLT loops: an index of requirements. The following XSLT code shows a named template that will achieve this for us.

```
<!-- Index Generation -->
<xsl:template name="index">
   <table>
   <xsl:for-each select="/fr/requirement">
     <xsl:sort select="@priority"/>
      <tr>
        <td>
          <xsl:number format="I."/>
        </td>
        <td>
          <a href="{concat('#',@id)}">
          <xsl:value-of select="name"/>
          </a>
        </td>
      </tr>
   </xsl:for-each>
   </table>
</xsl:template>
```

There are two new important pieces of information contained in this template:

1. **The use of attribute value templates:** note that instead of creating a new `a` element using `xsl:element` and then assigning an attribute to it using `xsl:attribute`, we just used a literal result element. Note also that the value of the `href` attribute is an XPath expression enclosed in curly braces {}; this means that the enclosed value must not be taken literally, but rather be evaluated and converted to a string.
2. **The use of the format attribute in xsl:number:** the output format of a number can be altered by using a pattern string as the

attribute to `xsl:number`. In this case, roman numerals are used, but expressions such as "1." indicate that the numeration done with Arabic numerals followed by a point, are also valid.

Figure 12.2 shows the outcome of invoking the above template when processing a requirements document.

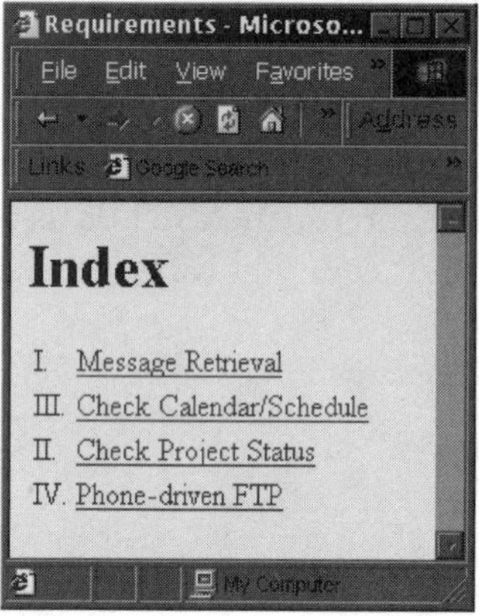

Figure 12.2
Requirements index.

Creating a Representation for Each Requirement

The following template uses XSLT conditionals, loops, and almost every other XSLT construction mentioned in Chapter 11 to create a suitable representation for each requirement. Most of the techniques used here are straightforward applications of the XSLT constructs. Some special details, however, like the recursive creation of the priority images, deserve extra attention and will be analyzed once the code is introduced.

```
<!-- this template is called for each requirement -->
<xsl:template name="req">
 <a name="{concat('#',@id)}"/> <!-- so the index links work -->
 <table border="1" width="100%">
  <tr>
    <td width="15%" valign="top" align="left">
```

NOTE

The same font effect can be achieved by other means, but for the sake of simplicity in the explanation, this method takes precedence.

```
<font face="Arial Black" size="1">ID</font>
        <xsl:value-of select="@id"/>
    </td>
    <td width="2%" valign="top" align="left">
        <font face="Arial Black" size="1">Priority</font>
        <!-- Insert as number copies of dot.gif that equals the
             priority of the requirement -->
        <xsl:call-template name="insert-dot">
          <xsl:with-param name="number" select="@priority"/>
        </xsl:call-template>
    </td>
    <td width="83%" colspan="2" bgcolor="#FFFF99"
        valign="top" align="left">
        <font face="Arial Black" size="3">
       <xsl:value-of select="name"/>
        </font>
    </td>
  </tr>
  <tr>
    <td width="66%" colspan="3" rowspan="2" valign="top"
    align="left">
        <font face="Arial Black" size="1">Description<br/></font>
        <font face="MS Sans Serif">
           <xsl:copy-of select="description/*"/>
        </font>
    </td>
    <td width="34%" valign="top" align="left">
        <font face="Arial Black" size="1">Inputs</font>
      <ul>
        <xsl:for-each select="input/entry">
          <li><font face="MS Sans Serif">
                <xsl:value-of select="."/>
              </font>
          </li>
        </xsl:for-each>
      </ul>
    </td>
  </tr>
  <tr>
    <td width="34%" valign="top" align="left">
      <font face="Arial Black" size="1">Outputs</font>
      <ul>
        <xsl:for-each select="output/result">
          <li><font face="MS Sans Serif">
                <xsl:value-of select="."/>
              </font>
          </li>
        </xsl:for-each>
      </ul>
    </td>
  </tr>
  <tr>
    <td width="66%" colspan="3" valign="top" align="left">
```

```
        <font face="Arial Black" size="1">Anomaly Description<br/>
      </font>
      <font face="MS Sans Serif">
         <xsl:copy-of select="anomaly/description/*"/>
      </font>
      <font face="Arial Black" size="1"><br/>
      Required behavior</font>
     <font face="MS Sans Serif">
         <xsl:copy-of select="anomaly/behavior/*"/>
     </font>
    </td>
    <td width="34%" valign="top" align="left" rowspan="2">
     <font face="Arial Black" size="1">Acceptance
      Criteria</font>
     <font face="MS Sans Serif">
         <xsl:copy-of select="behavior/*"/>
     </font>
    </td>
  </tr>
 </table>
</xsl:template>
```

As a simple inspection quickly reveals, there are at least two important points to review in the example above: the convenient use of `xsl:copy-of` and the call to a template called `insert-dot`.

USING XSL:COPY-OF

The use of `xsl:copy-of` is ideal for this particular example because it allows the inclusion of `b` and `i` elements within text paragraphs (both used identically in the source and the final XHTML), without having to create a template that copies each. Use this technique whenever the whole contents of an element can be replicated in the output, because it improves the readability of the code by decreasing the number of unnecessary templates.

REPEATING AN ACTION

The most interesting part of the previous exercise is the repeated print of dots to signify the priority of the requirement. It seems like a natural thing to do (after all, we are all used to the `for(i=0;i < priority; i++) { print…}` way of thinking) but it's really not that simple when you remember two facts:

- Variables are immutable (i.e. it is impossible to say i++ or i = i + 1).
- There are no number-based loop structures in XSLT. `xsl:for-each` is made to work over a collection of nodes, not a given number of times.

The solution is conceptually simple:

```
<!-- Recursive function to insert dots -->
<xsl:template name="insert-dot">
  <xsl:param name="number" select="5"/>
  <xsl:if test="$number &gt; 0">  <!-- have to escape the > char-
acter -->
    <img src="dot.gif"/>

     <xsl:call-template name="insert-dot">
          <xsl:with-param name="number" select="$number - 1"/>
     </xsl:call-template>

  </xsl:if>
</xsl:template>
```

The function is implemented recursively, having the single parameter `number`. The trivial case of the recursion is when the solution gets called with a number less than r equal to zero, in which case nothing is done. In any other case, the template prints one dot (inserts the `img` element for a dot) and calls itself with `number -1`.

This same technique can be applied to implement any iteration that needs a numeric argument to execute its value. It is based on XSLT basic constructs and can be easily replicated (once you know it!) but can be cumbersome. In the section about XSLT extensions, we will see how to expand the XSLT language to include classic procedural loops.

Putting It All Together

The following template ties together the pieces we have created, in order to produce one nice representation for all the requirements:

```
<xsl:stylesheet version="1.0"
            xmlns:xsl="http://www.w3.org/1999/XSL/Transform">

<xsl:template match="/fr">
<html>
   <head>
      <title>Requirements for
         <xsl:value-of select="header/project"/>
      </title>
   </head>
   <body>
     <h1>Requirements for
         <xsl:value-of select="header/project"/></h1>
     <h2>Index</h2>
     <xsl:call-template name="index"/>

     <h2>Individual Requirements</h2>
     <xsl:for-each select="requirement">
```

```
      <xsl:call-template name="req"/>
         <br/>
      </xsl:for-each>
   </body>
</html>
</xsl:template>

<xsl:template name="index">
   <!-- see contents of this template above -->
</xsl:template>


<xsl:template name="req">
   <!-- see contents of this template above -->
</xsl:template>

<!-- Recursive function to insert dots -->
<xsl:template name="insert-dot">
   <!-- see contents of this template above -->
</xsl:template>

</xsl:stylesheet>
```

The final document looks like that in Figure 12.3.

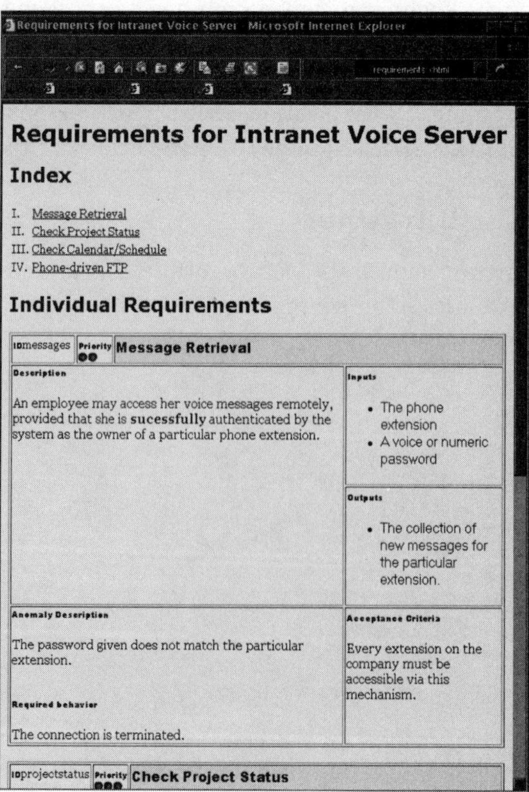

Figure 12.3 The final XHTML representation of the requirements document.

A Note on Transforming to PDF

One common desire among developers is to produce a form of the document that is suitable for printing. A popular way to do so is to create a file in a non-HTML format, such as TeX or PDF.

Producing formats like PDF out of XSLT transformations requires the use of output XML vocabularies and third-party tools we will cover in depth in other chapters. An explanation of those would deviate too much from the objective of this chapter, which is the advanced uses of XSLT. However, the CD includes a PDF translation for the requirements example, and the subject is addressed in Chapter 18, once the background information has been presented.

Non-textual Representations: Generating Graphics with SVG

In Chapter 11 we introduced one transformation that presented graphical data by means of a hack with CSS. Basically, the idea was to superimpose many instances of one picture over another in order to construct a plot for two-dimensional data. In this chapter we will really create images out of XML structured data using the Scalar Vector Graphics (SVG) standard, an XML vocabulary specifically created for the display of 2D and 3D graphics.

Graphical Representations

The issue we'll address in this section is the graphical representation of statistical data for server usage. In particular, we shall graph two things in a Cartesian model: the number of total hits in a particular span of time, and the number of "file-not-found" errors in that same period.

Modeling the Information

For the purposes of this section, we shall use a simplified version of the actual statistics kept by a particular Web server. The data on the XML instances will only include the number of hits during a particular time period as well as the number of 404 responses in that same period (404, as you probably know already, is the code returned by a Web server when a page requested is not found).

Creating the Document Type

The DTD for such information can be as simple as the following:

```
<!ELEMENT statistics  (span+)>

<!ENTITY % string_att   "CDATA">
<!ENTITY % description  "#PCDATA">

<!ATTLIST statistics
          generated_by  %string_att;  #REQUIRED>

<!ELEMENT span          (start, stop,
                         hits, hits_404)>

<!ENTITY % sec_att        "CDATA">
<!ENTITY % mili_att       "CDATA">
<!ENTITY % min_att        "CDATA">
<!ENTITY % hour_att       "CDATA">

<!ELEMENT start           (time)>
<!ELEMENT stop            (time)>
<!ELEMENT time            (%description;)>
<!ATTLIST time
          hour    %hour_att;       #IMPLIED
          min     %min_att;        #IMPLIED
          sec     %sec_att;        #IMPLIED
          mili    %mili_att;       #IMPLIED>

<!ELEMENT hits       (#PCDATA)>
<!ELEMENT hits_404   (#PCDATA)>
```

An Example

The following document shows an instance of the previous document type. It contains the access statistics for a hypothetical Web server during the afternoon of September 1, 2000:

```
<?xml version="1.0"?>
<!DOCTYPE statistics SYSTEM "stats.dtd">
<statistics generated_by="hypothetical_web_server">
  <span>
    <start>
      <time hour="3" min="30" sec="0">
      </time>
    </start>
```

```
    <stop>
      <time hour="4" min="45" sec="0">
      </time>
    </stop>
    <hits>400</hits>
    <hits_404>23</hits_404>
  </span>
  <span>
    <start>
      <time hour="4" min="45" sec="0">
      </time>
    </start>
    <stop>
      <time hour="6" min="39" sec="0">
      </time>
    </stop>
    <hits>421</hits>
    <hits_404>20</hits_404>
  </span>
  <span>
    <start>
      <time hour="6" min="39" sec="0">
      </time>
    </start>
    <stop>
      <time hour="7" min="2" sec="0">
      </time>
    </stop>
    <hits>332</hits>
    <hits_404>10</hits_404>
  </span>
</statistics>
```

Presenting the Data as SVG

Using vector graphics has many advantages over using pixel-based formats. In particular, problems such as resizing and rotating can be more elegantly and efficiently solved, without the traditional side-effects that come from those operations in pixel-based images.

In Figure 12.4, our final result for each document processed will be a collection of vector graphics, each showing the initial and end time for each time span (as analog clocks) along with a chart showing the total number of requests (as the complete circle) and the number of 404s (as a portion of the pie).

Future chapters will get into the details of the Scalable Vector Graphics format (SVG). For now, suffice it to say that this powerful graphics format, already a recommendation of the W3C, is an XML vocabulary for the expression and interchange of vector graphics. It includes elements for every type of basic figure you may require; for example, the following document would print a circle of radius 30 in the position (50,90) when interpreted with an SVG viewer:

```
<svg>
    <circle cx="50" cy="90" r="30"/>
</svg>
```

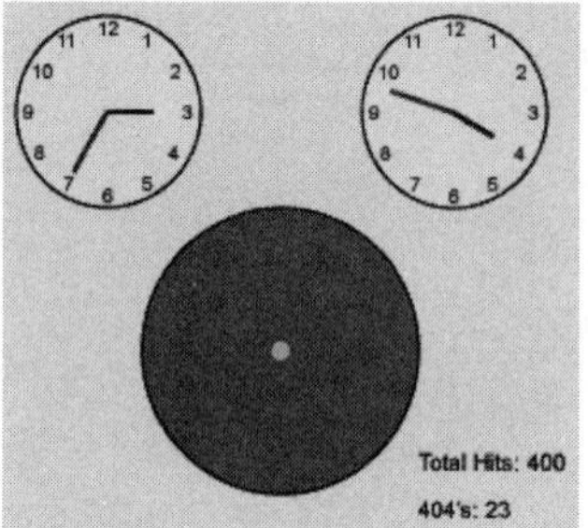

Figure 12.4
An SVG representation of the server usage data.

SVG is an ample and very complete format with dozens of elements and attributes for the display and manipulation of graphics. In our example we will confine ourselves to five of the many constructs in the language:

1. Text
2. Lines
3. Circles
4. Rotations
5. Translations

The structure of these elements is straightforward. Before you jump into the transformation, however, we recommend that you take the time to read one of the resulting SVG documents (the following, in particular, is the source code of Figure 12.4):

```
<?xml version="1.0" encoding="utf-8"?>

<svg>

<circle cx="50" cy="50" r="40" style="fill:white;stroke:black;"/>
<text x="65" y="23" style="font-size:8">1</text>
<text x="77" y="36" style="font-size:8">2</text>
<text x="82" y="53" style="font-size:8">3</text>
```

```
<text x="76" y="70" style="font-size:8">4</text>
<text x="65" y="83" style="font-size:8">5</text>
<text x="48" y="88" style="font-size:8">6</text>
<text x="31" y="83" style="font-size:8">7</text>
<text x="18" y="70" style="font-size:8">8</text>
<text x="13" y="53" style="font-size:8">9</text>
<text x="17" y="36" style="font-size:8">10</text>
<text x="28" y="23" style="font-size:8">11</text>
<text x="46" y="18" style="font-size:8">12</text>


<g transform="translate(50,50)">
  <g transform="rotate(210)">
    <line x1="0" y1="0" x2="0" y2="-29"
          style="stroke-width:2;stroke:red"/>
   </g>
   <g transform="rotate(90)">
     <line x1="0" y1="0" x2="0" y2="-20"
          style="stroke-width:2;stroke:black"/>
   </g>
 </g>
 <g transform="translate(150,0)">
  <circle cx="50" cy="50" r="40"
style="fill:white;stroke:black;"/>
  <text x="65" y="23" style="font-size:8">1</text>
  <text x="77" y="36" style="font-size:8">2</text>
  <text x="82" y="53" style="font-size:8">3</text>
  <text x="76" y="70" style="font-size:8">4</text>
  <text x="65" y="83" style="font-size:8">5</text>
  <text x="48" y="88" style="font-size:8">6</text>
  <text x="31" y="83" style="font-size:8">7</text>
  <text x="18" y="70" style="font-size:8">8</text>
  <text x="13" y="53" style="font-size:8">9</text>
  <text x="17" y="36" style="font-size:8">10</text>
  <text x="28" y="23" style="font-size:8">11</text>
  <text x="46" y="18" style="font-size:8">12</text>
  <g transform="translate(50,50)">
    <g transform="rotate(288)">
      <line x1="0" y1="0" x2="0" y2="-29"
            style="stroke-width:2;stroke:red"/>
    </g>
    <g transform="rotate(120)">
      <line x1="0" y1="0" x2="0" y2="-20"
         style="stroke-width:2;stroke:black"/>
    </g>
 </g>
</g>

  <circle cx="125" cy="150" r="60"
      style="fill:#B34DFB;stroke:black;"/>
    <text x="185" y="200" style="font-size:10;font-
color:#B34DFB">
     Total Hits: 400</text>
```

```
    <text x="185" y="220" style="font-size:10;font-color:yellow">
      404's: 23</text>
  <circle cx="125" cy="150" r="3.45"
          style="fill:yellow;stroke:yellow;"/>
</svg>
```

Transforming the Statistics to Multiple SVG Graphics

The following stylesheet produces as many SVG graphics as there are time spans in the statistics document.

```
<xsl:stylesheet version="1.0"
             xmlns:xsl="http://www.w3.org/1999/XSL/Transform"
             xmlns:xt="http://www.jclark.com/xt"
             extension-element-prefixes="xt">

<xsl:template match="/statistics">

<xsl:for-each select="span">
    <!-- for each span create an SVG file -->
  <xsl:variable
name="outputName">graph<xsl:number/>.svg</xsl:variable>
  <xt:document method="xml" href="{$outputName}">
   <svg>
    <!-- first position the start clock -->
    <xsl:call-template name="clock-skeleton"/>
    <xsl:call-template name="clock-hands">
      <xsl:with-param name="hour"   select="start/time/@hour"/>
      <xsl:with-param name="minute" select="start/time/@min"/>
    </xsl:call-template>

    <!-- now the end clock, avoiding superposition -->

    <g transform="translate(150,0)">
      <xsl:call-template name="clock-skeleton"/>
      <xsl:call-template name="clock-hands">
        <xsl:with-param name="hour"   select="stop/time/@hour"/>
        <xsl:with-param name="minute" select="stop/time/@min"/>
      </xsl:call-template>
    </g>

   <!-- now create the distribution pie -->
    <circle cx="125" cy="150" r="60"
            style="fill:#B34DFB;stroke:black;"/>
    <text x="185" y="200"
          style="font-size:10;font-color:#B34DFB">Total Hits:
         <xsl:value-of select="hits"/>
    </text>
    <text x="185" y="220" style="font-size:10;font-color:yel-
```

```
low">404's:
          <xsl:value-of select="hits_404"/>
    </text>

    <xsl:variable name="h"      select="hits"/>
    <xsl:variable name="h_404" select="hits_404"/>
    <xsl:variable name="lostRadius" select="($h_404 div $h)*60"/>

    <circle cx="125" cy="150" r="{$lostRadius}"
            style="fill:yellow;stroke:yellow;"/>


   </svg>
  </xt:document>
</xsl:for-each>

</xsl:template>

<!-- simply display the frame of the clock -->
<xsl:template name="clock-skeleton">
  <circle cx="50" cy="50" r="40"
style="fill:white;stroke:black;"/>
  <text x="65" y="23" style="font-size:8">1</text>
  <text x="77" y="36" style="font-size:8">2</text>
  <text x="82" y="53" style="font-size:8">3</text>
  <text x="76" y="70" style="font-size:8">4</text>
  <text x="65" y="83" style="font-size:8">5</text>
  <text x="48" y="88" style="font-size:8">6</text>
  <text x="31" y="83" style="font-size:8">7</text>
  <text x="18" y="70" style="font-size:8">8</text>
  <text x="13" y="53" style="font-size:8">9</text>
  <text x="17" y="36" style="font-size:8">10</text>
  <text x="28" y="23" style="font-size:8">11</text>
  <text x="46" y="18" style="font-size:8">12</text>
</xsl:template>

<xsl:template name="clock-hands">
  <xsl:param name="hour"/>
  <xsl:param name="minute"/>
  <xsl:variable name="hourAngle" select="($hour mod 12)*30"/>
  <xsl:variable name="minuteAngle" select="$minute*6"/>
  <g transform="translate(50,50)">
    <g transform="rotate({$minuteAngle})">
     <line x1="0" y1="0" x2="0" y2="-29"
           style="stroke-width:2;stroke:red"/>
    </g>
    <g transform="rotate({$hourAngle})">
     <line x1="0" y1="0" x2="0" y2="-20"
           style="stroke-width:2;stroke:black"/>
    </g>
  </g>
</xsl:template>

</xsl:stylesheet>
```

After using XT to run this stylesheet over an instance document with server statistics, the pictures shown in Figure 12.5 were produced.[2]

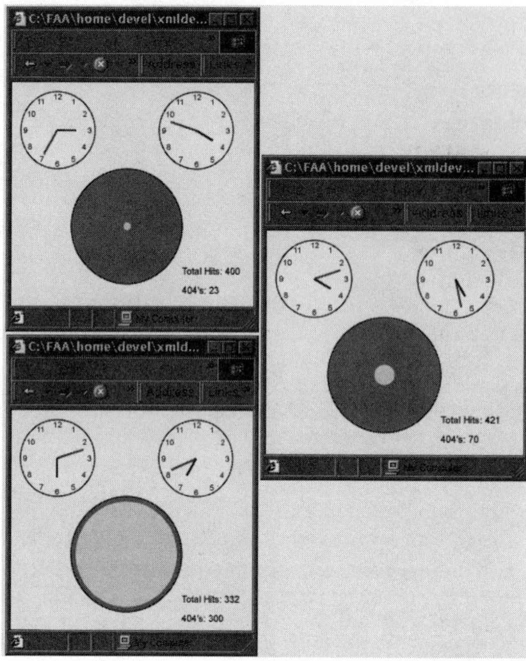

Figure 12.5
Resulting graphs.

In future chapters, many more examples of XSLT transformations will be presented. In particular, make sure to review the chapter on wireless application development, as it shows particularly relevant uses of XSLT as the core technology behind multi-device applications.

Stylesheet Reuse Techniques

So far, we have seen the reuse of XSLT constructs at the stylesheet level. We have made extensive use of named templates that encapsulate pieces of XSLT pretty much in the way functions encapsulate pieces of code in traditional languages. Now we must see how to reuse entire stylesheets, thus finding an equivalent to the use of traditional libraries.

[2] Please note that in order to see these pictures in your browser, an SVG plugin must be installed. The one used to render these examples can be downloaded from the Adobe Web site.

One Goal, Two Paths

XSLT provides two mechanisms to reuse a whole stylesheet as part of another:

1. Stylesheet inclusion
2. Stylesheet import

The stylesheet inclusion mechanism includes the templates of a stylesheet in another, in much the same way the traditional `#include` directive does in the C language. The `xsl:include` element—the syntactic mechanism for inclusion—can only appear as a top-level element (i.e. as a child of `xsl:stylesheet`) and only possesses one attribute: `href`. The value of `href` simply states the location of the included stylesheet:

```
<xsl:include href="included.xsl"/>
```

In case there are template conflicts between the included stylesheet and the original one, the original takes precedence. That is, `xsl:include` reuses a stylesheet without overriding.

`xsl:import`—the second form—has the same structure as `xsl:include`, but is semantically different in that it assigns a higher precedence to the imported stylesheets. In case of conflict, the template included with `xsl:import` takes precedence over the original defined in the stylesheet.

Extending XSLT

So far we have worked only with standard components of XSLT, aside from the XT extension for outputting multiple documents. In this section we shall see the mechanisms by which XSLT can be extended naturally to address particular problems not part of the original specification.

It is important to note that this section is about extending XSLT itself as a language; this is an advanced topic and should not be considered before acquiring a significant amount of experience with the basic mechanisms of XSLT.

When to Extend XSLT

Powerful and vast as it may be, XSLT has constructs that are limited and may not accommodate particular needs that may arise in your work. When such needs are recurrent and fundamental enough to be outside the reusability limits of a library of named templates (i.e. when you *really* need to extend the language, as opposed to just reusing things made on the language), you can use XSLT extensions.

XSLT extensions come in two flavors: extension functions and extension elements implemented in the XSLT processor; and pre-processed extension elements (special elements in a stylesheet that are translated via XSLT in order to produce another stylesheet with the desired behavior).

Extending XSLT, or any other language for that matter, is sometimes a tempting alternative that can lead to unnatural solutions, and adds an overhead of non-standardization. Always consider implementing your work with the basic set of constructs of XSLT before augmenting the language itself. That being said, let's see how to add new constructs to this powerful set of tools.

Non-Recursive Solutions

As became evident in the functional requirements section, dealing with the absence of a procedural loop mechanism in XSLT can sometimes be painful. Naturally (as was shown in that same example), procedural loops can always be replaced by recursive named templates; however, this might not seem natural in some cases.

Consider again, for example, our problem of outputting an arbitrary number of copies of the same element. In the pure XSLT version, this must be implemented as a recursion such as the following:

```
<!-- Recursive function to insert dots -->
<xsl:template name="n-copies">
  <xsl:param name="number">
  <xsl:if test="$number &gt; 0">  <!-- have to escape the > char-
acter -->
    <element/>

     <xsl:call-template name="n-copies">
         <xsl:with-param name="number" select="$number - 1"/>
     </xsl:call-template>

  </xsl:if>
</xsl:template>
```

```
<!-- a sample call -->
<xsl:call-template name="n-copies">
   <xsl:with-param number="5"/>
</xsl:call-template>
```

However, most people are used to non-recursive solutions in the form of constructs such as the traditional `for`; therefore a solution such as the following may seem much more appealing:

```
<ext:times n="5"> <!-- repeat the content n times -->
  <element/>
</ext>
```

The next section shows how to extend XSLT to include such a construct.

Implementing the `times` Construct

The most straightforward way to augment the XSLT language to include a `times` construct is by implementing a pre-processing stylesheet that translates the `times` element into a recursive equivalent.

Such stylesheet must transform a stylesheet like the following:

```
<xsl:stylesheet version="1.0"
        xmlns:xsl="http://www.w3.org/1999/XSL/Transform"
             xmlns:procedural="http://www.thefaactory.com/xslt/p"
                extension-element-prefixes="procedural">

<xsl:template match="/">
   <xsl:variable name="stars" select="movie/calification"/>

   <procedural:times n="$stars"/>
      <img src="star.gif"/>
   </procedural:times>

</xsl:template>
```

Into a stylesheet such as:

```
<?xml version="1.0" encoding="utf-8"?>

<xsl:stylesheet
                version="1.0"
             xmlns:xsl="http://www.w3.org/1999/XSL/Transform"
xmlns:procedural="http://www.thefaactory.com/xslt/p"
```

```
                xmlns:axsl="/1999/XSL/TransformAlias"
                extension-element-prefixes="procedural">

<!--Recursive function added by Iterator Compiler-->
<xsl:template xmlns:xsl="http://www.w3.org/1999/XSL/Transform"
              name="recursive-loop">

    <xsl:param name="n"/>
    <xsl:param name="contents"/>
    <xsl:if test="$n &gt; 0">
      <xsl:copy-of select="$contents"/>

      <xsl:call-template name="recursive-loop">
        <xsl:with-param name="n" select="$n - 1"/>
        <xsl:with-param name="contents" select="$contents"/>
      </xsl:call-template>
    </xsl:if>

</xsl:template>


<xsl:template match="/">
  <xsl:variable name="stars" select="movie/calification"/>
  <xsl:call-template name="recursive-loop">
    <xsl:with-param name="n" value="$stars"/>
    <xsl:with-param name="contents">

      <img src="star.gif"/>

    </xsl:with-param>
  </xsl:call-template>
</xsl:template>

</xsl:stylesheet>
```

Then, converting a source XML document becomes a two-step process like the following:

```
xalan -IN originalStyleSheet.xsl -XSL extensionCompiler.xsl -OUT
modifiedStylesheet.xsl
xalan -IN source -XSL modifiedStylesheet.xsl -OUT output.xml
```

The *extension compiler* stylesheet that performs the translation looks like the following:

```
<xsl:stylesheet version="1.0"
             xmlns:xsl="http://www.w3.org/1999/XSL/Transform"

xmlns:procedural="http://www.thefaactory.com/xslt/p"
                xmlns:axsl="/1999/XSL/TransformAlias"
                extension-element-prefixes="procedural">
```

```
<!-- ... rules for copying non-example elements ommited ... -->

<xsl:namespace-alias stylesheet-prefix="axsl" result-
prefix="xsl"/>

<xsl:template match="procedural:times">
    <axsl:call-template name="recursive-loop">
        <!-- pass the value of the n attribute as the first
parameter -->
        <axsl:with-param name="n" value="{@n}"/>
        <!-- pass the complete contents as the second parameter -->
        <axsl:with-param name="contents">
            <xsl:copy-of select="node()"/>
        </axsl:with-param>
    </axsl:call-template>
</xsl:template>

<xsl:template match="/xsl:stylesheet">
 <xsl:copy> <!-- just output the stylesheet element -->
  <xsl:comment>Recursive function added by Iterator
Compiler</xsl:comment>
  <axsl:template name="recursive-loop">
    <axsl:param name="n"/>
    <axsl:param name="contents"/>

    <axsl:if test="$n &gt; 0">
      <axsl:copy-of select="$contents"/>

      <axsl:call-template name="recursive-loop">
        <axsl:with-param name="n" select="$n - 1"/>
        <axsl:with-param name="contents" select="$contents"/>
      </axsl:call-template>
    </axsl:if>
  </axsl:template>


  <xsl:apply-templates/>
   <!-- ... rules for copying the rest of  elements ommited ... -->
 </xsl:copy>

</xsl:template>


</xsl:stylesheet>
```

There are several notable things about this example. The first is the `extension-element-prefixes` attribute on the `xsl:stylesheet` element: this is the form to declare all extensions to the language. The XSLT specification does not include anything else constraining extensions, but the fact that the namespace to which they are bound is declared in an `extension-element-prefixes` attribute, so that the processor can correctly interpret them as instructions and not as literal result elements.

In the case of extensions implemented in a particular processor (such as the Xalan multi-document extensions), this extension declaration is fundamental, for it tells the processor which prefixes are associated with extensions. In the case of extensions implemented as pre-processes, it is still good practice to declare extensions, because they improve readability and make absolutely clear the intention of each construct.

The `xsl:namespace-alias` mechanism serves as way to "escape" the special meaning of elements within the XSLT namespaces. It indicates that nodes with a particular prefix (`axsl`, in this case) must be output as elements with other prefixes (`xsl`). This allows the output of XSLT instructions that would otherwise be interpreted as members of the stylesheet.

A Note on Other Kinds of Extensions

As mentioned earlier, XSLT extensions can also come in the form of processor extensions that are understood only by particular implementations. Such extensions are well beyond the purpose of this book, but if you are interested in seeing them, you may do so by checking the original code of processors such as XT, which implement common extensions like the one used in this chapter to output several documents.

More Extensions

For more extensions, in particular a complete implementation of other forms of procedural loops, please look at the companion CD.

A Concise XSLT Reference

Table 12.1 shows all the constructs of the XSLT language. It is included as reference material, and is based directly on the contents of the XSLT specification. Because of their complexity and the fact that they are seldom used, some of the elements listed here are not treated in this chapter; you are invited to see the XSLT spec (see CD) for more information about them.

TABLE 12.1

A concise XSLT reference.

Element Syntax
<xsl:apply-imports />
<xsl:apply-templates select = node-set-expression mode = qname> <!-- Content: (xsl:sort | xsl:with-param)* --> </xsl:apply-templates>
<xsl:attribute name = { qname } namespace = { uri-reference }> <!-- Content: template --> </xsl:attribute>
<xsl:attribute-set name = qname use-attribute-sets = qnames> <!-- Content: xsl:attribute* --> </xsl:attribute-set>
<xsl:call-template name = qname> <!-- Content: xsl:with-param* --> </xsl:call-template>
<xsl:choose> <!-- Content: (xsl:when+, xsl:otherwise?) --> </xsl:choose>
<xsl:comment> <!-- Content: template --> </xsl:comment>

(continued on next page)

TABLE 12.1

A concise XSLT reference. (continued)

```
<xsl:copy
 use-attribute-sets = qnames>
 <!-- Content: template -->
</xsl:copy>
```

```
<xsl:copy-of
 select = expression />
```

```
<xsl:decimal-format
 name = qname
 decimal-separator = char
 grouping-separator = char
 infinity = string
 minus-sign = char
 NaN = string
 percent = char
 per-mille = char
 zero-digit = char
 digit = char
 pattern-separator = char />
```

```
<xsl:element
 name = { qname }
 namespace = { uri-reference }
 use-attribute-sets = qnames>
 <!-- Content: template -->
</xsl:element>
```

```
<xsl:fallback>
 <!-- Content: template -->
</xsl:fallback>
```

(continued on next page)

TABLE 12.1

A concise XSLT reference. (continued)

```
<xsl:for-each
  select = node-set-expression>
  <!-- Content: (xsl:sort*, template) -->
</xsl:for-each>
```

```
<xsl:if
  test = boolean-expression>
  <!-- Content: template -->
</xsl:if>
```

```
<xsl:import
  href = uri-reference />
```

```
<xsl:include
  href = uri-reference />
```

```
<xsl:key
  name = qname
  match = pattern
  use = expression />
```

```
<xsl:message
  terminate = "yes" | "no">
  <!-- Content: template -->
</xsl:message>
```

```
<xsl:namespace-alias
  stylesheet-prefix = prefix | "#default"
  result-prefix = prefix | "#default" />
```

```
<xsl:number
  level = "single" | "multiple" | "any"
  count = pattern
  from = pattern
```

(continued on next page)

TABLE 12.1 A concise XSLT reference. (continued)

```
  value = number-expression
  format = { string }
  lang = { nmtoken }
  letter-value = { "alphabetic" | "traditional" }
  grouping-separator = { char }
  grouping-size = { number } />
```

```
<xsl:otherwise>
  <!-- Content: template -->
</xsl:otherwise>
```

```
<xsl:output
  method = "xml" | "html" | "text" | qname-but-not-ncname
  version = nmtoken
  encoding = string
  omit-xml-declaration = "yes" | "no"
  standalone = "yes" | "no"
  doctype-public = string
  doctype-system = string
  cdata-section-elements = qnames
  indent = "yes" | "no"
  media-type = string />
```

```
<xsl:param
  name = qname
  select = expression>
  <!-- Content: template -->
</xsl:param>
```

```
<xsl:preserve-space
  elements = tokens />
```

(continued on next page)

TABLE 12.1

A concise XSLT reference. (continued)

```
<xsl:processing-instruction
  name = { ncname }>
  <!-- Content: template -->
</xsl:processing-instruction>
```

```
<xsl:sort
  select = string-expression
  lang = { nmtoken }
  data-type = { "text" | "number" | qname-but-not-ncname }
  order = { "ascending" | "descending" }
  case-order = { "upper-first" | "lower-first" } />
```

```
<xsl:strip-space
  elements = tokens />
```

```
<xsl:stylesheet
  id = id
  extension-element-prefixes = tokens
  exclude-result-prefixes = tokens
  version = number>
  <!-- Content: (xsl:import*, top-level-elements) -->
</xsl:stylesheet>
```

```
<xsl:template
  match = pattern
  name = qname
  priority = number
  mode = qname>
  <!-- Content: (xsl:param*, template) -->
</xsl:template>
```

```
<xsl:text
```

(continued on next page)

TABLE 12.1
A concise XSLT reference. (continued)

```
  disable-output-escaping = "yes" | "no">
  <!-- Content: #PCDATA -->
</xsl:text>
```

```
<xsl:transform
  id = id
  extension-element-prefixes = tokens
  exclude-result-prefixes = tokens
  version = number>
  <!-- Content: (xsl:import*, top-level-elements) -->
</xsl:transform>
```

```
<xsl:value-of
  select = string-expression
  disable-output-escaping = "yes" | "no" />
```

```
<xsl:variable
  name = qname
  select = expression>
  <!-- Content: template -->
</xsl:variable>
```

```
<xsl:when
  test = boolean-expression>
  <!-- Content: template -->
</xsl:when>
```

```
<xsl:with-param
  name = qname
  select = expression>
  <!-- Content: template -->
</xsl:with-param>
```

Summary

The XSLT language is a powerful declarative way of transforming XML documents. In Chapters 11 and 12 the structure and uses of the language were presented; in future chapters, the concepts outlined here will be of great importance as we use this essential specification in many XML problems.

CHAPTER 13

XML Schema

Introduction

Chapter 2 explained the details of XML DTDs, the most basic and common way of defining document types in XML. It also reviewed the many limitations of DTDs and promised a more powerful mechanism that would overcome them. This chapter treats precisely such a solution: XML Schema.[1]

XML Schema is not the only type-definition mechanism in the XML world besides DTDs, but the fact that it is addressed as a W3C recommendation makes it the de facto choice for all modeling problems beyond the reach of DTDs.

The chapter on XML Schema does two things: it presents a hands-on introduction to the use and concepts of XML schemas, and moves on to show advanced examples that can serve as a reference and inspiration for your own schemas, as well as methodologies and techniques to maximize this technology.

XML Schema: A Hands-on Approach

XML Schema is a type-definition mechanism that relies heavily on the concepts of object orientation and traditional data representation. XML Schema is created around the idea of types (such as integer, date, and Boolean) and instances of these types (e.g. the element *pi* is an instance of the *float* type).

Take for example, the following minimal schema, which describes a type called *tv-slot* (a certain lapse of time during which a particular TV show is aired):

```
<xsd:schema xmlns:xsd="http://www.w3.org/1999/XMLSchema">

<!-- The type definition -->
 <xsd:complexType name="TVSlot">
  <xsd:sequence>
   <xsd:element name="ShowName" type="xsd:string"/>
   <xsd:element name="day"      type="xsd:date"/>
   <xsd:element name="begin"    type="xsd:time"/>
```

[1] Even if you know for sure that you want XML Schemas for your project, please make sure you have a good understanding of the topics covered in Chapters 1 through 3, as this chapter assumes that knowledge, and no explanations of namespaces or XML validity are included here.

```
    <xsd:element name="end"      type="xsd:time"/>
  </xsd:sequence>
 </xsd:complexType>
```

Now, define that there must be an instance of the previous element:

```
<xsd:element name="slot" type="TVSlot"/>
</xsd:schema>
```

This small schema is already telling us at least four very important aspects of the XML Schema mechanism itself:

- XML Schema documents are written using XML. Instead of using another notation, with its own rules, XML schemas are well-formed XML documents, thus their learning and readability curves can be greatly improved.
- There are basic simple types that can be directly used for elements (e.g. `string`, `date`, and `time` in our example).
- There is a mechanism to construct complex types, declaring inside them elements of certain types. This is analogous to the constructions of classes like the following in OO languages (such as Java):

```
class TVSpot {
   String showName;
   Date   day;
   Time   beginning;
   Time   end;
}
```

- There is a clear distinction between creating a type and declaring an element of that type.

Now, let's refine the schema further in order to explore the details of the language.

Types

Types in XML Schema are divided into two categories: simple and complex. Simple types can only contain character data; they can't have attributes or element content. Complex types, on the other hand, can have any kind of combination of element content, character data, and attributes.

XML Schema provides a basic set of simple types that can be directly used (as we did in the previous example) to declare elements that conform to popular notions such as integer or date. Table 13.1 lists the complete set of basic types and their intended meaning.

TABLE 13.1

Built-in schema types (from the XML schema spec).

Simple Built-in Type	Example
string	"Confirm this is electric"
boolean	True, false, 1, 0
float	-INF, -1E4, -0, 0, 12.78E-2, 12, INF, NaN ("not a number"), equivalent to single-precision 32-bit floating point
double	-INF, -1E4, -0, 0, 12.78E-2, 12, INF, NaN, equivalent to double-precision 64-bit floating point
decimal	-1.23, 0, 123.4, 1000.00
timeInstant	1999-05-31T13:20:00.000-05:00 (May 31st 1999 at 1.20pm Eastern Standard Time, which is 5 hours behind Coordinated Universal Time)
timeDuration	P1Y2M3DT10H30M12.3S (1 year, 2 months, 3 days, 10 hours, 30 minutes, 12.3 seconds)
recurringInstant	--05-31T13:20:00 (May 31st every year at 1.20pm Coordinated Universal Time, format similar to timeInstant)
binary	100010
uri-reference	http://www.example.com/, http://www.example.com/doc.html#ID5
ID	is an XML 1.0 ID attribute type
IDREF	is an XML 1.0 IDREF attribute type
ENTITY	is an XML 1.0 ENTITY attribute type
NOTATION	is an XML 1.0 NOTATION attribute type
language	en-GB, en-US, fr, and other valid values for xml:lang as defined in XML 1.0
IDREFS	is an XML 1.0 IDREFS attribute type
ENTITIES	is an XML 1.0 ENTITIES attribute type
NMTOKEN	US, is an XML 1.0 NMTOKEN attribute type
NMTOKENS	"US UK", is an XML 1.0 NMTOKENS attribute type

continued on next page

TABLE 13.1
Built-in schema types (from the XML schema spec) (continued).

Simple Built-in Type	Example
Name	`ShipTo` (is an XML 1.0 Name type)
QName	Address (is an XML Namespace QName)
NCName	Address (is an XML Namespace NCName, i.e. is a QName without the prefix and colon)
integer	-126789, -1, 0, 1, 126789
non-positive-integer	-126789, -1, 0
negative-integer	-126789, -1
long	-1, 12678967543233
int	-1, 126789675
short	-1, 12678
byte	-1, 126
non-negative-integer	0, 1, 126789
unsigned-long	0, 12678967543233
unsigned-int	0, 1267896754
unsigned-short	0, 12678
unsigned-byte	0, 126
positive-integer	1, 126789
date	1999-05-31, ---05 (5th day of every month)
time	13:20:00.000, 13:20:00.000-05:00

The first and most popular use of built-in types is the direct declaration of elements and attributes that conform to them. The following is the declaration of a `show` type element that contains several subelements of built-in types.

```
<xsd:complexType name="Show">
 <xsd:sequence>
  <xsd:element   name="name"          type="xsd:string"/>
  <xsd:element   name="description"   type="xsd:string"/>
  <xsd:attribute name="show-id"       type="xsd:ID"/>
  <xsd:attribute name="first-aired"   type="xsd:date"/>
 </xsd:sequence>
</xsd:complexType>
```

Provided there is a declaration of the `show` element, as follows:

```
<xsd:element name="show" type="Show"/>
```

a valid element for this declaration[2] would look like the following:

```
<show show-id="nbc-18" first-aired="01/01/1990">
  <name>Seinfeld</name>
  <description>show about nothing</description>
<show>
```

This *complex type definition* shows two more important aspects of simple types:

- Attributes can be declared as conforming to a particular simple type. Since the values of simple types cannot include any element content, this not only makes perfect sense, but is a final solution to the syntactic limitations of mere internal entity aliasing in DTDs:[3]

```
<!-- The DTD equivalent for the first-aired attribute -->
<!ENTITY % date  "CDATA">
<!ATTLIST TVSlot
    first-aired %date;  REQUIRED>
```

- Attributes can still have the useful types defined in DTDs (`ID`, `NMTOKEN`, etc.), thus easing the transition between and interoperability of DTDs and XML Schema; they can also have the representation of concepts proven very useful in DTD creation (e.g. `ID` and `IDREF`).

Using Complex Types within Complex Types

So far we have seen only complex types that use subelments of simple types. However, in real life we wouldn't get too far with just that, so it's time to discuss nested complex types.

An element declaration, in its simplest form, is the union of an element name and a particular type:

---

[2] After we explore the language itself, we will take care of the mechanisms by which documents get associated with schemas (i.e. we will present the equivalent of the DOCTYPE declaration). For the moment, just assume that we are telling the parser explicitly what schema we are using.

[3] The technique used in this example is a useful and powerful one. It solves the problem of 80 percent of the applications: inform the reader of the DTD that this is intended to be a date. However, sometimes it is important to enforce syntactic checks of that intention from the parser itself, and that is when XML Schema is used.

```
<xsd:element   name="description"  type="xsd:string"/>
```

As long as the type is defined somewhere on the schema (or is a built-in simple type), the declaration can be made. Therefore, using a `show` type element in our initial `TV-Spot` type is as simple as the following:

```
<xsd:schema xmlns:xsd="http://www.w3.org/1999/XMLSchema">

<xsd:complexType name="Show">
 <xsd:sequence>
  <xsd:element   name="name"          type="xsd:string"/>
  <xsd:element   name="producer"      type="xsd:string"/>
  <xsd:attribute name="show-id"       type="xsd:ID"/>
 </xsd:sequence>
  <xsd:attribute name="first-aired"  type="xsd:date"/>

</xsd:complexType>

<xsd:complexType name="TVSlot">
 <xsd:sequence>
  <xsd:element name="show"      type="Show"/>
  <xsd:element name="day"       type="xsd:date"/>
  <xsd:element name="begin"     type="xsd:time"/>
  <xsd:element name="end"       type="xsd:time"/>
 </xsd:sequence>
</xsd:complexType>

<xsd:element name="slot" type="TVSlot"/>

</xsd:schema>
```

A valid document for this type will be as simple as the following:

```
<?xml version="1.0"?>
<slot>
  <show show-id="snl" first-aired="01/03/1974">
    <name>Saturday Night Live</name>
    <description>...<description>
  </show>
  <day>10/24/2001</day>
  <begin>23:00:00</begin>
  <end>23:58:00</end>
</slot>
```

A Better Solution

Even though the previous solution works as an illustration of complex types within other complex types, it fails to correctly model the problem because it leads to unnecessary redundancy.

Consider, for example, the case of a slightly improved schema with many `tv-slots`:

```
<xsd:schema xmlns:xsd="http://www.w3.org/1999/XMLSchema">

<xsd:complexType name="tvguide">
  <xsd:element name="slot"
               type="TVSlot"
               minOccurs="1"
            maxOccurs="*"/>
</xsd:complexType>
<!-- All other declarations of the previous example here -->
</xsd:schema>
```

If we were to use the definition of `TVSlot` given in the previous section, we would have to write many times the `show` subelement, even if the show is the same. This is a good opportunity to reuse the `ID` and `IDREF` techniques of DTDs in order to make a more maintainable and usable schema:

```
<xsd:schema xmlns:xsd="http://www.w3.org/1999/XMLSchema">

<xsd:complexType name="tvguide">
 <xsd:sequence>
  <xsd:element name="program"
               type="Show"
               minOccurs="0"
             maxOccurs="*"/>
  <xsd:element name="slot"
               type="TVSlot"
               minOccurs="1"
             maxOccurs="*"/>
 </xsd:sequence>
</xsd:complexType>


<xsd:complexType name="Show">
 <xsd:sequence>
  <xsd:element   name="name"          type="xsd:string"/>
  <xsd:element   name="description"   type="xsd:string"/>
 </xsd:sequence>
<xsd:attribute name="show-id"       type="xsd:ID"/>
<xsd:attribute name="first-aired"   type="xsd:date"/>

</xsd:complexType>

<xsd:complexType name="TVSlot">
 <xsd:sequence>
  <xsd:element   name="day"       type="xsd:date"/>
  <xsd:element   name="begin"     type="xsd:time"/>
  <xsd:element   name="end"       type="xsd:time"/>
```

```
 </xsd:sequence>
 <xsd:attribute name="show"     type="xsd:IDREF"/>

</xsd:complexType>

</xsd:schema>
```

Using this schema, we have more economic instances:

```
<?xml version="1.0"?>
<tvguide>
<show show-id="snl" first-aired="01/03/1974">
    <name>Saturday Night Live</name>
    <description>...<description>
</show>

<slot show="snl"/>
  <day>10/22/2001</day>
  <begin>23:00:00</begin>
  <end>23:58:00</end>
</slot>
<slot show="snl"/>
  <day>10/22/2001</day>
  <begin>23:00:00</begin>
  <end>23:58:00</end>
</slot>
</tvguide>
```

Facets

As mentioned in Chapter 2, one of the most obvious shortcomings of DTDs is the lack of mechanisms to control the format of character data inside an element. Consider, for example, the following DTD, whose only purpose is to define an element for software license keys (such as those asked for by installation applications in commercial products):

```
<!ELEMENT sw-key (#PCDATA)>
```

A valid instance of this element could indeed be a software key such as the following:

```
<sw-key>2222-IAG-32123</sw-key>
```

But the following totally unrelated (and conceptually misused) element is also valid:

```
<sw-key>
     This doesn't resemble anything like a software license key.
     But it is also valid according with the DTD.
</sw-key>
```

The solution to this problem is an XML Schema in the form of specially *restricted* simple types (after all, saying that something is of type `xsd:string` would not help us much here).

In order to restrict a particular simple built-in type, XML Schema defines *facets*, special aspects of the type that can be used to tailor it to a particular need. In the case of `xsd:string`, a particular facet called *pattern* can be used to restrict the string to our needs.

Facets come in the form of subelments inside the element declaration. In the case of the software key example, a facet would take the following shape:

```
<xsd:element name="vanilla-sw-key" type="xsd:string"/> <!--no
facet -->

<xsd:element name="vanilla-sw-key" type="xsd:string">
  <xsd:pattern value="/d{4}-[A-Z]{3}-/d{5}"/> <!óthe pattern
facet -->
</xsd:element>
```

The value of the pattern facet (stated in the value attribute) is a regular expression for the possible values of the string. If, and only if, a string matches the expression given (that is, if it is composed of four digits, then a hyphen, then three characters in the range of A to Z, and then five more digits), the string is valid.

Regular Expressions

The regular expression language used in patterns is very similar to that of Perl; however, a user requires no Perl experience whatsoever to understand it. A complete discussion of the theory of the pattern expression language is not within the scope of this chapter, but the following examples, shown in Table 13.2 will provide an idea of the possibilities and will prove useful when writing your own patterns.

Patterns are not the only facets in the XML Schema specification. Tables 13.3 and 13.4 summarize the facets available and the simple types to which they apply.

TABLE 13.2 Examples of XML Schema Patterns

Expression	Match(s)
a*x	x, ax, aax, aaax ....
a?x	ax, x
a+x	ax, aax, aaax ....
(a|b)+x	ax, bx, aax, abx, bax, bbx, aaax, aabx, abax, abbx, baax, babx, bbax, bbbx, aaaax ....
[abcde]x	ax, bx, cx, dx, ex
[a-e]x	ax, bx, cx, dx, ex
[-ae]x	-x, ax, ex
[ae-]x	ax, ex, -x
Chapter \d	Chapter 0, Chapter 1, Chapter 2...
Chapter\s\d	Chapter followed by a single whitespace character (space, tab, newline, etc), followed by a single digit
Chapter\s\w	Chapter followed by a single whitespace character (space, tab, newline, etc.), followed by a word character XML 1.0 letter or Digit)
[a-e-[bd]]x	ax, cx, ex
[^0-9]x	Any non-digit character followed by the character x
\Dx	Any non-digit character followed by the character x
.x	Any character followed by the character x
.*abc.*	1x2abc, abc1x2, z3456abchooray ....
ab{2}x	abbx
ab{2,4}x	abbx, abbbx, abbbbx
ab{2,}x	abbx, abbbx, abbbbx ....
(ab){2}x	Ababx

Notable Facets

Enumerating the syntax and uses of all the available facets for each type in the language is not feasible in this chapter. The recommended approach is to read the examples here (they cover the most widely used facets) and then refer to the tables and the specification for your particular needs.

Some notable facets include `minInclusive` and `maxInclusive` (and their counterparts `minExclusive` and `maxExclusive`). To see how these are used, suppose for example, that you want to model an element of a type that corresponds exactly with the Java notion of *short*.[4] You could do so by using the `minInclusive` and `maxExclusive` facets of the simple type `int` in the following way:[5]

```
<xsd:simpleType name="javaShort">
  <xsd:restriction base="xsd:integer">
    <xsd:minInclusive value="-32767"/>
    <xsd:maxExclusive value="32769"/>
  </xsd:restriction>
</xsd:simpleType>
```

Another important facet is precision. It is applicable to types derived from the simple type `decimal` (see types shown in Tables 13.3 and 13.4), and specifies the number of decimal positions in a particular number. For example, the following declaration states that the value of `decimalStature` (a value for the stature of a human being expressed in meters) can only have two decimal positions:

```
<xsd:simpleType name="decimalStature">
  <xsd:restriction base="xsd:decimal">
    <xsd:precision value="2"/>
  </xsd:restriction>
</xsd:simpleType>
```

Finally, and perhaps the single most useful facet in XML Schema, is `enumeration`. This allows a type to restrict its value to a set of particular instances of another type (just as in a programming language such as C). To illustrate, let's create an enumerated type for countries of Europe:

```
<xsd:simpleType name="EuropeanCountry">
  <xsd:restriction base="xsd:string">
    <xsd:enumeration value="Lithuania"/>
    <xsd:enumeration value="Germany"/>
    <xsd:enumeration value="France"/>
    <!--  etc.-->
  </xsd:restriction>
</xsd:simpleType>
```

---

[4] The schema spec also provides a short type (created exactly the same way) but its allowed values do not coincide with the Java notion of short.

[5] This declaration also illustrates the concept of *derivation by restriction*.

The following other example represents the enumerated type `donation` based on `integers`, which stipulates that donation to a particular charity can be made only for the quantities of 25.000, 50.000, or 100.000:

```
<xsd:simpleType name="Donation">
  <xsd:restriction base="xsd:integer">
    <xsd:enumeration value="25000"/>
    <xsd:enumeration value="50000"/>
    <xsd:enumeration value="100000"/>
  </xsd:restriction>
</xsd:simpleType>
```

TABLE 13.3

XML schema simple types versus facets.

Simple Types	Facets				
	Length	**minLength**	**maxLength**	**Pattern**	**Enumeration**
String	✔	✔	✔	✔	✔
Byte			✔	✔	
unsignedByte			✔	✔	
Binary	✔	✔	✔		✔
Integer			✔	✔	
positiveInteger			✔	✔	
negativeInteger			✔	✔	
nonNegativeInteger			✔	✔	
nonPositiveInteger			✔	✔	
Int			✔	✔	
unsignedInt			✔	✔	
Long			✔	✔	
unsignedLong			✔	✔	
Short			✔	✔	
unsignedShort			✔	✔	
Decimal			✔	✔	
Float			✔	✔	
Double			✔	✔	

continued on next page

TABLE 13.3

XML schema simple types versus facets (continued).

Simple Types	Facets				
	Length	minLength	maxLength	Pattern	Enumeration
Boolean			✔		
Time			✔	✔	
TimeInstant			✔	✔	
TimePeriod			✔	✔	
TimeDuration			✔	✔	
Date			✔	✔	
Month			✔	✔	
Year			✔	✔	
Century			✔	✔	
RecurringDay			✔	✔	
RecurringDate			✔	✔	
RecurringDuration			✔	✔	
Name	✔	✔	✔	✔	✔
Qname	✔	✔	✔	✔	✔
NCName	✔	✔	✔	✔	✔
UriReference	✔	✔	✔	✔	✔
Language	✔	✔	✔	✔	✔
ID	✔	✔	✔	✔	✔
IDREF	✔	✔	✔	✔	✔
IDREFS	✔	✔	✔		✔
ENTITY	✔	✔	✔	✔	✔
ENTITIES	✔	✔	✔		✔
NOTATION	✔	✔	✔	✔	✔
NMTOKEN	✔	✔	✔	✔	✔
NMTOKENS	✔	✔	✔		✔

Table 13.4 Other Facets.

Simple Types	Facets							
	maxinclusive	**maxExclusive**	**minInclusive**	**minExclusive**	**precision**	**scale**	**encoding**	**period**
duration								
Byte	✔	✔	✔	✔	✔	✔		
unsignedByte	✔	✔	✔	✔	✔	✔		
Binary						✔		
Integer	✔	✔	✔	✔	✔	✔		
positiveInteger	✔	✔	✔	✔	✔	✔		
negativeInteger	✔	✔	✔	✔	✔	✔		
nonNegativeInteger	✔	✔	✔	✔	✔	✔		
nonPositiveInteger	✔	✔	✔	✔	✔	✔		
Int	✔	✔	✔	✔	✔	✔		
unsignedInt	✔	✔	✔	✔	✔	✔		
Long	✔	✔	✔	✔	✔	✔		
unsignedLong	✔	✔	✔	✔	✔	✔		
Short	✔	✔	✔	✔	✔	✔		
unsignedShort	✔	✔	✔	✔	✔	✔		
Decimal	✔	✔	✔	✔	✔	✔		
Float	✔	✔	✔	✔				
Double	✔	✔	✔	✔				
Time	✔	✔	✔	✔			✔	✔
timeInstant	✔	✔	✔	✔			✔	✔
timePeriod	✔	✔	✔	✔			✔	✔
timeDuration	✔	✔	✔	✔				
Date	✔	✔	✔	✔			✔	✔
Month	✔	✔	✔	✔			✔	✔

Anonymous Types

So far, we have seen a common and straightforward way to design classes of documents: first, define types for the kinds of data you want to represent; then, declare elements of those types. The following example demonstrates the method applied to the problem of creating element types for movie titles:

```
<!-- first, the type definition -->
<xsd:complexType name="BasicMovie">
  <xsd:sequence>
   <xsd:element name="title" type="xsd:string"/>
   <xsd:element name="director" type="xsd:string"/>
   <xsd:element name="release"  type="xsd:date"/>
  </xsd:sequence>
  <xsd:attribute name="release"  type="xsd:date"/>
 </xsd:complexType>
<!-- now the element declaration -->
<xsd:element name="movie"  type="BasiMovie"/>
```

This method, despite its clarity and generality, can become tedious when one has many types that differ very little from each other and very few elements that use them. An abbreviated form called *anonymous types* is the solution for these cases.

In order to see the rationale behind anonymous types, take, for example, the problem of defining types for software copy keys, and suppose you want an element called *security* within which there is another element, a software key. The following elements will both be valid instances of our type:

```
<security>
  <Microsoft-Key>3322-AEG-3211</Microsoft-Key>
</security>
<security>
  <Adobe-Key>1234567ERT2312</Adobe-Key>
</security>
```

Since there are so many different types of keys, and each of them is going to have only one element, the schema could quickly become bloated with declarations such as the following:

```
<xsd:complex-type name="Adobe-Key-Type">
  <xsd:restriction base="xsd:string">
    <xsd:pattern value="\d{7}[A-Z]{3}\d{3}"/>
  </xsd:restriction>
</xsd:complex-type>
```

```
<xsd:element name="Adobe-Key" type="Adobe-Key-Type"/>
```

Instead, the two declarations could be rolled together, and the element could express the restrictions of the type itself. This is called *anonymous typing*.

```
<xsd:element name="Adobe-Key">
 <xsd:simpleType>
  <xsd:restriction base="xsd:string">
    <xsd:pattern value="\d{7}[A-Z]{3}\d{3}"/>
  </xsd:restriction>
 </xsd:simpleType>
 </xsd:element>
```

Naturally, the disadvantage of anonymous types is that they cannot be reused for other elements; use them only when you are confident that the type is not going to be reused (in the present or future versions of your schema).

Content Models

So far we have treated elements that are either simple typed or a sequence of subelements. Now it is time to explore other possibilities, such as empty elements, mixed content, and other advanced content models.

Specifying Options and Sequences in Content Models

In order to specify options in the content model of a complex type, we use the element `choice`, which specifies that only one of its children may appear in the content.

The following example shows a simple application equivalent to the DTD content model (A | B | C):

```
<xsd:complexType name="foo">
  <xsd:choice>
   <xsd:element name="A" type="AsType"/>
   <xsd:element name="B" type="BsType"/>
   <xsd:element name="C" type="CsType"/>
   <!-- etc -->
  </xsd:choice>
</xsd:complexType>
```

One very interesting fact about `choice` is that it can have as subelements constructs other than mere elements, providing the ability to finely control things out of reach in DTD such as attribute choices. The following example illustrates the point:

```
<xsd:complexType name="residence">
  <xsd:choice>
    <xsd:sequence>
       <xsd:attribute name="us-address"   type="xsd:string"/>
       <xsd:attribute name="us-address-2" type="xsd:string"/>
       <xsd:attribute name="us-address-3" type="xsd:string"
                      minOccurs="0"/>
    </xsd:sequence>
    <xsd:sequence>
       <xsd:attribute name="spanish-address"
type="xsd:string"/>
    </xsd:sequence>
  </xsd:choice>
</xsd:complexType>
```

Mixed Content

Traditionally with DTDs, mixed content (i.e. element content formed by both elements and character data) has been limited to specifying which elements can be interspersed with character data; no particular control over the order or cardinality of those elements could be made.

In XML Schema, one can specify as precisely as desired the contents of a mixed element. Take, for example, the following anonymous type:

```
<xsd:element name="paragraph">
 <xsd:complexType mixed="true">
  <xsd:choice>
     <xsd:element name="technical-review" type="xsd:string"/>
     <xsd:element name="review" type="xsd:string"/>
  </xsd:choice>
 </xsd:complexType>
</xsd:element>
```

Cardinalities

As mentioned previously, cardinalities can be specified via the `minOccurs` and `maxOccurs` attributes in element declarations.

```
<xsd:complexType name="cd-track">
    <xsd:sequence>
       <xsd:attribute name="track"   type="xsd:string"
                      minOccurs="1"  maxOccurs="*"/>
    </xsd:sequence>
</xsd:complexType>
```

It is worth highlighting that the default value of both `minOccurs` and `maxOccurs` is 1. Therefore, not specifying them dictates the existence of a required, single instance of the construct at hand.

Empty Elements

Empty element types can be specified by declaring a complex type with only attribute declarations as children.

Element and Attribute Reuse: Named Groups

One particularly useful technique of parameter entities in DTDs is the ability to reuse groups of element declarations such as the following:

```
<!ENTITY % reusableGroup   "heineken|quilmes|budweiser">
<!ELEMENT products (soap|fruit|(%reusableGroup;))>
```

In XML Schema, the same effect can be achieved by using named groups and references to them. A named group is merely a name assigned to a particular set of declarations involving `choice`, `sequence`, or `all`.[6]

```
<xsd:group name="products">
  <xsd:choice>
    <xsd:element name="soap" type="SoapType" />
    <xsd:element name="fruit" type="FruitType" />
      <xsd:choice>
        <xsd:element name="heineken"  type="BeerType" />
        <xsd:element name="quilmes"   type="BeerType" />
        <xsd:element name="budweiser" type="BeerType" />
      </xsd:choice>
  </xsd:choice>
</xsd:group>
```

Named group semantics do not change from those in unnamed counterparts (simple `choice`, `sequence`, and `all` elements without a name). Their only advantage is that they can be reused in much the same way we reused `%reusableGroup;` in the DTD:

```
<xsd:complexType name="grocerieList-draft">
  <xsd:group ref="products"/>
</xsd:complexType>
```

---

[6] `all` specifies that its contents must appear together or not at all.

Annotations

The XML Schema specification provides two comment elements for the benefit of the reader and the maintainability of the system:

- **Documentation**—Content targeted at the reader for explanation.
- **AppInfo**—Content targeted at either the reader or a program. This content specifies data about applications or stylesheets that may be relevant to a particular schema.

These elements most often appear inside an `annotation` element, which can itself appear at almost any point in a schema. The following example illustrates their use:

```
<xsd:complexType name="grocerieList-draft">
 <xsd:annotation>
  <xsd:documentation>Reusing a list of beers</xsd:documentation>
 </xsd:annotation>
  <xsd:group ref="products"/>
</xsd:complexType>
```

Summary

In this chapter we explored the basics of the XML Schema language. We have also outlined its general usage (create types, create elements, and attributes) and some comparisons with DTDs. However key concepts remaining include:

- Derivations by extension
- Derivations by restriction
- Uniqueness
- More on modularization and reuse

These concepts are better understood in a comparative setting, in which parallels to object orientation can be discussed, and comparisons with DTDs can be drawn. We'll do this in the next chapter.

CHAPTER 14

Advanced Data Modeling and XML Schemas

Introduction

XML Schema is a long and intricate specification, full of details and concepts that can be either a powerful tool or an unnecessary burden, depending on the type of application you need to develop. This chapter deals with such concepts by completing the catalog of constructs and syntax introduced in Chapter 13. It also discusses a customizable and extensible process to create document types and methods of applying the process order to create both XML schemas and DTDs.

The chapter is divided into two sections. The first addresses the remaining advanced concepts of XML Schema (derivation, uniqueness, modularization, and reuse); the second section summarizes the differences between DTDs and schemas.

Advanced XML Schema Concepts

This section presents the four advanced concepts not discussed in the original explanation of XML Schema in Chapter 13:

- Derivations and other advanced relationships
- Uniqueness
- Modularization
- Reuse

These concepts become especially relevant in light of a very data-oriented view of document construction, and in comparison to DTDs.

Derivations and Other Advanced Type Relationships

XML Schema is built around concepts such as *type* and *group*, as they are traditionally understood in a mathematical sense, especially within Object Orientation (OO) theory.

One of the most visible concepts borrowed from the object-oriented approach to systems modeling is that of subtyping (called type *derivation* in XML Schema). If you are familiar with an OO programming language, such as Java, chances are you are already familiar with derivation;[1] however, let's review the concept before continuing with its implementation in XML Schema.

Belonging and Other Relationships

Types may be related to others by different kinds of associations. The most common of these is the belonging ("*has a*") relationship, which we used several times in the previous chapter, and is illustrated in the following example. Consider the relationship depicted in Figure 14.1[2] between the types `Person` and `Ticket`, as they would be used in a movie theater application.

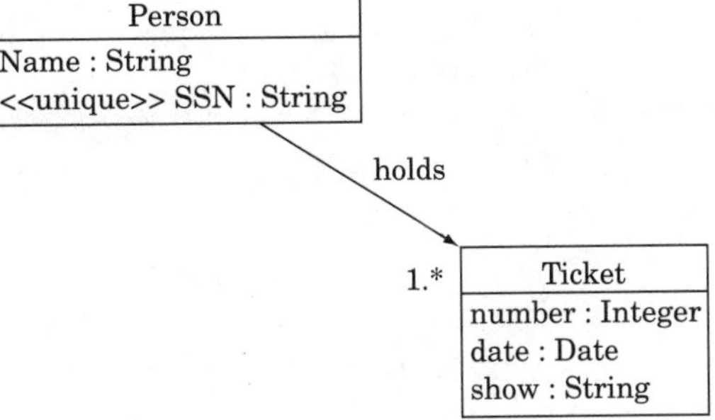

Figure 14.1 Person–ticket relationship.

This UML diagram illustrates a typical situation in which there is a belonging relationship between two types: a person in the system can have one or more tickets.

Traditionally, this kind of relationship has been implemented by nesting instances of the controlled/possessed type within instances of the dominant type. In order to dictate this relationship in the schema, one may write the following set of declarations:

```
<xsd:schema xmlns:xsd="http://www.w3.org/2000/10/XMLSchema">


<!-- ................ Main documentation ................ -->
<xsd:annotation>
 <xsd:documentation>
  Implementation of the Person and Ticket types for the
```

[1] From this point on, and for the sake of uniformity, we will refer to this concept as "derivation" even when talking about programming languages such as Java or design languages such as UML (where it is more commonly referred to as *subclassing*).

[2] Even though this particular diagram is fairly intuitive, it is recommended that you check Appendix D if you are not familiar with the UML notation.

```
  Movie theather example.
 </xsd:documentation>
</xsd:annotation>

<!-- ................   Ticket Type     ................ -->
<xsd:complexType name="TicketType">
 <xsd:element name="number" type="xsd:postitiveInteger"/>
 <xsd:element name="date"   type="xsd:date"/>
 <xsd:element name="show"   type="xsd:string"/>
</xsd:complexType>

<!-- ................   Person Type     ................ -->
<xsd:complexType name="PersonType">
 <xsd:element name="name"   type="xsd:string"/>
 <xsd:element name="ssn">
   <xsd:simpleType>
    <xsd:restriction base="xsd:string">
     <xsd:pattern value="\d{3}-\d{3}-\d{4}"/>
    </xsd:restriction>
   </xsd:simpleType>
 </xsd:element>

 <xsd:annotation>
  <xsd:documentation>
    Note how the relationship between the PersonType and the
    TicketType is stablished by stating that an instance of a
    PersonType may have a number of subelements of type
    TicketType
  </xsd:documentation>
 </xsd:annotation>

 <xsd:element name="ticket"
              type="TicketType"
              minOccurs="0"
              maxOccurs="*"/>

</xsd:complexType>

<!-- ................  Person List Type ................ -->
<xsd:complexType name="PersonListType">
 <xsd:element name="person"
              type="PersonType"
              minOccurs="0"
              maxOccurs="*"/>
</xsd:complexType>

<!-- ...............  (Root) Element Declaration ........ -->
<xsd:element name="ticketholders" type="PersonListType"/>

</xsd:schema>
```

An instance of the previous document type will look like the following:

```
<ticketHolders>
 <!-- Holden Caulfield's reservations for the NY film festival -->
 <person>
  <name>Holden Caulfield</name>
  <ssn>217-345-8989</ssn>
  <ticket>
    <number>16</number>
    <date>23/09/2000</date>
    <show>Fight Club</show>
  </ticket>
  <ticket>
    <number>22</number>
    <date>02/10/2000</date>
    <show>Annie Hall</show>
  </ticket>
  <ticket>
    <number>23</number>
    <date>03/10/2000</date>
    <show>L'Enfer</show>
  </ticket>
 </person>
</ticketHolders>
```

As you can see, the "has a" relationship between types can easily be expressed by stating the hierarchy among elements. This can easily be stated with DTDs and—except for cases with very precise cardinality requirements—rarely justifies the use of schemas. Take, for example, the following *equivalent* DTD for the movie ticket problem:

```
<!-- Auxiliary parameter entities -->
<!ENTITY  % string       "(#PCDATA)">
<!ENTITY  % positiveInt  "(#PCDATA)">
<!ENTITY  % date         "(#PCDATA)">

<!ELEMENT ticketHolders (person*)>
<!ELEMENT person        (name,ssn,ticket+)>
<!ELEMENT name          %positiveInt;>
<!ELEMENT ssn           %date;>


<!ELEMENT ticket        (number,date,show)>
<!ELEMENT number        %positiveInt;>
<!ELEMENT date          %date;>
<!ELEMENT show          %string;>
```

Not all relationships within types are as easily expressible in DTDs as this one. Some of them, especially those more object-oriented in nature, really justify the use of schemas in certain applications. Such is the case of the *derivation* relationship.

Derivation Relationship

Types A and B may be related by a derivation relationship if B *is an* A, but has some characteristics of its own that make it a specialized kind of A. One simple example is the classification of animals, shown in Figure 14.2, in which all the derived types are still animals, but the type is further refined to get more specialized definitions and characteristics applicable only to a certain group.

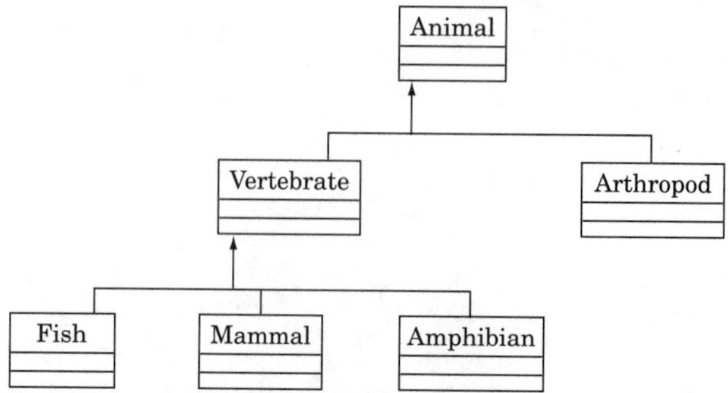

Figure 14.2
Animal hierarchy.

Capturing derivation relationships in DTDs is not always easy or natural. Suppose, for example, that you want to implement the persistence for a role-playing game that exhibits the type hierarchy of Figure 14.3.

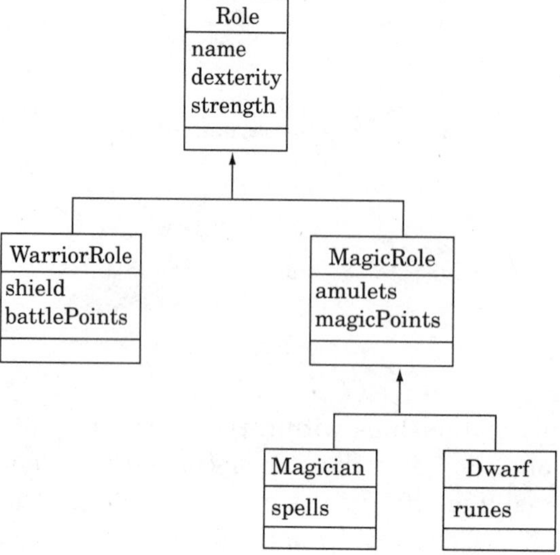

Figure 14.3
A role-playing game hierarchy.

The UML diagram of Figure 14.3 shows a very simple hierarchy in which all the roles come from a basic type, which defines the common attributes[3] present in every role. The types are further refined in other categories until we reach the leaf types, which include all the attributes of their parents, as well as some of their own (e.g. Dwarf contains name, dexterity, strength, magicPoints, amulets, and runes).

The goals of a type definition that implements this hierarchy are the following:

- Make explicit the fact that there is a relationship of derivation between types.
- Make explicit which types are related to which others (i.e. make the hierarchy itself explicit).
- Localize common data in a syntactic structure that is easy to understand and maintain.
- Provide a mechanism by which new types can be added to the hierarchy with a minimum of effort.
- The desirable ability to change a type's base (i.e. the type it is derived from).

With these goals in mind, let's analyze the following DTD solution:

```
<!-- Role Playing Game Persistance DTD -->

<!--
     Defines a DTD for the description of characters according
     to a hierarchy of roles.
-->

<!ENTITY % roleTraits  "name,
                        dexterity,
                        strength">

<!ENTITY % warriorTraits  "shield,
                           battlePoints">

<!ENTITY % magicTraits    "amulets,
                           magicPoints">

<!ELEMENT role  (%roleTraits;)>

<!ELEMENT warriorRole  (%roleTraits;,
```

[3] The term attribute is used here in the classical data-type sense, i.e. a characteristic or member of the type. Whether or not it is implemented as an XML attribute is something that will be decided later.

```
                              %warriorTraits;)>

<!ELEMENT magicRole     (%roleTraits;,
                         %magicTraits;)>

<!ELEMENT magician      (%roleTraits;,
                         %magicTraits;,
                         spells)>

<!ELEMENT dwarf         (%roleTraits;,
                         %magicTraits;,
                         runes)>

<!ENTITY  % string       "#PCDATA">
<!ENTITY  % positiveInt  "#PCDATA">
<!ENTITY  % date         "#PCDATA">

<!ELEMENT name           (%string;)>
<!ELEMENT dexterity      (%positiveInt;)>
<!ELEMENT strength       (%positiveInt;)>
<!ELEMENT shield         (%positiveInt;)>
<!ELEMENT battlePoints   (%positiveInt;)>
<!ELEMENT magicPoints    (%positiveInt;)>
<!ELEMENT amulet         (%string;)>
<!ELEMENT spells         (%positiveInt;)>
<!ELEMENT runes          (%positiveInt;)>

<!ENTITY % roleType      "(warriorRole|
                           magicRole|
                           magician|
                           dwarf)*">
<!ELEMENT personae       (%roleType;)>
```

Even though the previous DTD is elegant and useful (after all, it does solve the problem to a certain extent, as the following instance shows), it is not the most natural solution for a hierarchy problem, because it fails to represent a built-in language the relationship between the types. It must resort to parameter entities to simulate the structure, and most important, it is not very readable or extensible (in order to add a subtype of `dwarf`, at least four declarations should be touched).

```
<!DOCTYPE personae SYSTEM "roles.dtd">
<personae>
  <dwarf>
    <name>neiklot kuf</name>
    <dexterity>30</dexterity>
    <strength>12</strength>
    <amulets>mik</amulets>
    <magicpoints>10</magicpoints>
    <runes>2</runes>
  </dwarf>
```

```
  <warriorrole>
    <name>Noncerati</name>
    <dexterity>40</dexterity>
    <strength>25</strength>
    <shield>3</shield>
    <battlepoints>10</battlepoints>
  </warriorrole>
</personae>
```

It is out of limitations such as this that the XML Schema specification comes into use. The following two subsections will explain the mechanisms by which XML Schema (naturally) solves the extensibility problem.

XML SCHEMA DERIVATION BY EXTENSION

Derivation by extension is straightforward in XML Schema: create a new complex type, take an existing type as the base, and add the element and attribute declarations that refine the base type.

The following XML schema illustrates the use of derivation by extension in order to create the role hierarchy:

```
<xsd:schema xmlns:xsd="http://www.w3.org/2000/10/XMLSchema">

<!-- ................ Main documentation ................ -->
<xsd:annotation>
 <xsd:documentation>
  XML Schema Implementation of the role hierarchy
 </xsd:documentation>
</xsd:annotation>

<!-- ................    Base Role type     ................. -->
<xsd:complexType name="RoleType">
 <xsd:element name="name"        type="xsd:string"/>
 <xsd:element name="dexterity"   type="xsd:positiveInteger"/>
 <xsd:element name="strength"   type="xsd:positiveInteger"/>
</xsd:complexType>

<!-- ................    Warrior Type     ................. -->
<xsd:complexType name="WarriorType">
  <complexContent>
   <extension base="RoleType">
    <sequence>
     <element name="shield"          type="xsd:positiveInteger"/>
     <element name="battlePoints"    type="xsd:positiveInteger"/>
    </sequence>
   </extension>
  </complexContent>
</xsd:complexType>

<!-- ................    Magic Type     ................. -->
```

```
<xsd:complexType name="MagicType">
  <complexContent>
   <extension base="RoleType">
    <sequence>
     <element name="amulets"          type="xsd:string"/>
     <element name="magicPoints"      type="xsd:positiveInteger"/>
    </sequence>
   </extension>
  </complexContent>
</xsd:complexType>


<!-- ...............    Dwarf Type      ................. -->
<xsd:complexType name="DwarfType">
  <complexContent>
   <extension base="MagicType">
    <sequence>
     <element name="runes"           type="xsd:positiveInteger"/>
    </sequence>
   </extension>
  </complexContent>
</xsd:complexType>

<!-- other declarations here -->
</xsd:schema>
```

As this example shows, XML Schema is much better suited to the representation of derivation relationships and can be an instrumental tool when associations of this sort must be carved into type definitions.

XML SCHEMA DERIVATION BY RESTRICTION

In addition to derivation by extension, XML Schema provides a mechanism to derive new types from existing ones by means of *restricting* their original content models. This is called *derivation by restriction*.

In order to see how derivation by restriction works, imagine there is a new definition of the `dwarf` role, depicted in Figure 14.4, in which the runes are explicitly stated as elements (illustrating our previous discussion on "has a" relationships).

Now, let's model in XML Schema the new `dwarf` element:

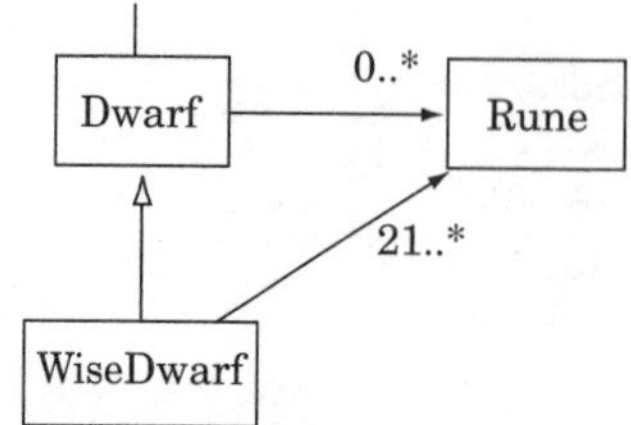

Figure 14.4 A new dwarf definition.

```
<xsd:complexType name="DwarfType">
  <xsd:complexContent>
   <xsd:extension base="MagicType">
    <xsd:sequence>
     <xsd:element name="rune" type="xsd:string"
                          minOccurs="0"
                          maxOccurs="*"/>
    </xsd:sequence>
   </xsd:extension>
  </xsd:complexContent>
</xsd:complexType>
```

By virtue of derivation by restriction, the trait imposed by `WiseDwarf` (namely the possession of at least 21 runes) can be modeled as follows:

```
<xsd:complexType name="WiseDwarfType">
 <xsd:complexContent>
   <xsd:restriction base="DwarfType">
    <xsd:element name="rune"  type="xsd:string"
                              minOccurs="21"
                              maxOccurs="*"/>
   </xsd:restriction>
  </xsd:complexContent>
</xsd:complexType>
```

Derivation by restriction can sometimes be obscure and confusing, especially because one may not be sure what is a valid restriction and what is not. Details and more examples of valid and invalid restrictions can be found in the specification itself, but you will be alright as long as your restrictions maintain what is known as the *substitutability principle*. This states that B is a valid derivation of A if, and only if, B can be used wherever A can be used.

For example, our `WiseDwarf/Dwarf` relationship holds the principle because a `dwarf` with 21 or more runes can be used wherever a `dwarf` with 0 or more runes can be used. On the other hand, the following schema shows an invalid restriction, because an element with more than one `wife` cannot be accepted where a monogamous one is expected:

```
 <xsd:schema xmlns:xsd="http://www.w3.org/2000/10/XMLSchema">

<!-- ........... Monogamous type ................ -->
<xsd:complexType name="Monogamous">
   <element name="wife"   type="xsd:string"
                          minOccurs="0"
                          maxOccurs="1"/>
</xsd:complexType>

<xsd:complexType name="InvalidRestriction">
```

```
 <xsd:complexContent>
   <xsd:restriction base="Monogamous">
    <xsd:element name="rune"  type="xsd:string"
                              minOccurs="0"
                              maxOccurs="2"/>
   </xsd:restriction>
  </xsd:complexContent>
</xsd:complexType>

</xsd:schema>
```

Uniqueness

We have already extensively explored the mechanism by which XML 1.0 DTDs define uniqueness: ID attributes. Useful as it may be, the DTD definition of uniqueness needs to be reviewed in light of advanced applications that require a more powerful definition, one that includes uniqueness of combinations and a more precise idea of scope.

The solution in XML Schema comes in the form of the `unique` element, which defines a two-part approach to the problem: first, there is a `selector` subelement whose value is an XPath expression, defining the scope of the uniqueness; then there are any number of `field` subelements, defining which elements or attributes must be uniquely combined.

The following example shows the application of this technique to the definition of a unique combination of date, show, and number for a movie ticket such as the one presented at the beginning of the chapter:

```
<!-- ...............     Ticket Type      ................ -->
<xsd:complexType name="TicketType">
 <xsd:element   name="number" type="xsd:postitiveInteger"/>
 <xsd:attribute name="date"   type="xsd:date"/>
 <xsd:element   name="show"   type="xsd:string"/>

 <xsd:unique name="ticketNumber">
   <selector>.</selector>
   <field>@date</field>
   <field>show</field>
   <field>number</field>
 </xsd:unique>

</xsd:complexType>
```

The existence of this mechanism—applicable to attributes and elements—doesn't rule out the possibility and widespread use of ID attributes. In fact, it is recommended that you use ID whenever possible because it allows a less painful port to DTDs (if needed).

Modularization and Reuse

In Chapter 2 we saw the use of internal parsed entities as a mechanism of modularization of DTD declarations. In this chapter we will introduce the mechanisms provided by the XML Schema standard for the reuse and modularization of its type definitions.

The first thing to note is that a schema document is an XML instance, and therefore there is nothing against the use of internal parsed entities as mechanisms of reuse. However, there are other mechanisms, the elements `include` and `import`.

Include

`Include` specifies the location of a schema that will be incorporated as part of the declarations in the calling document. The important detail about `include` is that the included declarations must have the same namespace as those in the calling document, otherwise they will be ignored.

The following example shows a classical invocation of `include`, as it would appear in the top level of an XML Schema:

```
<include
 schemaLocation="http://www.goethe.com/schemas/green.xsd"/>
```

Import

`Import` is analogous to `include` except for the fact that it allows the inclusion of declarations in namespaces other than that of the calling schema. For each `import` element both `namespace` and `schemaLocation` attributes can be provided, as shown in the following top-level element:

```
<import namespace="http://www.example.com/IPO"
        schemaLocation="http://www.zero.com/schema/math.xsd"/>
```

Now that we have finished our exploration of the major features and techniques of XML Schema, is time to draw a complete comparison between it and DTDs.

Comparison Between XML Schema and DTD (Rick Jelliffe)

The following table is the most complete summary of differences between XML Schema and DTD of which I know. It was originally developed by Rich Jelliffe[4] and is reproduced here (from the original location with his permission).

XML Markup Declarations	XML Schema	Comments
DOCTYPE Declaration	No equivalent header declaration.	An XML schema cannot specify which is the top-level element in any schema. The attribute schemaLocation can be used on elements in instances to nominate the location of a retrievable schema for that element associated with that namespace.
Internal and External Subset	No equivalent header declaration. There is no mechanism for overriding a declaration. (A SchemeSet element has been mooted to gather separate schema elements together.)	A schema for a single namespace can be composed from several distributed schema documents. Furthermore, instance may require reference to multiple schemas as it uses elements from different namespaces. A schema can be composed of several entities; the <import> and <include> mechanisms are also available.
ELEMENT Declaration	An <element> declaration creates a binding between a (namespaced) name and attributes, content models, and annotations.	The big difference between XML DTDs and XML Schemas is the tag/type distinction.
#PCDATA Declared Content Type	Supported as particle of simple	
ANY Declared Content Type	Supported as <any>	<any> has different wildcards, to support a richer range of possibilities. Note that <anyAttribute> is also available to allow wildcards on the possible attributes.
EMPTY Declared Content Type	Supported	Note that XML Schemas support an explicit null, as distinct from empty strings. In XML and SGML an implied attribute with no default can be taken as having a null value (actually, the value is to be implied by the application or processor) but this was not available for elements.

continued on next page

[4] Many thanks to Rick for this valuable contribution.

XML Markup Declarations	XML Schema	Comments
Content Model	Supported as <complexType>.	XML Schema keeps the XML Markup Declarations requirement for unambiguous content models. Note that XML Schemas maintain XML's model of mixed content, either allowing character data anywhere inside an element or nowhere.
, (Sequence Connector)	Supported; sequence compositor	
| (Alternative Connector)	Supported; disjunction compositor	
? (Optional)	Supported, through maxoccurs and minoccurs attributes	
+ (Required and Repeatable)	Supported, through maxoccurs and minoccurs attributes	
* (Optional and Repeatable)	Supported, through maxoccurs and minoccurs attributes	
( ) (Groups)	Supported	
ATTLIST Declaration	<attribute> declarations can be grouped into <attributeGroup> declarations.	
Multiple ATTLIST declarations	Not supported	(Do equivalence classes do something similar?)
CDATA Attribute Type	Supported as a built-in simple type "string"	Lexical constraints can be specified using regular expressions.
ID Attribute Type	Supported as a built-in simple type. The Key mechanism represents a major enhancement.	Lexical constraints on these names can be specified using regular expressions.
IDREF IDREFS Attribute Types	Supported as a built-in simple type. The Key mechanism represents a major enhancement.	Lexical constraints on these names can be specified using regular expressions.
NOTATION Attribute Type	Supported as a built-in simple type.	Lexical constraints on these names can be specified using regular expressions.
NMTOKEN NMTOKENS Attribute Types	Supported as a built-in simple type.	Lexical constraints on these names can be specified using regular expressions.

continued on next page

XML Markup Declarations	XML Schema	Comments
ENTITY ENTITIES Attribute Types	Supported as a built-in simple type	These are a kind of link, with declarations distinct from reference. Lexical constraints on these names can be specified using regular expressions.
Enumerations	Supported	
Attribute Defaults		
#FIXED Attributes		
#REQUIRED and #IMPLIED	Supported through the minOccurs attribute	
ENTITY Declaration	Not supported	Entities are declared in XML markup declarations.
ENTITY % Parameter Entity Declaration	Not supported	Parameter entities provide a low-level mechanism useful for many different purposes. XML schemas have tried to support first-class support for some of the most important: ■ the separation of <element> and <complexType> ■ attribute groups ■ named model groups ■ the type extension and restriction mechanisms ■ the <import> and <include> mechanism for composing schemas ■ the element equivalence class mechanism allows redefinition of element names Note that general entities can also be used to provide some of the other rarer uses of parameter entities. XML schemas 1.0 do not attempt to systematically reconstruct every possible use of parameter entities.
IGNORE/INCLUDE Marked Sections	Not supported	
NOTATION Declaration	Supported as a built-in simple type.	

continued on next page

XML Markup Declarations	XML Schema	Comments
Comment	The <documentation> subelement of the <annotation> element provides this functionality. (Comments can still be used.)	<documentation> elements are available to users of the schema. Comments are not part of the core information set of the document and may not be available or in a useful form.
PI	The <appinfo> subelement of the <annotation> element provides this functionality. (PIs can still be used.)	<appinfo> elements are available to users of the schema. PIs require knowledge of their notation to parse correctly. Extensions to the XML Schema can be made using <appinfo>, however an extension will not change the schema-validity of the document.

Summary

This chapter ends our exploration of XML Schema (and XML Schema vs. DTDs). XML Schema is a complex and controversial specification that may bring enormous power to complex applications that really need the constructs provided by it. It can also bring unnecessary complexity and overhead to a large number of applications which can be served just as well with DTDs. Also, XML Schema is a complex and extremely long specification (more than 200 printed pages). The material that has been covered in Chapters 13 and 14 is an overview designed to give you as much key information as possible, but it is recommended that you read at least part of the spec if you are planning to do serious development with it.

Chapters 13 and 14 have explored the syntax and uses of XML Schema constructs as well as a comparison with their DTD counterparts, where appropriate. Chapters in Part 4 (complete case studies) will treat the problem of choosing between DTDs and schemas with engineering criteria.

PART 4

Key XML Applications

CHAPTER 15

Wireless XML: WAP, VoiceXML, and Beyond

Introduction

As the power of phones, PDAs, and other wireless devices grows, the advent of an entire generation of wireless Web is finally materializing outside the labs and professional circles and into the mainstream.

This new environment imposes a new set of problems for the development and deployment of applications because it is based on devices far more limited than personal computers. In order to cope with such limitations, several efforts, especially the *Wireless Application Protocol* (WAP), have tried to construct a complete framework for the transmission of data over wireless networks and into small devices.

WAP is an ample specification, but it is not the whole picture in the wireless space. The first reason for this is that standards similar to WAP have a tremendous following outside the United States (e.g. Imode in Japan). The second reason is that wireless is not necessarily restricted to visual data (text and graphics). Technologies based on voice recognition/generation and infrared communications used within the context of cellular telephony are also considered part of the wireless space.

In order to provide a complete set of tools for the creation of real-world wireless applications, we'll tackle a broad spectrum of relevant technologies, architectures, and design criteria that are essential to this new space. These technologies include:

- WAP
- WML (XML application for wireless content in WAP)
- WMLScript
- VoiceXML

WAP

The Wireless Application Protocol is the result of years of development by the WAP Forum, a consortium formed by the most significant players in the wireless market (including Nokia and Ericsson).

WAP was developed to deliver Internet content in the wireless space while meeting the restrictions and shortcomings of a new kind of device (e.g. phones, PDAs, etc.) that differ from desktop computers in many fundamental ways because they have:

- More restricted memory
- More restricted computational power
- More restricted input devices
- More restricted output devices

Furthermore, these devices are connected using wireless networks that are not as reliable as traditional Internet connections. (We have all experienced the sudden loss of reception when getting in an elevator or going through a tunnel, for example.) Additional characteristics of today's wireless networks are:

- Less bandwidth
- Less connection stability
- Less predictability

The WAP specification attempts to create a complete framework for the creation of applications working over such limited devices and networks.

WAP Rationale

In the name of interoperability, scalability, efficiency, and security, the WAP Forum stated the following goals for the WAP effort:

- Leverage existing standards where possible.
- Define a layered, scaleable and extensible architecture.
- Support as many wireless networks as possible.
- Optimize for narrow-band bearers with potentially high latency.
- Optimize for efficient use of device resources (low memory/CPU usage/power consumption).
- Provide support for secure applications and communication.
- Enable the creation of Man Machine Interfaces (MMIs) with maximum flexibility and vendor control.
- Provide access to local handset functionality, such as logical indication for incoming calls.
- Facilitate network-operator and third-party service provisioning.
- Support multivendor interoperability by defining the optional and mandatory components of the specifications.
- Provide a programming model for telephony services and integration.

The WAP Model

Before going any further, let's look at the general model behind WAP applications. Figure 15.1 shows a diagram of what goes on behind the scenes of a client request in WAP (e.g. the request for a particular page).

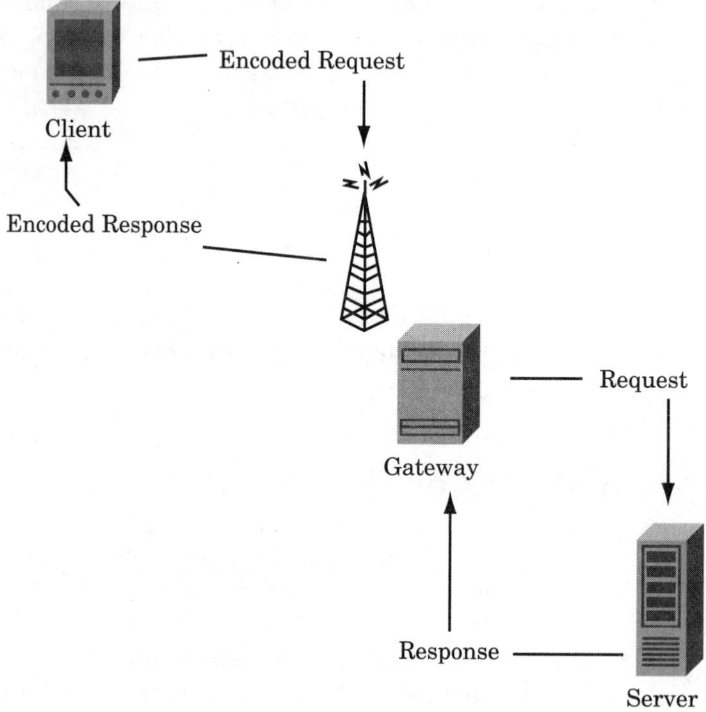

Figure 15.1 WAP model.

There are several important features about this model. Most of them become evident when we compare it with the traditional Web model, shown in Figure 15.2.

The most important features include:

- **The existence of a gateway**—In the WAP case, the client doesn't talk directly to the server; instead, it goes through the gateway, which forwards the request to the final destination server.
- **Encoding and compression of the data**—In the WAP case, the data are not passed directly to the client; instead, the gateway encodes the original server response and sends it to the client in a compressed format better suited to the restrictions mentioned in previous sections.

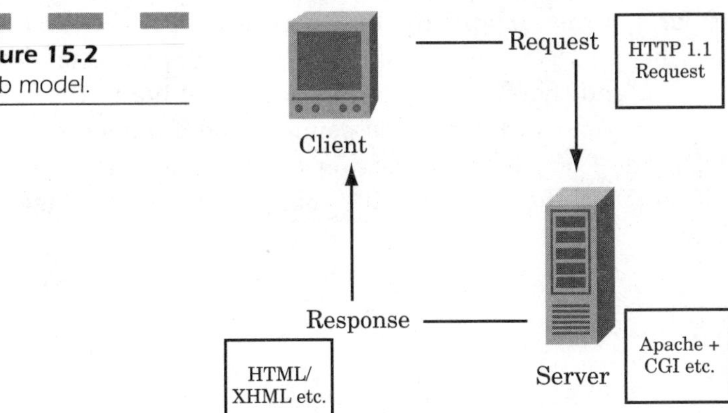

Figure 15.2 Web model.

- **Type of content**—The content provided by the server is not of the same type used for Web applications (i.e. it is not HTML); instead, the server replies with content marked up in WML, the *Wireless Markup Language*.

WAP Architecture

The WAP Forum decided that all levels of networking protocol for wireless applications should be recreated in light of the limitations of wireless connections. The result is the creation of a comprehensive protocol analogous to a good portion of traditional TCP/IP (it is a clean stack model that goes from a transport layer to an application layer). Figure 15.3 shows the complete architecture; the remainder of this section explains each layer.

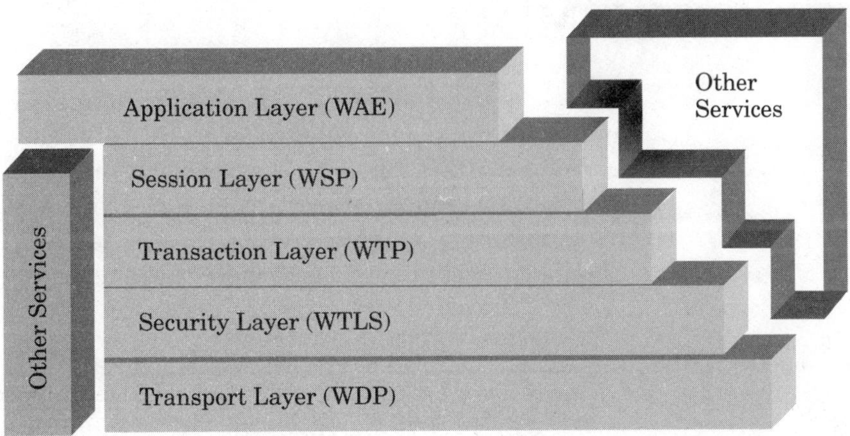

Figure 15.3 The WAP architecture.

The lower parts of the architecture are concerned with low-level network details, which are irrelevant to our discussion of application development with XML and therefore will not be addressed here. (If you are interested in them, you can refer to the pointers and documents on the companion CD.) The focus of our discussion will be application development and relevant XML use, which is the subject of the highest level of the stack: WAE.[1]

WAE

The highest level of the WAP stack is the *Wireless Application Environment* (WAE). It defines the languages and data types necessary for the creation of wireless applications over WAP.

WAE is essentially composed of two technologies:

- **WML**—The Wireless Markup Language, an XML application for the presentation of data on wireless devices.
- **WMLScript**—A scripting language based on ECMAScript (similar to JavaScript and other scripting languages used in browsers today).

An extra component of the WAE is the specification of particular data types for images, multipart messages, calendars, and electronic business cards (vCards). These are considered addenda to the core of the WAE and will be studied here only within the context of their applicability to WML and WMLScript.

WML

WML is, first of all, an XML application; therefore it shares the syntax and well-formedness rules of every XML vocabulary. The process of learning WML is the process of learning the structure and elements of the language and its semantics. However, before diving into the underlying paradigm of WML and its constructs, let's explore the simplest example in order to get a feeling for the language:

---

[1] Note also that the components of the WAE can be used over other services that are not necessarily WAP-enabled.

```
<?xml version="1.0"?>
<!DOCTYPE wml PUBLIC "-//PHONE.COM//DTD WML 1.1//EN"
               "http://www.phone.com/dtd/wml11.dtd" >
<!--  Basic "Hello World" example  -->

<wml>
    <card  title="Hello">
     <p>
         Hello World!
         <select>
          <option  onpick="samples.wml">XMLdevGuide
Samples</option>
          <option  onpick="wmlref.wml">WML Reference</option>
          <option  onpick="wmlscript.wml">WMLScript
Reference</option>
         </select>
     </p>
    </card>
</wml>
```

As you can see, the WML vocabulary is far from complex. The previous XML document defines a simple WML application, which displays the string "Hello World" and then a series of options for further navigation. When seen with a phone (or, in our case, with a phone emulator) the previous file will be interpreted as shown[2] in Figure 15.4.

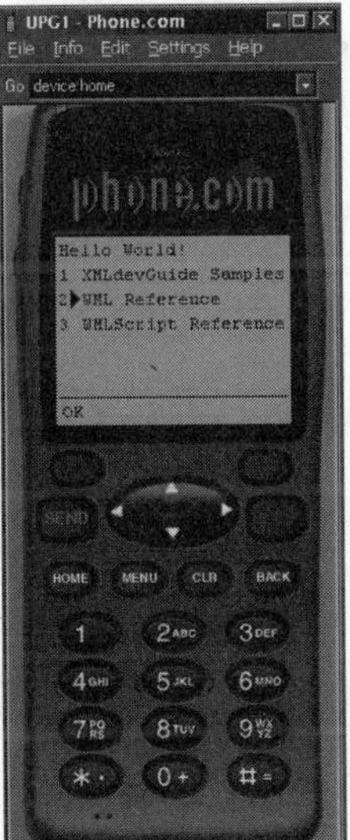

Figure 15.4 First WML application.

[2] All the phone figures in this chapter are taken from the Phone.com emulator included in UPSDK 4.0. Only Figure 15.4, however, contains a shot of the whole emulator window; the rest show only the phone screen.

Setting up a WML Development Environment

In order to get a working WML development environment, you must take the following steps:

- **Install a WAP Phone emulator**—In this book we will use the very popular Phone.com phone emulator, part of the Phone.com UPSDK. Please see the CD for instructions on how to get the installer.
- **Install a Web Server**—Throughout this book, the Apache Web server is used. Please refer to the CD for the Windows 9x/Linux installer. Even though the concepts and examples shown here are applicable to any other Web server, it is recommended that you use Apache.
- **Set up the WML MIME types**—As previously mentioned, one key difference between the interaction of a wireless client and its server versus that of a traditional client is the type of content served.

  Just to review, the response of a Web server always starts with a line describing the type of content being returned (e.g. `Content-type: text/html`, or `Content-type: image/gif`). The server figures out what to say in this first line based on the file extension of the file requested (e.g. `image/jpeg` if the file is `kustorika.jpg`).

  In order to specify which files correspond to which MIME types, the server provides a configuration file (`mime.types` in the case of Apache). In order to specify a relationship between the `text/vnd.wap.wml` and the files with `wml` extensions, simply add a line like the following to such files:

```
text/vnd.wap.wml        wml
```

  Likewise, for `wmlscript` files and `wbmps` (a graphic file format for WAP) you can add:

```
text/vnd.wap.wmlscript        wmls
image/vnd.wap.wbmp            wbmp
```

- **Put your wml files under the htdocs directory on the server and point the emulator to the correct URL**—If you put your "hello.wml" file under `apache/htdocs/wml`, you must set the emulator home to `http://yourservernameOrIP/wml/hello.wml`.

Alternatively, you can use the Nokia WAP development environment, which doesn't require a read from an HTTP server in order simulate the

WAP phone presentation. However, the server will be needed for the server-side dynamics examples.

WML Usage

As a markup language, WML seems to be constructed around three basic principles:

- Connections are expensive, time-consuming and unreliable. The more user screens (or data, in general) that can be sent in one transmission and stored in the phone for later retrieval, the better.
- The user interface in phones is extremely limited; event-based interfaces with very restricted keyboards (possibly even just an **OK** and a **CANCEL** button) are assumed.
- Screens are small and limited in character space. It is assumed that the best representation paradigm is a card, a small collection of paragraphs that gets presented automatically in a small screen.

The result of these principles is a markup language in which documents are composed as collections of cards that are sent to the client, so it can stack them up without having to make more requests to the server. The following *deck* (a standard name for a WML document) illustrates the point:

```
<?xml version="1.0"?>
<!DOCTYPE wml PUBLIC "-//PHONE.COM//DTD WML 1.1//EN"
             "http://www.phone.com/dtd/wml11.dtd" >


<!--  Basic "Hello World" example  -->

<wml>
    <card  id="first">
     <p>
       This is the first part of the message.
       If WML didn't use the card paradigm,
           the client would have to make a second request
           to get the <a href="#second">next part.</a>
     </p>
    </card>

    <card id="second">
    <p>
           The next part is also <b>a card</b>.
           As you can see, the paragraphs inside
```

```
            the cards are almost identical to those
            of HTML. <a href="#third">Next Card</a>
    </p>
    </card>

    <card id="third">
    <p>
            Just go back to the <a href="#first">beginning</a>
    </p>
    </card>
</wml>
```

Figure 15.5 shows how this deck appears in the client. Now that we have a basic idea of how WML decks are structured, let's see what else can be included in WML decks.

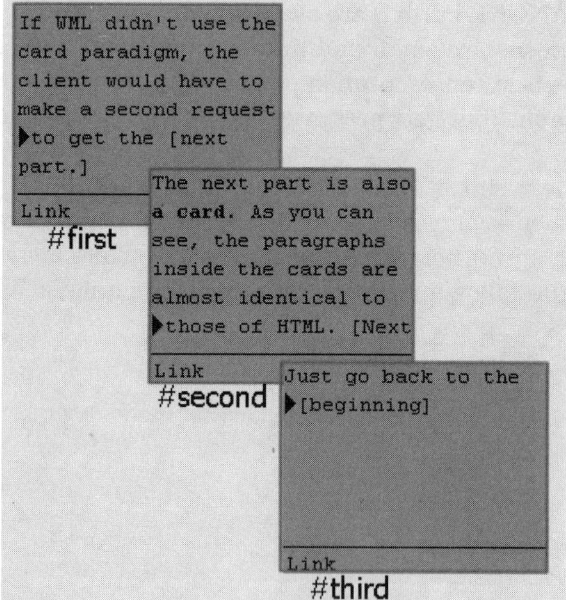

Figure 15.5 Multicard deck.

WML Complete

In this section we will go through every aspect of WML, first explaining its representation and semantics, then providing an example, and finally presenting a small snapshot of how it would look on a client device. All the code shown here is included on the companion CD. For the complete DTD, please also refer to Appendix C.

Format Tags within Paragraphs

Just like HTML, WML provides several format tags for the text inside a paragraph. The tags for this purpose are: `em`, `strong`, `b`, `I`, `u`, `big`, and `small`. The following is an example of their use:

```
<?xml version="1.0"?>
<!DOCTYPE wml PUBLIC "-//PHONE.COM//DTD WML 1.1//EN"
              "http://www.phone.com/dtd/wml11.dtd" >

<wml>
    <card  title="Hello World Example">
     <p>
     This is an example of normal text, plus
        <em>emphasized</em>, <strong>strong</strong>,
        <i>italic</i>, <b>bold</b>,<big>big</big> and
        <small>small</small>.
     </p>
    </card>
</wml>
```

As Figure 15.6 illustrates, there is a difference between the *official* semantics of tags and how they are actually presented in a particular device (see how text within `em`, `bold`, and `big` tags looks exactly the same). Since this is a pervasive issue with WML development, it is extremely important that you test your code on several platforms before release.[3]

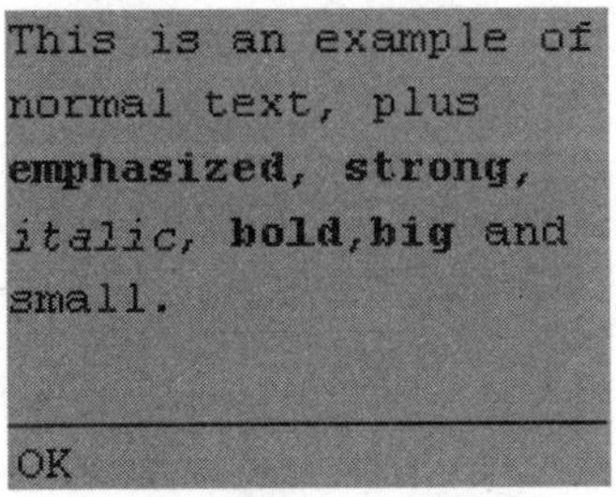

This is an example of
normal text, plus
emphasized, strong,
italic, **bold,big** and
small.

OK

Figure 15.6
WML text.

Tables

WML provides a basic mechanism for western tables, based on the same idea as HTML: table cell data (`td`) elements within table rows (`tr`). Each table cell may contain text, images, or links. Figure 15.7 shows a sample table.

[3] The Phone.com UPSDK includes several different phone profiles that can make this task easier.

Advanced table composition with attributes such as HTML's `rowspan` is not available; however, some other formatting capabilities are provided (e.g. alignment). The following deck shows an example of the possibilities available with WML tables:

```
<?xml version="1.0"?>
<!DOCTYPE wml PUBLIC "-//PHONE.COM//DTD WML 1.1//EN"
              "http://www.phone.com/dtd/wml11.dtd" >

<wml>
  <card>
    <p>
      <table align="L" columns="3">
     <tr>
       <td><b>Month</b></td>
       <td><b>In</b></td>
       <td><b>Out</b></td>
       <!-- note there is no such thing as HTML's th -->
     </tr>
     <tr>
       <td><i>Jan</i></td>
       <td>3</td>
       <td>2</td>
     </tr>
     <tr>
       <td><i>Feb</i></td>
       <td>6</td>
       <td>2</td>
     </tr>
     <tr>
       <td><i>Mar</i></td>
       <td>9</td>
       <td>2</td>
     </tr>
        <!-- rest of the months... -->
      </table>
    </p>
  </card>
</wml>
```

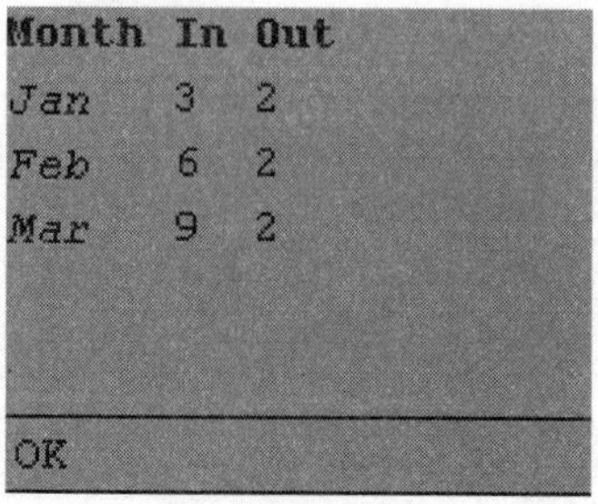

Month	**In**	**Out**
Jan	3	2
Feb	6	2
Mar	9	2

OK

Figure 15.7
WML tables.

Basic Linking

Basic linking is done via the a element. The semantics and structure of this element are analogous to that of HTML. The following example shows how to make links between cards and decks:

```
<?xml version="1.0"?>
<!DOCTYPE wml PUBLIC "-//PHONE.COM//DTD WML 1.1//EN"
             "http://www.phone.com/dtd/wml11.dtd" >

<wml>
    <card  id="ac">
     <p>
          The <b>a</b> element can be used to
          create links within <a href="#ot">cards </a>
     </p>
    </card>
    <card  id="ot">
     <p>
          The <b>a</b> element can be used to
          create links within <a href="another.wml">decks </a>
     </p>
    </card>
</wml>
```

Tasks

In WML, a task is a particular action, normally associated with a phone button or some other widget such as a soft key. A task in WML is composed of two parts:

- A do element specifies the type of task that is going to be performed (the client uses this information to decide how to present the task), and UI settings such as the label used to identify the task.
- A task element (either go, prev, noop, or refresh) defines the task itself. This element is a child of do.

The following first example of WML tasks shows a license agreement with two tasks: accept the license or go back. In most phones, these tasks would be associated with the OK and Cancel keys, displaying the corresponding labels over each of them as shown in Figure 15.8.

```
<?xml version="1.0"?>
<!DOCTYPE wml PUBLIC "-//PHONE.COM//DTD WML 1.1//EN"
             "http://www.phone.com/dtd/wml11.dtd" >
```

```
<!--  Voting example  -->

<wml>
    <card  id="ac">
      <do type="accept" label="Yes">
     <go href="#accepted"/>
      </do>
      <do type="unknown" label="Back">
        <prev/>
      </do>
      <p>
       The present license agreement... blah, blah
      </p>
    </card>

    <card id="accepted">
      <p>
       Thanks for accepting.
      </p>
    <do type="unknown" label="Go to Product">
      <go href="product.wml">
      </go>
    </do>
    </card>
</wml>
```

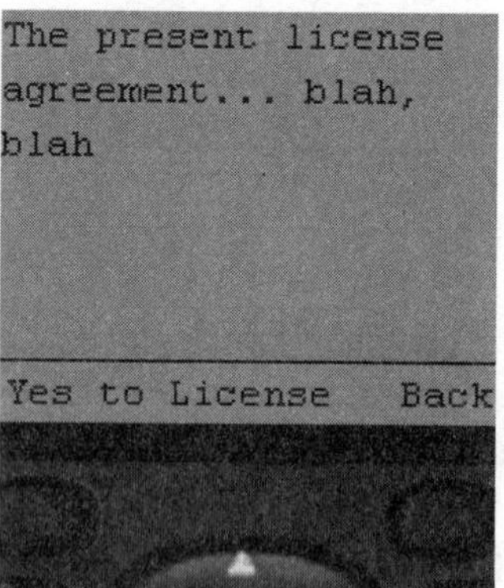

Figure 15.8 License agreement in phone content.

To complement the above code, Tables 15.1 and 15.2 show the possible values of the type attribute for do elements, and a description of each valid child, respectively:

TABLE 15.1

Predefined Do types from the WML specification.

Type	Description
accept	Positive acknowledgment (acceptance)
prev	Backward history navigation
help	Request for help
reset	Clearing or resetting state
Options	Request for options or additional operations
Delete	Delete item or choice
unknown	**A generic** `do` **element**
X-*, x-* vnd.*, VND.* and any combination of `[Vv][Nn][Dd].*`	Experimental and vendor-specific types

TABLE 15.2

Task elements ('Do' children).

Element	Description
Go	Direct to a particular URI
prev	Go Back to the previous item in the navigation history
Noop	No Operation. Do nothing
Refresh	Refresh the state of the client (analogous to traditional reload)

Using Templates

In order to specify common task elements among all the cards in a deck, the WML specification defines the `template` element, which appears as a top-level item in the deck.

The tasks defined inside a template are included in every card of the deck (unless they are overridden by a card definition). The following example shows how to add a common help button to all the cards in a deck using `template`.

```
<?xml version="1.0"?>
<!DOCTYPE wml PUBLIC "-//PHONE.COM//DTD WML 1.1//EN"
              "http://www.phone.com/dtd/wml11.dtd" >
<!--  Modified (template) Voting example  -->
```

```
<wml>
  <template>
    <do type="unknown" label="Help!">
    <!--
         if we would have used type="help", it wouldn't
         have been visible in many current phones.
      -->
      <go href="help.wml"/>
    </do>
  </template>

  <card  id="ac">
    <do type="accept" label="Yes">
     <go href="#accepted"/>
    </do>
    <p>
     The present license agreement... blah, blah
    </p>
  </card>

  <card id="accepted">
      <p>
       Thanks for accepting.
      </p>
    <do type="unknown" label="Go to Product">
      <go href="product.wml">
      </go>
    </do>
  </card>
</wml>
```

It is important to note again the gap between intended WML semantics and practical development (see Figure 15.9). For example, in this case it was preferable to use `type="unknown"` rather than `type="help"`, because the former forces the label to be visible in almost every WAP phone (whereas many models hide help-type do elements).

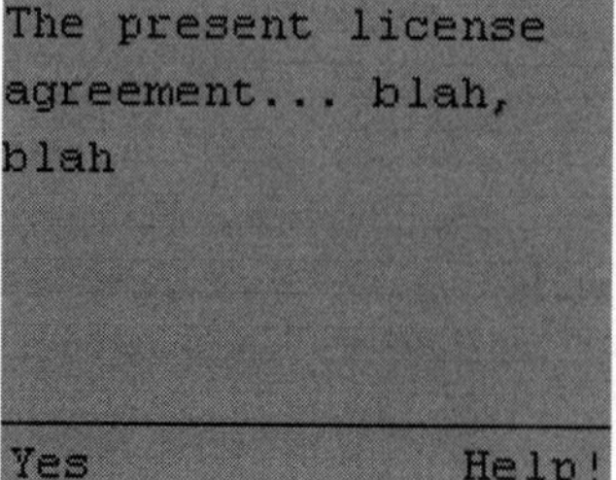

Figure 15.9 WML templates at work.

Setting Variables

Even though the true power of variables will only be used when we introduce WMLScript, we'll review the basic concepts of WML variables here.

A variable name in WML always starts with the `$` sign, followed by any combination of letters, underscores, and digits. In order to set a variable, one can use the `setvar` element, as shown in the following example (more useful applications of variables will be shown once we get to input elements and WMLScript processing):

```
<?xml version="1.0"?>
<!DOCTYPE wml PUBLIC "-//PHONE.COM//DTD WML 1.1//EN"
              "http://www.phone.com/dtd/wml11.dtd" >

<wml>
  <card id="ac">
    <p><b>Question 1</b>: What is celebrated in November 1st?</p>
    <do type="accept" label="Hallowmas">
     <go href="#answer"/>
     <setvar name="q1" value="Hallowmas"/>
    </do>
    <do type="accept" label="Halloween">
     <go href="#answer">
     <setvar name="q1" value="Hallowmas"/>
       </go>
    </do>
  </card>

  <card id="answer">
      <p>
        You answered "<b>$q1</b>".
        <!--
             See the section on WMLScript to see
             how to say whether it was wrong or not
         -->
      </p>
  </card>
</wml>
```

In order to escape the dollar sign, simply put together another one as follows:

```
<!--
    Assume there is a variable called $value with the
   price of a product
-->
<p> The value is $$$value </p>
```

Select Lists

WML provides a mechanism for selection lists akin to the `select` element in HTML. The following example illustrates the syntax:

```
<?xml version="1.0"?>
<!DOCTYPE wml PUBLIC "-//PHONE.COM//DTD WML 1.1//EN"
              "http://www.phone.com/dtd/wml11.dtd" >

<wml>
  <card id="age">
    <p>What is your age range?
     <select name="stage">
     <option value="kid">4-10</option>
     <option value="teen">11-19</option>
     <option value="young">20-40</option>
     <option value="mature">41-70</option>
     <option value="senior">71-</option>
      </select>
   </p>
    <do type="accept" label="Next">
      <go href="#kids">
      </go>
    </do>
  </card>
  <card id="kids">
    <p><i>You are a $stage person.</i>
       How many kids do you have?
       <select name="kids" value="0">
         <!-- This illustrates default values -->
     <option value="0">0</option>
     <option value="1">1</option>
     <option value="2">2</option>
     <option value="a lot of">3</option>
     <option value="too many">more</option>
      </select>
    </p>
    <do type="accept" label="Next">
      <go href="#result">
      </go>
    </do>
    <do type="prev">
      <prev/>
    </do>
  </card>
  <card id="result">
    <p>
       You are a <i>$stage</i> person.
       You have <i>$kids</i> kids.
   </p>
    <do type="prev">
      <prev/>
    </do>
  </card>
</wml>
```

Figure 15.10 shows the previous examples as seen in the Nokia 7110. The select and option elements have a number of other attributes;

some are illustrated in the comprehensive example, and a complete list is given with the DTD in Appendix C. However, when developing WML code, please remember that most of the "advanced" features of WML select lists (such as the "onpick" attribute in the option element) are not implemented by a number of phones.

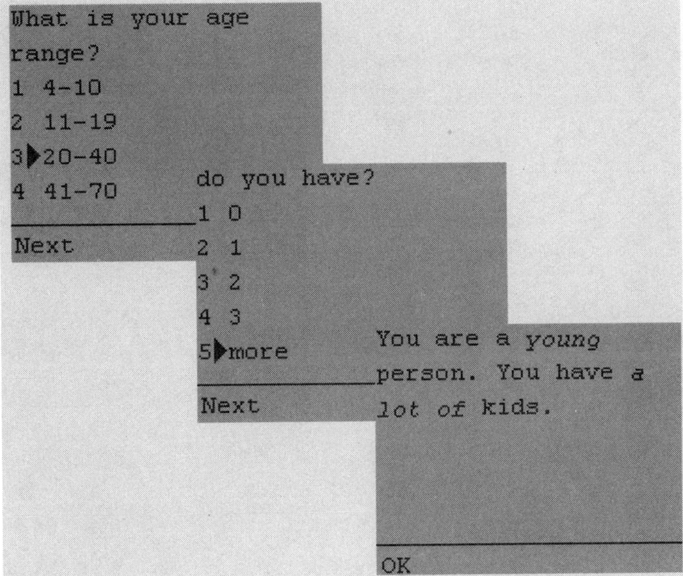

Figure 15.10
Select lists.

Input Elements

The `input` element is the text entry mechanism for WML applications. It is akin to its counterpart in HTML, but includes some attributes not found in the HTML version. The most important of these is the `format` attribute, which defines what kind of text is acceptable for the input. (A complete list of the possible values of `format` is given in Table 15.2.) The rest of the attributes are fairly intuitive and are clearly represented in the following example:

```
<?xml version="1.0"?>
<!DOCTYPE wml PUBLIC "-//PHONE.COM//DTD WML 1.1//EN"
              "http://www.phone.com/dtd/wml11.dtd" >

<wml>
  <card>
    <!-- The simplest form of input -->
    <p>What is your name?
       <input name="name"/>
```

```
    </p>
    <do type="accept" label="continue">
      <go href="#phone">
      </go>
    </do>
  </card>
  <card id="phone">
    <!-- An input with restricted format -->
    <p>Hi $name. <br/> What is your phone number?
       <input name="phone" format="NNN-NNN-NNNN"/>
       <!-- it is highly recommended that you test
            this in the emulator. It behaves quite nicely with
            formats.
         -->
    </p>
    <do type="accept" label="continue">
      <go href="#login">
      </go>
    </do>
  </card>
  <card id="login">
    <!-- Another example of format, plus optionality -->
    <p>What login would you like to have? <b>Up to 8
       characters</b>
       <input name="login"
              format="8m"
              emptyok="false"/>
    </p>
    <do type="accept" label="continue">
      <go href="#password">
      </go>
    </do>
  </card>
  <card id="password">
    <!-- format and hidden password -->
    <p>What login would you like to have? <b>Up to 8
       characters</b>
       <input name="password"
              type="password"
              format="8m"
          emptyok="false"/>
    </p>
    <do type="accept" label="continue">
      <go href="#results">
      </go>
    </do>
  </card>
  <card id="results">
    <p>Login: $login</p>
    <p>Password: [hidden]</p>
    <p>Name: $name</p>
    <p>Phone #: $phone</p>
  </card>
</wml>
```

Timer

Sometimes it is useful to specify actions that must be performed after a certain period of time. The most recurrent example is the `update` or `jump` from one card to another when the user has been inactive for a certain amount of time.

The `timer` element specifies an amount in tenths of a second. When the timer expires, an event is risen; if there is an `onevent` element ready to catch it—or if the card speficied an `ontimer` attribute—a task is performed. The following examples illustrate this point:

```
<?xml version="1.0"?>
<!DOCTYPE wml PUBLIC "-//PHONE.COM//DTD WML 1.1//EN"
              "http://www.phone.com/dtd/wml11.dtd" >

<wml>
  <card ontimer="/otherDeck.wml">
    <timer value="50"/>
    <p>This deck has moved. You will be redirected in 5 seconds.
    </p>
  </card>
</wml>
```

Timers can be tied to `onevent` elements, as follows:

```
<?xml version="1.0"?>
<!DOCTYPE wml PUBLIC "-//PHONE.COM//DTD WML 1.1//EN"
              "http://www.phone.com/dtd/wml11.dtd" >

<wml>
  <card>
    <onevent type="ontimer">
      <refresh>
        <!-- this will simply accumulate dots in the $i variable
-->
          <setvar name="i" value=".$i"/>
      </refresh>
    </onevent>
    <timer value="20"/>
    <p>$i</p>
    <p>The dots above show how many times this card has been
refreshed.
    </p>
    <p>It will continue to be refreshed every 2 seconds.</p>
  </card>
</wml>
```

Images—WBMP

From the WML point of view, all there is to say about images is that they might be presented using the `img` element. This provides all the attributes you would expect from a HTML-like tag of its nature, including height, width, align, and `alt` (for text representation in devices that don't support images). The following example shows a typical instance of this element:

```
<?xml version="1.0"?>
<!DOCTYPE wml PUBLIC "-//PHONE.COM//DTD WML 1.1//EN"
             "http://www.phone.com/dtd/wml11.dtd" >

<wml>
  <card>
    <p>A <em>WBMP</em> image:
      <img alt="cat" src="cat.wbmp"/>
    </p>
  </card>
</wml>
```

Close inspection of the above code reveals a somewhat odd extension for the image file loaded: `wbmp`. The reason for it is that WAP applications use their own file format for simple black and white bitmaps. This format is called WBMP (as shown in Figure 15.11) and both editors (such as the one included with the Nokia toolkit) and converters (such as the one developed by T.Hahn & A.Hierle of Infotiger) are readily available.

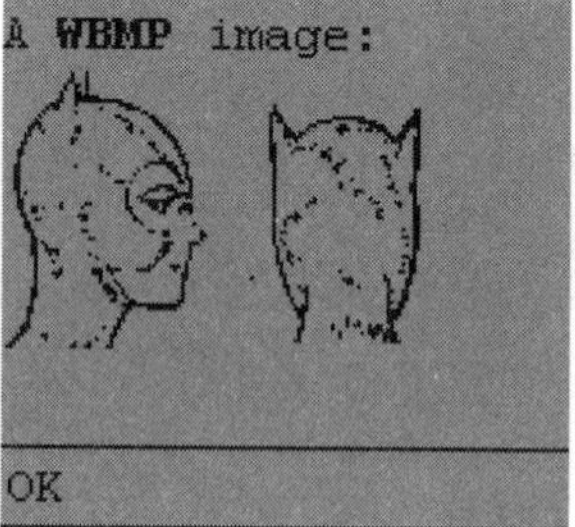

Figure 15.11
WBMP image.

Creating Server-side WML Applications

Now that we know the structure of the WML language, constructing WML applications that rely on server-side processing for their dynamics is as simple as putting together decks and CGI programs.

Architecture

From the developer's perspective, the general architecture of a server-oriented WAP application is as simple as that of traditional CGI applications for the Web, with the difference that we will be returning WML instead of HTML. Figure 15.12 shows the basic pattern, while the following section implements it in a small WML website.

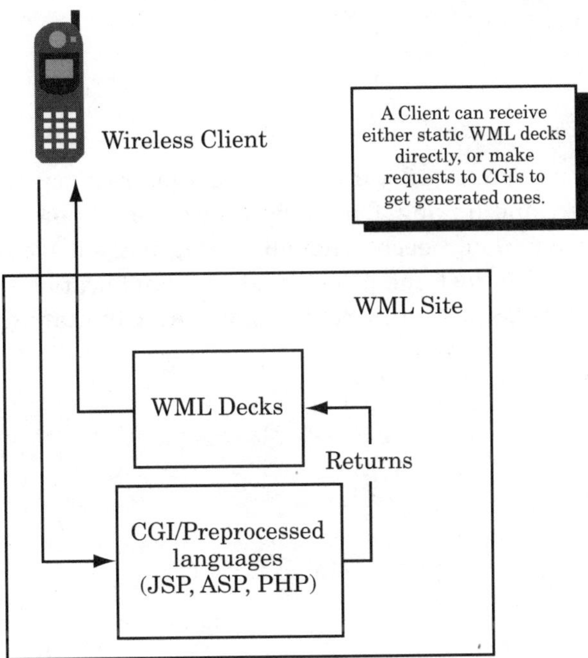

Figure 15.12 Architectural overview of server-oriented WML applications.

Example

The following decks summarize the applicability of the WML constructs shown in this chapter in a simple site. The site is composed of a splash screen, a news section, a download section, and a CGI that takes care of sending a file by email upon request.[4]

Splash Screen

The splash screen showcases the use of images and timers:

[4] An extended, multidevice variation of this application (serving WML, XHTML, and Voice) can be found in Chapter 19.

```
<?xml version="1.0"?>
<!DOCTYPE wml PUBLIC "-//PHONE.COM//DTD WML 1.1//EN"
              "http://www.phone.com/dtd/wml11.dtd" >

<wml>
  <card ontimer="news.wml">
    <timer value="50"/>
     <p>Welcome to the FAActory
      <img alt="logo" src="images/logo.wbmp"/>
    </p>
  </card>
</wml>
```

News

The news and software list pages illustrate basic formatting of decks, tables, and linking. One important detail is how the news is divided in more than one deck. Though conceptually it would be better to have them all in just one place, most WAP applications contain divided data like this because of current phone's space limitations.

```
<?xml version="1.0"?>
<!DOCTYPE wml PUBLIC "-//PHONE.COM//DTD WML 1.1//EN"
              "http://www.phone.com/dtd/wml11.dtd" >
<!-- Most recent news -->
<wml>
  <card>
    <p><b>Recent Updates</b>
     <table columns="2">
     <tr>
       <td><img alt="c++" src="images/arrow.wbmp"/></td>
       <td><a href="software.wml#xpath">XPath Tester 2.0
Released</a></td>
     </tr>
     <tr>
       <td><img alt="article" src="images/article.wbmp"/></td>
       <td><a href="www.xml.com">New Article on Groves</a></td>
     </tr>
     <tr>
       <td><img alt="article" src="images/article.wbmp"/></td>
       <td><a href="www.mcgrawhill.com">Info on XMLdev
Guide</a></td>
     </tr>
     <tr>
       <td><img alt="article" src="images/arrow.wbmp"/></td>
       <td><a href="software.wml#sax">SAX XLink Filters</a></td>
     </tr>
      </table>
    </p>
    <do type="unknown" label="More News">
```

```
      <go href="news2.wml">
      </go>
    </do>
  </card>
</wml>
```

`news2.wml` continues the list of updates:

```
<?xml version="1.0"?>
<!DOCTYPE wml PUBLIC "-//PHONE.COM//DTD WML 1.1//EN"
              "http://www.phone.com/dtd/wml11.dtd" >
<!-- Most recent news -->
<wml>
  <card>
    <p><b>Recent Updates</b>
     <table columns="2">
     <tr>
       <td><img alt="c++" src="images/cpp.wbmp"/></td>
       <td><a href="software.wml#cpp">C++ Tools</a></td>
     </tr>
     <tr>
       <td><img alt="article" src="images/article.wbmp"/></td>
       <td><a href="www.xml.com">SOAP</a></td>
     </tr>
     <tr>
       <td><img alt="article" src="images/arrow.wbmp"/></td>
       <td><a href="software.wml#sax">SAX Writer</a></td>
     </tr>
     <tr>
       <td><img alt="article" src="images/cpp.wbmp"/></td>
       <td><a href="software.wml#parsers">Parsers</a></td>
     </tr>
      </table>
    </p>
    <do type="unknown" label="More News">
      <go href="news.wml">
      </go>
    </do>
  </card>
</wml>
```

Figure 15.13 shows the first decks of our application.

Software Pages

The software pages show the available packages and provide the ability to call a CGI in the server in order to send the particular package to a given address. The CGI itself is irrelevant to this chapter, although some details about the way its invocation is constructed are interesting. Let's first examine the whole deck and then discuss the details.

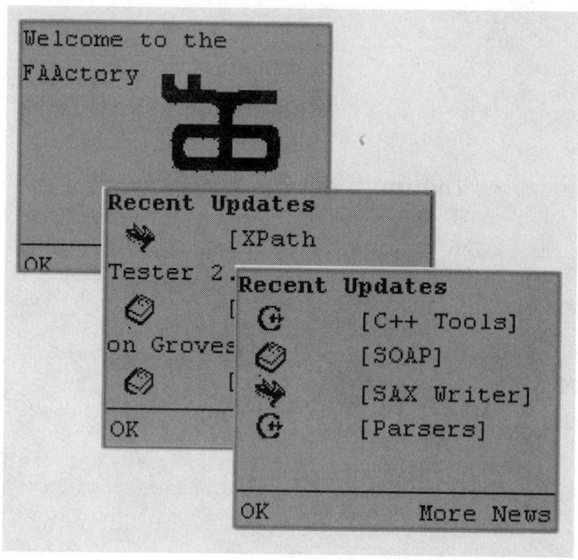

Figure 15.13
A WML site.

```
<?xml version="1.0"?>
<!DOCTYPE wml PUBLIC "-//PHONE.COM//DTD WML 1.1//EN"
              "http://www.phone.com/dtd/wml11.dtd" >
<!-- Most recent news -->
<wml>
  <card>
    <p><b>Software</b><br/>
     The following packages can be sent to you for free via
email.
     <select name="package"> <!-- no default value -->
     <option value="SAXWriter.zip">SAX Writer</option>
     <option value="Parsers.zip">Parsers</option>
     <option value="xpath.zip">XPath Tester</option>
     <option value="SAXFilters.zip">SAX XLink Filters</option>
      </select>
     <do type="accept">
     <go href="#send">
     </go>
      </do>
    </p>
  </card>
  <card id="send">
    <p>To receive the $package package, type your email
       address below:
       <input name="email"/>
    </p>
    <do type="accept">
      <go href="/cgi-
bin/sendPackage.cgi?to=$email&amp;package=$package">
      </go>
    </do>
```

```
  </card>
</wml>
```

What is interesting about the final go element is the way it uses variable names and standard XML entities to construct a valid URL to invoke the CGI. Since & is always resolved to the character &, if the user entered the address speer@i18.com and chose the Parsers option, then the URL constructed will be:

```
/cgi-bin/sendPackage.cgi?to=speer@i18.com&package=Parsers.zip
```

Since before calling the URL, the device must do URL escaping of the string, the final, invoked URL is:

```
/cgi-bin/sendPackage.cgi?to=speer%40i18.com&package=Parsers.zip
```

This example concludes our exploration of WML and its applicability in server-oriented applications. The following pages will explore client-side dynamics, by explaining the second fundamental part of the WAE, the WMLScript language.

WMLScript

So far we have seen WML applications that rely on server-side scripting for their dynamic behavior, but WAP also provides a language for the implementation of client-side logic: WMLScript. This is a procedural scripting language based on ECMAScript, and therefore very similar to JavaScript, VBScript, and other Web scripting languages.

WMLScript Structure

If you are already familiar with C, Perl, C++, Java, or any other similar language, you will find WMLScript extremely easy to learn. There are only a few key language features to keep in mind, and these are covered in the following sections.

General Usage and Structure

Unlike JavaScript in HTML, WMLScript programs are not embedded in WML decks. All invocations to WMLScript functions are done via linking elements as shown in the following example:

```
<?xml version="1.0"?>
<!DOCTYPE wml PUBLIC "-//PHONE.COM//DTD WML 1.1//EN"
              "http://www.phone.com/dtd/wml11.dtd" >
<wml>
  <card id="tickets" title="Tickets">
    <p>
        What is your age?
         <input name="age"/>
     How many tickets do you want to buy?:
         <input name="tix"/>
    </p>
    <do type="accept" label="Results">
      <go href="tickets.wmls#validate($tix,$age)"/>
    </do>
  </card>
  <card id="results" title="Result">
     <p>Your purchase was $status<br/>
     </p>
  </card>
</wml>
```

Conversely, the communication of results to the WML application can be performed via special variables in the WMLScript (namely the WMLBrowser object), as shown in the following code, or via function return values:

```
 extern function validate(numTickets,age)
{
     // If the person is older than 60 he can only get 1 ticket
     // If the person is younger than 30 he can get as many as 4
tickets
     // All other persons can have a maximum of 3 tickets
     if ((numTickets > 4) ||
            (numTickets > 3 && age > 29) ||
         (numTickets > 1 && age > 60) ||
            (numTickets < 1))
     {
          WMLBrowser.setVar("status", "Denied.");
     }
     else
          WMLBrowser.setVar("status", "Accepted. Enjoy the show");

     WMLBrowser.go("index.wml#results");
};
```

Variables and Data Types

WMLScript is a weakly typed language. This means there is no contract binding a particular variable to a type such as `int` or `float`. Depending on how you use them, variables will act as repositories of types as diverse as `string` or `URL`.

In order to use a variable, you first must declare it. In order to declare a variable, use the keyword `var` and a valid name (a combination of letters and numbers starting with a letter or underscore):

```
var a;          // Simple declaration
var b = 34;     // Declaration and initialization in one statement
```

Standard rules for variable scope and visibility (i.e. the rules almost all procedural languages since C have adopted) are applied, so things like variable redeclaration or access outside the declaring block are illegal.

Operators

All basic operators available in JavaScript (or Java) are available in WMLScript, retaining their semantics and precedence. These operators include binary arithmetic operators such as `+`, `-`, `*`, `/`, `%`, unary operators such as `++` and `--`, and logical operators such as `&&` and `||`.

Functions

Functions are the basic modularization unit in WMLScript. It may suffice to say that all the common definitions and ideas of functions in traditional scripting languages apply, though some of them are worth mentioning in detail:

- Functions cannot be nested.
- Function names must be unique.
- All parameters are passed by value.
- There are no optional arguments (i.e. the number of arguments passed must be exactly the number of arguments specified in the declaration).
- Functions always return a value. The default is the empty string.
- Functions can be either private or *extern*. Only if a function is declared as *extern*, may it be called from outside the script (say from a WML deck).

The general format for functions is the following:

```
extern function name( parameters )
{
```

```
  // body
  return x;
}; // note the ending ;
```

Examples

Now that we have reviewed the syntax of yet another procedural language, there are only two things left to cover: examples and the available libraries. This section deals with examples and the following section will summarize the contents of the WMLScript specification.

The following example shows another classical application of WMLScript: simple arithmetic.[5] It showcases a geometric calculator that can determine the area of a series of shapes:

```
// Calculate the area of a geometric figure
// @param figure defines the type of figure to calculate
// @param a defines the first parameter for the calculation
// @param b defines the second parameter for the calculation
//          (always provided, but ignored for spheres, squares
and circles)

extern function area(figure,a,b) {
  if(figure == 1) { // Square
        var length = a;
        WMLBrowser.setVar("area",(length * length));
        WMLBrowser.go("index.wml#results");
  }
  else if(figure == 2) { // Triangle
        var twidth = a; //only for readability and maintainabilty
purposes
        var theight = b;
        WMLBrowser.setVar("area",(twidth * theight / 2));
        WMLBrowser.go("index.wml#results");
  }
  else if(figure == 3) { // Rectangle
        var rwidth = a;
        var rheight = b;
        WMLBrowser.setVar("area",(rwidth * rheight));
        WMLBrowser.go("index.wml#results");
  }
  else if(figure == 4) { // Circle
        var cradius =a;
        WMLBrowser.setVar("area",(3.1416 * (cradius * cradius)));
        WMLBrowser.go("index.wml#results");
  }
```

[5] Because of the limitations of today's wireless devices (especially phones) for anything numeric-oriented that exceeds the complexity of these simplest applications, it is better to rely on server-side processing.

```
  else if(figure == 5) { // Sphere
        var sradius = a;
        WMLBrowser.setVar("area",(4 * 3.1416 * (sradius *
sradius)));
     WMLBrowser.go("index.wml#results");
  }
}
```

The following example shows a deck that uses this calculator to determine the area of a triangle:

```
<?xml version="1.0"?>
<!DOCTYPE wml PUBLIC "-//PHONE.COM//DTD WML 1.1//EN"
              "http://www.phone.com/dtd/wml11.dtd" >
<wml>
  <card id="triangle" title="triangle">
    <p>
        Width?
          <input name="w"/>
     Height?
          <input name="h"/>
    </p>
    <do type="accept" label="Results">
      <go href="area.wmls#area(2,$w,$h)">
      </go>
    </do>
  </card>

  <card id="results" title="Result">
    <p>The area of your triangle is <b>$area</b>
     </p>
  </card>
</wml>
```

WMLScript Core Libraries

The WMLScript specification determines a set of standard libraries that should be implemented by every compliant browser. Tables (15.3 through 15.8) list the functions on each library.[6]

In order to use a function, simply state the name of the library, a point, and the name of the function. e.g. `Float.pow(-2,43);`.

[6] For a more complete description of each page, refer either to the spec itself, or to an online guide such as www.w3schools.com where these tables are complemented with a navigable description of the whole API.

TABLE 15.3
Float library.

Function	Return Value	Description
`ceil()`	integer	Returns the nearest integer that is not smaller than a specified number
`floor()`	integer	Returns the nearest integer that is not larger than a specified number
int()	integer	Returns the integer part of a specified number
`maxFloat()`	floating-point	Returns the largest possible floating-point number
`minFloat()`	floating-point	Returns the smallest possible floating-point number
`pow()`	floating-point	Raises a number to the power of a second number and returns the result
`round()`	integer	Returns the nearest integer to a specified number
`sqrt()`	floating-point	Returns the square root of a specified number

TABLE 15.4
Lang library.

Function	Return Value	Description
`abort()`	none	Aborts a WMLScript and returns a message to the caller of the script
`abs()`	number	Returns the absolute value of a number
`characterSet()`	integer	Returns the character set supported by the WMLScript interpreter
`exit()`	none	Ends a WMLScript and returns a value to the caller of the script
`float()`	boolean	Returns true if floating-point numbers are support-ed and false if not
`isFloat()`	boolean	Returns true if a specified value can be converted into a floating-point number by the `parseFloat()` function and false if not
`isInt()`	boolean	Returns true if a specified value can be converted into an integer by the `parseInt()` function and false if not
`max()`	number	Returns the largest value of two numbers
`maxInt()`	integer	Returns the maximum possible integer value
`min()`	number	Returns the smallest value of two numbers

continued on next page

TABLE 15.4
Lang library (continued).

Function	Return Value	Description
`minInt()`	integer	Returns the minimum possible integer value
`parseFloat()`	floating-point	Returns a floating-point value defined by a string
`parseInt()`	integer	Returns an integer defined by a string
`random()`	integer	Returns a random integer between 0 and a specified number
`seed()`	string	Initializes the random number generator with a number and returns an empty string

TABLE 15.5
String library.

Function	Return Value	Description
`charAt()`	string	Returns a character that is placed in a specified position of a string
`compare()`	integer	Compares two strings, and returns an integer that tells if the two strings are identical, smaller or larger than the other string
`elementAt()`	string	Separates a string into elements, and then returns a specified element
`elements()`	integer	Returns the number of times a specified value appaers in a string
`find()`	integer	Returns the position of the first character in a string that matches another string
`format()`	string	Formats a value and returns the result
`insertAt()`	string	Separates a string into elements, inserts a specified value, and then returns the result
`isEmpty()`	boolean	Returns a Boolean value that is true if the string is empty, and false if not
`length()`	integer	Returns the length of a string
`removeAt()`	string	Separates a string into elements, removes an element, and then returns the result
`replace()`	string	Replaces a part of a string with a new string and returns the result
`replaceAt()`	string	Separates a string into elements, replaces an element, and then returns the result

continued on next page

TABLE 15.5
String library (continued).

Function	Return Value	Description
`squeeze()`	string	Reduces all white spaces to single spaces and returns the result
`subString()`	string	Returns a string that is a specified part of another string
`toString()`	string	Creates a string of a value and returns the result
`trim()`	string	Returns a string without leading and trailing

TABLE 15.6
URL library.

Function	Return Value	Description
`escapeString()`	string	Replaces special characters in a URL with an escape sequence and returns the result
`getBase()`	string	Returns the URL base
`getFragment()`	string	Returns the fragment in a URL
`getHost()`	string	Returns the host specified in a URL
`getParameters()`	string	Returns the parameters in the last path segment of a URL
`getPath()`	string	Returns the path specified in a URL
`getPort()`	string	Returns the port number specified in a URL
`getQuery()`	string	Returns the query part in a URL
`getReferer()`	string	Returns the referer
`getScheme()`	string	Returns the scheme in a URL
`isValid()`	boolean	Returns true if a URL has the right syntax, and false if not
`loadString()`	string/integer	Returns the content and the content type of a specified URL
`resolve()`	string	Returns an absolute URL from a base URL and a relative URL
`unescapeString()`	string	Replaces the escape sequences in a URL with characters and return the result

TABLE 15.7
Dialogs library.

Function	Return Value	Description
`alert()`	string	Displays a message, waits for a confirmation, and then returns an empty string
`confirm()`	boolean	Displays a message, waits for an answer, and then returns a Boolean value depending on which answer the user selected
`prompt()`	string	Displays a message, waits for an input, and then returns the user input

TABLE 15.8
WML browser library.

Function	Return Value	Description
`getCurrentCard()`	string	Returns the smallest relative URL of the current card
`getVar()`	string	Returns the value of a variable in the browser context
`go()`	string	Loads the content from the a specified URL
`newContext()`	string	Clears all variables of the WML context, and returns an empty string
`prev()`	string	The WML browser goes back to the previous WML card and returns an empty string
`refresh()`	string	Refreshes the current context
`setvar()`	boolean	Sets the value of a variable in the browser context, and returns true if the new value where implemented successfully and false if not

VoiceXML

VoiceXML, Voice eXtensible Markup Language, is an XML vocabulary used to create voice-based applications such as those found in phone banking systems and automated delivery services. VoiceXML applications feature synthesized speech, digitized audio, voice recognition, and touch-tone input.

VoiceXML Fundamentals

A VoiceXML application reflects a decision tree with input elements that may cause the interpreter to catch a voice or touch-tone response and may give back a taped or generated audio.

The following example shows the simplest (Hello World) VoiceXML application:

```
<!DOCTYPE vxml PUBLIC "-//Tellme Networks//Voice Markup Language
1.0//EN" "http://resources.tellme.com/toolbox/vxml-tellme.dtd">

<vxml
application="http://resources.tellme.com/lib/universals.vxml">
<form>
<block>
<audio src="http://resources.tellme.com/audio/misc/hello.wav">
 hello world
</audio>
<pause>500</pause>

<audio>
 good bye
</audio>

<pause>500</pause>

<goto next="_home"/>
</block>
</form>
</vxml>
```

Where Should We Go from Here with VoiceXML?

A complete discussion of VoiceXML would be too lengthy to undertake here. Instead, look at the hands-on example in Chapter 19 in which a voice interface is given to a particular application. It is also recommended that you look at the CD for VoiceXML examples and references.

Summary

This chapter presented the use of XML in the wireless application industry, particularly the WAE layer of WAP (WML and WMLScript languages). Several examples illustrated both the language constructs and their practical use.

Applications in the last section of the book will further expand on the languages presented here (including the briefly treated VoiceXML).

CHAPTER 16

XML and Databases

Introduction

The production of high-volume Web sites and countless other applications depends on the ability to store, query, and retrieve large amounts of data. Flexible and meaningful as they can be, plain XML documents by themselves are unfit for the performance requirements of traditional databases such as Oracle or PostgreSQL.

This chapter explores the relationship between XML and databases from the point of view of the applications developer, with a special focus on the practical alternatives for the implementation of real-world solutions. It does not review basic database concepts, but assumes an understanding of XML and concepts discussed in Chapters 4 and 6, particularly SAX.

The chapter is divided into several parts: the first is an explanation of the factors behind XML-database relationships and how they are reflected in five different types of solutions. The remaining sections explain each solution in detail, while providing examples of their implementations. In addition, a directory of the most relevant libraries and products, classified according to the type of solution, is provided at the end of the chapter.

The XML–Database Relationship

XML is particularly useful when it comes to data interoperability and semantics. It provides a clean and portable way of expressing data and metadata in a hierarchical document. Databases, on the other hand, are particularly useful when it comes to the storage and efficient retrieval of large volumes of data.

When creating industrial-sized Web XML applications (see examples in Chapter 19), or any application that deals with large volumes of data, the idea of maintaining plain XML documents as the persistence mechanism becomes less and less feasible, and the union of the two technologies—XML and traditional databases—becomes necessary.

This union can take many different forms, depending on the type of document you have, the particular goals of your application, and the degree to which you couple the application and the transformation process (i.e., the transformation between XML documents and database tables/objects).

Types of Documents

In the context of data persistence, it is customary to make the distinction between *document-oriented* XML and *data-oriented* XML.

Data-oriented XML exhibits very rigid structures, usually containing the XML representations of collections of similar objects made of attributes. In this type of document it is common to find PCDATA sections only in the leaf elements, and rare to find mixed content.

The following document is an example of data-oriented XML (a collection of CDs). Other examples would include shipment orders and XML-based configuration files.

```
<?xml version="1.0"?>
<!DOCTYPE cd_collection SYSTEM "cd.dtd">
<cd_collection>
  <title xml:space="preserve">A sample cut of a CD
collection</title>
  <cd id="a9362-43515-2">
    <title xml:space="preserve">In our sleep</title>
    <artist>Laurie Anderson &amp; Lou Reed</artist>
    <producer>Brian Eno</producer>
    <year>1995</year>
    <track number="1">In our sleep</track>
    <track number="2">...</track>
  </cd>
  <cd id="a9233-436432-3">
    <title xml:space="preserve">Trans-Europe Express</title>
    <artist>Kraftwerk</artist>
    <producer>Kraftwerk</producer>
    <year>1978</year>
    <track number="1">Europe Endless</track>
  </cd>
  <!-- ... more cds here ...-->
</cd_collection>
```

On the other hand, there is document-centric XML, in which the data represented are more oriented toward readability, the structure is less rigid, and mixed content abounds. This is the case of most Web pages, letters, and other documents encoded in XML. The following article snippet (written using the Docbook DTD) is representative of this type:

```
<!DOCTYPE article PUBLIC "-//Davenport//DTD DocBook V3.0//EN" [

<!ENTITY email          "fabio@viaduct.com">
<!ENTITY bulletType     "circle">
<!ENTITY version        "$Id: main.xml,v 1.5 2000/08/18
13:51:12 faa Exp $">
```

```
<!ENTITY status          "draft 1">
<!ENTITY project         "Introduction to XLink">
<!ENTITY abstract        SYSTEM  "abstract.xml">
<!ENTITY what            SYSTEM  "what.xml">
<!ENTITY intro            SYSTEM  "intro.xml">
<!ENTITY why             SYSTEM  "why.xml">
<!ENTITY how             SYSTEM  "how.xml">
<!ENTITY references      SYSTEM  "glossary.xml">
]>

<article>
  <artheader>
      <title>XLink (ex)plain(ed)</title>
      <title>An Introduction To XLink</title>
      <author><surname>Arciniegas
A.</surname><firstname>Fabio</firstname>
   </author>
  <!-- &abstract; -->
  </artheader>
  &intro;
  &what;
  &why;
  &how;
  &references;
</article>
```

abstract.xml:

```
<part id="intro-part">
<docinfo>
   <title>Abstract</title>
</docinfo>
<title>Abstract</title>

<chapter id="Main-Introduction">   <title>Introduction to Heqet:
A generic XML
editor for Gnome</title>
<para>
   Few technologies in the <a href="familiy">XML family</a>
   have deserved as wide an audience and as big an expectation as
   <emphasis>Xlink</emphasis>….
</para>
<!--… more here -->
```

The difference between data-oriented and document-oriented XML is fundamental for our purposes because it brings a key question into focus: are we interested in making persistent the ***data*** inside the XML instance, or are we interested in the XML instance itself?

In the case of document-oriented XML, chances are we are interested in the XML instance itself: the way the document is structured, its comments, the usage of entities, etc., which are all relevant to the problem.

On the other hand, in the case of data-oriented XML, we care mainly (if not only) about the data inside the document. Whether the document was composed by putting together five external entities or just one big XML file, is irrelevant;[1] so are comments, indentation, and sometimes even the order of the elements. (In a letter, the order of two paragraphs is certainly important. In an invoice, the order of the items may not be as relevant.)

Most applications in need of a database rely heavily on the data-oriented view in which the key factor is the efficient treatment of a high volume of very precise data (the inventory of a warehouse, or a collection of geographical data, for example). This chapter, therefore, will pay special attention to the tools and techniques needed to communicate data-oriented XML data to and from databases.

Coupling Degree

We also encounter the problem of determining how much the application will know about the underlying database. This issue, which is really a question about the degree of coupling between the application layer and the database, may range from total awareness (very high coupling) to absolute isolation of the two layers (very low coupling).

Very high coupling occurs when *custom classes* know about the database, make the connection and a query, and manually create XML out of the result sets.

Very low coupling occurs when the application level knows nothing about a different underlying representation; it simply calls the API provided by the XML server and obtains an XML document.

An intermediate level of coupling occurs when one uses middleware to connect to a traditional database (commonly relational such as PostgreSQL or MS Access) in order to obtain XML representation of the tables and vice versa.

A similar intermediate level of coupling will happen if one uses a parser that receives tables as its entry and sends SAX events as its output. This parser (which is, after all, another type of middleware) sits between the application and the database, providing a façade for the relational/OO database.

---

[1] This is in contrast to the data-oriented example, in which the entities are a key point in the modularization and usability of the document.

If we put together the two fundamental factors mentioned, we will have a map such as the one depicted in Figure 16.1.

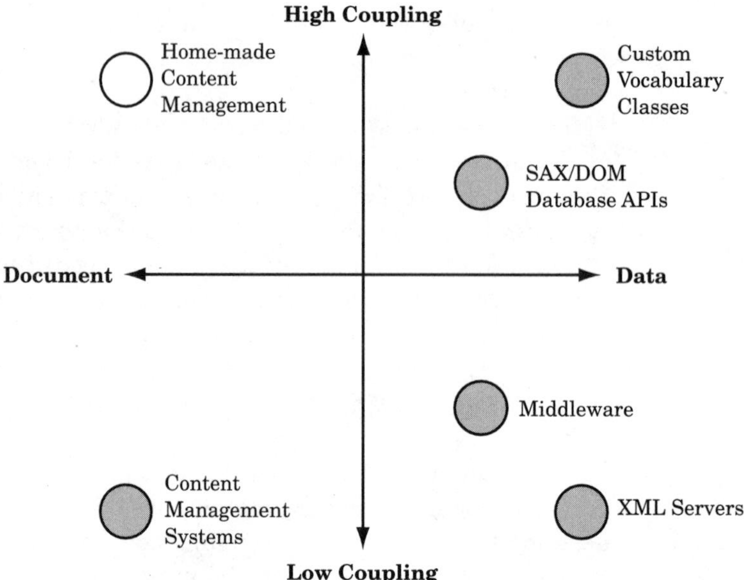

Figure 16.1 A map of the implementation alternatives for XML and databases.

Finding the right technology to use from this map depends on the third factor mentioned at the beginning of this chapter: the requirements of your application. The examples and theory of the next sections will put that fundamental element in perspective, will let you arrive at a decision about the type of technology for your project and its best use.

Custom Classes for Particular Vocabularies

The first, and simplest, way to create an XML document out of a database is to hardcode the logic for a specific vocabulary in a custom class. This custom class is highly coupled with both the database and the XML, and even though it presents advantages in performance (compared to the use of middleware, for example), it is definitely restricted and hardly extensible or maintainable.

However limited, such a quick in-house implementation is sometimes a useful hack. The following code shows the implementation of a custom class that retrieves from a table a set of records about movies:

```
import java.sql.  Connection;
import java.sql.  DriverManager;
import java.sql.  Statement;
import java.sql.  ResultSet;
import java.util. Properties;
import java.util. Properties;
import java.io.   FileInputStream;


public class CustomTable2XML {
    public static void main(String[] argv) {
     if (argv.length != 1) {
         System.out.println("Usage: java CustomTable2XML
                             PropertiesFile");
         System.exit(-1);
     }

     Connection conn = null;
     Statement stmt = null;
     ResultSet rs = null;
     Properties myDB = new Properties();
     try
     {
      myDB.load(new FileInputStream(argv[0]));
      Class.forName(myDB.getProperty("driver"));
          conn =
DriverManager.getConnection(myDB.getProperty("URL"),
                            myDB.getProperty("user"),
                            myDB.getProperty("password"));
          stmt = conn.createStatement();
          rs = stmt.executeQuery("SELECT * FROM " +
                                 myDB.getProperty("table"));
          createXMLDocument(rs);
     }
        catch(java.lang.ClassNotFoundException cnfe)
        {
         System.out.println("Driver not Found");
             System.exit(-1);
     }
       catch (java.sql.SQLException sqle)
       {
         System.out.println("Failed to connect with the database
                              (SQL) "
                              + sqle);
         System.exit(-1);
     }
       catch (java.lang.Exception e)
        {
```

```
        System.out.println("Failed to connect with the database "
+ e);
        System.exit(-1);
     }
    }

    // output to STDOUT the XML Representation of the Table
    public static void createXMLDocument(ResultSet rs) throws
    java.sql.SQLException, java.io.IOException
    {
     System.out.println("<?xml version=\"1.0\"?>");
     System.out.println("<!-- Custom Generated XML file from
                         Movies DB-->");
     System.out.println("<movies>");

     // The program knows exactly the structure of the table and
     // it has harcoded
     while(rs.next())
     {
         System.out.println("<dvd id='" + rs.getInt("DVDID") +
                               "'");
         System.out.println("     releasedDate='" +
            rs.getDate("Released" + toString()+"'>");
          System.out.println("    <title> " +
            rs.getString("DVDTitle")+"</title>");
         System.out.println("    <tagline> " +
            rs.getString("Tagline") + "</tagline>");
         System.out.println("    <category> " +
            rs.getString("Category") + "</category>");
         System.out.println("    <studio> " +
             rs.getString("Studio") + "</studio>");
         System.out.println("</dvd>");
        }
     System.out.println("</movies>");
    }
}
```

For the table shown in Figure 16.2 and the following properties file,

```
# CustomTable2XML property file
URL=jdbc:odbc:DTDs
user=
password=
table=Movies
driver=sun.jdbc.odbc.JdbcOdbcDriver
the result of invoking this program is the shown below:
C:\xmldb\customClasses>java CustomTable2XML properties.prop
<?xml version="1.0"?>
<!-- Custom Generated XML file from Movies DB-->
<movies>
<dvd id='1'
     releasedDate='1988-10-01'>
```

```
   <title> Dangerous Liaisons</title>
   <tagline> Lust, Seduction, Revenge. The Game as you've never
seen it played b
efore</tagline>
   <category> Drama</category>
   <studio> WB</studio>
</dvd>
<dvd id='2'
     releasedDate='1998-10-01'>
   <title> Rushmore</title>
   <tagline> Love. Expulsion. Revolution.</tagline>
   <category> Comedy</category>
   <studio> WB</studio>
</dvd>
<dvd id='3'
     releasedDate='1998-10-01'>
   <title> Being John Malkovich</title>
   <tagline> Ever wanted to be somebody else? Now you
can.</tagline>
   <category> Comedy</category>
   <studio> WB</studio>
</dvd>
</movies>
```

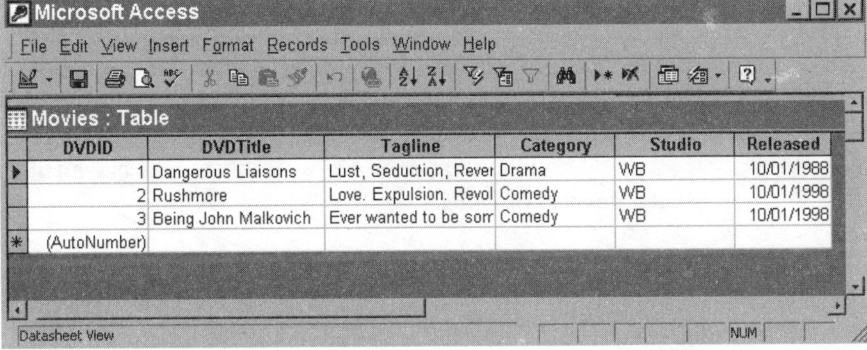

Figure 16.2
Movie table.

APIs for Database Isolation

Moving down in the scale of coupling there is an interesting solution: parsers that take arbitrary tables[2] as inputs and throw standard SAX events or DOM models as their output. From the point of view of the

[2] In this chapter we talk more frequently about tables and relationships than about objects. The reason is simple: the relational model is far more popular than the object model for databases. However, the concepts and examples can easily be applied to object databases.

rest of the application, there is no difference between this and the classical parser. All the database manipulation becomes isolated in the parser class, and the application can be concerned only with the handlers necessary to manage the incoming SAX events (Figure 16.3).

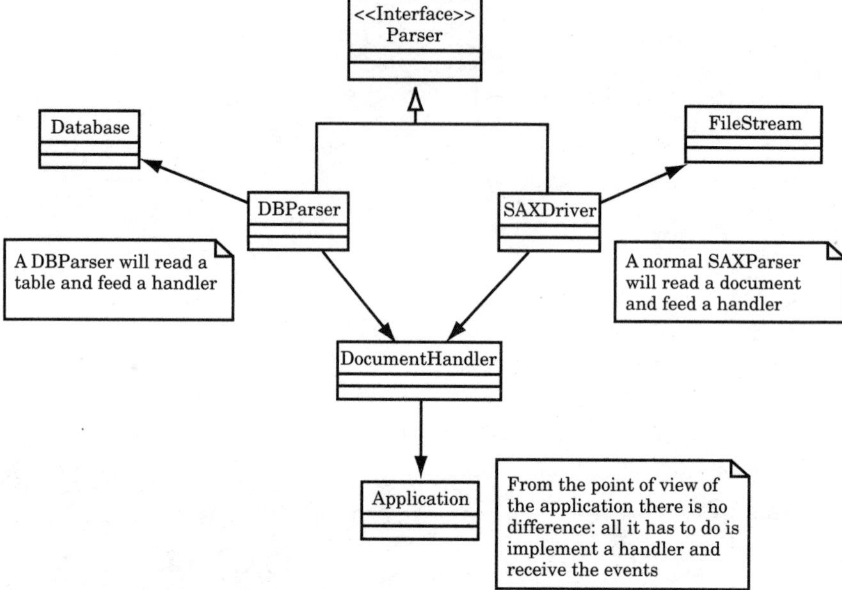

Figure 16.3 SAX API for databases.

The following code shows a `DBParser` class that implements the SAX parser interface:

```
import org.xml.sax.          *;
import org.xml.sax.helpers. LocatorImpl;
import org.xml.sax.helpers. AttributeListImpl;
import java.lang.           Integer;

import java.sql.            ResultSet;
import java.sql.            ResultSetMetaData;
import java.sql.            SQLException;
import java.io.             IOException;
import java.util.           Locale;
import java.util.           Vector;


public class DBParser implements Parser
{

    static HandlerBase s_defaulthandler =  new HandlerBase();
    EntityResolver  entityHandler    =   s_defaulthandler;
    DTDHandler      dtdHandler       =   s_defaulthandler;
```

```
DocumentHandler documentHandler =   s_defaulthandler;
ErrorHandler    errorHandler    =   s_defaulthandler;
```

First, all the methods from the parser interface must be implemented:

```
public void setEntityResolver(EntityResolver handler) {
    entityHandler = handler;
}

public void setDocumentHandler(DocumentHandler handler) {
    documentHandler = handler;
}

public void setErrorHandler(ErrorHandler handler) {
    errorHandler = handler;
}

public  void setDTDHandler (DTDHandler handler) {
    dtdHandler = handler;
}

public void parse (InputSource source)
 throws SAXException, IOException
 {
  throw new SAXException("DBParser must use a ResultSet as its
                          input");
 }

 public void parse (String systemId)
 throws SAXException, IOException
 {
  throw new SAXException("DBParser must use a ResultSet as its
                          input");
 }

public void setLocale (Locale locale)
  throws SAXException
  {
   // locales not implemented in this version.
     // Comply with SAX2 and throw an exception.
   throw new SAXException("No support for locales");
  }
```

Now that all the obligatory methods are implemented, we can get to the heart of our example: the actual `parse` method that allows the creation of SAX events from the a result set.[3]

---

3 This class can be easily modified to receive other database-oriented input such as a connection and a query statement.

This parse method receives four parameters:

- **ResultSet rs**—The ResultSet from which the XML will be produced
- **String rootName**—Specifies the name of the tag to be used as the root element
- **String rowTagName**—Each row of data is represented as an element of name rowTagName (whose subelements are actually the cells in the row). Specify the name of that row container element using this parameter.
- **Vector ra**—This vector contains the indices of the columns that must be represented as attributes. If the index of a column is not in this vector, the data will be represented as an element.

```
//*************************************************
// DBParser-Specific Methods
//*************************************************
public void parse(ResultSet rs,String rootName,
                  String rowTagName,Vector ra)
 throws SAXException,SQLException
{
 AttributeList emptyAL = new AttributeListImpl();
 ResultSetMetaData md = rs.getMetaData();
 int cols = md.getColumnCount();

 documentHandler.startDocument();
 documentHandler.startElement(rootName,emptyAL);

 while(rs.next())
     {
         AttributeListImpl atts = new AttributeListImpl();

      // get first those columns that must be represented as
      // attributes
      for(int i = 0; i < ra.size(); i++)
         {
       int col = ((Integer)ra.elementAt(i)).intValue();
       String atName =  md.getColumnLabel(col);
       String atValue = rs.getString(col);
       atts.addAttribute(atName,"CDATA",atValue);
      }

      documentHandler.startElement(rowTagName,atts);

      // now get those columns that must be represented as
      // subelements
      for(int i = 1; i <= cols; i++)
      {
       if(!ra.contains(new Integer(i)))
            {
         String eleName =  md.getColumnLabel(i);
```

```
                String eleContent = rs.getString(i);
                if (eleContent == null)
                 break;
                char[] eleContentCA = eleContent.toCharArray();

                documentHandler.startElement(eleName,emptyAL);
                documentHandler.characters(eleContentCA,0,
                                     eleContentCA.length);
                documentHandler.endElement(eleName);
            }
          }
          documentHandler.endElement(rowTagName);
      }

      documentHandler.endElement(rootName);
      documentHandler.endDocument();
     }
}
```

The following test program asks the parser to read the same table as the previous example, but instead of hardcoding the logic for the XML construction, it delegates the task to a SAX parser, to which it can hook any handler it wants,[4] just as if it were reading from an XML file:

```
import java.sql.  Connection;
import java.sql.  DriverManager;
import java.sql.  Statement;
import java.sql.  ResultSet;
import java.util. Properties;
import java.util. Vector;
import java.io.   FileInputStream;


public class TestSAXAPI {
    public static void main(String[] argv) {
     if (argv.length != 1) {
         System.out.println("Usage: java CustomTable2XML
                             PropertiesFile");
         System.exit(-1);
     }

     Connection conn = null;
     Statement stmt = null;
     ResultSet rs = null;
     Properties myDB = new Properties();
     try
```

[4] The test program uses the `SAXPrintHandler` class in order to write the events received as an XML document. This class was introduced in Chapters 4 and 5 and is included in the source code of the CD.

```
{
 myDB.load(new FileInputStream(argv[0]));
 Class.forName(myDB.getProperty("driver"));
     conn =
DriverManager.getConnection(myDB.getProperty("URL"),
                          myDB.getProperty("user"),
                          myDB.getProperty("password"));
     stmt = conn.createStatement();
     rs = stmt.executeQuery("SELECT * FROM " +
                                 myDB.getProperty("table"));
```

Note how conveniently the `DBParser` is used: specify that columns 1 and 5 should be represented as attributes, and the root element and row element names, and begin parsing. The registered handler will begin receiving the correct events.

```
 Vector representAsAtts = new Vector();
 representAsAtts.add(new Integer(1));
 representAsAtts.add(new Integer(5));
     DBParser myParser = new DBParser();

 SAXPrintHandlers ph = new SAXPrintHandlers();
 myParser.setDocumentHandler(ph);

 myParser.parse(rs,"movies","dvd",representAsAtts);
}
   catch(java.lang.ClassNotFoundException cnfe)
   {
    System.out.println("Driver not Found");
        System.exit(-1);
}
  catch (java.sql.SQLException sqle)
  {
    System.out.println("Failed to connect with the database
                      (SQL) " + sqle);
    System.exit(-1);
}
  catch (java.lang.Exception e)
   {
    System.out.println("Failed to connect with the database "
                      + e);
    System.exit(-1);
}
}

}
```

Since our handler is a `SAXPrintHandler` that will output back to XML the events it receives, the result is the following:

```
C:\ xmldb\SAXApi>java TestSAXAPI properties.prop
<movies>
<dvd DVDID="1" Studio="WB">
<DVDTitle>
Dangerous Liaisons</DVDTitle>
<Tagline>
Lust, Seduction, Revenge. The Game as you've never seen it played
before</Tagline>
<Category>
Drama</Category>
<Released>
1988-10-01 00:00:00</Released>
</dvd>
<dvd DVDID="2" Studio="WB">
<DVDTitle>
Rushmore</DVDTitle>
<Tagline>
Love. Expulsion. Revolution.</Tagline>
<Category>
Comedy</Category>
<Released>
1998-10-01 00:00:00</Released>
</dvd>
<dvd DVDID="3" Studio="WB">
<DVDTitle>
Being John Malkovich</DVDTitle>
<Tagline>
Ever wanted to be somebody else? Now you can.</Tagline>
<Category>
Comedy</Category>
<Released>
1998-10-01 00:00:00</Released>
</dvd>
</movies>
```

The SAX API for databases presents obvious improvements from the custom class approach. It decouples the XML building logic from the application and provides a reusable solution for database to XML construction.

The solution presented might be the correct approach for many projects. However, it has serious limitations, including the inability to go from XML to database (not to mention the fact that it's limited to a single table). The following section shows how full-blown middleware tools can be used to overcome such problems.

Middleware Tools

Robust and flexible implementations of complete APIs for the translation of XML to databases (and vice versa) are available in the form of open source and commercial middleware.

When bundled with a particular commercial database, middleware is advertised as an integral part of the product at hand, in which case the database is commonly termed "XML-enabled."

On the other hand, many noncommercial, vendor-independent packages provide the APIs needed to talk XML back and forth with standard relational databases (commonly via ODBC or JDBC). This section will show the rationale behind most commercial and free packages as well as their practical implementation in the open source middleware, xml-dbms by Ronald Bourret.

Templates versus Mapping

When faced with the problem of extracting meaningful XML data from a database, a general-purpose middleware package has two options:

- Allow the embedding of SQL statements in XML templates.
- Provide an explicit mapping between the fields in the database and XML elements.

In the first option, the input of the system would be an XML document with certain *replaceable* elements, which are translated by the middleware into XML representing the results of a query. For example, the following document specifies a query to the database in the `select` element:

```
<?xml version="1.0"?>
<songs>
   <description>A description of
                some of the jungle styles
   </description>
   <select name="style">SELECT name,description
                        FROM MusicStyles
                        WHERE type="Jungle"
   </select>
</songs>
```

When the document gets processed by the middleware, the `select` element is replaced and the following document is produced:

```
<?xml version="1.0"?>
<songs>
   <description>A description of
             some of the jungle styles
   </description>
   <style>
     <name>Jump-up</name>
     <description>Dance-oriented jungle based on
             hip-hop samples.
     </description>
   <style>
   <style>
     <name>Liquid Funk</name>
     <description> Funky danceable drum'n'bass
     </description>
   <style>
</songs>
```

In the second option (mapping), the inputs to the system are: 1) a mapping specifying how the XML elements and attributes are represented in the database and 2) either an XML document or a database. The result provided by the middleware will be either the database or an XML representation of the input data.

Template-based middleware is limited to database-to-XML transformations, in which mapping-based middleware is more applicable to two-way procedures. Also, mapping-based solutions are more widely available and documented. The following example of middleware usage will focus on a mapping-based API.

xml-dbms

The xml-dbms package, developed and maintained by Ronald Bourret, is a very good example of mapping-based APIs for the transformation of XML data into tables and vice versa. The xml-dbms model is based on the idea of a mapping language that permits the unambiguous, two-way translation of data. The structure of the typical xml-dbms application can be condensed in the following steps:

1. Create a map object out of a map document.
2. Pass the map object to either a `domToDBMS` or a `DMBSToDom` object.
3. Receive and manipulate the results of the translation.

The following subsections put these steps into concrete code.

Map Documents

A map document is an XML document conformant with the xml-dbms Map DTD.[5] Map documents provide the description for the mapping between constructs in the database (such as tables and columns) and constructs in XML (such as elements and attributes). The first and most common type of mapping expressed in a map document is that of element types to tables.

Before showing the element to table map, it is important to make a note: the `xml-dbms` mapping language is constructed around the idea that the XML first must be modeled as classes and attributes, and then that the model must be mapped into database constructs. Fortunately, the two things are done in the same map document, as the following sample illustrates:

```
<ClassMap>
   <ElementType Name="GeographicInfo"/>
   <ToClassTable>
      <Table Name="Places"/>
   </ToClassTable>
   ...property maps...
   ...related class maps...
</ClassMap>
```

Now that we have a relationship between a complex element type and a table, let's create a binding between the attributes and simple elements of the XML document and the columns of a table:

```
<PropertyMap>
   <Attribute Name="Altitude"/>
   <ToColumn>
      <Column Name="Altitude"/>
   </ToColumn>
</PropertyMap>
<PropertyMap>
   <Attribute Name="Latitud"/>
   <ToColumn>
      <Column Name="Latitude"/>
   </ToColumn>
</PropertyMap>


<PropertyMap>
   <ElementType Name="place"/>
   <ToColumn>
```

[5] Other middleware products define their own mapping languages.

```
        <Column Name="PlaceName"/>
     </ToColumn>
   </PropertyMap>
```

Other features of the xml-dbms map language include the mapping of inter-class relationships (i.e. modeling keys between tables to reflect hierarchies between elements):

```
<RelatedClass KeyInParentTable="placeID">
  <ElementType Name="PlaceDescription" />
  <CandidateKey Generate="No">
    <Column Name="placeID" />
  </CandidateKey>
  <ForeignKey>
   <Column Name="Part" />
  </ForeignKey>
</RelatedClass>
```

The three constructs shown here cover most of the things the majority of applications will ever need. However, for a complete description of all the options in the xml-dbms map language, please refer to the DTD and the xml-dbms documentation.

Creating a Map Object

Inside a Java program, the map document must be transformed into a map object. This is accomplished by using a *map factory*. Map factories are Java classes used to generate Map objects either from documents compliant with the xml-dbms language, or from DTDs (the section titled "Metadata Translation" explains the process used to create a map out of a DTD).

The following code shows how to create a Map object out of a map file:

```
   // Since the map is the bridge between document and database,
   // the constructor of the factory most get them both.
   factory = new MapFactory_MapDocument(conn, parser);

   // Create a Map from geo.map.
   map = factory.createMap(new InputSource(new
FileReader("geo.map")));
```

Passing the Map to dbsmToDOM and Retrieving the Data

Creating the XML representation of database data or vice versa is often a matter of only one line. The following code shows the transfer from a DB to XML; in the comprehensive example we will see the reverse.

```
// Create a new DBMSToDOM object.
   dbmsToDOM = new DBMSToDOM(map, new DF_Oracle());

   // Create a key and retrieve the data.
   key = {new Integer(123)};
   doc = dbmsToDOM.retrieveDocument("Sales", key);
```

Putting it All Together: A Comprehensive Example

So far we have seen solutions that take XML data *out of* the database (see custom classes and SAX API for databases). In this example, we will put the data inside an XML file into the database, using the `DOMtoDBMS` class of `xml-dbms`.

First of all, let's see the kind of document we want to process:

```
<?xml version="1.0"?>
<!-- Custom Generated XML file from Movies DB-->
<movies>
<dvd id='1'
     releasedDate='1988-10-01'>
   <title> Dangerous Liaisons</title>
   <tagline> Lust, Seduction, Revenge. The Game as you've never
seen it played before</tagline>
   <category> Drama</category>
   <studio> WB</studio>
</dvd>
<dvd id='2'
     releasedDate='1998-10-01'>
   <title> Rushmore</title>
   <tagline> Love. Expulsion. Revolution.</tagline>
   <category> Comedy</category>
   <studio> WB</studio>
</dvd>
<dvd id='3'
     releasedDate='1998-10-01'>
   <title> Being John Malkovich</title>
   <tagline> Ever wanted to be somebody else? Now you
can.</tagline>
   <category> Comedy</category>
   <studio> WB</studio>
</dvd>
</movies>
```

In order to provide the rules for the translation, here is the `dvd.map`:

```
<?xml version='1.0'?>
<!DOCTYPE XMLToDBMS SYSTEM "xmldbms.dtd" >
```

```
<XMLToDBMS Version="1.0">
   <Options>
   </Options>
   <Maps>
      <ClassMap>
         <ElementType Name="movies"/>
         <ToClassTable>
            <Table Name="dvd"/>
         </ToClassTable>
         <PropertyMap>
            <Attribute Name="id"/>
            <ToColumn>
               <Column Name="dvdid"/>
            </ToColumn>
         </PropertyMap>
         <PropertyMap>
            <Attribute Name="releaseDate"/>
            <ToColumn>
               <Column Name="release"/>
            </ToColumn>
         </PropertyMap>
         <PropertyMap>
            <ElementType Name="title"/>
            <ToColumn>
               <Column Name="title"/>
            </ToColumn>
         </PropertyMap>
         <PropertyMap>
            <ElementType Name="tagline"/>
            <ToColumn>
               <Column Name="tagline"/>
            </ToColumn>
         </PropertyMap>
         <PropertyMap>
            <ElementType Name="category"/>
            <ToColumn>
               <Column Name="category"/>
            </ToColumn>
         </PropertyMap>
         <PropertyMap>
            <ElementType Name="studio"/>
            <ToColumn>
               <Column Name="studio"/>
            </ToColumn>
         </PropertyMap>
      </ClassMap>
   </Maps>
</XMLToDBMS>
```

Finally, there is the `PutDVDs.java` program, which will use the `xml-dbms` middleware to put the XML file into the database:

```
import de.tudarmstadt.ito.xmldbms.DBMSToDOM;
import de.tudarmstadt.ito.xmldbms.DOMToDBMS;
import de.tudarmstadt.ito.xmldbms.Map;
import de.tudarmstadt.ito.xmldbms.helpers.KeyGeneratorImpl;
import de.tudarmstadt.ito.xmldbms.mapfactories.MapFactory_MapDoc-
ument;

// Other imports (of java.lang and org.apache )ommited

public class PutDVDs {
 public static void main (String[] argv) throws java.sql.SQLEx-
ception
 {
      Connection       conn1 = null, conn2 = null;
      Map              map;
      Document         doc;
      DOMToDBMS        domToDBMS;
      KeyGeneratorImpl keyGenerator = null;

      String mapFilename = argv[0];
      String xmlFilename = argv[1];
      try
      {
     if (argv.length != 2) {
         System.out.println("Usage: java PutDVDs mapfile xml-
                            file");
         System.exit(-1);
     }

         Class.forName("sun.jdbc.odbc.JdbcOdbcDriver");


         // Connect to the database.
         conn1 = DriverManager.getConnection("jdbc:odbc:DTDs");
         conn2 = DriverManager.getConnection("jdbc:odbc:DTDs");

         // Create and initialize a key generator
         keyGenerator = new KeyGeneratorImpl(conn1);
         keyGenerator.initialize();

         // Create the Map object and open the XML document.
         map = createMap(mapFilename, conn2);
         doc = openDocument(xmlFilename);

         // Create a new DOMToDBMS object and transfer the data.

         domToDBMS = new DOMToDBMS(map, keyGenerator, new
                     NQ_DOM2());
         domToDBMS.storeDocument(doc);
      }
      catch(Exception e)
      {
       System.out.println(e);
```

```
      }
      finally
      {
         if (conn1 != null) conn1.close();
         if (conn2 != null) conn2.close();
      }

   }

   static Map createMap(String mapFilename, Connection conn)
                        throws Exception
   {
      MapFactory_MapDocument    factory;

      // Create a new map factory and create the Map.
      factory = new MapFactory_MapDocument(conn, getSAXParser());
      return factory.createMap(new InputSource(getFileURL(map-
      Filename)));
   }

   static String getFileURL(String fileName)
   {
      File   file;

      file = new File(fileName);
      return "file:///" + file.getAbsolutePath();
   }

   static Parser getSAXParser()
   {
      return new SAXParser();
   }

   static Document openDocument(String xmlFilename) throws
                                Exception
   {

      DOMParser parser;

      // Instantiate the parser and set various options.
      parser = new DOMParser();
      parser.setFeature("http://xml.org/sax/features/namespaces",
                        true);

      // Parse the input file
      parser.parse(new InputSource(getFileURL(xmlFilename)));

      // Return the DOM tree
      return parser.getDocument();
   }
}
```

The result of running this program with `dvd.map` and `dvd.xml` as arguments is the population of a table with the content of the XML file, according to the specifications of the map. For more complex examples of `xml-dbms`, please refer to the documentation (especially to the `transfer.java` example, which illustrates advanced uses of all the topics covered here).

Metadata Translation

From the previous section on middleware, it is clear that having a mapping between a particular DTD and a database schema is a necessary input for most APIs that connect XML and databases.

The next question is, of course, how to deduce the database schema from the DTD. The following list shows the steps taken when implementing this process:[6]

1. For each element type with element or mixed content, create a table and a primary key column.
2. For each element type with mixed content, create a separate table in which to store the PCDATA, linked to the parent table through the parent's primary key.
3. For each single-valued attribute of that element type, and for each singly occurring child element type with PCDATA-only content, create a column in that table. If the child element type or attribute is optional, make the column nullable.
4. For each multivalued attribute and for each multiply-occurring child element type with PCDATA-only content, create a separate table to store values, linked to the parent table through the parent's primary key.
5. For each child element type with element or mixed content, link the parent element's table to the child element's table with the parent's primary key.

Conversely, a DTD can be generated from a database schema, by following these steps:

---

[6] When automatically implemented, these steps vary in detail depending on the source. This particular list has been transcribed from Roland Bourret's excellent article "XML and Databases."

1. For each table, create an element.
2. For each column in a table, create an attribute or a PCDATA-only child element.
3. For each primary key/foreign key relationship in which a column of the table contributes the primary key, create a child element.

Content Management Systems

So far we have explored almost all the solutions shown in the map of Figure 16.1. This section will present the most extreme document-oriented solution for XML persistence: Content Management Systems (CMS). The following section will present the most extreme data-oriented solution: XML servers.

CMS refers to a variety of products that deal with the problem of creating, editing, and maintaining versions of large numbers of documents. CMS are especially concerned with: (1) providing the end-user a powerful and easy interface for the management and composition of groups of documents and (2) the ability to scale along with the growth of the number of documents managed.

CMS are mostly end-user oriented and even when some of them provide accessible APIs; their view of the content is extremely dependent on the vendor[7] and very document-oriented in nature.

Because of these characteristics, we will limit the discussion of Content Management Systems to a list in the final products section of the most relevant XML CMS.

One final remark about CMS and the solutions map of Figure 16.1 must be made: as you can see, the highly coupled, home-made solution for content management is empty. Implementing an in-house product as big as a CMS is likely to be a waste of time and energy for most organizations.

XML (Database Application) Servers

XML servers are full application platforms that deliver and receive XML as their native communication (and sometimes persistence) mechanism.

---

[7] This might be changing with products such as IM by Interleaf, which claim a growing compliance with XML standards.

They provide APIs for the direct manipulation of the XML data and can be classified as the more encapsulated persistent solution for XML.[8]

Even though the borderline often gets blurry, XML servers differ from CMS in two fundamental aspects:

- XML servers are data oriented. They use XML because of its interoperability and extensibility advantages, but are mainly focused on data-related problems.
- XML servers are less user oriented in nature. Even when some of them provide user interfaces, their main target is application development, and therefore the exposure of APIs.

XML servers vary greatly in the type of interfaces they provide, so the best approach might be to go through the product list and learn the particular API of the server you choose. However, in order to provide some insight into their usage, the following code shows an API example from a database application server called `dbxml`:

```
import com.dbxml.core.corba.*;
import com.dbxml.core.corba.database.*;
import com.dbxml.orblet.*;
import org.omg.CosNaming.*;
import org.omg.CosNaming.NamingContextPackage.*;
import org.omg.CORBA.*;

import java.util.Properties;

public class APIExample {
   public static void main(String[] args) {
      try {
         Properties orbConfig = new Properties();

         /* Tell the orb where to find the naming service. These
           * parameters are the default for dbXML if your
           * configuration is different you must adjust this.
           */
         orbConfig.put("org.omg.CORBA.ORBInitialPort", "1997");
         orbConfig.put("org.omg.CORBA.ORBInitialHost",
                       "localhost");

         // create and initialize the ORB
         ORB orb = ORB.init(new String[0], orbConfig);
```

[8] That, of course, doesn't mean that they are the best solution for every XML-database problem. On the contrary, experience has shown that most middle-sized projects are better off with a middleware-based solution.

```
         // get the root naming context
         org.omg.CORBA.Object objRef =
         orb.resolve_initial_references("NameService");
         NamingContext ncRef =
NamingContextHelper.narrow(objRef);

         // resolve the Object Reference in Naming
         NameComponent nc = new NameComponent("Application", "");
         NameComponent path[] = {nc};
         Application app =
ApplicationHelper.narrow(ncRef.resolve(path));

         System.out.println("Application Name " + app.getName());

         // Run the examples
         listCollections(app);
         String oid = insertDocument(app);
         retrieveDocument(app, oid);
      } catch (Exception e) {
         System.out.println("ERROR : " + e) ;
         e.printStackTrace(System.out);
      }
   }

   /**
    * Lists all databases and their collections on the server
    */
   public static void listCollections(Application app) throws
Exception {
      // Get a list of databases
      String[] databases = app.listDatabases();
      int i = 0;
      while (i < databases.length) {
         System.out.println(databases[i] + ":");

         // Get all the collections for this database.
         Database database = app.getDatabase(databases[i]);
         String [] collections = database.listCollections();
         int j = 0;
         while (j < collections.length) {
            System.out.println("\t" + collections[j]);
            j++;
         }

         i++;
      }
   }

   /**
    * Insert a new document into a collection.
    */
   public static String insertDocument(Application app) throws
Exception {
```

```
        // Document must be a valid XML document.
        String document = "<?xml version=\"1.0\"?>\n
<test>Hello</test>";

        // The default install includes a test database with an ocs
collection
        Collection col =
app.getDatabase("test").getCollection("ocs");

        // CORBA requires the document to be an EncodedBuffer
        EncodedBuffer buf = new EncodedBuffer("", document.get-
Bytes());
        String oid = col.insertDocument(buf);
        System.out.println("Document OID: " + oid);
        return oid;
    }

    /**
        * Retrieve and print a stored document
        */
    public static void retrieveDocument(Application app, String
oid)
            throws Exception {
        // The default install includes a test database with an ocs
collection
        Collection col =
app.getDatabase("test").getCollection("ocs");
        System.out.println(oid);
        EncodedBuffer buffer = col.getDocument(oid);

        // The XML data is stored in buffer.buf
        System.out.println(new String(buffer.buf));
    }
}
```

Product List

As the final part of our exploration of XML-database techniques and technologies, this section presents a directory of some of the most relevant products on the market.

Tables 16.1 and 16.2 are designed to act only as a quick directory of products. Descriptions of each product can be found in the Ronald Bourret list of XML database products, available on the CD.

TABLE 16.1
Middleware products.

4ODS	FourThought	http://opentechnology.org/4Suite/
ASP2XML	Stonebroom	http://www.stonebroom.com/asp2xml.htm
Beanstalk	Transparency	http://www.transparency.com
Castor	exolab.org	http://castor.exolab.org/index.html
DatabaseDom	IBM	http://www.alphaworks.ibm.com/tech/databasedom
DataCraft	IBM	http://www.alphaworks.ibm.com/formula/datacraft
DB2XML	Volker Turau	http://www.informatik.fh-wiesbaden.de/~turau
DBIx::XML_RDB	Matt Sergeant	http://theory.uwinnipeg.ca/CPAN/
InterAccess	XML Software Corporation	http://www.xmlsoft.com.au/iaccess.html
Net.Data	IBM	http://www-4.ibm.com/software/data/net.data/
ODBC2XML	Intelligent Systems Research	http://members.xoom.com/gvaughan/odbc2xml.htm
XML-DB Link	Rogue Wave Software	http://www.roguewave.com/
XML-DBMS	Ronald Bourret	http://www.rpbourret.com/xmldbms/index.htm
XML Junction	Data Junction, Inc.	http://www.xmljunction.net
XLE	IBM	http://www.alphaworks.ibm.com/tech/xle

TABLE 16.2
XML servers and CMS.

Astoria	Chrystal Software	http://www.chrystal.com/products/astoria/astoria.htm
BladeRunner	Interleaf	http://www.xmlecontent.com/products/brintro.htm
Bluestone XML-Server	Bluestone	http://www.bluestone.com/
Cocoon	Apache.org	http://xml.apache.org/cocoon/sql.html
DataChannel Server	DataChannel	http://www.datachannel.com/
Documentum	Documentum, Inc.	http://www.documentum.com/

continued on next page

TABLE 16.2 XML servers and CMS (continued).

Dynabase	Inso	http://www.ebt.com/dynabase/
Epic	Arbortext	http://www.arbortext.com/Products/Epic/epic.html
Excelon	eXcelon Corp.	http://www.exceloncorp.com/products/excelon.html
Frontier	UserLand Software	http://frontier.userland.com/
GroveMinder	TechnoTeacher	http://www.techno.com/
Hynet Directive	Hynet Technologies	http://www.hynet.com/Products/main.html
Information	Interleaf Manager	http://www.xmlecontent.com/products/im.htm
Lasso	Blue World Communications	http://www.blueworld.com/blueworld/products/
LivePage Enterprise	Janna Systems	http://www.janna.com/
POET Suite	POET	http://www.poet.com/products/cms/cms.html
Rhythmyx	Percussion Software	http://www.percussion.com/
SigmaLink	STEP	http://www.step.de/sigmalink.htm
SIM	Progressive Information Technologies	http://www.simdb.com
Tamino	Software AG	http://www.softwareag.com/tamino/
Target 2000	Magnus	http://www.target2000.com/main.html
WSDOM XML-Portal	Radian Systems	http://www.radsys.com/products/portal.htm
XML Portal Server (XPS)	Sequoia Software Corp.	http://www.sequoiasw.com/xps/index.asp
XMLBase	eidon	http://www.eidon-products.com/sgmlxmlbase.htm

Summary

This chapter presented the different types of solutions for XML and database integration, classifying them according to their level of coupling with the database and the nature of the XML data.

Approaches ranging from hardcoded classes for particular vocabularies to SAX database APIs, middleware, and XML servers were all presented in both theory and context.

The concepts and classes defined in this chapter will be reused in following chapters as part of more complex applications.

CHAPTER 17

XML Server to Server: XML-RPC and B2B

Introduction

This chapter deals with one of the most interesting applications of XML available: Remote Procedure Calling and its use in business-to-business (B2B) communication. The technology treated is XML-RPC, a lightweight mechanism for remote procedure calls over HTTP, using XML. XML-RPC is a popular alternative to other, heavier and more complex mechanisms for distributed computing because of its extreme simplicity and accessibility. XML-RPC theory and structure is the subject of the first part of the chapter.

The second part of this chapter is a complete XML-RPC application, which uses the concepts discussed in the first part in order to create a service for DVD price comparisons.

Naturally, all the discussion around encoding and remote invocation of procedure calls using XML can lead to more possibilities in the B2B space. We'll revisit these issues in Chapter 20 where we discuss the relationship between RPC technologies (XML-RPC and SOAP).

XML-RPC

Before analyzing the syntax and semantics of XML-RPC, we should review the goals at hand.

Remote Procedure Call Fundamentals

RPC is the ability to perform the execution of a function (procedure) in a remote system. RPC had its beginning in the UNIX environment, in which a number of different implementations tried to solve the problem of distributing an application by having a client invoke the procedures of a server (Figure 17.1).

Different types of RPC have been around for almost as long as UNIX itself, and now some form of RPC is available for almost every operating system. Some of these forms of RPC are more widely used than others, but they all have in common the fact that they are dominated/defined by two basic variables:

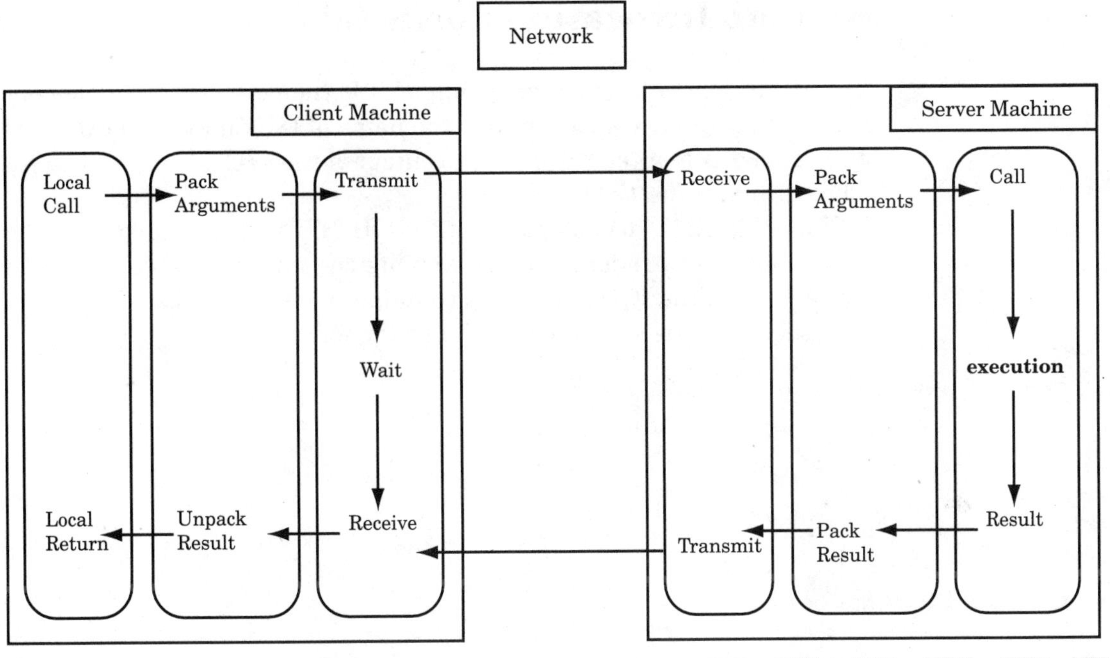

Figure 17.1 Traditional UNIX RPC.

- The format of the calls and responses.
- The way the calls are transported from one system to another.

Traditionally, the calls have been encoded in some form of binary format, while the underlying protocol has been specifically tailored. While this has worked reasonably well for years, the time has come to take the RPC ideas into the realm of the Web and open standards.

XML-RPC is the result of efforts to create a simple specification for RPC, characterized by a radical approach to the two variables mentioned:

- The format for encoding the calls is XML.
- The underlying communication is made using HTTP.

Before continuing to discuss the advantages of such an approach, let's investigate these statements by examining how an invocation and its response would look.

What an Invocation Looks Like

An XML-RPC invocation is very simple: it is composed of a root element called `methodCall`, which contains the name of the function to call, plus the arguments to it (encoded as the content of the `methodName` and `param` subelements, respectively).

Since this XML document is sent via HTTP `POST` to the server, the traditional `POST` headers (saying how big the message is, the name of the client, and the type of the data contained) are included.

In short, the invocation will look like the following:

```
POST /RPC2 HTTP/1.0
User-Agent: Autobahn/1.0 (Win98)
Host: gatubela.thefaactory.com
Content-Type: text/xml
Content-length: 232

<?xml version="1.0"?>
<methodCall>
   <methodName>StringUtils.palindrome</methodName>
   <params>
      <param>
         <value>
            <string>A Santa deified at NASA</string>
         </value>
       </param>
    </params>
</methodCall>
```

What this will do, when sent to the host is:

1. By virtue of the XML-RPC server,[1] the XML document will be processed and converted to an actual call in the system.
2. The call actually gets executed by the server (in this case, the server is a Java implementation of XML-RPC, so it will get transformed to a call like: `StringUtils.palindrome` ("A Santa deified at NASA");
3. The result of the call will be encoded as XML and sent back to the server.

[1] The XML-RPC server gets called because Apache (or any other Web server) can redirect the request to "RPC2" as stated in the first line of the message.

What a Response Looks Like

The return value of the call is encoded back as XML and sent to the client in the following form:

```
HTTP/1.0 200 OK
Server: Helma XML-RPC 1.0
Connection: close
Content-Type: text/xml
Content-Length: 143

<?xml version="1.0" encoding="ISO-8859-1"?>
<methodResponse>
     <params>
          <param>
            <value>
               <boolean>1</boolean>
            </value>
          </param>
     </params>
</methodResponse>
```

There are two important points to highlight about this response:

- The HTTP return code is 200. It will always be, regardless of the result of the procedure itself.
- The return value is also strongly typed. In our case, the value is true (boolean).

NOTE

The result is true because "A Santa deified at NASA" is indeed a palindrome. A palindrome is a string that reads the same backward and forward. Other examples are "ah, Satan sees Natasha!" and "I, man, am regal; a German am I".

Not all procedure calls are successful. Two types of problems may occur:

- For some reason, the XML-RPC communication itself fails. This is not actually classified as a proper XML-RPC problem, because things totally unrelated to the specification cause it. An example of this is the server's being down, or the HTTP server's not being configured to delegate XML-RPC calls.
- The invocation is unsuccessful because of errors in the call. This is an XML-RPC problem, and it usually happens when there is a wrong

number of arguments for the call or there is no function with that name actually registered in the system as a callable remote procedure.

What an Error Looks Like

When XML-RPC errors happen, instead of an HTTP error, the result will be a normal 200 response, but the content of the document will change, and instead of having a `params` element with the result, it will include a `fault` element with the description of the error:

```
HTTP/1.0 200 OK
Server: Helma XML-RPC 1.0
Connection: close
Content-Type: text/xml
Content-Length: 276

<?xml version="1.0" encoding="ISO-8859-1"?>
<methodResponse>
   <fault>
     <value>
       <struct>
          <member>
            <name>
              faultString
            </name>
            <value>java.lang.NoSuchMethodException</value>
          </member>
        <member>
        <name>
           faultCode
        </name>
        <value>
          <int>0</int>
        </value>
        </member>
      </struct>
    </value>
   </fault>
</methodResponse>
```

Testing XML-RPC Services

For the most part, you will not write XML-RPC directly. Instead, you will have a client/server toolkit for your preferred language; it will take care of translating calls like:

```
XMLRPCClient myClient = new XMLRPCClient("http://gatubela.
faactory.com");
Vector params = new Vector();
params.addElement("Nora, a raft! Is it far, Aaron?");
myClient.execute("StringUtil.Palindrome",params);
```

into the appropriate XML-RPC document and sending it to the HTTP server. Toolkits like this will be studied extensively in the following sections.

There are cases, however, when you need to test the remote procedures manually. One way to do it is to use Web-based XML-RPC clients such as the one by UserLand.com.[2] In these services you simply enter the XML document for the RPC call, as well as the connection parameters, and it will make the connection, returning a page with the response. Figure 17.2 shows the UserLand RPC "debug" page. By the end of this chapter, you will be able (among other things) to write a page with this functionality yourself.

Pros and Cons of XML-RPC

Using XML-RPC is an architectural decision for a project. It will have an impact on the way the project is made and define the limits of what can be done with it as a distributed application.

The main pros of implementing XML-RPC are:

- **Simplicity**—XML-RPC is arguably the simplest form of distributed computing available today.
- **Standards-based**—XML-RPC is based on two widely supported, totally available standards: HTTP and XML.
- **Internet-sensitive**—This rather cliché-sounding property is quite important. Other distributed computing alternatives such as CORBA or DCOM do not rely on HTTP for the transmission of the messages; instead, they have their own servers talking their own protocol.

  This has two main disadvantages: first, no matter how popular another RPC mechanism is, nothing beats the availability of Web servers. Getting and setting up a Web server is a trivial task nowadays, while the installation of other types of servers requires a steeper learning curve. Second, and most important, most firewalls allow the traffic through port 80 (HTTP) while they deny it to most other

[2] Testing the echo or the state name services in UserLand.com is a good idea at this point.

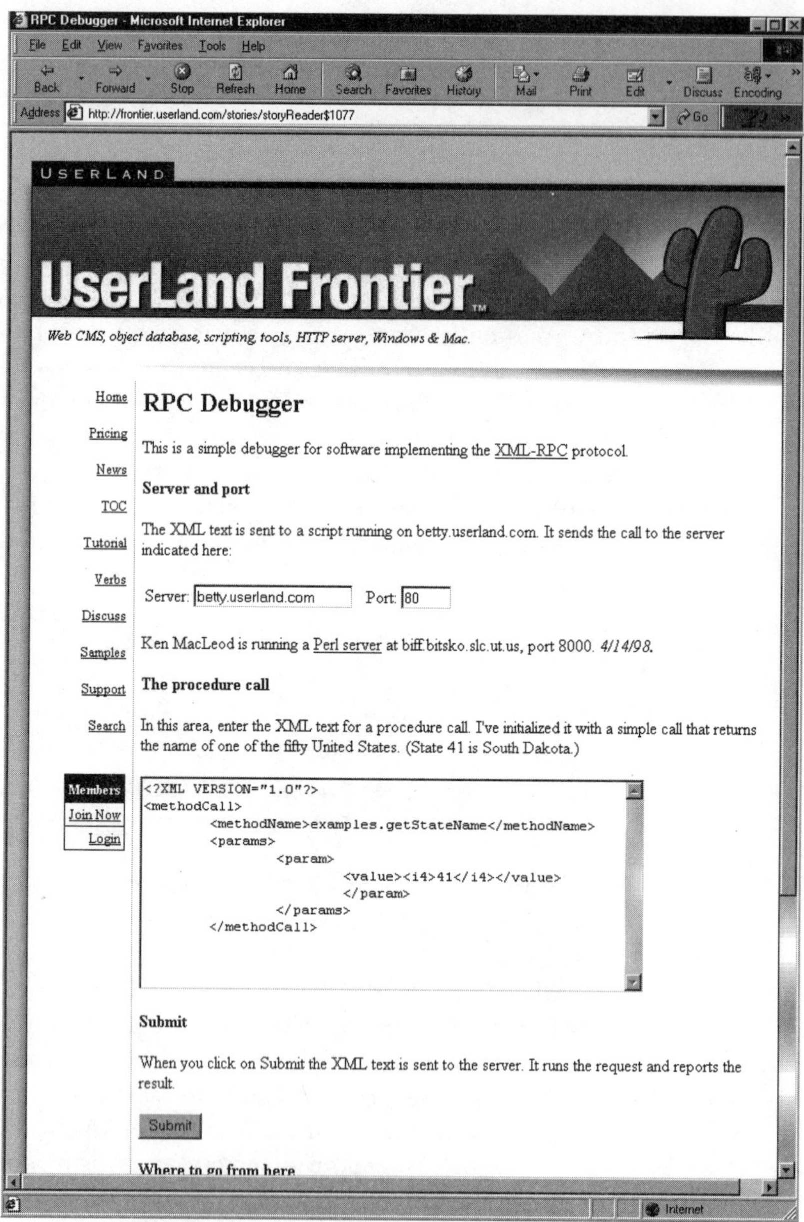

Figure 17.2
RPC debugger page.

ports. If you are using another mechanism, you will have to configure the firewall to allow the transmission of data via another port. When creating Internet-based distributed applications, one needs to connect to a wide variety of services; eliminating the problem of thinking about firewall restrictions is a major advantage for a protocol.

- **No stubs required**—Other RPC mechanisms need to know in advance the interfaces of the functions a server will provide in order to generate "stubs." The stubs are pieces of software that sit between the communication layer and the program, making possible the translation of the remote request into an actual call. Because of the simplicity of XML-RPC calls (no references, limited set of types, etc.), this is not needed.

On the other hand, there are several drawbacks to the use of XML-RPC:

- **Simplicity**—What works as an advantage can sometimes be a real problem when taken to an extreme. The simplicity of XML-RPC makes it unusable for large-scale projects in which features such as built-in encryption are needed.
- **Performance**—XML-RPC, because of its verbosity, can be significantly slower than alternatives such as CORBA or DCOM.
- **Scalability**—The lack of programming features such as asynchronous calls, references, and transactions pose scalability issues for XML-RPC.[3]

Deciding whether this might be the mechanism for the distributed computation of your system often comes down to a choice of complexity and robustness: do you really need those things not provided by XML-RPC such as built-in transactions? Is the simplicity of XML-RPC an advantage for your case or rather an inconvenient trap for extensibility problems? The answer for small to medium Internet-based applications seems to be that: XML-RPC precisely fits the needs. Beyond medium-sized requirements, chances are you might want to consider the traditional alternatives. The final decision, of course, depends on your particular scenario.

A Hands-on Introduction to XML-RPC Programming

As I mentioned before, should you decide to work with XML-RPC, you won't be writing XML documents directly, but instead you will be using

[3] Some XML-RPC users, however, seem to think that those restrictions have proven to be more beneficial (in terms of the learning curve) than damaging (in terms of scalability).

the interface provided by one of the many toolkits available (The "Implementation Toolkits" section contains pointers to tools in a number of programming languages such as Java, Perl, and Python).

The following section shows a typical use of these toolkits, by creating three components:

- The service itself
- The server that will listen to requests and delegate to the service
- The client

The Service

The service implemented is the palindrome checker of the first section. In Java, it can be implemented with the following code:

```
import java.lang.String;
import java.lang.Character;

public class StringUtil
{
    // Tests whether a phrase is palindrome or not.
    // i.e. whether it reads the same backwards or forward.

    public static boolean palindrome(String s)
    {
     String phrase = s.toLowerCase();
     // Begin with the indexes out of bounds, so the first
       // iteration is successful
     int i = -1;
     int j = phrase.length();
     boolean result = true; // assume they are palindrome
     char left = '.';
     char right = '.';
     while(j >= i && result)
         {
             left = phrase.charAt(++i);
         while(!Character.isLetter(left))
          left = phrase.charAt(++i);

             right = phrase.charAt(--j);
         while(!Character.isLetter(right))
          right = phrase.charAt(--j);
         result = left == right;
     }
     return result;
    }
    public static void main(String argv[])
    {
     System.out.println(palindrome(argv[0]));
```

```
    }
}
```

The Server

With the Java implementation of XML-RPC by UserLand, the process of creating a standalone HTTP server for XML-RPC is strikingly simple:

```
import helma.xmlrpc.WebServer;

// make an XML-RPC server for StringUtil

public class StringUtilServer
{
    public static void main(String argv[]) throws
java.io.IOException
    {
     WebServer ws = new WebServer(80);
       StringUtil myHandler = new StringUtil();
     ws.addHandler("MyStringUtil",myHandler);
    }
}
```

What happens here is: first, a new Web server is created and asked to listen to incoming requests on port 80.[4] Then, a Java object is registered to handle requests coming to `"MyStringUtil"`; this means that any RPC that looks for a method in `"MyStringUtil"` will be deflected to this object.

For small development projects, using the built-in Web server might be all right, but in general, chances are you'll want to integrate your XML-RPC with your normal Apache or Microsoft server. In order to do so, direct the requests to a program that uses the `XmlRpcServer` and reads the `POST` invocation from an input stream:

```
XmlRpcServer xmlrpc = new XmlRpcServer ();
xmlrpc.addHandler ("aHandler", new someHandler ());
// ...
byte[] result = xmlrpc.execute (request.getInputStream ());
response.setContentType ("text/xml");
response.setContentLength (result.length ());
OutputStream out = response.getOutputStream();
out.write (result);
out.flush ();
```

[4] When you do your own development and debugging, it is a good idea to stick with non-standard ports. Reserve 80 for deployment.

The Client

Finally, for the client, all we have to do is use the `XmlRpcClient` object to create a connection to the server and execute the call:

```
import helma.xmlrpc.XmlRpcClient;
import helma.xmlrpc.XmlRpc;
import java.util.Vector;

// make an XML-RPC server for StringUtil

public class StringUtilClient
{
    public static void main(String argv[])
                            throws java.io.IOException,
                                   java.lang.ClassNotFoundException
    {
       try
       {
     XmlRpcClient client = new
XmlRpcClient("http://localhost:80");
         Vector params = new Vector();
     if(argv.length > 0)
         params.addElement(argv[0]);
     else
         params.addElement("Camus sees sumac");

System.out.println(client.execute("Kabalah.palindrome",params));
       }
       catch(helma.xmlrpc.XmlRpcException e)
       {
     System.out.println("!" + e);
       }
    }
}
```

Figure 17.3 shows the client and server running on the same machine.

Similar code is possible in any of the languages with toolkits for XML-RPC (Java, Python, Perl, etc.). Please look at the toolkit section for more information on these.

A Close Look at the XML-RPC Specification

This section is based in the XML spec as published by UserLand in the www.xmlrpc.com site.[5]

---

[5] Copyright 1998-2000 UserLand Software, Inc.

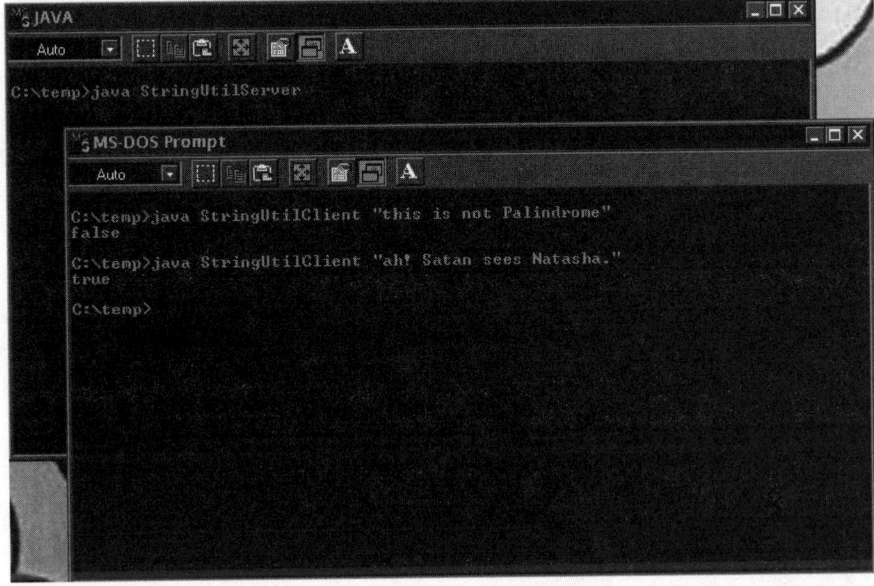

Figure 17.3 XML-RPC client and server.

Header Requirements

An HTTP POST request starts with a header of the form:

```
POST /RPC2 HTTP/1.0
User-Agent: Frontier/5.1.2 (WinNT)
Host: betty.userland.com
Content-Type: text/xml
Content-length: 181
```

In order for this header to be a valid XML-RPC header, the following conditions must be met:

- A `User-Agent` and `Host` must be specified.
- The `Content-Type` is `text/xml`.
- The `Content-Length` must be specified and must be correct.

The URI in the first line of the header is not restricted by the XML-RPC specification. However, using an identifier such as `/RPC2` helps when configuring servers in order to route RPC requests to the correct program.

Payload Format

The payload is an XML document with a `methodCall` root. `methodCall` must contain the following subelements:

- An obligatory methodName subelement, whose content is a free form string, identifying the method to be called. Note that this lack of constraint about methodName gives great flexibility to the mechanism; most times we will be using it to call methods in a class, but we could very well be giving the name of the file with a script to run.
- An optional set of param elements, wrapped in a params parent. Each param has a value, which is strongly typed according to the rules of the following section.

The following is an example of a typical payload:

```
<?xml version="1.0"?>
<methodCall>
   <methodName>Math.isPrime</methodName>
   <params>
      <param>
         <value><int>243</int></value>
      </param>
   </params>
</methodCall>
```

XML-RPC Types

The following are the allowed types of values in XML-RPC along with their respective examples and Java equivalents:

INT (OR I4)

An int is a four-byte signed integer:

```
<?xml version="1.0"?>
<methodCall>
   <methodName>Math.isPrime</methodName>
   <params>
      <param>
         <value><i4>243</i4></value>
      </param>
   </params>
</methodCall>
```

BOOLEAN

A boolean type can take one of two values: 0 (for false) and 1 (for true):

```
<?xml version="1.0"?>
<methodCall>
   <methodName>Logic.XOR</methodName>
   <params>
      <param>
```

```
            <value><boolean>1</boolean></value>
        </param>
        <param>
            <value><boolean>0</boolean></value>
        </param>
    </params>
</methodCall>
```

STRING

A simple ASCII string (this is arguably one of the less appealing limitations of XML-RPC):

```
<?xml version="1.0"?>
<methodCall>
    <methodName>StringUtil.reverse</methodName>
    <params>
        <param>
            <value><string>atiras eid</string></value>
        </param>
    </params>
</methodCall>
```

DOUBLE

A double-precision signed floating point number.

```
<?xml version="1.0"?>
<methodCall>
    <methodName>Math.log</methodName>
    <params>
        <param>
            <value><double>-232.221</double></value>
        </param>
    </params>
</methodCall>
```

DATETIME.ISO8601

A string representing time according to the 8601 standard:

```
<?xml version="1.0"?>
<methodCall>
    <methodName>Math.log</methodName>
    <params>
        <param>
            <value><double>19960704T14:08:55</double></value>
        </param>
    </params>
</methodCall>
```

BASE64

base64-encoded binary is especially useful for the transfer of images, sounds, or any other type of binary data embedded in an XML document. This is because a file encoded in base64 will not contain characters that could be interpreted as markup. The following example shows the base64 encoding for a small GIF image:

```
<?xml version="1.0"?>
<methodCall>
   <methodName>Images.submitToArchive</methodName>
   <params>
      <param>
         <value>
         <base64>
R0lGODlhHQAdALMAAO8QAPcxAPdCAPdKAPdSAPdaAPdrAPd7APelAP8IAP8YAP8hA
P/OAP/nAP//AP///ywAAAAAHQAdAEAE/lAhRyttGCHGz0FHIRqHYWhMY1kNA3rae7
jHMBAF47QqhrmgwgYY23gEugsHqNqBUr6oz7Cq7jKzBip08xgCwgPgUNG+NIOJg5A
YlISk8hLa48SgV5+jMEg2lXNLUlIBf1U+DB92HwYiBV5Whzs0HzBBBGSRgBx1KS8q
DAQEAQgYBQtkLZ43OBsbBWAeojksnIh2Q1G4CAUsPKopiTCDUQNUFz+eKLZ5gwpJh
z+KNEGOJQcCmsgtWYmXOCXQmnouLUNcJ9pyvI4FJB4lxnNWPIIVNDoN2E4e4ubLCG
wMECCAxJACChI0WZAg05IvJAbcU7AgIoFGbnA1o2FMwxuDOTLcNCH2b9mSIi9qCUo
GxNagRHJcYnBAZMPMQRLL6Ini4AABmyQbCFBzhcYjXCmaDeJjCFkgmcQiAAA7
         </base64>
        </value>
      </param>
   </params>
</methodCall>
```

STRUCTS

A structure is made out of members. Each member has a value, which can in turn be an instance of one of the scalar types above, or another structure, thus allowing the creation of complex recursive structures:

```
<?xml version="1.0"?>
<methodCall>
   <methodName>Images.submitToArchive</methodName>
   <params>
      <param>
          <value>
           <struct>
             <member>
              <name>lowerBound</name>
               <value><i4>18</i4></value>
              </member>
             <member>
              <name>upperBound</name>
               <value><i4>139</i4></value>
            </member>
          </struct>
        </value>
```

```
      </param>
   </params>
</methodCall>
```

ARRAYS

Arrays have a single data element, which contains all the values of the array. Arrays need not have homogeneous content (i.e. different values of the array can have different types, including structs).

```
<?xml version="1.0"?>
<methodCall>
   <methodName>Images.submitToArchive</methodName>
   <params>
      <param>
          <value>
            <array>
              <data>
                <value><i4>12</i4></value>
                <value><string>Egypt</string></value>
                <value><boolean>0</boolean></value>
                <value><i4>-31</i4></value>
              </data>
            </array>
         </value>
      </param>
   </params>
</methodCall>
```

Response Format

The response must come in the form of a methodResponse element, which can contain either a params element, with only one param (the result); or a fault element with two subelements: faultCode (an int) and faultString (a string).

```
HTTP/1.1 200 OK
Connection: close
Content-Length: 158
Content-Type: text/xml
Date: Fri, 13 Jul 1999 13:25:08 GMT
Server: Human Resources Rubbish Generator


<?xml version="1.0"?>
<methodResponse>
   <params>
      <param>
          <value>
            <string>We leverage the Synergy of our customers…
blah.</string>
```

```
            </value>
        </param>
    </params>
</methodResponse>
```

Regarding the HTTP headers, the following are the restrictions for the response:

- Unless there's a lower-level error, always return 200 OK.
- `Content-Length` is present and correct.
- The `Content-Type` is `text/xml`. `Content-Length` must be present and correct.

Finally, Table 17.1 shows the correspondence between XML-RPC and the Java implementation.

TABLE 17.1
XML-RPC vs Java types.

XML-RPC data type	Java Types
<i4> or <int>	int
<boolean>	boolean
<string>	java.lang.String
<double>	double
<dateTime.iso8601>	java.util.Date
<struct>	java.util.Hashtable
<array>	java.util.Vector
<base64>	byte[ ]

Now that we have covered the whole XML-RPC Spec, it is time to take a look at the available implementation toolkits and their use in a simple B2B application.

Implementation Toolkits

The following list is the most updated version of XML-RPC implementations at the time of this writing (October 2000):[6]

[6] It was obtained from the official xml-rpc.com site.

PYTHON
Author: PythonWare; [http://www.pythonware.com/products/xmlrpc]

JAVA
Author: Hannes Wallnöfer; [http://helma.at/hannes/xmlrpc/]; Author: Josh Lucas; [http://www.stonecottage.com/josh/rpcClient.html] (client only)

PERL
Author: Ken MacLeod; [http://bitsko.slc.ut.us/~ken/xml-rpc/]

TCL
Author: Steve Ball; [http://www.zveno.com/zm.cgi/in-tclxml/in-xmlrpc.html]
Author: Vitessa; [http://www.vitessa.net/opensource/] (client for Tcl 7.6)

ASP
Author: David Carter-Tod; [http://www.wc.cc.va.us/dtod/XMLRPC/]

COM
Author: Steven Livingstone; [http://www.deltabiz.com/xmlrpc/default.asp]

PHP
Author: Useful Inc.; [http://usefulinc.com/xmlrpc/]

ZOPE
Author: Zope 2.0 (built-in support); [http://www.zope.org/Members/Amos/XML-RPC]

APPLESCRIPT
Author: Late Night Software; [http://www.latenightsw.com/freeware/XMLTools2/xml-rpc.html]

REBOL
Author: Thomas Jensen; [http://www.obscure.dk/rebol/]
Author: Chris Langreiter; [http://www.langreiter.com/space/RXR]

A B2B Application Using XML-RPC: DVD Price Comparison

Before we close our discussion about XML-RPC, let's construct an XML-RPC application that will fulfill the following requirements:

- Given a particular string, a remote service will tell us the names and unique IDs of similar movies (e.g. for "shining" the server will return "the shining" with id "22212313" and "The making of the Shining" with id "23113142").
- From that list of movies, the user can select one, and several services across the net will be queried for the price they ask for the movie.

One particularly interesting thing about this application is that it shows how XML-RPC can be put to work in B2B applications where the promise of "programming to the interface, not to the implementation" can be finally achieved. Two different implementations of the service, one with a fixed price for all DVDs, and one that looks up the DVD in a database, are provided.

Architecture

The architecture of the system is portrayed in Figure 17.4. Basically, the idea is to have two JSP pages,[7] which query two different types of services: one for the movie data, and one for the price information. Different implementations of the service will have different ways of processing the request, but that is irrelevant for our clients, who only have to know about the interface of the services, not their inner-workings.

The DVDTitles Service

This service will provide three methods to the user:

- **HashTable getTitlesList(String candidateTitle)**—Given a candidate DVD title, the service returns a hashtable with all the matching titles from the database.

[7] They could easily have been ASP or PHP; we chose JSP to maintain continuity with the previous examples.

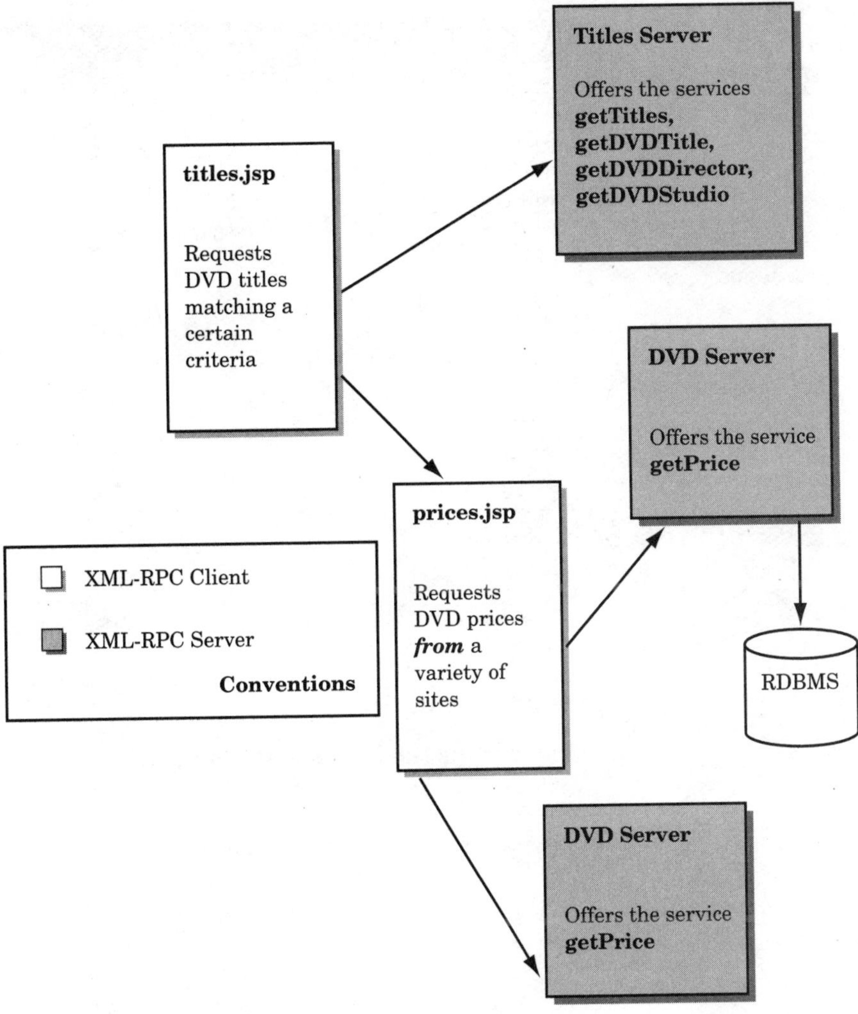

Figure 17.4 The DVD comparison system architecture.

- **int getDVDYear(String MovieID)**—Given a DVD, the service returns its release year.
- **String getDVDDirector(String MovieID)**—Given a DVD movie, the service returns its director.

All these services will be implemented using an underlying relational database. In this case we will use the simple Microsoft Access database whose only table is shown in Figure 17.5 (also included on the CD).

Figure 17.5
The DVDs database.

DVDs : Table

Field Name	Data Type	De
DVDId	AutoNumber	
DVDTitle	Text	
DVDYear	Number	
DVDDirector	Text	
DVDPrice	Number	

Field Properties

Implementation

The following is the implementation of the DVDTitles service:

```
import java.sql.  Connection;
import java.sql.  DriverManager;
import java.sql.  Statement;
import java.sql.  ResultSet;
import java.util. Properties;
import java.util. Vector;
import java.io.   FileInputStream;
import java.util. Hashtable;

public class DVDTitles
{
```

NOTE

In addition to the mentioned methods, this service must offer a constructor that reads the parameters of the `DataBase` *connection.*

```
    public DVDTitles(String DBProperties)
                   throws java.lang.Exception
    {
     try
```

```
    {
  myDB.load(new FileInputStream(DBProperties));
      Class.forName(myDB.getProperty("driver"));
      conn = DriverManager.getConnection
              (myDB.getProperty("URL"),
                     myDB.getProperty("user"),
                     myDB.getProperty("password"));
 }
    catch (java.lang.Exception e)
    {
     System.out.println("Failed to connect with the database
                        " + e);
     throw e;
 }
}
```

NOTE

This method is interesting because it shows a return type that is not scalar in XML-RPC. This return type (Hashtable) will be converted to the tag `struct`.

```
Hashtable getTitlesList(String candidateTitle)
                    throws java.lang.Exception
{
 try
 {
      Statement stmt = conn.createStatement();
      rs = stmt.executeQuery("SELECT DVDTITLE,DVDID FROM "
                          +  myDB.getProperty("table")
                +  "WHERE DVDTITLE LIKE"
                +  candidateTitle);
  Hashtable res = new Hashtable();
  while(rs.next())
  {
       res.put(rs.getString("DVDID"),
            rs.getString("DVDTITLE"));
  }
  return res;
 }
   catch (java.lang.Exception sqle)
   {
     System.out.println("SQL or NullPointer Exception:
                        " + sqle);
     throw sqle;
   }

 }

 int getDVDYear(String movieID)
              throws java.sql.SQLException
 {
  try
```

```
{
     Statement stmt = conn.createStatement();
     rs = stmt.executeQuery("SELECT DVDPRICE FROM "
                           + myDB.getProperty("table")
                 + "WHERE DVDID equals"
                 + movieID);

 return rs.getInt(0);
}
   catch (java.sql.SQLException sqle)
   {
     System.out.println("SQL Exception: " + sqle);
     throw sqle;
   }

}


String getDVDDirector(String movieID)
                     throws java.sql.SQLException
{
 try
 {
     Statement stmt = conn.createStatement();
     rs = stmt.executeQuery("SELECT DVDDIRECTOR FROM "
                           + myDB.getProperty("table")
                 + "WHERE DVDID equals"
                 + movieID);

 return rs.getString(0);
 }
   catch (java.sql.SQLException sqle)
   {
     System.out.println("SQL Exception: " + sqle);
     throw sqle;
   }

}

   Connection conn = null;
   ResultSet rs = null;
   Properties myDB = new Properties();
}
```

The DVDTitles Server

The server makes the `DVDTitle` service available to the world, using an `XMLRPCServer`. Note how a Web server is embedded in the class, in order to make it easier to deploy a standalone deliverable:

```
import helma.xmlrpc.WebServer;

// make an XML-RPC server for DVDTitles

public class DVDTitlesServer
{
```

In your projects you might want to do a more detailed management of exceptions. They are not the focus here, but you should take them into account.

```
public static void main(String argv[])
        throws java.lang.Exception
{
     if(argv.length != 2){
        System.out.println("Usage: java DVDTitleServer"
                           + " [port] [properties]");
          System.exit(-1);
     }
WebServer ws = new WebServer(new Integer(argv[0]).intValue());
ws.addHandler("DVDTitles",new DVDTitles(argv[1]));
     }
}
```

The DVDPage Client

The `DVDPage` client is a JSP page (or standalone application) that acts as the XML-RPC client for the `DVDTitle` service. It connects to the XML-RPC and queries the `getTitles` service.

The HTML portion of the page with the headers, etc. is not relevant for our purposes. The following is the XML-RPC connection that creates the table with the names and titles of all the matching movies:

```
import helma.xmlrpc. XmlRpcClient;
import helma.xmlrpc. XmlRpc;
import java.util.    Enumeration;
import java.util.    Hashtable;
import java.util.    Vector;
```

NOTE

Embed the code in your page if you want JSP. In this text, the connection is provided as a standalone application in order to support those who don't want to install a servlet engine. The CD, however, contains the equivalent JSP page (the XMLRPC and table code is identical).

```
public class DVDTitleClient
{
    public static void main(String argv[])
                            throws java.io.IOException,

java.lang.ClassNotFoundException
    {
       Vector params = new Vector();
       try
       {
     if(argv.length != 2){
         System.out.println("Usage: java DVDTitleClient"
                             + " [host:port] [title]");
             System.exit(-1);
        }

     XmlRpcClient client = new XmlRpcClient(argv[0]);

        params.addElement(argv[1]);

     Hashtable result = (Hashtable)

client.execute("DVDTitles.getTitleList",
                                               params);


System.out.println("<table><tr><th>ID</th><th>Title</th></tr>");
     for (Enumeration e = result.keys() ; e.hasMoreElements() ;) {

             String id = (String) e.nextElement();
             System.out.println("<tr><td>" + id
                   + "</td><td>" + result.get(id) + "</td>");
        }

     System.out.println("</table>");
       }
       catch(helma.xmlrpc.XmlRpcException e)
       {
     System.out.println("!" + e);
       }
    }
}
```

The DVDPrices Service

Two implementations of this service are provided. In the first, a look-up to the database is made. In the second, a store with only one price is implemented. From the point of view of our client, there is no impact whatsoever, because all it cares about is the interface provided.

DVDPricesSQL

```
import java.sql.  Connection;
import java.sql.  DriverManager;
import java.sql.  Statement;
import java.sql.  ResultSet;
import java.util. Properties;
import java.util. Vector;
import java.io.   FileInputStream;
import java.util. Hashtable;

public class DVDPricesSQL
{

    public DVDPricesSQL(String DBProperties)
                  throws java.lang.Exception
    {
     try
        {
      myDB.load(new FileInputStream(DBProperties));
         Class.forName(myDB.getProperty("driver"));
         conn =
DriverManager.getConnection(myDB.getProperty("URL"),
                          myDB.getProperty("user"),
                          myDB.getProperty("password"));
      }
        catch (java.lang.Exception e)
        {
         System.out.println("Failed to connect with the database "
                           + e);
         throw e;
     }
    }

    double getPrice(String movieID)
                 throws java.sql.SQLException
    {
     try
     {
         Statement stmt = conn.createStatement();
         rs = stmt.executeQuery("SELECT DVDPRICE FROM "
                             +  myDB.getProperty("table")
                  +  "WHERE DVDID equals"
                  +  movieID);

      return rs.getInt(0);
     }
       catch (java.sql.SQLException sqle)
       {
         System.out.println("SQL Exception: " + sqle);
         throw sqle;
       }

     }
```

```
    Connection conn = null;
    ResultSet rs = null;
    Properties myDB = new Properties();
}
```

DVDPricesFixed

```
public class DVDPricesFixed
{
// All DVDs for only 21.99!
    double getPrice(String movieID)
    {
     return 21.99;
    }
}
```

DVDPricesServer

The following program sets up two different Web and XML-RPC servers, one listening on port 8081 and responding with fixed prices, and the other on 8082, responding with the database information.

```
import helma.xmlrpc.WebServer;

public class DVDPricesServer
{
    public static void main(String argv[])
           throws java.lang.Exception
   {
     if(argv.length != 1){
         System.out.println("Usage: java DVDPricesServer"
                               + " [SQL properties]");
            System.exit(-1);
        }

     WebServer ws = new WebServer(8081);
     ws.addHandler("DVDPrices",new DVDPricesFixed());

     WebServer ws2 = new WebServer(8082);
     ws2.addHandler("DVDPrices",new DVDPricesSQL(argv[0]));
    }
}
```

DVDPricesClient

The client for the `DVDPrices` servers has an internal vector with a list of all the sites it must query for price information. The following code shows how it queries them all, without any concern for their implementation, and prints out the results:

```
import helma.xmlrpc. XmlRpcClient;
import helma.xmlrpc. XmlRpc;
import java.util.    Enumeration;
import java.util.    Hashtable;
import java.util.    Vector;


// make an XML-RPC Client for DVDPriceClient
// Embbed the code in your page if you want jsp.
// In this distrubution, it is provided as a standalone
// application in order to suppor people who don't want to
// install a servlet engine

public class DVDPricesClient
{
    public static void main(String argv[])
                                throws java.io.IOException,

java.lang.ClassNotFoundException
    {
       Vector params = new Vector();
       Vector hosts =  new Vector();
       hosts.addElement("http://localhost:8081");
       hosts.addElement("http://localhost:8082");
       try
       {
     if(argv.length != 2){
         System.out.println("Usage: java DVDTitleClient"
                                 + "  [movieId]");
             System.exit(-1);
        }

     for(int i = 0 ; i < hosts.size() ; i ++)
        {
         XmlRpcClient client = new XmlRpcClient(

(String)hosts.elementAt(i)
                                          );
              params.addElement(argv[0]);
              Double value =
(Double)client.execute("DVDPrices.getPrice",
                                                  params);
          double price = value.doubleValue();
          System.out.println("The price in site " +
                                (String)hosts.elementAt(i) +
                 "is " + value);

     }
       }
       catch(helma.xmlrpc.XmlRpcException e)
       {
     System.out.println("!" + e);
       }
    }
}
```

Summary

This chapter treated XML-RPC, its syntax, rationale, implementations, and applications. Further steps with XML-RPC and other distributed computing environments can be found in Chapter 20, where we discuss SOAP in regard to another B2B example.

PART 5

Comprehensive Case Studies

CHAPTER 18

Presentational XML: CSS2, XHTML, SVG, and SMIL

Introduction

Throughout this book, presentational XML vocabularies have been used in order to present the results of our programs (the interface) to our users. We've also explored design and implementation techniques in presentational problems. However, presentational XML has been, so far, merely an ancillary point in our discussion, yet another element to explain other technologies.

This chapter focuses on XML presentational vocabularies. Four key presentational technologies are treated: in Chapters 18 and 19 XML + Cascading Stylesheets, XHTML, Scalable Vector Graphics (SVG), and SMIL (Synchronized Multimedia Language). The first of them will be presented here, with a theory introduction, examples, and a guide. The other three will be presented in Chapter 19 as parts of a complete application for multimedia content in XML.

XML + CSS

In this section we will explore the Cascading Style Sheets language and its relationship with generic XML. Traditionally, CSS has been a powerful tool for HTML developers, because of its ability to decouple HTML tags from very specific formatting issues. The following sections will show how to leverage the use of CSS to the XML world and the tradeoffs involved in doing so.

NOTE

At this moment, there are three versions of CSS: CSS1, released in December 1996 as a W3C recommendation; CSS2, released in May 1998; and CSS3, which is still at the stage of candidate recommendation at the time of this writing (November 2000). The concepts in this chapter apply largely to both CSS1 and CSS2, but are mainly focused to CSS2. The first and second versions of CSS are implemented only partially by the different browsers available.

NOTE

For the examples, the original spelling of "Niblungs" has been preserved from the original George Bernard Shaw text (available free from the Gutemberg Project).

A Hands-On Introduction to XML+CSS

The following XML document shows a small paragraph of George Bernard Shaw's comments about the Ring of the Niblungs. It was marked up using Docbook version 4.1.2:

```
<?xml version="1.0"?>
<!DOCTYPE book PUBLIC "-//OASIS//DTD DocBook XML V4.1.2//EN"
                "http://www.oasis-
open.org/docbook/xml/4.0/docbookx.dtd">

<book>
  <chapter>
    <title>The Ring Of The Niblungs</title>
      <para>The Ring consists of four plays, intended to be
             performed on four successive evenings, entitled The
             Rhine Gold (a prologue to the other three),The
             Valkyries, Siegfried, and Night Falls On The Gods;
             or, in the original German, <emphasis>Das
             Rheingold</emphasis>, <emphasis>Die
             Walkure</emphasis>,
             <emphasis>Siegfried</emphasis>, and <emphasis>Die
             Gotterdammerung</emphasis>.
      </para>
  </chapter>
</book>
```

Now, suppose you want to display this document in a browser using CSS. In order to do so, you write a CSS stylesheet, which is composed of rules. Each rule has a pattern and a body (Figure 18.1). For each element of the document which matches the pattern, the body of the rule (i.e. a set of formatting instructions) is applied.

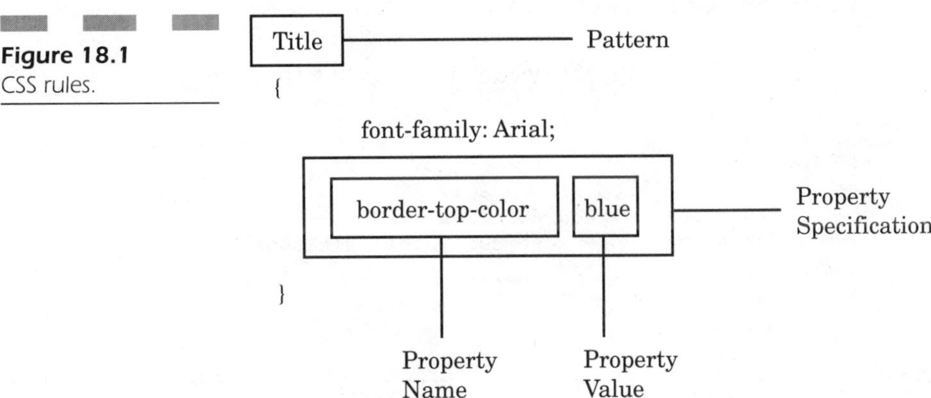

Figure 18.1
CSS rules.

The CSS stylesheet for our document can look like the following:

```
chapter
{
     display: block;
     background-color: #C0C0FF;
}
title
{
     display: block;
     font-family: Georgia;
     font-size: 30;
     color:   white;
     background-color: red;
     margin-left: 40pt;
}

para
    {
     display: block;
     color: black;
     font-family: Tahoma;
    }

emphasis
    {
     font-style: italic;
    }
```

The next natural step is to tie together the document and the stylesheet. This is achieved via the `xml:stylesheet` processing instruction. This PI can be included at the top of the document and may contain two attributes:

- href—The location of the stylesheet.
- type—The MIME type for the stylesheet. This can be text/css for CSS1 and CSS2 stylesheets.[1]

Once we add the PI, the document looks like the following:

```
<?xml version="1.0"?>
<!DOCTYPE book PUBLIC "-//OASIS//DTD DocBook XML V4.1.2//EN"
               "http://www.oasis-
open.org/docbook/xml/4.0/docbookx.dtd">
<?xml:stylesheet type="text/css" href="niblungs.css"?>
<book>
<!-- rest of the document unchanged -->
```

---

[1] The same technique can be used to associate XSLT stylesheets, using the appropriate MIME type (see Chapter 19).

When viewed with an XML-aware browser (such as Internet Explorer 5.5), the result is that shown in Figure 18.2.

Internet Explorer's default behavior is to fetch the DTD for a document if `DOCTYPE` is present. Docbook is a very large DTD and downloading it each time will undoubtedly slow your tests of the examples. An analogous file, with identical contents but no `DOCTYPE` in the prologue, is included on the CD as "niblungsSansDoctype.xml".

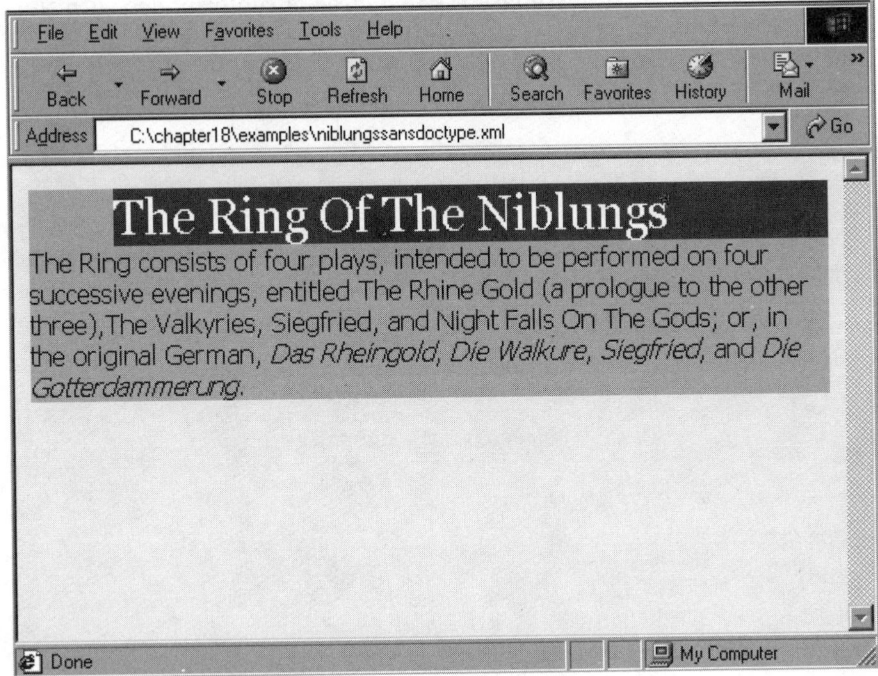

Figure 18.2 The Niblungs XML using CSS rendering.

XML + CSS Learning and Development Processes

Learning XML + CSS involves three steps:

- Understanding the basic syntax and mechanisms of the language (inheritance, modularization, etc.).
- Understanding the layout concepts behind the constructs of the language (boxes, nesting, etc.).
- Getting used to the vast number of properties provided by the language.

In the following sections we will see each of these points in the form of concise explanations and practical examples.

For the development of CSS stylesheets[2] you have several tools at your disposal (some of them are listed on the CD). This chapter will not delve into any of these tools, but you are encouraged to experiment with them, as they might be important time savers in your everyday XML development once you understand the inner workings of the language.

The Conformance/Portability Problem

Unfortunately, the degree of conformance with the specification between different implementations of CSS varies widely. The impact of this in projects with a wide audience is significant. Take, for example, the following document about a tennis tournament:

```
<?xml version="1.0" encoding="iso-8859-1"?>
<?xml-stylesheet type="text/css"
                 href="tennis.css"
                 media="screen"?>
<record xmlns:html="http://www.w3c.org/1999/xhtml">
   <player>Martina Hingis</player>
   <year>2000</year>

<tournament type="carpet">
   <name>Pan Pacific Open</name>
   <match round="2">
      <opponent>Raymond</opponent>
      <result win="yes">
          <set>
               <p>6</p>
               <o>3</o>
          </set>
          <set>
               <p>7</p>
               <o>5</o>
          </set>
      </result>
   </match>
   <match round="QF">
      <opponent>Kournikova</opponent>
      <result win="yes">
          <set>
               <p>6</p>
               <o>0</o>
          </set>
          <set>
               <p>6</p>
               <o>2</o>
          </set>
      </result>
   </match>
</tournament>
</record>
```

2 From now on, the acronym CSS will be used to denote CSS1 and CSS2 collectively. Where a differentiation of the version is needed, we will use the appropriate number.

Now take its stylesheet, which defines a very simple layout for the information, based on simple boxes and with a notable item: the use of different colors for the differentiation of winning and losing matches (result rules at the bottom):

```
@media screen, print
{
   tournament
   {
     display: block;
     margin-left: 40pt;
     font-family: Arial;
     font-size: 13pt;
   }

   player
   {
     display: inline;
     font-family: Verdana;
     font-size: 25pt;
     color: red;
   }

   year
   {
     display: inline;
     font-family: Verdana;
     font-size: 18pt;
     color: red;
   }

   tournament.name
   {
     display: block;
     margin-left: 42pt;
     font-family: Arial;
     font-size: 22pt;
     color: blue;
   }

   match
   {
     display: block;
     margin-left: 42pt;
     font-family: Arioso;
     font-size: 12pt;
     color: Green;
   }

   set
   {
     display: block;
  }
```

See how conditionals (for attributes) are expressed in a way similar to that of XPath.

```
result[win = "yes"]
   {
     color: red;
   }

   result[win = "no"]
   {
     color: blue;
   }

}
```

The result of displaying this document in two current browsers (Internet Explorer 5.5. and Mozilla Milestone 18) is shown in Figures 18.3 and 18.4.

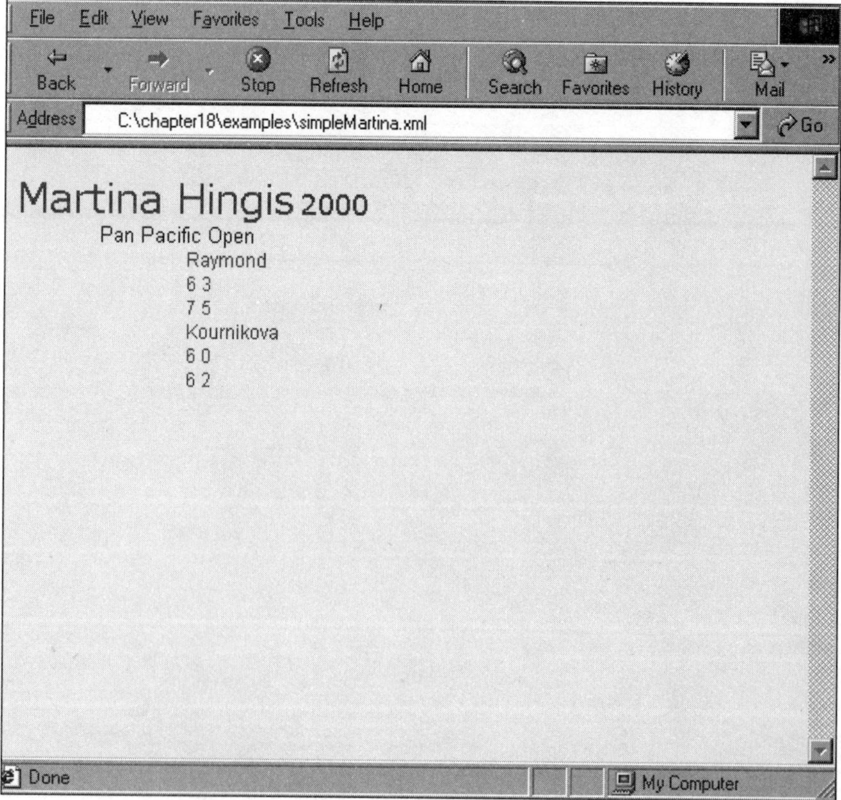

Figure 18.3
The martina.xml document in IE5.5.

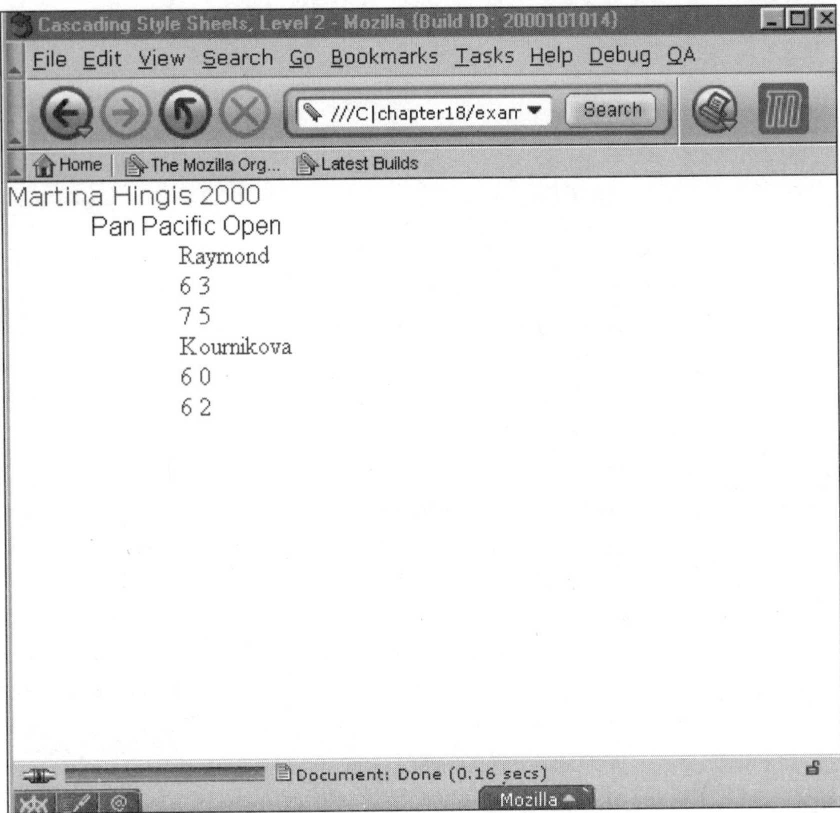

Figure 18.4
The martina.xml document in Mozilla M18.

As you can see, the rendering of the documents is not identical. Some of the items one would expect in the output are missing. For example, the colors are correctly represented in Mozilla, but they are not totally correct in IE5 (the names Raymond and Kournikova should be green and the scores red).

Glitches like this are not uncommon when working with CSS and one must be careful when deploying particularly robust applications, as they might compromise the portability of the product.

That being said, CSS is a very interesting language, full of options and helpful features for the precise rendering of information on browsers or printed media. The remaining part of this section formalizes some of the concepts behind CSS and its application in real-world XML projects.

Syntax and Mechanisms

This section will present the syntax and mechanisms of CSS; in particular, the ideas of rules, patterns, inheritance, and media selection. It is a condensed presentation of the most important sections about rules in the CSS2 specification.

Rules

Rules are the basic construction unit of CSS stylesheets. As shown previously, they are composed of a pattern and a body (Figure 18.1).

Patterns (Selectors)

When a processor goes through the document, applying the CSS stylesheet, it decides whether or not to apply a rule based on its selector. Selectors come in many flavors, but are all composed of the following elements:

- An initial simple selector.
- An optional list of more simple selectors, separated with combinators.

Simple Selectors

Simple selectors can be either `type` selectors or the `universal` selector.

A `type` selector matches the name of an element in the document. For example, the following rule applies a rather extreme color scheme to all `napier` elements in a document:

```
napier
{
     color: yellow;
     background-color: blue;
}
```

NOTE

It is important to remember that since XML is case sensitive, so are type selectors.

The universal selector is simply written as "*", and it matches the name of any element in the document.

Simple selectors can be immediately followed by zero or more attribute selectors, ID selectors, or pseudo-classes, in any order.

Attribute Selectors

It is very common to be interested in applying a style to an element only if it possesses some attribute—if an attribute has a certain value, etc. For such attribute-based selections, CSS provides an attribute selection mechanism.[3]

Attribute selectors may take four forms:

```
[att]
```

matches if the element possesses the attribute, regardless of its value. For example:

```
book[banned]
{
    color: red;
}
```

would present, in red, the element `<book banned="1978"/>`.

```
[att=val] or [att="val"]
```

matches if the element possesses the attribute `att`, and it has precisely a `val` value. For example:

```
artist[name="Fiona Apple"]
{
    color: blue;
}
```

```
[att~=val] or [att~="val"]
```

matches if the value of the element is a list of whitespace-separated words that includes `val`. For example, the following rule:

```
artist[name~="David"]
{
    color: red;
}
```

would match both `<artist name="David Bowie"/>` and `<artist name="David Byrne"/>`. Naturally, this type of selector becomes especially handy when used with attribute types such as `IDREFS` and `NMTOKENS`.

---

3 Actually, in CSS, the name attribute selector is sometimes confusing, because what is really being selected is the element that contains the attribute. The attribute selector is never used by itself; it is always a qualifier of a simple selector.

```
[att|=val] or [att|="val"]
```

matches if the value of the element is a list of hyphen-separated words that start with `val`. For example, the following rule:

```
*[xml:lang|="es"]
```

would match any language name that starts with es, such as `es-co` or `es-es`.[4]

It is important to note that more than one attribute selector can be added to a particular simple selector, as the following shows:

```
person[sex="female"][name~="Leni"]
{
    background-color: red;
}
```

ID Selectors

ID selectors allow the choosing of an element based on its ID attribute. In order to qualify a simple selector with an ID, add "#" followed by the expected ID. For example, the following rule:

```
SSN#212-215-4444
{
   letter-spacing: 0.5em;
}
```

would be applied to the SSN element with number 212-215-4444 in the following document:

```
<?xml version="1.0"?>
<!DOCTYPE persons [
     <!ELEMENT persons (person+)>
     <!ELEMENT person (SSN,name)>
     <!ENTITY % string          "#PCDATA">
     <!ENTITY % letter          "#PCDATA">
     <!ENTITY % english_def "xml:lang    NMTOKEN    'en'">

     <!ELEMENT name             (firstname,midinitial?,lastname)>
     <!ELEMENT firstname        (%string;)>
     <!ELEMENT midinitial       (%letter;)>
     <!ELEMENT lastname         (%string;)>
     <!ATTLIST name
```

4 As a matter of fact, this rather obscure attribute selector type was designed primarily for the language identification problem.

```
                %english_def;>

        <!ELEMENT SSN           (#PCDATA)>
        <!ATTLIST SSN
                number   ID     #REQUIRED>
]>

<persons>
<person>
  <SSN number="222-231-3525">Issued by the state of blah...</SSN>
  <name xml:lang="en">
    <firstname>Jhonny</firstname>
    <lastname>Mnemonic</lastname>
  </name>
</person>
<person>
  <SSN number="212-215-4444">Issued by the state of blah...</SSN>
  <name xml:lang="en">
    <firstname>Usnavy</firstname>
    <lastname>Litterman</lastname>
  </name>
</person>
</persons>
```

Note that the `ID` selector says nothing about the name of the `ID` attribute; that is inferred from the DTD. Since a vast majority of the documents on the Web lack DTD, relying on `ID` selectors might not be a good idea in many cases.

Pseudo-elements and Pseudo-classes

So far, we have seen ways to assign properties to elements, according to their position on the tree, or the characteristics of their attributes. This is all that's needed in most cases. However, sometimes one needs to identify elements using certain other criteria such as "The first child of an element" or "The element over which the mouse pointer is."

Pseudo-classes expand the range of addressable characteristics in an element (e.g. "is the mouse over the element?"). Similarly, *pseudo-elements* introduce a number of new concepts outside the document tree itself (e.g. "The first line of text", or "The first letter of a text").

The following paragraphs list all the pseudo-classes and pseudo-elements available.

THE :FIRST-CHILD PSEUDO-CLASS

`:first-child` matches an element if it is the first element of another.

```
chapter:first-chlid
```

```
{
    font-family: Tahoma;
}
```

THE LINK PSEUDO-CLASSES

CSS has a strong browser-oriented background; therefore, pseudo-classes such as `:link` and `:visited` are maintained in order to show purely browser-oriented features, such as differentiating the presentation of links which have been visited from those which have not.

```
A:link
{
  color: yellow;
}

A:visited
{
  color: red;
}
```

THE DYNAMIC PSEUDO-CLASSES

In the same vein as the link pseudo-classes, the dynamic pseudo-classes exist in order to provide custom behavior for common dynamic operations on browsers,[5] namely `:hover`, `:active`, and `:focus`.

The `:hover` pseudo-class applies while the user designates the element (e.g. when the mouse pointer is over a link). The `:active` pseudo-class applies while the user activates the element (e.g. between the mouse-down and mouse-up events). Finally, the `:focus` pseudo-class applies while the element has the focus (e.g. when a textbox is accepting keyboard events).

The section on XTHML (as well as the final example here) contains examples of the application of the dynamic pseudo-classes.

THE LANGUAGE PSEUDO-CLASS

The language pseudo-class is analogous to the `|=` attribute selector. It is used to discriminate according to the language property of the element.

```
para:lang("de")
{
    font-size: 20pt;
}
```

[5] Naturally, the specification refers not only to browsers, but generically to "Interactive User Agents."

Now that we have seen all the pseudo-classes, let's look at the three types of pseudo-elements.

THE :FIRST-LETTER PSEUDO-ELEMENT

The name of this pseudo-element is self-explanatory. The following rule expands our original stylesheet for the Niblungs in order to make the first letter a big, stylized capital:

```
para:first-letter { font-size: 300%;
                    font-family: Old English Text MT;
                        font-weight: bold; float: left;
    }
para
    {
      display: block;
      color: black;
      font-family: Tahoma;
    }
```

Figure 18.5 shows the result.

THE :FIRST-LINE PSEUDO-ELEMENT

Just like its `:first-letter` companion, the `:first-line` pseudo-element has very intuitive semantics. The following rule changes the first line of every paragraph to upper case:

```
para:first-line
{
     text-transform: uppercase;
}
```

Since `:first-line` and `:first-letter` are not exclusive, a stylesheet containing both can produce the result in Figure 18.6.

THE :BEFORE AND :AFTER PSEUDO-ELEMENTS

The last two types of pseudo-elements allow the inclusion of generated text before or after a matched element.

```
product[sale="yes"]:before
{
   content: "SALE!";
}
```

The final example contains more uses of this particular pseudo-element.

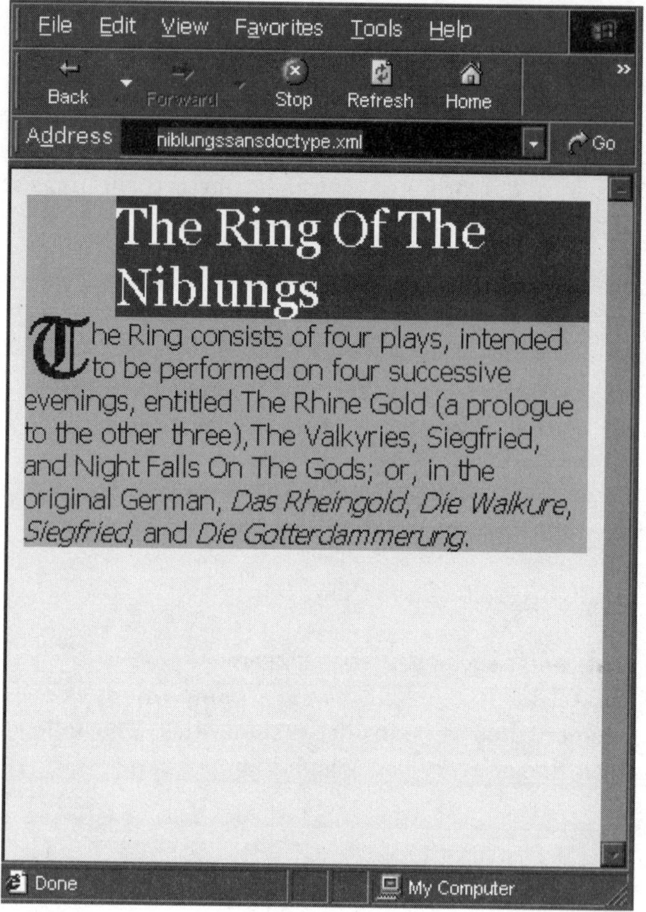

Figure 18.5 The :first-letter pseudo-element in use.

Complex Selectors

So far we have seen all the possibilities for simple selectors. Now it is time to compose selectors in order to specify relationships among them. There are three forms of relationships between elements in CSS: children, descendants, and siblings.[6]

Children are connected in rules using the > character, so in order to make a rule for all the paragraphs in a section, one could write the following:

```
section > para
{
```

[6] Therefore, complex selectors are classified as child, descendant, and adjacent sibling selectors.

Figure 18.6
The :first-line pseudo-element in use.

```
    letter-spacing: 0.3em;
}
```

Similarly, descendants are connected by whitespace, so in order to make a rule for all the paragraphs in a chapter, regardless of their section, one could write:

```
chapter[banned] para
{
    color: red;
}
```

Finally, the adjacent sibling selector uses the + character to separate selectors that share the same parent element and are contiguous. For example, the following rule states that a paragraph after an example should not be indented:

```
example + para
{
   text-indent: 0;
}
```

Table 18.1, taken from the CSS2 specification, summarizes the selector syntax.

TABLE 18.1
CSS selector syntax.

Pattern	Meaning
*	Matches any element
E	Matches any E element (i.e., an element of type E)
E F	Matches any F element that is a descendant of an E element
E > F	Matches any F element that is a child of an element E
E:first-child	Matches element E when E is the first child of its parent
E:link E:visited	Matches element E if E is the source anchor of a hyperlink of which the target is not yet visited (:link) or already visited (:visited)
E:active E:hover E:focus	Matches E during certain user actions
E:lang(c)	Matches element of type E if it is in (human) language c (the document language specifies how language is determined)
E + F	Matches any F element immediately preceded by an element E
E[foo]	Matches any E element with the “foo” attribute set (whatever the value)
E[foo=“warning”]	Matches any E element whose “foo” attribute value is exactly equal to “warning”
E[foo~=“warning”]	Matches any E element whose “foo” attribute value is a list of space-separated values, one of which is exactly equal to “warning”
E[lang|=“en”]	Matches any E element whose “lang” attribute has a hyphen-separated list of values beginning (from the left) with “en”
DIV.warning	HTML only. The same as DIV[class~=“warning”]
E#myid	Matches any E element ID equal to “myid”

Inheritance

In order to continue with our discussion of the syntax and mechanisms of CSS, we must introduce the notion of inheritance.

In the context of CSS, inheritance does not refer to a specific relationship between the rules, but rather an implied relationship in their application when treating nested elements. In other words you don't specify that a rule "inherits" from some other; instead, if a rule applies to an element, it will continue to apply to its subelements unless it is overwritten.

A simple example of this is the following stylesheet, in which the color property for the paragraph is applied not only to its own text, but to that of its subelements (like emphasis). Note that this doesn't prevent the subelements from having rules of their own.

```
paragraph
{
     color: red;
}
emphasis
{
     font-style: italic;
}
```

With the above stylesheet, an emphasis element inside a paragraph will show in red with italics.

Media

An `@media` rule specifies the target devices (separated by commas) of a set of rules. For example, using the `@media` rule, one can specify different rules for print or paper, all in the same stylesheet.

```
@media screen
{

  TITLE
  {
     display: block;
     font-family: Benguiat Bk BT;
     font-size: 26pt;
     color: blue;
     text-align: center;
  }

}
```

```
@media print
{

  TITLE
  {
     display: block;
     font-family: Arial;
     font-size: 25pt;
     color: black;
     text-align: center;
  }

}
```

In order to indicate the right media to use, the `xml-stylesheet` PI provides the media attribute:

```
<?xml-stylesheet href="play.css" type="text/css" media="screen"?>
```

CSS Visual Box Model

So far we have seen in detail *how* to create CSS rules, but we have only mentioned *what* to do with them. In order to make the most of CSS, we must understand the nature of its underlying model.

The whole CSS model is based on the idea of boxes. Each box has a *content* area and surrounding *padding*, *border*, and *margin* areas. (The different properties for the manipulation of those dimensions are shown in the example below and enumerated in the properties guide). Figure 18.7 shows these areas as graphically defined by the Specification.

Boxes may not only have visual properties of their own, like color, margins, etc., but they may contain other boxes. The properties of those boxes (like margins) are relative to their containing boxes.

Boxes can have different positioning schemes, namely normal flow, floats, and absolute positioning. The examples in this chapter show only normal flow of boxes, but you are encouraged to play with floating boxes or absolute position boxes to give your pages different effects.

Finally, there are the properties that can be applied in a particular rule. The number of available properties makes it impossible to go through each of them in this chapter; however, a complete enumeration of all properties (with brief descriptions) is included, and several key properties are shown in the following complete example.

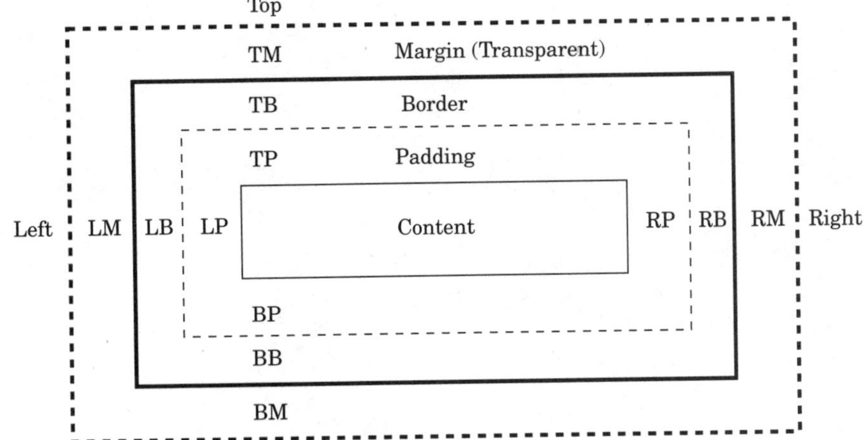

Figure 18.7
The Spec image for box dimensions.

Complete Example

The following example shows key elements of Web-oriented CSS formatting, including inline vs. block boxes, margins, fonts, and colors.

The example shows the visual formatting of the XML version of the play *Richard II* by William Shakespeare. (XML's father, Jon Bosak, made the original XML version of this and other Shakespeare plays.)

The XML Document

The original XML document is a collection of acts, each filled with speeches and stage directions. Additionally, a description of the personae and copyright information is given at the top. The following is an abridged version of the document:

```
<?xml version="1.0"?>
```

NOTE

The xml-stylesheet PI is included in order to link the play.css stylesheet to the document.

```
<?xml-stylesheet href="play.css" type="text/css" media="screen"?>

<PLAY>
<TITLE>The Tragedy of King Richard the Second</TITLE>

<FM>
```

```
<P>ASCII text placed in the public domain by Moby Lexical Tools,
1992.</P>
<P>SGML markup by Jon Bosak, 1992-1994.</P>
<P>XML version by Jon Bosak, 1996-1999.</P>
<P>The XML markup in this version is Copyright &#169; 1999 Jon
Bosak.
This work may freely be distributed on condition that it not be
modified or altered in any way.</P>
</FM>

<PERSONAE>
<TITLE>Dramatis Personae</TITLE>

<PERSONA>KING RICHARD, the Second. </PERSONA>

<PGROUP>
<PERSONA>JOHN OF GAUNT, Duke of Lancaster    </PERSONA>
<PERSONA>EDMUND OF LANGLEY, Duke of York  </PERSONA>
<GRPDESCR>uncles to the King.</GRPDESCR>
</PGROUP>

<PERSONA>HENRY, surnamed BOLINGBROKE, Duke of Hereford</PERSONA>
<PERSONA>son to John of Gaunt; afterwards King Henry
IV.</PERSONA>
<PERSONA>DUKE OF AUMERLE, son to the Duke of York.</PERSONA>
<PERSONA>THOMAS MOWBRAY, Duke of Norfolk.</PERSONA>
<PERSONA>DUKE OF SURREY</PERSONA>
<PERSONA>EARL OF SALISBURY</PERSONA>
<PERSONA>LORD BERKELEY</PERSONA>

<PGROUP>
<PERSONA>BUSHY</PERSONA>
<PERSONA>BAGOT</PERSONA>
<PERSONA>GREEN</PERSONA>
<GRPDESCR>servants to King Richard.</GRPDESCR>
</PGROUP>

<PERSONA>EARL OF NORTHUMBERLAND</PERSONA>
<PERSONA>HENRY PERCY, surnamed HOTSPUR, his son. </PERSONA>
<PERSONA>LORD ROSS</PERSONA>
<PERSONA>LORD WILLOUGHBY</PERSONA>
<PERSONA>LORD FITZWATER</PERSONA>
<PERSONA>BISHOP OF CARLISLE</PERSONA>
<PERSONA>Abbot Of Westminster</PERSONA>
<PERSONA>LORD MARSHAL</PERSONA>
<PERSONA>SIR STEPHEN SCROOP</PERSONA>
<PERSONA>SIR PIERCE OF EXTON</PERSONA>
<PERSONA>Captain of a band of Welshmen. </PERSONA>
<PERSONA>QUEEN to King Richard</PERSONA>
<PERSONA>DUCHESS OF YORK</PERSONA>
<PERSONA>DUCHESS OF GLOUCESTER</PERSONA>
<PERSONA>Lady attending on the Queen. </PERSONA>
<PERSONA>Lords, Heralds, Officers, Soldiers, two Gardeners,
Keeper, Messenger, Groom, and other Attendants. </PERSONA>
```

```
</PERSONAE>

<SCNDESCR>SCENE  England and Wales.</SCNDESCR>

<PLAYSUBT>KING RICHARD II</PLAYSUBT>

<ACT><TITLE>ACT I</TITLE>

<SCENE><TITLE>SCENE I.  London. KING RICHARD II's palace.</TITLE>
<STAGEDIR>Enter KING RICHARD II, JOHN OF GAUNT, with other
Nobles and Attendants</STAGEDIR>

<SPEECH>
<SPEAKER>KING RICHARD II</SPEAKER>
<LINE>Old John of Gaunt, time-honour'd Lancaster,</LINE>
<LINE>Hast thou, according to thy oath and band,</LINE>
<LINE>Brought hither Henry Hereford thy bold son,</LINE>
<LINE>Here to make good the boisterous late appeal,</LINE>
<LINE>Which then our leisure would not let us hear,</LINE>
<LINE>Against the Duke of Norfolk, Thomas Mowbray?</LINE>
</SPEECH>

<SPEECH>
<SPEAKER>JOHN OF GAUNT</SPEAKER>
<LINE>I have, my liege.</LINE>
</SPEECH>

<SPEECH>
<SPEAKER>KING RICHARD II</SPEAKER>
<LINE>Tell me, moreover, hast thou sounded him,</LINE>
<LINE>If he appeal the duke on ancient malice;</LINE>
<LINE>Or worthily, as a good subject should,</LINE>
<LINE>On some known ground of treachery in him?</LINE>
</SPEECH>

<SPEECH>
<SPEAKER>JOHN OF GAUNT</SPEAKER>
<LINE>As near as I could sift him on that argument,</LINE>
<LINE>On some apparent danger seen in him</LINE>
<LINE>Aim'd at your highness, no inveterate malice.</LINE>
</SPEECH>

<SPEECH>
<SPEAKER>KING RICHARD II</SPEAKER>
<LINE>Then call them to our presence; face to face,</LINE>
<LINE>And frowning brow to brow, ourselves will hear</LINE>
<LINE>The accuser and the accused freely speak:</LINE>
<LINE>High-stomach'd are they both, and full of ire,</LINE>
<LINE>In rage deaf as the sea, hasty as fire.</LINE>
</SPEECH>

<STAGEDIR>Enter HENRY BOLINGBROKE and THOMAS MOWBRAY</STAGEDIR>
… all other acts and speeches here (5363 lines) …
```

The CSS Stylesheet

The CSS stylesheet used to present the play in a browser is the following:

```
@media screen
{

  PLAY>TITLE
  {
     display: block;
     font-family: Benguiat Bk BT;
     font-size: 26pt;
     color: black;
     text-align: center;
  }

  FM
  {
     display: block;
     font-family: Arial;
     margin-left: 75pt;
     margin-right: 75pt;
     border-width: thin;
     font-size: 8pt;
     color: red;
  }

/** note the inheritance between personae and title (obvious in
the presentation of margins) **/
  PERSONAE
  {
     display: block;
     font-family: Garamond;
     color: black;
     margin-left: 15pt;
  }

  PERSONAE>TITLE
  {
     display: block;
     font-size: 18pt;
     color: black;
     margin-left: 10pt;
  }

  PGROUP>GRPDESCR
  {
     display: block;
     font-size: 10pt;
     color: black;
     margin-left: 32pt;
  }
```

```
  PERSONA
  {
     display: block;
     font-family: Garamond;
     color: black;
     margin-left: 15pt;
  }

  PERSONA:before
  {
     display: marker;
        content: url("bullet.gif");
  }
}
```

The above rules format the headers of the document, producing output such as the one in Figure 18.8 (using Mozilla M18).

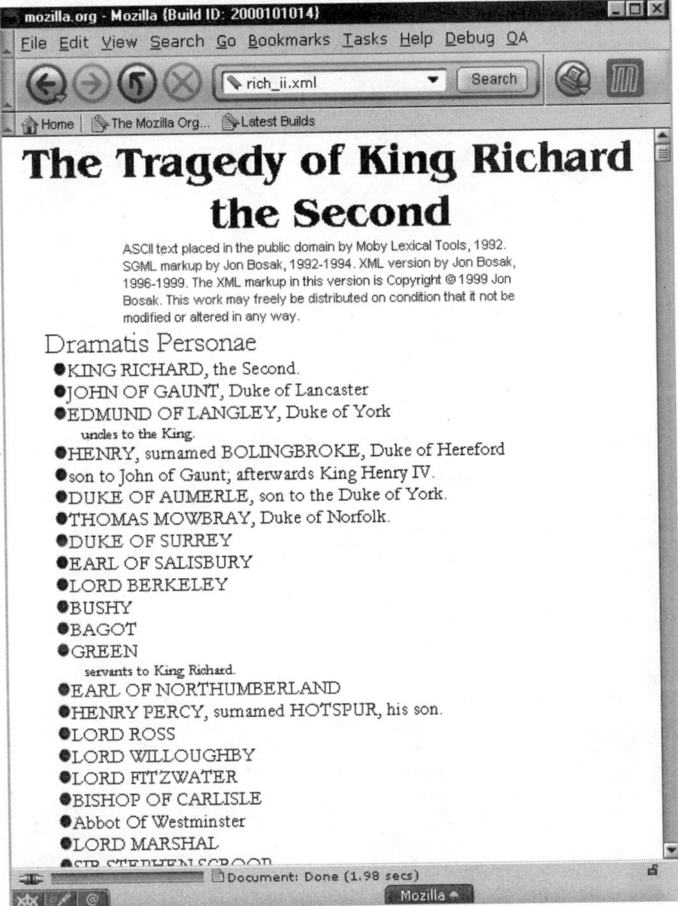

Figure 18.8 Headers and personae of the play.

Let's complement the CSS stylesheet with rules that present the acts and speeches:

```
ACT>TITLE
{
   display: block;
   font-family: Bakersville Old Face;
   font-size: 22pt;
   color: black;
   text-align: center;
}

PLAYSUBT
{
   display: block;
   font-family: Algerian;
   font-size: 26pt;
   color: black;
   text-align: center;
   margin-top: 18pt;
}

SCENE>TITLE
{
   display: block;
   font-family: Bakersville Old Face;
   font-size: 16pt;
   color: black;
   text-align: center;
      border: solid black;
}

SCNDESCR, STAGEDIR
{
   display: block;
   font-family: Times New Roman;
   font-size: 12pt;
   color: red;
   margin-left: 30pt;
   margin-top: 10pt;
}

SPEECH
{
   display: block;
   font-family: Times New Roman;
   font-size: 12pt;
   color: black;
   margin-left: 7pt;
   margin-top: 7pt;
}

SPEECH>SPEAKER
```

```
{
   display: inline;
   font-weight: bold;
}
```

The final result, as seen with Mozilla, is shown in Figure 18.9.

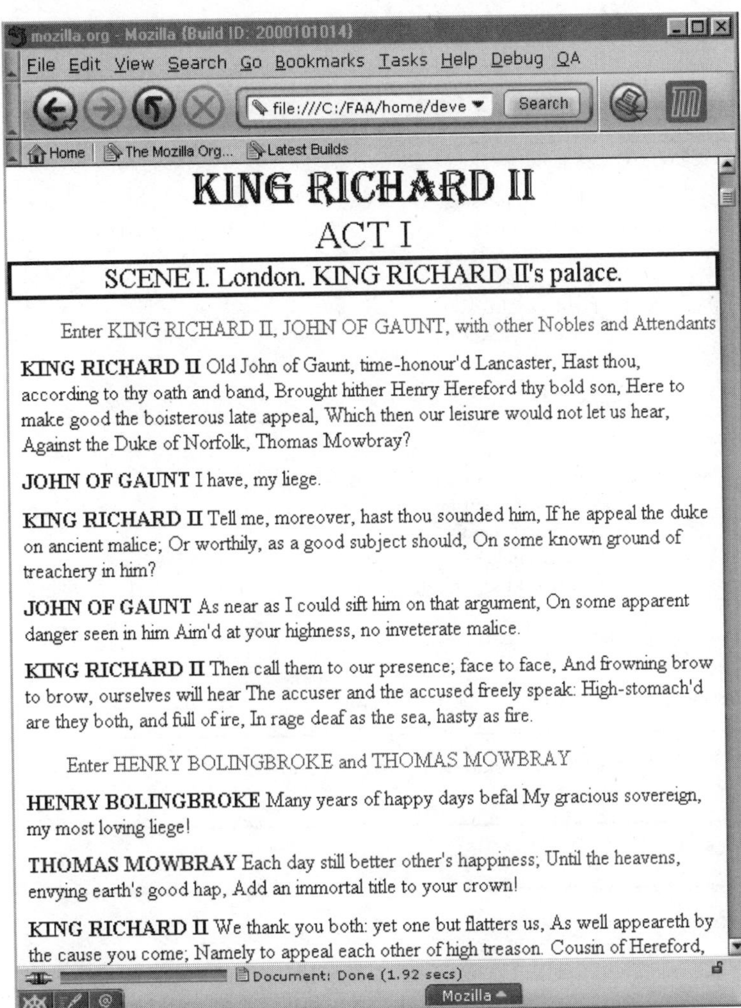

Figure 18.9
The acts of the play.

Summary

CSS has played a very important role in the development of a better HTML-based Web. Now, with XML, it is still relevant and useful, and even when it doesn't provide the flexibility and general power of XSLT, it can prove an essential tool for Web XML developers.

We conclude our CSS exploration by providing a complete enumeration of all the properties in the specification, for reference purposes.[7]

Property Index

Name	Values	Initial value	Applies to (Default: all)	Inherited?	Percentages (Default: N/A)
'azimuth'	<angle> | [[left-side | far-left | left | center-left | center | center-right | right | far-right | right-side] | | behind] | leftwards | rightwards | inherit	center		yes	
'background'	['background-color' | | 'background-image' | | 'background-position' 'background-repeat' | | 'background-attachment' | | 'background-position'] | inherit	XX		no	allowed on
'background-attachment'	scroll | fixed | inherit	scroll		no	
'background -color'	<color> | transparent | inherit	transparent		no	
'background-image"	<uri> | none | inherit	none		no	
'background-position'	[[<percentage> | <length>]{1,2} | [[top | center | bottom] | | [left | center | right]]] | inherit	0% 0%	block-level and replaced elements	no	refer to the size of the box itself

[7] This table has been taken from the original W3C CSS2 Recommendation.

Name	Values	Initial value	Applies to (Default: all)	Inherited?	Percentages (Default: N/A)
'background-repeat'	repeat | repeat-x | repeat-y | no-repeat | inherit	repeat		no	
'border'	['border-width' | | 'border-style' | | <color>] | inherit	see individual properties		no	
'border-collapse'	collapse | separate | inherit	collapse	'table' and 'inline-table' elements	yes	
'border-color'	<color>{1,4} | transparent | inherit	see individual properties		no	
'border-spacing'	<length><length>? | inherit	0	'table' and 'inline-table' elements	yes	
'border-style'	<border-style>{1,4} | inherit	see individual properties		no	
'border-top' 'border-right' 'border-bottom' 'border-left'	['border-top-width' | | 'border-style' | | <color>] | inherit	see individual properties		no	
"border-top-color' 'border-right-color' 'border-bottom-color' 'border-left-color'	<color> | inherit	the value of the 'color' property		no	
'border-top-style' 'border-right-style' 'border-bottom-style' 'border-left-style'	<border-style> | inherit	none		no	
'border-top-width' 'border-right-width' 'border-bottom-width' "border-left-width'	<border-width> | inherit	medium		no	
'border-width'	<border-width> {1,4} | inherit	see individual properties		no	

Name	Values	Initial value	Applies to (Default: all)	Inherited?	Percentages (Default: N/A)
'bottom'	<length> | <percentage> | auto | inherit	auto	positioned elements	no	refer to height of containing block
'caption-side'	top | bottom | left | right | inherit	top	'table-caption' elements	yes	
'clear'	none | left | right | both | inherit	none	block-level elements	no	
'clip'	<shape> | auto | inherit	auto	block-level and replaced elements	no	
'color'	<color> | inherit	depends on user agent		yes	
'content'	[<string> | <uri> | <counter> | attr(X) | open-quote | close-quote | no-open-quote | no-close-quote]+ | inherit	empty string	:before and :after pseudo-elements	no	
'counter-increment'	[<identifier> <integer>?]+ | none | inherit	none		no	
'counter-reset'	[<identifier> <integer>?]+ | none | inherit	none		no	
'cue'	['cue-before' || 'cue-after'] | inherit	XX		no	
'cue-after'	<uri> | none | inherit	none		no	
'cue-before'	<uri> | none | inherit	none		no	

Name	Values	Initial value	Applies to (Default: all)	Inherited?	Percentages (Default: N/A)
'cursor'	[[<uri> ,]* [auto | crosshair | default | pointer | move | e-resize | ne-resize | nw-resize | n-resize | se-resize | sw-resize | s-resize | w-resize | text | wait | help]] | inherit	auto		yes	
'direction'	ltr | rtl | inherit	ltr	all elements, but see prose	yes	
'display'	inline | block | list-item | run-in | compact | marker | table | inline-table | table-row-group | table-header-group | table-footer-group | table-row | table-column-group | table-column | table-cell | table-caption | none | inherit	inline		no	
'elevation'	<angle> | below | level | above | higher | lower | inherit	level		yes	
'empty-cells'	show | hide | inherit	show	'table-cell' elements	yes	
'float'	left | right | none | inherit	none	all but positioned elements and generated content	no	

<table>
<tr><th>Name</th><th>Values</th><th>Initial value</th><th>Applies to (Default: all)</th><th>Inherited?</th><th>Percentages (Default: N/A)</th></tr>
<tr><td>'font'</td><td>[['font-style' | | 'font-variant' | | 'font-weight']? 'font-size' [/ 'line-height']? 'font-family'] | caption | icon | menu | message-box | small-caption | status-bar | inherit</td><td>see individual properties</td><td></td><td>yes</td><td>allowed on 'font-size' and 'line-height'</td></tr>
<tr><td>'font-family'</td><td>[[<family-name> | <generic-family>],]* [<family-name> | <generic-family>] | inherit</td><td>depends on user agent</td><td></td><td>yes</td><td></td></tr>
<tr><td>'font-size"</td><td><absolute-size> | <relative-size> | <length> | <percentage> | inherit</td><td>medium</td><td>yes, the computed value is inherited</td><td></td><td>refer to parent element's font size</td></tr>
<tr><td>'font-size-adjust'</td><td><number> | none | inherit</td><td>none</td><td></td><td>yes</td><td></td></tr>
<tr><td>'font-stretch'</td><td>normal | wider | narrower | ultra-condensed | extra-condensed | condensed | semi-condensed | semi-expanded | expanded | extra-expanded | ultra-expanded | inherit</td><td>normal</td><td></td><td>yes</td><td></td></tr>
<tr><td>'font-style'</td><td>normal | italic | oblique | inherit</td><td>normal</td><td></td><td>yes</td><td></td></tr>
<tr><td>'font-variant'</td><td>normal | small-caps | inherit</td><td>normal</td><td></td><td>yes</td><td></td></tr>
</table>

Name	Values	Initial value	Applies to (Default: all)	Inherited?	Percentages (Default: N/A)
'font-weight'	normal | bold | bolder | lighter | 100 | 200 | 300 | 400 | 500 | 600 | 700 | 800 | 900 | inherit	normal		yes	
'height'	<length> | <percentage> | auto | inherit	auto	all elements but non-replaced inline elements, table columns, and olumn groups	no	see prose
'left'	<length> | <percentage> | auto | inherit	auto	positioned elements	no	refer to width of containing block
'letter-spacing'	normal | <length> | inherit	normal		yes	
'line-height'	normal | <number> | <length> | <percentage> | inherit	normal		yes	refer to the font size of the element itself
'list-style'	['list-style-type' | | 'list-style-position' | | 'list-style-image'] | inherit	XX	elements with 'display: list-item'	yes	
'list-style-image'	<uri> | none | inherit	none	elements with 'display: list-item'	yes	
'list-style-position'	inside | outside | inherit	outside	elements with 'display: list-item'	yes	

Name	Values	Initial value	Applies to (Default: all)	Inherited?	Percentages (Default: N/A)
'list-style-type'	disc | circle | square | decimal | decimal-leading-zero | lower-roman | upper-roman | lower-greek | lower-alpha | lower-latin | upper-alpha | upper-latin | hebrew | armenian | georgian | cjk-ideographic | hiragana | katakana | hiragana-iroha | katakana-iroha | none | inherit	disc	elements with 'display: list-item'	yes	
'margin'	<margin-width>{1,4} | inherit	XX		no	refer to width of containing block
'margin-top' 'margin-right' 'margin-bottom' 'margin-left'	<margin-width> | inherit	0		no	refer to width of containing block
'marker-offset'	<length> | auto | inherit	auto	elements with 'display: marker'	no	
'marks'	[crop | | cross] | none | inherit	none	page context	N/A	
'max-height'	<length> | <percentage> | none | inherit	none	all elements except non-replaced inline elements and table elements	no	refer to height of containing block
'max-width'	<length> | <percentage> | none | inherit	none	all elements except non-replaced inline elements and table elements	no	refer to width of containing block

Name	Values	Initial value	Applies to (Default: all)	Inherited?	Percentages (Default: N/A)
'min-height'	<length>	<percentage>	inherit	0	all elements except non-replaced inline elements and table elements	no	refer to height of containing block
'min-width'	<length>	<percentage>	inherit	UA dependent	all elements except non-replaced inline elements and table elements	no	refer to width of containing block
'orphans'	<integer>	inherit	2	block-level elements	yes	
'outline'	['outline-color'		'outline-style'		'outline-width']	inherit		see individual properties	no	
'outline-color'	<color>	invert	inherit	invert		no	
'outline-style'	<border-style>	inherit	none		no	
'outline-width'	<border-width>	inherit	medium		no	
'overflow'	visible	hidden	scroll	auto	inherit	visible	block-level and replaced elements	no	
'padding'	<padding-width>{1,4}	inherit	XX		no	refer to width of containing block
'padding-top' 'padding-right' 'padding-bottom' 'padding-left'	<padding-width>	inherit	0		no	refer to width of containing block
'page'	<identifier>	auto	auto	block-level elements	yes	

<table>
<tr><th>Name</th><th>Values</th><th>Initial value</th><th>Applies to (Default: all)</th><th>Inherited?</th><th>Percentages (Default: N/A)</th></tr>
<tr><td>'page-break-after'</td><td>auto | always | avoid | left | right | inherit</td><td>auto</td><td>block-level elements</td><td>no</td><td></td></tr>
<tr><td>'page-break-before'</td><td>auto | always | avoid | left | right | inherit</td><td>auto</td><td>block-level elements</td><td>no</td><td></td></tr>
<tr><td>'page-break-inside'</td><td>avoid | auto | inherit</td><td>auto</td><td>block-level elements</td><td>yes</td><td></td></tr>
<tr><td>'pause'</td><td>[[<time> | <percentage>]{1,2}] | inherit</td><td>depends on user agent</td><td></td><td>no</td><td>see descriptions of 'pause-before' and 'pause-after'</td></tr>
<tr><td>'pause-after'</td><td><time> | <percentage> | inherit</td><td>depends on user agent</td><td></td><td>no</td><td>see prose</td></tr>
<tr><td>'pause-before'</td><td><time> | <percentage> | inherit</td><td>depends on user agent</td><td></td><td>no</td><td>see prose</td></tr>
<tr><td>'pitch'</td><td><frequency> | x-low | low | medium | high | x-high | inherit</td><td>medium</td><td></td><td>yes</td><td></td></tr>
<tr><td>'pitch-range'</td><td><number> | inherit</td><td>50</td><td></td><td>yes</td><td></td></tr>
<tr><td>'play-during'</td><td><uri> mix? repeat? | auto | none | inherit</td><td>auto</td><td></td><td>no</td><td></td></tr>
<tr><td>'position'</td><td>static | relative | absolute | fixed | inherit</td><td>static</td><td>all elements, but not to generated content</td><td>no</td><td></td></tr>
<tr><td>'quotes'</td><td>[<string> <string>]+ | none | inherit</td><td>depends on user agent</td><td>yes</td><td></td><td></td></tr>
<tr><td>'richness'</td><td><number> | inherit</td><td>50</td><td>yes</td><td></td><td></td></tr>
<tr><td>'right'</td><td><length> | <percentage> | auto | inherit</td><td>auto</td><td>positioned elements</td><td>no</td><td>refer to width of containing block</td></tr>
</table>

Name	Values	Initial value	Applies to (Default: all)	Inherited?	Percentages (Default: N/A)
'size'	<length>{1,2} | auto | portrait | landscape | inherit	auto	the page context	N/A	
'speak'	normal | none | spell-out | inherit	normal		yes	
'speak-header'	once | always | inherit	once	elements that have table header information	yes	
'speak-numeral'	digits | continuous | inherit	continuous		yes	
'speak-punctuation'	code | none | inherit	none		yes	
'speech-rate'	<number> | x-slow | slow | medium | fast | x-fast | faster | slower | inherit	medium		yes	
'stress'	<number> | inherit	50		yes	
'table-layout'	auto | fixed | inherit	auto	'table' and 'inline-table' elements	no	
'text-align'	left | right | center | justify | <string> | inherit	depends on user agent and writing direction	block-level elements	yes	
'text-decoration'	none | [underline || overline || line-through || blink] | inherit	none		no (see prose)	
'text-indent'	<length> | <percentage> | inherit	0	block-level elements	yes	refer to width of containing block

Name	Values	Initial value	Applies to (Default: all)	Inherited?	Percentages (Default: N/A)
'text-shadow'	none | [<color> || <length> <length> <length>? ,]* [<color> || <length> <length> <length>?] | inherit	none		no (see prose)	
'text-transform'	capitalize | uppercase | lowercase | none | inherit	none		yes	
'top'	<length> | <percentage> | auto | inherit	auto	positioned elements	no	refer to height of containing block
'unicode-bidi'	normal | embed | bidi-override | inherit	normal	all elements, but see prose	no	
'vertical-align'	baseline | sub | super | top | text-top | middle | bottom | text-bottom | <percentage> | <length> | inherit	baseline	inline-level and 'table-cell' elements	no	refer to the 'line-height' of the element itself
'visibility'	visible | hidden | collapse | inherit	inherit		no	
'voice-family'	[[<specific-voice> | <generic-voice>],]* [<specific-voice> | <generic-voice>] | inherit	depends on user agent		yes	
'volume'	<number> | <percentage> | silent | x-soft | soft | medium | loud | x-loud | inherit	medium		yes	refer to inherited value
'white-space'	normal | pre | nowrap | inherit	normal	block-level elements	yes	
'widows'	<integer> | inherit	2	block-level elements	yes	

Name	Values	Initial value	Applies to (Default: all)	Inherited?	Percentages (Default: N/A)
'width'	<length> | <percentage> | auto | inherit	auto	all elements but non-replaced inline elements, table rows, and row groups	no	refer to width of containing block
'word-spacing'	normal | <length> | inherit	normal		yes	
'z-index'	auto | <integer> | inherit	auto	positioned elements	no	

CHAPTER 19

The Bug Tracking Application

Introduction

This chapter presents a complete example of an XML application for the tracking of bugs in a software product. It is a fairly complex Web application, showcasing some of the most relevant technologies in the XML space today; these include:

- Custom vocabularies for the development process (functional requirements)
- DTD construction techniques
- XSLT for the transformation of XML data
- WML for presentation on wireless devices
- XHTML/CSS for presentation on browsers
- SVG for the presentation of vector graphics
- Database/XML integration

One particularly interesting aspect of this application is how the ties to both XML and software engineering are enforced at every possible opportunity. For example, the application itself is XML based, but it aims to solve a software engineering problem. The implementation of the application is pure XML and so are some of the tools to create it (the requirements and UML diagrams for the application are encoded in XML too, for example).

This chapter is divided into four parts: (1) requirements, (2) analysis and design, (3) implementation of each module and (4) summary and post mortem.[1]

Requirements

As we mentioned earlier, in every step of the process in which we can apply XML, we will do so. Therefore, the requirements for our application are going to be encoded in XML, according to the Functional Requirements DTD.[2]

Before exploring the XML that underlies this section, let's take a look at the following output generated by the req2txt stylesheet (and therefore get an idea of what we must do with this application).

[1] If you feel something like automated XML testing is missing, please see the Hugin Framework on the Website.

[2] Developed by the author.

Requirements for XMLBugTrack (As Generated by req2txt.xsl)

XMLBugTrack is a bug report system accessible from Web browsers, WML devices (such as PDAs), and voice interfaces (phones). It uses several XML technologies such as XSLT, VoiceXML, XML/Databases, DOM, XHTML, and WML in order to achieve its objectives.

The exact requirements for the application are described in this document. If you want a complete description, browse the Requirements tables (shown in Figures 19.1 and 19.2). If you are only interested in the one-line description of the features, review the following summary.

Requirements Index

I. List Bugs as XHTML
II. List Bugs as WML
III. Bugs Submission/Persistence
V. Change the State of a Bug
VI. Graphic Bug Report
VII. Voice Bug Report

Individual Requirements

LIST BUGS AS XHTML [PRIORITY:1] [OPTIONAL:NO]

Upon request, returns a list of all the bugs and their attributes in the form of an XHTML 1.0 document.

LIST BUGS AS WML [PRIORITY:2] [OPTIONAL:NO]

Upon request, returns a list of all the bugs and their attributes in the form of a WML 1.1 document.

BUGS SUBMISSION/PERSISTENCE [PRIORITY:1][OPTIONAL:NO]

Each bug entry must be a simple description of a system bug as perceived by a user/programmer. The representation of the bugs, whatever it may be, must sensibly describe the following attributes for each bug: (1) description, (2) date, (3) type—UI, data integrity, security, etc.—and (4) importance, in a persistent way.

CHANGE THE STATE OF A BUG [PRIORITY:2] [OPTIONAL:NO]

A user may change the current state of a bug, thus signaling its fix (or at least the intention of fixing it).

GRAPHIC BUG REPORT [PRIORITY:3] [OPTIONAL:YES]
Each day, at the end of the day, the system must produce a graphic report of the bugs fixed vs. those submitted and pending.

VOICE BUG REPORT [PRIORITY:3] [OPTIONAL:YES]
Each day, at the end of the day, the system must produce a voice report of the bugs fixed vs. those submitted and pending. This report must be accessible via phone (as it is used by managers/developers who are on a trip and want quick access to statistics about the project).

Requirements for XMLBugTrack (As Generated by req2xhtml.xsl)

The original XML requirements document can also be treated using the req2html stylesheet, producing a much better, navigable representation of the requirements (as shown in Figures 19.1 and 19.2).

As a small exercise (and as a test of your environment), it is recommended that you generate this documentation from the original XML. You can do so by using the following command:[3]

```
java com.jclark.xsl.sax.Driver requirements.xml req2xhtml.xsl
reqs.html
```

or

```
xalan -IN requirements.xml -OUT reqs.html -XSL req2xhtml.xsl
```

Requirements for XMLBugTrack (Original XML)

All the above is generated from the following original requirements document:

```
<?xml version="1.0"?>
<!DOCTYPE fr
 PUBLIC "-//theFAActory//functionalRequirements DTD V2.0//EN"
 "fr\fr.dtd">
<fr>
  <header>
```

[3] For more details about XT and Xalan installation and usage see the chapters on XSLT.

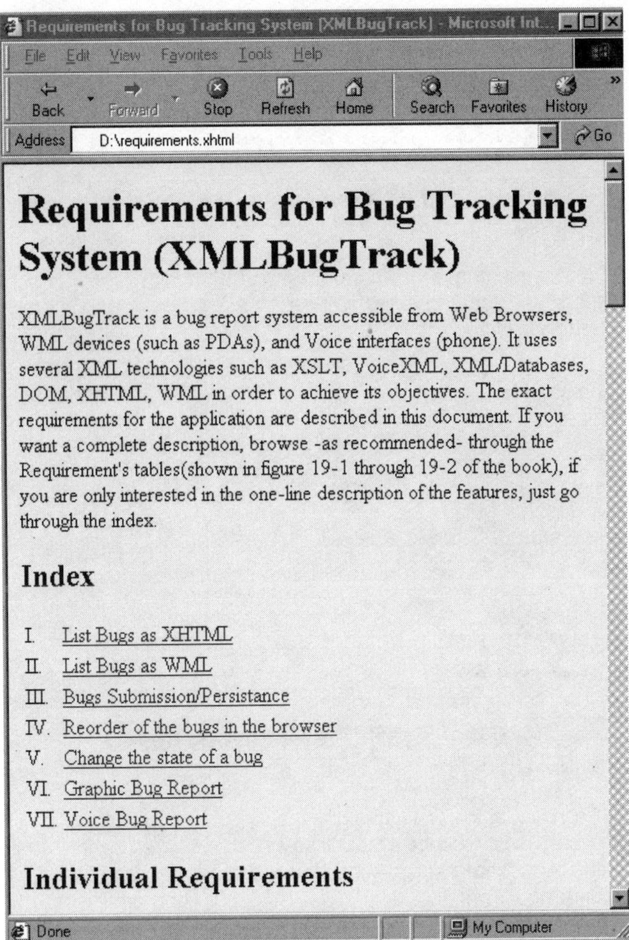

Figure 19.1 The XMLBugTrack requirements index.

```
<project>Bug Tracking System (XMLBugTrack)</project>
<description>
  <p>XMLBugTrack is a bug report system accessible from Web
     Browsers, WML devices (such as PDAs), and Voice
     interfaces (phone). It uses several XML technologies
     such as
     XSLT, VoiceXML, XML/Databases, DOM, XHTML, WML in order
     to achieve its objectives.
  </p>
  <p>The exact requirements for the application are described
     in this document. If you want a complete description,
     browse -as recommended- through the Requirement's tables
     (shown in Figures 19.1 and 19.2 of the book), if you are
     only interested in the one-line description of the
     features,
  just go through the index.</p>
```

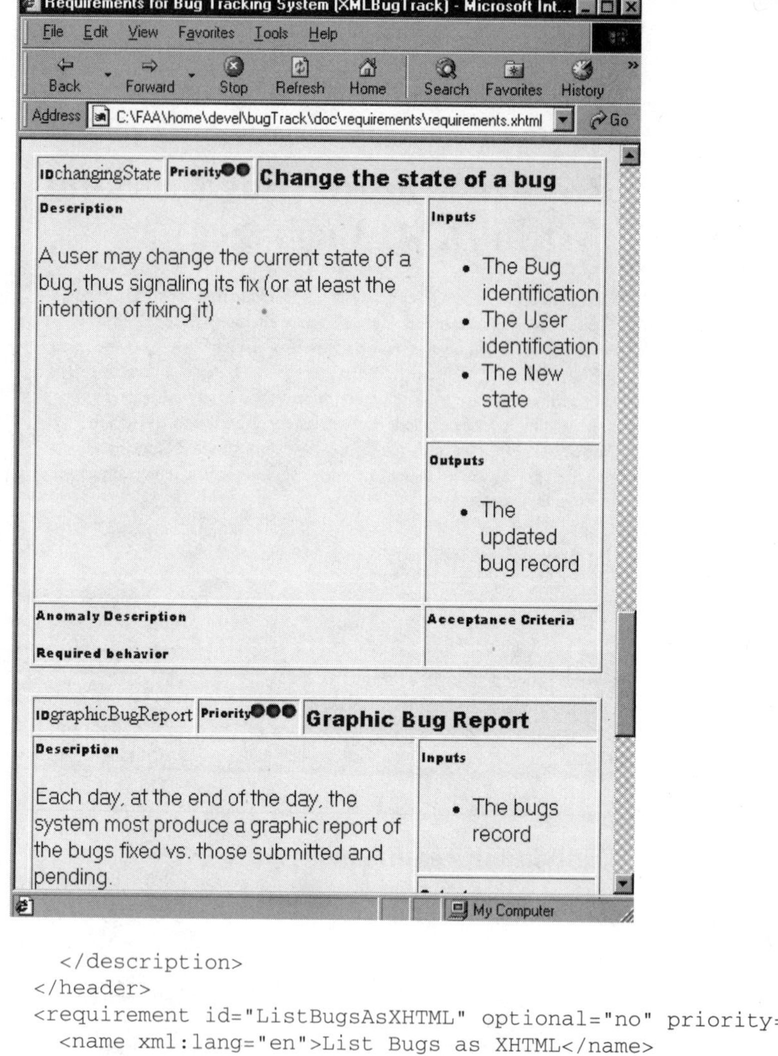

Figure 19.2 A portion of the XMLBugTrack requirements.

```
    </description>
  </header>
  <requirement id="ListBugsAsXHTML" optional="no" priority="1">
    <name xml:lang="en">List Bugs as XHTML</name>
    <description>
      <p>Upon request, return a list of all the bugs and their
         attributes in the form of an XHTML 1.0 document.</p>
    </description>
    <input>
      <entry>An HTTP request.</entry>
    </input>
    <output>
      <result>A bug list document conformant with XHTML
1.0</result>
    </output>
  </requirement>
  <requirement id="ListBugsAsWML" optional="no" priority="2">
```

```
  <name xml:lang="en">List Bugs as WML</name>
  <description>
    <p>Upon request, return a list of all the bugs and their
       attributes in the form of a WML 1.1 document.</p>
    <p>It is important to note that the selection of the
       correct format must be automatic.</p>
  </description>
  <input>
    <entry>An HTTP request.</entry>
  </input>
  <output>
    <result>A bug document conformant with WML 1.1</result>
  </output>
</requirement>
<requirement id="Persistance" optional="no" priority="1">
  <name xml:lang="en">Bugs Submission/Persistance</name>
  <description>
    <p>Each bug entry must be a simple description of a system
       bug as perceived by a user/programmer. The
       representation of the bugs, whatever it may be, must
       sensibly describe the following attributes for each bug:
       (1) description, (2)date, (3)type -UI,data
       integrity,security,etc-. and
    (4)importance, in a persistant way.
   </p>
  </description>
  <input>
    <entry>Bugs description</entry>
  </input>
  <output>
    <result>Persistance storage of each bug entry</result>
  </output>
</requirement>
<requirement id="ClientBugReorder" optional="yes" priority="3">
  <name xml:lang="en">Reorder of the bugs in the browser</name>
  <description>
    <p>Given a list of bugs, the user must be able to reorder
       them for reading in the browser, without having to re-
       fetch the data from the server. This requirement applies
       only to Web Browsers with DOM capabilities (not to wml
       browsers on phones or PDAs)</p>
  </description>
  <input>
    <entry>Sort criteria</entry>
  </input>
  <output>
    <result>Sorted document</result>
  </output>
</requirement>
<requirement id="changingState" optional="no" priority="2">
  <name xml:lang="en">Change the state of a bug</name>
  <description>
    <p>A user may change the current state of a bug, thus
```

```
            signaling its fix (or at least the intention of fixing
            it)</p>
        </description>
        <input>
          <entry>The Bug identification</entry>
          <entry>The User identification</entry>
          <entry>The New state</entry>
        </input>
        <output>
          <result>The updated bug record</result>
        </output>
      </requirement>
      <requirement id="graphicBugReport" optional="yes" priority="3">
        <name xml:lang="en">Graphic Bug Report</name>
        <description>
          <p>Each day, at the end of the day, the system most produce
             a graphic report of the bugs fixed vs. those submitted
             and pending. </p>
        </description>
        <input>
          <entry>The bugs record</entry>
        </input>
        <output>
          <result>Consolidated bug report using Scalar Vector
                  Graphics and XHTML</result>
        </output>
      </requirement>
      <requirement id="voiceBugReport" optional="yes" priority="3">
        <name xml:lang="en">Voice Bug Report</name>
        <description>
          <p>Each day, at the end of the day, the system most produce
             a voice report of the bugs fixed vs. those submitted and
             pending. This report must be accessible via phone (this
             is used for  managers/developers who are on a trip and
             want quick access to statistics about the project).</p>
        </description>
        <input>
          <entry>The bugs record</entry>
        </input>
        <output>
          <result>Consolidated bug report using VoiceXML</result>
        </output>
      </requirement>
    </fr>
```

Analysis and Design

The following sections will explore the general architecture and design for the BugTrack application. The architecture presents only a top-level view of the system in terms of components and relationships. The design materializes the architecture into a specific set of classes and interfaces. The rest of the chapter will show the implementation of the design.

Architectural View

Figure 19.3 shows the basic architecture for the BugTrack system.

Figure 19.3 BugTrack architecture.

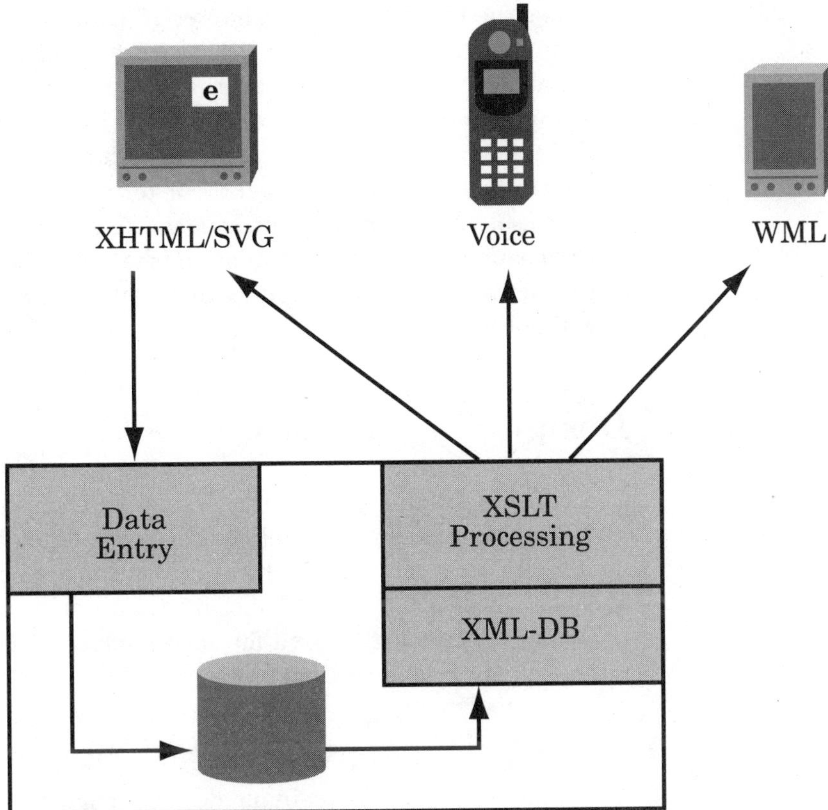

The system logic is composed of three server modules:

- **Data-gathering module**—Takes the bug description input from a browser and inserts it into a database.
- **Database to XML module**—Creates an XML representation of the bug data. Its output will be the XML document that the XSLT processor will take as its input.

- **XSLT Processor and Stylesheets**—Transforms the bug XML data into suitable representations for WML, VoiceXML, and SVG devices.

More details will arise as soon as we bring the architecture down to earth with the class design, but in the meantime there are already some key points to highlight:

- The output XML and the database query are decoupled. This is very important, because it makes the program more maintainable, putting to use the theory found in Chapter 16 (XML and Databases). Writing a simple JSP (or ASP, or PHP3) with hard-coded WML/XHTML and embedded SQL would make the program much more sensitive to changes in the database. More on this will be mentioned when we see the implementation of the database module.
- By means of a clean, one-point exit to the world, the addition of new devices is as simple as creating new XSLT stylesheets.
- By means of a clean encapsulation, the server side of this application can act as an isolated application, with clean inputs and outputs, without depending on blurry bindings to the client side.

Design

The following sections provide a design for each of the modules in the architecture, making it possible to see exactly the nature of each component, and how it interacts with the rest of the application. The diagrams and descriptions here do not discuss the implementation beyond mentioning the technologies used for each module. For such details, please refer to the following sections.

Database

The Database will have a simple design, representing only two types of data: users and bugs. A user has the following attributes:

- A name
- A login
- A password

A bug has the following attributes:[4]

- A description
- A submission date
- A type: UI, data integrity, data correctness, sability, integration
- A fix date
- An owner (name of the person responsible for fixing it)
- A state
- A modification date
- Platform
- Severity (0 = absolutely blocking to 10 = a superfluous enhancement request)

The database distributed on the CD is a small Microsoft Access database with two tables, one for each of the concepts above.

XML/Database Module

The XML database module is designed as a straightforward use of a SAX API for databases, as described in Chapter 16.

The following class diagram (Figure 19.4) shows the design of this module.

It is very important to note how this design decision significantly improves the quality of the application. If the presentation layer (XSLT) is decoupled from the database, several positive consequences occur. The most important of which are the following:

- The code to produce client representations is simpler and cleaner.
- The code to produce client representations is independent of the database; thus it is easier to maintain and modify.
- There is high reuse. Not only do we have a cleaner and more robust implementation, but the database code is already written and proved as an independent library.[5]

---

[4] Note that, as a result of analysis, more attributes are discovered. It is important to update the requirements document as a result of these findings. If you are using a version control system such as CVS, you will begin to see the benefits of holding your requirements as XML as soon as you can compare the two text files without the hassle a binary format would impose.

[5] The actual custom code needed to tailor the SAX database API for our needs will be more than one order of magnitude smaller than writing the database connection from scratch.

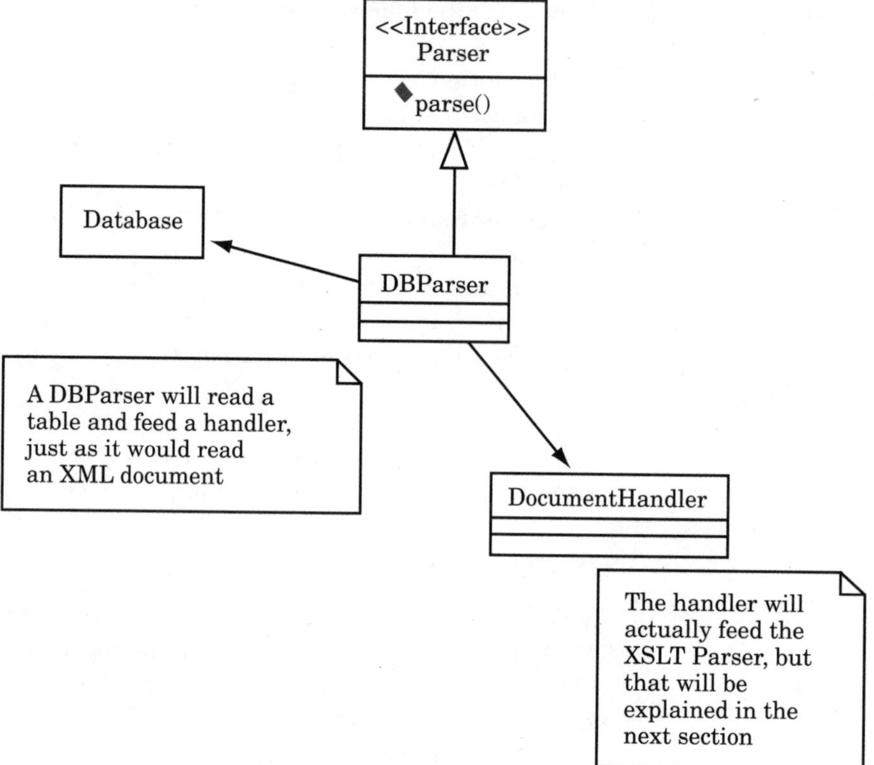

Figure 19.4 The database module design.

XSLT Processing Module

An XSLT processor, such as XT, uses SAX parsers to feed itself the source XML document to transform, and the stylesheet to transform it. Since we are already using a valid SAX parser that encapsulates the database and acts just like a normal source of SAX events, we can simply hook it up with the XSLT processor.

In order to prepare and administer the interaction between the parser and the XSLT processor (XT), a third class, `XSLTCoordinator` is included. Figures 19.5 and 19.6 show the structure of the module.

`XSLTCoordinator` will have the responsibility of creating the instances of both the parser and the XSLT processor, and administering the correct initialization data. In object-oriented design terms, this is an application of the Expert Pattern.

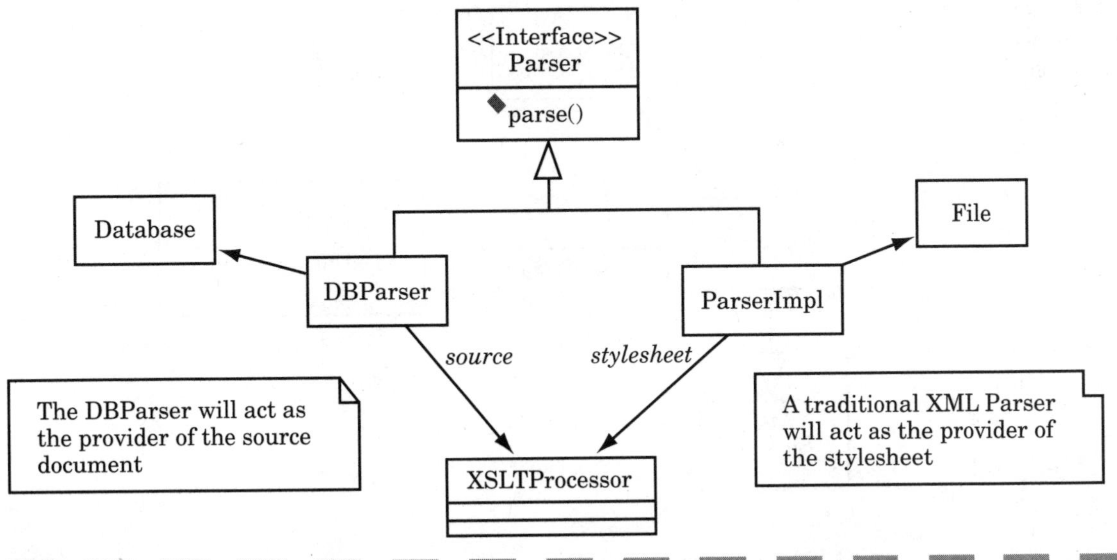

Figure 19.5 The XSLT processing module design.

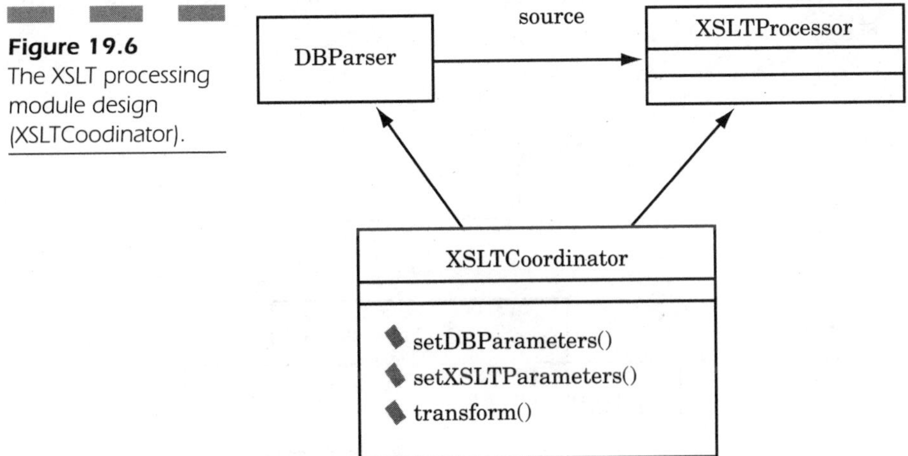

Figure 19.6 The XSLT processing module design (XSLTCoodinator).

Data Entry Module

The Data entry module is the simplest of them all. It is a classic servlet, which receives the bug data from a form and introduces it into the database. The data entry model interfaces with the client via a simple XHTML page with a data entry form. Figure 19.7 shows the diagram of this module's design.

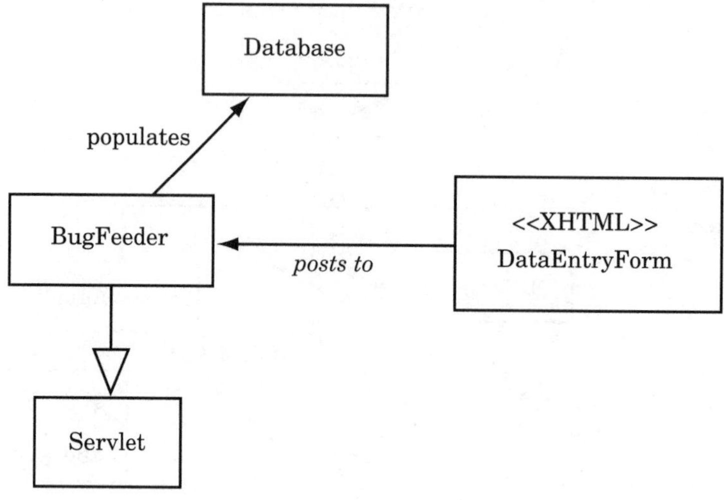

Figure 19.7
Data entry module.

XSLT Stylesheets

Finally, there are the XSLT stylesheets, a fundamental component of the system. These stylesheets are divided in two types: bug lists and reports. The following diagram (Figure 19.8) shows the structure of the stylesheets.

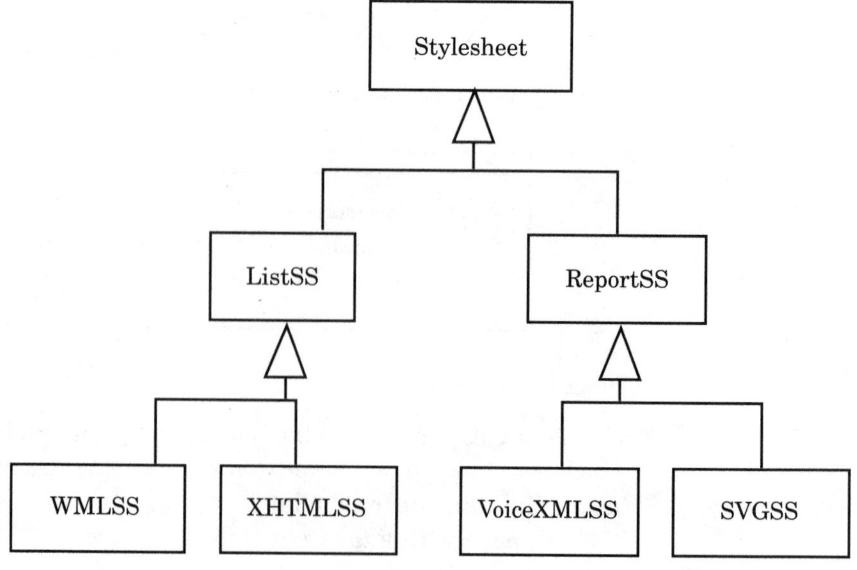

Figure 19.8
Stylesheets organization.

In total, four stylesheets are created:

- **Bug list for XHTML**—Used to present high-quality representations of the bug list with graphics and colors in a browser.
- **Bug list for WML**—Used to present a somewhat economical representation of the bug list for WML-enabled PDAs and phones.
- **SVG report**—An SVG set of graphics with the bug status distribution (as a pie chart) and the bug fixing productivity (as a Cartesian chart).
- **VoiceXML report**—A VoiceXML document with the same information as the SVG report, but suited for voice rendering.

COMPLETE CLASS MAP

Figure 19.9 shows the complete class diagram for the design of XML-BugTrack.

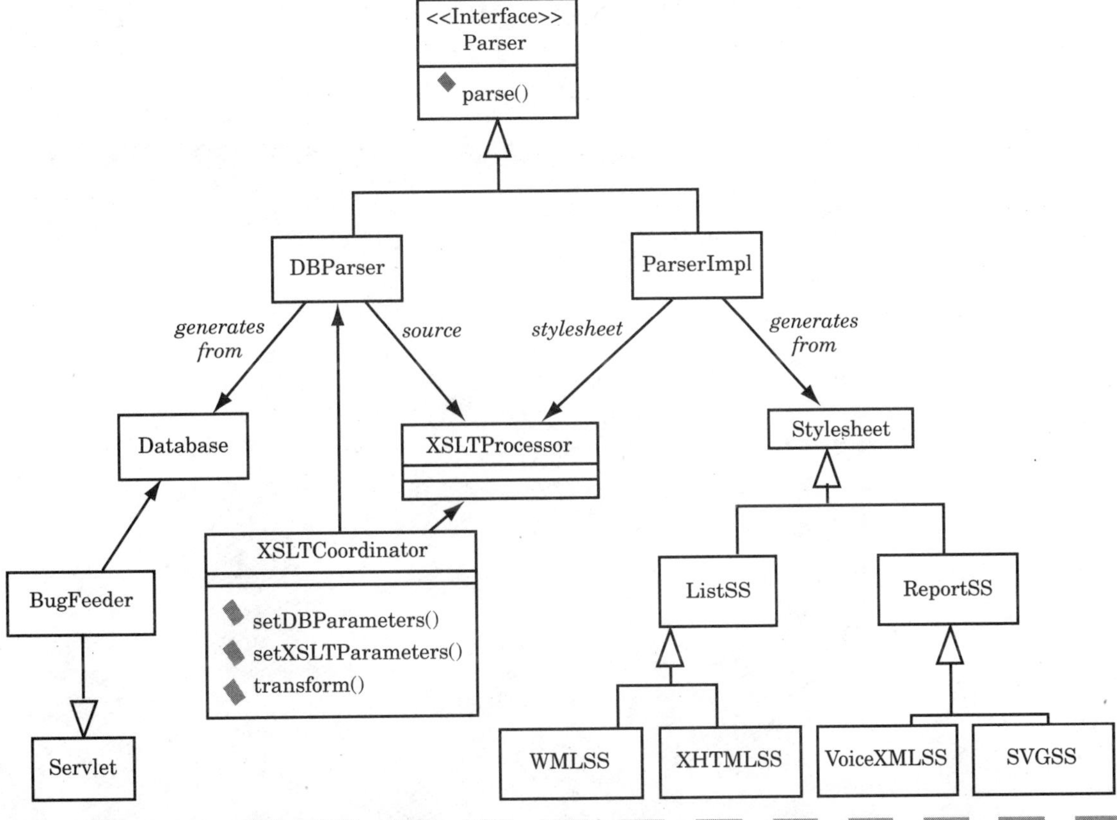

Figure 19.9 XMLBugTrack UML class diagram.

Implementation

The following sections show the most relevant aspects of the implementation of the Bug Tracker system. The complete code for this application is included on the CD.

Database Structure

The persistence layer is implemented as a simple, one-table, Microsoft Access relational database. The reason to create only one table is simple: the data entry will only happen using the Web interface inside the company's intranet; therefore, it is reasonable to relax the requirements (only for the purposes of this chapter) and skip user validation altogether.

Having user logins here would only derail us from our true objective, and if the need arises, the system can be trivially extended to support them.

The bugs table contains all the data outlined in the design. Figure 19.10 is a snapshot of the MS Access Design Table view, showing the actual table design.

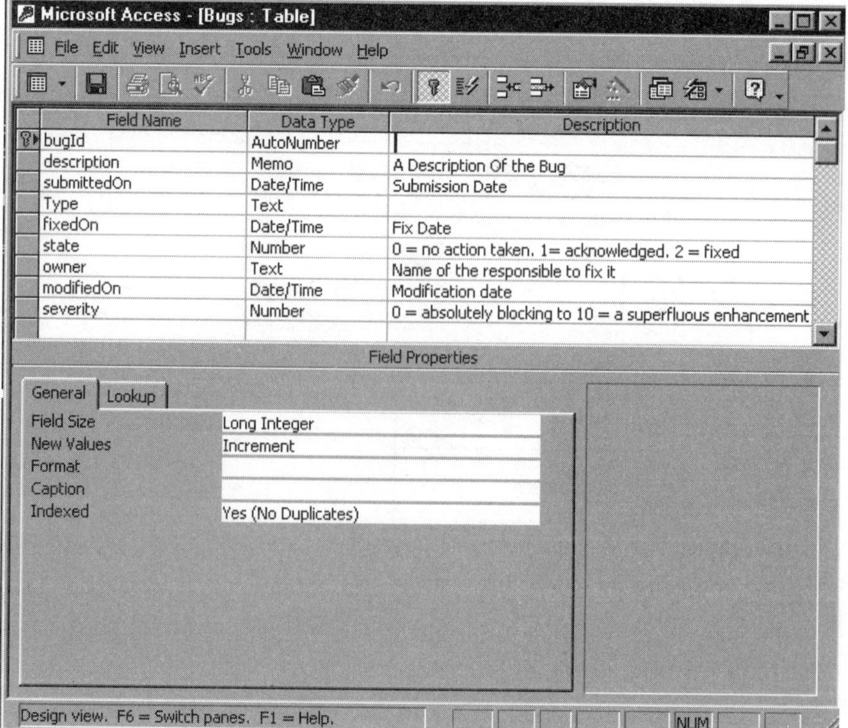

Figure 19.10
Table design.

On the other hand, Figure 19.11 shows some of the data populating the table.

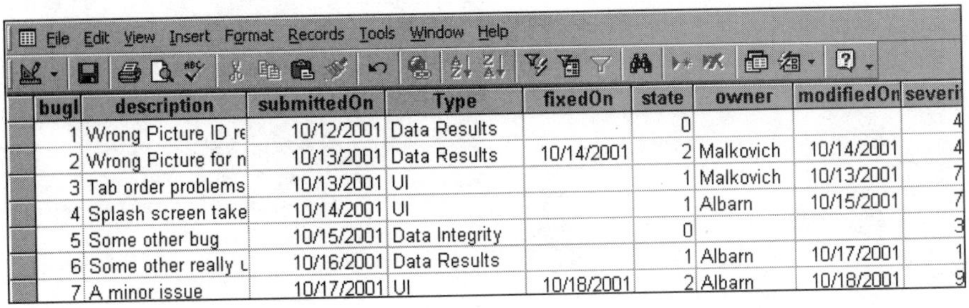

File Edit View Insert Format Records Tools Window Help

bugI	description	submittedOn	Type	fixedOn	state	owner	modifiedOn	severi
1	Wrong Picture ID re	10/12/2001	Data Results		0			4
2	Wrong Picture for n	10/13/2001	Data Results	10/14/2001	2	Malkovich	10/14/2001	4
3	Tab order problems	10/13/2001	UI		1	Malkovich	10/13/2001	7
4	Splash screen take	10/14/2001	UI		1	Albarn	10/15/2001	7
5	Some other bug	10/15/2001	Data Integrity		0			3
6	Some other really u	10/16/2001	Data Results		1	Albarn	10/17/2001	1
7	A minor issue	10/17/2001	UI	10/18/2001	2	Albarn	10/18/2001	9

Figure 19.11
Table contents.

Database to XML Connection and XSLT Processing

The whole application relies on the elegant and efficient solution to the problem of creating XML data from the database and transforming it on the fly.

One very efficient solution is the usage of a SAX API parser, which isolates the fact that the database itself exists, and presents the handlers with simple SAX events, even when it is really reading from relational tables.

The code for such a parser was presented in Chapter 16 and now is reused as a class library, by the real focus of this section: the `XSLTCoordinator` class, a simple control class that takes care of creating the `parser` and the `XSLT processor` and feeding both the adequate start data.

`XSLTCoordinator` offers two basic services:

- `transform(String stylesheetURL)`: Generates an end-user transformation using the given stylesheet.
- `setDatabaseProperties(Properties prop)`: Changes the database properties such as the default query to execute when creating the bug list. The default value is to return every bug in the database (this method is primarily included for extensibility reasons).

Before continuing, let's take a look at what are we expecting to get out of the database when we use the database SAX parser. The following document shows the XML output of reading the database with the class `com.faa.xml.databases.DBParser`:.

```
<bugList>
<bug bugId="1" Type="Data Results" state="0">
<description>
Wrong Picture ID returned for employees with ID &gt;
3423422</description>
<submittedOn>
2001-10-12 00:00:00</submittedOn>
</bug>
<bug bugId="2" Type="Data Results" state="2" owner="Malkovich">
<description>
Wrong Picture for non-employees</description>
<submittedOn>
2001-10-13 00:00:00</submittedOn>
<fixedOn>
2001-10-14 00:00:00</fixedOn>
<modifiedOn>
2001-10-14 00:00:00</modifiedOn>
<severity>
4</severity>
</bug>
<bug bugId="3" Type="UI" state="1" owner="Malkovich">
<description>
Tab order problems with entry form</description>
<submittedOn>
2001-10-13 00:00:00</submittedOn>
</bug>
<bug bugId="4" Type="UI" state="1" owner="Albarn">
<description>
Splash screen takes too long to appear and then stays for too
long</description>
<submittedOn>
2001-10-14 00:00:00</submittedOn>
</bug>
<bug bugId="5" Type="Data Integrity" state="0">
<description>
Some other bug</description>
<submittedOn>
2001-10-15 00:00:00</submittedOn>
</bug>
<bug bugId="6" Type="Data Results" state="1" owner="Albarn">
<description>
Some other really ugly bug</description>
<submittedOn>
2001-10-16 00:00:00</submittedOn>
</bug>
<bug bugId="7" Type="UI" state="2" owner="Albarn">
<description>
A minor issue</description>
<submittedOn>
2001-10-17 00:00:00</submittedOn>
<fixedOn>
2001-10-18 00:00:00</fixedOn>
<modifiedOn>
2001-10-18 00:00:00</modifiedOn>
```

```
<severity>
9</severity>
</bug>
</bugList>
```

Note that the use of general-purpose DBParser does not impose any ugliness in the final code, such as presenting everything as elements, or leaving flag data where nulls were found in the database. On the contrary, very simple code can be used for fine control of the XML produced; as a matter of fact, the following lines were all that was needed:

```
Vector representAsAtts = new Vector();
// Represent the first  column as an attribute
representAsAtts.add(new Integer(1));
representAsAtts.add(new Integer(4));
representAsAtts.add(new Integer(6));
representAsAtts.add(new Integer(7));
DBParser myParser = new DBParser();
```

NOTE

The invocation says: from the table `rs`*, create a document with root element* `bugList`*, in which each row is encapsulated in a* `bug` *element, where each column is an element, except for those columns specified in* `representAsAtts`*, which should be represented as attributes.*

```
myParser.parse(rs,"bugList","bug",representAsAtts);
```

Compare this (not only in terms of size and elegance, but also in terms of reusability and maintainability) with hard-coded JSPs or ASPs.

The CD contains a `TestDataBase` directory for this project, which will allow you to get the XML output in the screen, just as shown above. But that is only useful for testing purposes. We want to connect that SAX output with the XSLT processor. The following code shows how that is achieved with the `XSLTCoordinator` class:

```
import java.sql.  Connection;
import java.sql.  DriverManager;
import java.sql.  Statement;
import java.sql.  ResultSet;
import java.util. Properties;
import java.util. Vector;
import java.io.   FileInputStream;
import org.xml.sax.*;
import com.jclark.xsl.sax.*;
import java.io.FileOutputStream;
```

```
import java.io.IOException;
import java.io.File;
import java.io.FileDescriptor;
import java.net.URL;


public class XSLTCoordinator {

    public void XSLTCoordinator(String properties)
    {
     try
        {
         myDB.load(new FileInputStream(properties));
         Class.forName(myDB.getProperty("driver"));
        }
     catch (java.lang.Exception e)
        {
         System.out.println("wrong database params " + e);
        }
    }
```

NOTE

It is important to see that the key point in this code is only a few lines long: the coordinator gets a connection to the database and sets up the parser. That parser will be used by the XSLT processor as its source for SAX events.

```
    void setUpParser()
    {
     try {
         conn = DriverManager.
                   getConnection(myDB.getProperty("URL"),
                          myDB.getProperty("user"),
                          myDB.getProperty("password"));
         stmt = conn.createStatement();
         rs = stmt.executeQuery("SELECT * FROM " +
                                  myDB.getProperty("table"));

         Vector representAsAtts = new Vector();
         representAsAtts.add(new Integer(1));
         representAsAtts.add(new Integer(4));
         representAsAtts.add(new Integer(6));
         representAsAtts.add(new Integer(7));
         myParser = new DBParserFixedQuery();


myParser.setParseParameters(rs,"bugList","bug",representAsAtts);
    }
    catch (java.lang.Exception e)
         {
          System.out.println("Failed to connect with the database
```

```
                                " + e);
            System.exit(-1);
            }
    }

    boolean transform(String stylesheet)
    {
     try {
          XSLProcessorImpl xsl = new XSLProcessorImpl();
          setUpParser();
          String stylesheetParserClass =
                 "com.jclark.xml.sax.Driver";
          Object parserObj =

Class.forName(stylesheetParserClass).newInstance();
          xsl.setParser(myParser,(Parser)parserObj);
          xsl.setErrorHandler(new ErrorHandlerImpl());
          OutputMethodHandlerImpl outputMethodHandler =
           new OutputMethodHandlerImpl(xsl);
          xsl.setOutputMethodHandler(outputMethodHandler);
          File ss = new File(stylesheet);
          Destination dest =
             new FileDescriptorDestination(FileDescriptor.out);;
          outputMethodHandler.setDestination(dest);
          return transform(xsl,fileInputSource(ss));
     }
     catch (java.lang.Exception e) {
          System.err.println(e.toString());
     }
     return false;
    }

    boolean transform(XSLProcessor xsl,
                      InputSource stylesheetSource)
    {
     try {
          xsl.loadStylesheet(stylesheetSource);
          xsl.parse((InputSource)null);
          return true;
     }
     catch (java.lang.Exception e) {
          System.err.println(e.toString());
     }
     return false;
    }

    static class ErrorHandlerImpl implements ErrorHandler {
     public void warning(SAXParseException e) {
          System.out.println(e);
     }
     public void error(SAXParseException e) {
          System.out.println(e);
     }
```

```
    public void fatalError(SAXParseException e) throws
            SAXException {
        throw e;
    }
  }

  static public InputSource fileInputSource(File file) {
   String path = file.getAbsolutePath();
   String fSep = System.getProperty("file.separator");
   if (fSep != null && fSep.length() == 1)
       path = path.replace(fSep.charAt(0), '/');
   if (path.length() > 0 && path.charAt(0) != '/')
       path = '/' + path;
   try {
       return new InputSource(new URL("file", "",
             path).toString());
   }
   catch (java.net.MalformedURLException e) {
       /* According to the spec this could only happen if the
          file protocol were not recognized. */
       throw new Error("unexpected MalformedURLException");
   }
  }


  static Connection conn = null;
  static Statement stmt = null;
  static ResultSet rs = null;
  static Properties myDB = new Properties();
  DBParserFixedQuery myParser = null;
}
```

Once this is done, the rest of the system comes down to write the XSLT stylesheets. In order to test the `XSLTCoordinator` (and see how encapsulated the generation and transformations are), take a look at the `TestXSLTCoordinator` class:

```
public class TestXSLTCoordinator {
    public static void main(String[] argv) {
     if (argv.length != 1) {
         System.out.println("Usage: java TestDataBase
                             stylesheet");
         System.exit(-1);
     }

     try
     {
         XSLTCoordinator c = new
XSLTCoordinator("properties.prop");
         c.transform(argv[0]);
     }
       catch (java.lang.Exception e)
```

```
            {
            System.out.println("Failed to connect with the database
                                " + e);
            System.exit(-1);
         }
        }

}
```

When called from the command line like this:

```
java TestXSLTCoordinator test.xsl
```

it prints:

```
BUG Found! Wrong Picture ID returned for employees with ID >
3423422
BUG Found! Wrong Picture for non-employees
BUG Found! Tab order problems with entry form
BUG Found! Splash screen takes too long to appear and then stays
for too long
BUG Found! Some other bug
BUG Found! Some other really ugly bug
BUG Found! A minor issue
```

As you might have imagined already, the `test.xsl` stylesheet is only the following:

```
<xsl:stylesheet xmlns:xsl="http://www.w3.org/1999/XSL/Transform"
               xmlns:xt="http://www.jclark.com/xt"
         version="1.0"
               extension-element-prefixes="xt">
<xsl:output method="text"/>

<xsl:template match="bug">
BUG Found! <xsl:value-of select="description"/>
</xsl:template>

</xsl:stylesheet>
```

Returning the List of Bugs for Browsers

Now all we have to do is write the stylesheets for each presentation requirement. The remaining sections will show the XSLT required for each vocabulary and a snapshot of the result.[6]

[6] The submission of new bugs is implemented via a simple form. This is not relevant for the goals of the chapter, so it won't be included in the text. However, it is included on the CD.

The following is the first stylesheet, the list of bugs for XHTML browsers:

```
<xsl:stylesheet xmlns:xsl="http://www.w3.org/1999/XSL/Transform"
                xmlns:xt="http://www.jclark.com/xt"
         version="1.0"
                extension-element-prefixes="xt">
<xsl:output method="html"/>
<xsl:template match="bugList">
    <html>
        <head>
      <title> Bug Report </title>
     </head>
     <body>

     <p align="center">
           <font face="Franklin Gothic Heavy" size="7">Bug
            Report</font></p>
     <p align="left">
        <font face="Verdana" size="4">Statistics</font></p>
     <p align="left">
          <font face="Verdana">Total Bugs:
                         <xsl:value-of select="count(bug)"/>
       </font></p>

     <p align="left">
          <font face="Verdana"> Total Unresolved Bugs:
                         <xsl:value-of select="count(bug[@state =
                          '0'])"/>
          </font></p>

     <p align="left">
             <font face="Verdana"> Total Bugs Without An Owner:

                        <xsl:value-of select="count(bug)-
                         count(bug[@owner])"/>

       </font></p>


     <p align="left"><font face="Verdana" size="4">Bug
      List</font></p>

     <xsl:for-each select="bug">
        <xsl:call-template name="myBug"/>
     </xsl:for-each>
     </body>
   </html>
 </xsl:template>

 <xsl:template name="myBug">
    <table border="1" width="100%">
      <tr>
```

```
      <td width="33%" valign="top" colspan="2"><b>Severity</b>:
       <xsl:value-of select="severity"/>
     </td>
      <td width="34%" rowspan="4"
       valign="top"><b>Description</b>:
       <xsl:value-of select="description"/>
     </td>
    </tr>
    <tr>
      <td width="33%" valign="top" colspan="2"><b>State</b>:
         <xsl:value-of select="@state"/>
  </td>
    </tr>
    <tr>
      <td width="16%"><b>Submision Date</b>:
         <xsl:value-of select="submittedOn"/>
  </td>
      <td width="17%"><b>Last Update</b>:
         <xsl:value-of select="modifiedOn"/>
  </td>
    </tr>
    <tr>
      <xsl-if test="@state = '2'">
           <td width="33%" colspan="2"><b>
                   <xsl:value-of select="@owner"/> fixed on
                   <xsl:value-of select="fixedOn"/>.</b></td>
      </xsl-if>
    </tr>
  </table>
  <hr size="40"/>
 </xsl:template>
</xsl:stylesheet>
```

Figure 19.12 shows the result in Internet Explorer 5.5 (note that since the transform is made in the server, there is no dependence with the browser).

Returning the List of Bugs for WML Devices

The following is the XSLT stylesheet for WML devices:

```
<xsl:stylesheet xmlns:xsl="http://www.w3.org/1999/XSL/Transform"
                xmlns:xt="http://www.jclark.com/xt"
         version="1.0"
                extension-element-prefixes="xt">

<xsl:template match="bugList">

<wml>
  <card>
    <p><b> Bug Report </b> <br/>
```

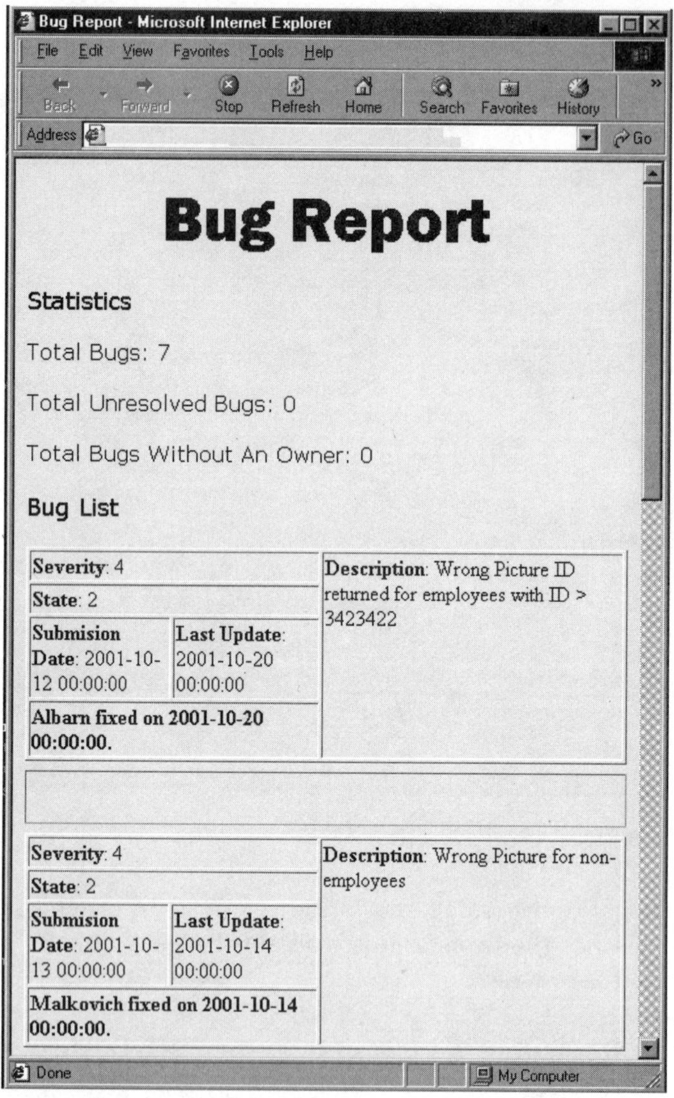

Figure 19.12 The XHTML bug list.

```
      Total Bugs: <xsl:value-of select="count(bug)"/><br/>
      Total Unresolved Bugs: <xsl:value-of select="count(bug[@state
                             = '0'])"/>
      Total Bugs Without An Owner: <xsl:value-of
                                   select="count(bug)-
                                   count(bug[@owner])"/>
    </p>
    <do type="accept" label="bugs">
      <go href="#a{bug[1]/@bugId}">
      </go>
```

```
    </do>
  </card>
     <xsl:for-each select="bug">
        <xsl:call-template name="myBug"/>
     </xsl:for-each>
</wml>
</xsl:template>

  <xsl:template name="myBug">
       <card id="a{@bugId}">
        <b>Severity</b>: <xsl:value-of select="severity"/> <br/>
        <b>Description</b>: <xsl:value-of select="description"/>
<br/>
        <b>State</b>: <xsl:value-of select="@state"/> <br/>
          <xsl:if test="following-sibling::bug">
         <do type="accept" label="more bugs">
           <go href="#a{following-sibling::bug/@bugId}">
           </go>
         </do>
          </xsl:if>
       </card>
  </xsl:template>
</xsl:stylesheet>
```

The result of this transformation is a WML document such as the following:

```
<?xml version="1.0" encoding="utf-8"?>
<wml>
<card>
<p>
<b>
 Bug Report </b>
<br/>

     Total Bugs: 7<br/>

     Total Unresolved Bugs: 0
     Total Bugs Without An Owner: 0</p>
<do type="accept" label="bugs">
<go href="#a1"/>
</do>
</card>
<card id="a1">
<b>Severity</b>: 4<br/>
<b>Description</b>: Wrong Picture ID returned for employees with
ID &gt; 3423422<br/>
<b>State</b>: 2<br/>
<do type="accept" label="more bugs">
<go href="#a2"/>
</do>
</card>
<card id="a2">
<b>
Severity</b>: 4<br/><b>
```

```
Description</b>: Wrong Picture for non-employees<br/>
<b>State</b>: 2<br/>
<do type="accept" label="more bugs">
<go href="#a3"/>
</do>
</card>
<card id="a3">
<b>Severity</b>: 7<br/>
<b>Description</b>: Tab order problems with entry form<br/>
<b>
State</b>: 2<br/>
<do type="accept" label="more bugs">
<go href="#a4"/>
</do>
</card>
<card id="a4">
<b>Severity</b>: 7<br/>
<b>Description</b>: Splash screen takes too long to appear and
then stays for too long<br/><b>
State</b>: 2<br/>
<do type="accept" label="more bugs">
<go href="#a5"/>
</do>
</card>
<card id="a5">
<b>Severity</b>: 3<br/>
<b>Description</b>: Some other bug<br/>
<b>State</b>: 2<br/>
<do type="accept" label="more bugs">
<go href="#a6"/>
</do>
</card>
<card id="a6">
<b>Severity</b>: 1<br/>
<b>Description</b>: Some other really ugly bug<br/>
<b>State</b>: 2<br/>
<do type="accept" label="more bugs">
<go href="#a7"/>
</do>
</card>
<card id="a7">
<b>Severity</b>: 9<br/>
<b>Description</b>: A minor issue<br/>
<b>State</b>: 2<br/>
</card>
</wml>
```

When viewed through a WAP phone (or an emulator in this case), the above document looks like Figures 19.13 and 19.14.

Figure 19.13
WML statistics output.

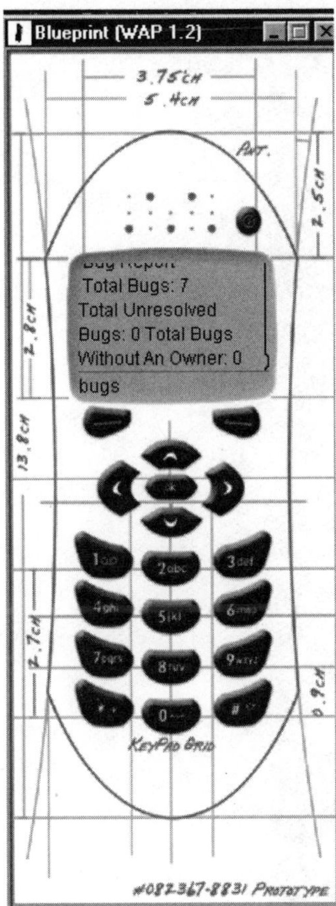

Generating a Daily Report of Bugs as Graphics (SVG and XHTML)

The following stylesheet creates an SVG graphic with the statistics for the day. It can automatically be sent every night to management via email.

SVG is a long and complex specification. The best way to learn it is by example. Please check the CD for more samples.

```
<xsl:stylesheet xmlns:xsl="http://www.w3.org/1999/XSL/Transform"
                xmlns:xt="http://www.jclark.com/xt"
        version="1.0"
                extension-element-prefixes="xt">

<xsl:template match="bugList">
<xsl:import name="sections.xsl"/>
```

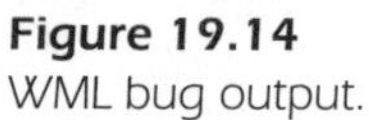

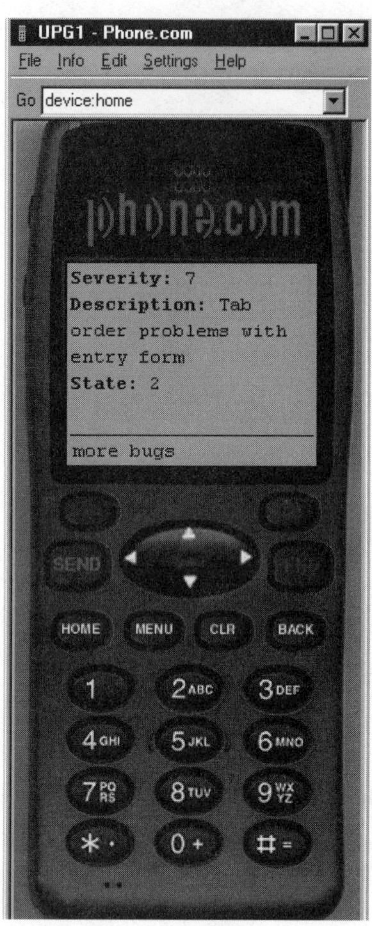

Figure 19.14
WML bug output.

```
<html>
<title>Daily Stats Bug Report</title>
<body bgcolor="#ffffff">

<embed name="pie" width="210" height="210" src="pie.svg"
       type="image/svg-xml"
       pluginspage="http://www.adobe.com/svg/viewer/install/"/>

</body>
</html>
<xt:document method="xml" href="pie.svg">
   <svg xml:space="preserve" width="9in" height="9in">>
   <g>
    <xsl:variable name="total"      select="count(bug)"/>
    <xsl:variable name="unresolved" select="count(bug[@state =
     '0'])"/>
    <xsl:variable name="orphan"     select="count(bug)-
```

```
     count(bug[@owner])"/>

    <circle cx="73" cy="73" r="70"
style="fill:white;stroke:black;"/>
    <text x="85" y="200" style="font-size:10;font-
color:#B34DFB">Total Bugs:
          <xsl:value-of select="$total"/>
    </text>
    <text x="85" y="180" style="font-size:10;font-
color:yellow">Unresolved:
          <xsl:value-of select="$unresolved"/>
    </text>
    <text x="85" y="160" style="font-size:10;font-
color:yellow">Without owner:
          <xsl:value-of select="$orphan"/>
    </text>

     <xsl:call-template name="sections.xsl"/>
   </g>

</svg>
</xt:document>
</xsl:template>
</xsl:stylesheet>
```

Figure 19.15 shows the output of the program (change the number of unresolved bugs in the database in order to get a more attractive output).

Generating a Daily Report of Bugs as Voice (VoiceXML)

A similar report (but this time for voice) is generated using VoiceXML. Again, this is a lengthy spec that can be best appreciated via examples. Please refer to the CD for more.

```
<xsl:stylesheet xmlns:xsl="http://www.w3.org/1999/XSL/Transform"
                xmlns:xt="http://www.jclark.com/xt"
          version="1.0"
                extension-element-prefixes="xt">

<xsl:template match="bugList">
<vxml>

<form id="bugs">
  <field name="wantbugs">

  <grammar>
  <![CDATA[
  [
  [dtmf-0 help] {<option "help">}
  [dtmf-1 bugs] {<option "dogs">}
```

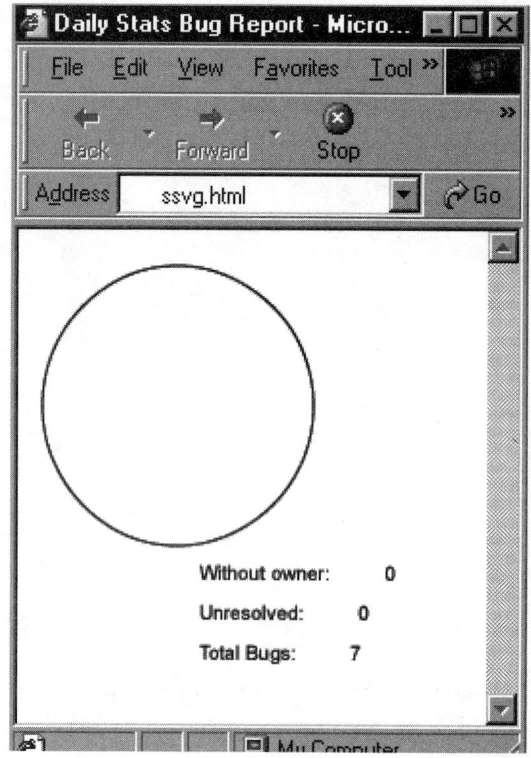

Figure 19.15 XHTML + SVG output.

```
]
]]>
</grammar>

<prompt>
  <audio>Say bugs or help</audio>
</prompt>

<nomatch>
  <audio>Sorry, I didn't understand</audio>
  <reprompt/>
</nomatch>

<noinput>
  <audio>Sorry, I didn't hear you</audio>
  <reprompt/>
</noinput>

<help>
  <audio>
   You can listen to the bug list by saying "Bugs"
  </audio>
  <reprompt/>
```

```
  </help>

  <default>
    <reprompt/>
  </default>

  <filled>
    <result name="dogs">
      <audio>I heard you say {wantbugs}</audio>
      <audio><xsl:value-of select
                ="count(bug)"/> Total Bugs.</audio>
      <audio><xsl:value-of select
                ="count(bug[@state = '0'])"/> Unresolved
Bugs.</audio>
      <audio><xsl:value-of select
             ="count(bug)-count(bug[@owner])"/> Without an
owner.</audio>
    </result>
  </filled>
  </field>

</form>
</vxml>
</xsl:template>
</xsl:stylesheet>
```

The result, when updated to a VoiceXML service such as TellMe Studio (www.tellme.com), is a simple application that responds to the word "bugs" with the list of bugs for the night.

Summary

In this chapter we saw how to make a robust and extensible XML application based on a database, keeping a clear distinction between the different modules of the system. We also explored the role of XML as a development tool for activities such as requirements gathering. The following chapter will explore even more development possibilities with XML, using another advanced example.

CHAPTER 20

Knowledge Management Application

Introduction

This chapter presents a complete example of an XML application for the gathering, display of., and search for technical annotations and summaries as a form of knowledge management.

Knowledge management is one of the key issues in the IT industry today. As knowledge becomes one of the selling points of a company (and a decisive factor behind its operations), the problem of gathering, maintaining, and effectively using knowledge becomes crucial.

In this chapter we will develop an application that serves one of the many aspects of *knowledge management* (KM): reading and learning logs. The application will provide the members of a team the means to record annotations, summaries, and comments about books, articles, conferences, etc. that might be relevant for future reference.

From those annotations, the system will be able to create searchable dictionaries and presentations for the rest of the company, thus expanding the possibilities and uses of knowledge that otherwise would be limited to an individual.

The XML technologies/techniques used are:

- DTDs.
- XLink for the creation of references and indexes.
- XPath in generated dictionaries.
- SMIL and HTML for the creation of presentations based on the data.
- CSS and XSLT on the client side.
- DOM and SAX2 for the programmatic creation of the underlying documents.
- SOAP for the programmatic, remote interface to the contents of the knowledge base.

Because of their nature, some of these points are treated with more detail here than others. Some are left to the CD/Website in order to avoid redundancy with previously written examples. Whether you are interested in those particular parts or not, it is recommended that you experiment with the application on the CD/Website and study the code.

What Is Knowledge Management?

Before we start, let's agree on the following definition: knowledge management is the systematic process of finding, selecting, organizing, distilling, and presenting information in a way that improves an employee's comprehension in a specific area of interest.

Our work in this chapter will create a basic KM system for the markup and manipulation of a document containing the user's annotations and comments from sources such as books or articles. From those documents, the system will be able to create dictionaries searchable with XPath, SMIL/HTML presentations, and arbitrary collections of annotations for printing.

To top it all off, these services will be available remotely using SOAP, so you can programmatically do operations such as selecting and printing the most relevant entries regarding topic X.

This chapter is about applied XML, not KM theory. However, we have made all possible effort to achieve a good balance between the purposes of this chapter as an XML learning tool and the actual usefulness of the application as a KM tool. The sections below follow the same development process as the previous chapter (requirements, analysis and architecture, design and implementation) in order to create our application.

Requirements

The following is the summary of the requirements returned by the req2txt.xsl stylesheet. The subsequent sections will cover the five key requirements.

- **Dictionary Creation [priority:1] [optional:no]**—From the annotations provided by the users, the system must create a searchable dictionary with definitions and references to concepts and keywords.
- **Edit and Enter Annotations [priority:1] [optional:no]**—The system must provide a sensible way to enter the XML data for a particular annotation. In other words, an editor for the Annotations Document Type must be provided.
- **SIML/HTML Presentation Creation [priority:2] [optional:yes]**—One common use for detailed notes, especially those taken with a broad audience in mind, is the creation of presentations. The system must provide the automatic creation of such PowerPoint™-like slides from annotation documents.
- **Browser Presentation [priority:1] [optional:yes]**—A sensible browser presentation must be provided for those documents which are to be individually browsed without being converted to presentations.

- **SOAP Interface to the application[priority:2] [optional:no]**—A programmatic, remote interface to the system must be provided. Even though it is not normally part of a functional requirement, this interface must be implemented using SOAP.

An HTML version of the requirements can be generated using the `req2html.xsl` stylesheet. The result is shown in Figure 20.1.

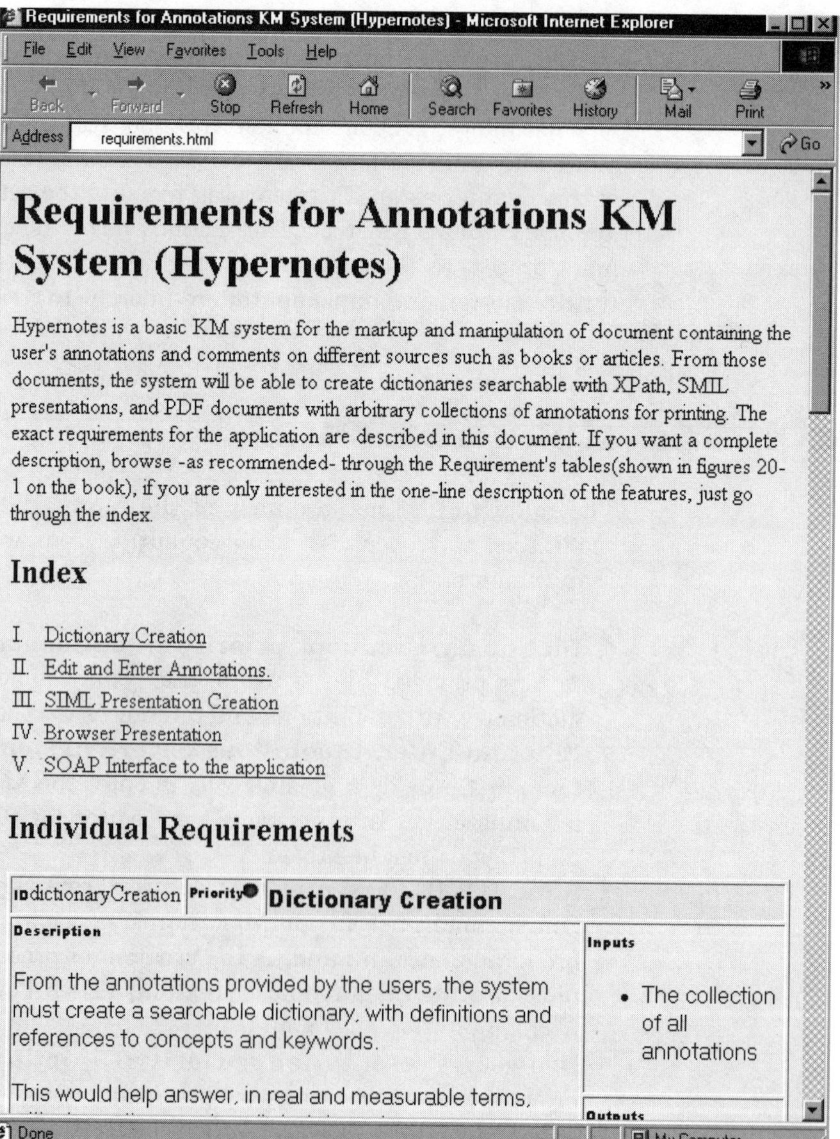
Requirements for Annotations KM System (Hypernotes) - Microsoft Internet Explorer
File Edit View Favorites Tools Help
Back Forward Stop Refresh Home Search Favorites History Mail Print
Address requirements.html
Go
Requirements for Annotations KM System (Hypernotes)
Hypernotes is a basic KM system for the markup and manipulation of document containing the user's annotations and comments on different sources such as books or articles. From those documents, the system will be able to create dictionaries searchable with XPath, SMIL presentations, and PDF documents with arbitrary collections of annotations for printing. The exact requirements for the application are described in this document. If you want a complete description, browse -as recommended- through the Requirement's tables(shown in figures 20-1 on the book), if you are only interested in the one-line description of the features, just go through the index.
Index
I. Dictionary Creation
II. Edit and Enter Annotations.
III. SIML Presentation Creation
IV. Browser Presentation
V. SOAP Interface to the application
Individual Requirements
ID dictionaryCreation
Priority
Dictionary Creation
Description
From the annotations provided by the users, the system must create a searchable dictionary, with definitions and references to concepts and keywords.
This would help answer, in real and measurable terms,
Inputs
The collection of all annotations
Outputs
Done
My Computer

Figure 20.1 The annotations KM system (xmlnotes).

For the sake of completeness, the XML document with the requirements for the project is included below:

```
<?xml version="1.0"?>
<!DOCTYPE fr
 PUBLIC "-//theFAActory//functionalRequirements DTD V2.0//EN"
 "fr\fr.dtd">
<fr>
  <header>
    <project>Annotations KM System (xmlnotes)</project>
    <description>
      <p>Xmlnotes is a basic KM system for the markup and
         manipulation of documents containing the user's
         annotations and comments on different sources such as
         books or articles. From those documents, the system will
         be able to create dictionaries searchable with XPath,
         SMIL presentations, and PDF documents with arbitrary
         collections of annotations for printing. </p>
      <p>The exact requirements for the application are described
         in this document. If you want a complete description,
         browse -as recommended- through the Requirement's
         tables(shown in Figure 20-1); if you are only interested
         in the one-line description of the features, just go
         through the index.</p>
    </description>
  </header>
  <requirement id="dictionaryCreation" optional="no"
   priority="1">
    <name xml:lang="en">Dictionary Creation</name>
    <description>
      <p>From the annotations provided by the users, the system
         must create a searchable dictionary with definitions and
         references to concepts and keywords.</p>
      <p>This would help answer, in real and measurable terms,
         critical questions such as "what do we know as an
         organization about X".</p>
    </description>
    <input><entry>The collection of all annotations
    </entry></input>
    <output><result>A searchable Dictionary with indexes and
     references to the definitions and emphasized terms in the
     original documents.
    </result></output>
  </requirement>
  <requirement id="enterAnnotations" optional="no" priority="1">
    <name xml:lang="en">Edit and Enter Annotations.</name>
    <description>
      <p>The System must provide a sensible way to enter the XML
         data for a particular annotation. In other words, an
         editor for the particular annotations Document Type must
         be provided.</p>
    </description>
```

```
    <input><entry>The components of the document through a user-
    friendly interface.
    </entry></input>
    <output><result>A conformant XML document that can be fed to
    the other parts of the system.
    </result></output>
  </requirement>
  <requirement id="PresentationCreation" optional="no"
  priority="2">
    <name xml:lang="en">SIML Presentation Creation</name>
    <description>
      <p>One common use for detailed notes, especially those
         taken with a broad audience in mind, is the creation of
         presentations.</p>
      <p>By virtue of having annotations marked-up as XML, the
         process of converting annotations to high-quality
         presentations is straight-forward (using XSLT).</p>
    </description>
    <input><entry>A particular set of notes (an XML document
    conformant with the annotations DTD).
    </entry></input>
    <output><result>A SIML Presentation with audio, text and pre-
    defined animation.
    </result></output>
  </requirement>
  <requirement id="browserPresentation" optional="no"
  priority="1">
    <name xml:lang="en">Browser Presentation</name>
    <description>
      <p>A sensible browser presentation must be provided for
         those documents which are to be individually browsed
         without being converted to presentations.</p>
    </description>
    <input><entry>A particular set of notes (an XML document
    conformant with the annotations DTD).
    </entry></input>
    <output><result>A browser view of it
    </result></output>
  </requirement>
  <requirement id="SOAP" optional="no" priority="2">
    <name xml:lang="en">SOAP Interface to the application</name>
    <description>
      <p>A programmatic, remote interface to the system must be
         provided. Even though it is not normally part of a
         functional requirement, it must be stressed here that
         this interface must be implemented using SOAP.</p>
    </description>
    <input><entry>
    </entry></input>
    <output><result>SOAP interface to the dictionary querying
    capabilities and SMIL creation.
    </result></output>
```

```
  </requirement>
</fr>
```

Architecture

The following architecture (Figure 20.2) is a high-level view of the system (from here on named xmlnotes), which shows, in terms of components and connectors, the basic parts of the solution for the requirements previously listed.

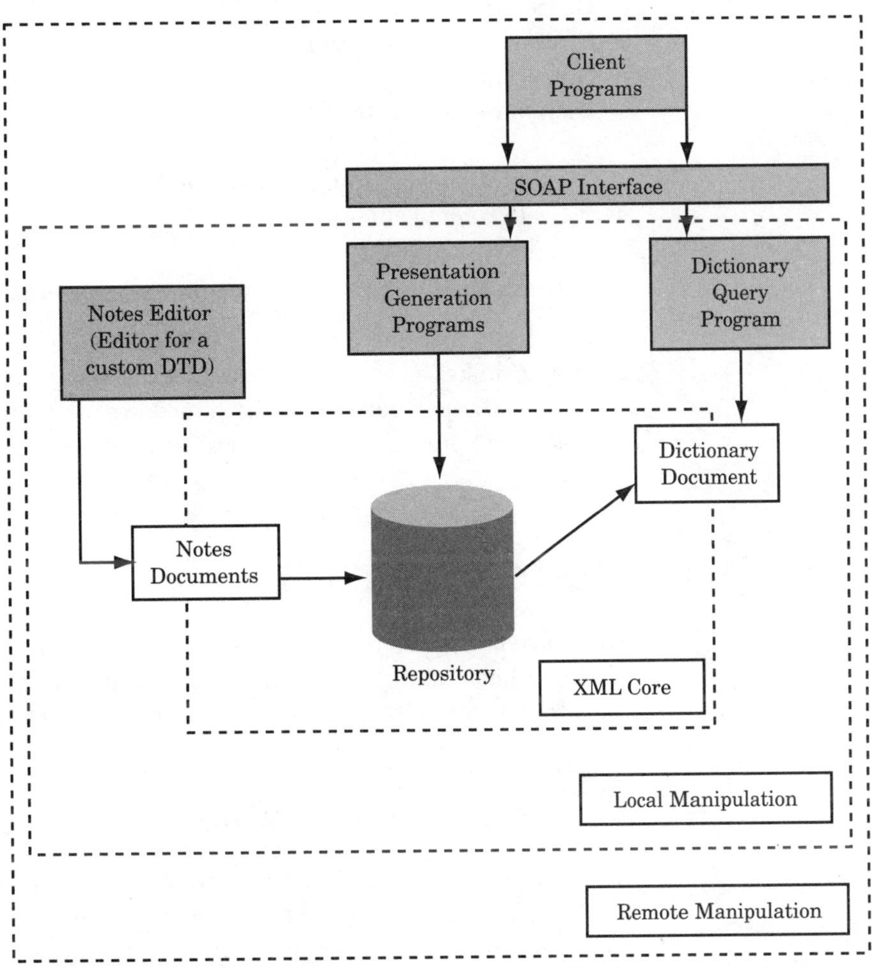

Figure 20.2 Architecture for the xmlnotes system.

The system is mainly composed of three levels: 1) the XML core—the documents that form the knowledge base of the company; 2) the local manipulation level, in which tools for the creation, population, and query of the core are provided; and 3) the remote manipulation level, which provides a SOAP interface to the second level, thus allowing the remote invocation of the services provided to local users.

The system, then, is composed of two types of documents: annotations and comments, and dictionary; and four different programs. Three of them are edition- and query-oriented (all them shown in the diagram) and the fourth program, because of its behind-the-scenes nature was not included in the diagram, but is essential for the system:

- Dictionary Query
- Presentation Generation
- Notes Editor
- Dictionary Generator

On top of these services, the SOAP interface will sit, providing its services to remote clients.

A Note on the Design and Implementation of the System

Due to the nature of the system (basically four very well-encapsulated pieces), it makes more sense (at least for the explanatory purposes of the book) to go through each of the main modules, designing and implementing, than trying to provide one huge class design diagram for the entire system.

Underlying DTDs

There are two types of documents to be designed: the annotations to an article or book, and the dictionary that binds collections of those annotations together as a coherent whole. Let's start with the annotations.

The Annotation DTD(s)

Even though it is true that the more complete and precise our markup is, the better our search mechanisms can perform, it is also true that the more requirements are imposed on the employee, the less frequent the system will be used.

To find a middle-ground solution, two DTDs were implemented: one, a transitional and very simple DTD that should be used only to introduce people to the system; and the other, a precise and rich DTD with many more options and expressive power, which should be the basis for serious organization data.

The SimpleNotes DTD

Even though it is possible to generate dictionaries from instances of the following DTD, its use is not encouraged and its only purpose is to give a quick and dirty introduction of loose notes for beginners.[1]

```
<!ELEMENT simpleNotes (title,
                       author,
                       originalAuthor,
                       notesGroup*)>
<!ATTLIST simpleNotes
          version        CDATA     #IMPLIED
       lastmodifiedCDATA          #IMPLIED>
<!ELEMENT originalAuthor    (#PCDATA)>
<!ELEMENT author    (#PCDATA)>
<!ELEMENT notesGroup      (title,intro?,(note|definiton)*)>
<!ATTLIST notesGroup
          name           ID         #REQUIRED>
<!ELEMENT title         (#PCDATA)>
<!ELEMENT intro         (#PCDATA)>
<!ELEMENT note          (title, p*)>
<!ELEMENT definition    (title, p*)>
<!ATTLIST note
          name           ID         #REQUIRED>
<!ELEMENT p             (#PCDATA| ul|
                         ol|
                         a|
                         img|
                         blockquote|
                         pre|
                         imp|
                         emp )* >
<!ELEMENT ul    (li*)>
<!ELEMENT ol    (li*)>
<!ELEMENT li    (#PCDATA|emp|imp|pre|blockquote)*>
<!ELEMENT a    (#PCDATA)>
<!ELEMENT img    (#PCDATA)>
<!ATTLIST img
          src  CDATA    #IMPLIED
          alt  CDATA    #IMPLIED>

<!ATTLIST a
          href  CDATA  #IMPLIED>
```

1 SMIL transformations are not provided for this document type. Only HTML+Javascript transformations are implemented for it.

```
<!ELEMENT blockquote   (pre)>
<!ELEMENT pre    (#PCDATA)>
<!ELEMENT imp    (#PCDATA)>
<!ELEMENT emp    (#PCDATA)>
```

The Booknotes DTD

The Booknotes DTD is a much more mature method of organizing annotations. Despite its name (which is only kept for historical reasons), instances of this document type can be used to annotate media other than books, and it is the center of our annotation system.

As you can see, this DTD takes elements from the theory presented for advanced DTDs (such as the use of parameter entity references in conditionals) as well as constructs from the XLink specification (such as the simple XLinks for the `relatedonline` element). The result is a robust way of expressing notes. The following is its definition:

```
<!--
     Name: booknotes
     Description: A DTD for notes made to a written work.
                  This DTD was Originally defined to express
                  notes to Umberto Eco's Foucault's Pendulum.
     Version : $Id: booknotes.dtd,v 1.2 2000/08/12 00:23:03
     Default Exp $
     Author: Fabio Arciniegas A.
-->

<!-- Typical use:

<!DOCTYPE booknotes PUBLIC "Fabio Arciniegas A.//DTD booknotes
V1.0//EN"
                           "booknotes.dtd">

-->

<!--
*****************************************************************
                Global Parameter entities
*****************************************************************
-->
  <!-- ***** Parameter entities used as conditionals ***** -->
     <!ENTITY % draft "INCLUDE">
     <!ENTITY % final "IGNORE">

<![%draft;[
  <!ENTITY % name "#PCDATA">
]]>

<![%final;[
```

```
  <!ENTITY % name "firstname,surname">
]]>

<!ENTITY % languageattribute "xml:lang    NMTOKEN    'en'">
<!ENTITY % referent           "term|person|book|concept|
                               artwork|name|mythrel|comment
                               organization|place|otherreferent">
<!ENTITY % number             "CDATA">
<!ENTITY % months
"jan|feb|mar|apr|may|jun|jul|aug|sep|oct|nov|dec">



<!--
****************************************************************
                  Elements and Attributes
****************************************************************
-->


<!ELEMENT booknotes (originalworkinfo,notesinfo,entry+)>
<!ATTLIST booknotes
          xmlns:xlink CDATA #FIXED
"http://www.w3.org/1999/xlink"
          xmlns       CDATA #FIXED
                      "http://www.thefaactory.com/booknotes">
<!ELEMENT originalworkinfo  (title,author,date,isbn?)>
<!ELEMENT notesinfo          (title,author,date)>
<!ELEMENT title              (#PCDATA)>
<!ATTLIST title
          %languageattribute;>
<!ELEMENT author             (%name;)>
<!ELEMENT date               (#PCDATA)>
<!ATTLIST date
          day    %number;   #IMPLIED
          month  (1|2|3|4|5|6|7|8|9|10|11|12|%months;|-)
#IMPLIED
          year   %number;   #REQUIRED>

<!--  ****** Referents ***** -->

<!ELEMENT entry   (name,daterange?,explanation,references)>
<!ELEMENT name    (#PCDATA)>
<!ATTLIST name
          %languageattribute;>
<!ELEMENT explanation (p+)>
<!ELEMENT p
(#PCDATA|emphasis|important|see|img|relatedonline|
                       relatedoutsidereferent)*>
<!ELEMENT references
(appearsin+,(see|relatedonline|relatedoutsidereferent)*)>
<!ATTLIST entry
          type       (%referent;)   #REQUIRED
```

```
          id          ID              #REQUIRED>

<!ELEMENT emphasis    (#PCDATA)>
<!ELEMENT important   (#PCDATA)>
<!ELEMENT daterange   (datefrom,dateto)>
<!ELEMENT datefrom                   (#PCDATA)>
<!ATTLIST datefrom
          day    %number;    #IMPLIED
          month  (1|2|3|4|5|6|7|8|9|10|11|12|%months;|-)
#IMPLIED
          year   %number;    #REQUIRED>
<!ELEMENT dateto                   (#PCDATA)>
<!ATTLIST dateto
          day    %number;    #IMPLIED
          month  (1|2|3|4|5|6|7|8|9|10|11|12|%months;|-)
#IMPLIED
          year   %number;    #REQUIRED>

<!ELEMENT see         (#PCDATA)>
<!ATTLIST see
          also        IDREF        #REQUIRED
       %languageattribute;>
<!ELEMENT img         (#PCDATA)>
<!ATTLIST img
          xlink:type (simple)  #FIXED   "simple"
          xlink:href CDATA     #REQUIRED>

<!-- Chapter and page of the book where its referenced -->
<!ELEMENT appearsin (#PCDATA)>
<!ATTLIST appearsin
          page        CDATA      #IMPLIED
          directly   (yes|no)    "yes"
          chapter     CDATA      #REQUIRED
       %languageattribute;>

<!ELEMENT relatedonline (#PCDATA)>
<!ATTLIST relatedonline
          xlink:type (simple)  #FIXED   "simple"
          xlink:href CDATA     #REQUIRED
       %languageattribute;>

<!-- A reference to a book, artwork, etc. that is not treated in
the notes nor is accessible on the web
-->
<!ELEMENT relatedoutsidereferent (#PCDATA)>
<!ATTLIST relatedoutsidereferent
          type        (%referent;)   #REQUIRED
       %languageattribute;>
```

SAMPLE DOCUMENTS

The following is a sample document for the `simpleNotes` DTD:

```
<simpleNotes>
  <title>AOP Primer</title>
  <bookauthor>Xerox Corporation</bookauthor>
  <noteGroup name="aopc">
     <title>Aspect-Oriented Programming Concepts</title>
     <definition name="whatiscrosscutting">
        <title>cross-cutting</title>
     An initial division of labor is achieved by means of
     objects. However, certain concerns are spread over many
     objects; the fact that this concerns touch in some way
     several components is called cross-cutting.
     </definition>
     <definition name="whatisaspect">
        <title>Aspect</title>
     <ul>
       <li>From the design point of view, is a cross-cutting
       concern.</li>
       <li>From the programming point of view, is a physical
       construct compromising variables, methods and waves, thus
       reflecting the design aspect.</li>
     </ul>
     </definition>
     <definition name="whatisweaving">
        <title>Weaving</title>
     Weaving is the systematic process of combining aspects and
     objects.
     </definition>
     <note name="moreinfo">
        <title>Getting more information</title>

     <A HREF="http://www.parc.xerox.com/aop">
     Aspect-Oriented Programming at Xerox PARC</A>

     <A HREF="http://www.parc.xerox.com/eca/pubs/by-topic.html">
     Publications from the Xerox PARC AOP project</A>

     <A HREF="http://www.parc.xerox.com/aop/ecoop98">
     Proceedings of the AOP workshop at ECOOP'98</A>

     <A HREF="http://www.parc.xerox.com/aop/icse98">
     Proceedings of the AOP workshop at ICSE'98</A>

     <A HREF="http://www.parc.xerox.com/aop/ecoop97">
     Proceedings of the AOP workshop at ECOOP'97</A>
     </note>
  </noteGroup>
  <!--other note groups here ->
</simpleNotes>
```

Much more interesting is the following document, an instance of the booknotes DTD:

```
<?xml version="1.0"?>
<!--
.....................................................................
                  FAA's Dictionary of Foucault's Pendulum.

.....................................................................
     Author: Fabio Arciniegas A.
fabio@viaduct.com

.....................................................................
     $Id: foucaults_pendulum.xml,v 1.5 2000/11/14 02:25:12
Default Exp $
 -->

<!DOCTYPE booknotes PUBLIC "Fabio Arciniegas A.//DTD booknotes
V1.0//EN"
                             "booknotes.dtd"
[
<!ENTITY recent "November 14, 2001">
]>
<booknotes xmlns:xlink="http://www.w3.org/1999/xlink"

xmlns="http://www.thefaactory.com/booknotes">
  <originalworkinfo>
    <title xml:lang="en">Il pendolo di Foucaoult</title>
    <author>Umberto Eco</author>
    <date month="jan" year="1988"></date>
  </originalworkinfo>
  <notesinfo>
    <title xml:lang="en">English Dictionary to Foucault's
Pendulum</title>
    <author>Fabio Arciniegas A.
&lt;faa@fabioarciniegas.com&gt;</author>
    <date year="2000">First entry: september 27 2000. Most
Recent: &recent;</date>
  </notesinfo>

  <entry type="person" id="anselm">
    <name xml:lang="en">Anselm, Saint</name>
    <daterange>
      <datefrom year="1033"/>
      <dateto year="1109"/>
    </daterange>
    <explanation>
      <p>Saint Anselm, a theologian and philosopher, was born in
         Circa in 1033. In 1078 he redacted
         his<relatedoutsidereferent type="book" xml:lang="en">
         Proslogium ("discourse") </relatedoutsidereferent> which
         contains his famous <emphasis>ontological
         argument</emphasis> which is based on the existence of
         degrees of <emphasis>goodness</emphasis>, and the
```

```
        ultimate "undeniable conclusion" of the ultimate
        goodness, God. </p>
      <p>Both he and his contemporary Gaunilo of Marmoutier serve
        as examples of <emphasis>"stupid"</emphasis> for
        <important>Belbo</important>'s typology since their
        arguments, though complex in nature, are completely
        delusional.</p>
    </explanation>
    <references>
      <appearsin directly="yes" chapter="10"
      xml:lang="en"></appearsin>
      <relatedonline xlink:type="simple"

xlink:href="http://goodcompanyclub.tripod.com/03_00forum.htm#Anse
lm"
      xml:lang="en">
      Anselm's favorite beverage or "Yohoo chocolate exists, God
      must too"
      </relatedonline>
    </references>
  </entry>

  <entry type="term" id="pantarei">
    <name>Panta Rei</name>
    <explanation><p>Panta Rei is a greek expression used by <see
    also="heraclitus" xml:lang="en">Heraclitus</see> to express
    the concept of <emphasis>perpetual change</emphasis> in the
    universe. According to Heraclitus, the only constant in the
    universe is change. Panta Rei means "<emphasis>everything
    flows</emphasis>".</p></explanation>
    <references>
      <appearsin directly="yes" chapter="1" xml:lang="en"/>
      <relatedoutsidereferent type="book" xml:lang="en">On
      Nature, by Heraclitus of Ephesus</relatedoutsidereferent>
    </references>
  </entry>

  <entry type="concept" id="ensof">
    <name>En-Sof</name>
    <explanation>
      <p>In the Hebrew Kabalah tradition, En-sof, which could be
        translated as "<emphasis>Infinite</emphasis>", is the
        primordial and perfect form of God, from which the ten
        <see also="sefirot" xml:lang="en">Sefirot</see>
        derive.</p>
    </explanation>
    <references>
      <appearsin directly="yes" chapter="1" xml:lang="en"/>
    </references>
  </entry>

  <entry type="person" id="heraclitus">
```

```
    <name>Heraclitus of Ephesus</name>
    <daterange>
      <datefrom year="540?"/>
      <dateto year="475?"/>
    <explanation>
      <p>Heraclitus of Ephesus was one of the founders of Greek
         <emphasis>Methaphysics</emphasis>. His philosophy is
         based on the principle of perpetual change, immanent to
         all things. His vision was later opposed by that of
         Parmenides, who argued the Universe is an indivisible
         and constant whole and any reference to change is
         self-contradictory.</p></explanation>
    <references>
      <appearsin directly="no" chapter="1" xml:lang="en"/>
    </references>
  </entry>
  <!-- 100+ more entries -->
</booknotes>
```

The Dictionary

The dictionary DTD defines the structure for a master index document that will be the target of all the queries in the system. The dictionary must have an entry for each term, person, book, concept, artwork, and place of the original documents, stating how it relates to other resources, as well as giving a definition of it.

The dictionary is based on two simple mechanisms: *XPointer expressions* to point to the correct elements in the original sources, and *redundant information* for the sake of time efficiency.

Both of these mechanisms are evident on the DTD: the first is obligatory on the `relatedX` elements, as the simple XLink must point to a particular location inside a document, not to a document as a whole. The second mechanism is pervasive throughout the DTD: entry counters, reference counters, aggregations by reference type, etc. are all pieces of data that could have been extracted from the dictionary itself. However, they are explicitly provided in order to minimize the access time of client routines[2] (e.g. it is far more efficient to fetch for the value of the XPath expression `/entryCount` than it is to count all the elements in the dictionary).

The following is the Dictionary DTD:

[2] Likewise the dictionary itself is a redundant way to express some of the data in the annotation documents, for the sake of efficiency.

```
    <!ENTITY % draft "INCLUDE">
  <!ENTITY % final "IGNORE">

<![%draft;[
  <!ENTITY % name "#PCDATA">
]]>

<![%final;[
  <!ENTITY % name "firstname,surname">
]]>

<!ENTITY % languageattribute "xml:lang    NMTOKEN    'en'">
<!ENTITY % referent              "term|person|book|concept|
                                  artwork|name|mythrel|comment|
                                  organization|place|otherreferent">
<!ENTITY % number                "CDATA">
<!ENTITY % months
"jan|feb|mar|apr|may|jun|jul|aug|sep|oct|nov|dec">


<!ELEMENT dictionary (header,entries)>
<!ELEMENT header     (entryCount,
                      termCount,
                      bookCount,
                      conceptCount,
                      organizationCount,
                      personCount,
                      placeCount)>
<!ELEMENT entries    (entry)+>
```

NOTE

Each bundle of references (`termReferences`*, etc.) is made obligatory, in order to simplify the implementation of some queries.*

```
<!ELEMENT entry              (name,termReferences,
                                   bookReferences,
                                   conceptReferences,
                                   personReferences,
                                   organizationReferences,
                                   placeReferences)>

<!ELEMENT termReferences    (entryRef*)>
<!ELEMENT bookReferences    (entryRef*)>
<!ELEMENT conceptReferences (entryRef*)>
<!ELEMENT placeReferences   (entryRef*)>
<!ELEMENT personReferences         (entryRef*)>
<!ELEMENT organizationReferences   (entryRef*)>

<!ELEMENT entryRef (#PCDATA) >
```

```
<!ATTLIST entryRef
          xlink:type (simple)  #FIXED   "simple"
          xlink:href CDATA     #REQUIRED>
```

A Sample Dictionary

An extremely small knowledge base (only two entries), could have a dictionary document such as the following:

```
<!DOCTYPE dictionary SYSTEM "dictionary.dtd">
<dictionary>
  <header>
    <entryCount>2</entryCount>
    <termCount>1</termCount>
    <bookCount>0</bookCount>
    <conceptCount>0</conceptCount>
    <organizationCount>0</organizationCount>
    <personCount>1</personCount>
    <placeCount>0</placeCount>
  </header>
  <entries>
    <entry>
      <name>Heraclitus of Ephesus</name>
      <termReferences>
     <entryRef xlink:type="simple"

xlink:href="hostDocument.xml#xpointer(//entry[id('pantarei')])">
         </entryRef>
      </termReferences>
      <bookReferences>
      </bookReferences>
      <conceptReferences>
      </conceptReferences>
      <personReferences>
      </personReferences>
      <organizationReferences>
      </organizationReferences>
      <placeReferences>
      </placeReferences>
    </entry>
    <entry>
      <name>Panta Rei</name>
      <termReferences>
      </termReferences>
      <bookReferences>
      </bookReferences>
      <conceptReferences>
      </conceptReferences>
```

NOTE

In the dictionary, both entries have references to each other, while in the original document only Panta Rei had a reference to Heraclitus.

```
<personReferences>
     <entryRef xlink:type="simple"

xlink:href="someother.xml#xpointer(//entry[id('heraclitus')])">
       </personReferences>
       <organizationReferences>
       </organizationReferences>
       <placeReferences>
       </placeReferences>
     </entry>
  </entries>
</dictionary>
```

Note that dictionaries serve pretty much the same use as indices in traditional databases. The reason why this and other DB parallels have been ignored is simple: what we are defining here can easily be ported to a database using encapsulation techniques such as the one shown in the previous chapter. The XML orientation here does not mean that everything must be in plain files.[3]

The dictionary generator is implemented as a series of simple SAX filters, very similar to those found in Chapter 5. Please refer to the CD for the actual code.

An Editor for the Annotation Documents

One attractive feature of the system is the inclusion of a custom editor for files of the type `booknote` DTD. Even though any editor could be used to generate these documents (e.g. XML spy, emacs), creating such a custom editor is a nice programming and UI design exercise, and has proved appealing in the past for similar projects.

The editor presented here is based on the Mediator pattern for DOM, described in Chapter 7 (Figure 20.3). The basic idea is to have a series of

[3] Here, for ease of implementation, the XML is actually in plain files. However, this need not be (nor should it be) the case for larger applications.

nodes (the entries), all coordinated by a central DOMMediator Class that takes care of updating them as the user interface changes.

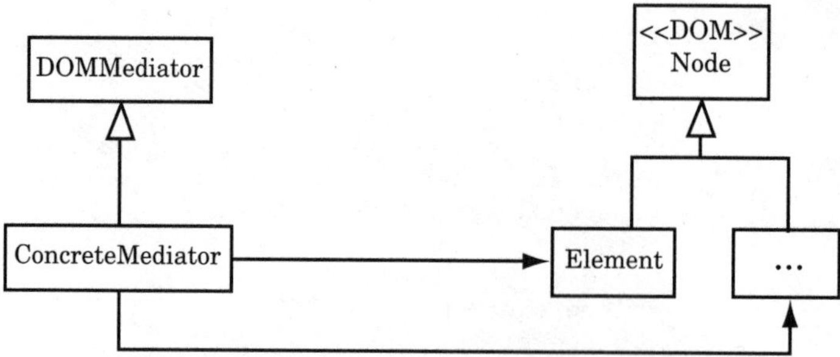

Figure 20.3 DOMMediator.

Programmatically, the application is very simple and could be described as the union of two basic procedures:

- Create the visual representation of the document, taking care of tying it back to the DOM document, so when the user clicks on the visual representation, the Mediator can easily know the location of the real node.
- Update the node whenever a UI item in the interface changes.

The first part can be easily implemented with the following methods:

```
import java.io.OutputStreamWriter;
import java.io.PrintWriter;
import java.io.UnsupportedEncodingException;

import org.w3c.dom.Attr;
import org.w3c.dom.Document;
import org.w3c.dom.NamedNodeMap;
import org.w3c.dom.Node;
import org.w3c.dom.NodeList;

public class DOMMediator {
    public static void main(String args[])
    {
          createVisualTree(myDocument);
    }
    public void createVisualTree(Node node)
    {

      if (node == null)
           return;

        int type = node.getNodeType();
```

```
        JTree current = null;

        switch (type)
         { // find what type of node we are dealing with

         case Node.DOCUMENT_NODE: {
               current = addNewVisualNode("Annotations", ICON_1);
               tieVisual(current,node);
          break;
         }

         case Node.ELEMENT_NODE: {
          if(node.getNodeName().compareTo("term"))
               {
               Node myDescription text =
                          node.getChildNodes().item(0).getValue();
               current = addNewVisualNode(myDescription,
               icon_term);
               tieVisual(current,node);
               }

          if(node.getNodeName().compareTo("organization"))
               {
               Node myDescription text =
                         node.getChildNodes().item(0).getValue();
               current = addNewVisualNode(myDescription,
                         icon_org);
               tieVisual(current,node);
               }
                   // similar ifs for person, place, etc
          break;
         }
         }

     // Now recurse through the children nodes
        NodeList children = node.getChildNodes();
        if (children != null) {
         int len = children.getLength();
            for (int i = 0; i < len; i++)
          createVisualTree(children.item(i));
        }
     }

     Document DOMTree;
     JTree    visualTree;
     JImage   icon_term; // and other icons for the other problems
     HashTable visualToDOM = new HashTable();
}
```

The second, easier, part of the application takes the form of UI handlers, fetching the right node and updating it to whatever the changed field requires. Here is one such implementation:

```
public Node findNode(JTreeNode visual)
{
 return (Node) visualToDOM(visual);
}
 public void changeTitle(JTreeNode visual)
{
  visualToDOM(visual).setValue(visual.getName());
}
```

SMIL/HTML for the Creation of Presentations

One of the services provided by the second layer of our application is the production of PowerPoint™-like presentations out of the annotation documents. The following rather complex transformation shows how to use the multiple output extension of XT and the XPath language in order to create numerous pages out of a single annotations file. More transformations for annotations can be found on the CD.

Snapshots of the Result

Before we get to the actual transformation, let's take a look at the final result. Figures 20.5 and 20.6 show some of the output.

```
<xsl:stylesheet xmlns:xsl="http://www.w3.org/1999/XSL/Transform"
                xmlns:xt="http://www.jclark.com/xt"
        version="1.0"
                extension-element-prefixes="xt">
<xsl:output method="text"/>

<xsl:template match="simplenotes">
  <xt:document method="html" href="index.html">
    <html>
        <head>
      <title> <xsl:value-of select="title"/> </title>
     </head>
     <FRAMESET ROWS="100,*" COLS="150,*" border="0">
       <FRAME SRC="logo.htm" NAME="logo"/>
       <FRAMESET COLS="550,*">
         <FRAME SRC="initialHeader.html" NAME="header"></FRAME>
         <FRAME SRC="initialNav.html" NAME="nav"></FRAME>
       </FRAMESET>
       <FRAME SRC="initialToc.html" NAME="toc"></FRAME>
       <FRAME SRC="initialBody.html" NAME="body"></FRAME>
```

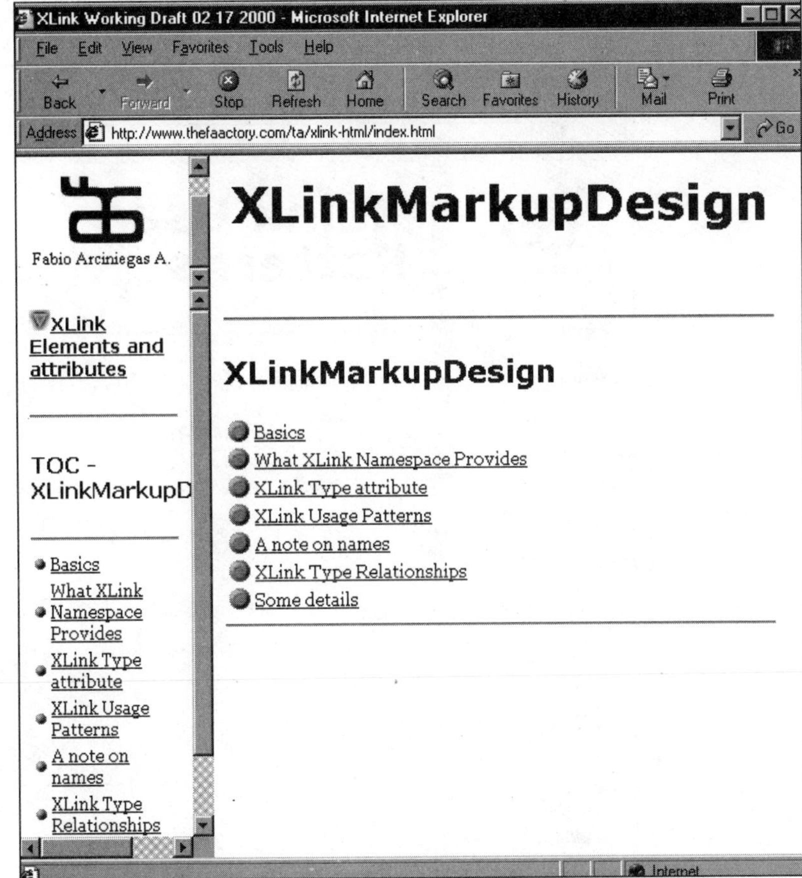

Figure 20.5 Annotation transformation output.

```
</FRAMESET>
   </html>
  </xt:document>

  <xsl:text>Created index.html: Main File.</xsl:text>
  <xsl:text>&#xA;</xsl:text>
  <!-- logo.html is not generated -->
  <xt:document method="html" href="initialHeader.html">
    <html>
     <body background="bodyBackground.jpg">
     </body>
    </html>
  </xt:document>

  <xt:document method="html" href="initialToc.html">
    <html>
     <body background="bodyBackground.jpg">
         <!-- Initial header is empty. -->
```

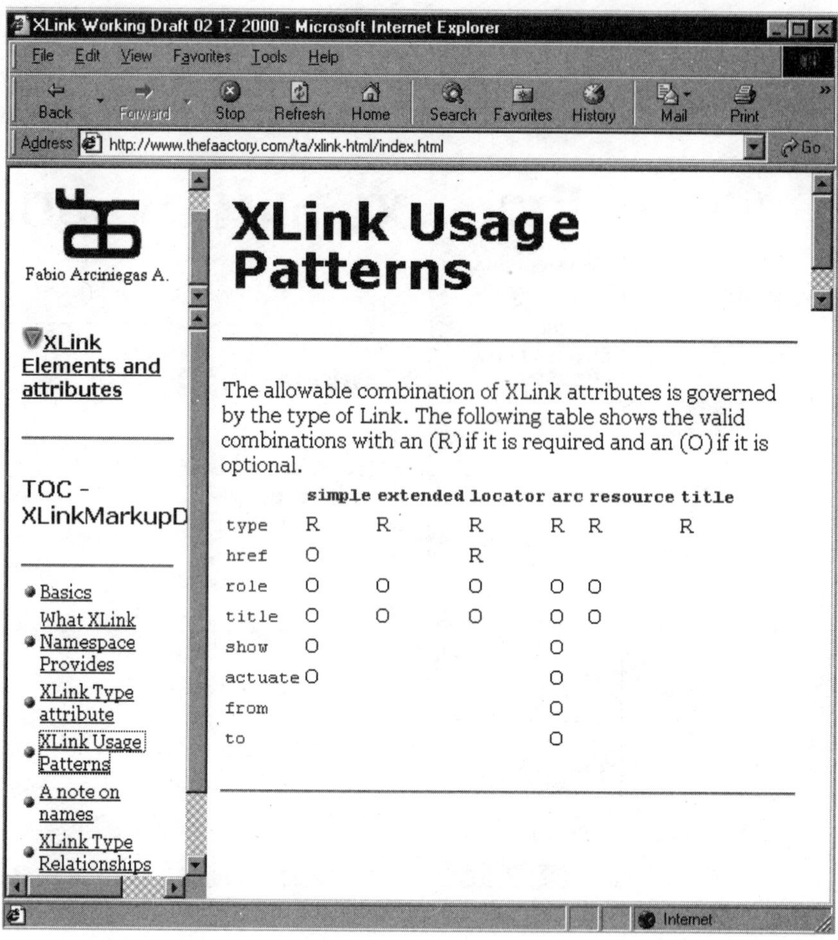

Figure 20.6 Annotation transformation output.

```
    </body>
   </html>
  </xt:document>


  <xt:document method="html" href="initialNav.html">
    <html>
     <body background="bodyBackground.jpg">
        <a href="{notegroup/@name}Nav.html"
         OnClick="top.header.location =
'{notegroup/@name}Header.html';
                  top.toc.location =
'{notegroup/@name}TOC.html';
                  top.body.location =
'{notegroup/@name}Body.html';"
         >
            <img src="start.gif" border="0"></img>
```

```
          <br/><small>Start Here</small>
        </a>
      </body>
    </html>
  </xt:document>


  <xt:document method="html" href="initialBody.html">
    <html>
     <!-- Generated by slider.xsl, Fabio Arciniegas A. 2000 -->
     <head>
       <title>TopTest</title>
       <link href="basic.css"  rel="stylesheet" type="text/css"/>
         </head>
     <body background="bodyBackground.jpg">
     <hr/>
     <center>
         <h1>  <xsl:value-of select="title"/>: Reading notes </h1>
         <h2>Fabio Arciniegas A.</h2>
         <h2>fabio@viaduct.com</h2>
        </center>
     <hr/>
     <center>
        <small>Copyright 2000, Fabio Arciniegas A.</small>
            <br/>
            <small>All rights Reserved.</small>
     </center>
     </body>
    </html>
  </xt:document>
  <xsl:apply-templates/>
</xsl:template>


<xsl:template match="notegroup">
  <xt:document method="html"
href="{concat(@name,'Header.html')}">
    <html>
     <head>
       <link href="basic.css"  rel="stylesheet" type="text/css"/>
     </head>
     <body background="bodyBackground.jpg">
       <table>
         <tr><td></td>
        <td><H1><xsl:value-of select="title"/></H1></td>
         </tr>
        </table>
     </body>
    </html>
  </xt:document>

  <xt:document method="html" href="{concat(@name,'TOC.html')}">
  <html>
```

```
    <head>
       <title>TOC - <xsl:value-of select="title"/></title>
       <link href="basic.css"  rel="stylesheet" type="text/css"/>
    </head>
    <body background="bodyBackground.jpg">
    <!-- Now put the previous and next notegroup  buttons -->
    <xsl:if test="following-sibling::notegroup">
         <h4>
              <a href="{following-
sibling::notegroup[1]/@name}TOC.html"
         OnClick="top.header.location = '{following-
sibling::notegroup[1]/@name}Header.html';
                   top.nav.location =    '{following-
sibling::notegroup[1]/@name}Nav.html';
                   top.body.location =    '{following-
sibling::notegroup[1]/@name}Body.html';"
         >
         <img src="darrow.gif" border="0"></img>
              <xsl:value-of select="following-
sibling::notegroup[1]/title"/>
         </a>
     </h4>
    </xsl:if>
    <xsl:if test="preceding-sibling::notegroup">
         <h4>
              <a href="{preceding-
sibling::notegroup[1]/@name}TOC.html"
         OnClick="top.header.location =
           '{preceding-sibling::notegroup[1]/@name}Header.html';
                   top.nav.location =
           '{preceding-sibling::notegroup[1]/@name}Nav.html';
                   top.body.location =
           '{preceding-sibling::notegroup[1]/@name}Body.html';"
         > <img src="uarrow.gif" border="0"></img>
              <xsl:value-of select="preceding-
sibling::notegroup[1]/title"/>
         </a>
     </h4>
    </xsl:if>

    </body>

   <hr/>
        <h3>TOC - <xsl:value-of select="title"/></h3>
              <hr/>
     <table>
                <xsl:for-each select="note|definition">
             <tr>
             <td>
               <img src="littleBullet.gif"></img>
             </td>
             <td><small>
              <a href="javascript:void(0)"
```

```
                OnClick="top.header.location =
'{./@name}Header.html';
                            top.nav.location =
'{./@name}Nav.html';
                              top.body.location =
'{./@name}Body.html';"
              >
                <xsl:value-of select="./title"/>
            </a>
            </small>
             </td>
            </tr>
          </xsl:for-each>
          </table>
        <hr/>
    </html>
  </xt:document>


  <xt:document method="html" href="{concat(@name,'Body.html')}">
    <html>
     <head>
       <title> <xsl:value-of select="title"/> </title>
         <link href="basic.css"  rel="stylesheet"
type="text/css"/>
        </head>
     <body background="bodyBackground.jpg">
       <hr/>
          <h2> <xsl:value-of select="title"/></h2>
          <h3> <xsl:value-of select="intro"/> </h3>
          <table>
               <xsl:for-each select="note|definition">
            <tr>
            <td>
              <img src="bullet.gif"></img>
            </td>
            <td>                      <a href="{./@name}Body.html"
                OnClick="top.header.location =
'{./@name}Header.html';
                                top.nav.location =
'{./@name}Nav.html';"
              >
                <xsl:value-of select="./title"/>
            </a>
             </td>
            </tr>
          </xsl:for-each>
          </table>
       <hr/>
      </body>
     </html>
   </xt:document>
```

```
  <xt:document method="html" href="{concat(@name,'Nav.html')}">
   <html>
     <body background="bodyBackground.jpg">
     </body>
   </html>
  </xt:document>
  <xsl:apply-templates/>
</xsl:template>


<xsl:template match="note/title">
  <!-- Ignore it -->
</xsl:template>

<xsl:template match="note">

  <!-- Generate the body -->
  <xt:document method="html"
href="{concat(@name,'Header.html')}">
   <html>
    <head>
      <link href="basic.css"  rel="stylesheet" type="text/css"/>
    </head>
    <body background="bodyBackground.jpg">
      <table>
        <tr><td></td>
       <td><H1><xsl:value-of select="title"/></H1></td>
        </tr>
       </table>
    </body>
   </html>
  </xt:document>

  <!-- Generate the body -->
  <xt:document method="html" href="{concat(@name,'Body.html')}">
    <html>
     <head>
       <title> <xsl:value-of select="title"/> </title>
         <link href="basic.css"  rel="stylesheet"
type="text/css"/>
        </head>
     <body background="bodyBackground.jpg">
       <hr/>
        <xsl:apply-templates/>
       <hr/>
     </body>
    </html>
  </xt:document>

  <!-- Generate navigation -->
  <xt:document method="html" href="{concat(@name,'Nav.html')}">
   <html>
```

```
<body background="bodyBackground.jpg">
<table>
<tr>
<xsl:if test="following-sibling::note">
   <td>
   <a href="{following-sibling::note[1]/@name}Nav.html"
    OnClick="top.header.location =
       '{following-sibling::note[1]/@name}Header.html';
              top.body.location =
       '{following-sibling::note[1]/@name}Body.html';"
         >
     <img src="rarrow.gif" border="0"> </img>
     </a>
       </td>
   </xsl:if>

   <xsl:if test="following-sibling::definition">
   <td>
   <a href="{following-sibling::definition[1]/@name}Nav.html"
    OnClick="top.header.location =
       '{following-sibling::definition[1]/@name}Header.html';
              top.body.location =
       '{following-sibling::definition[1]/@name}Body.html';"
         >
     <img src="rarrow.gif" border="0"> </img>
     </a>
       </td>
   </xsl:if>

<xsl:if test="preceding-sibling::note">
   <td>
   <a href="{preceding-sibling::note[1]/@name}Nav.html"
    OnClick="top.header.location =
       '{preceding-sibling::note[1]/@name}Header.html';
              top.body.location =
       '{preceding-sibling::note[1]/@name}Body.html';"
         >
     <img src="larrow.gif" border="0"> </img>
     </a>
       </td>
   </xsl:if>

   <xsl:if test="preceding-sibling::definition">
   <td>
   <a href="{preceding-sibling::definition[1]/@name}Nav.html"
    OnClick="top.header.location =
       '{preceding-sibling::definition[1]/@name}Header.html';
              top.body.location =
       '{preceding-sibling::definition[1]/@name}Body.html';"
         >
     <img src="larrow.gif" border="0"> </img>
     </a>
       </td>
```

```
          </xsl:if>
        </tr>
        </table>
        </body>
      </html>
    </xt:document>
</xsl:template>

<xsl:template match="imp">
      <em class="imp">
            <xsl:apply-templates/>
      </em>
</xsl:template>

<xsl:template match="emp">
      <em>
            <xsl:apply-templates/>
      </em>
</xsl:template>


<!-- For all the rest... there is xsl:copy-->
<xsl:template match="*|@*">
  <xsl:copy>
    <xsl:apply-templates select="@*"/>
    <xsl:apply-templates select="node()"/>
  </xsl:copy>
</xsl:template>
</xsl:stylesheet>
```

Summary

This chapter presented a medium-size knowledge management application based on XML. It showcased several key technologies such as XPath, DOM, SAX, and XSLT. This is a rather bulky application, and much can be learned from it. This chapter touched on the most crucial points of the architecture and design, and is expected to provide a good guide to the code. However, in order to get the most out of the application, it is strongly recommended that you experiment with it and study the code on the CD and the Website (http://www.thefaactory.com/xmldevguide).

APPENDIX A

XML SYNTAX REFERENCE

This appendix presents a summary of the syntax of XML documents and DTDs. It is intended as a quick lookup tool and doesn't replace Chapters 1 and 2, which go into further depth on the constructs presented here.

Elements and Attributes

Construct	Syntax	Example
Start tags	<name>	<redrum>
End tags	</name>	</redrum>
Empty element tags	<name/>	<danny/>
CDATA sections	<![CDATA[....]]>	<![CDATA[is 3 < Ψ and 4 < a ?]]>
Comments	<!-- comment -->	<!-- this is a comment -->
Elements	<tag> content </tag> – or – <tag/>	<mixed_element> <character_data_element> character data </character_data_element> some more character data </some_mixed_element>
Attributes	name= "value" – or – name='value' inside start or empty element tags	<foo year="2004">

DTD Declarations

<table>
<tr><th>Construct</th><th>Syntax</th><th>Example</th></tr>
<tr><td>Element declarations</td><td><!ELEMENT name (content_model)>
where content_model is one of:
#PCDATA
#PCDATA | element1 | element2
or any combination of elements or groups with the | and , operators, and the * ? modifiers (see Chapter 2 for complete description)</td><td><!ELEMENT a (#PCDATA)>
<!ELEMENT b (c | d)>
<!ELEMENT b (c | d | (e,f))*>
<!ELEMENT b (#PCDATA | c | d)></td></tr>
<tr><td>Attribute list declarations</td><td><!ATTLIST element_name attribute_name type optionality default>
(see Chapter 2 for a complete description)</td><td><!ATTLIST country population CDATA #REQUIRED>
<!ATTLIST dvd
id ID #REQUIRED
features NMTOKENS #IMPLIED
rating (G | PG | PG13 | R) "R"
onStock CDATA #FIXED "yes"></td></tr>
<tr><td>Parsed internal entity declarations</td><td><!ENTITY name "replacement"></td><td><!ENTITY bullet "diamond"></td></tr>
<tr><td>Parsed external entity declarations</td><td><!ENTITY name SYSTEM "location">
<!ENTITY name PUBLIC "identifier"></td><td><!ENTITY chapter2 SYSTEM "chap2.xml">
<!ENTITY chapter2 PUBLIC "Koobod"></td></tr>
<tr><td>Notation declarations</td><td><!NOTATION name PUBLIC "identifier"></td><td><!NOTATION vrml1 PUBLIC "VRML 1">
<!NOTATION vrml1 PUBLIC "VRML 1"></td></tr>
<tr><td>Unparsed entity declarations</td><td><!ENTITY name SYSTEM "system identifier" NDATA</td><td><!NOTATION jpeg PUBLIC "JPEG">
<!ENTITY unicorn
SYSTEM "http://www.thefaactory.com/unicorn.jpg"
NDATA jpeg>notation_name></td></tr>
<tr><td>Parameter entity declarations</td><td><!ENTITY % name "replacement"></td><td><!ENTITY % numer "#PCDATA"></td></tr>
</table>

Entity References

Construct	Syntax	Example
Parsed entities	&name;	&myText;
Parameter entities	%name; only within DTD	%float;
Unparsed entities as ENTITY or ENTITIES attribute value	<element entityAttribute= "name">	<fixedImage from="myEn"/>

APPENDIX B

XML 1.0 SPECIFICATION

This appendix presents a complete transcription of the XML 1.0 Specification. It is an essential reference tool that should be kept close at hand during the development of XML applications.

Even though the language itself has not suffered (and probably will not) any major modification since its inception, small errors and clarifications are occasionally published by the W3C. This chapter presents an updated version of the specification, but you are encouraged to check every couple of months for updates.

Extensible Markup Language (XML) 1.0 (Second Edition)

W3C Recommendation 6 October 2000

This Version

http://www.w3.org/TR/2000/REC-xml-20001006 (XHTML, XML, PDF, XHTML review version with color-coded revision indicators)

Latest Version

http://www.w3.org/TR/REC-xml

Previous Versions

http://www.w3.org/TR/2000/WD-xml-2e-20000814
http://www.w3.org/TR/1998/REC-xml-19980210

Editors

Tim Bray, Textuality and Netscape <tbray@textuality.com>
Jean Paoli, Microsoft <jeanpa@microsoft.com>
C. M. Sperberg-McQueen, University of Illinois at Chicago and Text Encoding Initiative <cmsmcq@uic.edu>
Eve Maler, Sun Microsystems, Inc. <eve.maler@east.sun.com>—Second Edition

Abstract

The Extensible Markup Language (XML) is a subset of SGML that is completely described in this document. Its goal is to enable generic SGML to be served, received, and processed on the Web in the way that is now possible with HTML. XML has been designed for ease of implementation and for interoperability with both SGML and HTML.

Status of this Document

This document has been reviewed by W3C Members and other interested parties and has been endorsed by the Director as a W3C Recommendation. It is a stable document and may be used as reference material or cited as a normative reference from another document. W3C's role in making the Recommendation is to draw attention to the specification and to promote its widespread deployment. This enhances the functionality and interoperability of the Web.

This document specifies a syntax created by subsetting an existing, widely used international text processing standard (Standard Generalized Markup Language, ISO 8879:1986(E) as amended and corrected) for use on the World Wide Web. It is a product of the W3C XML Activity, details of which can be found at **http://www.w3.org/XML**. The English version of this specification is the only normative version. However, for translations of this document, see **http://www.w3.org/XML/#trans.** A list of current W3C Recommendations and other technical documents can be found at **http://www.w3.org/TR**.

This second edition is not a new version of XML (first published 10 February 1998); it merely incorporates the changes dictated by the first-edition errata (available at **http://www.w3.org/XML/xml-19980210-errata**) as a convenience to readers. The errata list for this second edition is available at **http://www.w3.org/XML/xml-V10-2e-errata**.

Please report errors in this document to xml-editor@w3.org; archives are available.

Note

C. M. Sperberg-McQueen's affiliation has changed since the publication of the first edition. He is now at the World Wide Web Consortium, and can be contacted at **cmsmcq@w3.org**.

1 Introduction

Extensible Markup Language, abbreviated XML, describes a class of data objects called *XML documents* and partially describes the behavior of computer programs which process them. XML is an application profile or restricted form of SGML, the Standard Generalized Markup Language [ISO 8879]. By construction, XML documents are conforming SGML documents.

XML documents are made up of storage units called *entities*, which contain either parsed or unparsed data. Parsed data is made up of *characters*, some of which form *character data*, and some of which form markup. Markup encodes a description of the document's storage layout and logical structure. XML provides a mechanism to impose constraints on the storage layout and logical structure.

[Definition: A software module called an **XML processor** is used to read XML documents and provide access to their content and structure.] [Definition: It is assumed that an XML processor is doing its work on behalf of another module, called the *application*.] This specification describes the required behavior of an XML processor in terms of how it must read XML data and the information it must provide to the application.

1.1 Origin and Goals

XML was developed by an XML Working Group (originally known as the SGML Editorial Review Board) formed under the auspices of the World Wide Web Consortium (W3C) in 1996. It was chaired by Jon Bosak of

Sun Microsystems with the active participation of an XML Special Interest Group (previously known as the SGML Working Group) also organized by the W3C. The membership of the XML Working Group is given in an appendix. Dan Connolly served as the WG's contact with the W3C.

The design goals for XML are:

1. XML shall be straightforwardly usable over the Internet.
2. XML shall support a wide variety of applications.
3. XML shall be compatible with SGML.
4. It shall be easy to write programs which process XML documents.
5. The number of optional features in XML is to be kept to the absolute minimum, ideally zero.
6. XML documents should be human-legible and reasonably clear.
7. The XML design should be prepared quickly.
8. The design of XML shall be formal and concise.
9. XML documents shall be easy to create.
10. Terseness in XML markup is of minimal importance.

This specification, together with associated standards (Unicode and ISO/IEC 10646 for characters, Internet RFC 1766 for language identification tags, ISO 639 for language name codes, and ISO 3166 for country name codes), provides all the information necessary to understand XML Version 1.0 and construct computer programs to process it.

This version of the XML specification may be distributed freely, as long as all text and legal notices remain intact.

1.2 Terminology

The terminology used to describe XML documents is defined in the body of this specification. The terms defined in the following list are used in building those definitions and in describing the actions of an XML processor:

may

[Definition: Conforming documents and XML processors are permitted to but need not behave as described.]

must

[Definition: Conforming documents and XML processors are required to behave as described; otherwise they are in error.]

error

[Definition: A violation of the rules of this specification; results are undefined. Conforming software may detect and report an error and may recover from it.]

fatal error

[Definition: An error which a conforming *XML processor* must detect and report to the application. After encountering a fatal error, the processor may continue processing the data to search for further errors and may report such errors to the application. In order to support correction of errors, the processor may make unprocessed data from the document (with intermingled character data and markup) available to the application. Once a fatal error is detected, however, the processor must not continue normal processing (i.e., it must not continue to pass character data and information about the document's logical structure to the application in the normal way).]

at user option

[Definition: Conforming software may or must (depending on the modal verb in the sentence) behave as described; if it does, it must provide users a means to enable or disable the behavior described.]

validity constraint

[Definition: A rule which applies to all *valid* XML documents. Violations of validity constraints are errors; they must, at user option, be reported by *validating XML processors*.]

well-formedness constraint

[Definition: A rule which applies to all *well-formed* XML documents. Violations of well-formedness constraints are *fatal errors*.]

match

[Definition: (Of strings or names:) Two strings or names being compared must be identical. Characters with multiple possible representations in ISO/IEC 10646 (e.g. characters with both precomposed and base+diacritic forms) match only if they have the same representation in both strings. No case folding is performed. (Of strings and rules in the grammar:) A string matches a grammatical production if it belongs to the language generated by that production. (Of content and content models:) An element matches its declaration when it conforms in the fashion described in the constraint [*VC: Element Valid*].]

for compatibility

[Definition: Marks a sentence describing a feature of XML included solely to ensure that XML remains compatible with SGML.]

for interoperability

[Definition: Marks a sentence describing a non-binding recommendation included to increase the chances that XML documents can be processed by the existing installed base of SGML processors which predate the WebSGML Adaptations Annex to ISO 8879.]

2 Documents

[Definition: A data object is an **XML document** if it is *well-formed*, as defined in this specification. A well-formed XML document may in addition be *valid* if it meets certain further constraints.]

Each XML document has both a logical and a physical structure. Physically, the document is composed of units called *entities*. An entity may *refer* to other entities to cause their inclusion in the document. A document begins in a "root" or *document entity*. Logically, the document is composed of declarations, elements, comments, character references, and processing instructions, all of which are indicated in the document by explicit markup. The logical and physical structures must nest properly, as described in *4.3.2 Well-Formed Parsed Entities*.

2.1 Well-Formed XML Documents

[Definition: A textual object is a well-formed XML document if:]

1. Taken as a whole, it matches the production labeled *document*.
2. It meets all the well-formedness constraints given in this specification.
3. Each of the *parsed entities* which is referenced directly or indirectly within the document is *well-formed*.

Document

```
[1]   document   ::=   prolog element Misc*
```

Matching the document production implies that:

1. It contains one or more *elements*.
2. [Definition: There is exactly one element, called the *root*, or document element, no part of which appears in the *content* of any other element.] For all other elements, if the *start-tag* is in the content of another element, the *end-tag* is in the content of the same element. More simply stated, the elements, delimited by start- and end-tags, nest properly within each other.

[Definition: As a consequence of this, for each non-root element `C` in the document, there is one other element `P` in the document such that `C` is in the content of `P`, but is not in the content of any other element that is in the content of `P`. `P` is referred to as the *parent* of `C`, and `C` as a *child* of `P`.]

2.2 Characters

[Definition: A parsed entity contains *text*, a sequence of *characters*, which may represent markup or character data.] [Definition: A *character* is an atomic unit of text as specified by ISO/IEC 10646 [ISO/IEC 10646] (see also [ISO/IEC 10646-2000]). Legal characters are tab, carriage return, line feed, and the legal characters of Unicode and ISO/IEC 10646. The versions of these standards cited in *A.1 Normative References* were current at the time this document was prepared. New characters may be added to these standards by amendments or new editions. Consequently, XML processors must accept any character in the range specified for *Char*. The use of "compatibility characters," as defined in section 6.8 of [Unicode] (see also D21 in section 3.6 of [Unicode3]), is discouraged.]

Character Range

```
[2]   Char   ::=   #x9 | #xA | #xD | [#x20-      /* any Unicode character,
                   #xD7FF] | [#xE000-            excluding the surrogate
                   #xFFFD] | [#x10000-           blocks, FFFE, and FFFF. */
                   #x10FFFF]
```

The mechanism for encoding character code points into bit patterns may vary from entity to entity. All XML processors must accept the UTF-8 and UTF-16 encodings of 10646; the mechanisms for signaling which of the two is in use, or for bringing other encodings into play, are discussed later, in *4.3.3 Character Encoding in Entities*.

2.3 Common Syntactic Constructs

This section defines some symbols used widely in the grammar.

S (white space) consists of one or more space (#x20) characters, carriage returns, line feeds, or tabs.

White Space

```
[3]    S    ::=    (#x20 | #x9 | #xD | #xA)+
```

Characters are classified for convenience as letters, digits, or other characters. A letter consists of an alphabetic or syllabic base character or an ideographic character. Full definitions of the specific characters in each class are given in *B Character Classes*.

[Definition: A *Name* is a token beginning with a letter or one of a few punctuation characters, and continuing with letters, digits, hyphens, underscores, colons, or full stops, together known as name characters.] Names beginning with the string "`xml`", or any string which would match `(('X'|'x') ('M'|'m') ('L'|'l'))`, are reserved for standardization in this or future versions of this specification.

Note

The Namespaces in XML Recommendation [*XML Names*] assigns a meaning to names containing colon characters. Therefore, authors should not use the colon in XML names except for namespace purposes, but XML processors must accept the colon as a name character.

An *Nmtoken* (name token) is any mixture of name characters.

Names and Tokens

```
[4]    NameChar   ::=    Letter | Digit | '.' | '-' | '_' | ':' |
CombiningChar | Extender
[5]    Name   ::=    (Letter | '_' | ':') (NameChar)*
[6]    Names    ::=    Name (S Name)*
[7]    Nmtoken    ::=    (NameChar)+
```

```
[8]   Nmtokens   ::=   Nmtoken (S Nmtoken)*
```

Literal data is any quoted string not containing the quotation mark used as a delimiter for that string. Literals are used for specifying the content of internal entities (*EntityValue*), the values of attributes (*AttValue*), and external identifiers (*SystemLiteral*). Note that a *SystemLiteral* can be parsed without scanning for markup.

Literals

```
[9]    EntityValue    ::=   '"' ([^%&"] | PEReference | Reference)*
                            '"'
                            |  "'" ([^%&'] | PEReference |
                            Reference)* "'"
[10]   AttValue    ::=   '"' ([^<&"] | Reference)* '"'
                         |  "'" ([^<&'] | Reference)* "'"
[11]   SystemLiteral   ::=   ('"' [^"]* '"') | ("'" [^']* "'")
[12]   PubidLiteral   ::=   '"' PubidChar* '"' | "'" (PubidChar -
                            "'")* "'"
[13]   PubidChar   ::=   #x20 | #xD | #xA | [a-zA-Z0-9] | [-
                         '()+,./:=?;!*#@$_%]
```

Note:

Although the *EntityValue* production allows the definition of an entity consisting of a single explicit < in the literal (e.g., <!ENTITY mylt "<">), it is strongly advised to avoid this practice since any reference to that entity will cause a well-formedness error.

2.4 Character Data and Markup

Text consists of intermingled *character data* and markup. [Definition: **Markup** takes the form of *start-tags*, *end-tags*, *empty-element tags*, *entity references*, *character references*, *comments*, *CDATA section delimiters*, *document type declarations*, *processing instructions*, *XML declarations*, *text declarations*, and any white space that is at the top level of the document entity (that is, outside the document element and not inside any other markup).]

[Definition: All text that is not markup constitutes the *character data* of the document.]

The ampersand character (&) and the left angle bracket (<) may appear in their literal form *only* when used as markup delimiters, or within a *comment*, a *processing instruction*, or a *CDATA section*. If they are needed elsewhere, they must be *escaped* using either *numeric character references* or the strings “&” and “<” respectively. The right angle bracket (>) may be represented using the string “>”, and must, *for compatibility*, be escaped using “>” or a character reference when it appears in the string “]]>” in content, when that string is not marking the end of a *CDATA section*.

In the content of elements, character data is any string of characters that does not contain the start-delimiter of any markup. In a CDATA section, character data is any string of characters not including the CDATA-section-close delimiter, “]]>”.

To allow attribute values to contain both single and double quotes, the apostrophe or single-quote character (') may be represented as "'", and the double-quote character (") as """.

Character Data

```
[14]   CharData   ::=   [^<&]* - ([^<&]* ']]>' [^<&]*)
```

2.5 Comments

[Definition: **Comments** may appear anywhere in a document outside other *markup*; in addition, they may appear within the document type declaration at places allowed by the grammar. They are not part of the document's *character data*; an XML processor may, but need not, make it possible for an application to retrieve the text of comments. *For compatibility*, the string “--” (double-hyphen) must not occur within comments.] Parameter entity references are not recognized within comments.

Comments

```
[15]   Comment   ::=   '<!--' ((Char - '-') | ('-' (Char - '-')))*
                       '-->'
```

An example of a comment:

```
<!-- declarations for <head> & <body> -->
```

Note that the grammar does not allow a comment ending in --->. The following example is *not* well-formed.

```
<!-- B+, B, or B--->
```

2.6 Processing Instructions

[Definition: **Processing instructions** (PIs) allow documents to contain instructions for applications.]

Processing Instructions

```
[16]   PI   ::=   '<?' PITarget (S (Char* - (Char* '?>' Char*)))?
                  '?>'
[17]   PITarget   ::=   Name - (('X' | 'x') ('M' | 'm') ('L' |
                        'l'))
```

PIs are not part of the document's *character data*, but must be passed through to the application. The PI begins with a target (*PITarget*) used to identify the application to which the instruction is directed. The target names "XML", "xml", and so on are reserved for standardization in this or future versions of this specification. The XML *Notation* mechanism may be used for formal declaration of PI targets. Parameter entity references are not recognized within processing instructions.

2.7 CDATA Sections

[Definition: **CDATA sections** may occur anywhere character data may occur; they are used to escape blocks of text containing characters which would otherwise be recognized as markup. CDATA sections begin with the string "<![CDATA[" and end with the string "]]>":]

CDATA Sections

```
[18]   CDSect    ::=   CDStart CData CDEnd
[19]   CDStart   ::=   '<![CDATA['
[20]   CData     ::=   (Char* - (Char* ']]>' Char*))
[21]   CDEnd     ::=   ']]>'
```

Within a CDATA section, only the *CDEnd* string is recognized as markup, so that left angle brackets and ampersands may occur in their literal form; they need not (and cannot) be escaped using "<" and "&". CDATA sections cannot nest.

An example of a CDATA section, in which "<greeting>" and "</greeting>" are recognized as *character data*, not *markup*:

```
<![CDATA[<greeting>Hello, world!</greeting>]]>
```

2.8 Prolog and Document Type Declaration

[Definition: XML documents should begin with an **XML declaration,** which specifies the version of XML being used.] For example, the following is a complete XML document, *well-formed* but not *valid*:

```
<?xml version="1.0"?> <greeting>Hello, world!</greeting>
```

and so is this:

```
<greeting>Hello, world!</greeting>
```

The version number "1.0" should be used to indicate conformance to this version of this specification; it is an error for a document to use the value "1.0" if it does not conform to this version of this specification. It is the intent of the XML working group to give later versions of this specification numbers other than "1.0", but this intent does not indicate a commitment to produce any future versions of XML, nor if any are produced, to use any particular numbering scheme. Since future versions are not ruled out, this construct is provided as a means to allow the possibility of automatic version recognition, should it become necessary. Processors may signal an error if they receive documents labeled with versions they do not support.

The function of the markup in an XML document is to describe its storage and logical structure and to associate attribute-value pairs with its logical structures. XML provides a mechanism, the *document type declaration*, to define constraints on the logical structure and to support the use of predefined storage units. [Definition: An XML document is **valid** if it has an associated document type declaration and if the document complies with the constraints expressed in it.]

The document type declaration must appear before the first *element* in the document.

Prolog

```
[22]   prolog        ::=   XMLDecl? Misc* (doctypedecl Misc*)?
[23]   XMLDecl       ::=   '<?xml' VersionInfo EncodingDecl?
                           SDDecl? S? '?>'
[24]   VersionInfo   ::=   S 'version' Eq ("'" VersionNum "'" | '"'
                           VersionNum '"')/* */
[25]   Eq            ::=   S? '=' S?
[26]   VersionNum    ::=   ([a-zA-Z0-9_.:] | '-')+
[27]   Misc          ::=   Comment | PI | S
```

[Definition: The XML **document type declaration** contains or points to *markup declarations* that provide a grammar for a class of documents. This grammar is known as a document type definition, or **DTD**. The document type declaration can point to an external subset (a special kind of *external entity*) containing markup declarations, or can contain the markup declarations directly in an internal subset, or can do both. The DTD for a document consists of both subsets taken together.]

[Definition: A **markup declaration** is an *element type declaration*, an *attribute-list declaration*, an *entity declaration*, or a *notation declaration*.] These declarations may be contained in whole or in part within parameter entities, as described in the well-formedness and validity constraints below. For further information, see *4 Physical Structures*.

Document Type Definition

[28]	doctypedecl	::=	'<!DOCTYPE' *S* *Name* (*S* *ExternalID*)? *S*? ('[' (*markupdecl* | *DeclSep*)* ']' *S*?)? '>'	[VC: Root Element Type]
				[WFC: External Subset] /* */
[28a]	DeclSep	::=	*PEReference* | *S*	[WFC: PE Between Declarations] /* */
[29]	markupdecl	::=	elementdecl | AttlistDecl | EntityDecl | NotationDecl | PI | Comment	[VC: Proper Declaration/PE Nesting]
				[WFC: PEs in Internal Subset]

Note that it is possible to construct a well-formed document containing a *doctypedecl* that neither points to an external subset nor contains an internal subset.

The markup declarations may be made up in whole or in part of the *replacement text* of *parameter entities*. The productions later in this specification for individual nonterminals (*elementdecl*, *AttlistDecl*, and so on) describe the declarations after all the parameter entities have been *included*.

Parameter entity references are recognized anywhere in the DTD (internal and external subsets and external parameter entities), except in literals, processing instructions, comments, and the contents of ignored conditional sections (see *3.4 Conditional Sections*). They are also recognized in entity value literals. The use of parameter entities in the internal subset is restricted as described below.

VALIDITY CONSTRAINT: ROOT ELEMENT TYPE

The *Name* in the document type declaration must match the element type of the *root element*.

VALIDITY CONSTRAINT: PROPER DECLARATION/PE NESTING

Parameter-entity *replacement text* must be properly nested with markup declarations. That is to say, if either the first character or the last character of a markup declaration (*markupdecl* above) is contained in the replacement text for a *parameter-entity reference*, both must be contained in the same replacement text.

WELL-FORMEDNESS CONSTRAINT: PES IN INTERNAL SUBSET

In the internal DTD subset, *parameter-entity references* can occur only where markup declarations can occur, not within markup declarations. (This does not apply to references that occur in external parameter entities or to the external subset.)

WELL-FORMEDNESS CONSTRAINT: EXTERNAL SUBSET

The external subset, if any, must match the production for *extSubset*.

WELL-FORMEDNESS CONSTRAINT: PE BETWEEN DECLARATIONS

The replacement text of a parameter entity reference in a *DeclSep* must match the production *extSubsetDecl*.

Like the internal subset, the external subset and any external parameter entities referenced in a *DeclSep* must consist of a series of complete markup declarations of the types allowed by the non-terminal symbol *markupdecl*, interspersed with white space or *parameter-entity references*. However, portions of the contents of the external subset or of these external parameter entities may conditionally be ignored by using the *conditional section* construct; this is not allowed in the internal subset.

External Subset

```
[30]   extSubset       ::=   TextDecl? extSubsetDecl
[31]   extSubsetDecl   ::=   ( markupdecl | conditionalSect |   /* */
                             DeclSep)*
```

The external subset and external parameter entities also differ from the internal subset in that in them, *parameter-entity references* are permitted *within* markup declarations, not only *between* markup declarations.

An example of an XML document with a document type declaration:

```
<?xml version="1.0"?> <!DOCTYPE greeting SYSTEM "hello.dtd">
<greeting>Hello, world!</greeting>
```

The system identifier "hello.dtd" gives the address (a URI reference) of a DTD for the document.

The declarations can also be given locally, as in this example:

```
<?xml version="1.0" encoding="UTF-8" ?>
<!DOCTYPE greeting [
  <!ELEMENT greeting (#PCDATA)>
]>
<greeting>Hello, world!</greeting>
```

If both the external and internal subsets are used, the internal subset is considered to occur before the external subset. This has the effect that entity and attribute-list declarations in the internal subset take precedence over those in the external subset.

2.9 Standalone Document Declaration

Markup declarations can affect the content of the document, as passed from an *XML processor* to an application; examples are attribute defaults and entity declarations. The standalone document declaration, which may appear as a component of the XML declaration, signals whether or not there are such declarations which appear external to the *document entity* or in parameter entities. [Definition: An **external markup declaration** is defined as a markup declaration occurring in the external subset or in a parameter entity (external or internal, the latter being included because non-validating processors are not required to read them).]

Standalone Document Declaration

[32]	SDDecl	::=	*S* 'standalone' *Eq* (("'" ('yes' | 'no') "'") | ('"' ('yes' | 'no') '"'))	[VC: Standalone Document Declaration]

In a standalone document declaration, the value "yes" indicates that there are no *external markup declarations* which affect the information passed from the XML processor to the application. The value "no" indicates that there are or may be such external markup declarations. Note that the standalone document declaration only denotes the presence of external *declarations*; the presence, in a document, of references to external *entities*, when those entities are internally declared, does not change its standalone status.

If there are no external markup declarations, the standalone document declaration has no meaning. If there are external markup declarations but there is no standalone document declaration, the value "no" is assumed.

Any XML document for which `standalone="no"` holds can be converted algorithmically to a standalone document, which may be desirable for some network delivery applications.

VALIDITY CONSTRAINT: STANDALONE DOCUMENT DECLARATION

The standalone document declaration must have the value "no" if any external markup declarations contain declarations of:

- attributes with *default* values, if elements to which these attributes apply appear in the document without specifications of values for these attributes, or
- entities (other than `amp`, `lt`, `gt`, `apos`, `quot`), if *references* to those entities appear in the document, or
- attributes with values subject to *normalization*, where the attribute appears in the document with a value which will change as a result of normalization, or
- element types with *element content*, if white space occurs directly within any instance of those types.

An example XML declaration with a standalone document declaration:

```
<?xml version="1.0" standalone='yes'?>
```

2.10 White Space Handling

In editing XML documents, it is often convenient to use "white space" (spaces, tabs, and blank lines) to set apart the markup for greater readability. Such white space is typically not intended for inclusion in the delivered version of the document. On the other hand, "significant" white space that should be preserved in the delivered version is common, for example in poetry and source code.

An *XML processor* must always pass all characters in a document that are not markup through to the application. A *validating XML processor* must also inform the application which of these characters constitute white space appearing in *element content*.

A special *attribute* named `xml:space` may be attached to an element to signal an intention that in that element, white space should be preserved by applications. In valid documents, this attribute, like any other, must be *declared* if it is used. When declared, it must be given as an *enumerated type* whose values are one or both of "default" and "preserve." For example:

```
<!ATTLIST poem  xml:space (default|preserve) 'preserve'>

<!-- -->
<!ATTLIST pre xml:space (preserve) #FIXED 'preserve'>
```

The value "default" signals that applications' default white-space processing modes are acceptable for this element; the value "preserve" indicates the intent that applications preserve all the white space. This declared intent is considered to apply to all elements within the content of the element where it is specified, unless overriden with another instance of the `xml:space` attribute.

The *root element* of any document is considered to have signaled no intentions as regards application space handling, unless it provides a value for this attribute or the attribute is declared with a default value.

2.11 End-of-Line Handling

XML *parsed entities* are often stored in computer files which, for editing convenience, are organized into lines. These lines are typically separated by some combination of the characters carriage-return (`#xD`) and line-feed (`#xA`).

To simplify the tasks of *applications*, the characters passed to an application by the *XML processor* must be as if the XML processor normalized all line breaks in external parsed entities (including the document entity) on input, before parsing, by translating both the two-character sequence `#xD #xA` and any `#xD` that is not followed by `#xA` to a single `#xA` character.

2.12 Language Identification

In document processing, it is often useful to identify the natural or formal language in which the content is written. A special *attribute* named `xml:lang` may be inserted in documents to specify the language used in the contents and attribute values of any element in an XML document. In valid documents, this attribute, like any other, must be *declared* if it is used. The values of the attribute are language identifiers as defined by [IETF RFC 1766], *Tags for the Identification of Languages*, or its successor on the IETF Standards Track.

Note:

[IETF RFC 1766] tags are constructed from two-letter language codes as defined by [ISO 639], from two-letter country codes as defined by [ISO 3166], or from language identifiers registered with the Internet Assigned Numbers Authority [IANA-LANGCODES]. It is expected that the successor to [IETF RFC 1766] will introduce three-letter language codes for languages not presently covered by [ISO 639].

(Productions 33 through 38 have been removed.)
For example:

```
<p xml:lang="en">The quick brown fox jumps over the lazy dog.</p>
<p xml:lang="en-GB">What colour is it?</p>
<p xml:lang="en-US">What color is it?</p>
<sp who="Faust" desc='leise' xml:lang="de">
  <l>Habe nun, ach! Philosophie,</l>
  <l>Juristerei, und Medizin</l>
  <l>und leider auch Theologie</l>
  <l>durchaus studiert mit heißem Bemüh'n.</l>
</sp>
```

The intent declared with `xml:lang` is considered to apply to all attributes and content of the element where it is specified, unless overridden with an instance of `xml:lang` on another element within that content.

A simple declaration for `xml:lang` might take the form

```
xml:lang NMTOKEN #IMPLIED
```

but specific default values may also be given, if appropriate. In a collection of French poems for English students, with glosses and notes in English, the `xml:lang` attribute might be declared this way:

```
<!ATTLIST poem   xml:lang NMTOKEN 'fr'>
<!ATTLIST gloss  xml:lang NMTOKEN 'en'>
<!ATTLIST note   xml:lang NMTOKEN 'en'>
```

3 Logical Structures

[Definition: Each *XML document* contains one or more **elements**, the boundaries of which are either delimited by *start-tags* and *end-tags*, or, for *empty* elements, by an *empty-element tag*. Each element has a type, identified by name, sometimes called its "generic identifier" (GI), and may have a set of attribute specifications.] Each attribute specification has a *name* and a *value*.

Element

```
[39]   element   ::=   EmptyElemTag
                       | STag content ETag      [WFC: Element Type Match]
                                                [VC: Element Valid]
```

This specification does not constrain the semantics, use, or (beyond syntax) names of the element types and attributes, except that names beginning with a match to `(('X'|'x')('M'|'m')('L'|'l'))` are reserved for standardization in this or future versions of this specification.

WELL-FORMEDNESS CONSTRAINT: ELEMENT TYPE MATCH

The *Name* in an element's end-tag must match the element type in the start-tag.

VALIDITY CONSTRAINT: ELEMENT VALID

An element is valid if there is a declaration matching *elementdecl* where the *Name* matches the element type, and one of the following holds:

1. The declaration matches **EMPTY** and the element has no *content*.
2. The declaration matches *children* and the sequence of *child elements* belongs to the language generated by the regular expression in the content model, with optional white space (characters matching the nonterminal *S*) between the start-tag and the first child element, between child elements, or between the last child element and the end-tag. Note that a CDATA section containing only white space does not match the nonterminal *S*, and hence cannot appear in these positions.

3. The declaration matches *Mixed* and the content consists of *character data* and *child elements* whose types match names in the content model.
4. The declaration matches **ANY**, and the types of any *child elements* have been declared.

3.1 Start-Tags, End-Tags, and Empty-Element Tags

[Definition: The beginning of every non-empty XML element is marked by a **start-tag**.]

Start-tag

[40]	STag	::=	'<' *Name* (*S* *Attribute*)* *S*? '>'	[WFC: Unique Att Spec]
[41]	Attribute	::=	*Name Eq AttValue*	[VC: Attribute Value Type] [WFC: No External Entity References] [WFC: No < in Attribute Values]

The *Name* in the start- and end-tags gives the element's **type**. [Definition: The *Name-AttValue* pairs are referred to as the **attribute specifications** of the element], [Definition: with the *Name* in each pair referred to as the **attribute name**], and [Definition: the content of the *AttValue* (the text between the ' or " delimiters) as the **attribute value**.] Note that the order of attribute specifications in a start-tag or empty-element tag is not significant.

WELL-FORMEDNESS CONSTRAINT: UNIQUE ATT SPEC

No attribute name may appear more than once in the same start-tag or empty-element tag.

VALIDITY CONSTRAINT: ATTRIBUTE VALUE TYPE

The attribute must have been declared; the value must be of the type declared for it. (For attribute types, see *3.3 Attribute-List Declarations*.)

WELL-FORMEDNESS CONSTRAINT: NO EXTERNAL ENTITY REFERENCES

Attribute values cannot contain direct or indirect entity references to external entities.

WELL-FORMEDNESS CONSTRAINT: NO < IN ATTRIBUTE VALUES

The *replacement text* of any entity referred to directly or indirectly in an attribute value must not contain a <.

An example of a start-tag:

```
<termdef id="dt-dog" term="dog">
```

[Definition: The end of every element that begins with a start-tag must be marked by an **end-tag** containing a name that echoes the element's type as given in the start-tag:]

End-tag

```
[42]    ETag    ::=    '</' Name S? '>'
```

An example of an end-tag:

```
</termdef>
```

[Definition: The *text* between the start-tag and end-tag is called the element's **content**:]

Content of Elements

```
[43]    content   ::=    CharData? ((element | Reference |     /*
                         CDSect | PI | Comment) CharData?)*    */
```

[Definition: An element with no content is said to be **empty**.] The representation of an empty element is either a start-tag immediately followed by an end-tag, or an empty-element tag. [Definition: An **empty-element tag** takes a special form:]

Tags for Empty Elements

```
[44]    EmptyElemTag    ::=    '<' Name (S Attribute)*  [WFC: Unique
                               S? '/>'                   Att Spec]
```

Empty-element tags may be used for any element which has no content, whether or not it is declared using the keyword **EMPTY**. *For interoperability*, the empty-element tag should be used, and should only be used, for elements which are declared EMPTY.

Examples of empty elements:

```
<IMG align="left"
 src="http://www.w3.org/Icons/WWW/w3c_home" />
<br></br>
<br/>
```

3.2 Element Type Declarations

The *element* structure of an *XML document* may, for *validation* purposes, be constrained using element type and attribute-list declarations. An element type declaration constrains the element's content.

Element type declarations often constrain which element types can appear as *children* of the element. At user option, an XML processor may issue a warning when a declaration mentions an element type for which no declaration is provided, but this is not an error.

[Definition: An **element type declaration** takes the form:]

Element Type Declaration

[45]	elementdecl	::=	'<!ELEMENT' *S Name S contentspec S*? '>'	[VC: Unique Element Type Declaration]
[46]	contentspec	::=	'EMPTY' | 'ANY' | Mixed | children	

where the *Name* gives the element type being declared.

VALIDITY CONSTRAINT: UNIQUE ELEMENT TYPE DECLARATION

No element type may be declared more than once.

Examples of element type declarations:

```
<!ELEMENT br EMPTY>
<!ELEMENT p (#PCDATA|emph)* >
<!ELEMENT %name.para; %content.para; >
<!ELEMENT container ANY>
```

3.2.1 Element Content

[Definition: An element *type* has **element content** when elements of that type must contain only *child* elements (no character data), optionally separated by white space (characters matching the nonterminal *S*).][Definition: In this case, the constraint includes a **content model**, a simple grammar governing the allowed types of the child elements and the order in which they are allowed to appear.] The grammar is built on content particles (*cps*), which consist of names, choice lists of content particles, or sequence lists of content particles:

Element-content Models

```
[47]  children ::= (choice | seq) ('?' | '*' | '+')?
[48]  cp       ::= (Name | choice | seq) ('?' | '*' | '+')?      /* */
[49]  choice   ::= '(' S? cp ( S? '|' S? cp )+ S? ')'          /* */
                                                               [VC: Proper Group/PE Nesting]
                                                               /* */
[50]  seq      ::= '(' S? cp ( S? ',' S? cp )* S? ')'
                                                               [VC: Proper Group/PE Nesting]
```

where each *Name* is the type of an element which may appear as a *child*. Any content particle in a choice list may appear in the *element content* at the location where the choice list appears in the grammar; content particles occurring in a sequence list must each appear in the *element content* in the order given in the list. The optional character following a name or list governs whether the element or the content particles in the list may occur one or more (+), zero or more (*), or zero or one times (?). The absence of such an operator means that the element or content particle must appear exactly once. This syntax and meaning are identical to those used in the productions in this specification.

The content of an element matches a content model if and only if it is possible to trace out a path through the content model, obeying the sequence, choice, and repetition operators and matching each element in the content against an element type in the content model. *For compatibility*, it is an error if an element in the document can match more than one occurrence of an element type in the content model. For more information, see *E Deterministic Content Models*.

VALIDITY CONSTRAINT: PROPER GROUP/PE NESTING

Parameter-entity *replacement text* must be properly nested with parenthesized groups. That is to say, if either of the opening or closing parentheses in a *choice*, *seq*, or *Mixed* construct is contained in the replacement text for a *parameter entity*, both must be contained in the same replacement text.

For interoperability, if a parameter-entity reference appears in a *choice*, *seq*, or *Mixed* construct, its replacement text should contain at least one non-blank character, and neither the first nor last non-blank character of the replacement text should be a connector (| or ,).

Examples of element-content models:

```
<!ELEMENT spec (front, body, back?)>
<!ELEMENT div1 (head, (p | list | note)*, div2*)>
<!ELEMENT dictionary-body (%div.mix; | %dict.mix;)*>
```

3.2.2 Mixed Content

[Definition: An element *type* has **mixed content** when elements of that type may contain character data, optionally interspersed with *child* elements.] In this case, the types of the child elements may be constrained, but not their order or their number of occurrences:

MIXED-CONTENT DECLARATION

```
[51]   Mixed   ::=   '(' S? '#PCDATA' (S? '|' S?
                     Name)* S? ')*'
                     | '(' S? '#PCDATA' S? ')'       [VC: Proper
                                                      Group/PE Nesting]
                                                     [VC: No Duplicate
                                                      Types]
```

where the *Names* give the types of elements that may appear as children. The keyword **#PCDATA** derives historically from the term "parsed character data."

VALIDITY CONSTRAINT: NO DUPLICATE TYPES

The same name must not appear more than once in a single mixed-content declaration.

Examples of mixed content declarations:

```
<!ELEMENT p (#PCDATA|a|ul|b|i|em)*>
<!ELEMENT p (#PCDATA | %font; | %phrase; | %special; | %form;)* >
<!ELEMENT b (#PCDATA)>
```

3.3 Attribute-List Declarations

Attributes are used to associate name-value pairs with *elements*. Attribute specifications may appear only within *start-tags* and *empty-element tags*; thus, the productions used to recognize them appear in *3.1 Start-Tags, End-Tags, and Empty-Element Tags*. Attribute-list declarations may be used:

- To define the set of attributes pertaining to a given element type.
- To establish type constraints for these attributes.
- To provide *default values* for attributes.

[Definition: **Attribute-list declarations** specify the name, data type, and default value (if any) of each attribute associated with a given element type:]

Attribute-list Declaration

```
[52]   AttlistDecl    ::=   '<!ATTLIST' S Name AttDef* S? '>'
[53]   AttDef         ::=   S Name S AttType S DefaultDecl
```

The *Name* in the *AttlistDecl* rule is the type of an element. At user option, an XML processor may issue a warning if attributes are declared for an element type not itself declared, but this is not an error. The *Name* in the *AttDef* rule is the name of the attribute.

When more than one *AttlistDecl* is provided for a given element type, the contents of all those provided are merged. When more than one definition is provided for the same attribute of a given element type, the first declaration is binding and later declarations are ignored. *For interoperability*, writers of DTDs may choose to provide at most one attribute-list declaration for a given element type, at most one attribute definition for a given attribute name in an attribute-list declaration, and at least one attribute definition in each attribute-list declaration. For interoperability, an XML processor may at user option issue a warning when more than one attribute-list declaration is provided for a given element type, or more than one attribute definition is provided for a given attribute, but this is not an error.

ATTRIBUTE TYPES

XML attribute types are of three kinds: a string type, a set of tokenized types, and enumerated types. The string type may take any literal string as a value; the tokenized types have varying lexical and semantic constraints. The validity constraints noted in the grammar are applied after the attribute value has been normalized as described in *3.3 Attribute-List Declarations*.

ATTRIBUTE TYPES

```
[54]   AttType        ::=   StringType |
                            TokenizedType |
                            EnumeratedType
[55]   StringType     ::=   'CDATA'
[56]   TokenizedType  ::=   'ID'              [VC: ID]
                                              [VC: One ID per Element
                                              Type]
                                              [VC: ID Attribute Default]
                            | 'IDREF'         [VC: IDREF]
```

```
| | 'IDREFS'        [VC: IDREF]
| | 'ENTITY'        [VC: Entity Name]
| | 'ENTITIES'      [VC: Entity Name]
| | 'NMTOKEN'       [VC: Name Token]
| | 'NMTOKENS'      [VC: Name Token]
```

VALIDITY CONSTRAINT: ID

Values of type **ID** must match the *Name* production. A name must not appear more than once in an XML document as a value of this type; i.e., ID values must uniquely identify the elements which bear them.

VALIDITY CONSTRAINT: ONE ID PER ELEMENT TYPE

No element type may have more than one ID attribute specified.

VALIDITY CONSTRAINT: ID ATTRIBUTE DEFAULT

An ID attribute must have a declared default of **#IMPLIED** or **#REQUIRED**.

VALIDITY CONSTRAINT: IDREF

Values of type **IDREF** must match the *Name* production, and values of type **IDREFS** must match *Names*; each *Name* must match the value of an ID attribute on some element in the XML document; i.e. **IDREF** values must match the value of some ID attribute.

VALIDITY CONSTRAINT: ENTITY NAME

Values of type **ENTITY** must match the *Name* production, values of type **ENTITIES** must match *Names*; each *Name* must match the name of an unparsed entity declared in the DTD.

VALIDITY CONSTRAINT: NAME TOKEN

Values of type **NMTOKEN** must match the *Nmtoken* production; values of type **NMTOKENS** must match *Nmtokens*.

[Definition: **Enumerated attributes** can take one of a list of values provided in the declaration]. There are two kinds of enumerated types:

3.3.1 Enumerated Attribute Types

```
[57]  EnumeratedType  ::=  NotationType |
                           Enumeration
[58]  NotationType    ::=  'NOTATION' S '(' S?       [VC: Notation
                           Name (S? '|' S?            Attributes]
                           Name)* S? ')'
                                                      [VC: One Notation
                                                      Per Element Type]
```

```
[59]   Enumeration     ::=   '(' S? Nmtoken (S?        [VC: No Notation
                             '|' S? Nmtoken)* S?         on Empty
                             ')'                         Element]
                                                       [VC: Enumeration]
```

A **NOTATION** attribute identifies a *notation*, declared in the DTD with associated system and/or public identifiers, to be used in interpreting the element to which the attribute is attached.

VALIDITY CONSTRAINT: NOTATION ATTRIBUTES
Values of this type must match one of the *notation* names included in the declaration; all notation names in the declaration must be declared.

VALIDITY CONSTRAINT: ONE NOTATION PER ELEMENT TYPE
No element type may have more than one **NOTATION** attribute specified.

VALIDITY CONSTRAINT: NO NOTATION ON EMPTY ELEMENT
For compatibility, an attribute of type **NOTATION** must not be declared on an element declared **EMPTY**.

VALIDITY CONSTRAINT: ENUMERATION
Values of this type must match one of the *Nmtoken* tokens in the declaration.

For interoperability, the same *Nmtoken* should not occur more than once in the enumerated attribute types of a single element type.

3.3.2 Attribute Defaults

An *attribute declaration* provides information on whether the attribute's presence is required, and if not, how an XML processor should react if a declared attribute is absent in a document.

ATTRIBUTE DEFAULTS

```
[60]   DefaultDecl    ::=   '#REQUIRED'
                            | '#IMPLIED'
                            | (('#FIXED' S)?    [VC: Required
                            AttValue)             Attribute]
                                                [VC: Attribute Default
                                                  Legal]
                                                [WFC: No < in Attribute
                                                  Values]
                                                [VC: Fixed Attribute
                                                  Default]
```

In an attribute declaration, **#REQUIRED** means that the attribute must always be provided, **#IMPLIED** that no default value is provided. [Definition: If the declaration is neither **#REQUIRED** nor **#IMPLIED**, then the *AttValue* value contains the declared default value; the **#FIXED** keyword states that the attribute must always have the default value. If a default value is declared, when an XML processor encounters an omitted attribute, it is to behave as though the attribute were present with the declared default value.]

VALIDITY CONSTRAINT: REQUIRED ATTRIBUTE

If the default declaration is the keyword **#REQUIRED**, then the attribute must be specified for all elements of the type in the attribute-list declaration.

VALIDITY CONSTRAINT: ATTRIBUTE DEFAULT LEGAL

The declared default value must meet the lexical constraints of the declared attribute type.

VALIDITY CONSTRAINT: FIXED ATTRIBUTE DEFAULT

If an attribute has a default value declared with the **#FIXED** keyword, instances of that attribute must match the default value.

Examples of attribute-list declarations:

```
<!ATTLIST termdef
          id      ID       #REQUIRED
          name    CDATA    #IMPLIED>
<!ATTLIST list
          type    (bullets|ordered|glossary)  "ordered">
<!ATTLIST form
          method  CDATA    #FIXED "POST">
```

3.3.3 Attribute-Value Normalization

Before the value of an attribute is passed to the application or checked for validity, the XML processor must normalize the attribute value by applying the algorithm below, or by using some other method such that the value passed to the application is the same as that produced by the algorithm.

1. All line breaks must have been normalized on input to `#xA` as described in *2.11 End-of-Line Handling*, so the rest of this algorithm operates on text normalized in this way.
2. Begin with a normalized value consisting of the empty string.

3. For each character, entity reference, or character reference in the unnormalized attribute value, beginning with the first and continuing to the last, do the following:
   - For a character reference, append the referenced character to the normalized value.
   - For an entity reference, recursively apply step 3 of this algorithm to the replacement text of the entity.
   - For a white space character (`#x20`, `#xD`, `#xA`, `#x9`), append a space character (`#x20`) to the normalized value.
   - For another character, append the character to the normalized value.

If the attribute type is not CDATA, then the XML processor must further process the normalized attribute value by discarding any leading and trailing space (`#x20`) characters, and by replacing sequences of space (`#x20`) characters by a single space (`#x20`) character.

Note that if the unnormalized attribute value contains a character reference to a white space character other than space (`#x20`), the normalized value contains the referenced character itself (`#xD`, `#xA` or `#x9`). This contrasts with the case where the unnormalized value contains a white space character (not a reference), which is replaced with a space character (`#x20`) in the normalized value and also contrasts with the case where the unnormalized value contains an entity reference whose replacement text contains a white space character; being recursively processed, the white space character is replaced with a space character (`#x20`) in the normalized value.

All attributes for which no declaration has been read should be treated by a non-validating processor as if declared **CDATA**.

Following are examples of attribute normalization. Given the following declarations:

```
<!ENTITY d "&#xD;">
<!ENTITY a "&#xA;">
<!ENTITY da "&#xD;&#xA;">
```

the attribute specifications in the left column below would be normalized to the character sequences of the middle column if the attribute `a` is declared **NMTOKENS** and to those of the right columns if `a` is declared **CDATA**.

Attribute specification	a is NMTOKENS	a is CDATA
a="		
xyz"	x y z	#x20 #x20 x y z
a="&d;&d;A&a;&a;B&da;"	A #x20 B	#x20 #x20 A #x20 #x20 B #x20 #x20
a=	#xD #xD A #xA	#xD #xD A
"

A

 B
" | #xA B #xD #xA | #xa #xA B #xd #xD |

Note that the last example is invalid (but well-formed) if a is declared to be of type **NMTOKENS**.

3.4 Conditional Sections

[Definition: **Conditional sections** are portions of the *document type declaration external subset* which are included in, or excluded from, the logical structure of the DTD based on the keyword which governs them.]

Conditional Section

```
[61]  conditionalSect     ::=  includeSect | ignoreSect
[62]  includeSect         ::=  '<![' S? 'INCLUDE' S? '[' extSubsetDecl ']]>'   /* */
                                                     [VC: Proper Conditional Section/PE Nesting]
[63]  ignoreSect          ::=  '<![' S? 'IGNORE' S? '[' ignoreSectContents* ']]>'   /* */
                                                     [VC: Proper Conditional Section/PE Nesting]
[64]  ignoreSectContents  ::=  Ignore ('<![' ignoreSectContents ']]>' Ignore)*
[65]  Ignore              ::=  Char* - (Char* ('<![' | ']]>') Char*)
```

VALIDITY CONSTRAINT: PROPER CONDITIONAL SECTION/PE NESTING

If any of the "<![", "[", or "]]>" of a conditional section is contained in the replacement text for a parameter-entity reference, all of them must be contained in the same replacement text.

Like the internal and external DTD subsets, a conditional section may contain one or more complete declarations, comments, processing instructions, or nested conditional sections, intermingled with white space.

If the keyword of the conditional section is **INCLUDE**, then the contents of the conditional section are part of the DTD. If the keyword of the conditional section is **IGNORE**, then the contents of the conditional section are not logically part of the DTD. If a conditional section with a keyword of **INCLUDE** occurs within a larger conditional section with a keyword of **IGNORE**, both the outer and the inner conditional sections are ignored. The contents of an ignored conditional section are parsed by ignoring all characters after the "[" following the keyword, except conditional section starts "<![" and ends "]]>", until the matching conditional section end is found. Parameter entity references are not recognized in this process.

If the keyword of the conditional section is a parameter-entity reference, the parameter entity must be replaced by its content before the processor decides whether to include or ignore the conditional section.

An example:

```
<!ENTITY % draft 'INCLUDE' >
<!ENTITY % final 'IGNORE' >

<![%draft;[
<!ELEMENT book (comments*, title, body, supplements?)>
]]>
<![%final;[
<!ELEMENT book (title, body, supplements?)>
]]>
```

4 Physical Structures

[Definition: An XML document may consist of one or many storage units. These are called **entities**; they all have **content** and are all (except for the *document entity* and the *external DTD subset*) identified by entity **name**.] Each XML document has one entity called the *document entity*, which serves as the starting point for the *XML processor* and may contain the whole document.

Entities may be either parsed or unparsed. [Definition: A **parsed entity's** contents are referred to as its *replacement text*; this *text* is considered an integral part of the document.]

[Definition: An **unparsed entity** is a resource whose contents may or may not be *text*, and if text, may be other than XML. Each unparsed entity has an associated *notation*, identified by name. Beyond a requirement that an XML processor make the identifiers for the entity and notation available to the application, XML places no constraints on the contents of unparsed entities.]

Parsed entities are invoked by name using entity references; unparsed entities by name, given in the value of **ENTITY** or **ENTITIES** attributes.

[Definition: **General entities** are entities for use within the document content. In this specification, general entities are sometimes referred to with the unqualified term *entity* when this leads to no ambiguity.] [Definition: **Parameter entities** are parsed entities for use within the DTD.] These two types of entities use different forms of reference and are recognized in different contexts. Furthermore, they occupy different namespaces; a parameter entity and a general entity with the same name are two distinct entities.

4.1 Character and Entity References

[Definition: A **character reference** refers to a specific character in the ISO/IEC 10646 character set, for example one not directly accessible from available input devices.]

Character Reference

```
[66]    CharRef   ::=    '&#' [0-9]+ ';'
                       | '&#x' [0-9a-fA-F]+ ';'   [WFC: Legal Character]
```

WELL-FORMEDNESS CONSTRAINT: LEGAL CHARACTER

Characters referred to using character references must match the production for *Char*.

If the character reference begins with `"&#x"`, the digits and letters up to the terminating; provide a hexadecimal representation of the character's code point in ISO/IEC 10646. If it begins just with `"&#"`, the digits up to the terminating `;` provide a decimal representation of the character's code point.

[Definition: An **entity reference** refers to the content of a named entity.] [Definition: References to parsed general entities use ampersand (`&`) and semicolon (`;`) as delimiters.] [Definition: Parameter-entity references use percent-sign (`%`) and semicolon (`;`) as delimiters.]

Entity Reference

[67]	Reference	::=	*EntityRef* | *CharRef*	
[68]	EntityRef	::=	'&' *Name* ';'	[WFC: Entity Declared] [VC: Entity Declared] [WFC: Parsed Entity] [WFC: No Recursion]
[69]	PEReference	::=	'%' *Name* ';'	[VC: Entity Declared] [WFC: No Recursion] [WFC: In DTD]

WELL-FORMEDNESS CONSTRAINT: ENTITY DECLARED

In a document without any DTD, a document with only an internal DTD subset which contains no parameter entity references, or a document with `"standalone='yes'"`, for an entity reference that does not occur within the external subset or a parameter entity, the *Name* given in the entity reference must *match* that in an *entity declaration* that does not occur within the external subset or a parameter entity, except that well-formed documents need not declare any of the following entities: `amp`, `lt`, `gt`, `apos`, `quot`. The declaration of a general entity must precede any reference to it which appears in a default value in an attribute-list declaration.

Note that if entities are declared in the external subset or in external parameter entities, a non-validating processor is *not obligated to* read and process their declarations; for such documents, the rule that an entity must be declared is a well-formedness constraint only if *`standalone='yes'`*.

VALIDITY CONSTRAINT: ENTITY DECLARED

In a document with an external subset or external parameter entities with `"standalone='no'"`, the *Name* given in the entity reference must *match* that in an *entity declaration*. For interoperability, valid documents should declare the entities `amp`, `lt`, `gt`, `apos`, `quot`, in the form specified in *4.6 Predefined Entities*. The declaration of a parameter entity must precede any reference to it. Similarly, the declaration of a general entity must precede any attribute-list declaration containing a default value with a direct or indirect reference to that general entity.

WELL-FORMEDNESS CONSTRAINT: PARSED ENTITY

An entity reference must not contain the name of an *unparsed entity*. Unparsed entities may be referred to only in *attribute values* declared to be of type **ENTITY** or **ENTITIES**.

WELL-FORMEDNESS CONSTRAINT: NO RECURSION

A parsed entity must not contain a recursive reference to itself, either directly or indirectly.

WELL-FORMEDNESS CONSTRAINT: IN DTD

Parameter-entity references may only appear in the *DTD*.

Examples of character and entity references:

```
Type <key>less-than</key> (&#x3C;) to save options.
This document was prepared on &docdate; and
is classified &security-level;.
```

Example of a parameter-entity reference:

```
<!-- declare the parameter entity "ISOLat2"... -->
<!ENTITY % ISOLat2
        SYSTEM "http://www.xml.com/iso/isolat2-xml.entities" >
<!-- ... now reference it. -->
%ISOLat2;
```

4.2 Entity Declarations

[Definition: Entities are declared thus:]

Entity Declaration

```
[70]   EntityDecl ::=   GEDecl | PEDecl
[71]   GEDecl     ::=   '<!ENTITY' S Name S EntityDef S? '>'
[72]   PEDecl     ::=   '<!ENTITY' S '%' S Name S PEDef S? '>'
[73]   EntityDef  ::=   EntityValue | (ExternalID NDataDecl?)
[74]   PEDef      ::=   EntityValue | ExternalID
```

The *Name* identifies the entity in an *entity reference* or, in the case of an unparsed entity, in the value of an **ENTITY** or **ENTITIES** attribute. If the same entity is declared more than once, the first declaration encountered is binding; at user option, an XML processor may issue a warning if entities are declared multiple times.

4.2.1 Internal Entities

[Definition: If the entity definition is an *EntityValue*, the defined entity is called an **internal entity**. There is no separate physical storage object, and the content of the entity is given in the declaration.] Note that some processing of entity and character references in the *literal entity value* may be required to produce the correct *replacement text*: see *4.5 Construction of Internal Entity Replacement Text*.

An internal entity is a *parsed entity*.

Example of an internal entity declaration:

```
<!ENTITY Pub-Status "This is a pre-release of the
 specification.">
```

4.2.2 External Entities

[Definition: If the entity is not internal, it is an **external entity**, declared as follows:]

EXTERNAL ENTITY DECLARATION

[75]	ExternalID	::=	'SYSTEM' *S SystemLiteral* | 'PUBLIC' *S PubidLiteral S SystemLiteral*	
[76]	NDataDecl	::=	*S* 'NDATA' *S Name*	[VC: Notation Declared]

If the *NDataDecl* is present, this is a general *unparsed entity*; otherwise it is a parsed entity.

VALIDITY CONSTRAINT: NOTATION DECLARED

The *Name* must match the declared name of a *notation*.

[Definition: The *SystemLiteral* is called the entity's **system identifier**. It is a URI reference (as defined in [IETF RFC 2396], updated by [IETF RFC 2732]), meant to be dereferenced to obtain input for the XML processor to construct the entity's replacement text.] It is an error for a fragment identifier (beginning with a # character) to be part of a system identifier. Unless otherwise provided by information outside the scope of this specification (e.g. a special XML element type defined by a particular DTD, or a processing instruction defined by a particular application specification), relative URIs are relative to the location of the resource within which the entity declaration occurs. A URI might thus be relative to the *document entity*, to the entity containing the *external DTD subset*, or to some other *external parameter entity*.

URI references require encoding and escaping of certain characters. The disallowed characters include all non-ASCII characters, plus the excluded characters listed in Section 2.4 of [IETF RFC 2396], except for the number sign (#) and percent sign (%) characters and the square bracket characters re-allowed in [IETF RFC 2732]. Disallowed characters must be escaped as follows:

1. Each disallowed character is converted to UTF-8 [IETF RFC 2279] as one or more bytes.
2. Any octets corresponding to a disallowed character are escaped with the URI escaping mechanism (that is, converted to `%HH`, where `HH` is the hexadecimal notation of the byte value).
3. The original character is replaced by the resulting character sequence.

[Definition: In addition to a system identifier, an external identifier may include a **public identifier**.] An XML processor attempting to retrieve the entity's content may use the public identifier to try to generate an alternative URI reference. If the processor is unable to do so, it must use the URI reference specified in the system literal. Before a match is attempted, all strings of white space in the public identifier must be normalized to single space characters (`#x20`), and leading and trailing white space must be removed.

Examples of external entity declarations:

```
<!ENTITY open-hatch
         SYSTEM "http://www.textuality.com/boilerplate/Open-
Hatch.xml">
<!ENTITY open-hatch
         PUBLIC "-//Textuality//TEXT Standard open-hatch boiler-
plate//EN"
         "http://www.textuality.com/boilerplate/OpenHatch.xml">
<!ENTITY hatch-pic
         SYSTEM "../grafix/OpenHatch.gif"
         NDATA gif >
```

4.3 Parsed Entities

4.3.1 The Text Declaration

External parsed entities should each begin with a **text declaration**.

TEXT DECLARATION

```
[77]   TextDecl   ::=   '<?xml' VersionInfo? EncodingDecl S? '?>'
```

The text declaration must be provided literally, not by reference to a parsed entity. No text declaration may appear at any position other than the beginning of an external parsed entity. The text declaration in an external parsed entity is not considered part of its *replacement text*.

4.3.2 Well-Formed Parsed Entities

The document entity is well-formed if it matches the production labeled *document*. An external general parsed entity is well-formed if it matches the production labeled *extParsedEnt*. All external parameter entities are well-formed by definition.

WELL-FORMED EXTERNAL PARSED ENTITY

```
[78]   extParsedEnt   ::=   TextDecl? content
```

An internal general parsed entity is well-formed if its replacement text matches the production labeled *content*. All internal parameter entities are well-formed by definition.

A consequence of well-formedness in entities is that the logical and physical structures in an XML document are properly nested; no *start-tag*, *end-tag*, *empty-element tag*, *element*, *comment*, *processing instruction*, *character reference*, or *entity reference* can begin in one entity and end in another.

4.3.3 Character Encoding in Entities

Each external parsed entity in an XML document may use a different encoding for its characters. All XML processors must be able to read entities in both the UTF-8 and UTF-16 encodings. The terms "UTF-8" and "UTF-16" in this specification do not apply to character encodings with any other labels, even if the encodings or labels are very similar to UTF-8 or UTF-16.

Entities encoded in UTF-16 must begin with the Byte Order Mark described by Annex F of [ISO/IEC 10646], Annex H of [ISO/IEC 10646-2000], section 2.4 of [Unicode], and section 2.7 of [Unicode3] (the ZERO WIDTH NO-BREAK SPACE character, `#xFEFF`). This is an encoding signature, not part of either the markup or the character data of the XML document. XML processors must be able to use this character to differentiate between UTF-8 and UTF-16 encoded documents.

Although an XML processor is required to read only entities in the UTF-8 and UTF-16 encodings, it is recognized that other encodings are used around the world, and it may be desired for XML processors to read entities that use them. In the absence of external character encoding information (such as MIME headers), parsed entities which are stored in an encoding other than UTF-8 or UTF-16 must begin with a text declaration (see *4.3.1 The Text Declaration*) containing an encoding declaration:

4.3.4 Encoding Declaration

```
[80]  EncodingDecl ::=  S 'encoding' Eq ('"'
                        EncName '"' | "'"
                        EncName "'" )
[81]  EncName      ::=  [A-Za-z] ([A-Za-z0-   /* Encoding name
                        9._] | '-')*             contains only Latin
                                                 characters */
```

In the *document entity*, the encoding declaration is part of the *XML declaration*. The *EncName* is the name of the encoding used.

In an encoding declaration, the values `"UTF-8"`, `"UTF-16"`, `"ISO-10646-UCS-2"`, and `"ISO-10646-UCS-4"` should be used for the various encodings and transformations of Unicode/ISO/IEC 10646, the values `"ISO-8859-1"`, `"ISO-8859-2"`, ... `"ISO-8859-n"` (where *n* is the part number) should be used for the parts of ISO 8859, and the values `"ISO-2022-JP"`, `"Shift_JIS"`, and `"EUC-JP"` should be used for the various encoded forms of JIS X-0208-1997. It is recommended that character encodings registered (as *charsets*) with the Internet Assigned Numbers Authority [IANA-CHARSETS], other than those just listed, be referred to using their registered names; other encodings should use names starting with an "x-" prefix. XML processors should match character encoding names in a case-insensitive way and should either interpret an IANA-registered name as the encoding registered at IANA for that name or treat it as unknown (processors are, of course, not required to support all IANA-registered encodings).

In the absence of information provided by an external transport protocol (e.g. HTTP or MIME), it is an *error* for an entity including an encoding declaration to be presented to the XML processor in an encoding other than that named in the declaration, or for an entity which begins with neither a Byte Order Mark nor an encoding declaration to use an encoding other than UTF-8. Note that since ASCII is a subset of UTF-8, ordinary ASCII entities do not strictly need an encoding declaration.

It is a fatal error for a *TextDecl* to occur other than at the beginning of an external entity.

It is a *fatal error* when an XML processor encounters an entity with an encoding that it is unable to process. It is a fatal error if an XML entity is determined (via default, encoding declaration, or higher-level protocol) to be in a certain encoding but contains octet sequences that are not legal in that encoding. It is also a fatal error if an XML entity contains no encoding declaration and its content is not legal UTF-8 or UTF-16.

Examples of text declarations containing encoding declarations:

```
<?xml encoding='UTF-8'?>
<?xml encoding='EUC-JP'?>
```

4.4 XML Processor Treatment of Entities and References

The table below summarizes the contexts in which character references, entity references, and invocations of unparsed entities might appear and the required behavior of an *XML processor* in each case. The labels in the leftmost column describe the recognition context:

REFERENCE IN CONTENT
As a reference anywhere after the *start-tag* and before the *end-tag* of an element; corresponds to the nonterminal *content*.

REFERENCE IN ATTRIBUTE VALUE
As a reference within either the value of an attribute in a *start-tag*, or a default value in an *attribute declaration*; corresponds to the nonterminal *AttValue*.

OCCURS AS ATTRIBUTE VALUE
As a *Name*, not a reference, appearing either as the value of an attribute which has been declared as type **ENTITY**, or as one of the space-separated tokens in the value of an attribute which has been declared as type **ENTITIES**.

REFERENCE IN ENTITY VALUE
As a reference within a parameter or internal entity's *literal entity value* in the entity's declaration; corresponds to the nonterminal *EntityValue*.

REFERENCE IN DTD
As a reference within either the internal or external subsets of the DTD, but outside of an EntityValue, AttValue, PI, Comment, SystemLiteral,

PubidLiteral, or the contents of an ignored conditional section (see *3.4 Conditional Sections*).

	Entity Type				
	Parameter	**Internal General**	**External Parsed General**	**Unparsed**	**Character**
Reference in Content	Not recognized	Included if validating	Included	Forbidden	Included
Reference in Attribute Value	Not recognized	Included in literal	Forbidden	Forbidden	Included
Occurs as Attribute Value	Not recognized	Forbidden	Forbidden	Notify	Not recognized
Reference in EntityValue	Included in literal	Bypassed	Bypassed	Forbidden	Included
Reference in DTD	Included as PE	Forbidden	Forbidden	Forbidden	Forbidden

4.4.1 Not Recognized

Outside the DTD, the `%` character has no special significance; thus, what would be parameter entity references in the DTD are not recognized as markup in *content*. Similarly, the names of unparsed entities are not recognized except when they appear in the value of an appropriately declared attribute.

4.4.2 Included

[Definition: An entity is **included** when its *replacement text* is retrieved and processed, in place of the reference itself, as though it were part of the document at the location the reference was recognized.] The replacement text may contain both *character data* and (except for parameter entities) *markup*, which must be recognized in the usual way. (The string `"AT&T;"` expands to `"AT&T;"` and the remaining ampersand is not recognized as an entity-reference delimiter.) A character reference is **included** when the indicated character is processed in place of the reference itself.

4.4.3 Included If Validating

When an XML processor recognizes a reference to a parsed entity, in order to *validate* the document, the processor must *include* its replacement text. If the entity is external, and the processor is not attempting to validate the XML document, the processor *may*, but need not, include the entity's replacement text. If a non-validating processor does not include the replacement text, it must inform the application that it recognized, but did not read, the entity.

This rule is based on the recognition that the automatic inclusion provided by the SGML and XML entity mechanism, primarily designed to support modularity in authoring, is not necessarily appropriate for other applications, in particular document browsing. Browsers, for example, when encountering an external parsed entity reference, might choose to provide a visual indication of the entity's presence and retrieve it for display only on demand.

4.4.4 Forbidden

The following are forbidden, and constitute *fatal* errors:

- the appearance of a reference to an *unparsed entity*.
- the appearance of any character or general-entity reference in the DTD except within an *EntityValue* or *AttValue*.
- a reference to an external entity in an attribute value.

4.4.5 Included in Literal

When an *entity reference* appears in an attribute value, or a parameter entity reference appears in a literal entity value, its *replacement text* is processed in place of the reference itself as though it were part of the document at the location the reference was recognized, except that a single or double quote character in the replacement text is always treated as a normal data character and will not terminate the literal. For example, this is well-formed:

```
<!--  -->
<!ENTITY % YN '"Yes"' >
<!ENTITY WhatHeSaid "He said %YN;" >
```

while this is not:

```
<!ENTITY EndAttr "27'" >
<element attribute='a-&EndAttr;>
```

4.4.6 Notify

When the name of an *unparsed entity* appears as a token in the value of an attribute of declared type **ENTITY** or **ENTITIES**, a validating processor must inform the application of the *system* and *public* (if any) identifiers for both the entity and its associated *notation*.

4.4.7 Bypassed

When a general entity reference appears in the *EntityValue* in an entity declaration, it is bypassed and left as is.

4.4.8 Included as PE

Just as with external parsed entities, parameter entities need only be *included if validating*. When a parameter-entity reference is recognized in the DTD and included, its *replacement text* is enlarged by the attachment of one leading and one following space (`#x20`) character; the intent is to constrain the replacement text of parameter entities to contain an integral number of grammatical tokens in the DTD. This behavior does not apply to parameter entity references within entity values; these are described in *4.4.5 Included in Literal*.

4.5 Construction of Internal Entity Replacement Text

In discussing the treatment of internal entities, it is useful to distinguish two forms of the entity's value. [Definition: **The literal entity value** is the quoted string actually present in the entity declaration, corresponding to the non-terminal *EntityValue*.] [Definition: The **replacement text** is the content of the entity, after replacement of character references and parameter-entity references.]

The literal entity value as given in an internal entity declaration (*EntityValue*) may contain character, parameter-entity, and general-entity references. Such references must be contained entirely within the literal entity value. The actual replacement text that is *included* as described above must contain the *replacement text* of any parameter entities referred to, and must contain the character referred to, in place of any character references in the literal entity value; however, general-entity references must be left as-is, unexpanded. For example, given the following declarations:

```
<!ENTITY % pub    "&#xc9;ditions Gallimard" >
<!ENTITY   rights "All rights reserved" >
<!ENTITY   book   "La Peste: Albert Camus,
&#xA9; 1947 %pub;. &rights;" >
```

then the replacement text for the entity "book" is:

```
La Peste: Albert Camus,
© 1947 Éditions Gallimard. &rights;
```

The general-entity reference "&rights;" would be expanded should the reference "&book;" appear in the document's content or an attribute value.

These simple rules may have complex interactions; for a detailed discussion of a difficult example, see *D Expansion of Entity and Character References*.

4.6 Predefined Entities

[Definition: Entity and character references can both be used to **escape** the left angle bracket, ampersand, and other delimiters. A set of general entities (amp, lt, gt, apos, quot) is specified for this purpose. Numeric character references may also be used; they are expanded immediately when recognized and must be treated as character data, so the numeric character references "<" and "&" may be used to escape < and & when they occur in character data.]

All XML processors must recognize these entities whether they are declared or not. For interoperability, valid XML documents should declare these entities, like any others, before using them. If the entities lt or amp are declared, they must be declared as internal entities whose replacement text is a character reference to the respective character (less-than sign or ampersand) being escaped; the double escaping is required for these entities so that references to them produce a well-formed result. If the entities gt, apos, or quot are declared, they must be declared as internal entities whose replacement text is the single character being escaped (or a character reference to that character; the double escaping here is unnecessary but harmless). For example:

```
<!ENTITY lt     "&#38;#60;">
<!ENTITY gt     "&#62;">
```

```
<!ENTITY amp     "&#38;#38;">
<!ENTITY apos    "&#39;">
<!ENTITY quot    "&#34;">
```

4.7 Notation Declarations

[Definition: **Notations** identify by name the format of *unparsed entities*, the format of elements which bear a notation attribute, or the application to which a *processing instruction* is addressed.]

[Definition: **Notation declarations** provide a name for the notation, for use in entity and attribute-list declarations and in attribute specifications, and an external identifier for the notation which may allow an XML processor or its client application to locate a helper application capable of processing data in the given notation.]

Notation Declarations

[82]	NotationDecl	::=	'<!NOTATION' *S Name S* (*ExternalID* | *PublicID*) *S*? '>'	[VC: Unique Notation Name]
[83]	PublicID	::=	'PUBLIC' *S PubidLiteral*	

VALIDITY CONSTRAINT: UNIQUE NOTATION NAME

Only one notation declaration can declare a given *Name*.

XML processors must provide applications with the name and external identifier(s) of any notation declared and referred to in an attribute value, attribute definition, or entity declaration. They may additionally resolve the external identifier into the *system identifier*, file name, or other information needed to allow the application to call a processor for data in the notation described. (It is not an error, however, for XML documents to declare and refer to notations for which notation-specific applications are not available on the system where the XML processor or application is running.)

4.8 Document Entity

[Definition: The **document entity** serves as the root of the entity tree and a starting-point for an *XML processor*.] This specification does not specify how the document entity is to be located by an XML processor; unlike other entities, the document entity has no name and might well appear on a processor input stream without any identification at all.

5 Conformance

5.1 Validating and Non-Validating Processors

Conforming *XML processors* fall into two classes: validating and non-validating.

Validating and non-validating processors alike must report violations of this specification's well-formedness constraints in the content of the *document entity* and any other *parsed entities* that they read.

[Definition: **Validating processors** must, at user option, report violations of the constraints expressed by the declarations in the *DTD*, and failures to fulfill the validity constraints given in this specification.] To accomplish this, validating XML processors must read and process the entire DTD and all external parsed entities referenced in the document.

Non-validating processors are required to check only the *document entity*, including the entire internal DTD subset, for well-formedness. [Definition: While they are not required to check the document for validity, they are required to **process** all the declarations they read in the internal DTD subset and in any parameter entity that they read, up to the first reference to a parameter entity that they do *not* read; that is to say, they must use the information in those declarations to *normalize* attribute values, *include* the replacement text of internal entities, and supply *default attribute values*.] Except when `standalone="yes"`, they must not *process entity declarations* or *attribute-list declarations* encountered after a reference to a parameter entity that is not read, since the entity may have contained overriding declarations.

5.2 Using XML Processors

The behavior of a validating XML processor is highly predictable; it must read every piece of a document and report all well-formedness and validity violations. Less is required of a non-validating processor; it need not read any part of the document other than the document entity. This has two effects that may be important to users of XML processors:

- Certain well-formedness errors, specifically those that require reading external entities, may not be detected by a non-validating processor. Examples include the constraints entitled *Entity Declared*, *Parsed Entity*, and *No Recursion*, as well as some of the cases described as *forbidden* in *4.4 XML Processor Treatment of Entities and References*.

- The information passed from the processor to the application may vary, depending on whether the processor reads parameter and external entities. For example, a non-validating processor may not *normalize* attribute values, *include* the replacement text of internal entities, or supply *default attribute values*, where doing so depends on having read declarations in external or parameter entities.

For maximum reliability in interoperating between different XML processors, applications which use non-validating processors should not rely on any behaviors not required of such processors. Applications which require facilities such as the use of default attributes or internal entities which are declared in external entities should use validating XML processors.

6 Notation

The formal grammar of XML is given in this specification using a simple Extended Backus-Naur Form (EBNF) notation. Each rule in the grammar defines one symbol, in the form

```
symbol ::= expression
```

Symbols are written with an initial capital letter if they are the start symbol of a regular language, otherwise with an initial lower case letter. Literal strings are quoted.

Within the expression on the right-hand side of a rule, the following expressions are used to match strings of one or more characters:

```
#xN
```

where `N` is a hexadecimal integer, the expression matches the character in ISO/IEC 10646 whose canonical (UCS-4) code value, when interpreted as an unsigned binary number, has the value indicated. The number of leading zeros in the `#xN` form is insignificant; the number of leading zeros in the corresponding code value is governed by the character encoding in use and is not significant for XML.

```
[a-zA-Z], [#xN-#xN]
```

matches any *Char* with a value in the range(s) indicated (inclusive).

`[abc], [#xN#xN#xN]`

matches any *Char* with a value among the characters enumerated. Enumerations and ranges can be mixed in one set of brackets.

`[^a-z], [^#xN-#xN]`

matches any *Char* with a value *outside* the range indicated.

`[^abc], [^#xN#xN#xN]`

matches any *Char* with a value not among the characters given. Enumerations and ranges of forbidden values can be mixed in one set of brackets.

`"string"`

matches a literal string *matching* that given inside the double quotes.

`'string'`

matches a literal string *matching* that given inside the single quotes.

These symbols may be combined to match more complex patterns as follows, where `A` and `B` represent simple expressions:

`(expression)`

`expression` is treated as a unit and may be combined as described in this list.

`A?`

matches `A` or nothing; optional `A`.

`A B`

matches `A` followed by `B`. This operator has higher precedence than alternation; thus `A B | C D` is identical to `(A B) | (C D)`.

`A | B`

matches `A` or `B` but not both.

```
A - B
```

matches any string that matches `A` but does not match `B`.

```
A+
```

matches one or more occurrences of `A`. Concatenation has higher precedence than alternation; thus `A+ | B+` is identical to `(A+) | (B+)`.

```
A*
```

matches zero or more occurrences of `A`. Concatenation has higher precedence than alternation; thus `A* | B*` is identical to `(A*) | (B*)`.

Other notations used in the productions are:

```
/* ... */
```

comment.

```
[ wfc: ... ]
```

well-formedness constraint; this identifies by name a constraint on *well-formed* documents associated with a production.

```
[ vc: ... ]
```

validity constraint; this identifies by name a constraint on *valid* documents associated with a production.

A References

A.1 Normative References

IANA-CHARSETS

(Internet Assigned Numbers Authority) *Official Names for Character Sets*, ed. Keld Simonsen et al. See ftp://ftp.isi.edu/in-notes/iana/assignments/character-sets.

IETF RFC 1766

IETF (Internet Engineering Task Force). *RFC 1766: Tags for the Identification of Languages*, ed. H. Alvestrand. 1995. (See http://www.ietf.org/rfc/rfc1766.txt.)

ISO/IEC 10646

ISO (International Organization for Standardization). ISO/IEC 10646-1993 (E). *Information technology — Universal Multiple-Octet Coded Character Set (UCS) — Part 1: Architecture and Basic Multilingual Plane*. [Geneva]: International Organization for Standardization, 1993 (plus amendments AM 1 through AM 7).

ISO/IEC 10646-2000

ISO (International Organization for Standardization). *ISO/IEC 10646-1:2000. Information technology — Universal Multiple-Octet Coded Character Set (UCS) — Part 1: Architecture and Basic Multilingual Plane.* [Geneva]: International Organization for Standardization, 2000.

Unicode

The Unicode Consortium. *The Unicode Standard, Version 2.0*. Reading, Mass.: Addison-Wesley Developers Press, 1996.

Unicode3

The Unicode Consortium. *The Unicode Standard, Version 3.0*. Reading, Mass.: Addison-Wesley Developers Press, 2000. ISBN 0-201-61633-5.

A.2 Other References

Aho/Ullman

Aho, Alfred V., Ravi Sethi, and Jeffrey D. Ullman. *Compilers: Principles, Techniques, and Tools*. Reading: Addison-Wesley, 1986, rpt. corr. 1988.

Berners-Lee et al.

Berners-Lee, T., R. Fielding, and L. Masinter. *Uniform Resource Identifiers (URI): Generic Syntax and Semantics*. 1997. (Work in progress; see updates to RFC1738.)

Brüggemann-Klein

Brüggemann-Klein, Anne. Formal Models in Document Processing. Habilitationsschrift. Faculty of Mathematics at the University of Freiburg, 1993. (See ftp://ftp.informatik.uni-freiburg.de/documents/papers/brueggem/habil.ps.)

Brüggemann-Klein and Wood

Brüggemann-Klein, Anne, and Derick Wood. *Deterministic Regular Languages*. Universität Freiburg, Institut für Informatik, Bericht 38, Oktober 1991. Extended abstract in A. Finkel, M. Jantzen, Hrsg., STACS 1992, S. 173-184. Springer-Verlag, Berlin 1992. Lecture Notes in Computer Science 577. Full version titled *One-Unambiguous Regular Languages* in Information and Computation 140 (2): 229-253, February 1998.

Clark

James Clark. Comparison of SGML and XML. (See http://www.w3.org/TR/NOTE-sgml-xml-971215.)

IANA-LANGCODES

(Internet Assigned Numbers Authority) Registry of Language Tags, ed. Keld Simonsen et al. (See http://www.isi.edu/in-notes/iana/assignments/languages/.)

IETF RFC2141

IETF (Internet Engineering Task Force). *RFC 2141: URN Syntax*, ed. R. Moats. 1997. (See http://www.ietf.org/rfc/rfc2141.txt.)

IETF RFC 2279

IETF (Internet Engineering Task Force). *RFC 2279: UTF-8*, a transformation format of ISO 10646, ed. F. Yergeau, 1998. (See http://www.ietf.org/rfc/rfc2279.txt.)

IETF RFC 2376

IETF (Internet Engineering Task Force). *RFC 2376: XML Media Types*. ed. E. Whitehead, M. Murata. 1998. (See http://www.ietf.org/rfc/rfc2376.txt.)

IETF RFC 2396

IETF (Internet Engineering Task Force). *RFC 2396: Uniform Resource Identifiers (URI): Generic Syntax*. T. Berners-Lee, R. Fielding, L. Masinter. 1998. (See http://www.ietf.org/rfc/rfc2396.txt.)

IETF RFC 2732

IETF (Internet Engineering Task Force). *RFC 2732: Format for Literal IPv6 Addresses in URL's*. R. Hinden, B. Carpenter, L. Masinter. 1999. (See http://www.ietf.org/rfc/rfc2732.txt.)

IETF RFC 2781

IETF (Internet Engineering Task Force). *RFC 2781: UTF-16, an encoding of ISO 10646*, ed. P. Hoffman, F. Yergeau. 2000. (See http://www.ietf.org/rfc/rfc2781.txt.)

ISO 639

(International Organization for Standardization). ISO 639:1988 (E). *Code for the representation of names of languages*. [Geneva]: International Organization for Standardization, 1988.

ISO 3166

(International Organization for Standardization). ISO 3166-1:1997 (E). *Codes for the representation of names of countries and their subdivisions — Part 1: Country codes* [Geneva]: International Organization for Standardization, 1997.

ISO 8879

ISO (International Organization for Standardization). *ISO 8879:1986(E). Information processing — Text and Office Systems — Standard Generalized Markup Language (SGML).* First edition — 1986-10-15. [Geneva]: International Organization for Standardization, 1986.

ISO/IEC 10744

ISO (International Organization for Standardization). *ISO/IEC 10744-1992 (E). Information technology — Hypermedia/Time-based Structuring Language (HyTime).* [Geneva]: International Organization for Standardization, 1992. Extended Facilities Annexe. [Geneva]: International Organization for Standardization, 1996.

WEBSGML

ISO (International Organization for Standardization). *ISO 8879:1986 TC2. Information technology — Document Description and Processing Languages*. [Geneva]: International Organization for Standardization, 1998. (See http://www.sgmlsource.com/8879rev/n0029.htm.)

XML Names

Tim Bray, Dave Hollander, and Andrew Layman, editors. *Namespaces in XML*. Textuality, Hewlett-Packard, and Microsoft. World Wide Web Consortium, 1999. (See http://www.w3.org/TR/REC-xml-names/.)

B Character Classes

Following the characteristics defined in the Unicode standard, characters are classed as base characters (among others, these contain the alphabetic characters of the Latin alphabet), ideographic characters, and combining characters (among others, this class contains most diacritics). Digits and extenders are also distinguished.

Characters

```
[84]   Letter      ::=   BaseChar | Ideographic
[85]   BaseChar    ::=   [#x0041-#x005A] | [#x0061-#x007A]
                         | [#x00C0-#x00D6] | [#x00D8-#x00F6]
                         | [#x00F8-#x00FF] | [#x0100-#x0131]
                         | [#x0134-#x013E] | [#x0141-#x0148]
                         | [#x014A-#x017E] | [#x0180-#x01C3]
                         | [#x01CD-#x01F0] | [#x01F4-#x01F5]
                         | [#x01FA-#x0217] | [#x0250-#x02A8]
                         | [#x02BB-#x02C1] | #x0386 | [#x0388-
                         #x038A] | #x038C | [#x038E-#x03A1]
                         | [#x03A3-#x03CE] | [#x03D0-#x03D6]
                         | #x03DA | #x03DC | #x03DE | #x03E0
                         | [#x03E2-#x03F3] | [#x0401-#x040C]
                         | [#x040E-#x044F] | [#x0451-#x045C]
                         | [#x045E-#x0481] | [#x0490-#x04C4]
                         | [#x04C7-#x04C8] | [#x04CB-#x04CC]
                         | [#x04D0-#x04EB] | [#x04EE-#x04F5]
                         | [#x04F8-#x04F9] | [#x0531-#x0556]
                         | #x0559 | [#x0561-#x0586] | [#x05D0-
```

```
#x05EA] | [#x05F0-#x05F2] | [#x0621-
#x063A] | [#x0641-#x064A] | [#x0671-
#x06B7] | [#x06BA-#x06BE] | [#x06C0-
#x06CE] | [#x06D0-#x06D3] | #x06D5
| [#x06E5-#x06E6] | [#x0905-#x0939]
| #x093D | [#x0958-#x0961] | [#x0985-
#x098C] | [#x098F-#x0990] | [#x0993-
#x09A8] | [#x09AA-#x09B0] | #x09B2
| [#x09B6-#x09B9] | [#x09DC-#x09DD]
| [#x09DF-#x09E1] | [#x09F0-#x09F1]
| [#x0A05-#x0A0A] | [#x0A0F-#x0A10]
| [#x0A13-#x0A28] | [#x0A2A-#x0A30]
| [#x0A32-#x0A33] | [#x0A35-#x0A36]
| [#x0A38-#x0A39] | [#x0A59-#x0A5C]
| #x0A5E | [#x0A72-#x0A74] | [#x0A85-
#x0A8B] | #x0A8D | [#x0A8F-#x0A91]
| [#x0A93-#x0AA8] | [#x0AAA-#x0AB0]
| [#x0AB2-#x0AB3] | [#x0AB5-#x0AB9]
| #x0ABD | #x0AE0 | [#x0B05-#x0B0C]
| [#x0B0F-#x0B10] | [#x0B13-#x0B28]
| [#x0B2A-#x0B30] | [#x0B32-#x0B33]
| [#x0B36-#x0B39] | #x0B3D | [#x0B5C-
#x0B5D] | [#x0B5F-#x0B61] | [#x0B85-
#x0B8A] | [#x0B8E-#x0B90] | [#x0B92-
#x0B95] | [#x0B99-#x0B9A] | #x0B9C
| [#x0B9E-#x0B9F] | [#x0BA3-#x0BA4]
| [#x0BA8-#x0BAA] | [#x0BAE-#x0BB5]
| [#x0BB7-#x0BB9] | [#x0C05-#x0C0C]
| [#x0C0E-#x0C10] | [#x0C12-#x0C28]
| [#x0C2A-#x0C33] | [#x0C35-#x0C39]
| [#x0C60-#x0C61] | [#x0C85-#x0C8C]
| [#x0C8E-#x0C90] | [#x0C92-#x0CA8]
| [#x0CAA-#x0CB3] | [#x0CB5-#x0CB9]
| #x0CDE | [#x0CE0-#x0CE1] | [#x0D05-
#x0D0C] | [#x0D0E-#x0D10] | [#x0D12-
#x0D28] | [#x0D2A-#x0D39] | [#x0D60-
#x0D61] | [#x0E01-#x0E2E] | #x0E30
| [#x0E32-#x0E33] | [#x0E40-#x0E45]
| [#x0E81-#x0E82] | #x0E84 | [#x0E87-
#x0E88] | #x0E8A | #x0E8D | [#x0E94-
#x0E97] | [#x0E99-#x0E9F] | [#x0EA1-
#x0EA3] | #x0EA5 | #x0EA7 |
[#x0EAA-#x0EAB] | [#x0EAD-#x0EAE]
| #x0EB0 | [#x0EB2-#x0EB3] | #x0EBD
| [#x0EC0-#x0EC4] | [#x0F40-#x0F47]
| [#x0F49-#x0F69] | [#x10A0-#x10C5]
| [#x10D0-#x10F6] | #x1100 | [#x1102-
#x1103] | [#x1105-#x1107] | #x1109
| [#x110B-#x110C] | [#x110E-#x1112]
| #x113C | #x113E | #x1140 | #x114C
| #x114E | #x1150 | [#x1154-#x1155]
| #x1159 | [#x115F-#x1161] | #x1163
| #x1165 | #x1167 | #x1169 | [#x116D-
#x116E] | [#x1172-#x1173] | #x1175
```

```
                               | #x119E | #x11A8 | #x11AB | [#x11AE-
                               #x11AF] | [#x11B7-#x11B8] | #x11BA
                               | [#x11BC-#x11C2] | #x11EB | #x11F0
                               | #x11F9 | [#x1E00-#x1E9B] | [#x1EA0-
                               #x1EF9] | [#x1F00-#x1F15] | [#x1F18-
                               #x1F1D] | [#x1F20-#x1F45] | [#x1F48-
                               #x1F4D] | [#x1F50-#x1F57] | #x1F59
                               | #x1F5B | #x1F5D | [#x1F5F-#x1F7D]
                               | [#x1F80-#x1FB4] | [#x1FB6-#x1FBC]
                               | #x1FBE | [#x1FC2-#x1FC4] | [#x1FC6-
                               #x1FCC] | [#x1FD0-#x1FD3] | [#x1FD6-
                               #x1FDB] | [#x1FE0-#x1FEC] | [#x1FF2-
                               #x1FF4] | [#x1FF6-#x1FFC] | #x2126
                               | [#x212A-#x212B] | #x212E | [#x2180-
                               #x2182] | [#x3041-#x3094] | [#x30A1-
                               #x30FA] | [#x3105-#x312C] | [#xAC00-
                               #xD7A3]
[86]  Ideographic     ::=      [#x4E00-#x9FA5] | #x3007 | [#x3021-
                               #x3029]
[87]  CombiningChar   ::=      [#x0300-#x0345] | [#x0360-#x0361]
                               | [#x0483-#x0486] | [#x0591-#x05A1]
                               | [#x05A3-#x05B9] | [#x05BB-#x05BD]
                               | #x05BF | [#x05C1-#x05C2] | #x05C4
                               | [#x064B-#x0652] | #x0670 | [#x06D6-
                               #x06DC] | [#x06DD-#x06DF] | [#x06E0-
                               #x06E4] | [#x06E7-#x06E8] | [#x06EA-
                               #x06ED] | [#x0901-#x0903] | #x093C
                               | [#x093E-#x094C] | #x094D | [#x0951-
                               #x0954] | [#x0962-#x0963] | [#x0981-
                               #x0983] | #x09BC | #x09BE | #x09BF
                               | [#x09C0-#x09C4] | [#x09C7-#x09C8]
                               | [#x09CB-#x09CD] | #x09D7 | [#x09E2-
                               #x09E3] | #x0A02 | #x0A3C | #x0A3E
                               | #x0A3F | [#x0A40-#x0A42] | [#x0A47-
                               #x0A48] | [#x0A4B-#x0A4D] | [#x0A70-
                               #x0A71] | [#x0A81-#x0A83] | #x0ABC
                               | [#x0ABE-#x0AC5] | [#x0AC7-#x0AC9]
                               | [#x0ACB-#x0ACD] | [#x0B01-#x0B03]
                               | #x0B3C | [#x0B3E-#x0B43] | [#x0B47-
                               #x0B48] | [#x0B4B-#x0B4D] | [#x0B56-
                               #x0B57] | [#x0B82-#x0B83] | [#x0BBE-
                               #x0BC2] | [#x0BC6-#x0BC8] |
                               [#x0BCA-#x0BCD] | #x0BD7 | [#x0C01-
                               #x0C03] | [#x0C3E-#x0C44] | [#x0C46-
                               #x0C48] | [#x0C4A-#x0C4D] | [#x0C55-
                               #x0C56] | [#x0C82-#x0C83] |
                               [#x0CBE-#x0CC4] | [#x0CC6-#x0CC8]
                               | [#x0CCA-#x0CCD] | [#x0CD5-#x0CD6]
                               | [#x0D02-#x0D03] | [#x0D3E-#x0D43]
                               | [#x0D46-#x0D48] | [#x0D4A-#x0D4D]
                               | #x0D57 | #x0E31 | [#x0E34-#x0E3A]
                               | [#x0E47-#x0E4E] | #x0EB1 | [#x0EB4-
                               #x0EB9] | [#x0EBB-#x0EBC] | [#x0EC8-
```

```
                                #x0ECD] | [#x0F18-#x0F19] | #x0F35
                                | #x0F37 | #x0F39 | #x0F3E | #x0F3F
                                | [#x0F71-#x0F84] | [#x0F86-#x0F8B]
                                | [#x0F90-#x0F95] | #x0F97 | [#x0F99-
                                #x0FAD] | [#x0FB1-#x0FB7] | #x0FB9
                                | [#x20D0-#x20DC] | #x20E1 | [#x302A-
                                #x302F] | #x3099 | #x309A
[88]    Digit          ::=     [#x0030-#x0039] | [#x0660-#x0669]
                                | [#x06F0-#x06F9] | [#x0966-#x096F]
                                | [#x09E6-#x09EF] | [#x0A66-#x0A6F]
                                | [#x0AE6-#x0AEF] | [#x0B66-#x0B6F]
                                | [#x0BE7-#x0BEF] | [#x0C66-#x0C6F]
                                | [#x0CE6-#x0CEF] | [#x0D66-#x0D6F]
                                | [#x0E50-#x0E59] | [#x0ED0-#x0ED9]
                                | [#x0F20-#x0F29]
[89]    Extender       ::=     #x00B7 | #x02D0 | #x02D1 | #x0387
                                | #x0640 | #x0E46 | #x0EC6 | #x3005
                                | [#x3031-#x3035] | [#x309D-#x309E]
                                | [#x30FC-#x30FE]
```

The character classes defined here can be derived from the Unicode 2.0 character database as follows:

- Name start characters must have one of the categories Ll, Lu, Lo, Lt, Nl.
- Name characters other than Name-start characters must have one of the categories Mc, Me, Mn, Lm, or Nd.
- Characters in the compatibility area (i.e. with character code greater than `#xF900` and less than `#xFFFE`) are not allowed in XML names.
  - Characters which have a font or compatibility decomposition (i.e. those with a "compatibility formatting tag" in field 5 of the database—marked by field 5 beginning with a "<") are not allowed.
  - The following characters are treated as name-start characters rather than name characters, because the property file classifies them as Alphabetic: `[#x02BB-#x02C1]`, `#x0559`, `#x06E5`, `#x06E6`.
  - Characters `#x20DD–#x20E0` are excluded (in accordance with Unicode 2.0, section 5.14).
  - Character `#x00B7` is classified as an extender, because the property list so identifies it.
  - Character `#x0387` is added as a name character, because `#x00B7` is its canonical equivalent.
  - Characters ':' and '_' are allowed as name-start characters.
  - Characters '-' and '.' are allowed as name characters.

C XML and SGML (Non-Normative)

XML is designed to be a subset of SGML, in that every XML document should also be a conforming SGML document. For a detailed comparison of the additional restrictions that XML places on documents beyond those of SGML, see [Clark].

D Expansion of Entity and Character References (Non-Normative)

This appendix contains some examples illustrating the sequence of entity- and character-reference recognition and expansion, as specified in *4.4 XML Processor Treatment of Entities and References*.

If the DTD contains the declaration

```
<!ENTITY example "<p>An ampersand (&#38;#38;) may be escaped
numerically (&#38;#38;#38;) or with a general entity
(&amp;amp;).</p>" >
```

then the XML processor will recognize the character references when it parses the entity declaration, and resolve them before storing the following string as the value of the entity `"example"`:

```
<p>An ampersand (&#38;) may be escaped
numerically (&#38;#38;) or with a general entity
(&amp;amp;).</p>
```

A reference in the document to `"&example;"` will cause the text to be reparsed, at which time the start- and end-tags of the p element will be recognized and the three references will be recognized and expanded, resulting in a p element with the following content (all data, no delimiters or markup):

```
An ampersand (&) may be escaped
numerically (&#38;) or with a general entity
(&amp;).
```

A more complex example will illustrate the rules and their effects fully. In the following example, the line numbers are solely for reference.

```
1 <?xml version='1.0'?>
2 <!DOCTYPE test [
3 <!ELEMENT test (#PCDATA) >
4 <!ENTITY % xx '&#37;zz;'>
5 <!ENTITY % zz '&#60;!ENTITY tricky "error-prone" >' >
6 %xx;
7 ]>
8 <test>This sample shows a &tricky; method.</test>
```

This produces the following:

- in line 4, the reference to character 37 is expanded immediately, and the parameter entity "xx" is stored in the symbol table with the value "%zz;". Since the replacement text is not rescanned, the reference to parameter entity "zz" is not recognized. (And it would be an error if it were, since "zz" is not yet declared.)
- in line 5, the character reference "<" is expanded immediately and the parameter entity "zz" is stored with the replacement text "<!ENTITY tricky "error-prone" >", which is a well-formed entity declaration.
- in line 6, the reference to "xx" is recognized, and the replacement text of "xx" (namely "%zz;") is parsed. The reference to "zz" is recognized in its turn, and its replacement text ("<!ENTITY tricky "error-prone" >") is parsed. The general entity "tricky" has now been declared, with the replacement text "error-prone".
- in line 8, the reference to the general entity "tricky" is recognized, and it is expanded, so the full content of the test element is the self-describing (and ungrammatical) string *This sample shows a error-prone method.*

E Deterministic Content Models (Non-Normative)

As noted in 3.2.1 Element Content, it is required that content models in element type declarations be deterministic. This requirement is *for compatibility* with SGML (which calls deterministic content models "unambiguous"); XML processors built using SGML systems may flag non-deterministic content models as errors.

For example, the content model ((b, c) | (b, d)) is non-deterministic, because given an initial b the XML processor cannot know which b in the model is being matched without looking ahead to see which element follows the b. In this case, the two references to b can be collapsed into a single reference, making the model read (b, (c | d)). An initial b now clearly matches only a single name in the content model. The processor doesn't need to look ahead to see what follows; either c or d would be accepted.

More formally: a finite state automaton may be constructed from the content model using the standard algorithms, e.g. algorithm 3.5 in section 3.9 of Aho, Sethi, and Ullman [Aho/Ullman]. In many such algorithms, a follow set is constructed for each position in the regular expression (i.e., each leaf node in the syntax tree for the regular expression); if any position has a follow set in which more than one following position is labeled with the same element type name, then the content model is in error and may be reported as an error.

Algorithms exist which allow many but not all non-deterministic content models to be reduced automatically to equivalent deterministic models; see Brüggemann-Klein 1991 [Brüggemann-Klein].

F Autodetection of Character Encodings (Non-Normative)

The XML encoding declaration functions as an internal label on each entity, indicating which character encoding is in use. Before an XML processor can read the internal label, however, it apparently has to know what character encoding is in use—which is what the internal label is trying to indicate. In the general case, this is a hopeless situation. It is not entirely hopeless in XML, however, because XML limits the general case in two ways: each implementation is assumed to support only a finite set of character encodings, and the XML encoding declaration is restricted in position and content in order to make it feasible to autodetect the character encoding in use in each entity in normal cases. Also, in many cases other sources of information are available in addition to the XML data stream itself. Two cases may be distinguished, depending on whether the XML entity is presented to the processor without, or with, any accompanying (external) information. We consider the first case first.

F.1 Detection Without External Encoding Information

Because each XML entity not accompanied by external encoding information and not in UTF-8 or UTF-16 encoding *must* begin with an XML encoding declaration, in which the first characters must be '<?xml', any conforming processor can detect, after two to four octets of input, which of the following cases apply. In reading this list, it may help to know that in UCS-4, '<' is "#x0000003C" and '?' is "#x0000003F", and the Byte Order Mark required of UTF-16 data streams is "#xFEFF". The notation ## is used to denote any byte value except that two consecutive ##s cannot be both 00.

With a Byte Order Mark:

00 00 FE FF	UCS-4, big-endian machine (1234 order)
FF FE 00 00	UCS-4, little-endian machine (4321 order)
00 00 FF FE	UCS-4, unusual octet order (2143)
FE FF 00 00	UCS-4, unusual octet order (3412)
FE FF ## ##	UTF-16, big-endian
FF FE ## ##	UTF-16, little-endian
EF BB BF	UTF-8

Without a Byte Order Mark:

00 00 00 3C 3C 00 00 00 00 00 3C 00 00 3C 00 00	UCS-4 or other encoding with a 32-bit code unit and ASCII characters encoded as ASCII values, in respectively big-endian (1234), little-endian (4321) and two unusual byte orders (2143 and 3412). The encoding declaration must be read to determine which of UCS-4 or other supported 32-bit encodings applies.
00 3C 00 3F	UTF-16BE or big-endian ISO-10646-UCS-2 or other encoding with a 16-bit code unit in big-endian order and ASCII characters encoded as ASCII values (the encoding declaration must be read to determine which).
3C 00 3F 00	UTF-16LE or little-endian ISO-10646-UCS-2 or other encoding with a 16-bit code unit in little-endian order and ASCII characters encoded as ASCII values (the encoding declaration must be read to determine which).
3C 3F 78 6D	UTF-8, ISO 646, ASCII, some part of ISO 8859, Shift-JIS, EUC, or any other 7-bit, 8-bit, or mixed-width encoding which ensures that the characters of ASCII have their normal positions, width, and values; the actual encoding declaration must be read to detect which of these applies, but since all of these encodings use the same bit patterns for the relevant ASCII characters, the encoding declaration itself may be read reliably.
4C 6F A7 94	EBCDIC (in some flavor; the full encoding declaration must be read to tell which code page is in use).

Other	UTF-8 without an encoding declaration, or else the data stream is mislabeled (lacking a required encoding declaration), corrupt, fragmentary, or enclosed in a wrapper of some kind.

Note

In cases above which do not require reading the encoding declaration to determine the encoding, section 4.3.3 still requires that the encoding declaration, if present, be read and that the encoding name be checked to match the actual encoding of the entity. Also, it is possible that new character encodings will be invented that will make it necessary to use the encoding declaration to determine the encoding, in cases where this is not required at present.

This level of autodetection is enough to read the XML encoding declaration and parse the character-encoding identifier, which is still necessary to distinguish the individual members of each family of encodings (e.g. to tell UTF-8 from 8859, and the parts of 8859 from each other, or to distinguish the specific EBCDIC code page in use, and so on).

Because the contents of the encoding declaration are restricted to characters from the ASCII repertoire (however encoded), a processor can reliably read the entire encoding declaration as soon as it has detected which family of encodings is in use. Since in practice, all widely used character encodings fall into one of the categories above, the XML encoding declaration allows reasonably reliable in-band labeling of character encodings, even when external sources of information at the operating-system or transport-protocol level are unreliable. Character encodings such as UTF-7 that make overloaded usage of ASCII-valued bytes may fail to be reliably detected.

Once the processor has detected the character encoding in use, it can act appropriately, whether by invoking a separate input routine for each case, or by calling the proper conversion function on each character of input.

Like any self-labeling system, the XML encoding declaration will not work if any software changes the entity's character set or encoding without updating the encoding declaration. Implementors of character-encoding routines should be careful to ensure the accuracy of the internal and external information used to label the entity.

F.2 Priorities in the Presence of External Encoding Information

The second possible case occurs when the XML entity is accompanied by encoding information, as in some file systems and some network protocols. When multiple sources of information are available, their relative priority and the preferred method of handling conflict should be specified as part of the higher-level protocol used to deliver XML. In particular, please refer to [IETF RFC 2376] or its successor, which defines the `text/xml` and `application/xml` MIME types and provides some useful guidance. In the interests of interoperability, however, the following rule is recommended.

- If an XML entity is in a file, the Byte-Order Mark and encoding declaration are used (if present) to determine the character encoding.

G W3C XML Working Group (Non-Normative)

This specification was prepared and approved for publication by the W3C XML Working Group (WG). WG approval of this specification does not necessarily imply that all WG members voted for its approval. The current and former members of the XML WG are:

- Jon Bosak, Sun (Chair)
- James Clark (Technical Lead)
- Tim Bray, Textuality and Netscape (XML Co-editor)
- Jean Paoli, Microsoft (XML Co-editor)
- C. M. Sperberg-McQueen, U. of Ill. (XML Co-editor)
- Dan Connolly, W3C (W3C Liaison)
- Paula Angerstein, Texcel
- Steve DeRose, INSO
- Dave Hollander, HP
- Eliot Kimber, ISOGEN
- Eve Maler, ArborText
- Tom Magliery, NCSA
- Murray Maloney, SoftQuad, Grif SA, Muzmo and Veo Systems
- MURATA Makoto (FAMILY Given), Fuji Xerox Information Systems

- Joel Nava, Adobe
- Conleth O'Connell, Vignette
- Peter Sharpe, SoftQuad
- John Tigue, DataChannel

H W3C XML Core Group (Non-Normative)

The second edition of this specification was prepared by the W3C XML Core Working Group (WG). The members of the WG at the time of publication of this edition were:

- Paula Angerstein, Vignette
- Daniel Austin, Ask Jeeves
- Tim Boland
- Allen Brown, Microsoft
- Dan Connolly, W3C (Staff Contact)
- John Cowan, Reuters Limited
- John Evdemon, XMLSolutions Corporation
- Paul Grosso, Arbortext (Co-Chair)
- Arnaud Le Hors, IBM (Co-Chair)
- Eve Maler, Sun Microsystems (Second Edition Editor)
- Jonathan Marsh, Microsoft
- MURATA Makoto (FAMILY Given), IBM
- Mark Needleman, Data Research Associates
- David Orchard, Jamcracker
- Lew Shannon, NCR
- Richard Tobin, University of Edinburgh
- Daniel Veillard, W3C
- Dan Vint, Lexica
- Norman Walsh, Sun Microsystems
- François Yergeau, Alis Technologies (Errata List Editor)
- Kongyi Zhou, Oracle

I Production Notes (Non-Normative)

This Second Edition was encoded in the *XMLspec DTD* (which has *documentation* available). The HTML versions were produced with a combination of the *xmlspec.xsl*, *diffspec.xsl*, and *REC-xml-2e.xsl* XSLT stylesheets. The PDF version was produced with the *html2ps* facility and a distiller program.

APPENDIX C

KEY PRESENTATIONAL DTDS

Few things are as useful as a printed reference of fundamental DTDs (even if you are working with a DTD-aware editor such as XML-Spy or Emacs). This appendix provides the complete DTDs—augmented with some personal comments but unaltered otherwise—of some of the most widely used vocabularies in this book.

Aside from their reference function, these DTDs serve as real-life examples of the techniques discussed in the book (e.g. the use of entity parameters to model synonyms for character data). The vocabularies listed are the latest versions (as of November 2000):

- WML
- XHTML
- SMIL

WML

```
<!--

Wireless Markup Language (WML) Document Type Definition.
WML is an XML language. Typical usage:
<?xml version="1.0"?>
<!DOCTYPE wml PUBLIC "-//WAPFORUM//DTD WML 1.2//EN"
"http://www.wapforum.org/DTD/wml12.dtd">
<wml>
...
</wml>

-->
<!ENTITY % length "CDATA"> <!-- [0-9]+ for pixels or [0-9]+"%"
for percentage length -->
```

```
<!ENTITY % vdata "CDATA"> <!-- attribute value possibly
containing variable references -->
<!ENTITY % HREF "%vdata;"> <!-- URI, URL or URN designating a
hypertext node. May contain variable references -->
<!ENTITY % boolean "(true|false)">
<!ENTITY % number "NMTOKEN"> <!-- a number, with format [0-9]+ -->
<!ENTITY % coreattrs "id ID #IMPLIED
class CDATA #IMPLIED">
<!ENTITY % ContentType "%vdata;"> <!-- media type. May contain
variable references -->
<!ENTITY % emph "em | strong |b |i |u |big |small">
<!ENTITY % layout "br">
<!ENTITY % text "#PCDATA | %emph;">
<!-- flow covers "card-level" elements, such as text and images -->
<!ENTITY % flow "%text; | %layout; | img | anchor |a |table">
<!-- Task types -->
<!ENTITY % task "go | prev | noop | refresh">
<!-- Navigation and event elements -->
<!ENTITY % navelmts "do | onevent">
<!--================= Decks and Cards =================-->
<!ELEMENT wml ( head?, template?, card+ )>
<!ATTLIST wml
xml:lang NMTOKEN #IMPLIED
%coreattrs;
>
<!-- card intrinsic events -->
<!ENTITY % cardev
"onenterforward %HREF; #IMPLIED
onenterbackward %HREF; #IMPLIED
ontimer %HREF; #IMPLIED"
>
<!-- card field types -->
<!ENTITY % fields "%flow; | input | select | fieldset">
<!ELEMENT card (onevent*, timer?, (do |p |pre)*)>
<!ATTLIST card
title %vdata; #IMPLIED
newcontext %boolean; "false"
ordered %boolean; "true"
xml:lang NMTOKEN #IMPLIED
%cardev;
%coreattrs;
>
<!--================= Event Bindings =================-->
<!ELEMENT do (%task;)>
<!ATTLIST do
type CDATA #REQUIRED
label %vdata; #IMPLIED
name NMTOKEN #IMPLIED
optional %boolean; "false"
xml:lang NMTOKEN #IMPLIED
%coreattrs;
>
<!ELEMENT onevent (%task;)>
<!ATTLIST onevent
```

```
type CDATA #REQUIRED
%coreattrs;
>
<!--================= Deck-level declarations =================-->
<!ELEMENT head ( access | meta )+>
<!ATTLIST head
%coreattrs;
>
<!ELEMENT template (%navelmts;)*>
<!ATTLIST template
%cardev;
%coreattrs;
>
<!ELEMENT access EMPTY>
<!ATTLIST access
domain CDATA #IMPLIED
path CDATA #IMPLIED
%coreattrs;
>
<!ELEMENT meta EMPTY>
<!ATTLIST meta
http-equiv CDATA #IMPLIED
name CDATA #IMPLIED
forua %boolean; "false"
content CDATA #REQUIRED
scheme CDATA #IMPLIED
%coreattrs;
>
<!--================= Tasks =================-->
<!ELEMENT go (postfield | setvar)*>
<!ATTLIST go
href %HREF; #REQUIRED
sendreferer %boolean; "false"
method (post|get) "get"
enctype %ContentType; "application/x-www-form-urlencoded"
accept-charset CDATA #IMPLIED
%coreattrs;
>
<!ELEMENT prev (setvar)*>
<!ATTLIST prev
%coreattrs;
>
<!ELEMENT refresh (setvar)*>
<!ATTLIST refresh
%coreattrs;
>
<!ELEMENT noop EMPTY>
<!ATTLIST noop
%coreattrs;
>
<!--================= postfield =================-->
<!ELEMENT postfield EMPTY>
<!ATTLIST postfield
name %vdata; #REQUIRED
```

```
value %vdata; #REQUIRED
%coreattrs;
>
<!--================= variables =================-->
<!ELEMENT setvar EMPTY>
<!ATTLIST setvar
name %vdata; #REQUIRED
value %vdata; #REQUIRED
%coreattrs;
>
<!--================= Card Fields =================-->
<!ELEMENT select (optgroup|option)+>
<!ATTLIST select
title %vdata; #IMPLIED
name NMTOKEN #IMPLIED
value %vdata; #IMPLIED
iname NMTOKEN #IMPLIED
ivalue %vdata; #IMPLIED
multiple %boolean; "false"
tabindex %number; #IMPLIED
xml:lang NMTOKEN #IMPLIED
%coreattrs;
>
<!ELEMENT optgroup (optgroup|option)+ >
<!ATTLIST optgroup
title %vdata; #IMPLIED
xml:lang NMTOKEN #IMPLIED
%coreattrs;
>
<!ELEMENT option (#PCDATA | onevent)*>
<!ATTLIST option
value %vdata; #IMPLIED
title %vdata; #IMPLIED
onpick %HREF; #IMPLIED
xml:lang NMTOKEN #IMPLIED
%coreattrs;
>
<!ELEMENT input EMPTY>
<!ATTLIST input
name NMTOKEN #REQUIRED
type (text|password) "text"
value %vdata; #IMPLIED
format CDATA #IMPLIED
emptyok %boolean; "false"
size %number; #IMPLIED
maxlength %number; #IMPLIED
tabindex %number; #IMPLIED
title %vdata; #IMPLIED
accesskey %vdata; #IMPLIED
xml:lang NMTOKEN #IMPLIED
%coreattrs;
>
<!ELEMENT fieldset (%fields; | do)* >
<!ATTLIST fieldset
```

```
title %vdata; #IMPLIED
xml:lang NMTOKEN #IMPLIED
%coreattrs;
>
<!ELEMENT timer EMPTY>
<!ATTLIST timer
name NMTOKEN #IMPLIED
value %vdata; #REQUIRED
%coreattrs;
>
<!--================= Images =================-->
<!ENTITY % IAlign "(top|middle|bottom)" >
<!ELEMENT img EMPTY>
<!ATTLIST img
alt %vdata; #REQUIRED
src %HREF; #REQUIRED
localsrc %vdata; #IMPLIED
vspace %length; "0"
hspace %length; "0"
align %IAlign; "bottom"
height %length; #IMPLIED
width %length; #IMPLIED
xml:lang NMTOKEN #IMPLIED
%coreattrs;
>
<!--================= Anchor =================-->
<!ELEMENT anchor ( #PCDATA | br | img | go | prev | refresh )*>
<!ATTLIST anchor
title %vdata; #IMPLIED
accesskey %vdata; #IMPLIED
xml:lang NMTOKEN #IMPLIED
%coreattrs;
>
<!ELEMENT a ( #PCDATA | br | img )*>
<!ATTLIST a
href %HREF; #REQUIRED
title %vdata; #IMPLIED
accesskey %vdata; #IMPLIED
xml:lang NMTOKEN #IMPLIED
%coreattrs;
>
<!--================= Tables =================-->
<!ELEMENT table (tr)+>
<!ATTLIST table
title %vdata; #IMPLIED
align CDATA #IMPLIED
columns %number; #REQUIRED
xml:lang NMTOKEN #IMPLIED
%coreattrs;
>
<!ELEMENT tr (td)+>
<!ATTLIST tr
%coreattrs;
>
```

```
<!ELEMENT td ( %text; | %layout; | img | anchor |a )*>
<!ATTLIST td
xml:lang NMTOKEN #IMPLIED
%coreattrs;
>
<!--================ Text layout and line breaks
================-->
<!ELEMENT em (%flow;)*>
<!ATTLIST em
xml:lang NMTOKEN #IMPLIED
%coreattrs;
>
<!ELEMENT strong (%flow;)*>
<!ATTLIST strong
xml:lang NMTOKEN #IMPLIED
%coreattrs;
>
<!ELEMENT b (%flow;)*>
<!ATTLIST b
xml:lang NMTOKEN #IMPLIED
%coreattrs;
>
<!ELEMENT i (%flow;)*>
<!ATTLIST i
xml:lang NMTOKEN #IMPLIED
%coreattrs;
>
<!ELEMENT u (%flow;)*>
<!ATTLIST u
xml:lang NMTOKEN #IMPLIED
%coreattrs;
>
<!ELEMENT big (%flow;)*>
<!ATTLIST big
xml:lang NMTOKEN #IMPLIED
%coreattrs;
>
<!ELEMENT small (%flow;)*>
<!ATTLIST small
xml:lang NMTOKEN #IMPLIED
%coreattrs;
>
<!ENTITY % TAlign "(left|right|center)">
<!ENTITY % WrapMode "(wrap|nowrap)" >
<!ELEMENT p (%fields; | do)*>
<!ATTLIST p
align %TAlign; "left"
mode %WrapMode; #IMPLIED
xml:lang NMTOKEN #IMPLIED
%coreattrs;
>
<!ELEMENT br EMPTY>
<!ATTLIST br
%coreattrs;
```

```
>
<!ELEMENT pre "(#PCDATA |a |br |i |b |em |strong | input | select
)*">
<!ATTLIST pre
xml:space CDATA #FIXED "preserve"
%coreattrs;
>
<!ENTITY quot "&#34;"> <!-- quotation mark -->
<!ENTITY amp "&#38;#38;"> <!-- ampersand -->
<!ENTITY apos "&#39;"> <!-- apostrophe -->
<!ENTITY lt "&#38;#60;"> <!-- less than -->
<!ENTITY gt "&#62;"> <!-- greater than -->
<!ENTITY nbsp " "> <!-- non-breaking space -->
<!ENTITY shy "&#173;"> <!-- soft hyphen (discretionary hyphen) -->
```

XHTML (strict)

```
<!--
   Extensible HTML version 1.0 Strict DTD

   This is the same as HTML 4.0 Strict except for
   changes due to the differences between XML and SGML.

   Namespace = http://www.w3.org/1999/xhtml

   For further information, see: http://www.w3.org/TR/xhtml1

   Copyright (c) 1998-2000 W3C (MIT, INRIA, Keio),
   All Rights Reserved.

   This DTD module is identified by the PUBLIC and
   SYSTEM identifiers:

   PUBLIC "-//W3C//DTD XHTML 1.0 Strict//EN"
   SYSTEM "http://www.w3.org/TR/xhtml1/DTD/xhtml1-strict.dtd"

   $Revision: 1.1 $
   $Date: 2000/01/26 14:08:56 $

-->

<!--========== Character mnemonic entities ===================-->

<!ENTITY % HTMLlat1 PUBLIC
   "-//W3C//ENTITIES Latin 1 for XHTML//EN"
   "xhtml-lat1.ent">
%HTMLlat1;

<!ENTITY % HTMLsymbol PUBLIC
   "-//W3C//ENTITIES Symbols for XHTML//EN"
```

```
   "xhtml-symbol.ent">
%HTMLsymbol;

<!ENTITY % HTMLspecial PUBLIC
   "-//W3C//ENTITIES Special for XHTML//EN"
   "xhtml-special.ent">
%HTMLspecial;

<!--================== Imported Names
====================================-->

<!ENTITY % ContentType "CDATA">
    <!-- media type, as per [RFC2045] -->

<!ENTITY % ContentTypes "CDATA">
    <!-- comma-separated list of media types, as per [RFC2045] -->

<!ENTITY % Charset "CDATA">
    <!-- a character encoding, as per [RFC2045] -->

<!ENTITY % Charsets "CDATA">
    <!-- a space separated list of character encodings, as per
[RFC2045] -->

<!ENTITY % LanguageCode "NMTOKEN">
    <!-- a language code, as per [RFC1766] -->

<!ENTITY % Character "CDATA">
    <!-- a single character from [ISO10646] -->

<!ENTITY % Number "CDATA">
    <!-- one or more digits -->

<!ENTITY % LinkTypes "CDATA">
    <!-- space-separated list of link types -->

<!ENTITY % MediaDesc "CDATA">
    <!-- single or comma-separated list of media descriptors -->

<!ENTITY % URI "CDATA">
    <!-- a Uniform Resource Identifier, see [RFC2396] -->

<!ENTITY % UriList "CDATA">
    <!-- a space separated list of Uniform Resource Identifiers -->

<!ENTITY % Datetime "CDATA">
    <!-- date and time information. ISO date format -->

<!ENTITY % Script "CDATA">
    <!-- script expression -->

<!ENTITY % StyleSheet "CDATA">
    <!-- style sheet data -->
```

```
<!ENTITY % Text "CDATA">
    <!-- used for titles etc. -->

<!ENTITY % FrameTarget "NMTOKEN">
    <!-- render in this frame -->

<!ENTITY % Length "CDATA">
    <!-- nn for pixels or nn% for percentage length -->

<!ENTITY % MultiLength "CDATA">
    <!-- pixel, percentage, or relative -->

<!ENTITY % MultiLengths "CDATA">
    <!-- comma-separated list of MultiLength -->

<!ENTITY % Pixels "CDATA">
    <!-- integer representing length in pixels -->

<!-- these are used for image maps -->

<!ENTITY % Shape "(rect|circle|poly|default)">

<!ENTITY % Coords "CDATA">
    <!-- comma separated list of lengths -->

<!--============== Generic Attributes ========================-->

<!-- core attributes common to most elements
  id       document-wide unique id
  class    space separated list of classes
  style    associated style info
  title    advisory title/amplification
-->
<!ENTITY % coreattrs
 "id          ID              #IMPLIED
  class       CDATA           #IMPLIED
  style       %StyleSheet;    #IMPLIED
  title       %Text;          #IMPLIED"
  >

<!-- internationalization attributes
  lang        language code (backwards compatible)
  xml:lang    language code (as per XML 1.0 spec)
  dir         direction for weak/neutral text
-->
<!ENTITY % i18n
 "lang        %LanguageCode; #IMPLIED
  xml:lang    %LanguageCode; #IMPLIED
  dir         (ltr|rtl)      #IMPLIED"
  >

<!-- attributes for common UI events
  onclick     a pointer button was clicked
  ondblclick  a pointer button was double clicked
```

```
  onmousedown a pointer button was pressed down
  onmouseup   a pointer button was released
  onmousemove a pointer was moved onto the element
  onmouseout  a pointer was moved away from the element
  onkeypress  a key was pressed and released
  onkeydown   a key was pressed down
  onkeyup     a key was released
-->
<!ENTITY % events
 "onclick     %Script;       #IMPLIED
  ondblclick  %Script;       #IMPLIED
  onmousedown %Script;       #IMPLIED
  onmouseup   %Script;       #IMPLIED
  onmouseover %Script;       #IMPLIED
  onmousemove %Script;       #IMPLIED
  onmouseout  %Script;       #IMPLIED
  onkeypress  %Script;       #IMPLIED
  onkeydown   %Script;       #IMPLIED
  onkeyup     %Script;       #IMPLIED"
  >

<!-- attributes for elements that can get the focus
  accesskey   accessibility key character
  tabindex    position in tabbing order
  onfocus     the element got the focus
  onblur      the element lost the focus
-->
<!ENTITY % focus
 "accesskey   %Character;    #IMPLIED
  tabindex    %Number;       #IMPLIED
  onfocus     %Script;       #IMPLIED
  onblur      %Script;       #IMPLIED"
  >

<!ENTITY % attrs "%coreattrs; %i18n; %events;">

<!--=================== Text Elements
=====================================-->

<!ENTITY % special
   "br | span | bdo | object | img | map">

<!ENTITY % fontstyle "tt | i | b | big | small">

<!ENTITY % phrase "em | strong | dfn | code | q | sub | sup |
                  samp | kbd | var | cite | abbr | acronym">

<!ENTITY % inline.forms "input | select | textarea | label
| button">

<!-- these can occur at block or inline level -->
<!ENTITY % misc "ins | del | script | noscript">

<!ENTITY % inline "a | %special; | %fontstyle; | %phrase;
```

```
| %inline.forms;">

<!-- %Inline; covers inline or "text-level" elements -->
<!ENTITY % Inline "(#PCDATA | %inline; | %misc;)*">

<!--================== Block level elements
=================================-->

<!ENTITY % heading "h1|h2|h3|h4|h5|h6">
<!ENTITY % lists "ul | ol | dl">
<!ENTITY % blocktext "pre | hr | blockquote | address">

<!ENTITY % block
     "p | %heading; | div | %lists; | %blocktext; | fieldset
| table">

<!ENTITY % Block "(%block; | form | %misc;)*">

<!-- %Flow; mixes Block and Inline and is used for list items
etc. -->
<!ENTITY % Flow "(#PCDATA | %block; | form | %inline;
| %misc;)*">

<!--============== Content models for exclusions ===============-->

<!-- a elements use %Inline; excluding a -->

<!ENTITY % a.content
   "(#PCDATA | %special; | %fontstyle; | %phrase; |
%inline.forms; | %misc;)*">

<!-- pre uses %Inline excluding img, object, big, small,
sup or sup -->

<!ENTITY % pre.content
   "(#PCDATA | a | br | span | bdo | map | tt | i | b |
      %phrase; | %inline.forms;)*">

<!-- form uses %Block; excluding form -->

<!ENTITY % form.content "(%block; | %misc;)*">

<!-- button uses %Flow; but excludes a, form and form controls -->

<!ENTITY % button.content
   "(#PCDATA | p | %heading; | div | %lists; | %blocktext; |
    table | %special; | %fontstyle; | %phrase; | %misc;)*">

<!--=========== Document Structure ===========================-->

<!-- the namespace URI designates the document profile -->

<!ELEMENT html (head, body)>
<!ATTLIST html
```

```
  %i18n;
  xmlns       %URI;          #FIXED
'http://www.w3.org/1999/xhtml'
  >

<!--=========== Document Head ===================================-->

<!ENTITY % head.misc "(script|style|meta|link|object)*">

<!-- content model is %head.misc; combined with a single
     title and an optional base element in any order -->

<!ELEMENT head (%head.misc;,
     ((title, %head.misc;, (base, %head.misc;)?) |
      (base, %head.misc;, (title, %head.misc;))))>

<!ATTLIST head
  %i18n;
  profile     %URI;          #IMPLIED
  >

<!-- The title element is not considered part of the flow of text.
       It should be displayed, for example as the page header or
       window title. Exactly one title is required per document.
    -->
<!ELEMENT title (#PCDATA)>
<!ATTLIST title %i18n;>

<!-- document base URI -->

<!ELEMENT base EMPTY>
<!ATTLIST base
  href        %URI;          #IMPLIED
  >

<!-- generic metainformation -->
<!ELEMENT meta EMPTY>
<!ATTLIST meta
  %i18n;
  http-equiv  CDATA          #IMPLIED
  name        CDATA          #IMPLIED
  content     CDATA          #REQUIRED
  scheme      CDATA          #IMPLIED
  >

<!--
  Relationship values can be used in principle:

   a) for document specific toolbars/menus when used
      with the link element in document head e.g.
        start, contents, previous, next, index, end, help
   b) to link to a separate style sheet (rel="stylesheet")
   c) to make a link to a script (rel="script")
   d) by stylesheets to control how collections of
```

```
      html nodes are rendered into printed documents
   e) to make a link to a printable version of this document
      e.g. a PostScript or PDF version (rel="alternate"
media="print")
-->

<!ELEMENT link EMPTY>
<!ATTLIST link
  %attrs;
  charset     %Charset;      #IMPLIED
  href        %URI;          #IMPLIED
  hreflang    %LanguageCode; #IMPLIED
  type        %ContentType;  #IMPLIED
  rel         %LinkTypes;    #IMPLIED
  rev         %LinkTypes;    #IMPLIED
  media       %MediaDesc;    #IMPLIED
  >

<!-- style info, which may include CDATA sections -->
<!ELEMENT style (#PCDATA)>
<!ATTLIST style
  %i18n;
  type        %ContentType;  #REQUIRED
  media       %MediaDesc;    #IMPLIED
  title       %Text;         #IMPLIED
  xml:space   (preserve)     #FIXED 'preserve'
  >

<!-- script statements, which may include CDATA sections -->
<!ELEMENT script (#PCDATA)>
<!ATTLIST script
  charset     %Charset;      #IMPLIED
  type        %ContentType;  #REQUIRED
  src         %URI;          #IMPLIED
  defer       (defer)        #IMPLIED
  xml:space   (preserve)     #FIXED 'preserve'
  >

<!-- alternate content container for non script-based rendering -->

<!ELEMENT noscript %Block;>
<!ATTLIST noscript
  %attrs;
  >

<!--=============== Document Body ===============================-->

<!ELEMENT body %Block;>
<!ATTLIST body
  %attrs;
  onload          %Script;   #IMPLIED
  onunload        %Script;   #IMPLIED
  >
```

```
<!ELEMENT div %Flow;>  <!-- generic language/style container -->
<!ATTLIST div
  %attrs;
  >

<!--=================== Paragraphs
=======================================-->

<!ELEMENT p %Inline;>
<!ATTLIST p
  %attrs;
  >

<!--============== Headings ===================================-->

<!--
  There are six levels of headings from h1 (the most important)
  to h6 (the least important).
-->

<!ELEMENT h1  %Inline;>
<!ATTLIST h1
   %attrs;
   >

<!ELEMENT h2 %Inline;>
<!ATTLIST h2
   %attrs;
   >

<!ELEMENT h3 %Inline;>
<!ATTLIST h3
   %attrs;
   >

<!ELEMENT h4 %Inline;>
<!ATTLIST h4
   %attrs;
   >

<!ELEMENT h5 %Inline;>
<!ATTLIST h5
   %attrs;
   >

<!ELEMENT h6 %Inline;>
<!ATTLIST h6
   %attrs;
   >

<!--============= Lists =====================================-->

<!-- Unordered list -->
```

```
<!ELEMENT ul (li)+>
<!ATTLIST ul
  %attrs;
  >

<!-- Ordered (numbered) list -->

<!ELEMENT ol (li)+>
<!ATTLIST ol
  %attrs;
  >

<!-- list item -->

<!ELEMENT li %Flow;>
<!ATTLIST li
  %attrs;
  >

<!-- definition lists - dt for term, dd for its definition -->

<!ELEMENT dl (dt|dd)+>
<!ATTLIST dl
  %attrs;
  >

<!ELEMENT dt %Inline;>
<!ATTLIST dt
  %attrs;
  >

<!ELEMENT dd %Flow;>
<!ATTLIST dd
  %attrs;
  >

<!--============== Address ====================================-->

<!-- information on author -->

<!ELEMENT address %Inline;>
<!ATTLIST address
  %attrs;
  >

<!--============== Horizontal Rule ===========================-->

<!ELEMENT hr EMPTY>
<!ATTLIST hr
  %attrs;
  >

<!--============== Preformatted Text =========================-->
```

```
<!-- content is %Inline; excluding "img|object|big|small|sub|sup" -->

<!ELEMENT pre %pre.content;>
<!ATTLIST pre
  %attrs;
  xml:space (preserve) #FIXED 'preserve'
  >

<!--============== Block-like Quotes =========================-->

<!ELEMENT blockquote %Block;>
<!ATTLIST blockquote
  %attrs;
  cite        %URI;           #IMPLIED
  >

<!--============== Inserted/Deleted Text =====================-->

<!--
  ins/del are allowed in block and inline content, but its
  inappropriate to include block content within an ins element
  occurring in inline content.
-->
<!ELEMENT ins %Flow;>
<!ATTLIST ins
  %attrs;
  cite        %URI;           #IMPLIED
  datetime    %Datetime;      #IMPLIED
  >

<!ELEMENT del %Flow;>
<!ATTLIST del
  %attrs;
  cite        %URI;           #IMPLIED
  datetime    %Datetime;      #IMPLIED
  >

<!--============== The Anchor Element ========================-->

<!-- content is %Inline; except that anchors shouldn't be nested -->

<!ELEMENT a %a.content;>
<!ATTLIST a
  %attrs;
  charset     %Charset;       #IMPLIED
  type        %ContentType;   #IMPLIED
  name        NMTOKEN         #IMPLIED
  href        %URI;           #IMPLIED
  hreflang    %LanguageCode;  #IMPLIED
  rel         %LinkTypes;     #IMPLIED
  rev         %LinkTypes;     #IMPLIED
  accesskey   %Character;     #IMPLIED
  shape       %Shape;         "rect"
```

```
  coords      %Coords;        #IMPLIED
  tabindex    %Number;        #IMPLIED
  onfocus     %Script;        #IMPLIED
  onblur      %Script;        #IMPLIED
  >

<!--================= Inline Elements ===========================-->

<!ELEMENT span %Inline;> <!-- generic language/style container -->
<!ATTLIST span
  %attrs;
  >

<!ELEMENT bdo %Inline;>  <!-- I18N BiDi over-ride -->
<!ATTLIST bdo
  %coreattrs;
  %events;
  lang        %LanguageCode; #IMPLIED
  xml:lang    %LanguageCode; #IMPLIED
  dir         (ltr|rtl)      #REQUIRED
  >

<!ELEMENT br EMPTY>   <!-- forced line break -->
<!ATTLIST br
  %coreattrs;
  >

<!ELEMENT em %Inline;>   <!-- emphasis -->
<!ATTLIST em %attrs;>

<!ELEMENT strong %Inline;>   <!-- strong emphasis -->
<!ATTLIST strong %attrs;>

<!ELEMENT dfn %Inline;>   <!-- definitional -->
<!ATTLIST dfn %attrs;>

<!ELEMENT code %Inline;>   <!-- program code -->
<!ATTLIST code %attrs;>

<!ELEMENT samp %Inline;>   <!-- sample -->
<!ATTLIST samp %attrs;>

<!ELEMENT kbd %Inline;>  <!-- something user would type -->
<!ATTLIST kbd %attrs;>

<!ELEMENT var %Inline;>   <!-- variable -->
<!ATTLIST var %attrs;>

<!ELEMENT cite %Inline;>   <!-- citation -->
<!ATTLIST cite %attrs;>

<!ELEMENT abbr %Inline;>   <!-- abbreviation -->
<!ATTLIST abbr %attrs;>
```

```
<!ELEMENT acronym %Inline;>   <!-- acronym -->
<!ATTLIST acronym %attrs;>

<!ELEMENT q %Inline;>   <!-- inlined quote -->
<!ATTLIST q
  %attrs;
  cite        %URI;          #IMPLIED
  >

<!ELEMENT sub %Inline;> <!-- subscript -->
<!ATTLIST sub %attrs;>

<!ELEMENT sup %Inline;> <!-- superscript -->
<!ATTLIST sup %attrs;>

<!ELEMENT tt %Inline;>   <!-- fixed pitch font -->
<!ATTLIST tt %attrs;>

<!ELEMENT i %Inline;>   <!-- italic font -->
<!ATTLIST i %attrs;>

<!ELEMENT b %Inline;>   <!-- bold font -->
<!ATTLIST b %attrs;>

<!ELEMENT big %Inline;>   <!-- bigger font -->
<!ATTLIST big %attrs;>

<!ELEMENT small %Inline;>   <!-- smaller font -->
<!ATTLIST small %attrs;>

<!--================= Object ====================================-->
<!--
  object is used to embed objects as part of HTML pages.
  param elements should precede other content. Parameters
  can also be expressed as attribute/value pairs in the
  object element itself when brevity is desired.
-->

<!ELEMENT object (#PCDATA | param | %block; | form | %inline;
| %misc;)*>
<!ATTLIST object
  %attrs;
  declare     (declare)      #IMPLIED
  classid     %URI;          #IMPLIED
  codebase    %URI;          #IMPLIED
  data        %URI;          #IMPLIED
  type        %ContentType;  #IMPLIED
  codetype    %ContentType;  #IMPLIED
  archive     %UriList;      #IMPLIED
  standby     %Text;         #IMPLIED
  height      %Length;       #IMPLIED
  width       %Length;       #IMPLIED
  usemap      %URI;          #IMPLIED
  name        NMTOKEN        #IMPLIED
```

```
  tabindex    %Number;        #IMPLIED
  >

<!--
  param is used to supply a named property value.
  In XML it would seem natural to follow RDF and support an
  abbreviated syntax where the param elements are replaced
  by attribute value pairs on the object start tag.
-->
<!ELEMENT param EMPTY>
<!ATTLIST param
  id          ID              #IMPLIED
  name        CDATA           #IMPLIED
  value       CDATA           #IMPLIED
  valuetype   (data|ref|object) "data"
  type        %ContentType;   #IMPLIED
  >

<!--=============== Images ========================================-->

<!--
   To avoid accessibility problems for people who aren't
   able to see the image, you should provide a text
   description using the alt and longdesc attributes.
   In addition, avoid the use of server-side image maps.
   Note that in this DTD there is no name attribute. That
   is only available in the transitional and frameset DTD.
-->

<!ELEMENT img EMPTY>
<!ATTLIST img
  %attrs;
  src         %URI;           #REQUIRED
  alt         %Text;          #REQUIRED
  longdesc    %URI;           #IMPLIED
  height      %Length;        #IMPLIED
  width       %Length;        #IMPLIED
  usemap      %URI;           #IMPLIED
  ismap       (ismap)         #IMPLIED
  >

<!-- usemap points to a map element which may be in this document
  or an external document, although the latter is not widely sup-
ported. -->

<!--============== Client-side image maps =====================-->

<!-- These can be placed in the same document or grouped in a
     separate document although this isn't yet widely supported. -->

<!ELEMENT map ((%block; | form | %misc;)+ | area+)>
<!ATTLIST map
  %i18n;
  %events;
```

```
  id          ID              #REQUIRED
  class       CDATA           #IMPLIED
  style       %StyleSheet;    #IMPLIED
  title       %Text;          #IMPLIED
  name        NMTOKEN         #IMPLIED
  >

<!ELEMENT area EMPTY>
<!ATTLIST area
  %attrs;
  shape        %Shape;         "rect"
  coords       %Coords;        #IMPLIED
  href         %URI;           #IMPLIED
  nohref       (nohref)        #IMPLIED
  alt          %Text;          #REQUIRED
  tabindex     %Number;        #IMPLIED
  accesskey    %Character;     #IMPLIED
  onfocus      %Script;        #IMPLIED
  onblur       %Script;        #IMPLIED
  >

<!--=========== Forms ===========================================-->
<!ELEMENT form %form.content;>   <!-- forms shouldn't be nested -->

<!ATTLIST form
  %attrs;
  action       %URI;           #REQUIRED
  method       (get|post)      "get"
  enctype      %ContentType;   "application/x-www-form-urlencoded"
  onsubmit     %Script;        #IMPLIED
  onreset      %Script;        #IMPLIED
  accept       %ContentTypes;  #IMPLIED
  accept-charset %Charsets;    #IMPLIED
  >

<!--
  Each label must not contain more than ONE field.
  Label elements shouldn't be nested.
-->
<!ELEMENT label %Inline;>
<!ATTLIST label
  %attrs;
  for          IDREF           #IMPLIED
  accesskey    %Character;     #IMPLIED
  onfocus      %Script;        #IMPLIED
  onblur       %Script;        #IMPLIED
  >

<!ENTITY % InputType
  "(text | password | checkbox |
    radio | submit | reset |
    file | hidden | image | button)"
   >
```

```
<!-- the name attribute is required for all but submit & reset -->

<!ELEMENT input EMPTY>     <!-- form control -->
<!ATTLIST input
  %attrs;
  type        %InputType;     "text"
  name        CDATA           #IMPLIED
  value       CDATA           #IMPLIED
  checked     (checked)       #IMPLIED
  disabled    (disabled)      #IMPLIED
  readonly    (readonly)      #IMPLIED
  size        CDATA           #IMPLIED
  maxlength   %Number;        #IMPLIED
  src         %URI;           #IMPLIED
  alt         CDATA           #IMPLIED
  usemap      %URI;           #IMPLIED
  tabindex    %Number;        #IMPLIED
  accesskey   %Character;     #IMPLIED
  onfocus     %Script;        #IMPLIED
  onblur      %Script;        #IMPLIED
  onselect    %Script;        #IMPLIED
  onchange    %Script;        #IMPLIED
  accept      %ContentTypes; #IMPLIED
  >

<!ELEMENT select (optgroup|option)+>  <!-- option selector -->
<!ATTLIST select
  %attrs;
  name        CDATA           #IMPLIED
  size        %Number;        #IMPLIED
  multiple    (multiple)      #IMPLIED
  disabled    (disabled)      #IMPLIED
  tabindex    %Number;        #IMPLIED
  onfocus     %Script;        #IMPLIED
  onblur      %Script;        #IMPLIED
  onchange    %Script;        #IMPLIED
  >

<!ELEMENT optgroup (option)+>   <!-- option group -->
<!ATTLIST optgroup
  %attrs;
  disabled    (disabled)      #IMPLIED
  label       %Text;          #REQUIRED
  >

<!ELEMENT option (#PCDATA)>     <!-- selectable choice -->
<!ATTLIST option
  %attrs;
  selected    (selected)      #IMPLIED
  disabled    (disabled)      #IMPLIED
  label       %Text;          #IMPLIED
  value       CDATA           #IMPLIED
  >
```

```
<!ELEMENT textarea (#PCDATA)>     <!-- multi-line text field -->
<!ATTLIST textarea
  %attrs;
  name        CDATA          #IMPLIED
  rows        %Number;       #REQUIRED
  cols        %Number;       #REQUIRED
  disabled    (disabled)     #IMPLIED
  readonly    (readonly)     #IMPLIED
  tabindex    %Number;       #IMPLIED
  accesskey   %Character;    #IMPLIED
  onfocus     %Script;       #IMPLIED
  onblur      %Script;       #IMPLIED
  onselect    %Script;       #IMPLIED
  onchange    %Script;       #IMPLIED
  >

<!--
  The fieldset element is used to group form fields.
  Only one legend element should occur in the content
  and if present should only be preceded by whitespace.
-->
<!ELEMENT fieldset (#PCDATA | legend | %block; | form | %inline;
| %misc;)*>
<!ATTLIST fieldset
  %attrs;
  >

<!ELEMENT legend %Inline;>     <!-- fieldset label -->
<!ATTLIST legend
  %attrs;
  accesskey   %Character;    #IMPLIED
  >

<!--
 Content is %Flow; excluding a, form and form controls
-->
<!ELEMENT button %button.content;>  <!-- push button -->
<!ATTLIST button
  %attrs;
  name        CDATA          #IMPLIED
  value       CDATA          #IMPLIED
  type        (button|submit|reset) "submit"
  disabled    (disabled)     #IMPLIED
  tabindex    %Number;       #IMPLIED
  accesskey   %Character;    #IMPLIED
  onfocus     %Script;       #IMPLIED
  onblur      %Script;       #IMPLIED
  >

<!--================== Tables ================================-->

<!-- Derived from IETF HTML table standard, see [RFC1942] -->
```

```
<!--
 The border attribute sets the thickness of the frame around the
 table. The default units are screen pixels.

 The frame attribute specifies which parts of the frame around
 the table should be rendered. The values are not the same as
 CALS to avoid a name clash with the valign attribute.
-->
<!ENTITY % TFrame
"(void|above|below|hsides|lhs|rhs|vsides|box|border)">

<!--
 The rules attribute defines which rules to draw between cells:

 If rules is absent then assume:
     "none" if border is absent or border="0" otherwise "all"
-->

<!ENTITY % TRules "(none | groups | rows | cols | all)">

<!-- horizontal placement of table relative to document -->
<!ENTITY % TAlign "(left|center|right)">

<!-- horizontal alignment attributes for cell contents

  char        alignment char, e.g. char=':'
  charoff     offset for alignment char
-->
<!ENTITY % cellhalign
  "align      (left|center|right|justify|char) #IMPLIED
   char       %Character;     #IMPLIED
   charoff    %Length;        #IMPLIED"
  >

<!-- vertical alignment attributes for cell contents -->
<!ENTITY % cellvalign
  "valign     (top|middle|bottom|baseline) #IMPLIED"
  >

<!ELEMENT table
     (caption?, (col*|colgroup*), thead?, tfoot?, (tbody+|tr+))>
<!ELEMENT caption  %Inline;>
<!ELEMENT thead    (tr)+>
<!ELEMENT tfoot    (tr)+>
<!ELEMENT tbody    (tr)+>
<!ELEMENT colgroup (col)*>
<!ELEMENT col      EMPTY>
<!ELEMENT tr       (th|td)+>
<!ELEMENT th       %Flow;>
<!ELEMENT td       %Flow;>

<!ATTLIST table
  %attrs;
  summary    %Text;         #IMPLIED
```

```
  width       %Length;        #IMPLIED
  border      %Pixels;        #IMPLIED
  frame       %TFrame;        #IMPLIED
  rules       %TRules;        #IMPLIED
  cellspacing %Length;        #IMPLIED
  cellpadding %Length;        #IMPLIED
  >

<!ENTITY % CAlign "(top|bottom|left|right)">

<!ATTLIST caption
  %attrs;
  >

<!--
colgroup groups a set of col elements. It allows you to group
several semantically related columns together.
-->
<!ATTLIST colgroup
  %attrs;
  span        %Number;        "1"
  width       %MultiLength;   #IMPLIED
  %cellhalign;
  %cellvalign;
  >

<!--
 col elements define the alignment properties for cells in
 one or more columns.

 The width attribute specifies the width of the columns, e.g.

     width=64        width in screen pixels
     width=0.5*      relative width of 0.5

 The span attribute causes the attributes of one
 col element to apply to more than one column.
-->
<!ATTLIST col
  %attrs;
  span        %Number;        "1"
  width       %MultiLength;   #IMPLIED
  %cellhalign;
  %cellvalign;
  >

<!--
    Use thead to duplicate headers when breaking table
    across page boundaries, or for static headers when
    tbody sections are rendered in scrolling panel.

    Use tfoot to duplicate footers when breaking table
    across page boundaries, or for static footers when
    tbody sections are rendered in scrolling panel.
```

```
    Use multiple tbody sections when rules are needed
    between groups of table rows.
-->
<!ATTLIST thead
  %attrs;
  %cellhalign;
  %cellvalign;
  >

<!ATTLIST tfoot
  %attrs;
  %cellhalign;
  %cellvalign;
  >

<!ATTLIST tbody
  %attrs;
  %cellhalign;
  %cellvalign;
  >

<!ATTLIST tr
  %attrs;
  %cellhalign;
  %cellvalign;
  >


<!-- Scope is simpler than headers attribute for common tables -->
<!ENTITY % Scope "(row|col|rowgroup|colgroup)">

<!-- th is for headers, td for data and for cells acting as both -->

<!ATTLIST th
  %attrs;
  abbr        %Text;        #IMPLIED
  axis        CDATA         #IMPLIED
  headers     IDREFS        #IMPLIED
  scope       %Scope;       #IMPLIED
  rowspan     %Number;      "1"
  colspan     %Number;      "1"
  %cellhalign;
  %cellvalign;
  >

<!ATTLIST td
  %attrs;
  abbr        %Text;        #IMPLIED
  axis        CDATA         #IMPLIED
  headers     IDREFS        #IMPLIED
  scope       %Scope;       #IMPLIED
  rowspan     %Number;      "1"
  colspan     %Number;      "1"
```

```
%cellhalign;
%cellvalign;
>
```

SMIL

```
<!--

    This is the XML document type definition (DTD) for SMIL 1.0.

    Date: 1998/06/15 08:56:30

    Authors:
        Jacco van Ossenbruggen <jrvosse@cwi.nl>
        Sjoerd Mullender       <sjoerd@cwi.nl>

    Further information about SMIL is available at:

          http://www.w3.org/AudioVideo/

-->

<!-- Generally useful entities -->
<!ENTITY % id-attr "id ID #IMPLIED">
<!ENTITY % title-attr "title CDATA #IMPLIED">
<!ENTITY % skip-attr "skip-content (true|false) 'true'">
<!ENTITY % desc-attr "
        %title-attr;
        abstract        CDATA   #IMPLIED
        author          CDATA   #IMPLIED
        copyright       CDATA   #IMPLIED
">

<!--============== SMIL Document ==============================-->
<!--
     The root element SMIL contains all other elements.
-->
<!ELEMENT smil (head?,body?)>
<!ATTLIST smil
        %id-attr;
>

<!--============== The Document Head ==========================-->
<!ENTITY % layout-section "layout|switch">

<!ENTITY % head-element "(meta*,((%layout-section;), meta*))?">

<!ELEMENT head %head-element;>
<!ATTLIST head %id-attr;>
```

```
<!--=============== Layout Element ==============================-->
<!--
     Layout contains the region and root-layout elements defined
     by smil-basic-layout or other elements defined an external
     layout mechanism.
-->
<!ELEMENT layout ANY>
<!ATTLIST layout
        %id-attr;
        type CDATA      "text/smil-basic-layout"
>


<!--=============== Region Element ==============================-->
<!ENTITY % viewport-attrs "
        height              CDATA    #IMPLIED
        width               CDATA    #IMPLIED
        background-color    CDATA    #IMPLIED
">

<!ELEMENT region EMPTY>
<!ATTLIST region
        %id-attr;
        %title-attr;
        %viewport-attrs;
        left                CDATA    "0"
        top                 CDATA    "0"
        z-index             CDATA    "0"
        fit                 (hidden|fill|meet|scroll|slice)
"hidden"
        %skip-attr;
>

<!--=============== Root-layout Element ========================-->
<!ELEMENT root-layout EMPTY>
<!ATTLIST root-layout
        %id-attr;
        %title-attr;
        %viewport-attrs;
        %skip-attr;
>


<!--=============== Meta Element================================-->
<!ELEMENT meta EMPTY>
<!ATTLIST meta
        name    NMTOKEN #REQUIRED
        content CDATA   #REQUIRED
        %skip-attr;
>

<!--=============== The Document Body ==========================-->
<!ENTITY % media-object
```

```
"audio|video|text|img|animation|textstream|ref">
<!ENTITY % schedule "par|seq|(%media-object;)">
<!ENTITY % inline-link "a">
<!ENTITY % assoc-link "anchor">
<!ENTITY % link "%inline-link;">
<!ENTITY % container-content "(%schedule;)|switch|(%link;)">
<!ENTITY % body-content "(%container-content;)">

<!ELEMENT body (%body-content;)*>
<!ATTLIST body %id-attr;>

<!--=============== Synchronization Attributes ==================-->
<!ENTITY % sync-attributes "
        begin   CDATA   #IMPLIED
        end     CDATA   #IMPLIED
">

<!--=============== Switch Parameter Attributes =================-->
<!ENTITY % system-attribute "
        system-bitrate              CDATA                #IMPLIED
        system-language             CDATA                #IMPLIED
        system-required             NMTOKEN              #IMPLIED
        system-screen-size          CDATA                #IMPLIED
        system-screen-depth         CDATA                #IMPLIED
        system-captions             (on|off)             #IMPLIED
        system-overdub-or-caption   (caption|overdub)    #IMPLIED
">

<!--============== Fill Attribute ===============================-->
<!ENTITY % fill-attribute "
        fill    (remove|freeze)    'remove'
">


<!--=============== The Parallel Element =======================-->
<!ENTITY % par-content "%container-content;">
<!ELEMENT par    (%par-content;)*>
<!ATTLIST par
        %id-attr;
        %desc-attr;
        endsync CDATA           "last"
        dur     CDATA           #IMPLIED
        repeat  CDATA           "1"
        region  IDREF           #IMPLIED
        %sync-attributes;
        %system-attribute;
>

<!--============== The Sequential Element =====================-->
<!ENTITY % seq-content "%container-content;">
<!ELEMENT seq    (%seq-content;)*>
<!ATTLIST seq
        %id-attr;
        %desc-attr;
```

```
        dur     CDATA            #IMPLIED
        repeat  CDATA            "1"
        region  IDREF            #IMPLIED
        %sync-attributes;
        %system-attribute;
>

<!--============== The Switch Element =======================-->
<!-- In the head, a switch may contain only layout elements,
     in the body, only container elements. However, this
     constraint cannot be expressed in the DTD (?), so
     we allow both:
-->
<!ENTITY % switch-content "layout|(%container-content;)">
<!ELEMENT switch (%switch-content;)*>
<!ATTLIST switch
        %id-attr;
        %title-attr;
>

<!--============== Media Object Elements =====================-->
<!-- SMIL only defines the structure. The real media data is
     referenced by the src attribute of the media objects.
-->

<!-- Furthermore, they have the following attributes as defined
     in the SMIL specification:
-->
<!ENTITY % mo-attributes "
        %id-attr;
        %desc-attr;
        region     IDREF            #IMPLIED
        alt        CDATA            #IMPLIED
        longdesc   CDATA            #IMPLIED
        src        CDATA            #IMPLIED
        type       CDATA            #IMPLIED
        dur        CDATA            #IMPLIED
        repeat     CDATA            '1'
        %fill-attribute;
        %sync-attributes;
        %system-attribute;
">

<!--
     Most info is in the attributes; media objects are empty or
     contain associated link elements:
-->
<!ENTITY % mo-content "(%assoc-link;)*">
<!ENTITY % clip-attrs "
        clip-begin      CDATA   #IMPLIED
        clip-end        CDATA   #IMPLIED
">

<!ELEMENT ref           %mo-content;>
```

```
<!ELEMENT audio          %mo-content;>
<!ELEMENT img            %mo-content;>
<!ELEMENT video          %mo-content;>
<!ELEMENT text           %mo-content;>
<!ELEMENT textstream     %mo-content;>
<!ELEMENT animation      %mo-content;>

<!ATTLIST ref            %mo-attributes; %clip-attrs;>
<!ATTLIST audio          %mo-attributes; %clip-attrs;>
<!ATTLIST video          %mo-attributes; %clip-attrs;>
<!ATTLIST animation      %mo-attributes; %clip-attrs;>
<!ATTLIST textstream     %mo-attributes; %clip-attrs;>
<!ATTLIST text           %mo-attributes;>
<!ATTLIST img            %mo-attributes;>

<!--============== Link Elements ===============================-->

<!ENTITY % smil-link-attributes "
        %id-attr;
        %title-attr;
        href            CDATA                   #REQUIRED
        show            (replace|new|pause)     'replace'
">


<!--============== Inline Link Element ========================-->
<!ELEMENT a (%schedule;|switch)*>
<!ATTLIST a
        %smil-link-attributes;
>


<!--============== Associated Link Element ====================-->
<!ELEMENT anchor EMPTY>
<!ATTLIST anchor
        %skip-attr;
        %smil-link-attributes;
        %sync-attributes;
        coords          CDATA                   #IMPLIED
>
```

APPENDIX D

UML QUICK REFERENCE

The Unified Modeling Language (UML) is a standard language for writing software designs. UML may be used to visualize, specify, construct, and document a software system. In this book we use it extensively for the static modeling of complex data types and object-oriented systems.

UML defines numerous types of diagrams, each suited for a particular type of view of the system. In this book we use the two more popular types of diagrams on UML:

- Use case diagrams
- Class diagrams

The following sections show the rationale and rules for each of them.

Class Diagrams

A class diagram is a visual representation of the static view of a system in terms of the classes that compose it. A class diagram is formed by two things:

- Classes
- Relationships (either dependencies, associations or generalizations)

Classes are represented by boxes divided in three compartments: the topmost division holds the name of the class, the middle division holds the attributes of the class[1], and the last division holds the operations (or methods) of the class. Showing the two lower divisions is optional.

[1] The term *attribute* is used here in the classical data-type sense, i.e. a characteristic or member of the type.

Figure D.1 shows a classical example of the depiction of a class in UML.

Figure D.1
A sample class.

Ticket
number : Integer date : Date show : String
reserve()

Classes may be connected by *relationships*. A relationships can be one of three types:

- **Dependency**—A relationship that states that a change in one class may affect another that uses it (the reverse is not necessarily true). An example of this could be the relationship between "wheels" and "car".
- **Generalization**—A relationship between a general class (called the parent) and a more specific type. This is normally implemented in OO languages as inheritance. A simple example could be the relationship between "animal" and "invertebrate".
- **Association**—An association is a structural relationship between types (e.g. "author" writes for "editor"). When the association represents "whole/part" relationships, it is called aggregation.

Figure D.2 shows an example of a class diagram with several relationships in it.

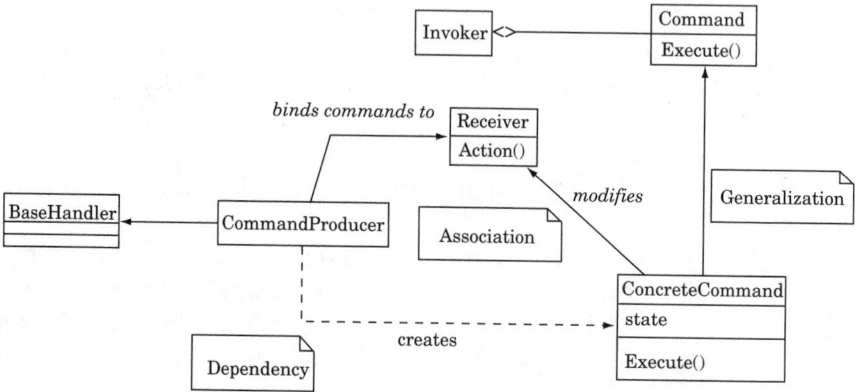

Figure D.2
A sample class diagram.

Use Case Diagrams

Use case diagrams capture the behavior of the system from a very high level, avoiding any type of actual specification other than the description of the contexts in which actors interact with the system. In other words, use case diagrams help visualize the scenarios in which a system is used. They help understand the system since they avoid the actual implementation in terms of classes and associations and limit themselves to the presentation of high-level users and their actions with respect to the system.

Use case diagrams involve three things:

- Use cases
- Actors
- Dependency, generalization, and association relationships

Figure D.3 shows the symbolisms used for each kind of component in this particular type of diagram.

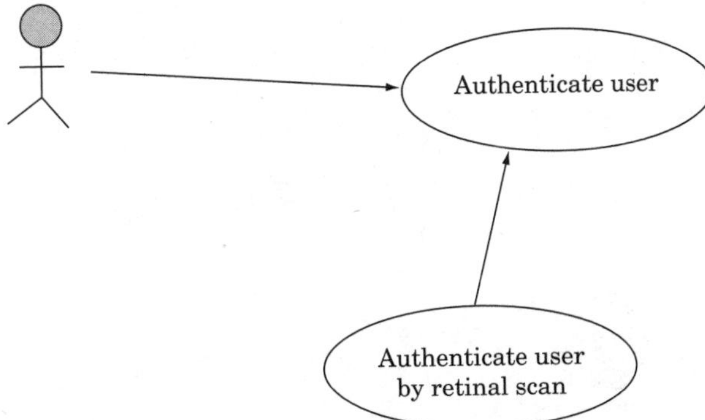

Figure D.3
A sample use case diagram.

APPENDIX E

KEY CUSTOM-MADE DTDS

Introduction

This appendix presents a compilation of the most important custom DTDs used throughout the book.

Besides their reference function, these DTDs serve as real-life examples of the techniques discussed in the book (e.g., the use of entity parameters to model synonyms for character data). The Vocabularies listed are the latest versions (as of November 2000):

- Functional Requirements DTD
- Helper Entities
- Reading Notes DTD

Functional Requirements

```
<!-- Name: FunctionalRequirements.dtd                                -->
<!-- Description: DTD for the description of a series of
Functional Requirements  -->
<!-- Version : 2.0 -->
<!-- Author: Fabio Arciniegas A.                                        -->

<!ELEMENT fr (header,requirement+)>

<!ELEMENT header (author*,version?,project,description)>


<!-- ******** Metadata about the requirements ********** -->
```

```
<!ENTITY % string       "#PCDATA">
<!ENTITY % character    "#PCDATA">
<!ENTITY % letter       "#PCDATA">
<!ENTITY % number_att   "CDATA">

<!ENTITY % english_def "xml:lang    NMTOKEN    'en'">

<!ELEMENT author        (firstname,midinitial?,lastname)>
<!ELEMENT firstname     (%string;)>
<!ELEMENT midinitial    (%letter;)>
<!ELEMENT lastname      (%string;)>
<!ATTLIST name
        %english_def;>

<!ELEMENT version (#PCDATA)>

<!ATTLIST version
        release       %number_att;   #IMPLIED
        subordinate   %number_att;   #IMPLIED>

<!ELEMENT project (%string;)>


<!-- Type definition for requirements -->
<!ELEMENT requirement (name,description,
                      uses*,extends*,
                      input,output,
                      anomaly*,acceptance*)>

<!ELEMENT name  (%string;)>
<!ATTLIST requirement
        id        ID              #REQUIRED
        optional  (yes|no)        #REQUIRED
        priority  (0|1|2|3|4|5)   #REQUIRED
>

<!-- a description is composed by paragraphs, describing
     the problem
-->
<!ELEMENT description (p+)>
<!ELEMENT p           (#PCDATA|b|i)*>
<!ELEMENT b           (#PCDATA)>
<!ELEMENT i           (#PCDATA)>

<!-- A requirement may use or extend others (see example) -->
<!ELEMENT uses EMPTY>
<!ATTLIST uses
        req  IDREF #REQUIRED>

<!ELEMENT extends EMPTY>
<!ATTLIST extends
        req      IDREF #REQUIRED>

<!ELEMENT input  (entry*)>
```

```
<!ELEMENT output (result*)>


<!ELEMENT entry   (%string;)>
<!ELEMENT result  (%string;)>

<!ELEMENT anomaly (description,behavior)>
<!ELEMENT behavior (p+)>

<!-- The description of the acceptance criteria -->
<!ELEMENT acceptance (p+)>
```

Helper Entities

```
<!--
     Name: FAA Standard Entities
     Description: This file contains standard definitions for
                  elements, attributes and types commonly used on
                  DTDs.
     Rationale: XML Schema and other languages define rich types
               to represent data such as "positive float" in XML.
               Using such langs is frequently an advantage, but
               sometimes using traditional XML 1.0 DTDs is a
               must. In such cases, techniques like the use of
               parameter entities declaring aliases for basic DTD
               types means a great improvement on readability and
               maintainabilty.

     Version :
     $Id: FAA-Standard-Entities.dtd,v 1.2 2000/08/12 00:23:03
Default Exp $
     Author: Fabio Arciniegas A.
-->

<!-- Typical use:

<!ENTITY % faa-standard-entities SYSTEM "FAA-Standard-Entities.dtd">

%faa-standard-entities;

-->

<!--
***************************************
                 Global Parameter entities
****************************************
-->
  <!-- ***** Parameter entities for common Language Attributes
***** -->
  <!-- Use inside ATTLIST declarations -->
```

```
    <!ENTITY % english_def "xml:lang    NMTOKEN    'en'">
    <!ENTITY % french_def  "xml:lang    NMTOKEN    'fr'">
    <!ENTITY % german_def  "xml:lang    NMTOKEN    'ge'">


  <!-- ***** Parameter entities and elements for some basic *****
-->
    <!ENTITY % string_att      "CDATA">
    <!ENTITY % letter_att      "CDATA">
    <!ENTITY % number_att      "CDATA">

    <!ENTITY % string          "#PCDATA">
    <!ENTITY % character       "#PCDATA">
    <!ENTITY % letter          "#PCDATA">



  <!-- *** Parameter entities and elements for date
representation *** -->

    <!ENTITY % year_att        "CDATA">
    <!ENTITY % day_att         "CDATA">
    <!ENTITY % months_att      "(jan|feb|mar|apr|may|jun|
                                jul|aug|sep|oct|nov|dec|
              1|2|3|4|5|6|7|8|9|10|11|12)">

    <!ENTITY % description    "#PCDATA">

    <!ELEMENT date             (%description;)>
    <!ATTLIST date
         day    %number_att;       #IMPLIED
         month  %months_att;      #IMPLIED
         year   %number_att;       #REQUIRED>

    <!ATTLIST date
           year        %year_att;            (%description;)>

    <!ELEMENT datefrom                 (#PCDATA)>
    <!ATTLIST datefrom
         day    %number_att;  #IMPLIED
         month  %months_att;   #IMPLIED
         year   %number_att;   #REQUIRED>

    <!ELEMENT dateto                 (#PCDATA)>
    <!ATTLIST dateto
         day    %number_att;   #IMPLIED
         month  %months_att;   #IMPLIED
         year   %number_att;   #REQUIRED>


  <!-- *** Parameter entities and elements for time
representation *** -->
```

```
<!ENTITY % sec_att        "CDATA">
<!ENTITY % mili_att       "CDATA">
<!ENTITY % min_att        "CDATA">
<!ENTITY % hour_att       "CDATA">

<!ELEMENT time            (%description;)>
<!ATTLIST time
     hour    %hour_att;      #IMPLIED
     min     %min_att;      #IMPLIED
     sec     %sec_att;       #IMPLIED
     mili    %mili_att;      #IMPLIED>


<!-- *** Parameter entities and elements for text-oriented
problems ** -->
    <!ELEMENT p          (#PCDATA|emphasis|important)*>
    <!ELEMENT emphasis   (#PCDATA)>
    <!ELEMENT important  (#PCDATA)>


<!-- *** Parameter entities and elements for name
representation ** -->

    <!ELEMENT name             (firstname,midinitial?,lastname)>
    <!ELEMENT firstname        (%string;)>
    <!ELEMENT midinitial       (%letter;)>
    <!ELEMENT lastname         (%string;)>
    <!ATTLIST name
             %english_def;>

<!-- *** Parameter entities and elements for simple links *** -->
    <!ELEMENT a                (ANY)>
    <!ATTLIST a
        xlink:type (simple)  #FIXED   "simple"
        xlink:href CDATA     #REQUIRED
     %languageattribute;>


<!-- *** Parameter entities and elements for images *** -->
    <!ELEMENT img        (#PCDATA)>
    <!ATTLIST img
             xmlns:xlink CDATA
"http://www.w3c.org/1999/XLink"
             xlink:type  (simple)  #FIXED   "simple"
             xlink:href  CDATA     #REQUIRED>
```

Reading Notes DTD (Simple Version)

```
<!ELEMENT readingnotes (title, bookauthor, chapter*)>
<!ATTLIST readingnotes
        version       CDATA     #IMPLIED
```

```
      lastmodifiedCDATA          #IMPLIED>
<!ELEMENT bookauthor    (#PCDATA)>
<!ELEMENT chapter       (title,intro?,(note)*)>
<!ATTLIST chapter
          name           ID         #REQUIRED>
<!ELEMENT title         (#PCDATA)>
<!ELEMENT intro         (#PCDATA)>
<!ELEMENT note          (title, p*)>
<!ATTLIST note
          name           ID         #REQUIRED>
<!ELEMENT p     (#PCDATA| ul|
                    ol|
                a|
                img|
                blockquote|
                pre|
                imp|
                emp )* >
<!ELEMENT ul    (li*)>
<!ELEMENT ol    (li*)>
<!ELEMENT li    (#PCDATA|emp|imp|pre|blockquote)*>
<!ELEMENT a    (#PCDATA)>
<!ELEMENT img    (#PCDATA)>
<!ATTLIST img
          src  CDATA    #IMPLIED
          alt  CDATA    #IMPLIED>

<!ATTLIST a
          href  CDATA   #IMPLIED>

<!ELEMENT blockquote   (pre)>
<!ELEMENT pre    (#PCDATA)>
<!ELEMENT imp    (#PCDATA)>
<!ELEMENT emp    (#PCDATA)>
```

INDEX

Note: Boldface numbers indicate illustrations; italic t indicates a table.

E

I

J

K

L

M

T

Z

ABOUT THE AUTHOR

FABIO ARCINIEGAS A. is a software engineer with ample XML development experience, including the design and construction of several important Java, C++, and Perl XML projects such as Hugin, the Simple API for SAX Databases, and the definition of design patterns for the serialization of objects into XML.

Fabio is also a frequent author on publications such as xml.com. He can be reached at faa@thefaactory.com and faa@fabioarciniegas.com.

ABOUT THE CD

The CD contains all the code shown in the book, including complete programs that were abridged in the printed text because of space issues. It also contains the following tools used for the development and test of the examples:

- Expat: C parser
- XP: Java parser
- Aelfred: Java parser
- JDK 1.2
- Active Perl for windows 5.6
- XML4C by IBM: Suite of C++ parsers and tools for XML
- XML4J by IBM: Suite of C++ parsers and tools for XML
- Adobe Acrobat SVG viewer
- Phone.com emulator
- Apache Server for Windows
- XML Spy
- All XML tools developed at the FAActory mentioned in the text (viewers, DOM tools and other utilities by the author)
- Xalan and Xerces: Parser and XSLT processors by the Apache project
- Emacs with psgml
- XT: XSLT processor by James
- Docbook DTD and Stylesheets
- OpenJade

NOTE

In the case of tools that were not re-distributable on the CD because of copyright issues, direct pointers to their location on the web are provided.

All the tools and code samples are organized by chapter, subject, and type.

SOFTWARE AND INFORMATION LICENSE

The software and information on this diskette (collectively referred to as the "Product") are the property of The McGraw-Hill Companies, Inc. ("McGraw-Hill") and are protected by both United States copyright law and international copyright treaty provision. You must treat this Product just like a book, except that you may copy it into a computer to be used and you may make archival copies of the Products for the sole purpose of backing up our software and protecting your investment from loss.

By saying "just like a book," McGraw-Hill means, for example, that the Product may be used by any number of people and may be freely moved from one computer location to another, so long as there is no possibility of the Product (or any part of the Product) being used at one location or on one computer while it is being used at another. Just as a book cannot be read by two different people in two different places at the same time, neither can the Product be used by two different people in two different places at the same time (unless, of course, McGraw-Hill's rights are being violated).

McGraw-Hill reserves the right to alter or modify the contents of the Product at any time.

This agreement is effective until terminated. The Agreement will terminate automatically without notice if you fail to comply with any provisions of this Agreement. In the event of termination by reason of your breach, you will destroy or erase all copies of the Product installed on any computer system or made for back-up purposes and shall expunge the Product from your data storage facilities.

LIMITED WARRANTY

McGraw-Hill warrants the physical diskette(s) enclosed herein to be free of defects in materials and workmanship for a period of sixty days from the purchase date. If McGraw-Hill receives written notification within the warranty period of defects in material or workmanship, and such notification is determined by McGraw-Hill to be correct, McGraw-Hill will replace the defective diskette(s). Send request to:

Customer Service
McGraw-Hill
Gahanna Industrial Park
860 Taylor Station Road
Blacklick, OH 43004-9615

The entire and exclusive liability and remedy for breach of this Limited Warranty shall be limited to replacement of defective diskette(s) and shall not include or extend to any claim for or right to cover any other damages, including but not limited to, loss of profit, data, or use of the software, or special, incidental, or consequential damages or other similar claims, even if McGraw-Hill has been specifically advised as to the possibility of such damages. In no event will McGraw-Hill's liability for any damages to you or any other person ever exceed the lower of suggested list price or actual price paid for the license to use the Product, regardless of any form of the claim.

THE McGRAW-HILL COMPANIES, INC. SPECIFICALLY DISCLAIMS ALL OTHER WARRANTIES, EXPRESS OR IMPLIED, INCLUDING BUT NOT LIMITED TO, ANY IMPLIED WARRANT OF MERCHANTABILITY OR FITNESS FOR A PARTICULAR PURPOSE. Specifically, McGraw-Hill makes no representation or warranty that the Product is fit for any particular purpose and any implied warranty of merchantability is limited to the sixty day duration of the Limited Warranty covering the physical diskette(s) only (and not the software or information) and is otherwise expressly and specifically disclaimed.

This Limited Warranty gives you specific legal rights, you may have others which may vary from state to state. Some states do not allow the exclusion of incidental or consequential damages, or the limitation on how long an implied warranty lasts, so some of the above may not apply to you.

This Agreement constitutes the entire agreement between the parties relating to use of the Product. The terms of any purchase order shall have no effect on the terms of this Agreement. Failure of McGraw-Hill to insist at any time on strict compliance with this Agreement shall not constitute a waiver of any rights under this Agreement. This Agreement shall be construed and governed in accordance with the laws of New York. If any provision of this Agreement is held to be contrary to law, that provision will be enforced to the maximum extent permissible and the remaining provisions will remain in force and effect.